DIVERSITY, CRIME, AND JUSTICE IN CANADA

DIVERSITY, CRIME, AND JUSTICE IN CANADA

Edited by
Barbara Perry

OXFORD
UNIVERSITY PRESS

OXFORD
UNIVERSITY PRESS

8 Sampson Mews, Suite 204, Don Mills, Ontario M3C 0H5
www.oupcanada.com

Oxford University Press is a department of the University of Oxford.
It furthers the University's objective of excellence in research, scholarship, and education by publishing worldwide in

Oxford New York

Auckland Cape Town Dar es Salaam Hong Kong Karachi Kuala Lumpur Madrid
Melbourne Mexico City Nairobi New Delhi Shanghai Taipei Toronto

With offices in

Argentina Austria Brazil Chile Czech Republic France Greece
Guatemala Hungary Italy Japan Poland Portugal Singapore
South Korea Switzerland Thailand Turkey Ukraine Vietnam

Oxford is a trade mark of Oxford University Press in the UK and in certain other countries

Published in Canada by Oxford University Press

Library and Archives Canada Cataloguing in Publication

Diversity, crime, and justice in Canada / edited by Barbara Perry.

Includes bibliographical references and index.
ISBN 978-0-19-543233-6

1. Social justice—Canada. 2. Criminal justice, Administration of—Canada.
3. Cultural pluralism—Canada. I. Perry, Barbara J. (Barbara Jean),

HM671.D59 2011   303.3'720971   C2011-900395-3

Cover image: Hill Street Studios/Gary Kious GettyImages

This book is printed on permanent (acid-free) paper ∞.

Printed and bound in the United States of America.

2 3 4 —15 14 13

Contents

Part Three Justice for Diversity   309

List of Tables and Figures

Contributors

Shahid Alvi is an associate dean and professor of Social Science and Humanities at the University of Ontario Institute of Technology. His current research interests include violence against immigrant women, youth crime, research methods, communities and crime, and the links between violence and culture. His recent publications focus on the psychological and physical abuse of poor minority women, second-generation crime prevention through environmental design, women's victimization in public housing, feminist routine activities theory, fear of crime, and youth in prison. He recently completed a research project on the victimization of the urban homeless in Durham Region. Currently, he is analyzing data from another recently completed project on immigrant women's quality of life, particularly their experiences of racism. He has also been consulted by a number of communities on public safety issues. Dr Alvi is the 2002 recipient of the Critical Criminologist of the Year Award from the American Society of Criminology's Critical Criminology Division.

Gillian Balfour (Ph.D.) is an associate professor in the Department of Sociology at Trent University in Peterborough, Ontario. She has published 'Re-Imagining a Feminist Criminology' in the *Canadian Journal of Criminology and Criminal Justice*; co-edited (with Elizabeth Comack) *Criminalizing Women: Gender and (In)Justice in Neo-liberal Times*; and co-authored (with Elizabeth Comack) *The Power to Criminalize: Violence, Inequality and the Law*. Her research interests are in the victimization and criminalization of Aboriginal women and state violence against women.

Carla Cesaroni is an associate professor in the Faculty of Social Science and Humanities at the University of Ontario Institute of Technology. She received her Ph.D. from the University of Toronto. Her research seeks to examine the stress and adjustment of incarcerated individuals. Additionally, she is interested in the role of punishment in the criminal justice system and in the public psyche. For the last decade she has studied the experiences of adolescent males serving custodial sentences. She is currently conducting a comparative study of the experiences of girls and boys in custody.

Jane Dickson-Gilmore is currently an associate professor in the Department of Law at Carleton University, where she teaches such subjects as Aboriginal community and restorative justice, conflict resolution, and introductory law and legal studies. Active in First Nations communities, she has served as an advisor for the Oujé-Bougoumou Cree First Nation and the Grand Council of the Cree/Cree Regional Authority on community justice. Dr Dickson-Gilmore has been called upon to present before the Standing Committee of Justice and Human Rights, has acted as an expert witness in proceedings before the Federal Court and Canadian Human Rights Commission, and is a member of Legal Aid Ontario's Aboriginal Issues Advisory Committee. She is the author of numerous academic publications and has received several academic awards.

Ellen Faulkner is an instructor of criminal justice and criminology at the G. Raymond Chang School of Continuing Education, Ryerson University. Her areas of research are hate crime, diversity in the legal profession, and policing. Her publications include *Victim No More: Women's Resistance to Law, Culture and Power* (with Gayle MacDonald).

Joan Harbison is an associate professor at Dalhousie University's School of Social Work, where she teaches courses on critical perspectives on aging and health service delivery. Her research and publications address issues of service delivery, legislation, and the rights of older people. She leads an interdisciplinary research team that includes members from the disciplines of social work, sociology, and criminology and law.

Denise Helly is a senior researcher at Institut National de Recherche Scientifique. She was trained in anthropology (Ph.D., La Sorbonne, 1975), sociology, political science, and sinology and specializes in studies on ethnic minorities, citizenship, nationalism, policies of cultural pluralism and of immigration, discrimination, and state and religious regimes. She has conducted several surveys on the integration of immigrants in Quebec, published 10 books and numerous articles covering topics such as Chinese overseas, Chinese in Canada, Canadian multiculturalism, Quebec policy toward cultural minorities, citizenship and nation, social cohesion, Muslims in Canada and Europe, and temporary migrant workers.

Bryan Hogeveen is an associate professor at the University of Alberta. He has published widely on a number of his academic interests, which include socio-legal theory, violence, martial arts in society, young offenders and the law, and justice. In 2009 he published (with Joanne Minaker) *Youth, Crime & Society: Issues of Power and Justice* with Pearson. Dr Hogeveen has been invited to share his ideas with both national and international audiences. He recently returned from giving the keynote address at the Provincial University of Rio de Janeiro. He is currently undertaking a three-year research project, funded by the Social Sciences and Humanities Research Council, that considers neoliberalism's impact on Canada's Prairie provinces.

Karim Ismaili is an associate dean and professor of criminal justice in the College of Humanities and Social Sciences at Kennesaw State University. Previously, he was inaugural chair of the Department of Criminal Justice at Ryerson University. His areas of teaching, research, and publishing include criminal justice policy and analysis, criminological theory, crime and inequality, and post-9/11 crime and security developments.

Heidi Janz is a postdoctoral fellow and co-investigator for the Defining Disability Ethics Project at the University of Alberta's John Dossetor Health Ethics Centre. She has been pursuing academic work in Disability Studies and Disability Ethics since 1995.

Yasmin Jiwani is an associate professor in the Department of Communication Studies at Concordia University, Montreal. Her doctorate in Communication Studies from Simon Fraser University examined issues of race and representation in Canadian television news. Her recent publications include *Discourses of Denial: Mediations of Race, Gender and Violence* and an edited collection, *Girlhood: Redefining the Limits*. Her work has appeared in *Social Justice*, *Violence against Women*, the *Canadian Journal of Communication*, the *Journal of Popular Film & Television*, *Topia*, the *International Journal of Media and Cultural Politics*, the *University of Toronto Quarterly*, and numerous anthologies. Her research interests include meditations of race, gender, and violence in the context of war stories, femicide reporting in the press, and representations of women of colour in popular and mainstream media.

Karen Mock is a registered psychologist, educator, and consultant on human rights, diversity, and hate crime. Formerly executive director of the Canadian Race Relations Foundation and of the League for Human Rights of B'nai Brith Canada, she taught for 15 years at the university level. Dr Mock was the principal advisor to the Western Judicial Education Centre and has worked with several policing services on training programs relevant to racism and hate crime, as well as with various public and private sector agencies on policies and practices for creating an equitable and barrier-free workplace. Having received many awards and honours for her work, Dr Mock has been recognized by Canadian courts and human rights tribunals as an expert on hate groups, racism, discrimination, and antisemitism. She chaired the Hate Crime Community Working Group, which produced the report *Addressing Hate Crime in Ontario* for the attorney general and the minister of community safety and corrections in 2006, and served as senior policy advisor to the minister of education for the development and delivery of Ontario's Equity and Inclusive Education Strategy, launched in 2009. Since 2005 she has been special advisor to the Ontario judicial ad hoc committees on 'Combating Hatred in the 21st Century'.

Akwasi Owusu-Bempah is a doctoral student at the Centre of Criminology, University of Toronto. His research examines racially biased policing in Canada, the United States, and the United Kingdom; public perceptions of criminal (in) justice; youth gang involvement; and immigration and crime. His dissertation investigates black males' perceptions of and experiences with the criminal justice system in Canada. He has recently published in the *Journal of International Migration and Integration* and the *Canadian Journal of Law and Society*. He has also recently won awards for community service and for academic merit from the Association of Black Law Enforcers and the American Society of Criminology.

Barbara Perry is a professor and associate dean in the Faculty of Social Science and Humanities at the University of Ontario Institute of Technology. She has written extensively in the areas of diversity and hate crime, including five books on the latter topic, among them: *In the Name of Hate: Understanding Hate Crime* and *Silent Victims: Hate Crime against Native Americans*. Her latest book deals with disparate policing in Native American communities. Dr Perry continues to work in the area of hate crime and has begun to contribute to the limited scholarship on hate crime in Canada. Here, she is particularly interested in anti-Muslim violence, hate crime against Aboriginal people, and the community impacts of hate crime.

Valerie Pruegger (M.Sc.) has taken her specialty in cross-cultural and organizational psychology to the business world, where she has developed and facilitated diversity organizational change processes and workshops on intercultural communication for a variety of volunteer, government, and private sec-

tor organizations. She has served as a consultant to police agencies across Canada and internationally; has written policy papers on hate/bias crime and community policing for the federal government and the Royal Canadian Mounted Police; is a member of the Justice, Policing and Security domain of Metropolis; and sits on the Alberta Hate Crimes Committee. Currently, she teaches Psychology and the Law in the Department of Psychology at the University of Calgary and is employed as a Research Social Planner by The City of Calgary, where she examines social issues and makes recommendations for changes to social policy and programming, particularly with reference to systemic discrimination and immigration.

Dick Sobsey is a professor emeritus of educational psychology at the University of Alberta, where he also serves as associate director of the J. P. Das Developmental Disabilities Centre and as a core member of the John Dossetor Health Ethics Centre. He has conducted research on violence against people with disabilities since the 1980s.

Scot Wortley has been a professor at the Centre of Criminology, University of Toronto, since 1996. In 2001 he was appointed the Justice and Law domain leader at the Centre of Excellence for Research on Immigration and Settlement (CERIS). In 2007 he was appointed by Metropolis to the position of national priority leader for research on Justice, Policing and Security. His current research projects explore street gangs in Toronto; gang intervention/gang prevention programs in the Toronto area; the relationship between immigration and crime; criminal offending and victimization in Jamaica; racial differences in perceptions of and experiences with the Canadian criminal justice system; criminal offending and victimization among Toronto high school students and street youth; and racial profiling and police use of force in Ontario. Professor Wortley has also conducted research on youth violence as part of the Toronto District School Board's School Community Safety Advisory Panel (chaired by Julian Falconer) and the Ontario government's Roots of Youth Violence Inquiry (chaired by Roy McMurtry and Alvin Curling). He has published in various academic journals, and recently he published the edited volume *Crime and Criminal Justice in the Caribbean* with researchers from the University of the West Indies.

Li Zong is an associate professor of sociology at the University of Saskatchewan and an affiliated researcher of the Prairie Metropolis Centre (PMC) in Canada. He is also a research fellow at the Institute for Empirical Social Science Research at Xi'an Jiaotong University and an adjunct professor for Tianjin Academy of Educational Science, Xi'an Jiaotong University, Lanzhou University, Qingdao Binhai University, and Norwest University for Nationalities in China. His research projects have been funded by the Social Sciences and Humanities Council of Canada (SSHRC), the Prairie Metropolis Centre, the federal Department of Canadian Heritage, and other funding agencies. His ongoing research projects include occupational attainment and social mobility of foreign-trained professional immigrants in Canada, covert racism and racial inequality, and China's economic reform and social change. He has co-authored a book on sociology and published articles and reviews in refereed journals on the issues of immigrants, new racism, multiculturalism, transnational Chinese business, civil society and social transformation, and race and ethnic relations. He has also contributed many chapters to published books.

Preface and Acknowledgments

Diversity, Crime, and Justice in Canada is first and foremost inspired by my students. They are hungry not only for knowledge of historical and contemporary patterns of social exclusion, but also for strategies to intervene in these patterns. My goal with this book was to bring together Canada's leading scholars in the area of diversity and justice to provide their insights for the students. I have been teaching courses on diversity and justice for nearly 20 years. In that time, changes in both the academic context and within the justice system have made such courses more rather than less relevant to students' education. Recent years have seen dramatic shifts in the demographics of Canadian colleges and universities. What were once enclaves of white male privilege have become increasingly diverse, both in terms of faculty and the student body. Remarkably, women are now over-represented in many programs, albeit traditionally 'feminine' ones such as social science, education, and nursing. People of colour are likewise represented at a much higher rate than even a decade ago. However, they still lag behind in proportional terms, and continue to experience depressed retention rates. Given the unwelcoming climate they experience in such institutions, this should come as no surprise.

There is evidence that formerly all-white, largely male preserves have been breached not only by white women, but also by men and women of colour. In addition, heightened concern about identity and its political articulation have given minorities visibility and clout beyond their numbers. In short, the voices on campus have become more numerous and more diverse. In particular, the need to meet the demands of the newly represented has become more pressing. Calls for curricular innovation have been met with dramatic changes in educational programs and curricula. Consequently, most campuses have made more or less concentrated efforts to accommodate the plurality of interests, largely through recruitment and curricular reform. Hence, more people of colour as well as women have been offered positions on faculty, in order to lend expertise and to act as role models for students. Additionally, there has been a remarkable increase in the number of programs such as Women's Studies, Equity Studies, African American Studies, or Aboriginal Studies, programs that bring these issues to the centre rather than the periphery. In addition, many universities have integrated diversity-related courses into their core or Liberal Studies requirements. Programs like those in the Faculty of Social Science and Humanities at my institution—the University of Ontario Institute of Technology—have, in fact, embedded issues of **inequality**, **oppression**, and **social justice** throughout the curriculum. We see such concerns as an integral focus for those who seek to enter careers in the criminal or social justice fields. It is no longer possible to ignore the role that identity plays in one's relationship to justice.

Consequently, I offer this text as a starting point for explorations of the nexus of diversity, criminal justice, and social justice. As the final chapter will make especially clear, social and criminal justice are intimately connected, such that neither can be achieved independent of the other. The other chapters also illustrate these links concretely, drawing connections between the life experiences of diverse communities and their vulnerability to victimization and criminalization.

This book has obviously been a collaborative effort. I am particularly grateful to Oxford University Press and my editors Rebecca Ryoji and Phyllis Wilson for recognizing the value of the stories told in the text. I hope they will be proud of what we've accomplished here. Of course, the contributors are the key to the success of the project. I value the remarkable work that they have done here. They have written chapters that will engage, inform, and hopefully motivate students to challenge patterns of injustice wherever they confront them. On a related note, I must thank the students from my graduate class on Contemporary Justice Issues and my undergraduate students in Social Justice and Conflict who reviewed various chapters to provide a student perspective on the text. It seems from their comments that we hit the mark! Thanks for that affirmation.

I am lucky to work in an environment that keeps me motivated. My colleagues in the Faculty of Social Science and Humanities share my vision of an inclusive and respectful Canada, but also of a truly just 'justice' system. The energy and inspiration I derive from them is empowering and energizing. I also have the good fortune to have parents who have supported me along my academic journey. The loss of my father in the midst of writing this text reminded me how much they have both meant to me over the years and how much his quiet support will be missed. Finally, as always, my biggest fan and supporter has been my husband, Michael Groff. He keeps me smiling—most days!

Dedication

To Daddy

For the students and those they will empower

Conceptualizing Difference

Every structure must be built on a solid foundation. This opening section is thus intended to provide the conceptual and theoretical foundations upon which the remainder of the text is built. An important note is that the first two chapters were circulated to the other contributors early in the process to maximize the consistency of themes across chapters. Within this broad schema, however, each author was encouraged to take his or her own creative approach to the presentation of the material. Nonetheless, a number of consistent themes link most of the chapters theoretically. In particular, readers will see that all the authors have woven into their chapters issues of history and context, power and powerlessness, and social and political action. This parallel structure across chapters represents one of the unique features of the book and is meant to facilitate comparison across groups within the relevant courses.

The opening chapter provides the context for the contemporary nexus of diversity, crime, and justice. In particular, it places the discussion within the context of the Canadian ideology of multiculturalism. This is a controversial popular mythology, both in terms of the demographics it describes and the practices meant to support it. Indeed, it is in the context of justice issues that the gap between theory and practice is most dramatic. Thus, the chapter also explores this disconnect, providing some preliminary insights into the ways in which differences in identity shape differential experiences with justice.

As the title of chapter 2 suggests, the key organizing theme for the book is the notion that difference is socially constructed, such that differences matter because of the relative value placed on them. The meanings assigned to one's identity, then, shape one's life experiences, relative positions of power, and, specific to the substantive issue at hand, interactions with crime and criminal justice. This chapter lays out the theoretical framework of the text, mapping the notion of how difference structures experience generally. Chapter 2 ends with a discussion of some of the key mechanisms—for example, language, stereotypes, media and legislation—by which we construct and reinforce rigid hierarchies around an array of identities. Chapter 3 takes up the theme, focusing explicitly on cultural representations of racialized Others that enable disparate treatment, including within the context of justice.

The argument is made in chapter 2 that difference implies a standard, a norm against which others are judged. Chapter 4 lays out that standard, or dominant identity, as it is represented in Canada. Specifically, it speaks to the experiences and roles of white middle-class men in defining difference and in defining who and what is to be considered 'criminal'. It addresses the notion of the 'typical' as opposed to the 'stereotypical' offender, as well as how this is (mis)represented in crime statistics and in the popular imagination.

1 An Introduction: Considering Diversity and Justice in Canada

BARBARA PERRY

In January 2008, 30 black jail guards at Toronto Jail walked off the job to protest lack of action on dozens of racially threatening letters they had been receiving from colleagues.

In September 2008, a gay man walking with his partner was verbally berated before being beaten so badly that he had to have his jaw wired.

In November 2008, a report released by the United Nations Committee on the Elimination of Discrimination against Women observed that, in Canada, 'hundreds of cases involving Aboriginal women who have gone missing or been murdered in the past two decades have neither been fully investigated nor attracted priority attention, with the perpetrators remaining unpunished.'

In December 2008, Conservative politicians indicated that they would once again attempt to repeal Canada's Civil Marriage Act.

Collectively, this small sampling of incidents from the months preceding the writing of this book speaks to the persistence of differential access to and experiences with the justice system in Canada. And they are testimony to the need for focused attention on issues of **diversity** in the context of Canadian justice. Examples like these highlight the important fact that difference matters in Canada, to the extent that one's identity has significant implications for one's experience – and expectations – of justice. Whether victims, offenders, practitioners, or equity seekers, *individuals* come into contact with the law carrying with them *collective* identities that figure prominently in their subsequent encounters. It is this intersection of (in)equality and (in)justice that this text explores.

However, before moving to the heart of this text – diversity and justice – I share a few thoughts on the broader patterns of diversity that characterize the Canadian landscape.

Patterns of Diversity in Canada—The *Vertical Mosaic* Revisited

More than forty years ago—in 1965—**John Porter** wrote the Canadian classic *The Vertical Mosaic*. Few pieces of scholarship have had such an overwhelming influence on an entire field of study. It both inspired and shaped a generation of writing on issues of **social stratification**, **power**, and **hierarchy** that continues to resonate today. Contrary to the popular wisdom of the day, Porter maintained that Canada was not, in fact, a classless egalitarian society. Rather, he argued forcefully, it was riddled with multiple fault lines, particularly along the dimensions of class and ethnicity. I will let Porter's words speak for themselves in defining what he meant by the 'vertical mosaic' as applied to Canadian society:

> In a society which is made up of many cultural groups there is usually some relationship between a person's membership in these groups and his class position and, consequently, his chances of reaching positions of power. Because the Canadian people are often referred to as a mosaic composed of different ethnic groups, the title, *The Vertical Mosaic*, was originally given to the chapter which examines the relationship between ethnicity and social class. As the study proceeded, however, the hierarchical relationship between Canada's many cultural groups became a recurring theme in class and power. (Porter, 1965, pp. xii–xiii)

This conceptualization of Canada's structures of power subsequently became a key starting point for both parallel and competing analyses. Interestingly, while this particular quote opens with at least an implicit understanding of what has come to be recognized as **intersectionality**, many of the social identities that have come to the fore in Canadian scholarship remain invisible in Porter's work—note, for example, the very gendered use of the masculine pronoun!

Nonetheless, contemporary social scientists are indebted to Porter for opening up a fruitful field of study in Canada. This text is part of that lineage and represents part of an increasing body of literature on diversity in the context of criminal justice specifically. In what follows, ethnicity and class are joined by other categories of difference as the authors explore how identity conditions people's expectations and experiences of 'justice'.

Porter was writing well before Canada embarked on its official journey toward what has since become one of its globally heralded characteristics: **multiculturalism**. Equally praised, criticized, and ridiculed, the mantra of multiculturalism has formed the basis for Canada proclaiming itself as being among the most diverse and inclusive countries of its peers. Beginning with a formal multiculturalism policy in 1971 and institutionalized in the **Canadian Multiculturalism Act** of 1988, this guiding principle has become a hallmark of Canadian identity. But that is not to say that it is unproblematic. Multiculturalism both constitutes and is constituted by a dynamic, shifting, and often ambiguous culture, so it too suffers from the same embedded flaws and limitations. Audrey Kobyashi (1999, p. 33) highlights the inherently complex nature of the beast:

> Canadian multiculturalism is an aspiration and an **ideology**, a national discourse and a personal project, a way of life and a structural framework. It is contested, transformative and transforming, a product of collective imagination and an ideal that fuels the imagination. The imaginative plane of multiculturalism is diverse, fragmented, complicated and

extensive, and as a result often incoherent or incomprehensible. To a large extent this fragmented picture represents the contradictions that arise from a diverse society, in which ideological and cultural divisions, riven with unequal power relations, create conflicts of interest and frustrate the postmodern dream of living harmoniously in our diversity.

In an attempt to capture the complexity and multidimensional nature of Canadian multiculturalism, **Augie Fleras** has crafted a model that portrays the notion as (1) an empirical fact; (2) an ideology; (3) a formal policy; (4) a set of practices; and (5) a critical discourse.

The rhetoric of multiculturalism emerged in the late 1960s and early 1970s in the context of changing demographics in Canada and as a means of learning to live with the resultant differences that were evolving. In this sense, it was a response to the recognition of the *empirical fact* of Canadian diversity. Like most Western nations, Canada had been host to the growth of new social movements that signalled the growing visibility of long-marginalized and -silenced voices: women, gay men and lesbians, religious minorities, as well as labour interests. Added to this were the rapid demographic changes provoked by 1960s immigration reform, which would forever change the nature of Canadian racial and ethnic relations.

Prior to the 1960s, Canada's immigration policy had largely excluded immigrants who did not hail from white European nations. With the legislative reforms came a sudden and dramatic influx of those who were 'different'. Consequently, Canada stands today as one of the most demographically diverse nations in the world. Consider that the 1901 Census documented only 25 different ethnic groups in Canada; by the 2006 Census, this number had leapt to over 200, with 11 such groups numbering more than 1 million members. Between 2001 and 2006 alone, Canada's visible minority population grew by nearly 30 per cent. And in 2006 South Asians surpassed Chinese as the largest visible minority group, with blacks ranking third. What is particularly interesting is that these visible minority groups are themselves ethnoculturally diverse. For instance, black Canadians identified themselves as Caribbean (52 per cent), African (42.4 per cent), British (11.6 per cent), Canadian (10.9 per cent), and French (4.1 per cent) (Statistics Canada, 2007). It is these features of a modern nation that multiculturalism is said to address.

The *ideology* of multiculturalism provides the conceptual framework for how these differences are to be managed. It conveys an idealized image of the preferred means by which we live and interact in this plural society. It is an ideology that values and encourages diversity and is usually associated with the liberal view that we should be tolerant, non-discriminatory, and respectful of others. Fleras and Elliott (2002, p. 37) enumerate a series of catch-phrases that capture the heart of this vision: 'Take differences seriously!' 'Diversity within unity!' '(Multi) cultural relativism!' 'Respect others!' 'Active acceptance!' 'Mosaic!' 'Inclusiveness!'

Keep in mind that this liberal statement of values reflects an ideal. While it is a powerful discourse that promises inclusion, it nonetheless preserves persistent patterns of exclusion. As such, the ideology of multiculturalism responds to the 'strong pressure to conceal, evade and distort; if it did not do these things—that is, if (Canada) did not write its own national myths to paper over its cultural contradictions—it might well dissolve as a nation, and multiculturalism serves as such a myth' (Fleras & Elliott, 2002, p. 36).

Nonetheless, the ideology of multiculturalism has been institutionalized in public *policy*. It was adopted as official policy in Canada in 1971, that is, as a policy of multiculturalism within a bilingual framework. While the Multiculturalism Act of 1988 is an explicit statement of principle, the tenets of multiculturalism have also been embedded in other policy venues, such as the **Charter of Rights** (1982) and the Employment Equity Act (1986). Moreover, an array of federally funded programs in support of multiculturalism has also emerged. In 1984, a parliamentary committee report, *Equality Now*, called not for just statutes, but also for the establishment of a national research institute on multiculturalism and race relations issues—what would become the Canadian Race Relations Foundation. In addition, Canadian Heritage supports multicultural programs, such as heritage languages, multicultural councils, and ethnic programs.

Chronology of Federal Policies Relevant to Multiculturalism

1947 Passage of the first-ever **Canadian Citizenship Act**
1960 Passage of the **Canadian Bill of Rights**
1963 Establishment of the Royal Commission on Bilingualism and Biculturalism
1969 Book IV of the Bilingualism and Biculturalism Commission Report emphasizes the bilingual and multicultural nature of Canada.
1969 Introduction of the **Official Languages Act**
1971 Introduction of Canada's Multiculturalism Policy
1977 Passage of the **Canadian Human Rights Ac**t
1982 Adoption of the **Canadian Charter of Rights and Freedoms**
1984 Special parliamentary committee report, *Equality Now*, calls for a Multiculturalism Act and establishment of a national research institute on multiculturalism and race relations issues.
1986 Passage by Parliament of the **Employment Equity Act**
1988 Passage of the **Canadian Multiculturalism Act**
1996 Government establishes the Canadian Race Relations Foundation.
1997 Renewed Multiculturalism Program announced

Theoretically, multicultural *practice* would involve the fair and equitable treatment of all, whether by individuals, groups, or institutions. Regardless of background, Canadian citizens, residents, and visitors could expect to go about their lives free from the threat of discrimination. And, after 30 or more years of official multiculturalism, there are signs of declining racism, sexism, and other forms of inequality. For the most part, key institutions—the labour force, the justice system, the schools, and so on—have all shown signs of having greater awareness of and paying more attention to issues of inclusion and fairness. Compared to the 1970s, they are more responsive to and representative of the communities they serve in terms of both employment and service delivery. Nonetheless, there remains a deep divide between the ideology of multiculturalism and its practice. Progress has been intermittent and uneven, as it 'intermingles with inertia to create a confusing picture that speaks volumes about the politics of putting principles into practice. In other words, institutions may have come a long way from an exclusionary past; nonetheless, they still have a long way to go before inclusion is a reality' (Fleras, 2010, p. 318).

So, for example, while more Aboriginal youths complete high school, they still lag far behind their peers; while same-sex marriage has been legalized, members of the LGBT community still face ongoing harassment and victimization; and while women are more likely to earn seven-figure salaries, they are also more likely to live in poverty, especially if they are single mothers. Illustrative examples such as these highlight the limitations of the ideology of multiculturalism. They are indicators of the extent to which the rhetoric of inclusion trumps the reality of exclusion. The chapters that follow question Canada's commitment to and ability to fully recognize the values of multiculturalism, specifically within the halls of justice.

This is not to say that multiculturalism should then be rejected as a legitimate and progressive political project. It can be turned on its head to be exploited as a *critical discourse*, or as a transformative form of politics. Rather than reproducing current power relations, it would challenge them, working toward a meaningful redistribution of power and resources (Fleras, 2010). Fleras characterizes traditional Canadian multiculturalism as an ideology and practice that depoliticizes diversity. From a more radical perspective, multicultural discourse can instead have the capacity to consciously politicize diversity in a way that recognizes and empowers those who have long been excluded. It would name and challenge group difference, group privilege, and the ways in which existing relations of power perpetuate and shape these. This text is, in fact, part of that project.

Diversity in the Criminal Justice System

One context in which the national myth of multiculturalism is most dramatically challenged is within the justice system. Here, we see how identity shapes the nature and dynamics of the experiences of victims, offenders/suspects, and service providers. To begin, there can be no denying that there are dramatic differences in people's risk of **victimization**, depending on their group membership. Generally, young men are most susceptible to victimization of virtually every description, with the exceptions of intimate partner violence and sexual assault, which leave so many women and girls at risk. In 2006, 83 per cent of reported victims of 'spousal assault' were women; that same year continued the trend, with the rate of spousal homicide for women three to five times that for men (Ogrodnik, 2006). Brennan and Taylor-Butts (2008) report that, in 2004, women experienced sexual assault at nearly five times the rates as men (3,248 and 664 per 100,000, respectively). Moreover, for both types of violence, Aboriginal women are at higher risk than non-Aboriginal women (Chartrand & McKay, 2006).

Age, too, is a major determinant of risk, in that youth between 15 and 24 years of age are 1.5 times more likely than those aged 25 to 34, and 19 times more likely than those 65 and older, to be victims of violent crime (Statistics Canada, 2007). Even in the context of sexual assault, young people are more at risk. In 2007, for example, girls aged 15 to 24 reported sexual assault at a rate almost 18 times greater than that recorded for Canadians aged 55 years and older (5,563 versus 315 per 100,000 population). More dramatic still, police data suggest that over half (58 per cent) of sexual assault victims in 2007 were children; those under 12 accounted for 25 per cent of sexual assault victims (Brennan & Taylor-Butts, 2008).

In recent years, increasing attention has been paid to violence that is in itself motivated by bias against the victim's group. This has come to be known as **hate crime**. Like most other Western nations, Canada has had its share of bias-motivated violence throughout its history. From the periodic assaults on First Nations communities, to the riotous attacks on Chinese labourers in the 1880s, to the recent spate of anti-Semitic violence in Montreal and Toronto, our country has proven itself to be less welcoming than its international image would suggest. Indeed, the presence of such violence gives lie to the 'myth of multiculturalism' that is so deeply embedded in our national psyche. As the Right Honourable Beverly McLachlin (2003) stated in her LaFontaine-Baldwin address, 'In Canada, we vaunt our multi-cultural society, yet still racism, anti-Semitism and religious intolerance lurk in our dark corners.'

The available data sources on hate crime in Canada are limited. The annual General Social Survey (GSS) and the Ethnic Diversity Survey each include some rather weak questions on hate crime. There have also been a number of Justice Canada and Statistics Canada reports that attempt to measure hate crime. For example, in a survey involving 12 major police forces across Canada covering some 43 per cent of the national volume of crime, there were 921 incidents of hate crime recorded for 2001 and 2002, some 57 per cent of which were designated as motivated by race/ethnicity and some 43 per cent by religion (Silver, Milhorean, & Taylor-Butts, 2004). Additionally, the Canadian General Social Survey showed for 1999 that about 4 per cent of self-reported criminal-victimization incidents were believed by victims to be motivated by hate. This amounted to some 273,000 incidents, the vast majority of which were believed to be associated with race/ethnicity (43 per cent), religion (37 per cent), or culture (18 per cent) (Silver, Milhorean, & Taylor-Butts, 2004). The most frequent victims were Jews (25 per cent), blacks (17 per cent), Muslims (11 per cent), South Asians (10 per cent), gays and lesbians, multi-ethnic/racial people, east and southeast Asians, and Arabs/West Asians, each of whom accounted for just under 10 per cent of the victims.

Traditionally marginalized and disadvantaged groups of Canadians have also long been over-represented in offence statistics. In Canada, particular attention has been paid to the experiences of Aboriginal people, who consistently fill our prisons and jails at numbers well beyond their share in the population. Consider the summary data presented below:

Aboriginal Adults (2005–6)
- 4 per cent of the total Canadian adult population (2006 Census)
- 24 per cent of admissions to provincial/territorial sentenced custody
- 18 per cent of admissions to federal prisons
- 19 per cent of admissions to remand
- 21 per cent of male prisoner population
- 30 per cent of female prisoner population
- In Manitoba, Aboriginal people accounted for 71 per cent of sentenced admissions in 2005/2006 (and make up 16 per cent of the outside population), up from 58 per cent in 1996/1997.
- In Saskatchewan, Aboriginal adults make up 79 per cent of the total prisoner population (15 per cent of outside population).

Aboriginal Women (2004–5)

- In the provincial system, 30 per cent of female prisoners are Aboriginal (2004–5).
- In the federal system, 25 per cent of female prisoners are Aboriginal (2005–6 stat). This has increased steadily since 1997, when Aboriginal women made up 15 per cent of federal female prisoners.
- In Saskatchewan, Aboriginal women account for 87 per cent of all female admissions.
- In Manitoba and the Yukon, Aboriginal women account for 83 per cent of all female admissions.
- In Alberta, Aboriginal women account for 54 per cent of all female admissions.
- In British Columbia, Aboriginal women account for 29 per cent of all female admissions (prisonjustice.ca, 2008; see also Babooram, 2008).

Conservative commentators would argue that these patterns arise because Aboriginal people, like other people of colour generally, are more prone to criminal behaviour. More sympathetic accounts point to systemic patterns of racism in the broader society and the justice system to explain the disparity. Indeed, multiple inquiries over the years have arrived at the same conclusion as that of the 1996 Royal Commission on Aboriginal Peoples:

> All the inquiries concur that Aboriginal people who encounter the justice system are confronted with both *overt and systematic discrimination* and that this discrimination is one reason why many Aboriginal persons have not received due justice. (Royal Commission on Aboriginal Peoples, 1996, p. 16)

Much the same could be said of other racialized communities in Canada. This is perhaps most obvious in the persistence of the **over-policing** of communities of colour, which might take such forms as **racial profiling**, harassment, and other related forms of 'stop and search'. These behaviours can be traced back in part to stereotypical views wherein 'the crimes of the individual came to be seen as the crimes of the community' (Whitfield, 2004, p. 158). Whitfield's observation reflects the apparent reality of law enforcement assumptions about the connection between race and criminality, assumptions that are ultimately used to justify selective intervention. The first faulty assumption is that it is members of minority communities that commit the majority of crimes and thus warrant greater scrutiny. The second, and related, assumption is that most members of these same groups engage in criminal activity, and thus racial profiling is likely to result in a 'hit', that is, in the discovery of wrongdoing (Leadership Conference on Civil Rights, 2000).

The stop-and-search practices noted above are part and parcel of a broader pattern of behaviours now known collectively as racial profiling. Reports by Amnesty International (2004) and the Ontario Human Rights Commission (OHRC, 2003) provide useful definitions of the term:

> Racial profiling occurs when law enforcement agents rely solely on race, ethnicity, national origin, or religion in deciding whom to target for criminal investigation. (Amnesty International, 2004)

> Any action undertaken for reasons of safety, security or public protection that relies on stereotypes about race, colour, ethnicity, ancestry, religion, or place of origin rather than on reasonable suspicion, to single out an individual for greater scrutiny or different treatment. (OHRC, 2003, p. 6)

Both reports also recognize that racial profiling occurs in multiple and diverse contexts. Contemporary scholarship has tended to focus on vehicular profiling, although this has begun to shift with the increased tendency to profile those deemed to be of Middle Eastern descent in the aftermath of the September 11 attacks. It is possible to recognize an array of types of profiling; people may be assessed while driving; while walking; while travelling through airports; while shopping; while at home; and while travelling to and from places of worship (Amnesty International, 2004). Profiling of all kinds is disturbingly common and affects people from multiple communities, including First Nations, Asian Canadians, black Canadians, Canadian Muslims, as well as visitors to this country.

A 2002 Leadership Conference on Civil Rights report entitled *Justice on Trial: Racial Disparities in the American Criminal Justice System* documents the widespread disparities faced by African Americans and Hispanic Americans in the United States specifically. However, similar dynamics and impacts face Canadians as well. Importantly, the report also highlights the cumulative consequences of these inequities. Four key areas are identified:

1. disempowerment of minority communities;
2. exacerbation of minority hostility toward and distrust of the justice system;
3. impact on minority communities in terms of economics and public health; and
4. loss of national ideals.

A later report from Amnesty International stresses similar debilitating effects, arguing that the 'human impact' of disparate police behaviours culminates in diminished trust in police and disempowered and disenfranchised communities (Amnesty International, 2004). Interestingly, a 2003 Ontario Human Rights Commission inquiry on the 'human cost' of racial profiling specifically saw fit to devote a component of the inquiry and report to the specific experiences of Aboriginal people in Ontario. This was justified with reference to the unique historical and political situation of Canada's First Nations and to the recognition that they were not 'just another ethnic minority group' but rather constituted nations unto themselves. Regardless of the race of the affected community, however, the inquiry came to similar conclusions as those in the American reports. Racial profiling has devastating effects on the emotional, psychological, financial, physical, and even cultural well-being of not just the affected individuals but their communities as well (OHRC, 2003).

In light of the above, and in light of the persistently contentious relationship between the justice system and minority communities, it should come as no surprise that women, people of colour, and members of other marginalized communities are dramatically under-represented in most justice-related professions. Interestingly, women were beginning to enter the legal profession and policing in unprecedented numbers by the late 1970s. However, by the mid-1990s, they were leaving justice professions at a similarly fast pace (Krakauer & Chen, 2003), owing largely to the sexist and patriarchal environments in which they found themselves. In the legal profession, specifically, women now make up the majority of law school graduates, but they remain under-represented in the profession itself, as they face ongoing barriers to engagement in the field.

A 2002 report traces the representation of women, visible minorities, Aboriginal people, and immigrants across Canada's justice-related professions (Goudreau, 2002). The patterns of **under-representation** are remarkably consistent across all of these groups. The only group represented near or above their proportion of the population (2 per cent) was Aboriginal peoples, who constituted just over 2 per cent of the total justice personnel. However, much of this is accounted for by their relatively large numbers in the category of security personnel, one of the lowest paying and lowest prestige of the all justice-related careers. Typically, members of the disadvantaged communities in the justice-related professions were under-represented; had higher levels of education; and earned lower incomes than the population of justice professionals as a whole. Moreover, the areas in which they were employed in high numbers were generally low-paying, low-prestige jobs such as security personnel, clerical court workers, and legal secretaries.

Fearing lack of sympathy, comprehension, or commitment on the part of justice professionals, many of the communities most dramatically affected by the justice system have opted to establish organizations and agencies that serve the needs of their communities with considerably more sensitivity. Communities across the nation have begun to establish their own advocacy and action groups as supplements—or more often alternatives—to criminal justice agencies; these are intended to represent and protect the interests—and often the rights—of diverse groups. Traditionally silenced communities have begun to mobilize their growing numerical strength into political and social power. Women's shelters and rape crisis centres, once seen as 'radical' ideas, are now widely dispersed and funded by governments and private sources alike. Social and cultural organizations, for example, are indispensable mechanisms by which to ease the transition for newcomers. Such programs more generally represent the interests of marginal groups through community organizing, social functions, and the provision of services and service links to legal, social, and medical agencies. Other organizations seek to protect the civil rights of all Canadians by engaging in legal consultations, civil rights litigation, and educational services. In response to the harassment and violence often suffered by diverse groups, many anti-violence and civil rights groups have emerged in recent years. Grassroots organizing will continue to play a vital role within the justice system so long as prevailing structures of inequality remain intact.

Organization of the Text

Part 1 of this text lays out the conceptual and theoretical foundations of the book. As the title of chapter 2 suggests, the key organizing theme is the notion that difference is socially constructed in that differences matter because of the relative value placed on them. The meanings assigned to one's identity, then, shape one's life experiences, relative positions of power, and—specific to the context at hand—interactions with crime and criminal justice. Chapter 3 expands this analysis, looking specifically at the ways in which representations of identity (e.g., stereotypes, media images, etc.) facilitate the subsequent stigmatization, and often criminalization, of marginalized groups. Chapter 4 begins the exploration of the concrete ways in which 'difference matters' in the context of criminal justice by tracing the standard or dominant identity against which all others are judged—that is, the experience and role of white, middle-class men in particular in defining difference and in defining what is criminal. It addresses the notion of the 'typical' as opposed to 'stereotypical' offender, as well as how this affects crime statistics.

Part 2 constitutes the substantive heart of the text. Here, specific groups are examined with respect to their visibility to and contact with the justice system. What makes this treatment unique is that each substantive chapter in this section addresses consistent themes, allowing comparison between diverse groups. Each chapter opens with a conceptual overview of the group in question that includes historical experiences, cultural trends, and so forth. Each chapter addresses issues facing the group members in terms of victimization, criminalization/offending, and service provision within the criminal justice system. Within this framework, each author takes his or her own creative approach to presenting the material. Nonetheless, there are consistent themes linking the chapters theoretically, largely derived from chapter 2. In particular, the authors weave into their chapter issues such as history and context, intersectionality, power and powerlessness, and social and political action.

There is no art or science to the selection of identities that make up the core of this text. And, I am certain, my choices will not please everyone. There will be those who suggest I've been too inclusive and those who will suggest just the opposite: that I've not been inclusive enough. To these, add a third camp: those who would argue that, by naming communities, I fall into the trap of essentializing identity and denying the multiplicity of simultaneous identity positions. What I've attempted to do is to at least move beyond the 'holy trinity' of race, class, and gender, which have formed the core of so much scholarship around diversity and justice. Thus, I share with British criminologist Basia Spalek (2008, pp. 5–6) the insistence that

> a critical focus upon gender, 'race'/ethnicity, religion/spirituality, sexual orientation, disability and ageing might start to make visible discriminatory norms that help reproduce discrimination and oppression, as it seems that a modernist agenda has largely failed to give sufficient voice to these broader norms.

I do not deny the importance of intersectionality, as will be evident from chapter 2. It is not always clear whether or which elements of identity shape experiences in any given context. For example, Doug Meyer's (2008) interviews with victims of anti-LGBT violence suggest that even victims are not always certain whether it is their sexuality, gender, or race that motivates their assailants. That said, I have asked contributors to explore discrete communities while also encouraging them to account for the ways in which those communities are shaped by differences within as well as without. How, for instance, does class intervene in racial dynamics, or religion in gender dynamics? Such considerations constitute through-lines across the text.

Part 3, the final section of the text, recognizes and in fact celebrates the notion that if difference is socially constructed, then the flip side is that it can be reconstructed. Thus, with the book's first two parts having established the nature and dynamics of disparate experiences within the criminal justice system, this concluding section addresses means by which those disparities can be minimized. Some, but not all, of the initiatives are grounded in criminal justice reform. However, these must also be contextualized within concrete efforts to reconstruct difference in positive relational terms and within a social justice framework.

Chapter 17 leads the way. One way to minimize disparities in criminal justice experiences is to enhance communication and thus understanding between communities and to break down damaging and disparaging stereotypes. It is also imperative that those working with diverse communities be aware of culturally distinct patterns of verbal and non-verbal communication (e.g., eye contact) and barriers to effective intercultural communication.

One context for enhancing awareness of the dynamics of inequality within the justice system lies in the realm of anti-racism/anti-oppression training. Thus, chapter 18 provides insight into this strategy. Increasingly, trainers have become aware of the need to provide focused pre- and in-service education for criminal justice personnel. This includes broad approaches to diversity generally, but also more specialized training relevant to particular contexts/crimes (e.g., hate crime). The chapter will also explore some of the important caveats learned to date with respect to the appropriate means of delivering such training to personnel who are typically adult learners.

The concluding chapter takes up the theme of social equity as a prerequisite for reducing disparity in criminal justice. It sums up recurring themes and encourages the reader to think about alternative ways to respond to offending, victimization, and service provision. In particular, it stresses the importance of social justice (economic, political, cultural) for enhancing just and humane responses to crime.

Key Terms

Canadian Charter of Rights and Freedoms	Fleras, Augie	multiculturalism	social justice
	hate crime	oppression	social stratification
Canadian Multiculturalism Act	hierarchy	over-policing	under-representation
	ideology	Porter, John	The Vertical Mosaic
	inequality	power	victimization
diversity	intersectionality	racial profiling	white male privilege

Questions for Critical Thought

1.   In what ways and along what lines can Canada be considered a diverse or multicultural society?

2.   Some commentators suggest that multiculturalism is divisive and pulls the country apart. What arguments can you think of both to support and to challenge this perspective?

3.   How do contemporary criminal justice patterns and practices challenge the principles of multiculturalism?

Additional Readings

Fleras, A., & Elliott, J. (2002). *Engaging diversity: Multiculturalism in Canada*. Toronto: Nelson Thomson Learning.

Porter, J. (1965). *The vertical mosaic: An analysis of social class and power in Canada*. Toronto: University of Toronto Press.

Statistics Canada. (2007). *Canada's ethnocultural mosaic, 2006 Census: National picture*. Ottawa: Statistics Canada. Retrieved April 29, 2009, from www12.statcan.ca/English/census06/analysis.ethnicorigin/cultural.cfm

Websites of Interest

Canadian Centre for Diversity: www.centrefordiversity.ca

Canadian Heritage: www.pch.gc.ca

Statistics Canada: www.statcan.gc.ca

References

Amnesty International. (2004). *Threat and humiliation: Racial profiling, domestic security, and human rights in the United States*. New York: Amnesty International.

Babooram, A. (2008). *The changing profile of adults in custody, 2006/2007*. Ottawa: Statistics Canada.

Brennan, S., & Taylor-Butts, A. (2008). *Sexual assault in Canada, 2004 and 2007*. Ottawa: Statistics Canada. Catalogue no. 85F0033M—no. 19.

Chartrand, L., & McKay, C. (2006). *A review of research on criminal victimization and First Nations, Métis and Inuit Peoples 1990 to 2001*. Ottawa: Policy Centre for Victim Issues, and Research and Statistics Division, Department of Justice Canada.

Fleras, A. (2010). *Unequal relations* (6th ed.). Toronto: Pearson.

Fleras, A., & Elliott, J. (2002). *Engaging diversity: Multiculturalism in Canada*. Toronto: Nelson Thomson Learning.

Goudreau, J. (2002). *A statistical profile on persons working in justice-related professions in Canada*.

Ottawa: Canadian Centre for Justice Statistics, Statistics Canada. Catalogue no. 85-555-XIE.

Johnson, H. (2006). *Measuring violence against women: Statistical trends 2006*. Ottawa: Statistics Canada. Catalogue no. 85-570-XIE.

Kobyashi, A. (1999). Employment equity in Canada: The paradox of tolerance and denial. In C. James (Ed.), *Possibilities and limitations: Multicultural policies and programs in Canada* (pp. 154–162). Halifax: Fernwood.

Krakauer, L., & Chen, C. (2003). Gender barriers in the legal profession: Barriers for career development of female law students. *Journal of Employment Counseling, 40*(2), 65–79.

Leadership Conference on Civil Rights. (2000). *Justice on trial: Racial disparities in the American criminal justice system*. Washington: LCCR.

McLachlin, B. (2003). *The civilization of difference*. LaFontaine-Baldwin Address. Toronto: Institute for Canadian Citizenship.

Meyer, D. (2008). Interpreting and experiencing anti-queer violence: Race, class, and gender differences among LGBT hate crime victims. *Race, Gender & Class, 15*(3–4), 262–282.

Ogrodnik, L. (2006). In *Family violence in Canada: A statistical profile, 2006*. Ottawa: Canadian Centre for Justice Statistics, Statistics Canada. Catalogue no. 85-224-XIE.

Ontario Human Rights Commission. (2003). *Paying the price: The human cost of racial profiling*. Toronto: Ontario Human Rights Commission.

Porter, J. (1965). *The vertical mosaic: An analysis of social class and power in Canada*. Toronto: University of Toronto Press.

Royal Commission on Aboriginal Peoples. (1996). *Bridging the cultural divide: A report on Aboriginal People and criminal justice*. Ottawa: Royal Commission on Aboriginal People.

Scott, J. (1995). The rhetoric of crisis in higher education. In M. Berubé & C. Nelson (Eds), *Higher education under fire: Politics, economics, and the crisis of the humanities* (pp. 293–304). New York: Routledge.

Silver, W., Milhorean, K., & Taylor-Butts, A. (2004). *Hate crime in Canada*. Ottawa: Statistics Canada. Catalogue no. 85-002-XPE.

Spalek, B. (2008). *Communities, identities and crime*. Bristol, UK: Policy Press.

Statistics Canada. (2007). *Canada's Ethnocultural Mosaic, 2006 Census: National Picture*. Ottawa: Statistics Canada. Retrieved April 29, 2009, from www12. statcan.ca/English/census06/analysis.ethnicorigin/ cultural.cfm

Whitfield, J. (2004). *Unhappy dialogue: The Metropolitan Police and black Londoners in post-war Britain*. Devon, UK: Willan.

2 Framing Difference

BARBARA PERRY

Difference Is Socially Constructed

Both historical and contemporary patterns of stratification in Canada challenge the ideology of **multiculturalism** discussed in the opening chapter. These patterns suggest that, far from being the epitome of inclusion and equity, this is a nation grounded in deeply embedded notions of difference that have been used to justify and construct intersecting hierarchies along lines of **sexuality, race, gender**, and class, to name but a few. In other words, difference has been socially constructed but in ever-changing ways across time and space. Nonetheless, these constructions have reinforced similarly changing practices of **exclusion** and **marginalization**.

Biology is not destiny. Rather, in our culture, biology is the hook on which we hang our assumptions about the holder of a given set of characteristics. In other words, difference is not biologically given, but socially constructed. We tend to assume that there is some inherent, immutable, and universal **essence** that differentiates groups of people. This 'essentialist' interpretation of difference assumes that 'reality exists independently of our perceptions of it; i.e., that there are real and important (essential) differences among categories of people' (Pincus 2006, p. 12).

The secret to the success of these social constructs is that they are virtually invisible, to the extent that the divisions appear natural; they are taken for granted. Omi and Winant (1994, p. 60) express this notion with respect to race, although it is an equally useful assessment of gender or sexual identity:

> Everyone learns some combination, some version, of the rules of racial classification, and of her own racial identity, often without obvious teaching or conscious inculcation. Thus we are inserted in a comprehensively racialized social structure. Race becomes 'common sense'—a way of comprehending, explaining and being in the world.

The systems of classification to which Omi and Winant refer tend to presume mutually exclusive categories of belonging. They assume an either/or understanding of identity: one is either a man or a woman; either white or black or Asian or Native; either Christian or Jew or Muslim. Given this conceptualization of identity, one is forced to choose a 'side'. In some contexts, the choice is given, since differences in race or gender, for example, are assumed to be innate, biological—that is, natural. Whatever the case, discrete boundaries are assumed. One can belong only to one side of the equation; the borders are held to be impermeable.

A remarkable example of this comes from the life story of Gregory Williams, author of *Life on the Color Line*. Williams shares his own experience of the imposed 'color-line' in North America. Keep in mind that Williams is now a celebrated academic, a holder of five degrees and three honorary degrees. Born in the 1940s in Virginia, he attended all-white schools and participated in whites-only activities and locales. When he was 10 years old, he moved to Indiana with his recently divorced father. During the course of their journey north, Williams learned how racial identity could be imposed from without. His father explained to his two sons that they were 'no longer white'. Rather, because they had a paternal grandmother who was black, in Indiana, they too would be considered black. Thus, 'In Virginia, you were white boys. In Indiana, you're going to be colored boys. I want you to remember that you're the same today that you were yesterday. But people in Indiana will treat you differently' (Williams, 1995, p. 33). His father's words did indeed preface a dramatic change in the way that Williams and his family were perceived and treated. They did indeed 'become' black.

This example illustrates the complexity of the notion of race in North America. On the one hand, Williams and his family were forced into an either/or situation. They could be black or white; there was no other option in the middle. In this way, the racial boundaries were preserved intact, albeit differently depending on the state. Yet the fact that Williams and his family suddenly became black also highlights an alternate interpretation of difference. The very fact that one's racial identity can so easily be revised depending on context suggests that it is not inherent in the individual, but is in fact socially constructed. What the essentialist view of difference fails to recognize is that what makes difference important are the meanings that are applied. What we take to be the essence of a given group is a product of the culture and the time in which we live. In Williams's case, the move from one state to another suddenly made him black.

This example also highlights the importance of context in the meanings assigned to difference. Race, class, and gender—all markers of difference—have long been used to signify key categories of social differentiation. But the significance and definitions of most lines of demarcation have varied considerably across time and place. Today, for example, women are assumed to be 'fashion plates', whereas 'in Victorian England, it was men who wore wigs, high heels, stockings and frilly blouses' precisely as signs of masculinity (Wonders, 2009, p. 11). And while skin colour is key to determining race in Canada, in many Latin American countries hair colour and texture are more important. My favourite example of the slippery nature of social categories comes from South Africa:

> Nearly 800 South Africans became officially members of a different race group last year, according to figures quoted in Parliament and based on the Population Registration Act. They included 518 colored who were officially reclassified as white, 14 whites who became

colored, 7 Chinese who became white, 2 whites who became Chinese, 3 Malays who became white, 1 white who became an Indian, 50 Indians who became colored, 54 coloreds who became Indian, 17 Indians who became Malay, 4 coloreds who became Chinese, 1 Malay who became Chinese, 89 blacks who became colored, 5 coloreds who became black. (Uys, 1988, 27)

Like Gregory Williams, hundreds of South Africans became something different literally overnight. In neither case had anything changed but the ways in which people were identified by others. If race had been a biologically given essence, such events could never have taken place. Similarly, if difference were absolute, we would not have to work so hard to maintain distinctions: we would not have to dress little girls in pink and give them dolls to play with or dress little boys in blue and give them trucks to play with. We would not have to post 'Whites Only' signs. Little girls and boys would come to their gender roles naturally, with no tutoring if these differences were in fact organic; people of colour would know where they could and could not go.

You can see how identity is not constant and immutable, but rather is subject to dramatic variation across time and place. The ways in which we define and assess differences today may not have been the case historically or be the case in other locales. As a final illustration, consider homosexuality. Today in Canada, homosexual behaviour is legal, as is same-sex marriage, largely as a result of the broadening of the social acceptance of homosexuality. Until the 1970s, however, same-sex relationships were stigmatized and same-sex behaviour was criminalized. In the United States, the remaining pieces of sodomy legislation—most commonly used to censure same-sex behaviour—have only recently been struck down; and same-sex 'unions' are legal in only five states.

The cultural specificity of definitions of sexuality becomes even clearer if we look beyond North America and beyond the contemporary era. The **stigmatization** of homosexuality is not historically or cross-culturally universal. Biery (1990, p. 10) suggests that what we now refer to as homosexuality really 'began in the nineteenth century when the word was used for the first time.' However, 'a label does not give birth to something. Same-sex affection and eroticism have existed since the beginning of recorded history—and probably long before that.'

Same-sex relationships have flourished in cultures as diverse as Ancient Greece, Medieval England, and contemporary Polynesia. Moreover, the social and moral assessment of such behaviour varies dramatically by time, place, and culture. More so than most cultural groups in North America, Aboriginal people have long held flexible, fluid views of sexuality. Behaviour is more likely to be evaluated according to the appropriateness of the context rather than according to the behaviour itself. Thus, there is no rigid proscription against homosexuality. On the contrary, many Aboriginal traditions refer to the 'Two Spirited' as those who are valued because of their inherent combination of both the male and the female spirits (Tafoya, 1997, p. 8).

Some Asian cultures have traditionally shared, to a certain degree, this tolerant outlook on sexual diversity. Historically, same-sex relationships permeated the upper echelons of Japanese society, including the wealthy urban classes, Buddhist clergy, and the military. In fact, *nanshoku* (male colours) or shudo (way of companions) was so intimately connected to the warrior society that it was often referred to as the 'pastime' of the Samurai. However, while this tradition was readily accepted for centuries, it seems to have become latent since the turn of the century, a phenomenon Miller (1995) attributes to the Westernization of Japan—a process that included a transition in sexual morality.

Difference, then, is not constant. It changes with political, social, and cultural shifts in definitions of what is right and wrong. Additionally, it is interesting to note that difference is not simply something that is created 'out there'. Each of us conspires, consciously or not, to recreate difference either in line with or in contrast to what is generally demanded of us. Race, gender, and sexuality—all the dimensions of identity discussed throughout this text—represent what West and Fenstermaker (1997) refer to as an '**ongoing accomplishment**' (see also Messerschmidt, 1993, 1997; Perry, 2001). Identity is created through conscious, reflective pursuit and must be established and re-established under varied conditions. However, it is important to keep in mind that while each of us plays a key role in mediating difference in our daily lives, our 'ability to define these classifications in [our] own way is always limited' (Newman, 2007, pp. 38–39). In other words, identity construction is an activity concerned with 'managing situated conduct' (West & Zimmerman, 1987, p. 127) according to socially normative expectations of what constitutes, for example, the essence of one's race or gender.

The construction of identity is an interactional accomplishment by which actors perform their 'manliness' or 'womanliness', their 'whiteness' or 'blackness' or 'Asian-ness'. They do so with an eye to how their behaviour will be interpreted or evaluated by others. Central to this understanding is the notion of 'accountability'. At all times, in all situations, actors are concerned with whether their behaviour will be seen to be in accordance with approved standards for their assigned identity. Consequently, '[t]o the extent that members of society know their actions are accountable, they will design their actions in relation to how they might be seen and described by others' (West & Fenstermaker, 1997, p. 25). Since this enactment is situated within existing relations of power, the conduct will generally repeat and thus support those relations (Winant, 1997, p. 505). Conventional culture is consumed with ensuring our awareness of and commitment to traditional notions of gender, sexuality, race, and so on. Movies, advertising, the legal order, even the organization of department stores take for granted the essential differences between such groups. It is in this context that we are continually expected to account for our gendered behaviour, for example.

Difference Assumes a Standard or Norm

The most significant aspect about this positioning of self and other is the fact that it implies the **normativity** of a **hegemonic** form, what Lorde (1995, p. 192) refers to as a '**mythical norm**':

> Somewhere, on the edge of consciousness, there is what I call a *mythical norm*, which each of us within our hearts knows 'that is not me.' In America, this norm is usually defined as white, thin, male, young, heterosexual, Christian and financially secure. It is with this mythical norm that the trappings of power reside within this society.

In Canada, difference has historically been constructed in negative relational terms. A dominant norm such as that suggested by Lorde has been established, against which all others are (unfavourably) judged. This is the case whether we speak in terms of race, class, gender, sexuality, beauty, or any other element of identity. So it is those who are not white or male or Christian or moneyed who are marked or stigmatized as different. They are the alien Others who fall outside the standardized boundaries.

Also implicit in this construction of difference is the assumption of a good/bad opposition. Not only are the Others different; by definition they are also aberrant, deviant, inferior. Structures of oppression operate through a set of dualisms—such as good/evil, superior/inferior, strong/weak, dominant/subordinate—wherein the second half of the binary is always marked as a deficiency relative to the superior capacities and privileges of the norm.

In contrast to these polar opposites, we must keep in mind that different is not inherently inferior. That evaluation is imposed on the Other by the dominant forces in the culture. The marking of the Other as deviant is an interpretive act: 'It is assigning a value to a particular difference in a way that discredits an individual or group to the advantage of another that transforms mere difference into deficiency' (Rothenberg, 1995, p. 11).

The marking of difference as deficiency is a social, political process that has the effect of creating hierarchies along divisions such as race, sexuality, and class. Once a group has been defined as inferior or defective or substandard, it is necessarily assigned a subordinate place in society. This construction of the Other facilitates the unequal distribution of resources and power in such a way that it appears natural and justifiable. Racism, sexism, and homophobia are predicated upon such negative valuations of difference. Women, for example, are deemed inferior by virtue of their 'weakness' or 'irrationality'; Asians by virtue of their 'hyper-rationality'.

This 'oppressive meaning of difference', as Young (1995) expresses it, suggests that social systems prioritize some versions of identity over others, so that subordinate individuals and groups are sure to stay in that position. MacKinnon's observations with respect to gender might just as easily be applied to race or class for example: 'gender is not difference; gender is hierarchy. . . . [T]he idea of gender difference helps keep male dominance in place' (cited in Rothenberg, 1992, p. 60).

Difference Matters

As early as the 1920s, pioneering sociologists William Thomas and Dorothy Thomas uttered a phrase that continues to resonate today: 'If [people] define situations as real, they are real in their consequences' (Thomas & Thomas, 1928, p. 572). So it is with the social construction of difference. Regardless of the fact that it is socially constructed, difference is perceived as real. Importantly, it is because difference is perceived as real that it *matters*—that is, how we see ourselves and are seen by others dramatically affects our life experiences. Our identities often determine the type of education we receive, the type of health care available to us, or the ways in which others respond to us.

Often, what we know, or think we know, about others reflects **prejudice**—a tendency to prejudge, typically in negative terms. Prejudicial attitudes tend to be unfavourable judgments of people because of their group membership. Newman (2007, p. 158) makes the claim that virtually every 'non-normative' group is subject to prejudice such that 'if there's a group of people that is distinctive and identifiable, it's inevitable that someone will find these people unfit, unapproachable, or undesirable.'

Prejudice refers to an attitudinal response to difference; it may have little or no impact unless it becomes manifest in behaviour motivated by negative perceptions of the Other. When prejudice motivates differential treatment, it crosses the line into **discrimination**. This is the behavioural counterpart or outcome of prejudice and refers to behaviours and actions that disadvantage some groups relative to others. Typically, when we think of discrimination, we think of individual actions that one might take against another—a landlord refusing to rent to a gay couple, for example. However, such behaviours are the least of the problems. Discrimination is especially problematic and far-reaching in its effect when it is institutional or structural.

Institutional discrimination refers to 'established laws, customs, policies and practices that systematically reflect and produce inequalities in society' (Newman, 2007, p. 181). There is intent to treat groups differently and in such a way as to reinforce existing relations of power. South African apartheid, for example, was a rigid system of inclusions and exclusions that legally restricted the options of non-whites; and immigration legislation that precludes particular classes of people, or people from particular countries, is intended to exclude and marginalize.

Slightly different is **structural discrimination**, which reflects policies and practices that, on the surface, appear race, gender, class, or nation neutral but nonetheless have disparate effects on different groups. For most of the twentieth century, for example, women were not officially excluded from policing, but rigid weight and height requirements meant that they generally did not have access to this field. The provision of benefits to married partners has tradition-ally meant that gay couples were not afforded the same protections. In such cases, the *intent* to discriminate may not have been present, but the effect was nonetheless inequitable.

One site where it is readily apparent that 'difference matters'—where prejudice and discrimin-ation shape our experiences—is in the context of labour, both reproductive and productive. Despite dramatic strides in women's position in society, they remain the primary caregivers for children, as well as, increasingly, for aging parents. The traditional **public/private-sphere** split remains: women are expected to dominate the home, while men are expected to dominate in business and politics. For example, the 2001 Census reveals that 550,000 women but only 62,000 men were single parents. Moreover, women make up nearly half of the labour force (46 per cent) but tend to remain segregated in relatively low-paid service sector positions. In the 2008 federal election, less than one-quarter of the candidates were women and less than one-third of the winning candidates were women. Even more dramatic is women's representation in powerful executive positions. In 2008, women accounted for only 5.8 per cent (37 of 535) of top executives in Canada's largest 100 companies (CNW Group, 2008). Here, then, one can see how gender places men and women differently with respect to their relationships to both reproduct-ive and productive labour and to family and public sector institutions.

Earlier, I wrote about the presumed essential differences between groups. Because categorical differences between groups are assumed to be accompanied by differences in capacities, there are also dramatic discrepancies in the place and treatment of groups in the context of labour. Thus, the social division of labour represents a valuable support for prevailing structures of inequality along multiple lines, including race, class, gender, and—certainly—country of origin (Connell, 1987, 1995; Pharr, 1995). Moreover, '[t]he method is quite complex: limit education and training opportunities for women and people of color and then withhold adequate paying jobs with the excuse that people of color and women are incapable of filling them' (Pharr, 1995, p. 483).

The essentialist definition of difference discussed earlier affects the social division of labour. On the basis of presumed abilities (or lack thereof), those who are marked as different or inferior or deficient are correspondingly assigned productive and reproductive roles that are held to be in line with their 'natural' tendencies. Predictably, the opportunities are limited to a very narrow range of relatively powerless positions, thereby maintaining and reinforcing their workers' subordinate place. Moreover, **job segregation** into low-wage employment ensures the unequal distribution of income, which is also a hallmark of these relations of domination. Access to material resources—including education, employment, income level—places groups and individuals in relation to one another within the racialized, or gendered, or class hierarchies.

Differential access to and involvement in the labour force persists in Canada. I wrote earlier about women's workplace involvement. We might also consider the patterns of racial differences in employment. Canada's First Nations communities have long been disadvantaged with respect to employment opportunities. A 2007 report by Luffman and Sussman reveals that this remains the case but that the patterns differ regionally:

> Provinces with the highest percentage of Aboriginal people—Manitoba and Saskatchewan—had Aboriginal unemployment rates of about 18 per cent and 22 per cent respectively. This was more than four times the unemployment rate of the non-Aboriginal population in both these provinces. Aboriginal unemployment rates were also high in the Atlantic provinces (where the proportion of Aboriginal people is lower), ranging from 20 per cent in Nova Scotia to 32 per cent in Newfoundland and Labrador. (Luffman & Sussman, 2007)

Moreover, differences in employment rates correspond to differences in employment categories. Especially in the West, Aboriginal Canadians are largely to be found in three types of work: sales and service; trades; and clerical work.

Some of the most dramatic patterns of labour force disparity are to be found among recent immigrants. The 2001 Census found that 65.8 per cent of recent immigrants were employed, in contrast to 81.8 per cent of the Canadian-born population; and their unemployment rate was twice that of Canadian-born workers. In addition, thousands of immigrants are **underemployed**. Immigrants continue to come to this country with relatively high levels of education and experience, yet find themselves in jobs for which they are significantly overqualified. There is a grain of truth to the **stereotype** of the foreign-born and -trained doctor driving a taxi on Canada's streets: 'More than one-half (52 per cent) of recent immigrants with a university degree worked in a job requiring only high school education at some point during the six-year period. This was almost twice the proportion of 28 per cent among their Canadian-born counterparts' (Li, Gervais, & Duval, 2006, p. 8).

Of course, one's position in the labour force is related not only to race, gender, and citizenship status, but also to class. Like Americans, Canadians consider themselves to be living in a relatively classless society, or at the very least in a uniformly middle-class society. Yet recall the continuing relevance of Porter's vertical mosaic as discussed in the opening chapter. Ours is clearly a society stratified by class. Indeed, the polarization of Canada's rich and poor has increased rather than dissipated in recent years. A 2007 report from the Canadian Centre for Policy Alternatives tells us that the gap reached a 30-year high in 2004, such that 'the earnings of the richest 10 per cent of Canada's families raising children was 82 times that earned by the poorest 10 per cent. That is approaching triple the ratio of 1976, which was around 31 times' (Yalnizyan, 2007, p. 3). According to the report, the rich truly are getting richer—30 per cent higher than over a generation ago—and the poor truly are getting poorer—their share of total earnings has dropped from 27 per cent to 20.5 per cent in spite of their working more hours.

Class position shapes myriad aspects of life, from whether and where people take vacations, to the educational attainment of children, to the kinds of food people eat, to the types of leisure activities they can engage in. Consider involvement in Canada's national sport: hockey. A current television commercial shows a young—possibly 12-year-old—boy seeking a job at a diner, where the owner asks him whether he shouldn't be playing hockey or something. The boy replies that this is what he's trying to do. The ad is intended to highlight the fact that one-third of Canadian families cannot afford to have their children engage in the nation's favourite winter pastime. Indeed, with equipment and registration fees, a season's worth of hockey can cost in the thousands. When a parent earning minimum wage must make the choice between paying rent and buying a new pair of skates, the prospective Edmonton Oiler loses out. Contrast this with a family earning above $100,000 a year; this family does not have to make such difficult choices.

Just as identity shapes one's employment and income, so too does it shape the nature and dynamics of one's engagement with the justice system. Indeed, difference matters dramatically in this context, to the extent that it determines whether and in what ways an individual comes into contact with the justice system: as victim, offender, or service provider. This issue was noted briefly in chapter 1, and it is the focus of the greater part of this book. As the contributors to this volume will have a great deal to say on this subject, I will say here only that the justice system is one context in which the implications of difference are, perhaps, the most dramatic.

Difference Involves Relations of Power

The ways in which we construct difference are not random or idiosyncratic; rather they arise out of and reinforce **relations of power**. Indeed, we are not all equally endowed with the power to define which differences matter in which ways. On the contrary, 'he who has the biggest stick has the better chance of imposing his definition of reality' (Berger & Luckmann, 1966, p. 109). Gendered language aside, Berger and Luckmann's assessment remains true. Those in society with the most power—however defined—are in the strongest position to define the realities of difference and thereby create and recreate 'systems of dominance and power that determine where and how important resources like income, wealth, and access to education and health care are distributed' (Newman, 2007, p. 37).

As the preceding quotation implies, the importance of power as a cornerstone of the politics of difference goes beyond purely economic concerns. Power is a much broader concept, encompassing 'the ability to impose a definition of the situation, to set the terms in which events are understood and issues discussed, to formulate ideas and define morality, in short, to assert hegemony' (Connell, 1995, p. 107). Power, then, consists of the ability to set the terms of discourse and action and impose a particular type of order. Again, we might link this to the negative politics of difference in that it seeks to effectively deny the authority of marked Others. Consequently, relations of power might be conceptualized in economic, social, political, or cultural terms. It is because it is manifest in such a range of locations that power becomes such an important structural feature of the relations within and between groups.

Oppression is one of the primary concepts social scientists use to describe the process by which power is employed to create and sustain difference. Simply put, oppression might be understood as a 'dynamic process by which one segment of society achieves power and privilege through the control and exploitation of other groups, which are burdened and pushed down into the lower levels of the social order' (Pincus, 2006, p. 14). In short, oppression is a means of ensuring those on top stay on top, keeping subordinate groups in their place of inferiority. Think of the literal interpretation of the term from the Latin—*ob*, against; and *premere*, to press—to press against. More generally, we use the term to imply the process of pushing down those one seeks to dominate. It is experienced as a series of limitations on one's ability to act freely—as a series of constraints on one's freedom. The classic analogy that helps us understand this complex notion is Marilyn Frye's depiction of a 'birdcage':

> If you look very closely at just one wire in the cage, you cannot see the other wires. If your conception of what is before you is determined by this myopic focus, you could look at one wire, up and down the length of it, and be unable to see why a bird would not just fly around the wire any time it wanted to go somewhere. . . . It is only when you step back, stop looking at the wires one by one, microscopically, and take a macroscopic view of the whole cage, that you can see why the bird does not go anywhere; and then you will see it in a moment. . . . It is perfectly *obvious* that the bird is surrounded by a network of systematically related barriers no one of which would be the least hindrance to its flight, but which, by their relations to each other, are as confining as the solid walls of a dungeon. (Frye, 2007, pp. 31–32)

And so it is with the oppression of subordinate groups in society, the members of whom are systematically oppressed by myriad practices that cross-cut their lives. It is not one event or one set of experiences that creates their disempowerment, but rather the cumulative impact of several mutually reinforcing processes. Think about the oppression of women as a class. You might look at their under-representation in political office; *or* their under-representation in upper-management positions; *or* their extensive patterns of intimate partner victimization; *or* their increased likelihood of being low-income single parents; *or* their representation as sexual objects in the mass media. If you were to consider the effects of any one of these phenomena, you might not understand how it works to 'keep women in their place'. Yet if you were to consider the cumulative effect of this system of barriers, you would readily recognize how they work together to this end.

Specifically, this systematic disadvantaging of women can be referred to as **sexism**. Parallel patterns of oppression characterize experiences along other dimensions of differ-ence. Hence, **racism** refers to the disadvantaging of people of colour; **heterosexism** refers to privileging heterosexuality above other sexualities; **anti-Semitism** refers to the dispar-ate treatment and placement of those of the Jewish faith; and so on. In each of these cases, systematic relations of power contribute to the privileging of an identifiable dominant group relative to a subordinate group. Some might argue that people of colour can be racist or that women can be sexist. While it is true that they might hold particular prejudices or engage in biased behaviour, this does not constitute *racism* or *sexism*. These are characterized by the systemic application of power in such a way as to advantage one group relative to another. In other words, '[n]ot everyone has the power to act on the basis of those prejudices. As long as Euro-Americans continue to control the major political, economic, and social insti-tutions in this country, including the criminal justice system, they have the institutional resources to discriminate, whereas people of color do not' (Zatz & Mann, 2006, p. 4). For instance, black people as a group are not in a position to constrain the choices and actions of white people as a group; nor are workers as a group in a position to thwart the capacities of capitalists as a group. In these examples, neither black people nor workers have the social, economic, political, or cultural power to affect the life chances of white people or capitalists, respectively.

Differences Are Multiple and Overlapping

Throughout this chapter, and indeed this book, the emphasis is on the diverse experiences of discrete groups. However, this should not blind us to the fact that while each of the identities that we discuss retains its own specificity and internal (il)logic, they are also interlocking struc-tures of domination (Crenshaw, 1994; Anderson & Hill Collins, 1995; West & Fenstermaker, 1997). Thus, it is both the independent and combined effects of these dimensions that condi-tion actions, interactions, opportunities, and privilege. Nonetheless, the salience and impact of these interactive structures of power are situationally specific. In different contexts, in different institutional settings, one structure may be more visible or dramatic in its impact or different combinations might prevail. In other words, from situation to situation, the nature and depth of the interactive effects of race, class, sexuality, gender, and age, for example, will be distinct.

Hence, while gender may come to the fore in the context of the family, the combination of race and gender may be more salient in the criminal justice system or sexuality may be the most relevant dimension at a Gay Pride Parade.

This concept has come to be known as **intersectionality**. We simultaneously occupy multiple subject positions or identities. So I am at once a woman, white, middle class, and a professor. I am relatively advantaged by each of these dimensions, with the exception of my gender. So I might expect, over my lifetime, to earn less than my male counterparts but perhaps more than colleagues who are people of colour. Kimberlé Crenshaw (1994) was among the first scholars to highlight academic neglect of the 'intersection of racism and patriarchy'. We might add other categories of difference to this equation such that we attend not only to the intersection of racism and patriarchy, but also to that of heterosexuality, class, religion, and disability. All women do not experience their gender in the same ways; they experience it through the prisms of the other elements of their identity. Similarly, to be 'working class' is to experience life differently depending on one's ethnicity, religion, or sexuality.

Consider women's experience of gendered violence. Women of colour may be uniquely vulnerable to this form of violence because of their multiply determined structural disempowerment. As a second illustration, consider how anti-gay violence crosscuts ethnicity. Violence perpetrated against gays by men of colour crosses the axes of race, gender, and sexuality. In other words, regardless of race or ethnicity, masculinity, in particular, assumes heterosexuality. bell hooks (1990, 1992, 1994, 1995) returns again and again to the tendency of black males to demand compulsory heterosexuality. In this sense, gay men, especially black and Latino gay men, are further marginalized within their racial communities, since they are simultaneously 'race traitors' and 'gender traitors'. Gay men of colour are outsiders on all three of the axes of identity—gender, sexual, and racial. Ultimately, then, our identities and life chances are dramatically affected not by one element of who we are, but by multiple, crosscutting, and sometimes contradictory positions.

Difference Can Be Reconstructed

One of the themes that has dominated this chapter is that difference is socially constructed. As you will see in the next section, difference is supported by an array of facilitative mechanisms, such as stereotypes, language, legislation, and job segregation. It is apparent, for instance, that stereotyping Aboriginal people as 'savages', criminalizing the sexuality of gay men and lesbians, and excluding Asians from citizenship have served to maintain the stigmatized outsider identity of these Others. It is also apparent that these Others have been defined negatively in terms of their relationship to some dominant norm—that is, that 'black' is defined as inherently inferior to 'white', Jewish to Christian, gay to straight. Nonetheless, there is reason to hope. To the extent that difference is socially constructed, it can also be socially reconstructed. In other words, as a society, we can redefine the ways in which difference 'matters'. We can strive for a just and democratic society in which the full spectrum of diversity addressed here is re-evaluated in a positive and celebratory light.

In other words, an insurgent politics of difference can conceivably reconstruct both the cultural and institutional supports for particular ways of doing and valuing difference. Such changes, of course, will not occur magically or out of the beneficence of the state or some imagined hegemonic bloc. On the contrary, they will require the concentrated efforts of grass-roots mobilizations. The new social movements that did the transformative labour of the last half of the twentieth century must continue to extend the early gains in the workplace, in the home, and in the public imagination. The remaining structures and supports for oppressive constructions of difference must be undercut through movements oriented around the positive politics of difference.

We would do well to heed Young's (1990) advice that we embrace a positive politics of difference. This would involve much more than efforts to assimilate Others or merely tolerate their presence. Rather, it would challenge us to celebrate our differences. Of course, this would require that much of our current way of ordering the world be radically altered. It would mean that we must cease to define 'different' as inferior and see it instead as simply not the same. As Minow (1990, p. 377) states so elegantly, 'Changing the ways we classify, evaluate, reward, and punish may make the differences we had noticed less significant . . . irrelevant or even a strength. The way things are is not the only way things could be.'

This pursuit of a positive politics of difference is not an abolitionist project. Nor should it be allowed to become one. The heart of the agenda is not oriented around colour (or gender) blindness or neutrality. Both the liberal assimilationist and radical abolitionist models run the risk of occluding the persistent reality of oppression and disadvantages that accrue to difference. Only by acknowledging difference can we recognize its effects. Consequently, our goal must be a transformative politics that empowers difference: 'I am just what they say I am—a Jewboy, a colored girl, a fag, a dyke, or a hag—and proud of it. No longer does one have the impossible project of trying to become something one is not, under circumstances where the very trying reminds one of who one is' (Young, 1990, p. 166). This is doing difference differently, under different ground rules where enacting one's identity is not an occasion for potential rebuke. Rather, doing difference becomes a risk-free expression of one's culture, perspectives, and insights.

To engage in such a powerful politics is to resist the temptation to ask all Others to conform to an artificial set of norms and expectations. It is to reclaim and value the natural heterogeneity of this nation rather than force a false homogeneity. It is to refuse to denigrate the culture and experiences of black people, women, or gay men and lesbians, for example. It is to learn and grow from the strength and beauty that alternative cultures have to offer.

Given the historical and contemporary processes revealed in this book, reconstructing the meaning and value associated with difference will be no easy task. It will require dramatic changes in attitudes and behaviours throughout society. Each contributor to this volume—and especially those featured in the concluding section—has been asked to consider policies and practices that will facilitate the creation of an alternative vision of difference that will preclude the exclusion and disempowerment of the Other.

Mechanisms for Constructing Difference

In this chapter, I have mentioned in passing at various points that difference is created and maintained through a number of diverse mechanisms and sites. In the next few pages, I will touch briefly on what I see to be some of the key strategies. The list is clearly not exhaustive, but it reflects my own perspective. Moreover, the discussion is intended to provide only a skeletal introduction to the themes taken up in the rest of the book. I leave it to the authors in Part 2 to give these bones some flesh as they address the concrete experiences of particular groups.

The strategies and sites that I discuss below constitute integral parts of our legal and non-legal **culture**. Cultural artifacts and practices intersect with other structural patterns to give rise to relations of inequality. Speaking of the production of culture, Fiske contends that 'all meanings of self, of social relations, all the discourses and texts that play such important cultural roles can circulate only in relation to the social system . . . Culture . . . and meanings . . . are centrally involved in the distribution and possible redistribution of various forms of social power' (cited in Apple, 1997, p. 124). Culture, then, is crucial to shaping the social construction of patterns of inequality. It is in the realm of culture that we find the meanings, the significance, and the roles assigned to self and Other.

Culture is a vast complex that spans the breadth from political discourse, to ideological constructs, to media representations, to religious dogma. In the most coherent and perhaps authoritarian cultures, each of these would correspond exactly. However, in Western culture—presumed to be more open and democratic—the fit is much looser. Nonetheless, even in Canada and the United States, it is possible to detect a relatively consistent discursive formation as described by Goldberg (1990, p. 297):

> a totality of ordered relations and correlations—of subjects to each other and to objects; of economic production and reproduction, cultural symbolism, and signification; of laws and moral rules; of social, political, economic or legal inclusion and exclusion. The socio-discursive formation consists of a range of rules: 'is's' and 'oughts', 'do's' and 'dont's', 'cans' and 'cannots', 'thou shalts' and 'thou shalt nots'.

Culture acts to spread and in fact normalize particular representations of groups independently and in relation to others—in ways that reinforce hierarchical patterns. Thus, those characteristics of groups, those natural predispositions discussed previously, find expression in cultural processes. As I discuss below, they are institutionalized in the language we use, in ideologies and stereotypes of racial or gender inferiority, in laws that marginalize or exclude particular groups and individuals, and in media depictions that demonize the Other.

Language

Language is a key means by which we transmit our culture. Moreover, it is the main way in which we communicate about—and thus construct—difference. The very words we choose and use shape our individual and collective realities. They suggest relationships, place, and status, both implicitly and explicitly. For many years now, I have asked students in my diversity courses to read Robert Moore's (2007) article on racism in the English language, along with Nilsen's (1993) parallel article on sexist language and Gans's (2007) article on the language of class. Together, these are remarkably thought-provoking pieces of scholarship that often change the way students think about and use language. As there is significant overlap, I will primarily use Moore's article to illustrate the power of language to differentiate between groups in ways that reinforce presumed relations of power. What I offer is a very brief synopsis, but I heartily recommend that you read each of the articles to get the full flavour.

Moore offers a catalogue of mechanisms by which the English language perpetuates racist values and beliefs. The first among these, **obvious bigotry**, refers to the derogatory language that is still used in reference to marginalized social groups. We are all familiar with the common slurs used to refer to diverse racialized communities, women, and members of the LGBT community. I need not repeat those here. Yet other groups—the elderly, people with disabilities, even poor people—are also frequently subject to less than complimentary labels. In spite of widespread recognition of the offensiveness of these terms, such epithets continue to be used, particularly behind closed doors. **Gendered language**, too, is a form of bigotry. When we use 'he' or 'his' to describe the generic person, that person becomes male. Gendered language is an exclusive rather than inclusive means of communicating ideas. Some forms of bigoted language are so deeply embedded in our culture that we are not even aware of their connotations and so continue to use them. While we would generally not even consider using the 'N' word in public, many of us have no such qualms about such terms as 'welshed on the deal' (resident of Wales) or getting 'gypped' (Gypsy).

Colour symbolism refers to the colour terms used to describe particular groups. Most obvious, of course, are black and white, but we have also used the terms 'red', 'brown', and 'yellow' to refer to specific racial groups. We tend not to think carefully about the connotations of these terms in the way we use them. Clearly, 'white' suggests purity and cleanliness and 'black' the polar opposite—darkness and filth. 'Brown' has similar connotations, and 'yellow' suggests disease. The adoption of these signifiers was itself a political and cultural process of differentiation emphasizing the 'rightness of whiteness' (Moore, 2007, p. 368).

The use of the *passive tense* in describing the experiences of subordinate groups is a means of rendering the experiences and their implications invisible. So, for example, 'history texts will discuss how European immigrants came to the United States seeking a better life and expanded opportunities, but will note that *"slaves were brought here"*' (Moore, 2007, p. 370) in a way that minimizes the destructive impacts of a brutal slave trade orchestrated by white merchants. Nilsen offers a slightly different take on passive/active roles with respect to men and women, drawing attention, first, to traditional Western marriage ceremonies, which include the father of the bride giving her away, and then to women's virginity, which she 'loses' because he has 'taken' it. In both cases, women's agency or ability to act consciously and independently is denied.

Much of the language that we use to describe the Other is value laden. Gans (2007) highlights the inherent bias in the use of the term 'underclass' to describe the poor, for example. He argues that the term has come to have decidedly racial and evaluative undertones, implying that its members are predominantly black and thoroughly 'undeserving' by virtue of the inherent characteristics of sloth and laziness. Similarly, we commonly use the phrase 'underdeveloped' to describe Third World nations in a way that implies some failure on their part, rather than their hyper-exploitation by richer nations.

Value-laden language is akin to what Moore (2007) refers to as **loaded words** or phrases that often distort the nature of relationships between groups. A classic example is the use of the word 'discover' with reference to Columbus's experience in what is now North America. To refer to it in such a way denies the prior existence of rich and sophisticated cultures from coast to coast. Since the September 11 terrorist attacks, Muslims have found themselves subjects of similarly loaded language, as media reports feature the excessive use of such words as 'fundamentalist' or 'extremist'.

Finally, we often use *qualifying adjectives* in speaking of traditionally marginalized groups. It is not uncommon to hear others refer to their 'black' doctor, 'male' nurse, or 'coherent' elder. The use of such descriptors implies some deviation from the norm or from what we expect. We see another side of this in media reports that call attention to 'black suspects' but not their white counterparts. Here, stereotypes are reaffirmed rather than challenged.

Stereotypes

The kinds of language patterns noted above both reflect and create stereotypes that come to define difference. Applying stereotypes is a typical, virtually universal strategy for marginalizing, if not stigmatizing, the Other. By *stereotype*, we mean an overgeneralization about the traits shared by members of a group. It reflects the tendency to assume that everyone who occupies a particular identity position will carry with them the same anticipated set of behaviours, beliefs, values, or other characteristics. Stereotypes provide a shorthand by which we can make sense of the world and our place in it. They allow us to easily place people into pre-arranged categories so that we 'know' what to expect of them when we interact. Moreover, they are relatively resistant to change, regardless of evidence to the contrary. Those people who do not fit the mould will be taken to be exceptions to the rule.

The realm of stereotypes and popular images justifies and underlies the differential treatment of subordinate groups. In line with an essentialist understanding of difference, the overriding theme is that of inscribed traits wherein 'the stereotypes confine them to a nature which is often attached in some way to their bodies, and which thus cannot easily be denied' (Young, 1990, p. 59). The very process of racializing First Nations communities, for example, is itself essential to the denial of nationhood. Hundreds of self-sufficient, autonomous nations are reduced to a single homogeneous collective known as 'Indians'. They are reduced in status to just another minority group, sharing undifferentiated characteristics—and typically unflattering characteristics at that.

Stereotypes that distinguish the Other from the dominant norm noted above are grounded in what are held to be the identifying features of the secondary group(s). They help to distance white from not white; male from female; Christian from non-Christian; able-bodied from disabled. The latter among each of these pairings are to be feared, ridiculed, and loathed for their differences as recognized in the popular psyche. Almost invariably, the stereotypes are loaded with disparaging associations suggesting inferiority, irresponsibility, immorality, and non-humanness, for example. Consequently, they provide both motive and rationale for existing hierarchies. Acting upon these interpretations allows dominant group members to recreate 'their' norm of superiority while castigating the Other for their presumed traits and behaviours.

Once identified as Other, no minority racial group can escape the application of labels that are held to apply to the group as a whole. Most communities of colour share the unfortunate fate of being characterized as dishonest and deceitful. In extreme cases, the whole group—and especially males—may be painted as criminal, as violent, thieving, sexual predators. Several racial groups are also identified as lazy and unambitious. The high unemployment rates of these groups are taken as a sign of their unwillingness to work, rather than as a sign of the structural discrimination that precludes them from rewarding and high-paying jobs. Gay men are not to be trusted as teachers or scout leaders, since the common stereotype holds them to be 'diseased' at best, pedophiles at worst.

Individuals enter each social interaction carrying with them the baggage that holds these stereotypical images, and criminal justice practitioners are certainly no exception to this pattern. Police, for example, represent the front-line troops in the effort to maintain the social order. As such, they carry into their interactions with diverse groups the same stockpile of stereotypes and images that shapes the broader patterns of cultural imperialism. Neugebauer (2000, p. 87) argues that police use racial identity as a resource to the extent that they 'generalize situations in terms of fixed racist stereotypes located in both the occupational and the popular culture.' Consequently, the discriminatory practices that follow from these attitudes are in large part an outcome of negative stereotypes retained by law enforcement. Thus, it is not uncommon for people of colour, for example, to report name-calling and racial slurs directed at them by police officers (Neugebauer, 2000; Perry, 2009).

Where youth—especially youth of colour—are involved, the labelling takes a slightly different tone, mirroring the more general tendency to presume gang affiliation among young men of colour. A Native American youth whom I interviewed in Montana claimed, with a circle of peers nodding their heads in agreement, that 'if they see a bunch of us together, they think we're in a gang or doing drugs or getting ready to do something wrong. They don't treat us right.' In short, they suspected that police were always ready to think the worst of them, to diminish their worth by reverting to gross and inaccurate generalizations about Native Americans.

It is not just potential suspects who may fall prey to negative images. Victims, too, are often viewed through the same uncomplimentary lens. It is a truism within criminology that, from a law enforcement perspective, there are deserving victims and undeserving victims.; that is, there are those whose victimization can and should be taken seriously and those whose parallel experiences should not. Too often people of colour are thought to fall into the latter category. Somehow, injury, loss, or damage that affects them is less serious and thus less worthy of either immediate or concentrated attention. So entrenched is the vision of racialized groups as inherently suspect that law enforcement seems reluctant to acknowledge them as victims. They can be only one or the other from this perspective—either victims or offenders—and it is much more in line with the stereotypical Other to see them as somehow at fault. Should they present themselves as victims, it can only be because they have somehow brought it upon themselves— they have provoked their victimization or deserved it by virtue of their own behaviour.

Media Images

The disparate treatments of criminals and victims are reinforced by the popular media. The diverse media are important sites from which our perceptions of difference and crime are derived. It is from the movies, newspapers, even cartoons, for example, that many of us first learn about the 'essential' differences between groups. There, discriminatory language and stereotypes abound. The media descriptions and labels attached to crime and justice are themselves complicit in the social construction of difference, especially with respect to class. Corporate wrongdoings, for example, are typically much more harmful and widespread in their impact than most index crimes. Toxic waste seeps into our groundwater, affecting extensive environmental chains of flora and fauna. The impacts are geographically broad and long-lasting. Yet such offences are much more likely to be described as 'regulatory violations' than as crimes. We refer to 'industrial accidents' as opposed to 'brutal murders', 'misappropriation of funds' rather than 'theft', and 'collateral damage' rather than 'assault'. Each of the dualisms suggests that the social harms committed by the powerful are somehow less threatening and damaging than their counterparts on the streets.

There are identifiable ways by which media shape our reality. First, 'the media often provide our first and only point of contact with the world out there' (Fleras & Elliott, 2002, p. 181). In spite of the growing diversity of our nation, many people have little or no contact with those who are not like them—who are not white, Christian, or heterosexual, for example. Thus, the only knowledge they have is gained through various media sources. To the extent that media perpetuate stereotypes, what people thus 'know' may not be an accurate reflection of the Other. Based as they often are on simplified and stereotypical caricatures of particular groups, media images 'miscast' the Other:

> This miscasting seems to have fallen into a pattern: minorities have been trivialized as irrelevant or inferior, *or* demonized as a social menace and threat to society, *or* scapegoated as problem people creating social problems, *or* ridiculed for being too different or not different enough, *or* "projected" through the prism of Eurocentric fears and fantasies, *or* subjected to double-standards that lampoon minorities regardless of what they do or don't do. (Fleras & Elliott, 2002, p. 160)

The media define for us what is culturally acceptable and desirable. They reinforce notions of normativity and deviance, thereby supporting prevailing ideologies and hierarchies. As noted previously, these definitions can be very rigid, allowing little room for variation. It is through the media, for example, that young girls learn about the standards of beauty to which they should aspire. Typically, these are standards that preclude those who are not white, who are not underweight, and who do not have any visible disability. Similarly, the media shapes our understanding of acceptable and unacceptable relationships. The emphasis is on heterosexual monogamous relationships. However, the media also teach us lessons about preserving the 'colour line' through their representations of intimate interracial relationships. The prevailing trend has been either to deny their existence by rendering them invisible or to portray them as unnatural border crossings. As bell hooks reminds us, 'True love in television and movies is almost always an occurrence between those who share the same race. When love happens across boundaries as in *The Bodyguard*, *Zebraland*, or *A Bronx Tale*, it is doomed for no apparent reason and/or has tragic consequences' (hooks, 1995, p. 113). The moral of such stories is that difference is inviolable; border crossing is unnatural and unacceptable.

Legislation

Oftentimes, lessons about what is acceptable and unacceptable are embedded in the law of the land. Returning to the question of interracial relationships, it is important to keep in mind that **miscegenation** has been explicitly outlawed in most Western nations. The United States was especially renowned for its legal strictures against interracial relationships (i.e., miscegenation); as early as 1662, Virginia became the first state in the New World to enact legislation prohibiting miscegenation. It would take over 300 years for such prohibitions to be repealed by edict of the Supreme Court of America in 1967. In the intervening years, legal regulation of interracial relationships in the United States would take myriad, often contradictory, forms, allowing 'sexual transgress' between white men and some women of colour but not others, while generally banning similar relationships between white women and any men of colour. As late as the twentieth century, it was a federal offence in the United States to transport white women across state lines for immoral purposes, with the result that black men travelling with white women were subject to criminal prosecution. Moreover, in 1924 Virginia enacted the provocatively titled 'Bill to Preserve the Integrity of the White Race', which prohibited any white/non-white union. By the time of the 1967 *Loving* decision, 11 states still had anti-miscegenation legislation on the books.

The law can effectively exclude or restrict the actions and options of particular groups, just as immigration and naturalization laws have historically prevented many Asians from entry or from attaining citizenship. Exclusive policies raise questions about the particular groups' legitimacy and place in Canadian society; in some cases, they explicitly define their 'outsider' status. In other words, the law is a dramatic form of political and cultural expression that 'draws the boundaries that divide us into groups, with momentous effects on our individual identities' (Karst, 1993, p. 2). The law is implicated in the shaping and valuing of difference. It is an integral part of the field in which difference is constructed and reaffirmed, an integral mechanism by which the boundaries between Us and Them are policed.

The law plays a crucial role, too, in the **criminalization** of particular groups. Most critical criminologists would argue that the criminal law is in fact constructed according to white, middle-class norms, with the explicit intent to constrain the 'dangerous classes' by closely regulating and in fact outlawing their behaviours. Like difference, crime is also socially constructed.

Few behaviours are universally considered taboo. Michalowski (1985, p. 15), for example, reminds us that it is a myth that 'there exists some universally consistent definition of theft and violence as criminal acts.' On the contrary, both as a category and as a social phenomenon in and of itself, crime is 'dynamic and in a state of constant movement and change, rather than static and fixed' (Bowling, 1993, p. 238).

For the most part, then, crime reflects conscious politicized choices about which behaviours are to be allowed and which are not, and does so in such a way as to reinforce hierarchies of power. Crime is relative; it is historically and culturally contingent. For example, what we take as hate crime in Canada today may be, in another time, in another place, standard operating procedure. Across the Western world, until the 1980s it was perfectly acceptable and legal to assault, even rape, one's wife, thereby reflecting the gendered order. In Canada, spousal rape was not criminalized until 1982; and in the United States, some states continue to allow for mitigated sentencing in the case of marital rape.

The law is also complicit in the criminalization of racialized communities. Indeed, Jiwani's (2002) engaging title 'The Criminalization of "Race", the Racialization of Crime' infers the link between the two. The classic text *Policing the Crisis* (Hall et al., 1978) clearly articulated the racialization of social problems, whereby people of colour are framed as an inherent threat to public safety and thus (over)policed accordingly. They have been 'historically the targets of **moral panics** and continue to be stereotyped as the criminal "other"' (Mirchandi & Chan, 2002, p. 15). Symons (2002) provides an intriguing example. Looking at Montreal police practice, she observes that they identify five 'ethnic' gangs in the city: Jamaican, Haitian, Asiatic, extreme right, and Latino. What is interesting here is that all but the 'extreme right' gang are identified by ethnic or racial affiliation; the outlier is defined by activity, in spite of the fact that it, too, tends to be identifiable according to racial membership. The extreme right across the Western world is by and large a white movement. Thus, the categorization contributes to 'the racialization of the street gang issue' and the criminalization of ethnic minorities, but not white ethnic groups (117).

In the chapters that follow, scholars from across Canada will apply much more concretely the conceptual issues I have raised here. They will examine the ways in which diverse groups have been subject to very similar patterns of marginalization, victimization, and criminalization, while also acknowledging the ongoing efforts to resist and overturn these patterns.

Key Terms

anti-Semitism
colour symbolism
criminalization
culture
discrimination
essentialism
gender
gendered language
hegemony
heterosexism

institutional
    discrimination
intersectionality
job segregation
loaded words
marginalization
media images
miscegenation
moral panic
multiculturalism

mythical norm
normativity
obvious bigotry
ongoing accomplish-
ment
oppression
prejudice
public/private sphere
race
racism
relations of power

sexism
sexuality
social construction
    of difference
stereotype
stigmatization
structural
    discrimination
underemployed

Questions for Critical Thought

1. Define and differentiate among individual, institutional, and structural discrimination. Provide concrete examples of each.

2. What is meant by the 'social construction' of race? Of gender? Of class? Illustrate your response with reference to historical and cultural differences in the meanings/implications of the terms.

3. Define 'stereotype' in your own words. Why do stereotypes persist? Identify ads/commercials that seem to reflect popular stereotypes of two to three different groups.

Additional Readings

Chan, W., & Mirchandi, K. (Eds.). (2002). *Crimes of colour: Racialization and the criminal justice system in Canada*. Toronto: Broadview Press.

Newman, D. (2007). *Identities and Inequalities*. Boston: McGraw-Hill.

Yalnizyan, A. (2007). *The rich and the rest of us: The changing face of Canada's growing gap*. Toronto: Canadian Centre for Policy Alternatives.

Websites of Interest

Beyond Prejudice: www.beyondprejudice.com

Canadian Race Relations Foundation: www.crr.ca

Media Awareness Network: www.media-awareness.ca

References

Amnesty International. (2004). *Threat and humiliation: Racial profiling, domestic security, and human rights in the United States.* New York: Amnesty International.

Anderson, M., & Hill Collins, P. (1995). Preface to Part 4. In M. Anderson & P. Hill Collins (Eds), *Race, class and gender: An anthology* (pp. 350–362). Belmont, CA: Wadsworth.

Apple, M. (1997). Consuming the Other: Whiteness, education and cheap French fries. In M. Fine, L. Weis, L. Powell, & L. Mun Wong (Eds), *Off white: Readings on race, power and society* (pp. 121–128). New York: Routledge.

Babooram, A. (2008). *The changing profile of adults in custody, 2006/2007.* Ottawa: Statistics Canada. Retrieved January 8, 2009, from www.statcan.gc.ca/pub/85-002-x/2008010/article/10732-eng.pdf

Berger, P.L., & Luckmann, T. (1966). *The social construction of reality.* Garden City, NY: Anchor.

Biery, R. (1990). *Understanding homosexuality: The pride and the prejudice.* Austin: Edward-William Publishing Company.

Bowling, B. (1993). Racial harassment and the process of victimization. *British Journal of Criminology, 33*(2), 231–250.

Brennan, S., & Taylor-Butts, A. (2008). *Sexual assault in Canada 2004 and 2007.* Ottawa: Statistics Canada. Retrieved January 8, 2009, from www.statcan.gc.ca/pub/85f0033m/85f0033m2008019-eng.pdf

Chartrand, L., & McKay, C. (2006). *A review of research on criminal victimization and First Nations, Métis and Inuit Peoples 1990 to 2001.* Ottawa: Department of Justice Canada. Retrieved January 8, 2009, from www.justice.gc.ca/eng/pi/rs/rep-rap/2006/rr06_vic1/index.html

CNW Group. (2008). *Fewer women holding top executive positions in Canada.* Retrieved January 2, 2009, from www.newswire.ca/en/releases/archive/January2008/15/c8967.html

Connell, R. (1987). *Gender and power.* Stanford, CA: Stanford University Press.

Connell, R. (1995). *Masculinities.* Berkeley: University of California Press.

Crenshaw, K. (1994). Mapping the margins: Intersectionality, identity and violence against women of color. In M. Albertson Fineman & R. Mykitiuk (Eds), *The public nature of private violence* (pp. 93–118). New York: Routledge.

Fleras, A., & Elliott, J. 2002. *Engaging diversity: Multi-culturalism in Canada.* Toronto: Nelson Thomson Learning.

Frye, M. (2007). Oppression. In P. Rothenberg (Ed.), *Race, class, and gender in the United States* (7th ed., pp. 154–157). New York: Worth.

Gans, P. (2007). Deconstructing the underclass. In P. Rothenberg (Ed.), *Race, class, and gender in the United States* (7th ed., pp. 102–107). New York: Worth.

Goldberg, D. T. (1990). The social formation of racist discourse. In D. T. Goldberg (Ed.), *Anatomy of racism* (pp. 295–318). Minneapolis: University of Minnesota Press.

Goudreau, J-P. (2002). *A statistical profile of persons working in justice-related professions in Canada, 1996.* Ottawa: Statistics Canada. Retrieved January 10, 2009, from http://dsp-psd.tpsgc.gc.ca/Collection-R/Statcan/85-555-XIE/0009685-555-XIE.pdf

Hall, S., Critcher, C., Jefferson, T., Clarke, T., & Roberts, B. (1978). *Policing the crisis.* London: Macmillan.

hooks, b. (1990). *Yearning.* Boston: South End Press.

hooks, b. (1992). *Black looks.* Boston: South End Press.

hooks, b. (1994). *Outlaw Culture.* New York: Routledge.

hooks, b. (1995). *Killing rage: Ending racism.* New York: Henry Holt and Company.

Jiwani, Y. (2002). The criminalization of 'race', the racialization of crime. In W. Chan & K. Mirchandi (Eds.), *Crimes of colour: Racialization and the criminal justice system in Canada* (pp. 67–86). Toronto: Broadview Press.

Karst, K. (1993). *Law's promise, law's expression.* New Haven, CT: Yale University Press.

Krakauer, L., & Chen, C. (2003). Gender barriers in the legal profession: Implications for career development of female law students. *Journal of Employment Counseling, 40*(2), 65–79.

Leadership Conference on Civil Rights. (2002). *Justice on trial: Racial disparities in the American criminal justice system.* Washington: LCCR.

Li, C., Gervais, G., & Duval, A. (2006). *The dynamics of overqualification: Canada's underemployed university graduates.* Ottawa: Statistics Canada. Retrieved January 2, 2009, from www.statcan.gc.ca/pub/11-621-m/2006039/4054348-eng.htm

Lorde, A. (1995). Age, race, class and sex: Women redefining difference. In J. Arthur & A. Shapiro (Eds), *Campus wars: Multiculturalism and the politics of difference* (pp. 191–198). Boulder, CO: Westview.

Luffman, J., & Sussman, D. (2007). The Aboriginal labour force in Western Canada. *Perspectives on labour and income, 8*(1). Retrieved January 2, 2009, from www.statcan.gc.ca/pub/75-001-x/10107/9570-eng.htm#aut

McLachlin, B. (2003). *The civilization of difference.* LaFontain-Baldwin Symposium Lecture, Halifax.

Messerschmidt, J. (1993). *Masculinities and crime.* Lanham, MD: Rowman and Littlefield.

Messerschmidt, J. (1997). *Crime as structured action.* Thousand Oaks, CA: Sage.

Michalowski, R. (1985). *Order, law and crime.* New York: Random House.

Miller, N. (1995). *Out of the past: Gay and lesbian history from 1969 to the present.* New York: Vintage Press.

Minow, M. (1990). *Making all the difference: Inclusion, exclusion and American law.* Ithaca, NY: Cornell University Press.

Mirchandi, K., & Chan, W. (2002). From race and crime to racialization and criminalization. In W. Chan & K. Mirchandi (Eds), *Crimes of colour: Racialization and the criminal justice system in Canada* (pp. 9–22). Toronto: Broadview Press.

Moore, R. B. (2007). Racist stereotyping in the English language. In M. Andersen & P. Hill Collins (Eds), *Race, class and gender: An anthology* (6th ed., pp. 365–375). Belmont, CA: Thomson-Wadsworth.

Neugebauer, R. (2000). Kids, cops and colour: The social organization of police-minority youth relations. In R. Neugebauer (Ed.), *Criminal injustice: Racism in the criminal justice system* (pp. 83–108). Toronto: Canadian Scholars' Press.

Newman, D. (2007). *Identities and inequalities.* Boston: McGraw-Hill.

Nilsen, A. (1993). Sexism in English: A 1990s update. In V. Cyrus (Ed.), *Experiencing race, class and gender in the United States* (pp. 159–165). Mountain View, CA: Mayfield.

Ogrodnik, L. (2008). *Family violence in Canada: A statistical profile.* Ottawa: Statistics Canada. Retrieved January 8, 2009, from www.statcan.gc.ca/pub/85-224-x/85-224-x2008000-eng.pdf

Omi, M., & Winant, H. (1994), *Racial formation in the United States* (2nd ed.). New York: Routledge.

Ontario Human Rights Commission. (2003). *Paying the price: The human cost of racial profiling.* Toronto: Ontario Human Rights Commission.

Perry, B. (2001). *In the name of hate: Understanding hate crime.* New York: Routledge.

Perry, B. (2009). *Policing race and place: Under- and over-policing in Indian Country.* Lanham, MD: Lexington.

Pharr, S. (1995). Homophobia as a weapon of sexism. In P. Rothenberg (Ed.), *Race, class and gender in the United States* (3rd ed., pp. 481–490). New York: St Martin's Press.

Pincus, F. (2006). *Understanding diversity.* Boulder, CO: Lynne Rienner.

prisonjustice.ca. (2008). *Facts and statistics.* www.prisonjustice.ca/politics/facts_stats.html

Rothenberg, P. (1992). The construction, deconstruction and reconstruction of difference. In R. Baird & S. Rosenbaum (Eds), *Bigotry, prejudice and hatred* (pp. 47–64). Buffalo: Prometheus.

Rothenberg, P. (1995). Introduction. In P. Rothenberg (Ed.), *Race, class and gender in the United States* (3rd ed., pp. 1–12). New York: St Martin's Press.

Rowe, M. (2004). *Policing, race and racism.* Devon, UK: Willan.

Royal Commission on Aboriginal Peoples. (1996). *Bridging the cultural divide: A report on Aboriginal People and criminal justice.* Ottawa: Royal Commission on Aboriginal People.

Silver, W., Mihorean, K., & Taylor-Butts, A. (2004). *Hate crime in Canada.* Catalogue no. 85-002-XPE, vol. 24, no. 4. Ottawa: Statistics Canada.

Statistics Canada. (2005, November 24). General Social Survey. *The Daily.* Retrieved January 8, 2009, from www.statcan.gc.ca/daily-quotidien/051124/dq051124b-eng.htm

Stone, V., & Tuffin, R. (2000). *Attitudes of people from minority ethnic communities towards a career in the police service.* London: Home Office.

Symons, G. (2002). Police constructions of race and gender in street gangs. In W. Chan & K. Mirchandi (Eds), *Crimes of colour: Racialization and the criminal justice system in Canada* (pp. 115–126). Toronto: Broadview Press.

Tafoya, T. (1997). Native gay and lesbian issues: Two spirited. In B. Greene (Ed.), *Ethnic and cultural diversity among lesbians and gay men* (pp. 1–10). Thousand Oaks, CA: Sage.

Thomas, W. I., & Thomas, D. 1928. *The child in America.* New York: Knopf.

Uys, P. D. (1988, September 23). Chameleons thrive under apartheid. *The New York Times*, p. 27(N).

West, C. (1994). *Race matters.* New York: Vintage.

West, C., & Fenstermaker, S. (1993). Power, inequality and the accomplishment of gender: An ethnomethodological view. In P. England (Ed.), *Theory on gender/feminism on theory* (pp. 151–174). Hawthorne, NY: Aldine de Gruyter.

West, C., & Fenstermaker, S. (1995). Doing difference. *Gender and Society, 9*(1), 8–37.

West, C., & Zimmerman, D. (1987). Doing gender. *Gender and Society, 1*(2), 125–151.

Whitfield, J. (2004). *Unhappy dialogue: The Metropolitan Police and black Londoners in post-war Britain*. Devon, UK: Willan.

Williams, G. (1995). *Life on the color line: The true story of a white boy who discovered he was black*. New York: Dutton.

Winant, H. (1997). Where culture meets structure. In D. Kendall (Ed.), *Race, class and gender in a diverse society* (pp. 27–38). Boston: Allyn and Bacon.

Wonders, N. (2009). Conceptualizing difference. In the Criminology and Criminal Justice Collective of Northern Arizona University (Eds), *Investigating difference* (pp. 10–22). Upper Saddle River, NJ: Prentice Hall.

Young, I. M. (1990). *Justice and the politics of difference*. Princeton, NJ: Princeton University Press.

Young, I. M. (1995). Social movements and the politics of difference. In J. Arthur & A. Shapiro (Eds), *Campus wars: Multiculturalism and the politics of difference* (pp. 199–225). Boulder, CO: Westview.

Yalnizyan, A. (2007). *The rich and the rest of us: The changing face of Canada's growing gap*. Toronto: Canadian Centre for Policy Alternatives. Retrieved January 2, 2009, from www.growinggap.ca/files/RichandtheRestofUs.pdf

Zatz, M., & Mann, C. (2006). The power of images. In C. Mann, M. Zatz, & N. Rodriquez (Eds), *Images of color, images of crime* (3rd ed., pp. 1–14). Los Angeles: Roxbury.

3 | Mediations of Race and Crime: Racializing Crime, Criminalizing Race[1]

YASMIN JIWANI

[Whiteness] is not an essential racial category that contains a set of fixed meanings, but a strategic deployment of power. It comprises the construction and occupation of a central space from which to view the world, and from which to operate in the world. This space of whiteness contains a limited but varied set of normalizing positions from which that which is not white can be made into the abnormal; by such means whiteness constitutes itself as a universal set of norms by which to make sense of the world. When faced with a crisis—that is, a situation that demands solution—whiteness can withdraw into its self-constructed normality and never question its assumptions that the abnormal—that is, that which threatens whiteness—is what must change in order to resolve the crisis.

(Fiske, 1996, p. 42)

Introduction

No 'barbaric cultural practices' here: New Citizenship Guide; 'When you become a citizen, you're not just getting a travel document into hotel Canada', minister says.

(Stone, 2009)

As the above headline indicates, there is a sense among political elites such as the current minister of Citizenship, Immigration and Multiculturalism, Jason Kenney, that immigrants are the source of 'barbaric cultural practices' that are inherently criminal in nature. In the same article, Minister Kenney states, 'It's no secret that we've seen instances of culturally rooted abuse of women, so-called "honour killings", forced marriages, and spousal abuse, and even female genital mutilation' (Stone, 2009). Kenney's assertion reverberates with the many stereotypes of immigrants and, most especially, immigrants of colour that associate them with 'barbaric' practices. To point the finger at racialized minority groups because of a small number of incidents involving specific acts of violence is to disregard the larger and prevalent patterns of violence that occur throughout Canadian society. To take just the most obvious example, this would be akin to stating that because violence occurs on the ice in the context of hockey games in Canada, such barbaric practices are emblematic of all Canadian hockey players. Violence in the hockey arena occurs in a controlled environment and between equals, and while hockey is undoubtedly violent, the violence that occurs within that sphere is not used to cast blame on all those who participate in the sport or to label them as innately violent.

In this chapter, I begin by examining how the mainstream media works to criminalize particular groups and communities. Within this context, I outline and utilize the different discursive ways in which racism is communicated and show how race is conjoined with this notion of 'barbarity' to imply that only some groups have an inherent proclivity to crime or are engaged in specific kinds of crime. I then chart the contours of these **racialized discourses** in mainstream print media, focusing particularly on examples from the *Globe and Mail*. The media constitute cultural screens onto which images of the Other—the different and stigmatized group or collective—are projected. The ensuing mediated landscapes, I suggest, provide us with an imagined sense of self—an imagined national identity to which we cling all the more ferociously when confronted with apparitions of threat. This is most apparent in the figure of the terrorist, the iconic representation of the threat that has fuelled **moral panics** and media hysteria since the events of 9/11. I conclude with an examination of how the discourse of terrorism is tied to notions of threat and security and how these notions work in concert to legitimize surveillance and fortify the current law-and-order agenda. Religion, as in Islam, has become racialized since 9/11. I begin, however, by mapping the discourses of race and racism that are integral to and interwoven in mediated accounts.

Discourses of Race and Racism

As chapter 2 outlines, notions of race are not fixed in biology but instead have a social significance. They are 'social facts' in that they influence the lives and realities of those who are racialized, or marked with the attributes of being racially different. Hence, while race is not a fixed category, it is the use to which it is put as a 'floating signifier', to quote Stuart Hall (Media Education Foundation, 1997), that is of relevance. In other words, as a sign, race constitutes different meanings at different historical junctures. Nonetheless, the defining features of racialized identities are, as Hall (1990) neatly summarizes, organized around a **grammar of race**. The power coordinates within this grammar are as follows: (a) within the relations of subordination and domination, the racialized group assumes the position of subordination; (b) behaviours attributed to the subordinate are naturalized in that they are regarded as being inherent to the individuals within that group; (c) the behaviours and norms of the subordinated group are evacuated of all historical traces and references such that how that group came to evolve or embrace particular ways of seeing or behaving are emptied of their historical significance and removed from time.

Race, Goldberg (2009) argues, has become a privatized affair in this **neo-liberal** context. This privatization, I contend, is linked to the contemporary discourse on race and racism, wherein it is no longer 'polite' or 'cool' to make explicitly racist statements, although these are made quite often. Rather, the dominant tendency is to deploy an **inferential** form of racism, wherein 'naturalized representations of events and situations relating to race, whether "factual" or "fictional" . . . have racist premises and propositions inscribed in them as a set of unquestioned assumptions. These enable racist statements to be formulated without ever bringing into awareness the racist predicates on which these statements are grounded' (Hall, 1990, pp. 12–13).

The news headline that opens this introduction is an example of an inferential form of racism. The racist predicates are only made clear when the term 'barbaric' is transposed into the current Canadian context to refer to acts that are equally violent, though not deemed to be barbaric in the sense of being outside the realm of civilized conduct. The fact that violence against women is a recurrent and prevalent phenomenon in Canadian society is evacuated from the minister's statement and not brought into 'awareness' or made explicit by the reporter. Rather, he simply depicts 'others' as engaging in these forms of gendered violence. Similarly, Canada's lack of response to or neglect of the more than 520 cases of Aboriginal women missing or murdered is constitutive of a barbaric practice. Yet this, too, is not brought out or juxtaposed with Kenney's statement, which is then left to stand alone as an accusatory labelling of all immigrant groups coming to the country.

Inferential racism also relies on the use of coded language to communicate race. This is part of the tendency to privatize and hide race behind a veil of civility or what Goldberg refers to as '**cordial racism**': 'It is civil society's racism without responsibility, civility fronting for terms of extended dismissal. Structural dislocation, exclusion, debilitation, racially indexed, are buried, but buried alive. Racial reference vaporizes, racisms evaporating into the very air we breathe' (2009, p. 343). Such coded language is most apparent in the media's coverage of immigrant groups and immigration in general. Here, immigrants are not described as racialized minorities or people of colour—but they are assumed to be such. Karim (1993) notes that the term 'immigrant' has become synonymous with illegal migrants, bogus refugee claims, and unassimilable others. Likewise, Razack (1998) has observed that culture becomes a way of talking 'race'. In the same vein, 'gangs' and 'gang warfare' have become coded for race and racialized groups (see Jiwani, 2006).

Immigrants, thus conceived, are racialized. They become raced figures, carrying the burden of connotations placed on their culture, country of origin, language, and religion. At the same time, as raced figures, immigrants are the perpetual outsiders, never quite 'fitting in' or being fully assimilable. Their difference can be tolerated as long as it can be commodified in the form of ethnic food, exotic fashions, and erotic practices. Where such commodification cannot be contained, the immigrant figure represents a multi-dimensional threat—in a discourse that fits with whatever happens to be the currency of societal risk at the time. Williams (1996) observed that racialized people in the criminal justice system were often asked about their immigrant status and court transcripts often referenced their foreign origins. Even in the case of the Toronto 18, the group of youths arrested on charges of alleged terrorism in Toronto in June 2006, the media underscored their Canadian births as if to highlight that these were not foreign born, but rather second-generation youth of immigrant parentage.

The dominance of whiteness is **exnominated** in these contexts (Fiske, 1996). It stands as the invisible and normative background against which the others are defined and their differences rendered salient. The dominance of whiteness then reinforces the darkening of the Other, a process that is inherent to and constitutive of nation-making (Pratt, 2002; Thobani, 2002).

Van Dijk offers a very useful formulation of the ways in which immigrant groups are represented in the press. He posits that media interlocutors deploy positive self-group and negative out-group representations in their strategies of expression. This **strategy of polarization** can be conceptualized as an ideological square:

1. Emphasize our good properties/actions
2. Emphasize their bad properties/actions
3. Mitigate our bad properties/actions
4. Mitigate their good properties/actions

(van Dijk, 1998, p. 33)

The basis of the ideological square is an 'us'/'them' binary, thus, 'we' are law-abiding, while 'they' are not; 'we' are reasonable, while 'they' are not, and so forth.

In his analysis of racism in the press, van Dijk (1991, 1993) observes that immigrants tend to be constructed as threats to the social, political, economic, and cultural order. In the sections below, I trace these constructions as they are manifested in the Canadian mainstream press. However, before offering these examples, I return to Hall's work concerning media representations.

Historically Sedimented Knowledge

In his seminal work on representations, Hall (1990, 1997) draws attention to the role of the common stock of knowledge that includes historical as well as contemporary forms of cognition and consciousness. However, these different forms or kinds of knowledge are constitutive of common sense. Hall's use of 'common sense' is derived from Gramsci's work. In this regard, common-sense knowledge is not a unified system, but rather a 'rag bag' of conflicting information. He notes that

> contemporary forms of common sense are shot through with the debris and traces of previous, more developed ideological systems; and their reference point is what passes, without exception, as the wisdom of *our* particular age and society, overcast with the glow of traditionalism. It is precisely its 'spontaneous' quality, its transparency, its 'naturalness', its refusal to be made to examine the premises on which it is founded, its resistance to change or to correction, its effect of instant recognition, and the closed circle in which it moves which makes common sense, at one and the same time, 'spontaneous', ideological and unconscious. You cannot learn, through common sense, *how things are*: you can only discover *where they fit* into the existing scheme of thing. In this way, its very taken-for-grantedness is what establishes it as a medium in which its own premises and presuppositions are being rendered invisible by its apparent transparency. (Hall 1979, pp. 325–326)

Stereotypes are part and parcel of this common-sense stock of knowledge, and the stereo-type of the immigrant as being prone to crime and as having an inherent, biological propensity towards crime has been well documented historically. This is so even in cases that are geograph-ically and historically distant, as in, for example, the infamous case of Jack the Ripper in 1880s England, wherein the Ripper was first thought to be an immigrant Jew (Walkowitz, 1982). Closer to home, numerous scholars have commented on the criminalization of immigrants in Canada (Backhouse, 1999; Barnes, 2002; Henry et al., 1995; Flynn & Crawford, 1998; Jakubowski, 1999; Williams, 1996; Wortley, 2002). However, the existing literature highlights how it is *racialized* immigrants who tend to be criminalized (see Mahtani & Mountz, 2002). **Racialization** can be defined as a process by which particular groups, because of their perceived or putative differ-ences, are associated with negatively valued characteristics, traits, and associated behaviours. Historically, this has included the Italian community and its stereotypical connection to organ-ized crime; the Polish and Russian communities have also been indicted in the same way. During World War II, Japanese Canadians were interned in camps in the western provinces as a result of their appearance and connection to the enemy nation. As I have argued elsewhere, 'Those at the bottom are considered to be the most prone to crime, are seen as less credible and deserving, and are often perceived by the dominant society as dispossessed and disposable' (Jiwani, 2002, p. 69).

Over-Policed and Under-Protected

Underpinning the criminalization of racialized groups is the scrutiny to which they are subjected—the over-policing of their communities. Over-policing is based on stereotypes that police officers hold of these communities (see Ungerleider, 1992; Henry et al., 1995). The charge of racial profiling is also based on the currency of these stereotypes informing police percep-tions and judgments about the behaviours of others (Closs & McKenna, 2006; Tator & Henry, 2006; Satzewich & Shaffir, 2009).[2] These perceptions are not simply confined to the police; rather, they permeate all the different sectors of the criminal justice system (see Thornhill, 2008; Williams, 1996). Further, I would argue that, within each regional area, specific groups are targeted in terms of over-policing and increased incarceration. Speaking particularly of anti-black racism, Williams notes in the report of the Commission on Systemic Racism in the Ontario Criminal Justice System that

> the higher incarceration rate of black convicted men in [the study's] sample is partly due to discretion being exercised more harshly against black than white men who share the same personal and case characteristics (direct discrimination). Differences in rates of unemployment, detention before trial, not-guilty pleas and prosecution by indictment also contributed to disparity in sentencing outcomes. Thus the indirect (systemic) impact of these apparently neutral factors was more frequent resort to prison sentences for black than white men. (1996, p. 14)

Concomitantly with the over-policing of racialized immigrant communities is the under-protection of these same communities, resulting in their enhanced vulnerabilities to systemic and racialized gendered violence. For instance, in a study of the missing and murdered Aboriginal women in the Downtown Eastside of Vancouver, Jiwani and Young (2006) observed how the stereotypical framing of these women as drug-addicted sex workers effectively delimited the kind of assistance and intervention that they or their families could obtain from the police. In a previous study involving a survey of women's shelters and anti-violence organizations in British Columbia, Jiwani and Buhagiar (1997) found that police were often reluctant to respond. And in the case of the murder of nine family members in Vernon, BC, the Royal Canadian Mounted Police (RCMP) did not intervene despite the complaints articulated by one of the victims prior to the shooting. Jiwani (2006) details the ways in which the family of nine was represented in the media—representations that underscored their immigrant and South Asian cultural origins. Underlying this tendency towards not responding or failing to protect racialized minority groups and individuals is the sense of their perceived deservedness/undeservedness or worthiness/unworthiness as victims. Rigakos (1995) observed this phenomenon at work in his analysis of the non-enforcement of protection orders on the part of the police, where female complainants were not taken seriously and their claims of violence and threat trivialized. As Van Zoonen argues, the 'power of discourse lies not only in its capacity to define what is a social problem, but also in its prescriptions of how an issue should be understood, the legitimate views on it, the legitimacy and deviance of the actors involved, the appropriateness of certain acts, etc.' (1994, p. 40).

Mediating Race and Crime

> The reality of race in any society is, so to speak, to coin a phrase, 'mass-mediated'.
>
> (Hall, 1989)

In *Discipline and Punish*, Foucault (1978/1995) describes the **panoptic** function of society as condensed in the disciplinary functions of surveillance. This surveillance manifests itself today in a myriad of ways: from the cameras positioned at traffic intersections to the surveillance technologies used to chart internet communications. Foucault puts it most succinctly when he emphasizes the individualizing power of the panoptic regime:

> In a disciplinary regime . . . as power becomes more anonymous and more functional, those on whom it is exercised tend to be more strongly individualized; it is exercised by surveillance rather than ceremonies, by observation rather than commemorative accounts, by comparative measures that have the 'norm' as reference rather than genealogies giving ancestors as points of reference; by 'gaps' rather than by deeds. (p. 193)

Hence, anyone who deviates from the 'norm' is likely to be considered deviant, and where that deviance is neither a legitimized form of deviance (see Foucault, 1978/1995) nor a deviance that can be utilized by those in power, it is likely to be put under surveillance. The critical aspect of surveillance is that it licenses a cumulative stock of knowledge to be gathered about particular individuals and groups. This knowledge base then permits the construction of profiles, such as, for example, those of serial killers (see Warf & Waddell, 2002) or, as Razack (2008a) has observed, those of terrorists. That these profiles are often far-fetched and based on threads drawn together from scant and flimsy sources has been previously documented (Tanovich, 2006). Nonetheless, such profiles have tremendous power in legitimizing state intervention in the form of arrests, incarceration, and deportations.

Complementing the panoptic regimes of the state's surveillance structure is the **synoptic** power of the mass media. While the panopticon, as Mathiesen has argued, authorizes the 'few to see the many', the synopticon permits the 'many to see the few', so that 'a large number focuses on something in common which is condensed' (1997, p. 219). The power of the synopticon, Mathiesen observes, is most apparent in the mass media. As nodal points of power, the media selectively pull together and offer viewers both prescriptive and descriptive images of Others (Bannerji, 1986). These images then describe the world out there or the multiplicity of worlds that exist while simultaneously prescribing normative values and behaviours. Stereotypical constructions of racialized Others are part of what is communicated through the synopticon, along with morality tales about how not to behave or the consequences of social transgressions. Within this context, the media **prime** audiences to be receptive to certain kinds of messages, including, for example, the associations between black people and crime (Dixon & Linz, 2000; Dixon, Azocar, & Casas, 2003; Entman, 1990; Oliver, 2003). Dixon, Azocar, and Casas define 'priming' as the invocation of 'schemas or cognitive structures [that] influence the interpretation of new information such that recently and/or frequently activated ideas come to mind more easily than ideas that have not been activated once perceivers encounter similar stimuli' (2003, p. 502). In other words, schemas organized around or involving stereotypes of racialized others as prone to criminality are likely to be activated if the viewer/audience is consistently presented with stories linking race and crime. Other studies—for instance, those of Dixon and Linz (2000, 2002)—have consistently found a pattern of blacks being over-represented as perpetrators of crime in television newscasts, thereby priming audiences to associate blacks with criminality.

This association between stereotypes and priming plays a key role in the phenomenon of **racial profiling** (Tator & Henry, 2006). Such profiling is widespread in the criminal justice system. For instance, in their survey of Toronto high school students' encounters with the police, Wortley and Tanner (2005) found that black students were more frequently stopped and searched than were students from other racial groups. These findings have been corroborated by other studies in different jurisdictions (e.g., Closs & McKenna, 2006). In his analysis of racial profiling, Tanovich (2006) has observed that such profiling has targeted Aboriginal peoples as well and that while there is little evidence to support it, profiling continues to be used because of its resonance with deeply entrenched stereotypes. These stereotypes are also constitutive of **media template**s—templates that Kitzinger describes as 'rhetorical shorthand, helping journalists and audiences to make sense of fresh news stories. They are instrumental in shaping narratives around particular social problems, guiding public discussion not only about the past, but also the present and the future' (2000, p. 61).

If we apply van Dijk's schema to representations of different racialized groups and communities, we would likely find a clustering of stereotypical portrayals in different domains of social life. The law-and-order agendas of conservative political parties (as exemplified in the current political climate in Canada) tend to fall within the realm of the social, having the same impact on the social order as threats to national security do in the form of terrorism. Each of these domains, with its corresponding constructed threat, is defined in criminal terms as well. For instance, under threats to the economic order, one could add money-laundering schemes, piracy, thievery, stealing jobs, jumping the queue, taking undue and unfair advantage of welfare benefits, and the like. Within the realm of the cultural, such threats often congeal in the form of the unassimilable immigrant whose cultural ways and norms deviate from the normative order. Where such differences are criminalized (e.g., abortion, the wearing of veils), those transgressing the normative order are defined as criminals. The cultural order can also include threats that are perceived to be culturally detrimental or invasive, as with, for instance, the recent focus on Muslims and other ethnic minority groups as threats to Quebec's cultural sovereignty (evident in many of the sentiments that were articulated at the various hearings of the Commission on Reasonable Accommodation). Hence, the typical stereotypes that abound in each one of these categorical domains include refugees and illegal immigrants, who are perceived to be stealing jobs and exploiting welfare and other benefits; racialized immigrants from cultures that are deemed to be 'unlike' those of the majority population and thus unassimilable; and immigrants whose religious traditions lead them, in stereotypical terms, to commit criminal acts that threaten the safety of the nation and its citizens.

Media Topography: Mediascapes of Race and Crime on Page A1 of the Globe and Mail

To determine how immigrants and racialized Others are constructed and their representations mediated, I examined all of the headlines that were printed in the *Globe and Mail* on page A1 over a period of one year (from October 2008 to October 2009). My decision to focus on headlines on the front page had to do with their salience—they are the most noticeable and captivating. Van Dijk (1993) argues that headlines are cognitive organizers. They summarize the issue and, while reflecting the dominant perspective, present it in a condensed way that makes sense. Moreover, the kind of media topography presented here allows us to apprehend the **actuarial gaze** that is often fixed on marginalized and racialized communities. Such a gaze reveals a 'visual organization and institutionalization of threat perception and prophylaxis, which cross cuts politics, public health, public safety, policing, urban planning and media practice' (Feldman, 2005, p. 206). While the media topography of the front pages of the *Globe and Mail* examined here lacks the visual dimension (there are no photographs included and neither is the layout of stories in terms of their proximity and juxtaposition described), the headlines themselves unveil the predominant constructions of threat that are being highlighted.

In total, there were 282 headlines that appeared on these front pages. Removing all those that dealt with summaries (i.e., 'What is in the Globe today') as well as those not directly related to crime resulted in 166 headlines. Of these, 75 pertained to international issues or affairs occurring in countries other than Canada. The international headlines were further broken down so that it could be determined which countries were seen as important to the press and its perceived and intended audience. These countries not only represent Canada's involvement, but also signify the source countries for many of the immigrants. The number of headlines pertaining to each country is summarized below:

Afghanistan	39 (terrorism related and pertaining to Canadian military activities)
African countries	15 (relating to hostage taking and Al-Qaeda operatives)
India	5 (terrorist bombings)
Pakistan	3 (related to the Afghan mission)
Israel	2 (pertaining to its war on Gaza)
Jamaica	2 (plane hijackings)
Korea	2 (nuclear power issue)
Iran	4 (corrupt elections and nuclear ambitions)
Iraq	2 (on violence)
Mexico	2 (on gangs and meeting with Harper)
Italy	1 (immunity for president)
USA	13 (mostly dealing with Obama)
Total	75

As evident in other studies (e.g., Dahlgren & Chakrapani, 1982; Hackett, 1989), source countries that are part of the developing world are presented as inherently problematic; they are sites marked by chaos, disorder, corruption, and disaster. Of the countries on the list, there are only two aside from the United States that would qualify as industrialized, wealthy, and primarily white: Israel (because of its Ashkenazi Jewish elite) and Italy. I have compiled all African countries into one category not to level the differences between them, but to underscore the well-entrenched notion of Africa as the 'dark continent'. Here, Africa represents the darkness under which Al-Qaeda and similar groups are able to hide and engage in terrorist activities. This kind of representation—of Africa as the dark continent nurturing all manner of savagery—has been commented upon by numerous scholars (Hammond & Jablow, 1977).

Of the 166 headlines, another 30 dealt with white-collar crimes, as signified by the Mulroney-Schreiber money exchange (the Oliphant Inquiry) as well as various ponzi schemes. A number of headlines dealt with femicides, including headlines concerning the cases of Stephanie Rengal, Victoria Stafford, and Wendy Ladner-Beaudry in British Columbia. There were also headlines about missing children, including headlines relating to Brandon Crisp, an Alberta girl who was found, and a headline pertaining to missing Aboriginal girls. Furthermore, seven other headlines dealt with Aboriginal issues. Separating out the above-mentioned headlines and those dealing with First Nations groups and issues culminated in a total of 51 headlines that dealt directly with racialized and immigrant groups. These are itemized in Table 3.1.

This mapping of the front page outlines the ways in which immigrant and racialized groups are depicted, and underscores the links between these representations and crimes. If we cluster

Table 3.1 Number of Headlines Relating to Specific Racialized Groups

Mexicans	3 refugee-related
	1 on Mexican Gang
Tamils	1 on Tamil protest in Toronto
	3 on Tamil refugee headlines
Black (African/Afro-Caribbean)	2 related to HIV cases
	2 related to Jane Creba shooting in Toronto
South Asian women and girls	2 related to the murder of Reena Virk
	1 on a divorce case (woman had to pay alimony to abusive spouse)
Chinese—aberrant crimes	2 on the beheading that occurred on the Greyhound bus
	1 on store owner who defended himself but was charged
	1 on cyber crime
Korean	3 on the same boy who used martial arts to defend himself against racist remark and physical abuse at school
Polish immigrant	Taser inquiry
Muslim males *including South Asian, Ethiopian, Sudanese, Saudi, and others who were not named*	12 headlines in total dealing with home-grown terrorists—jihadists, Muslims held in home countries, familicide, defamation charge against school, custody and access case, terrorism charges
Gangs and youth violence	15 headlines. Gangs are colour-coded by geography, nationality/culture and thus racialized.

the crimes according to van Dijk's schema, we arrive at the following scenario in Table 3.2.

Not fitting these schemata is the one case of the Korean boy who utilized his martial-arts skills to counter the racist bullying he was experiencing at school; rather, this story stands out as a special case that demonstrates the boy's fair use of his skills in his defence against provocation.

Victims and Perpetrators

If we further break down these components along the axis of victims and perpetrators, it is apparent that there are more perpetrators than victims. However, in the victim category, there are worthy and unworthy victims. Those who are perceived as worthy are typically represented as not being culpable for the actions taken against them or the circumstances in which they have found themselves. They are also positioned as subjects warranting our sympathy. A good example of this is the portrayal of Robert Dziekanski, the Polish immigrant who was killed by tasers used against him by police. Unworthy victims, by contrast, while acknowledged as victims still bear some culpability for their circumstances and actions. Thus, unworthy victims include those who put themselves in harm's way despite being aware of the conditions of illegality (e.g., illegal refugees, Canadians of colour held in hostage situations overseas, and those who have been detained unnecessarily for some alleged connection to terrorism). Interestingly, those Canadians of colour who were detained in African countries, such as those in Ethiopia and Sudan, were not regarded as worthy victims to the same extent as were white Canadian diplomats similarly held as hostages in other

Table 3.2 Race and Crime

Threats	Social	Cultural	Economic
Muslims	Jihadists Terrorism	Familicide—domestic violence/murder	Economic costs of policing and intervening in other countries where Canadian Muslims are being confined
Black and other youth of colour	Gangs, murder	Violations in the form of shooting innocent bystanders	Costs incurred from policing gangs and using resources that provincial governments require to control the situation
Black	HIV infections Murders—shootings	Innocent victims getting shot: e.g., the Creba case in Toronto	Economic costs of policing
South Asian women	Victimized others	Marrying abusive spouses Hanging around with wrong crowd—unassimilable	
Chinese	Aberrant crimes, as in beheading—outside the normatively defined kinds of murders Cybercrime Self-defence	Aberrant crime as in beheading—seen as particularly strange and backward; a Chinese store-owner who took it upon himself to defend his store against theft.	Costs of cybercrime
Refugees–Mexicans and Tamils	Illegal immigrants—not abiding by laws Mexican gangs and their impact here Tamil protest as disturbing the peace/normalcy	Not sharing dominant cultural frameworks	Costs of monitoring and ensuring conformity to immigration rules

African countries. Stories concerning South Asian women and girls underscored their victim status as subjects of patriarchal violence and 'girl on girl' violence (see Jiwani, 2006; Razack, 1998).

In contrast to the 30 white-collar crime headlines, which included charges of corruption in various government departments and corporations, the headlines pertaining to racialized and immigrant groups dealt more with social and culturally coded crimes, the economic aspects of which were largely left either unstated or assumed. By far, the largest categories of race-related representations fell under the headings of 'gangs' and 'Muslims'. These two categories convey contemporary concerns and anxieties about terrorism and social disorder/chaos.

In *The Colour of Justice* (2006), Tanovich has extensively documented the racialization of gangs in Canada, drawing attention to the role of racial profiling. He argues that the increased surveillance of communities of colour results in correspondingly high numbers of stops and seizures. Gangs, while common across all racial groups, are most commonly apprehended in communities of colour because of the profiling of these communities and their over-policing. While racial profiling is the material reality of the practice of discriminatory policy and heightened surveillance, another factor is how the police themselves view gangs from racialized communities. In her research on the Montreal police, Symons (2002) found that officers consistently referred to gangs composed of racialized youth in terms of their country of origin. In contrast, white supremacist gangs were simply described and referred to in terms of their practices. She notes that police 'also speak about a "culture of violence" that the youth left behind in their "war-torn" country of origin (immigrant status being taken for granted)', and further that they regard ethnocultural communities as the 'Other' and that 'the "we/they" dichotomy is clearly articulated in both language and practice' (p. 119).

Yet, the racialization of crimes is not simply confined to the realm of policing; it is also evident in the court systems (Tanovich, 2008). In fact, the emphasis on policing can be understood in terms of the police being the primary definers of crime (Hall et al., 1978). Nevertheless, judicial prejudice notwithstanding, there is, as Tanovich (2008) notes, a certain reluctance to factor in or name 'race' and racism as playing a role in criminal cases that are brought before the courts.

In the section below, I return to the other significant category of coverage in the media topography outlined above, this time focusing on Muslims, given that religion has now become racialized through its association with Islam and the myth of a clash of civilizations, a view promulgated and amplified by the mass media (Boggs & Pollard, 2006; Jiwani, 2004; Said, 1981; Shaheen, 2001).

The Terrorist Other

[T]he transnational figure of the 'terrorist' suggests that such a figure is beyond redemption and thus is of such high risk to the nation and the state as to be incarcerated immediately or to be destroyed. The flip side of this danger is thus the 'security' and happiness and freedom to be felt by the incarceration of such bodies designated as 'risk producing'.

(Grewal, 2003, p. 539)

The threat of terrorism—as that rooted in amorphous terror cells spread across both Canada and the United States—has been widely articulated in numerous media formats, ranging from TV news documentaries to popular films and television crime dramas, including the infamous *24* and its Canadian counterpart, *The Border*. We are, as Altheide (2007) puts it, 'primed' for any future attacks—we know the language, we have been taught to read the signs, and we are even disciplined enough to report on each other should the threat of terrorism rear its head. This priming, agenda setting, and shaping of public discourse can be directly attributed to the mass media, and have, I would suggest, not only spawned a climate of fear, but have also created a structure of anxiety (see Brunsdon, 1998)—an anxiety that the media feeds into and attempts to appease by pressing for quick-fix solutions and turning to the state to provide these requisite solutions.

In 2003, the RCMP, along with other state authorities, apprehended at gun point 17 South Asian men, several of whom were in bed sleeping at the time. These men were arrested on charges of engaging in terrorist activity. In all, 23 South Asian males were arrested. Although allegations of terrorism were subsequently dropped, 21 were deported. 'Operation Thread', as it was called, seemed to pivot around some flimsy evidence. The common factor was that most of these men were named Mohamed, and a further questionable common denominator connecting them was their enrolment at the Ottawa Business School, which operated as a shell according to the press coverage (see Odartey-Wellington, 2004; Khan, 2008). In 2006, another group of men, the Toronto 18, were arrested. Again, the common factor was their Muslim identity. Muslims, Dossa (2008) points out, have been constructed as '[l]ethal entities'. In the immediate aftermath of the Toronto 18's arrest, journalist Robert Fisk (2006) wrote in the *Independent* that the national Canadian press coverage 'indulged in an orgy of finger-pointing that must reduce the chances of any fair trial and, at the same time, sow fear in the hearts of the country's more than 700,000 Muslims. In fact, if I were a Canadian Muslim right now, I'd already be checking the airline timetables for a flight out of town.' Fisk's article was titled 'How Racism Has Invaded Canada,' suggesting that this is a new phenomenon when in fact it is as old as the nation itself.

At the base of these arrests is the cluster of stereotypes parsing a particular profile. This profile, as Razack (2008b) describes it, based on the accumulated stock of knowledge of state security agencies, is comprised of the following features: the men (and they are all men) come from a specific region that is noted for its religious extremism (the religion being Islam); they 'attended the same university programs during the same period of time' (quoted in Razack 2008b, 11); and they 'share similar educated middle-class backgrounds' (ibid.). Razack adds that this sleeper-cell profile emphasizes the fact that the men are 'linked to each other; appear to reside in clusters of 4 or 5 young males and appear to change their address with other clusters' (ibid.). It is this notion of 'clusters' and 'cells' that Razack underscores in her analysis, drawing attention to its semiotic anchoring within a biological paradigm as if these cells or clusters are like 'foreign bodies who band together in small units and who threaten as do clusters of cancer cells, the healthy social body' (ibid.). It is worth recalling that in the United States, over 1,200 Muslim men were detained by the authorities in the immediate aftermath of 9/11 (Kellner, 2003). In Canada, the Canadian Council on American-Islamic Relations and the Canadian Muslim Civil Liberties Association recorded 110 incidents of threats, harassment, attacks on property and assaults against Muslims (Bahdi, 2003). Tanovich (2006), drawing from data cited by the Canadian Islamic Congress, points to a 1,600 per cent increase in hate crimes against Muslims and those looking like Muslims since September 11.

That aside, the Muslim threat has pushed the envelope for heightened security and surveillance laws, a move that works in concert with the law-and-order agenda of conservative political parties. Zedner (2005) argues that 'the more ill-defined the threat, the greater the potential to tip the balance in favour of tougher security measures, to detain and hold suspects on the slightest of grounds, to carry out covert searches, and to suspend normal protections associated with due process and a fair trial' (p. 512). This is akin to the state of the concentration camp, described by philosopher Agamben (1998) as a 'state of exception'. Agamben clarifies this idea when he states, 'Insofar as the state of exception is "willed", it inaugurates a new juridico-political paradigm in which the norm becomes indistinguishable from the exception. The camp is thus the structure in which the state of exception—the possibility of deciding on which founds sovereign power—is realized *normally*' (170). Razack (2008a) develops this thesis further by demonstrating the different social and legal realms from which Muslims have been 'cast out'. Indeed, Bahdi (2003) observes that, post-9/11, race and religion have become a proxy for risk. She reasons that '[o]ver time, we become comfortable with our prejudices and determinations of risk become even more inextricably linked with stereotypes about Arabs and Muslims so that Arabness and Muslimness itself becomes a substitute for risk' (p. 308).

In Conclusion—Remaking Docile Citizens

In charting the contours of the terrain of racialized crimes and criminalized races, it becomes obvious that underpinning these constructions of Others as threats is the national imaginary defining the self. I return again to Foucault (1978/1995) and his notion of the disciplined self—the subject formation that is cultivated and nurtured to accord with, if not fit into, the existing neo-liberal order. Within this context, the reasonable citizen is contrasted against her or his unreasonable counterpart. The legacy of the Enlightenment, with its binary juxtapositions of reason and emotion, rational and irrational, continues to undergird systems of classification and order, thereby casting out those who are defined as Others. Indeed, can racialized Others truly belong to the nation? Hage (1998) responds to this question in the negative; yet despite this, he argues that such Others attempt to accumulate as much of a sense of belonging as they can. This comes through most clearly in the heightened patriotism that is demanded of racialized others and the constant requirement imposed on them to prove their worth and loyalty to the nation.

Within law, the concept of the 'reasonable person' has been interrogated with some success to reveal its gendered and racial biases (Bhandar, 1997; Devlin, 1995). Within contemporary neo-liberal discourse, the reasonable person has become transmuted into the preferred immigrant or the assimilable immigrant—the 'good' Muslim (Mamdani, 2004) and the docile, tax-paying citizen who makes little or no demand on the state and its various apparatuses of power. This privileged position is then held up as the state to which all others must aspire if they are to enjoy even a limited and conditional acceptance into the nation. However, this skilful veiling of difference covers up the kinds of crimes that are normalized and taken for granted, that do not have the same grit or patina of dirt and contagion, such as crimes that are white collar and coded in the language of civility, explained away as greed (a 'rational' response to the capitalist system and its emphasis on the accumulation of wealth) rather than essentialized as an inherent proclivity on the part of a particular racial group. Against the backdrop of this white normalcy, all other crimes become crimes of colour, reinforcing the status quo. Thus, it is worth noting that one never speaks of 'white on white' crime (Tanovich, 2006) or of the Christian fundamentalism of terrorists such as Timothy McVeigh, or of the religious affiliation of the Columbine school shooters. Labels, as Hall et al. (1995) note, 'not only place and identify those events, they assign events to a context. Thereafter the use of the label is likely to mobilize this whole referential context, with all its associated meanings and connotations' (p. 19).

Key Terms

actuarial gaze	inferential racism	panoptic	racial profiling
cordial racism	media templates	prime/priming	strategy of
exnominated	moral panics	racialization	polarization
grammar of race	neo-liberal	racialized discourses	synoptic

Questions for Critical Thought

1. What are the different discursive ways in which racism is communicated by the mainstream media to criminalize particular groups and communities?
2. What is an inferential form of racism?
3. What does the figure of the terrorist suggest about the threat of terrorism?
4. How does the media's portrayal of immigrant groups as threats to the social order connect with discourses and policies concerning national security?
5. In what other ways do media technologies perform a synoptic and panoptic function?
6. Define and discuss inferential and cordial racism. Can you give other examples of this?
7. How does exnomination work?
8. What is the strategy of polarization?
9. What is an actuarial gaze?
10. Define and discuss the term 'neo-liberalism'. In what ways is it related to discourses of crime?

Additional Readings

Altheide, D. L. (2009). The Columbine shootings and the discourse of fear. *American Behavioral Scientist, 52*(10), 1354–1370.

Del Zotto, A. C. (2002). Weeping women, wringing hands: How the mainstream media stereotyped women's experiences in Kosovo. *Journal of Gender Studies, 11*(2), 141–150.

Jiwani, Y., & Young, M. L. (2006). Missing and murdered women: Reproducing marginality in news discourse. *Canadian Journal of Communication, 31*(4), 895–917.

Louw, P. E. (2003). The 'War against Terrorism', a public relations challenge for the Pentagon. *Gazette: The International Journal for Communication Studies, 65*(3), 211–230.

Mahtani, M. (2001). Representing minorities: Canadian media and minority identities. *Canadian Ethnic Studies, 33*(3), 93–133.

Parameswaran, R. (2006). Military metaphors, masculine modes, and critical commentary, deconstructing journalists' inner tales of September 11. *Journal of Communication Inquiry, 30*(1), 42–64.

Smolash, W. N. (2009). Mark of Cain(Ada): Racialized security discourse in Canada's national newspapers. *University of Toronto Quarterly, 78*(2), 745–763.

Tanovich, D. (2008). The charter of whiteness: Twenty-five years of maintaining racial injustice in the Canadian criminal justice system. *Supreme Court Law Review, 40*(2d), 655–686.

Zine, J. (2009). Unsettling the nation: Gender, race and Muslim cultural politics in Canada. *Studies in Ethnicity and Nationalism, 9*(1), 146–193.

Websites of Interest

Prism magazine: www.prism-magazine.com

FREDA Centre for Research on Violence against Women and Children: http://fredacentre.com

Canadian Race Relations Foundation: www.crr.ca

Stop Racism and Hate Collective: www.stopracism.ca/content/canadian-anti-racism-education-and-research-society-caers

Endnotes

1. The research for this chapter was made possible by a grant from the Social Sciences and Humanities Research Council. I would especially like to thank Ainsley Jenicek and Alan Wong for their research assistance.
2. However, Satzewich and Shaffir ascribe the practice of racial profiling to police professionalism—the culture of policing. This is a debatable point, as it simply takes for granted that those who are over-policed because of a long-standing and socialized practice are not racialized or that the racial aspect is a neutral element in the process of identification and discrimination.

References

Agamben, G. (1998). *Homo sacer, sovereign power and bare life* (D. Heller-Roazen, Trans.). Stanford, CA: Stanford University Press.

Altheide, D. L. (2007). The mass media and terrorism. *Discourse & Communication, 1*(3), 287–308.

Backhouse, C. (1999). *Colour-coded: A legal history of racism in Canada, 1900–1950*. Toronto: University of Toronto Press.

Bahdi, R. (2003). No exit: Racial profiling and Canada's war against terrorism. *Osgoode Hall Law Journal, 41*(2–3), 293–316.

Bannerji, H. (1986). Now you see us/Now you don't. *Video Guide, 8*(40), 1–4.

Barnes, A. (2002). Dangerous duality: The net effect of immigration and deportation on Jamaicans in Canada. In W. Chan & K. Mirchandani (Eds), *Crimes of colour: Racialization and the criminal justice system in Canada* (pp. 191–203). Peterborough, ON: Broadview Press.

Bhandar, B. (1997, October 12). *Race, identity and difference in the courts: Overcoming judicial 'bias'.* Paper presented at the BC Provincial Court Judges Conference, Vancouver.

Boggs, C., & Pollard, T. (2006). Hollywood and the spectacle of terrorism. *New Political Science, 28*(3), 335–351.

Brunsdon, C. (1998). Structure of anxiety: Recent British television crime fiction. *Screen, 39*(3), 223–243.

Closs, W. J., & McKenna, P. F. (2006). Profiling a problem in Canadian police leadership: The Kingston Police Data Collection Project. *Canadian Public Administration, 49*(2), 143–60.

Dahlgren, P., & Chakrapani, S. (1982). The third world on TV news: Western ways of seeing the 'Other'. In W. C. Adams (Ed), *Television coverage of international affairs* (pp. 45–65). Norwood, NJ: Ablex.

Devlin, R. F. (1995). We can't go on together with suspicious minds: Judicial bias and racialized perspective in R.V.R.D.S. (Case Comm.). *Dalhousie Law Journal, 18*, 408–435.

Dixon, T. L., Azocar, C.L., & Casas, M. (2003). The portrayal of race and crime on television network news. *Journal of Broadcasting & Electronic Media, 47*(4), 498–523.

Dixon, T. L., & Linz, D. (2000). Race and the misrepresentation of victimization on local television news. *Communication Quarterly, 27*(5), 547–573.

Dixon, T. L., & Linz, D. (2002).Television news, prejudicial pretrial publicity, and the depiction of race. *Journal of Broadcasting & Electronic Media, 46*(1), 112–136.

Dossa, S. (2008). Lethal Muslims: White-trashing Islam and the Arabs. *Journal of Muslim Minority Affairs, 28*(2), 225–236.

Entman, R. M. (1990). Modern racism and the image of blacks in local television news. *Critical Studies in Mass Communication, 7,* 332–345.

Feldman, A. (2005). On the actuarial gaze, from 9/11 to Abu Ghraib. *Cultural Studies, 19*(2), 203–226.

Fisk, R. (2006). How racism has invaded Canada. *The Independent.* Retrieved November 10, 2009, from www.aljazeerah.info/Opinion%20editorials/2006%20 Opinion%20Editorials/June/11%20o/How%20 Racism%20Has%20Invaded%20Canada%20By%20 Robert%20Fisk.htm

Fiske, J. (1996). *Media matters: Race and gender in U.S. politics* (rev. ed). Minneapolis: University of Minnesota Press.

Flynn, K., & Crawford, C. (1998). Committing 'race treason': Battered women and mandatory arrest in Toronto's Caribbean community. In K. D. Bonnycastle & G. S. Rigakos (Eds), *Unsettling truths: Battered women, policy, politics and contemporary research in Canada* (pp. 91–102). Vancouver: Collective Press.

Foucault, M. (1978/1995). *Discipline and punish, the birth of the prison.* New York: Vintage Books.

Goldberg, D. T. (2009). *The threat of race, reflections on racial neoliberalism.* Oxford: Wiley-Blackwell.

Grewal, I. (2003).Transnational America: Race, gender and citizenship after 9/11. *Social Identities, 9*(4), 535–561.

Hackett, R. A. (1989). Coups, earthquakes and hostages? Foreign news on Canadian television. *Canadian Journal of Political Science, 22*(4), 809–825.

Hage, G. (1998). *White nation: Fantasies of white supremacy in a multicultural society.* New York and Australia: Routledge and Pluto Press.

Hall, S. (1979). Culture, the media and the 'ideological effect'. In J. Curran, M. Gurevitch, & J. Woollacott (Eds), *Mass communication and society* (pp. 315–347). London: E. Arnold in association with the Open University Press.

Hall, S. (1989). Convocation address, University of Massachusetts at Amherst.

Hall, S. (1990). The whites of their eyes, racist ideologies and the media. In M. Alvarado & J. O. Thompson (Eds), *The Media Reader* (pp. 9–23). London: British Film Institute.

Hall, S. (1997). The work of representations. In S. Hall (Ed.), *Representation, cultural representation and signifying practices* (pp. 15–74). London: Sage in association with the Open University Press.

Hall, S., Critcher, C., Jefferson, T., & Roberts, B. (1978). *Policing the crisis: Mugging, the state, law and order.* London: Macmillan Press.

Hammond, D., & Jablow, A. (1977). *The myth of Africa.* New York: Library of Social Sciences.

Henry, F., Tator, C., Mattis, W., & Rees, T. (1995). *The colour of democracy: Racism in Canadian society.* Toronto: Harcourt Brace.

Jakubowski, L. M. (1999). Managing Canadian immigration: Racism, ethnic selectivity, and the law. In E. Comack et al. (Eds), *Locating law: Race/class/gender connections* (pp. 98–124). Halifax: Fernwood.

Jiwani, Y. (2002). The criminalization of 'race', the racialization of crime. In W. Chan & K. Mirchandani (Eds), *Crimes of colour: Racialization and the criminal justice system in Canada* (pp. 67–86). Peterborough, ON: Broadview Press.

Jiwani, Y. (2004). Gendering terror: Representations of the Orientalized body in Quebec's post-September 11 English-language press. *Critique: Critical Middle Eastern Studies, 13*(3), 265–291.

Jiwani, Y. (2006). *Discourses of denial: Mediations of race, gender and violence.* Vancouver: University of British Columbia Press.

Jiwani, Y., & Buhagiar, L. (1997). *Policing violence against women in relationships: An examination of police response to violence against women in British Columbia.* Vancouver: FREDA Centre for Research on Violence against Women and Children.

Jiwani, Y., & Young, M. L. (2006). Missing and murdered women: Reproducing marginality in news discourse. *Canadian Journal of Communication, 31*(4), 895–917.

Karim, K. H. (1993). Constructions, deconstructions, and reconstructions: Competing Canadian discourses on ethnocultural terminology. *Canadian Journal of Communication, 18*(2).

Kellner, D. (2003). *From 9/11 to terror war, the dangers of the Bush legacy.* Lanham, MD: Rowman and Littlefield.

Khan, A. (2008). *Threadbare, a film about Canada's 'War on Terror'.* Montreal.

Kitzinger, J. (2000). Media templates: Patterns of association and the (re)construction of meaning over time. *Media, Culture and Society, 22*(1), 61–84.

Mahtani, M., & Mountz, A. (2002). Immigration to British Columbia: Media representations and public opinion. *Research Centre on Immigration and Integration in the Metropolis,* Working Paper Series.

Mamdani, M. (2004). *Good Muslim, bad Muslim: America, the Cold War and the roots of terror.* New York: Pantheon.

Mathiesen, T. (1997). The viewer society, Michel Foucault's 'panopticon' revisited. *Theoretical Criminology, 1*(2), 215–234.

Media Education Foundation. (1997). Race, the floating

signifier with Stuart Hall (Transcript). Retrieved October 8, 2009, from www.mediaed.org/assets/products/407/transcript_407.pdf

Odartey Wellington, F. (2004). *The Al-Qaeda sleeper cell that never was: The Canadian news media, state security apparatus, and 'operation thread'.* Unpublished master's thesis, Concordia University.

Oliver, M. B. (2003). African American men as 'criminal and dangerous': Implications of media portrayals of crime on the 'criminalization' of African American men. *Journal of African American Studies, 7*(2), 3–18.

Pratt, G. (2002). Between homes: Displacement and belonging for second generation Filipino-Canadian youths. *Research on Immigration and Integration in the Metropolis,* Working Paper Series, no. 02-13.

Razack, S. (1998). *Looking white people in the eye: Gender, race, and culture in courtrooms and classrooms.* Toronto: University of Toronto Press.

Razack, S. (2008a). *Casting out: The eviction of Muslims from Western law and politics.* Toronto: University of Toronto Press.

Razack, S. (2008b). The camp: A place where law has declared that the rule of law does not operate. *RaceLink,* 9–17.

Rigakos, G. S. (1995). Constructing the symbolic complainant: Police sub-culture and the non-enforcement of protection orders for battered women. *Violence and Victims,* no. 10, 227–247.

Said, E. (1981). *Covering Islam: How the media and experts determine how we see the rest of the world.* New York: Pantheon Books.

Satzewich, V., & Shaffir, W. (2009). Racism versus professionalism: Claims and counter-claims about racial profiling. *Canadian Journal of Criminology and Criminal Justice, 51*(2), 199–226.

Shaheen, J. G. (2001). *Reel bad Arabs: How Hollywood vilifies a people.* New York: Olive Branch Press.

Stone, L. (2009, November 13). No 'barbaric cultural practices' here: New citizenship guide; 'When you become a citizen, you're not just getting a travel document into Hotel Canada,' minister says. *Gazette* (Montreal), p. A12.

Symons, G. L. (2002). Police constructions of race and gender in street gangs. In W. Chan & K. Mirchandani (Eds), *Crimes of colour: Racialization and the criminal justice system in Canada* (pp. 115–125). Peterborough, ON: Broadview Press.

Tanovich, D. (2006). *The colour of justice: Policing race in Canada.* Toronto: Irwin Law.

Tanovich, D. (2008). The charter of whiteness: Twenty-five years of maintaining racial injustice in the Canadian criminal justice system. *Supreme Court Law Review, 40*(2d), 655–686.

Tator, C., & Henry, F. (2006). *Racial profiling in Canada, challenging the myth of 'a few bad apples'.* Toronto: University of Toronto Press.

Thobani, S. (2002). Closing the nation's doors to immigrant women: The restructuring of Canadian immigration policy. *Atlantis, 24*(2), 16–26.

Thornhill, E. (2008). So seldom for us, so often against us: Blacks and the law in Canada. *Journal of Black Studies, 38*(3), 321–337.

Ungerleider, C. (1992). *Issues in police intercultural and race relations training in Canada.* Ottawa: Solicitor General of Canada.

van Dijk, T. A. (1991). *Racism and the press.* London: Routledge.

van Dijk, T. A. (1993). *Elite discourse and racism.* Vol. 6 of *Race and Ethnic Relations.* Newbury Park, CA: Sage.

van Dijk, T. A. (1998). Opinions and ideologies in the press. In A. Bell & P. Garrett, *Approaches to media discourse* (pp. 21–63). Oxford: Blackwell.

van Zoonen, L. (1994). *Feminist media studies.* Thousand Oaks, CA: Sage.

Walkowitz, J. R. (1982). Jack the Ripper and the myth of male violence. *Feminist Studies, 8*(3), 543–574.

Warf, B., & Waddell, C. (2002). Heinous spaces, perfidious places: The sinister landscapes of serial killers. *Social & Cultural Geography, 3*(3), 323–45.

Williams, T. (1996, May 21–23). *Report of the Commission on Systemic Racism in the Ontario Criminal Justice System: Summary of key findings.* Paper presented as background notes for the Ontario Court of Justice (Provincial Division) Annual Convention.

Wortley, S. (2002). Misrepresentation or reality?: The depiction of race and crime in the Toronto print media. In B. Schissel & C. Brooks (Eds), *Marginality & Condemnation: An Introduction to Critical Criminology* (pp. 55–82). Halifax: Fernwood.

Wortley, S., & Tanner, J. (2005). Inflammatory rhetoric? Baseless accusations? A response to Gabor's critique of racial profiling research in Canada. *Canadian Journal of Criminology and Criminal Justice, 47*(3), 581–609.

Zedner, L. (2005). Securing liberty in the face of terror: Reflections from criminal justice. *Journal of Law and Society, 32*(4), 507–33.

The Mythical Norm

Barbara Perry

Whiteness. Masculinity. Heterosexuality. There can be no stronger markers of **privilege** in Canada or, indeed, in most Western nations. To pick up a theme from chapter 2, our collective favouring of these key identities matters to the extent that it ensures advantages for those occupying these positions. Conversely, those outside the narrow boundaries of what it is to be 'white' and/or 'male' and/or 'straight' are typically disadvantaged along multiple dimensions. Lorde's (1995, p. 192) classic characterization of the '**mythical norm**', also cited in chapter 2, bears repeating: 'Somewhere, on the edge of consciousness, there is what I call a mythical norm, which each of us within our hearts knows "that is not me." . . . [T]his norm is usually defined as white, thin, male, young, heterosexual, Christian and financially secure. It is with this mythical norm that the trappings of power reside within this society.'

With power comes privilege, by which we generally mean advantages that accrue to individuals by virtue of their group membership rather than through their own individual effort. Typically, privilege refers to ***unearned* advantages** that work to maintain or reinforce the systematic systems of power described in chapter 2. This is in contrast to ***earned* advantages** that are, in fact, garnered by dint of effort. The difference is that those who are privileged are typically empowered by their social position in and of itself. Mullaly (2010, p. 289) offers an amusing illustration: 'Bush was born on third base, but to this day believes he hit a triple.' In other words, he succeeded not because of his skill set, or intellect, but because he enjoyed the advantages of his white, male, upper-class position. Those occupying privileged positions have relatively unfettered access to the means and opportunities to maintain if not enhance their status.

Privilege—or lack thereof—thus shapes our life chances. However, it is also the case that privilege is typically rendered invisible. It is simply the norm, the way the world is. Such **invisibility** means that the identity of the privileged largely remains unremarked. Only the Other is raced or gendered, such that race and gender are applied only to their identities, not to whites and males. For Canadians as much as for Americans, identity revolves around 'a conception of America (or Canada) that defines what it is not' (Wellman, 1993, p. 245). The Canadian is not raced, is not black or Asian, is *not* even ethnic. As I noted in chapter 2, language reinforces this exclusive categorizing to the extent that the norm of whiteness is implicit in such terms as 'black author', 'Pakistani doctor', or in the distinction between white 'hired hands' and black 'servants'. The same could be said of gender, whereby a 'woman doctor' is somehow distinct from the generic term 'doctor'.

Peggy McIntosh's work has been among the most influential in helping us to better comprehend the invisibility of privilege. She writes of the '**invisible knapsacks**' of 'special provisions, maps, passports, codebooks, visas, clothes, tools and blank checks' that the privileged carry with them (McIntosh, 2002, p. 97). These are not unusual or extreme tools, but rather ordinary, everyday conditions or experiences that, as a white person, she could count on to facilitate her journey through the day. She illustrates this through her own knapsack of white privilege, listing 26 items, including:

- I can go shopping alone most of the time, pretty well assured that I will not be followed or harassed.
- When I am told about our national heritage or about 'civilization', I am shown that people of my colour made it what it is.
- I can be sure that my children will be given curricular materials that testify to the existence of their race.
- I can do well in a challenging situation without being called a credit to my race.
- I can choose blemish cover or bandages in 'flesh' colour and have them more or less match my skin. (McIntosh, 2002, pp. 98–99)

Mullaly (2010, pp. 300–308) extends the knapsack analogy to consider a broad array of privileges, including upper class ('I do not worry about how an emergency might affect me financially'); male ('I never worry about being paid less than my female counterparts'); heterosexual ('I don't have to worry about people trying to "cure" me of my heterosexuality'); traditional family ('My children do not have to answer questions about why they have two different-sex parents'); non-disability ('I can succeed without people being surprised because they have low expectations of my ability to contribute to society'); and young adult/middle age ('I am assured that people will not consider me as incapable of having a sex life or that if I do, it must be because I am a "dirty old man"').

Fruits of Privilege

An obvious hallmark of racism as a structure of domination is the restriction of the power of non-white racial groups. To this end, racial minorities have historically been limited in terms of social, political, and economic power (the latter will be explicitly addressed in the next section). In 1965, Kenneth Clark suggested the boundaries within which racial minorities circulated. His metaphor remains apt now, 30 years later: 'The dark ghetto's invisible walls have been erected by the white society, by those who have power, both to confine those who have no power and to perpetuate their powerlessness. The dark ghettos are social, political, educational, and—above all—economic colonies' (cited in Pinkney, 1994, p. 7). The ghetto to which Clark refers is not only a geographical location. It is, metaphorically, a social process by which minorities are marginalized—ghettoized—relative to legitimate sources of empowerment. The sorts of racial constructions and categorizations discussed earlier are the stuff of which social exclusions are built, to the extent that they legitimate discrepancies in access to opportunities and privilege. The power that is wielded—physical and social—by whites is exercised in such a way as to 'develop, evolve, nurture, spread, impose, and enforce the very myths . . . that underlie racism' (Fernandez, 1996, p. 160).

Historically in Canada, power has been cautiously guarded by the imposition of restrictions on **citizenship** and its correspondent **rights**. The significance of this is that '[t]o possess citizenship is to be a full member of the community and to enjoy the civil, political and social rights which constitute membership' (Cook, 1993, p. 156). Thus, restrictions on citizenship constitute restrictions on one's ability to engage fully in society. Whether through formal policy or informal practice, racialized minorities have consistently been disenfranchised and thereby limited in voice and position. **Slavery**, for example, was first and foremost a means of denying the humanity and thus eligibility for citizenship of black men and women. This institution constructed whiteness as personhood and blackness as property—chattel. At the very moment when democracy and liberty were heralded, slavery sentenced blacks to a right-less existence. Consequently, blacks were restricted from the exercise of political (e.g., voting, holding office), civil (e.g., restricted from giving testimony against whites), and social (e.g., access to public buildings, right to choose one's employment) empowerment until well into the twentieth century.

While not subject to slavery, most other racial minority groups have nonetheless suffered a similar lack of access to citizenship resources. For example, not only were Aboriginal people denied voting rights and other forms of political expression, but efforts were made to **deculturate** them by removing children from their families and placing them in foster homes or boarding schools where they could be recreated in the image of the dominant white culture. The earliest Asian immigrants were welcomed as a source of cheap labour but were nonetheless excluded from enjoying privileges of citizenship by a series of federal and provincial bills. Indeed, Chinese residents were not given the vote until 1947.

While no ethnic or racial group is legally excluded from attaining Canadian citizenship at this time, it does not necessarily follow that all groups are able to enjoy the privileges associated with this status. Racial minorities continue to be marginalized by their inability to gain full access to political, civil, and social rights, such that inclusion is still constituted of and by 'whiteness,' not 'colour'. Collectively, Aboriginal sovereignty continues to be thwarted by the failure of the state to recognize treaty rights. As a group, Aboriginal people are limited in political and economic terms. Similarly, housing and mortgage discrimination continues to be a determining factor in the persistence of racial and ethnic segregation (Hacker, 1995; Smith, 1995). And, while the political power of minorities has increased somewhat over the past couple of decades, all such groups are still under-represented in the formal machinery of politics. For example, the ongoing DiverseCity research project in Toronto found that in 2009 only 13 per cent of Greater Toronto Area (GTA) leaders were visible minorities, compared to their concentration of 49.5 per cent of the population (Diversity Institute, 2009).

Gendered relations of power follow similar patterns of advantage and disadvantage. Indeed, Canada remains a male supremacist society wherein gender difference is constructed as gender inferiority and, ultimately, gender disadvantage. Consequently, women garner less power, prestige, and economic reward than men, who have consistently retained leadership and control in government, commerce, and family matters (Lorber, 1994). This is readily apparent in the legal history that has helped shape gendered relations of power. Male privilege has long been guaranteed by legal proscriptions and silences that have simultaneously excluded women from involvement in the public sphere while failing to protect them in the context of their private lives (Taub & Schneider, 1990).

On the one hand, legal exclusions on women's enfranchisement, ownership of property, and employment (e.g., law, medicine) have meant that, until well into the twentieth century, women were unable to participate fully in politics or the economy. Even today, restrictions on access to abortion or to social security provisions limit the participatory power of women. On the other hand, the law has also enabled the subordination of women within the home. The same nineteenth- and twentieth-century provisions that limited (married) women's owner-ship of property meant that married women, in particular, ceded autonomy to their husbands upon marriage. The historical tendency to exclude from criminal proceedings husbands' rapes or assaults on wives similarly ensured the dominance of men, who were merely exercis-ing their 'marital rights'. The continued failure to recognize the value of women's domestic labour through some form of income support likewise helps to maintain women's economic dependence on men, both during and subsequent to marriage. This is exacerbated by inequit-able divorce settlements and the intractable wage disparities between men and women.

The **gendered division of labour** is manifest in a number of identifiable patterns, including **wage differentials, job segregation**, and uneven patterns of **reproductive labour** in the home. Each of these can be traced back to the deeply embedded ideologies of 'gender appropriate' labour. Not only is the work that women do devalued, it has also traditionally been viewed as secondary. Labour inside the home is invisible and unrecognized; that outside the home is merely something she does until married or to earn pin money. In contrast, 'men's work' is deemed essential to the operation of both the national and family economy. His is the 'real' work that earns a 'real' pay cheque. Consequently, women's labour tends to be both under-acknowledged and underpaid (if not unpaid), while that of men tends to be highly recognized in both social and economic terms.

The gendered division of labour is also reproduced in the household. In spite of the dramatic increase in women's labour force participation, they continue to bear a disproportionate share of the burden of homemaking. The parallel construction of a gendered division of labour in the home means that 'just as there is a wage gap between men and women in the workplace, there is a "leisure gap" between them at home. Most women work one shift at the office or factory and a "second shift" at home' (Hochschild, 1995, p. 444). Consequently, traditional male privilege tends also to be reproduced in the home: women's unequal structural and economic power finds its counterpart in her unequal access to personal power within the home. Thus, her primary role is still presumed to be caring for the family. It is women's 'essence', after all, to nurture. This expectation lies at the heart of the sexual division of labour. What Connell (1987) refers to as **emphasized femininity** is enacted through women's commitment to household labour: cleaning, cooking, and attending to the needs of husband and children alike. Regardless of the reality, the idealized image of femininity might resemble something from the black-and-white episodes of *Pleasantville* or *Leave It to Beaver* or the full-colour television ads of today. A nicely dressed Mommy mops the (already spotless) floor of a tidy and ordered house, then prepares a full-course meal for her provider husband and well-behaved and well-coiffed children. She is overseeing the children's homework one moment, the next she is a fiery vixen satisfying her husband's sexual fantasies.

Of course, this is a simplified and monolithic vision. There is remarkable variation across class, race, and ethnicity with respect to the extent to which women are held accountable to the ideal. For example, Coltrane's (1995) interviews with dual-income Chicano couples found an asymmetrical division of labour to be more prevalent among both lower-class and upper-middle-class couples than among white-collar working-class Chicanos. Barnes's (1985) examination of African American couples suggests also that men at the extremes of educational and occupational hierarchies rejected housework as a threat to their masculinity.

Privileged Differently: Marginalized White Ethnicities/ Masculinities

The closing comments in the previous section should act as a reminder that no particular identity is truly homogeneous. Rather, there is dramatic variation within groups as well as between groups. However, it is typically the case that differences within what we consider to be whiteness, in particular, are largely invisible. As we too often do with racial groups generally, we tend to homogenize whiteness and assume that all white males, for example, derive the same benefits from their racial categorization. As Webster (2008, p. 294) rightly points out:

> The key problem seems to be a general difficulty in social science in conceiving whiteness or white ethnicity other than in terms of privilege, power and superiority over other ethnicities. Whiteness as an ethnicity appears as an empty signifier devoid of content or meaning except insofar as it racializes other 'visible minorities'.

All white males are not (socially) created equal. On the contrary, by virtue of their class and ethnic identities, there are those whites who in fact share the disadvantage of their more typically 'raced' counterparts. As Rothenberg (2002, p. 3) reminds us, white privilege 'is not the same for all people with white-looking skin.' Indeed, the historical racialization of physiologically 'white' Europeans is a powerful illustration of the shifting boundaries of whiteness and its associated privileges. Recent academic titles like *How the Irish Became White* (Ignatiev, 1996), *Whiteness of a Different Colour* (Jacobson, 1999), and *How Jews Became White Folk* (Brodkin, 1998) all suggest that, over time and space, particular ethnic groups have in fact been barred from the fruits of white privilege. Indeed, 'acquired in the course of collective and individual history, white ethnicity is about becoming, being and staying "white", and its distinctiveness becomes realized in specific social and spatial locations' (Webster, 2008, p. 295). Thus, in the opening years of the twentieth century, many Europeans—Italians, Greeks, Irish, for example—were considered 'not quite white' and treated accordingly, with lower wages, limited access to prestigious jobs and educational opportunities, and a social status subordinate to their 'wholly white'—i.e., Anglo-Saxon—counterparts. Signs warning 'Italians need not apply' were nearly as common as those warning 'Negroes need not apply.' Members of these groups suffered many of the same stereotypes, biases, hostilities, and discriminatory patterns of behaviour as black Americans of the day. They ranked only slightly higher on the racial hierarchy. It was largely through concentrated labour action that their 'contributions' were recognized as worthy of racial inclusion.

Class and ethnicity, in particular, continue to shape the relative privileges of diverse white people. The designation of 'white trash' stigmatizes poor whites. And Eastern Europeans, especially newcomers, continue to be perceived with some negativity. Moreover, when we turn to gender, similar trends emerge; not all men, for example, profit equally from the dominance of 'men-as-a-class'. No less important than the hierarchy among white ethnics is the 'denial of authority to some groups of men' (Connell, 1987, p. 109). Significantly, there exists a hierarchy of masculinities in which some men are subordinated to others. Relations of power operate between masculinities and femininities, but also between an array of masculinities. Not all men share in the ability to exercise control at either the macro- or micro-social level. Below a hegemonic or dominant masculinity there is arrayed a series of subordinated masculinities. Working-class men are subordinate to capitalists; black men to white; homosexuals to heterosexuals. Goffman (1963, p. 128) may have only slightly overstated the case when he identified ideal—or **hegemonic—masculinity** as

> a young, married, white, urban, northern, heterosexual Protestant father, of college education, fully employed, of good complexion, weight and height, and a recent record in sports. . . . Any male who fails to qualify in any of these ways is likely to view himself—during moments at least—as unworthy, incomplete and inferior.

The crucial point here is that the non-qualifiers not only feel inferior, but are so judged. This is the standard according to which the hierarchy of masculinities is created, resulting in stigmatized and marginalized 'out-groups'.

The politics of privilege also work themselves out in the context of the criminal justice system. Identities shape quite dramatically the experiences we can expect in the context of victimization, offending, and service provision. As these issues are addressed at length in the chapters in Part 2, I will make only fleeting comments here.

Victimization

Since at least the 1960s, those carefully crafted hierarchies of privilege noted here and in chapter 2 have been under threat. Winant (1997, p. 41) shares this contention, observing that, traditionally, Western society constituted 'a nearly monolithic racial hierarchy, in which everyone knew his place. Today, nobody knows where he or she fits in the . . . racial order.' The traditional primacy and privilege of whiteness and of masculinity have been seriously challenged, if not eroded, since the onset of the civil rights movement. As Winant's assertion suggests, we are now in the midst of a cultural shift in which identity politics have thrown into question the historical correlation of whiteness, masculinity, and privilege. Minority groups have asserted claims to inclusion and participation, that is, to the status of Canadian. Such challenges to hegemonic cultural identities have, not surprisingly, engendered considerable anxiety and hostility.

One effect of these changes has been that white men have been led to perceive themselves as disproportionately at risk of victimization. This is, of course, at its extreme within the **white supremacist movement**, whose members fear that European Canadians face extinction on many levels, both literally and figuratively. Black crime and immigrant crime, for example, are taken as evidence of a conspiracy to eliminate white Canadians physically. And the justice system is complicit in this, since 'the guilty often go unpunished or the innocent are persecuted, not on the basis of any evidence, but based upon the racial composition of the jury' (National Alliance, *American Dissident Voices*, online). This is a sentiment shared by the National Alliance's Kevin Strom (online), who asks:

> How often are White people the victims of diverse juries who decide against the White accused or for the non-White accused because of a perception that we Whites have got it coming to us? . . . The lack of justice, the racial group think of hate Whitey, the non-White crime, the increase in the population of non-Whites, and the decrease and aging of the White population are all going to accelerate and reinforce each other.

However, even among the general population, fear of black crime, especially, remains a constant. Chapter 8, for example, illustrates this through recent survey findings that highlight the fear of **inter-racial crime**. However, the reality is that most crime is **intra-racial** rather than inter-racial—that is, victims are most likely to be victimized by members of their own race. Moreover, regardless of offender, it is people of colour who are typically most vulnerable to victimization and certainly to racial violence. Indeed, black Canadians continue to be at greatest risk of hate crime victimization (Walsh & Dauvergne, 2009; Dauvergne, 2010).

Another common misperception is that women are more vulnerable to victimization than are men. Again, this is not typically the case. Just as most violence is intra-racial, so too is most violence male on male. Of course, there are discrete contexts in which this is not the case. By far the majority of victims of sexual assault are women. Similarly, the vast majority of victims of domestic and familial violence are women and girls. This is notwithstanding recent claims of the 'symmetry of violence', by which is meant that women are as likely to use violence in intimate relationships as men.

Offending/Criminalization

The standard opening gambit for courses on race and crime asks students to imagine, or even draw, their image of the **typical offender**. All too often, the resultant figure sports dark hair and dark skin. Indeed, public opinion surveys still reveal that Canadians tend to equate crime with race, and especially with black Canadians. The media do little to dispel this construct. Indeed, images of the 'predatory Other' are reinforced by media representations of crime. Recall the earlier discussion of how our language 'races' only those who are not white. So, too, is this the case in the context of crime, whereby reference is commonly made to the 'black suspect' but rarely to the 'white suspect'. Mirchandi and Chan (2002, p. 15) remind us that the '**racialized** nature of social problems in Canada is a trend that is neither new nor original. Racialized groups have been historically the targets of moral panics and continue to be stereotyped as the criminal "other".'

Yasmin Jiwani (chapter 3, this volume) draws explicit attention to the tendency to conflate race with crime. Mirchandi and Chan (2002) draw a similar connection between the mutually constitutive processes of racialization and criminalization, referring to the 'merging' of the two. In particular, they argue that racialized communities have been over-criminalized. Similarly, Holdaway's (1996; Holdaway & Barron, 1997) extensive work on black police officers in the United Kingdom explicitly examines the racialization of British police, by which he means the 'ways in which "race" is constructed within the relationships between the police and black and Asian people' (Holdaway, 1996, p. 23). Thus, he, too, links the process of racialization with the process of criminalization.

Yet, objectively, crime statistics paint a different picture of the 'typical offender'. Consistently, across the Western world, the prototypical offender is a young, white male. Sadly, relevant data in Canada are hard to come by, given that we do not collect data on race within the justice system (see chapters 5–9 of this volume). However, we have ample statistical evidence of the very high proportion of crime committed by youth and young adults (chapter 15) and the very low proportion of crime committed by women and girls (e.g., Kong & AuCoin, 2008; chapter 12, this volume). At a glance, the limited 'official' data on race seems to lend credence to the criminogenic nature of Aboriginal peoples, at least in some provinces. Nationally, they constitute fewer than 20 per cent of the incarcerated population. Yet in some provinces and territories, they make up well over half of the prison population. In Manitoba, they account for about 75 per cent of the federally incarcerated population, and in Saskatchewan a remarkable 76 per cent. However, it is fool-hardy to assume that this has anything to do with the inherent nature of Aboriginal peoples; rather, it has far more to do with their historical and contemporary conditions of life, as Jane Dickson-Gilmore makes clear in chapter 5 of this volume. Moreover, even in terms of incarceration, whites dominate the population. In chapter 8, Scot Wortley documents the racial distribution of national prison populations, showing that whites constitute approximately two-thirds of inmates. The next highest concentration is among Aboriginal people, who make up less than 20 per cent, with all other racial groups under 10 per cent. Even by this rough standard, then, the typical offender is not a person of colour, but white.

There are, moreover, two areas in which white men excel as offenders: **corporate crime** and **hate crime**. In his discussion of 'varieties of real men', Jim Messerschmidt (1993, p. 133) highlights the ways in which the raced and gendered nature of corporations 'ensure[s] white men positions of power, where corporate crimes originate'. Indeed, in Canada, such positions of power are clearly occupied by a very narrow slice of the population. They are about two-thirds male (*The Daily*, 2006), and 90 per cent white (*Catalyst*, 2008), and the distribution is even more skewed at the most senior levels. Thus, the corporation and its related legal and illegal activities are the purview of white males.

In chapter 11, Bryan Hogeveen alludes to the impacts of corporate crime on society and on individuals. Corporate crime accounts for far more harm and monetary loss than typical street crimes, yet it is largely invisible as a targeted social problem. For example, Jeffry Reiman (2007) estimates—conservatively—that in 2003 white-collar crime as a whole accounted for approximately $418 billion in direct costs in the United States. This stands in dramatic contrast to the $17 billion in loss attributed to traditional property crimes as reported in the Uniform Crime Report.

Social and individual losses are corporate gains. The sorts of offences carried out by corporate offenders serve the purpose of lining the pockets of shareholders and agents both by increasing profits and reducing costs. On the one hand, fraud (e.g., Bernie Madoc), tax evasion, securities theft, and so on derive direct cash benefits. On the other hand, cost reduction activities are more indirect in their contribution to the bottom line, often involving such things as failure to comply with health and safety standards or failure to address known product defects (e.g., Toyota's sticky accelerators).

Just as corporate crime reinforces economic relations of power, so too does hate crime reinforce social and cultural relations of power. Challenges to social constructions of difference threaten the carefully moulded perceptions about how the world should be and what each person's or each group's place should be in that world. When confronted with such novelties, one means by which to 'put things right' is through violence. Consequently, hate crime provides a context in which the perpetrator can reassert his or her privileged identity and at the same time punish the victim(s) for the individual or collective performance of his or her identity. In other words, hate-motivated violence is used to sustain the privilege of the dominant group and to police the boundaries between groups by reminding the Others of their place. Perpetrators thus recreate their own masculinity, or whiteness, for example, while punishing the victims for their deviant identity performance.

Violence can also be used as a mechanism to reinforce gendered identities. At least with respect to domestic violence, men's perceived sense of ownership continues to provide a context for the victimization of women. The structured inequality of women leaves them vulnerable to the presumption of male control by whatever means necessary. It establishes an environment in which men freely manipulate the terms of a relationship. Violence becomes one such means by which he can prove that he is 'the man' and therefore in control. And, as with racially motivated violence, gender-motivated violence often emerges in the context of what is perceived by men as a loss of relative position. Challenges to the collective privilege of men are often met with aggressive attempts to reassert the 'natural' dominance of men. It is, in these terms, a reactive expression of insecurity in the face of reconstituted femininities.

It is no coincidence that violent crime perpetrated against women has risen so steadily in the four decades that correspond to the rise of the women's movement. As women have collectively striven to redefine themselves as autonomous actors, some men have been compelled to meet the challenge by resorting to the readily available resource of violence. Marc Lepine is a case in point. On 6 December 1989, Lepine entered a classroom at Montreal's École Polytéchnique, systematically separated the male and female engineering students, and opened fire on the women. Before he killed himself, Lepine murdered 14 women and seriously injured 9 others. In his verbal harangue during the shooting and in his suicide note, Lepine made it clear that his assault was intended to punish the 'uppity' feminists he held responsible for his personal failures—in particular, his inability to get into engineering school. Lepine's response was extreme but nonetheless illustrative of the male response to the erosion of white male privilege.

Intuitively, this analysis implies that domestic violence perpetrated against women of colour may be especially problematic, as noted in chapter 2. Women of colour are multiply disadvantaged by gender, race, and often class, and thus highly vulnerable to violence. That this is the case is also suggested by recent trends toward increasing domestic violence among Aboriginal people, for example (McGillivray & Comaksey, 2004). The traditionally egalitarian nature of these people has been distorted by their more recent history of racial discrimination and disempowerment. Racial and economic disadvantage, coupled with the incursion of European gender ideals, has dramatically altered the place of Aboriginal women. Increasingly, like their white counterparts, these women are expected to perform the rituals of domestic femininity as a complement to the male performance of patriarch.

Another intriguing Canadian illustration of this trend can be found in Asian and South Asian communities. In contrast to what is often a very traditional division of labour and power in their homeland, Asian and South Asian immigrants to Canada find that their abilities to maintain the boundaries are compromised. Asian and South Asian women in this country are more likely to be employed, albeit in low-wage occupations, than either their counterparts at home or their male partners in Canada (see chapters 7 and 9, this volume). Consequently, they assume an elevated position in the family as breadwinner and decision maker—a clear threat to the masculinity, authority, and place of their husbands. As in the parallel white patriarchal family, violence can come to represent a levelling influence. Asian immigrant males' inability to sustain traditional patriarchal identities and women's challenges to an idealized and subordinate femininity have resulted in elevated rates of family violence among these families (chapter 9). Such violence is a readily available means to resurrect 'normal' relations of power whereby women are reminded that, regardless of their economic contributions, their true place is in the kitchen, their true occupation the care and nurturing of the family.

Service Provision

There is no denying that the criminal justice system is an entity largely made by and for white, middle-class men. It has long been an institution that has helped to define and reinforce white, middle-class norms. We saw earlier in this chapter and in chapter 2 how the law, generally, has been used to support the privileges that accrue to white men. Moreover, the law has both material and ideological effects. On the one hand, the law itself can effectively exclude or restrict the participation of particular groups in the ongoing activities and processes of society—for example, restrictions on women's ability to practise medicine. The law can also—by its silences—exclude groups from protections afforded others, such as in the failure to include gays or women in hate crime or civil rights legislation. The latter examples have both material and ideological effects in that such exclusions leave the unnamed groups vulnerable to bias-motivated attacks while simultaneously sending the message that they are unworthy of protection and therefore legitimate victims. Law and legal ruminations are discursive practices by which Self and Other are constructed and arranged hierarchically.

There is an endless array of examples of legislation and policy that maintain the relative positions of the privileged and not-so-privileged: anti-abortion policies limit women's autonomy; social security restrictions endanger and exclude immigrants; Aboriginal policy marginalizes First Nation populations. In their own way, each of these pieces serves to marginalize or subordinate the groups in question. They raise questions about particular groups' legitimacy and place in Canadian society.

In the context of the criminal justice system specifically, the insider status of the privileged is reinforced by employment patterns. For the most part, criminal justice is 'white man's work'. There has, sadly, been little relevant scholarship in Canada on this issue—this in spite of the dramatic under-representation of visible minorities in justice-related jobs in Canada, well under 10 per cent. An additional barrier to understanding these patterns is that, even internationally, the literature focuses largely on policing to the exclusion of other categories of workers. Thus, as an illustration of the broader trends, I focus here on policing, drawing largely on work arising out of the United Kingdom. The emerging literature on the presence and impact of racism against black police officers in the UK is consistent and convincing, and can thus provide some insight here. Recent studies of both resigned or serving officers in the UK show the extent to which officers perceived racist behaviour and policies as a normative part of their careers. Holdaway's (2004, p. 856) succinct summary of the collective findings of research spanning the 1980s and 1990s indicates that such experiences covered the spectrum from individual acts of racism to the systemic patterns associated with **institutional racism**:

> Ethnic-minority officers' experience was of frequent prejudice and discrimination, expressed through joking, banter, exclusion from full membership of their work team, little confidence in the willingness or ability of immediate and more senior supervisors to deal with the difficulties they faced, and an acceptance of the virtual inevitability of racism in the police workforce.

Consistently, Holdaway's respondents, and those queried in similar studies found that officers from black and minority ethnic (BME) communities felt that they were seen first as black or Asian and then as police officers. Their racial status could never quite allow them to fully integrate into their professional status; they were prohibited by virtue of their race from joining the 'brotherhood'. Daily reminders in the form of racial jokes and epithets combined with the more subtle forms of exclusion to render them perpetual outsiders (Holdaway, 1996; Holdaway & Barron, 1997).

In light of the above, and in light of the persistently contentious relationship between police and BME communities, it should come as no surprise that black men and women are dramatically under-represented in policing in most Western nations. A significant contributing factor to the difficulties in recruiting black officers is the paucity of role models because of the elevated attrition rates of black officers. Holdaway's (1996; Holdaway & Barron, 1997) work on resignations is seminal in this context. Holdaway and Barron (1997) offer their observation that virtually all black and Asian officers who had resigned from policing did so because of their experiences of prejudice and racism, which ranged from the persistent use of stereotypes and racialized language to outright insults and harassment. What cemented their decision was the lack of action on the part of superiors—that is, the occupational culture of racism was condoned by an indifferent administration. A more recent study on retention (Cooper & Ingram, 2004) indicates that racism within the police service continues to drive officers out. Among the BME officers surveyed, half agreed that discrimination—whether against them or against other BME officers or BME communities—conditioned their decision to leave, either by resignation or transfer.

One of the discriminatory practices that undoubtedly influences officers' perceptions of their workplace is the limited potential for advancement. Perceived limits on progression through the ranks are major disincentives to recruitment of people of colour. And indeed there is substantial evidence to bear this out. It was not until 2003 that the first black chief constable was appointed (in Kent). This late occurrence is indicative of the broader patterns of slow progression for black and Asian officers in the police service. Additionally, it is apparent that promotion is very slow in coming to those who apply. Bland et al. (1999) found that it took 5 months and 18 months longer for Asian and black officers, respectively, to be promoted than for their white counterparts.

Just as the raced nature of policing keeps people of colour out, so too does its gendered nature work to exclude women. Police work embodies the ideals of aggressive masculinity: toughness, bravery, strength. Consequently, women are deemed unfit for such work, 'since traditionally they are viewed as weak, indecisive, emotionally unstable and timid' (Erez & Tontodonato, 1992, p. 241). When women enter the world of law enforcement, the masculinity of the role becomes questionable. Susan Martin's work has aptly demonstrated the threat posed to men's status and self-image as women increasingly enter the traditional male stronghold of policing. It is felt to be imperative, therefore, that males reassert their masculinity and their power by subordinating women. Sexual harassment is one resource for this work of 'doing gender'. It allows men to reassert the gendered and sexualized distinction between men and women.

Women who enter policing are perceived to be violating the code of femininity. A police academy training officer is reported to have told a female recruit that 'this is my personal opinion; I don't think you should be in this job. You should go home and have babies' (Wexler

& Logan, 1983, p. 50). This sentiment is shared by another male officer who asserted that '[a] woman can't be refined and be a police officer too. Women give up some of their femininity to work this job' (Martin, 1992, p. 294). Women are assigned a certain 'essence' that demands adherence to a very narrow conception of how femininity is to be enacted—and engagement in policing is not part of it. Kanter's (1977) work in organizational cultures has relevance here. Women are held to be accountable to three primary modes of femininity: mother, sex object, kid sister. Should they refuse any of these and adopt alternative gendered identities, they are assigned the identity of 'iron maiden' and thus denigrated and harassed.

In response, women police officers attempt to reconstruct their femininity. Martin (1992) draws an interesting distinction between police*women* and *police*women as a means of characterizing the different femininities female police officers typically enact. Police*women* attempt to maintain accountability to traditional femininity 'by acquiescing to stereotypic feminine roles and seeking sex-typed assignments' (p. 293). These women recreate traditional femininity within the masculine field by engaging in 'women's work' (e.g., domestic violence cases, juvenile offenders) and by exploiting their own sexuality.

In contrast, *police*women construct something of an oppositional femininity by which they assert traits associated with the police culture: aggression, professionalism, and toughness, for example (Martin, 1992). However, this too is often met with further harassment and defamation (e.g., 'dyke', 'bitch'). Rather than interpret this as a kind of femininity, male officers fear that such a construction of identity by a woman further blurs the boundaries between men and women.

To be sure, recent years have seen concentrated attempts on the part of criminal justice agencies to change the demographics of their staff. In particular, we have seen aggressive recruitment from traditionally excluded communities. While still below their representation within the labour force, the proportion of visible minorities in the police departments of Canada's largest and most diverse cities increased as much as fourfold over the 1990s. Between 1990 and 1997, for example, the proportion of visible-minority officers in Ottawa increased from 2.3 to 8.3 per cent, while in Edmonton, the change was from 2 to 5.3 per cent (Jain, Singh, & Agocs, 2006). The Toronto Police Service has been especially aggressive in recruiting from among key equity groups in the first decade of the twenty-first century, such that one-half of new recruits in 2006 were from those communities and one-third were from visible-minority groups specifically (BMO Financial Group, 2008). Nationally, women have also made some advances, growing from a proportion of one in eight (1999) to one in five (2009) (*The Daily*, 2009).

The strategies that have contributed to this growth have been innovative and varied. Jain, Singh, and Agocs (2008), for example, catalogue both traditional and more creative approaches. Among the former are the use of traditional media outlets and employee referrals. In line with the desire for better-educated recruits, college and university recruiting has increased dramatically, while reliance on high school contacts has declined. Similarly, the focus has shifted from using mainstream media outlets to advertising in diverse community publications and venues. Some agencies are also working more closely with community organizations, soliciting their advice on how best to make inroads within under-represented groups. The Toronto Police

Service has also begun to recruit at ethnic community events and to hold celebrations of diversity that themselves become recruitment opportunities.

Summary

This chapter has sought to highlight the historical and contemporary contours of white male privilege and their implications for criminal justice concerns. It opened with a discussion of what is meant by the idea of white male privilege, but then problematized the concept by addressing the ways in which not all white men are created equal. There are distinctions among and between white men's position and status, dependent on such factors as ethnicity, class, and sexuality.

Nonetheless, there are identifiable ways in which white men as an identifiable collective reap the benefits of their privilege, both inside and outside the home, across virtually all social institutions. In particular, they occupy positions of power economically, politically, and socially. This means, too, that they have different experiences in the context of criminal justice. Specifically, young white men tend to account for most crime; white males tend to be less vulnerable to victimization and especially to racial violence than their non-white peers, but more vulnerable than women regardless of the women's race; and, finally, white males are dominant as service providers across the continuum of criminal justice professions, including such roles as judges, lawyers, and police officers.

Key Terms

citizenship	hegemonic	masculinity	slavery
corporate crime	masculinity	McIntosh, Peggy	'typical' offender
deculturation	heterosexuality	'mythical norm'	unearned advantage
earned advantage	institutional racism	power	wage differential
emphasized feminity	inter- and intra-racial	privilege	whiteness
gendered division of	crime	racialization of crime	white supremacist
labour	'invisible knapsack'	reproductive labour	movement
hate crime	job segregation	rights	

Questions for Critical Thought

1. McIntosh lists the 'privileges' attributed to her solely on the basis of her race; Mullaly provides examples of other kinds of privileges. Do a parallel analysis of three kinds of privilege associated with identities other than whiteness.
2. What mechanisms reinforce white male privilege? Provide concrete examples. How might white male privilege be deconstructed?
3. What sorts of recruitment strategies might be effective in creating more diverse and thus more representative criminal justice agencies?

Additional Readings

Brodkin, K. (1998). *How Jews became white folk and what that says about race in America*. New Brunswick, NJ: Rutgers University Press.

Crenshaw, K. (1994). Mapping the margins: Intersectionality, identity and violence against women of colour. In M. Albertson Fineman & R. Mykitiuk (Eds), *The public nature of private violence* (pp. 93–118). New York: Routledge.

McIntosh, P. (2002). White privilege: Unpacking the invisible knapsack. In P. Rothenberg (Ed.), *White privilege: Essential readings on the other side of racism* (pp. 97–102). New York: Worth.

Mullaly, B. (2010). *Challenging oppression and confronting privilege*. Toronto: Oxford University Press.

Webster, C. (2008). Marginalized white ethnicity, race and crime. *Theoretical Criminology, 12*(3): 293–312.

Websites of Interest

Corporate Crime Reporter: www.corporatecrimereporter.com

Mirrors of Privilege: Making Whiteness Visible: www.youtube.com/watch?v=pAljja0vi2M&feature=related

White Privilege: http://whitepriv.blogspot.com

References

Barnes, A. S. (1985). *The black middle class family*. Bristol, IN: Wyndham Hall Press.

Bland, N., Mundy, G., Russell, J., & Tuffin, R. (1999). *The career progression of minority ethnic police officers*. London: Home Office.

BMO Financial Group. Canada's best diversity employers. www.canadastop100.com/diversity

Brodkin, K. (1998). *How Jews became white folk and what that says about race in America*. New Brunswick, NJ: Rutgers University Press.

Catalyst. (2008). Quick takes: Visible minorities. www.catalyst.org/publication/243/visible-minorities

Coltrane, S. (1995). Stability and change in Chicano men's family lives. In M. Kimmel & M. Messner (Eds), *Men's lives* (pp. 469–484). Needham Heights, MA: Allyn and Bacon.

Connell, R. (1987). *Gender and power*. Stanford, CA: Stanford University Press.

Cook, D. (1993). Racism, citizenship and exclusion. In D. Cook & B. Hudson (Eds), *Racism and criminology* (pp. 136–157). London, UK: Sage.

Cooper, C., & Ingram, S. (2004). *Retention of police officers: A study of resignations and transfers in ten forces*. London: Home Office.

The Daily. (2006, March 7). Women in Canada. Statistics Canada.

The Daily. (2009, December 14). Police personnel and expenditures. Statistics Canada.

Dauvergne, M. (2010). Police-reported hate crime in Canada, 2008. *Juristat, 30*(2). Ottawa: Statistics Canada. Catalogue no. 85-002-X.

Diversity Institute. (2009). Diversecity counts: A snapshot of diversity in the Greater Toronto Area. Toronto: Diversity Institute, Ryerson University.

Erez, E., & Tontodonato, P. (1992). Sexual harassment in the criminal justice system. In I. Moyer (Ed.), *The changing roles of women in the criminal justice system* (pp. 227–252). Prospect Heights, IL: Waveland.

Fernandez, J. (1996). The impact of racism on whites in corporate America. In B. Bowser and R. Hunt (Eds), *Impacts of racism on white Americans*. Thousand Oaks, CA: Sage.

Goffman, E. (1963). *Stigma: Notes on the management of spoiled identity*. New York: Touchstone Books.

Hacker, A. (1995). *Two nations: Black and white, separate, hostile, unequal*. New York: Ballantine Books.

Hochschild, A. (1995). The second shift: Employed women are putting in another day of work at home. In M. Kimmel & M. Messner (Eds), *Men's Lives* (pp. 443–447). Needham Heights, MA: Allyn and Bacon.

Holdaway, S. (1996). *The racialisation of British policing*. Basingstoke, UK: Macmillan.

Holdaway, S. (2004). The development of black police associations: Changing articulations of race within the police. *British Journal of Criminology, 44*, 854–865.

Holdaway, S., & Barron, A.-M. (1997). *Resigners? The experience of black and Asian police officers*. Basingstoke, UK: Macmillan.

Ignatiev, N. (1996). *How the Irish became white*. New York: Routledge.

Jacobson, M. (1999). *Whiteness of a different colour: European immigrants and the alchemy of race*. Boston: Harvard University Press.

Jain, H., Singh, P., & Agocs, C. (2008). Recruitment, selection and promotion of visible-minority and aboriginal police officers in selected Canadian police services. *Canadian Public Administration, 43*(1): 46–74.

Kanter, R. (1977). *Men and women of the corporation*. New York: Basic Books.

Kong, R., & AuCoin, K. (2008). Female offenders in Canada. *Juristat 28*(1). Ottawa: Statistics Canada. Catalogue no. 85-002-XIE.

Leadership Conference on Civil Rights. (n.d.). *Justice on trial: Racial disparities in the American criminal justice system*. Washington, DC: LCCR. Retrieved on November 10, 2005, from www.civilrights.org/publications/reports/cj/

Lorber, J. (1994). *Paradoxes of Gender*. New Haven, CT: Yale University Press.

Lorde, A. (1995). Age, race, class and sex: Women redefining difference. In J. Arthur & A. Shapiro (Eds), *Campus wars: Multiculturalism and the politics of difference* (pp. 191–198). Boulder, CO: Westview.

McGillivray, A., & Comaskey, B. (2004). *Black eyes all of the time: Intimate violence, Aboriginal women, and the justice system*. Toronto: University of Toronto Press.

McIntosh, P. (2002). White privilege: Unpacking the invisible knapsack. In P. Rothenberg (Ed.), *White privilege: Essential readings on the other side of racism* (pp. 97–102). New York: Worth.

Martin, S. (1992). The changing status of women officers: Gender and power in police work. In I. Moyer (Ed.), *The changing roles of women in the criminal justice system* (pp. 281–305). Prospect Heights, IL: Waveland.

Messerschmidt, J. (1993). *Masculinities and crime*. Lanham, MD: Rowman and Littlefield.

Mirchandi, W., & Chan, K. (2002). From race and crime to racialization and criminalization. In W. Mirchandi & K. Chan (Eds), *Crimes of colour* (pp. 9–24). Peterborough, ON: Broadview Press.

Mullaly, B. (2010). *Challenging oppression and confronting privilege*. Toronto: Oxford University Press.

National Alliance. *American dissident voices*. www.natall.com/free-speech

Pinkney, A. (1994). *White hate crimes*. Chicago: Third World Press.

Reiman, J. (2007). *The rich get richer and the poor get prison* (8th ed.). Boston: Pearson/Allyn and Bacon.

Rothenberg, P. (2002). Introduction. In P. Rothenberg (Ed.), *White privilege: Essential readings on the other side of racism* (pp. 1–8). New York: Worth.

Smith, R. (1995). *Racism in the post-civil rights era*. Albany NY: SUNY Press.

Taub, N., & Schneider, E. (1990). Women's subordination and the role of law. In D. Kairys (Ed.), *The politics of law* (pp. 151–176). New York: Pantheon.

Walsh, P., & Dauvergne, M. (2009). Police-reported hate crime in Canada, 2007. *Juristat, 29*(2). Ottawa: Statistics Canada. Catalogue no. 85-002-X.

Webster, C. (2008). Marginalized white ethnicity, race and crime. *Theoretical Criminology, 12*(3): 293–312.

Wellman, D. (1993). *Portraits of white racism*. Cambridge, UK: Cambridge University Press.

Wexler, J., & Logan, D. (1983). Sources of stress among women police officers. *Journal of Police Science and Administration, 11*(1), 46–53.

Winant, H. (1997). Where culture meets structure. In D. Kendall (Ed.), *Race, class and gender in a diverse society* (pp. 27–38). Boston: Allyn and Bacon.

Categories
of Difference

The core of this section addresses the particular experiences that an array of communities have had with social and criminal justice. As noted in the opening chapter, the selection of identity groups will not please everyone. There will be those who will be critical of the categories left out and the categories left in. What I have attempted to do is provide insights into those communities that are most visible demographically but also in terms of their contact with the justice system.

I asked each contributor to this section to follow a consistent format, opening with a conceptual overview of the group in question that includes historical experiences, cultural trends, and so on. One thing that these chapters make clear is that disproportionate vulnerability to victimization and criminalization is embedded in broader and deeper patterns of systemic discrimination in other realms. We see, for example, how stereotypes render racialized groups vulnerable to the undue attention of police, and how un- and underemployment make crime a viable option. We also see how historical and contemporary practices of patriarchy leave women at an elevated risk of intimate violence. It is important for the reader to be aware of these conditioning factors.

What makes this volume unique in terms of coverage is that it does not fall into the trap of focusing only on the 'holy trinity' of race, class, and gender. It is grounded in a much more inclusive understanding of diversity, such that it also touches on identities grounded in religion, ability, sexuality, and age. Like many racialized communities, for example, Muslims and those within LGBT communities are at an elevated risk of hate crime. People with disabilities are often misunderstood and thus mistreated by criminal justice personnel. The very young and the very old are vulnerable to familial abuse. The chapters thus uncover remarkable consistencies across groups.

Several contributors address the experiences of racialized communities. This is always a problematic topic, given the paucity of 'official' data on race and justice in Canada, as will become evident in the chapters that follow. Several authors make mention of this fact and 'apologize' for their inability to provide more concrete data. Fortunately, there has been a recent flurry of scholarly research in this area, so that authors are able to draw on very current findings to flesh out their observations.

Given the evident failure of the justice system to treat all comers equitably, this section makes it clear that one of the areas that must be addressed is that of service provision. There is little evidence that the communities noted here have been proportionately integrated into the justice system as front-line personnel. Women and people of colour continue to be under-represented as police officers, judges, or correctional officers, for example. In short, the system that is meant to serve them does not reflect their perspectives and interests. Similarly, there is a shortage of culturally specific programs within the justice system. The strongest areas in this respect are perhaps Aboriginal services and services for female victims of intimate violence. Yet even these are inadequate. Consequently, several authors highlight the importance of grassroots initiatives devised and designed by the affected communities.

A final conclusion that might be drawn from these chapters is that a great deal of work remains to be done before we can fully understand the nature of victimization, offending, and criminalization in Canada. With very little data or scholarship to guide them, the authors in this book have done a masterful job of articulating emerging patterns. It is to be hoped that the evidence of dramatic disparities presented here will inspire further analysis by the next generation of race/justice scholars in Canada.

5 Aboriginal People in Canada: Culture, Colonialism, and Criminal Justice

JANE DICKSON-GILMORE

All Aboriginal people are victims, at least in an historical sense, of colonization and dispossession. The vast majority continue to live in conditions of appalling disadvantage. Despite this, the vast majority of Aboriginal people in both urban and rural areas of Australia have never been arrested by the police for any offence.

(Weatherburn, Fitzgerald, & Hua, 2003, p. 70)

... the quantity and quality of law enforcement the citizens receive, both as victim and as suspect, reflects the underlying pattern of social stratification in society.

(Norris, Fielding, & Kemp, 1994, p. 62)

It is not uncommon to hear Canadians, whether in the media or casual conversation, refer to 'the Canadian Indian', as if there were only one such person, and all those falling under the label live the same sort of lives in very similar cultural contexts. And yet such a homogeneous view is belied by the remarkable diversity and complexity of First Nations and Aboriginal people who reside within Canadian borders (Drost, 2001). While Canada struggles with bilingualism, Aboriginal people speak over 60 different languages across 52 different cultural groups, from the Haida of British Columbia's West Coast, through the Crees and Blackfoot of the Prairies, the Mohawks and Algonquin of central Canada, and on to the Micmac of the East Coast and the Inuit of the Far North.

Within these cultures are a similar variety of communities and individuals residing in both rural and urban settings, at all levels of the socio-economic spectrum, and within social, political, and economic contexts characterized by considerable and ongoing change. For example, in 1951, only 6.7 per cent of Aboriginal people lived in cities; by 2001, 49 per cent lived in cities. Today, approximately 71 per cent of Aboriginal people reside off-reserve, and 59 per cent (Newhouse & Peters, 2003) live in large cities such as Edmonton, Regina, and Winnipeg, or in smaller urban centres. The exodus from **reserves** is not surprising. While some reserves, such as the Mohawk reserve at Kahnawake, Quebec, are prosperous, positive places in which to live, these are the exception to a more general rule of a reserve life characterized by poverty, blocked opportunity, and ill health. According to the **Assembly of First Nations**, the political body representing **status Indians** in Canada, conditions on far too many reserves closely resemble those we normally associate with the Third World (Assembly of First Nations, n.d.). Housing is substandard from the point of construction, and many homes lack even the most basic of amenities, such as indoor plumbing. Overcrowding is rampant (Assembly of First Nations, n.d.), and in July 2009, 116 communities had received warnings that their water supplies were compromised and presented significant risks to human health (Blatchford, 2009). Poor living environments cultivate disease and despair. Rates of tuberculosis, a disease Canada once congratulated itself for eradicating within its borders, are 8 to 10 times higher on reserves than outside them, and the H1N1 epidemic hit reserve communities much harder than non-Aboriginal communities, especially in rural and isolated areas. First Nations, while constituting only 4 per cent of the Canadian population, account for 16 per cent of new HIV/AIDS diagnoses (Assembly of First Nations, n.d.).

The disarray and dysfunction that challenge a remarkable percentage of the 609 Indian bands and communities across Canada are rooted in the history of **dispossession** and state-induced marginalization of Aboriginal people. Although the early period of the Aboriginal-newcomer relationship was characterized by a balance fostered by mutual need and shared interests, as the dependence of the newcomers on their Aboriginal partners in trade and warfare diminished, so did the ability of Aboriginal leaders to press newcomer governments to respect the **treaties** and keep their promises. First Nations came to be seen as impediments to **colonization** and progress, and were treated accordingly. State policies sought to 'civilize' and 'christianize' Aboriginal people, and by 1850 the federal government moved to define and control virtually all aspects of Indian life through legislation that culminated in the modern **Indian Act** (R.S.C., 1985, c-I-5). The goals of this early legislation were clear: Aboriginal people were to be **assimilated** into Canadian life; they were to be transformed from 'red men' to 'white', and this transition was to be achieved through **residential schooling**, land surrenders, and relegation onto reserves, as well as the imposition of non-Aboriginal models of family, social life, spirituality, and governance, which facilitated the erosion of indigenous cultures and societies.

The systematic deconstruction of Aboriginal life was devastating for many Aboriginal people, who saw within the state's rejection of their lifestyles and cultures a rejection of their personhood and humanity. Caught between a traditional heritage undermined by colonialism and colonization and a 'new world' that seemed reluctant to make a place for them, Aboriginal people stood firm against the state and struggled to create lives in the often untenable middle ground of reserve life. The strains of that struggle are evident in their modern communities, however, as many are beset with high rates of school leaving among youth, high unemployment, dissolution of the family unit, and high rates of single-parent, female-head-of-household families, especially in the cities (Dickson-Gilmore & La Prairie, 2005). Perhaps most telling, however, are the numbers of suicides among Aboriginal people: rates of suicide among Aboriginals between the ages of 10 and 24 years of age are estimated to be five to six times higher than among non-Aboriginal Canadians in the same age range (Assembly of First Nations, n.d.; Allard, Wilkins, & Berthelot, 2004).

Faced with the poverty, disease, and marginalization that characterizes myriad Indian reserves, it is not surprising that many Aboriginal people who cannot physically escape the reserve will try to escape through drugs and alcohol. Yet these offer only limited release and often exacerbate the stresses and strains of life on the margins, leading to high rates of family and partner violence and conflict, as well as other harms. These events foster high rates of conflict with the law, which feed into the gross over-representation of Aboriginal people at all levels of the Canadian criminal justice system. Although adult Aboriginal people comprise only 2 per cent of the Canadian population, they constitute 17 per cent of the federal adult prison population; in some provincial institutions, rates of **over-representation** are much worse. For example, in 2006 in Saskatchewan, where the adult Aboriginal population comprises 8 per cent of the provincial adult population, Aboriginal adults accounted for 76 per cent of admissions to adult institutions; in the Northwest Territories, where Aboriginal adults make up 54 per cent of the adult population, a full 93 per cent of adult admissions to provincial correctional institutions were Aboriginal.

Attempts to understand the high rates of over-representation of Aboriginal people within Canadian courts and prisons coalesce into four broad streams of analysis and argument. The first posits that Aboriginal people find themselves disproportionately caught up in criminal justice processes because they experience **differential criminal justice processing** that arises from racial discrimination on the part of those who work in the system, as well as from a fundamental discord between traditional indigenous modes of conflict management and resolution and those endemic to Western law. Here, argument relies largely upon the compelling qualitative reports of the inappropriate and outright criminal treatment of some Aboriginal people caught up in the system. These are the stories of Minnie Sutherland, an Aboriginal woman left for dead by a hit-and-run driver, only to be discovered by police. The police, assuming her lack of consciousness was caused by alcohol rather than an automobile accident, took her to a detox centre that refused to admit a 'drunk Indian'. She was later left in a jail cell to 'dry out' and was then released. Sutherland died seven days later from head injuries caused in the accident. Other, perhaps more famous, cases include the experiences of Donald Marshall, Jr, and Fred Quilt, such practices as the 'Starlight Tours' (Reber & Renaud, 2006),[1] and the failure of the police to investigate adequately the disappearances of over 500 Aboriginal women over the past decade.[2]

As an attempt to explain over-representation, the 'culture-clash' position and the issue of racism it reifies are certainly among the most prominent and well-publicized lines of argument. However, while it is unquestionable that discrimination and, in some contexts, outright racism constitute *one part* of a larger configuration of factors feeding into over-representation, the current research indicates strongly that racism is neither the sole nor even the major part of the problem—at least in the system, if not in society. In fact, the available data suggest that the involvement of Aboriginal people in the criminal justice and correctional systems cannot be attributed to racial bias alone. For example, one of the most critical gaps in information about the causes of over-representation is the role of police in charging. While anecdotal accounts abound, there are very few data collected through participant observation or any other kind of systematic research strategy that can assist us in arguing for shifts in police practice. As a result, while reports of police wrong-doing emerge in the media, it is impossible to say much with confidence about the role of the police in over-representation generally, or more interestingly, about whether they play a role in the regional variation in over-representation observed across the country.

The situation facing Aboriginal accused at court is also unclear, as research into such matters as prosecutorial decision making is largely absent in Canada Where data does exist, it indicates that unintended discrimination may be a bigger problem than consciously racist tendencies on the part of system actors. In like fashion, there is very little good comparative sentencing research that could illuminate the question of whether discrimination and racism have an impact on Aboriginal defendants at the point of sentencing. What limited research has been done on this question tends toward a common position—namely, that while carceral sentences may be used more often for Aboriginal offenders, this may be more an issue of *risk* than discrimination. Insofar as Aboriginal offenders are more likely to have longer records and therefore present higher-risk profiles at sentencing, they are more likely to receive sentences of incarceration.

While there is little well-constructed research at this time to support the culture clash/racism argument, there is a growing body of work that challenges that argument and compels researchers to look for other explanations for over-representation. For example, research focusing on sentence length as part of the explanation of over-representation has produced a substantial body of evidence that appears to confirm the somewhat unexpected possibility that Aboriginal offenders tend to receive shorter sentences than non-Aboriginal offenders. This finding is consistent across both federal institutions and some provincially sentenced offenders as well. For example, as early as 1982, Correctional Services Canada (CSC) data showed that native admissions tended to be very similar or marginally shorter, than their non-Native counterparts with the same admitting offence (Moyer, 1987). Since that time, similar findings have been generated in other studies, particularly in research involving federal offenders (York, 1995; Shaw, 1991).

Research that looks into sentencing at the provincial level suggests that the situation there is more complex but has also produced outcomes that may help us understand why Aboriginal defendants receive shorter sentences in spite of their longer, and often more challenging, offending histories. Clark (1989) and Hagan (1975), in dated but nonetheless interesting work, discovered that many judges were aware of the difficult conditions facing Aboriginal accused and that this may influence the nature of the sentences they hand down. This is intriguing, as it suggests that the 1996 changes to the Canadian Criminal Code (R.S.C. 1985, c. C-46) provisions around sentencing contained in s. 718.2(e), which compel judges to consider such factors and actively to seek to treat Aboriginal offenders in more culturally informed and appropriate ways, may have been, at least in part, largely redundant.

Indeed, this amendment, which was intended as a means to achieve more appropriate sentencing and as a support for Aboriginal decarceration, appears not only to have been redundant, but also to have been unable to reduce over-representation. In the wake of s. 718.2(e), interpretations of the section by the Supreme Court of Canada in **R. v. Gladue** ([1999] 1 S.C.R. 688), *R. v. Wells* ([2000] S.C.C. 10), and a succession of cases that considered the 'unique circumstances' of Aboriginal offenders and 'all available sanctions other than imprisonment' have failed to reduce over-representation in any significant measure. This is largely due to the Court's reasoning that where serious or violent offences are involved, sentences handed down to Aboriginal offenders are likely to be the same or similar to those meted out to non-Aboriginal offenders, notwithstanding the 'unique circumstances' of Aboriginal accused. Given the disproportionate rate at which Aboriginal offenders commit serious violent crimes against the person—acts that must be contextualized within often lengthy and substantial offending histories—it is unlikely that s. 718.2(e) could have significantly affected prison populations.

It is possible that s. 718.2(e) and *Gladue*'s most significant impact lies not in the numbers of Aboriginal offenders kept out of prison, but rather in the remarkable number of Aboriginal offenders whose offences were unlikely to have resulted in incarceration but who have become caught up in the 'quasi-incarceration' implicit in conditional sentences involving **restorative justice** and healing programs. Discouraged by s. 718.2(e) from relying on traditional sentencing options, judges have turned to conditional sentences and, in so doing, have pulled into the system significant numbers of Aboriginal offenders who might otherwise have received the comparatively less onerous and restrictive sentences of probation, fines, or suspended sentences (Rudin & Roach, 2000). The irony is not lost that, in attempting to keep Aboriginal offenders out of prison, the state and courts have simply found other ways to constrain ever greater numbers of Aboriginal people for having committed an ever-greater range of offences.

At present, the bulk of the research focusing on racism and discrimination as explanations for over-representation supports the position that Aboriginal offenders in the Canadian criminal justice system are more likely to experience positive, rather than negative, discrimination in regard to sentencing, especially in terms of such factors as sentence length. As observed earlier, where disparities in sentences do exist, they can be explained to some degree by the seriousness of the offences committed by Aboriginal offenders (Hann & Harman, 1992) and the generally higher recidivism rates characterizing Aboriginal offenders (York, 1995), both of which speak to the perceived risks presented by Aboriginal offenders seeking early release. Risk profiles are further exacerbated by the socio-demographic realities to which many Aboriginal offenders return upon release and that may influence the formulation of viable release plans, especially for the most disadvantaged status Indian offenders. It may be the case that status offenders, who are the most disadvantaged with regard to those socio-demographic factors (poverty and blocked opportunities, early exposure to substance abuse and violence, etc.) that may encourage greater conflict with the law, are less likely to obtain early release for precisely the same reasons that contributed to their landing in prison in the first place. This would seem to suggest that if we wish to reduce the over-representation of Aboriginal people within the criminal justice system, we would do well to look to ameliorating the socio-demographic conditions that both foster greater levels of conflict and disorder in communities and render them less salutary places for offenders to return to for healing and reintegration.

The second and third lines of research and analysis that attempt to explain over-representation focus, respectively, on higher Aboriginal offending levels and the commission by Aboriginal people of the type of offences that are more likely to result in carceral sentences. There is considerable overlap in these positions, so we shall consider them together.

There is, unfortunately, much quantitative support for these explanations. The Aboriginal population does appear to manifest a higher per capita involvement in conflict and disorderly activities, including those much more serious offences. For example, on the two factors that are most likely to result in carceral sentences (seriousness of offence and prior record), Weatherburn et al. (2004) found Aboriginal people in Australia much more likely than non-Aboriginals to be arrested for offences likely to result in imprisonment and to have a prior record of serious offences. A self-report study of Aboriginal and non-Aboriginal secondary school students corroborated the offence and prior history data. Aboriginal students reported committing significantly more offences over a 12-month and five-year period than their non-Aboriginal peers, and this was the case in every category of crime (Weatherburn et al., 2004).

It is difficult to counter such realities, and yet at the same time it is crucial that the numbers be contextualized within the larger socio-demographic situation of Aboriginal people. Although such a contextual analysis cannot change the data, it can add two important dimensions to the discussion. First, it is important that Canadians be dissuaded from the common misperception that the problems facing Aboriginal people are essentially 'of their own making', and that thus successive Canadian governments, and those who support them and their policies, are somehow limited in their responsibility to ameliorate the problems that render too many Aboriginal communities inherently more criminogenic than non-Aboriginal communities. Second, it seems quite clear that more than two decades of research on the system and system reform have availed us little, and that attending to the socio-demographic elements of offending patterns may shift the discussion away from one focused on criminal justice to one focused on social justice—or more specifically, on how the absence of the latter leads to over-representation in the former. While it is difficult to understand or develop ameliorative policy based on the quantitative picture of over-representation, when the numbers are informed by the knowledge that there are disproportionate numbers of Aboriginal youth falling into the age range most likely to encounter conflict with the law and that these youth face poverty, blocked opportunity, and early exposure to violence, we can move beyond the data to develop policy aimed at the situations that encourage those numbers. In fact, when we look at the overall portrait of some Aboriginal communities in Canada, it seems logical to enquire why offending rates are not higher.

An additional difficulty with focusing on offending rates to explain over-representation resides in the reality that it may not be offending per se that is the problem, but rather how we choose to respond to offending. In other words, offending doesn't actually cause over-representation; rather, over-representation is caused by our choosing to respond to offending in a particular way. Insofar as Aboriginal offenders present different profiles from non-Aboriginal offenders, they tend to be responded to differently, and this leads to over-representation and perceptions of bias in the system. However, inasmuch as the differences arise from the application of similar criteria (i.e., offence type, prior offending history) and processes to all offenders, this begs the question of the direction and shape that should inform efforts to reform, especially given the putative absence of negative discrimination as indicated by much of the quantitative research.

The fourth and final explanatory stream asserts that Aboriginal people are disproportionately caught up in the criminal justice system largely because Canada adheres to criminal justice policies and practices that have a differential impact on Aboriginal offenders because of their socio-economic conditions. Explanations of over-representation that fall within this category generally assert that over-representation is caused at least in part by discrimination as opposed to racism. In this regard, these explanations are superior to much of the culture clash/racism arguments, which seem often to disregard rather important distinctions between racism and discrimination and to fail to see them as distinct, if sometimes overlapping, phenomena. Racism involves overt and conscious attitudes of bias that are willingly and knowingly translated into both physical and psychological violence against members of targeted groups; discrimination, while no less devastating in impact, tends to arise from the unconscious implementation of structures or policies that were not intended to be discriminatory but, owing to the manner in which they interact with larger social structures, create disadvantage for members of certain groups. And while the impacts of discrimination and racism are equally devastating for those on the receiving end, it may be that different types of prejudice require quite different policy approaches to ameliorate them.

This category of efforts to explain over-representation falls very much in line with 'life chances arguments', which assert that 'when an individual's life chances are poor, their likelihood of coming into conflict with the law will be increased' (La Prairie, 1994). It remains unclear whether that likelihood is influenced more by the nature of the law, its biases and processes, the risks implicit in a life lived on the margins, or some combination of these factors. What is clear, however, is that the larger socio-demographic context in which far too many Aboriginal children are raised—one characterized by poverty, early exposure to violence, substance abuse, and generally more dysfunctional social patterns—not only limits their life chances generally, but also encourages the likelihood of conflict with the law. Indeed, given the severity of conditions in some communities, a criminal lifestyle looks like a fairly rational choice. Thus the socio-demographic argument not only informs the 'why' of much Aboriginal offending, wherein the absence of social justice paves the way for a far greater intrusion of criminal justice agencies, but also explains the differential impact of those agencies' activities in Aboriginal lives.

While it cannot be doubted that factors such as poverty affect access to justice, the reality presented by quantitative data suggesting positive discrimination against some Aboriginal offenders in regard to some aspects of the system suggests that two considerations must inform efforts to explain over-representation within this category of explanations. First, it may be that, in some jurisdictions at least, judges not only are aware of the disadvantaged backgrounds of Aboriginal accused, but actively account for those factors in their sentencing of these offenders. Thus it may be that socio-demographics are to some degree already controlled for in terms of their contribution to over-representation. Second, if this factor has been controlled for at the point of sentencing, then it may be that our most productive reform efforts could now be directed toward a much earlier point in the process; that is, if socio-demographics influence an individual's choice—or lack of choice—to engage in acts of conflict and disorder, then it may be toward socio-demographic change that we should direct our reforms, not toward the criminal justice system, which can neither control nor change those choices or the acts that follow from them. If this is accurate, then those explanations of over-representation that focus on criminal justice system reform may be distracting attention from the much more necessary reform of the very factors to which proponents of system reform attribute much of the responsibility both for rates of conflict and disorder among Aboriginal people and for the system that reacts in inadequate and discriminatory ways to those offenders, owing to their location on the larger socio-economic ladder. Of course, insofar as such an approach would involve massive social policy change and the meaningful redress of historical treaties and human rights abuses among Aboriginal peoples, it is unlikely to find favour with the state and many of those it represents. Thus it may be that it is here, in the space between criminal justice reform and social justice reform, that we can locate the origins of restorative justice—the reform that promises to restore and transform entire communities by changing the way criminal justice is administered to their membership.

The current focus on restorative justice as a means of undermining over-representation probably has a great deal to do with the difficult fact that most other policy initiatives seem to have had limited, if any, impact on the doing of justice in Aboriginal contexts. Efforts to 'indigenize' the criminal justice system by involving more Aboriginal people in its administration have had disappointing results, as only a small number of Aboriginal people seem to be attracted to careers in social control—a factor undoubtedly encouraged by the limitations of the system within which they must function and the challenges they meet there. Cross-cultural training of non-Aboriginal justice workers to acquaint them with the realities facing Aboriginal victims, witnesses, and offenders has also had limited results, as unseating stereotypes that, while pejorative, serve a purpose for those who hold them is a difficult task and one whose impacts are rarely enduring. And as we have seen above, sentencing reforms and the courts have proven unable to usurp patterns of over-representation that find their origins outside the system, in the early years of offenders' lives and in the families and communities in which they are shaped and formed.

The creation of fully indigenized courts, staffed and administered by Aboriginal people, while presenting a compelling superficial measure of change, must nonetheless continue to administer laws through a legal structure that remains foreign and intimidating to many Aboriginal people. And while having justice done for and to you by your own people may somehow soften the impact of retributive processes, Aboriginal courts, like the non-Aboriginal structures they emulate, are limited in their ability to overcome either the risk/need profiles of most Aboriginal offenders or the life conditions and chances that encourage them. In an effort to overcome the limitations of juridical processes, criminal courts in Canada often invoke such restorative initiatives as **sentencing circles**, or diversions of Aboriginal defendants into more culturally appropriate healing or talking circles or community conferences; in similar fashion, Correctional Services Canada has developed a series of Healing Lodges, which are intended to house Aboriginal offenders in more culturally friendly contexts more conducive to healing and rehabilitation. These reforms have assumed many shapes and directions. It is beyond the parameters of this brief chapter to discuss all of them, and thus we will look briefly at the most popular and well known of restorative initiatives in Aboriginal justice: sentencing circles.

Sentencing circles originated in the Yukon Territory in the Kwanlin Dun First Nation as a joint initiative undertaken with the Yukon Territorial Court under Judge Barry Stuart. They were first formally reported in the case of *R. v. Moses* ([1992] Y.J. No. 50 DRS. 93-00327; 11 C.R. (4th) 357). In their initial incarnation, sentencing circles sought to overcome the formality and barriers of traditional sentencing hearings in criminal courts by reorganizing the physical structure of the courtroom. Participants in sentencing were to be seated in a large circle that would include the victim and the offender, as well as their communities of care, the lawyers, and the judge; with the participants arranged thus on an equal footing, with no bench to separate them, the sentencing would be reached through a dialogue with the entire circle contributing their thoughts and preferences regarding a proper sentence for the accused.[3] At the conclusion of the dialogue, the circle's recommendations would be considered actively by the judge and, if appropriate, confirmed within the accused's sentence. In many cases, the goal of the circle was not just to offer victim and offender a safe context in which to share their experiences of the conflict event in a manner facilitative of healing for all, but also to communicate to the offender that he or she would remain part of the community, notwithstanding the conflict. Ideally, the intention was to craft a sentence in the circle that kept the offender out of prison, thereby reducing over-representation, and, by healing and community support, rehabilitated the offender and ended recidivism.

Although circles were initially touted as having reduced recidivism by nearly 80 per cent and thus to be a superior form of 'Aboriginal justice', they are not without their detractors. Some commentators have expressed the concerns that, while sentencing circles give an appearance of power sharing between system and the community, the reality is that the decision about sentencing remains only and ultimately with the judge. Thus the power given to the community is more illusory than real. As observed by one judge in northern Canada,

> The public must be made to understand that the court retains both authority and jurisdiction to impose whatever sentence the judge, rather than the circle, decides or recommends in any particular case. In other words, the circle, representing the community of the accused in the entire process, and the prosecutor, representing the larger public in the court proceedings, may assist and advise the judge, but the judge and the judge alone must decide what sentence should be imposed. (McNamara, 2000)

In addition, there are considerable concerns about the ability of communities to be 'just' with one another in the management and resolution of disputes. In the limited but growing research and commentary questioning the impact of communities on circles, there are increasingly questions of whether 'the community can be an appropriate vehicle for equitable, effective and efficient change' (Clairmont, 1996). The reality is that many Aboriginal communities are, thanks to the colonial process, characterized by dysfunctional power structures and social relationships, and unless these are fully understood and carefully controlled for, the potential for them to be replicated within the circle is significant. This is especially so given that many of the cases dealt with in the circles are very difficult ones involving partner and family violence— conflicts that distort power relationships, destroy trust, and thus resist the very sort of open discussion required by circles. The potential for circles to 're-victimize' victims is distressingly high and increasingly borne out by the research.[4]

In an effort to control for re-victimization in circles, the courts have developed a series of rules that must be applied when a community is seeking a circle sentencing. The rules, outlined in the case of *R. v. Joseyounen* ([1995] 6 W.W.R. 438), specify, among other things, that before a circle can be held, the judge must attempt to determine whether the victim suffers from 'battered wife syndrome', since if she does, it would make it very difficult for her to participate in the circle's deliberations; the judge must also ensure that 'respected, non-political community leaders' are available and willing to participate in the circle, a condition that would resist the intrusion of negative community and family politics.

There are also concerns about the potential for sentencing disparity in circle sentences, insofar as the circle's goal is to craft a sentence to meet the unique needs of each offender. The risk that such sentencing might lead to very different sentences for similar offences, and thereby cause unfairness, is real and has been voiced by Roberts and La Prairie (1996) and others. Similarly, there is the concern that the pressure that is placed on communities to participate in sentencing circles might lead them to overlook the fact that many communities might lack the resources, both human and other, to meet the needs of offenders who remain in the community to serve their sentences. There are serious questions about whether Aboriginal communities, many of which already struggle daily with the stresses and strains of poverty and marginalization, can rightly be asked to take on the very demanding roles involved in the supervision and rehabilitation of offenders.

That said, sentencing circles and other restorative initiatives can have positive impacts for the community insofar as they offer Aboriginal people an opportunity to take responsibility for acts of conflict and disorder in their communities. The act of stepping up to the challenge is not easy in communities that experience the daily stress of many Aboriginal communities, and those who do so experience considerable, and sometimes quite novel, feelings of accomplishment and self-respect. These are not small things when one is surrounded by the legacies of colonialism and marginalization, and they can constitute important early steps in the road to true self-government. Given this, it is important that those who would promote circles and all other forms of restorative justice in Aboriginal communities be completely transparent about the limitations of what can be achieved by these processes. For example, while there can be little doubt that sentencing circles can assist in community building, we now have good research confirming that the promises around reductions in recidivism by circles are simply not true. An evaluation of circles released in the spring of 2008 from Australia confirmed that those who were sentenced via circle sentencing did not experience any different or better outcomes with regard to recidivism than those who did not experience circle sentencing. Thus, while it is possible that the 'personal reflection' that is central to circle and other restorative processes has some intrinsic value, the researchers found that this is '[n]ot enough to reduce the risk of reoffending. Offenders also need to be given opportunities to address the factors that get them involved in crime, particularly drug and alcohol abuse' (Weatherburn et al., 2008). Thus, while restorative initiatives such as sentencing circles can have some ameliorative impacts, this evaluation reminds us that if we truly wish to reduce rates of conflict and disorder in communities, we should focus our efforts on the conditions in communities that create offenders in the first place.

There is a wealth of evidence to support the position that if we wish to reduce the number of Aboriginal (and other) people in the courts and prisons of Canada, we should direct as much policy and resources as possible toward building communities. By focusing on making communities happy, healthy, and functional to be in, we enhance their inhabitants' life chances and radically reduce the likelihood that they will come into conflict with the law. Much Aboriginal justice policy for the past half-century has focused on 'fixing' the system so that Aboriginal disputants, victims, and offenders will fit into it better and thus experience better justice. This approach has had few, if any, ameliorative impacts, and it is not clear at this time that the considerable support given to restorative justice will prove much better at reducing over-representation and healing offenders, victims, and their communities. Indeed, we are now more than a decade into restorative justice, and the rate at which Aboriginal people are drawn into courts and sent to prison has shown no sign of diminishing.

It may be, then, that instead of concentrating on achieving better criminal justice, we should work to achieve greater social justice with and for Aboriginal people. Let us honour treaties, respect our promises, and work with communities to raise healthy, optimistic children who have the same life chances as all Canadians. This is an achievable and far more rational approach, given the dubious track record of the victim blaming and system tinkering that have dominated policy responses to date. It will, however, require not only a substantial change in how Canadians perceive the 'Indian problem', but also a pronounced shift in how we respond to the challenges facing Aboriginal communities. We must change our psyches before we can change the cycle of poverty, the marginalization, and the over-representation. We have the means and resources, both human and monetary, to embark on a serious, ethical partnership with Aboriginal people to effect meaningful social change. What we lack, however, is something far more potent—namely, the will to change what can be changed and the determination to see those changes made real. This is something that cannot be done by fiat, legal reform, or the courts. It involves changing one mind at a time. Let yours be one of the first to open to a new way of seeing our country and the First Peoples who share it with us.

Key Terms

Assembly of First
    Nations

assimilation

colonization

differential criminal
    justice processing

dispossession

Indian Act

over-representation

R. v. Gladue

reserves

residential schools

restorative justice

sentencing circles

status Indian

treaties

Questions for Critical Thought

1. How does the history of colonization affect Aboriginal peoples' current vulnerability to offending and criminalization?

2. Describe and distinguish between the four competing explanations for Aboriginal over-representation in the justice system. Which is the most powerful explanation?

3. What are the strengths and limitations of restorative justice initiatives as potential solutions to the problems of Aboriginal offending?

Additional Readings

Dickson-Gilmore, J., & La Prairie, C. (2005). *Will the circle be unbroken? Aboriginal communities, restorative justice and the challenges of conflict and change.* Toronto: University of Toronto Press.

Reber, S., & Renaud, R. (2006). *Starlight tour: The last lonely night of Neil Stonechild.* Toronto: Random House.

Victimization and offending among the Aboriginal population in Canada. (2006). *Juristat 26*(3), 1.

Weatherburn, D. (2008). Circle sentencing evaluation. www.lawlink.nsw

Websites of Interest

Aboriginal Canada Portal: www.aboriginalcanada.gc.ca/acp/site.nsf/eng/index.html

Amnesty International—Stolen Sisters Project: www.amnesty.ca/stolensisters/amr 2000304.pdf

Assembly of First Nations: www.afn.ca

Endnotes

1. The practice of some police in Saskatchewan of picking up intoxicated Aboriginals in the city, driving them to the outskirts of town, and leaving them without shoes or jackets, often in the depths of winter, to find their way back to the centre of town. The practice was revealed in the winter of 1990, when 17-year-old Neil Stonechild was found frozen to death on the outskirts of Saskatoon and was later discovered to have been a victim of a starlight tour (www.cbc.ca/news/background/aboriginal/starlighttours.html; Reber & Renaud, 2006).

2. For more information about these women and the campaign to recover them, consult the Stolen Sisters Project of Amnesty International at www.amnesty.ca/stolensisters/amr2000304.pdf

3. As observed by Judge Stuart in the *Moses* case, 'By arranging the court in a circle without desks or tables, with all participants facing each other, with equal access and equal exposure to each other, the dynamics of the decision-making process [is] profoundly changed. . . . The circle significantly breaks down the dominance that traditional courtrooms accord lawyers and judges. In a circle, the ability to contribute, the importance and credibility of any input is not defined by seating arrangements. The audiences change' ([1992] Y.J. No. 50 D.R.S. 93-00327; 11 C.R. (4th) 357). Given that rearranging the furniture may not realign the power relationships in the circle, in Ontario sentencing circles occur via the diversion of an offender into the circle, which takes place in the absence of lawyers and court personnel and usually under the supervision and support of a community justice worker.

4. The possibility that restorative processes cannot escape dysfunctional power relations within communities or families and the implications of this for 'healing' have been well documented by researchers such as Crnkovich (1995), Green (1998), Anderson (1999), and Clairmont (1996).

References

Allard, Y. E., Wilkins, R., & Berthelot, J. M. (2004). Premature mortality in health regions with high Aboriginal populations. www.statscan.gc.ca/studies-etudes/82-003/archive/2004/67-65.eng.pdf

Anderson, C. (1999). Governing Aboriginal justice in Canada: Constructing responsible individuals and communities through 'tradition'. *Crime, Law and Social Change, 31*(4), 303–326.

Assembly of First Nations. (n.d). *Fact Sheet: The reality for First Nations in Canada.* www.afn.ca

Blatchford, A. (2009, August 30). Canada's potable water problem. *Canadian Press.* http://janegoodall.ca/canadaspotablewaterproblem.php

Clairmont, D. (1996). Alternative justice issues for Aboriginal justice. Ottawa: Department of Justice, Aboriginal Justice Directorate. *Journal of Legal Pluralism, 36*, 125–157.

Clark, S. (1989). *The Mikmaq and criminal justice in Nova Scotia.* Halifax: Government Printer.

Crnkovich, M. (1995). *The role of the victim in the criminal justice system: Circle sentencing in Inuit communities.* Banff, AB: Canadian Institute for the Administration of Justice Conference.

Dickson-Gilmore, J., & La Prairie, C. (2005). *Will the circle be unbroken? Aboriginal communities, restorative justice and the challenges of conflict and change.* Toronto: University of Toronto Press.

Drost, H. (2001). *Labour market relations and income distribution of Aboriginal residents in Canada's metropolitan areas.* Presentation at the Policy Conference on Options for Aboriginal People in Canada's Cities, Regina.

Green, R. G. (1998). *Justice in Aboriginal communities: Sentencing alternatives.* Saskatoon: Purich.

Hagan, J. (1975). Law, order, and sentencing: A study of attitude in action. *Sociometry 38*(2), 375–384.

Hann, R., & Harman, W. (1992). *Predicting release risk for Canadian penitentiary inmates.* Ottawa: Ministry of the Solicitor General.

La Prairie, C. (1994). *Seen but not heard: Aboriginal people in the inner city.* Ottawa: Department of Justice.

McNamara, L. (2000). Appellate Court scrutiny of circle sentencing. *Manitoba Law Journal, 27,* 209–240.

Minister of Industry, Ottawa. (2008). *Aboriginal peoples in Canada in 2006: Inuit, Métis and First Nations, 2006 Census.* www.statcan.ca

Moyer, S. (1987). Homicides involving adult subjects 1962–1984: A comparison of Native and non-Natives. Ottawa: Ministry of the Solicitor General.

Newhouse, D., & Peters, E. (2003). *Not strangers in these parts: Urban Aboriginal people.* Canada: Policy Research Initiative.

Norris, C., Fielding, N., Kemp, C., & Fielding, J. (1993). *The status of this demeanor: An analysis of the influence of social status on being stopped by the police.* Draft paper prepared for the British Criminology Conference, University of Wales, Cardiff. In Carol La Prairie, *Seen but not heard: Aboriginal people in the inner city.* Ottawa: Department of Justice, 1994.

Reber, S., & Renaud, R. (2006). *Starlight tour: The last lonely night of Neil Stonechild.* Toronto: Random House.

R. v. Joseyounen [1995] 6 W.W.R. 438.

R. v. Moses [1992] Y.J. No.50 DRS 93-00327; 11 C.R. (4th) 357.

R. v. Wells [2000] S.C.C. 10.

Roach, K., & Rudin, J. (2000, July). Gladue: The judicial and political reception of a promising decision. *Canadian Journal of Criminology, 42*(3), 355–388.

Roberts, J., & La Prairie, C. (1996). Sentencing circles: Some unanswered questions. *Criminal Law Quarterly, 39,* 69–83.

Shaw, M. (1991). *Survey of federally sentenced women: Report to the Task Force on Federally Sentenced Women on the prison survey.* Ottawa: Solicitor General Canada.

Weatherburn, D., Fitzgerald, J., & Hua, J. (2004). Reducing Aboriginal over-representation in prison. *Australian Journal of Public Administration 62*(3), 65–73.

York, P. (1995). *The Aboriginal federal offender: A comparative analysis between Aboriginal and non-Aboriginal offenders.* Ottawa: Correctional Services Canada.

6 | Immigration, Immigrants, and the Shifting Dynamics of Social Exclusion in Canada[1]

KARIM ISMAILI

Introduction

Immigration has been central to nation building and social development in Canada (Li, 2003, p. 15). Often heralded as an example of Canada's tolerant, progressive, and humanitarian nature, it has evolved into a cornerstone of the nation's mythology. To the casual observer, the frequent statements made by leaders in government, business, and industry extolling the virtues of immigration and celebrating the contributions of this population to Canadian society would seem entirely consistent with Canada's reputation as a nation that both welcomes and values immigrants. Unfortunately, the lived experience of many immigrants sharply contrasts with this widely held impression. Immigrant lives in Canada often feature struggle, **discrimination,** and a variety of vexing social problems. The ability to gain a foothold in Canadian society is differentiated by race, ethnicity, class, and gender, and the consequence of this reality is profound for individuals, communities, and the nation as a whole. This chapter will examine the historical and contemporary context of immigration in Canada. By exploring immigration patterns, anti-immigration sentiments, and immigrant interactions with the criminal justice system, it will uncover how the national mythology surrounding immigration blinds the populace to some of the more problematic aspects of Canadian society.

Immigration Patterns

A nation cannot be fully understood unless one examines the complex set of historical forces that have shaped it. A troubling feature of the contemporary discourse on immigration, however, is how frequently it ignores the fact that centuries before immigrants ever arrived in what is now Canada, this was a land inhabited and settled by Aboriginal peoples. While the focus of this chapter is on immigration and immigrants, it is important to recognize at the outset the place and contributions of substantial numbers of *non-immigrants* to Canada. To not do so would render this population invisible (Perry et al., 2009, p. 88).

The **colonization** of North America by France and Britain in the seventeenth century brought the first immigrants to Canada. French and British artisans, fur traders, and missionaries competed to establish settlements and outposts across the land and vied to become the dominant cultural, linguistic, economic, and military power. Although the British conquest of 1760 established that the governance of the two immigrant groups would be placed firmly under British rule, it did not eliminate the French-British rivalry that has become an enduring feature of Canadian society (Li, 2003, p. 16). Sarah Wayland has argued that the founding of Canada by two distinct settler nations is one reason why it 'may never possess the unified sense of peoplehood that characterizes a true nation' (1997, p. 34). She notes that the British North America Act of 1867—an act of the British Parliament that created Canada as a self-governing British dominion—retained existing French cultural features such as language, the civil code, and the educational system in those parts of the dominion where they had already been established by law or custom. This not only set the tone for a collectivist notion of rights in Canada, but also made the acceptance of a pluralistic society more acceptable (p. 34). And while this may be true, it is also evident that, as the charter groups of Canada, the French and British were 'able to set the conditions of entry and rules of accommodation for subsequent immigrant groups' (Li, 2003, p. 16).

Since 1867, the Canadian government's decisions concerning who should be allowed into the country have been guided by two questions: 'Are certain immigrants better suited than others for certain kinds of jobs?' and 'Are certain immigrants better candidates than others for participation in Canadian social and political life?' According to McCalla and Satzewich, 'the answers to these two questions have constituted the basis for the processes of immigrant inclusion and exclusion, immigrant allocation in the labor force, and immigrants' treatment in Canadian society' (2002, 33).

Peter Li (2003, chap. 2) observes **four phases of immigration** to Canada, each one shaped by economic, demographic, social, political, and ideological forces. During the first phase, from 1867 to 1895, Canada maintained a laissez-faire approach to immigration, letting market forces of supply and demand dictate migration flows in order to facilitate domestic production, build the transportation infrastructure, and enable western expansion for agricultural settlement. The main concern of the first Immigration Act of 1869 was how to limit the influx of British paupers (McCalla & Satzewich, 2002, p. 33). By 1881, the Canadian census indicated that 90 per cent of the population were of either British, French, or Native origin. The remaining 10 per cent were comprised of newcomers from central and western Europe and China (Wayland, 1997, p. 36). By the 1880s, concerns about the class background of immigrants were supplemented by concerns over non-white immigrants. In 1885, Canada began to impose a $50 **head tax** on virtually every Chinese immigrant. By 1904, the tax had grown to $500, which was added to the $200 landing fee that was imposed on every Asian in 1903 (McCalla & Satzewich, 2002, p. 34). In this first phase of immigration, an institutionalized pattern emerged in Canada whereby a distinction was made between *preferred* and *non-preferred* immigrants (Kruger et al., 2004).

The second immigration phase began in 1896 and moved through to the outbreak of World War I in 1914. Driven by improved agricultural production in the prairies, high-priced staples, reduced rates for transportation, the advent of industrialization, and growing consumer demand for goods in Europe, the period brought the highest levels of immigration to Canada in its history (Li, 2003, p. 18). Under the leadership of Interior Minister Clifford Sifton, 2.5 million immigrants entered Canada during this period (Wayland, 1997, p. 38). Most arrived from the nations of eastern and southern Europe, with the United States, Britain, and northern and western Europe also contributing to the population influx. Despite an acute labour shortage, 'Canada maintained an immigration policy that used race as a basis to restrict non-whites who were deemed socially questionable and racially undesirable' during this period (Li, 2003, p. 19). Limits on the immigration of non-whites were both formal (e.g., through the implementation of the Asian head tax) and informal (e.g., American and Caribbean blacks were permitted to apply for immigration but faced numerous obstacles and were routinely rejected, and the stipulation of a continuous passage to Canada effectively eliminated South Asians for immigration consideration). As a measure of anti-immigrant sentiment, a series of demonstrations in Vancouver led to riots and other acts of violence in ethnic neighbourhoods in 1907. It is clear, as Thobani has said, that this second immigration phase 'sought to tightly restrict the immigration of Third World peoples for permanent settlement. . . . European immigrants were actively and aggressively recruited to replenish the nation' (2000, p. 36).

This pattern continued into the third immigration phase, from 1915 to the end of World War II in 1945. As in the past, a preferred immigration hierarchy was strictly enforced, with British and American immigrants at the top, followed by northern Europeans, who in turn were followed by central, southern, and eastern Europeans. Jews and non-white immigrants were not welcome (Li, 2003, p. 21). During World War I, Canada implemented a series of laws that restricted the rights of foreigners and placed unemployed 'aliens' in internment camps. Government officials were particularly concerned that immigrants were behind the nationwide strikes of 1917 and 1918. If not directly accused of spreading Bolshevik doctrine, immigrants were widely believed to be sympathetic to its basic tenets (Wayland, 1997, p. 40). Growing public anxiety and widespread anti-immigrant sentiment led to clampdowns on organized labour, press freedoms, and immigrant rights, this despite the fact that most immigrant arrivals during the period were from Britain and the United States. Anti-immigrant sentiment grew in the 1920s and 1930s, leading to large numbers of immigrant deportations, heightened levels of anti-Semitism, and laws and regulations that prohibited immigrants from entering certain professions. Following the attack on Pearl Harbor in December 1941, 22,000 Japanese Canadians were rounded up and placed in internment camps, a decision rooted in fear and anxiety, but also a result of the broader anti-immigrant sentiment of the period. At a time when the United States accepted 240,000 Jews from wartorn Europe, Canada accepted fewer than 4,000. The two world wars and the Great Depression had a significant impact on overall immigration levels. As Wayland notes, between 1900 and 1930, nearly 5 million immigrants entered Canada. That number dropped to 200,000 between 1930 and 1945 (1997, p. 41).

The post–World War II period represents the final immigration phase. A major pronouncement by Prime Minister McKenzie King in 1947 set the tone for what was to follow. In a statement to the House of Commons, King 'indicated that the government viewed immigration as a source of population and economic growth, but did not want to alter the fundamental composition of the Canadian population as a result of immigration' (Li, 2003, p. 23). The result was an expansion in the intake of immigrants from the United States and Europe coupled with tight controls of immigrants from Asia. Changes to the Immigration Act in 1952 eliminated race and country of origin as means of categorizing preferred and non-preferred immigrants. However, this shift did not eliminate discrimination. By specifying that nationality, ethnic group affiliation, occupation, lifestyle, unsuitability with regard to Canada's climate, and perceived inability to become assimilated into Canadian society were all valid reasons to deny immigration applications, the Act 'merely reformulated how discrimination was understood by government officials' (Kruger et al., 2004, p. 74).

Larger social, political, and economic developments rendered the orientation of the 1952 Immigration Act unsustainable. According to Wayland, four factors contributed to a shift away from the traditional conception of immigration rooted in the Act: Quebec's desire to liberalize immigration policy and play a stronger role in immigration recruitment; interestgroup pressure on governments to take a more active role in global **refugee** problems; the sense that Canada's immigration policy was undermining its standing in both the United Nations and the Commonwealth; and, finally, the passage of the Bill of Rights in 1960, which necessitated changes in immigration policy for Canada to retain credibility on matters of human rights (1997, p. 44). In addition, as the economy of western Europe improved and the nations of eastern Europe restricted the mobility of their people, it became clear that Canada would need to attract immigrants from other parts of the world (Kruger et al., 2004, p. 74). In 1962, the existing system of preferred immigration from Europe and the United States was abandoned and replaced in 1967 with a **points system**. The points system represented an effort to apply non-discriminatory and selective criteria to determine eligibility for immigration, with points awarded for occupation, education, language, skills, and age. As such, it ushered in a transformation in the method of immigrant selection and a redefinition of those deemed to be preferred and non-preferred immigrants.

The shift toward non-European sources of immigrants that began in the late 1960s dramatically changed the makeup of Canada. As has been discussed, immigrants arriving in Canada before 1970 were overwhelmingly from Europe and the United States. Only 10.2 per cent of arrivals to Canada during this period were racial or visible minorities. This figure increased to 51.8 per cent for arrivals in the 1970s, 65.4 per cent for arrivals in the 1980s, and approximately 75 per cent for arrivals in the 1990s. Racial or visible minorities constituted less than 1 per cent of the total Canadian population in 1971 (Reitz & Banerjee, 2007, p. 489). That proportion grew to 4.7 per cent of the population in 1981 and 16.2 per cent of the population in 2006. According to Statistics Canada, current trends indicate that racial or visible minorities will make up one-fifth of the Canadian population in 2017 (Fenlon, 2008).

Fuelled by a dramatic growth in the numbers of immigrants from Asia, Africa, the Caribbean, South and Central America, and the Middle East, the ethno-racial diversity absorbed by Canada during a relatively short period of time has raised a number of challenges. First and foremost among these is how to both identify and mitigate the impact of the various structural and systemic barriers that create inequality in Canadian society for immigrants, especially for racial and visible minorities. A second challenge concerns how to balance the integration of immigrant populations with the explicit Canadian constitutional commitment to **multicultural-ism**. This, in turn, raises questions of how to enhance social cohesiveness while also nurturing immigrant feelings of belonging. A third challenge reflects the reality that just under 96 per cent of Canada's visible-minority population reside in metropolitan areas, with most clustered in three cities: Toronto, Vancouver, and Montreal (Fenlon, 2008). This extremely high concentration means that municipalities are faced with significant demands for services and play a vital role in ensuring that populations are not excluded or marginalized from mainstream society and its various institutions. Finally, crises—whether social, political, economic, or military— can have a particularly significant impact on the lives of immigrants. As will be seen shortly, all this not only affects levels of public support for immigration and diversity in the population, but also raises the spectre of discriminatory treatment of and violence against immigrants, as they are often scapegoated as the cause of a variety of social ills.

The Contemporary Context of Immigration in Canada

Immigrants fall into two broad categories: those who are self-reliant and able to make their way in their newly adopted homeland with the aid of existing entitlements and those who require additional assistance because of their socio-economic position, their inability to communicate in the majority language, or their status as victims owing to some sort of misfortune. Those in the latter group often require housing, language training, employment counselling, medical assistance, and income support (Agrawal et al., 2007, p. 110). Beyond addressing these basic needs, receiving nations also have a responsibility to foster the full and equal participation of newcomers in the economic, social, cultural, and political dimensions of life in their new country. This commitment to **social inclusion** necessitates the identification and removal of barriers that lead to **social exclusion** in each of these domains (Omidvar & Richmond, 2003, p. 1).

Recent research indicates that many immigrants are experiencing significant difficulties integrating into Canadian society. Particularly noteworthy are the difficulties immigrants have encountered in the labour market over the past 25 years. Omidvar and Richmond (2003) report higher levels of discrimination against visible-minority workers (both immigrants and Canadian born), higher levels of gender-based wage discrimination against female immigrants, and lower overall earnings during this period, especially when compared with such statistics for those who arrived in Canada between 1945 and 1985—this, despite the fact that recent immigrants to Canada are better educated and better skilled than their previous counterparts. In addition to being underemployed, immigrants experience higher levels of poverty than in the past, are more likely to be dependent on social assistance, and are increasingly affected by urban social problems. As Reitz and Banerjee (2007) note, these conditions not only heighten immigrant feelings of social exclusion, they also have implications for social cohesion in Canada. The troubling rise in racial discrimination and inequality and its temporal association with the shift toward immigration from non-European source nations are of concern to many who advocate on behalf of immigrants, as well as to those who study social policy. Among the latter are criminologists who explore the implications of these and other developments for crime, victimization, the operation of the criminal justice system, and service provision. It is to this work we will now turn.

Immigrants as Offenders

The role that the media plays in reinforcing and fostering the perception of a relationship between immigrants and criminality cannot be underestimated. Anti-immigrant sentiments are most apparent in the treatment of racial and visible minorities (Jiwani, 2002, p. 75), leading some to argue that the immigrant-crime connection is the outcome of a media-driven **moral panic** (see Costelloe, 2009). Wortley (2009, p. 349) traces the recent history of this phenomenon in Canada back to 1994 when a black male assailant murdered a white female in Toronto. The media commentary following the tragedy not only highlighted the fact that the offender was a black citizen of Jamaica (he had arrived in Canada at a young age, but did not obtain Canadian citizenship), it also implicated the entire immigration system as being too lenient, leaving the impression that future acts of violence by immigrants were inevitable. The association between immigrants and crime became cemented in the public mind.

According to national public opinion data, 21 per cent of Canadian citizens surveyed in 1995 either agreed or strongly agreed that immigrants increase crime; that number grew to 27 per cent of those surveyed in 2003 (Simon & Sikich, 2007, p. 960). This finding supports Jiwani's (2002, p. 75) assertion that immigrants in Canada are perceived to be 'a social threat in terms of their proclivity to crime', a finding that is strengthened by the fact that race/immigrant-specific crime data are not collected by the criminal justice system, making it difficult to arrive at such a conclusion with any degree of confidence. As will be seen in the following pages, the casting of immigrants as criminal threats is a complex social phenomenon involving myths and fears that are often manifested as exaggerated reactions to difference. This problem is neither new to Canada nor a uniquely Canadian attribute. It is, however, vital to both understand and address this phenomenon in light of the significant demographic changes described earlier in the chapter as well as in light of recent events that have served to heighten the perception of immigrants as criminal threats in the culture.

Explanations for Immigrant Criminality

Although research on the relationship between immigrants and crime is relatively limited and subject to significant national and international variation due to differences in the information collected and disseminated by governments, criminologists have advanced a number of explanations for a possible immigration-crime connection. According to Wortley (2009), these explanations can be organized into four frameworks: the **importation model**, the **strain model**, the **cultural conflict model**, and the **bias model**. The importation model contends that some individuals decide to migrate from one country to another with the clear intention to commit crime within the receiving nation. This rational actor model has been advanced to explain criminal activity linked to international organized-crime syndicates, criminal gangs, and terrorist networks and organizations, has led to the adoption of restrictive immigration policies with respect to those nations seen to be the source of criminal offenders, and has provided the foundation for the tough crime control policies often used against those engaged in criminal conduct.

The strain model posits that crime committed by immigrants is a result of their being marginalized and excluded from the various mainstream opportunities and resources available in the receiving nation. Discrimination in employment, housing, education, and a host of other arenas leads to deprivation, which in turn pushes people into crime. Unlike the importation model, which places blame directly on the individuals involved in crime, the strain model presents a structural explanation in pointing to the social and economic causes of immigrant criminality.

The cultural conflict model highlights the problems that can emerge when immigrants engage in behaviour that is culturally and legally acceptable in their country of origin but is illegal in their newly adopted homeland. In such situations, immigrants may be unaware of the receiving nation's prohibition of the behaviour, or they may be unable to resist the cultural pressure to continue the behaviour that emanates from the larger immigrant group itself. The potential for cultural conflict abounds in modern society and can be seen in both private and public realms. While education on social and legal norms is often presented as a solution to cultural conflict, this becomes complicated in Western democratic nations that value the exercise of individual freedoms and/or have an explicit commitment to multiculturalism.

Finally, rather than explaining any over-representation of immigrants or ethnic minorities in crime statistics as being the result of differences in criminal behaviour, the bias model contends that this over-representation reflects discrimination within the criminal justice system. As Wortley notes, 'certain immigrant/ethnic minority groups may be over-represented in crime statistics because, compared to the native born, they are more likely to come under intense police surveillance (racial profiling), more likely to be arrested by the police, and more likely to be convicted and given tough sentences by the criminal courts' (2009, p. 35). Such discriminatory treatment against racial and visible minorities has been identified around the world, though precise patterns and outcomes vary from nation to nation. In any event, reducing its incidence requires reforms directed at the everyday practices, beliefs, and biases that produce institutional and systemic discrimination.

Recent Research on Immigrant Criminality

In an influential 2006 opinion editorial published in the *New York Times,* Robert J. Sampson, a professor of sociology at Harvard University, argued that increased immigration to the United States was a major factor associated with the crime drop of the 1990s. According to Sampson, 'immigrants appear in general to be less violent than people born in America, particularly when they live in neighborhoods with high numbers of other immigrants' (Sampson, 2006, p. A27). His finding, based on research conducted in 180 Chicago neighbourhoods, runs counter to the widely held belief that a concentration of immigrants and an influx of foreigners will 'drive up crime rates, because of the assumed propensities of these groups to commit crimes and settle in poor, presumably disorganized communities' (Sampson, 2006, p. A27). It is consistent, however, with a growing body of American research that has found immigrants to be more law-abiding than the native born (see Wortley, 2009, p. 350). According to 2000 US Census data on incarcerated males, foreign-born people commit fewer crimes per capita than American citizens. Indeed, those born in the United States commit crimes at a rate that is approximately four times greater than that for the foreign born. Moreover, recent research confirms that immigrants provide a stabilizing effect in communities, both reducing crime rates and increasing the economic viability of the area (Costelloe, 2009, p. 220).

Similar results challenging existing stereotypes have been noted in Canada. For example, Wortley and Tanner's (2006, p. 34) research on urban youth gangs found that immigration status was not related to criminal gang membership. Research conducted by Hagan et al. (2008) found that both first- and second-generation immigrant youth were less likely to engage in deviant behaviour than those born in Canada. And Yeager (2002) found that the vast majority of immigrants (97.5 per cent of the sample examined) who were granted a rehabilitation waiver under the Immigration Act were not re-arrested in a 3.5-year period following their entry into Canada (the waivers are issued by the minister of Citizenship and Immigration to immigration applicants with foreign criminal histories). Yeager concludes from his research that it is 'important to exercise care in discussing crime and immigration, as it is a subject easily prone to the creation of "moral panics" and resulting repressive legislation which particularly impacts persons of color' (p. 188).

Although the research described above challenges the notion that immigrants represent a significant criminal threat, it would appear that Yeager's warning has not been heeded in Canada. In fact, the convergence between criminal and immigration law that has taken place in recent years has only served to emphasize the presumed danger that immigrants pose for society, reflecting a general orientation toward a crime control policy rooted in the importation model of immigrant crime (Barnes, 2009, p. 434; see Pratt, 2005, chap. 8; Chan, 2005). The result, as described by Lucas, is an immigration system built on a criminal justice/enforcement model with dramatic **net-widening** potential (2005, p. 324). Nowhere is this more evident than in the expansion in the range of crimes defined as dangerous for the purposes of **deportation**. As noted by Pratt, such crimes now include fraud, forgery, and minor drug offences, making the reliability of the classification highly problematic (2005, pp. 142–143). As we will see in the section that follows, these and other developments have not only shaped how the immigrant population is institutionally defined, perceived, and ultimately controlled, but have also structured public perception, paving the way for the new discourse of immigrant 'threat' that has taken hold in the post 9/11 period.

Immigrants as National Security Threats

In the wake of the 11 September 2001 terrorist attack, it was predicted that attitudes toward immigration in the United States and Canada would likely become less favourable owing to the economic and social consequences of the attack. It was also predicted that national identity and attachment among members of the host population would be strengthened, leading to tighter and more clearly defined in-group boundaries (Esses et al., 2002, pp. 72–73). According to Esses et al., '[u]nder conditions of threat, people are more likely to see the out-group in more homogenous ("they are all alike") and in negative stereotypical ways (e.g., "they are dangerous")' (2002, p. 74). In such an environment, unfavourable public attitudes toward immigration and immigrants can grow, generating pressure to 'develop more restrictive immigration policies and procedures that are seen as protecting members of the national in-group' (p. 80).

The decade-long shift toward policies that emphasize protection from external and internal security threats in both the United States (see Ismaili, 2010) and Canada suggests that this prediction has come true, although evidence of a direct relationship between public pressure and policy outcomes remains mixed. According to Murphy (2007, p. 451), a 'securitized' environment has emerged in Canada, an environment driven by presentations from governments and the media of a variety of threats in a highly dramatized and persuasive form of public discourse. In the aftermath of the 9/11 attack, commentary—much of it unsubstantiated—'warned that Canada had become a hiding place for sleeper terrorist cells, a haven for illegal and smuggled immigrants, a source of illegal passports, a conduit for terrorist money-laundering and fundraising, the creator of a dangerously liberal immigration system, and the keeper of an under-policed border which posed a security threat to its powerful neighbor, the United States' (Murphy, 2007, p. 452). In this context of moral panic, immigration was framed as a security concern, with Middle Eastern, West Asian, and Muslim peoples viewed as 'implicit objects of suspicion and potential threat' (Vukov, 2003, p. 345; Bahdi, 2003). This recasting of immigrants and refugees as potential security risks and 'enemies within' has only served to heighten feelings of marginalization, exclusion, and criminalization. As French has stated, '[w]hether it is called **risk management** or **racial profiling**, the practice of singling out communities, of classing groups of people as deserving of increased scrutiny because of their race, ethnicity, or apparent community affiliation, is prevalent' in Canada (2007, p. 60). And while racial and visible minorities have always been subjected to scrutiny, the spectre of terrorism has made such scrutiny more menacing and consequential. With security now firmly in the foreground of political attention, past mentalities that classified refugees and migrants as preferred or non-preferred based on factors such as race, religion, or country of origin have been resurrected (Kruger et al., 2004, p. 77).

It should not be assumed that Canadians fully endorse the post-9/11 security orientation toward immigration and national security policy. In the immediate aftermath of the attacks, public support for greater scrutiny of individuals of Arab origin was high. At the same time, however, a large majority of Canadians voiced concerns over the possibility of retaliation against members of the same population. Indeed, within weeks of the attack Canadian views moderated, 'signaling a return to tolerance that contradicts governmental interpretations of increasing public fears' (Kruger et al., 2004, p. 85). That tolerance has grown over time, with most Canadians supportive of a non-interference pact among the various racial and ethnic groups living in Canada. This contradiction has led Kruger et al. to argue that 'a significant gap in perception exists regarding the nature and extent of the threat posed to Canada's security. There is a lack of communication and a discrepancy in perspectives between governing institutions and the Canadian public. The continued evolution of security responses suggests a disregard of alternative views' (p. 86). In a society with large numbers of new and recent immigrants, this discrepancy and disregard has serious consequences. As was evident in the days following the 9/11 attacks, the **security threat** paradigm of governance can leave immigrants vulnerable to its darker and more troubling manifestations, especially during times of crisis.

Immigrants as Victims

According to an analysis of data from the Canadian census and the General Social Survey (GSS), immigrants in 2004 experienced 68 violent incidents (i.e., sexual assault, robbery and assault) per 1,000 population in Canada. This was considerably lower than the 116 per 1,000 violent victimization rate reported for the Canadian-born population and is similar to findings reported in 1999. Even when risk factors are controlled (e.g., age, sex, marital status, number of evening activities, and proximity of crime), 'immigrants run roughly 30 per cent less risk than non-immigrants for being a victim of violent crime' (Statistics Canada, 2008, p. 11). In all other respects, the characteristics of the violent crimes experienced by immigrants and the Canadian-born population are similar. Like the Canadian-born population, immigrants reported only one-third (32 per cent) of violent incidents to the police. While immigrants may well experience less personal violence than the Canadian-born population, this represents a very narrow, albeit significant, category of victimization. For example, the same 2004 GSS found that nearly 1 in 5 immigrants had experienced discrimination in the preceding five years, with 70 per cent attributing it to their ethnic origin, culture, or skin colour. By way of comparison, 1 in 10 of the Canadian-born population reported discrimination, with 38 per cent attributing it to one or more of the factors cited above. It is also noteworthy that despite having a significantly lower risk of violent victimization, immigrants report slightly higher levels of fear than the Canadian born (Statistics Canada, 2008, p. 14). Although it remains unclear whether these latter two findings are related, such insights point to how our level of understanding can be improved through analysis guided by both an expansive definition of victimization and a sensitivity to the lived immigrant experience.

Recent Canadian studies have uncovered some of the **hidden dimensions of victimization** to which immigrants are particularly vulnerable. For example, the RCMP has conservatively estimated that 600 women and children are trafficked into Canada each year for the purpose of sexual exploitation. An additional 800 are trafficked to work in other markets, such as the drug trade, domestic work, or the garment industry. It has also been reported that immigrants are being trafficked from Canada into the United States (Hanley et al., 2006, p. 82). In each of these examples, immigrants are at the mercy of their smugglers. They fear and experience not only violence, but also repercussions from authorities owing to their precarious legal status. The clandestine nature of human trafficking makes it difficult to estimate the full extent of the victimization experienced by immigrants caught in its web, but for the reasons described above, it can be assumed to encompass a variety of troubling dimensions and is subject to significant under-reporting.

The **under-reporting of victimization** is a phenomenon that also affects the estimated 200,000 undocumented immigrants already residing in Canada (Magalhaes et al. 2010, p. 132). The pervasive fear of official scrutiny—including the possibility of deportation—makes this population extremely vulnerable to exploitation and abuse in both public (e.g., the workplace) and private (e.g., the home) settings. The inability to redress situations involving unsafe work conditions, unpaid salaries, long workdays, harassment, and sexual exploitation, among other things, is directly related to the immigrants' undocumented status and points to additional forms of victimization largely ignored in official statistics. While many of these situations may not be considered criminal in a narrow legal sense, the experience for the immigrant is one of victimization nonetheless.

Immigrants who do become victims of crime face significant obstacles to securing fair treatment through the criminal justice system. As described by Davis et al. (2001), immigrants may arrive in their new country from places where authorities are viewed as oppressors. The lack of trust that develops in such contexts can be transferred to the new environment, reducing the likelihood that immigrants will feel comfortable interacting with the justice system, even when victimized. Language barriers, cultural differences, fear of retaliation, and lack of knowledge about how the justice system works may also factor into the under-reporting of immigrant victimization. The impact of these and other realities is particularly acute for women and children, who may be further marginalized due to the cultural norms of the specific immigrant community (see Tyyska & Dinshaw, 2009). It should also be noted that immigrant women are especially vulnerable to abuse because many are dependent on their spouses for economic support or for the relationships that will enable them to acquire the necessary legal status in Canada.

The consequences of under-reporting victimization carry with them broad social implications. If immigrants do not report their victimization—whether criminal or not—the problem can grow, endangering more and more people. This, in turn, diminishes the ability of society to reduce victimization and brings into question whether the justice system can be said to be responsive to the essential needs of immigrants. As noted by Davis et al., 'it is not enough to know that crimes against immigrants often go unreported, but also what the crimes are and how serious their effect is on the victims and the community' (2001, p. 194). And while there is little doubt that the criminal justice system can play a vital role in helping immigrants overcome the many obstacles described here, the success or failure of any initiative will in large part be determined by how this population perceives the system itself.

A recent study by Wortley and Owusu-Bempah suggests the complexity of the relationship between race, immigration status, and attitudes toward the criminal justice system (2009, p. 469). Their survey of white, black, and Chinese people living in Toronto found that recent immigrants—those in Canada for less than 5 years—along with those who had lived in Canada for more than 20 years, evaluated the police more highly than those who had lived in the country between 5 and 20 years. Recent immigrants also evaluated the criminal courts more highly than the Canadian born or those who had lived in Canada for a long period of time (pp. 457–458). While recent immigrants were found to be less likely to perceive bias in the criminal justice system when compared to the Canadian born, perceptions of discrimination in this population increased the longer the time spent in the country (p. 459). On the basis of these findings, the authors conclude that recent immigrants have among the best opinions of Canadian criminal justice institutions, but that the longer they reside in Canada, the worse their opinion of the police and the courts becomes (p. 466). While the attitudinal shift may be related to personal experiences, vicarious learning, the influence of media coverage, or any other intervening factor(s), the overall trend is noteworthy. The limited geographic reach of the survey, the narrow range of immigrant groups examined, and the general lack of research on immigrant perceptions of the justice system make it difficult to generalize beyond the study (while the overall findings are consistent with the 2004 GSS, more supporting research is required to take them to be definitive; see Statistics Canada 2008, p. 12). Nevertheless, it would appear that the decline of confidence in the criminal justice system that immigrants to Canada experience after having lived in the country for more than five years should give policy-makers pause, especially since perceptions of discrimination begin to increase in the same population at the same time.

The preceding discussion has highlighted some of the many forms of victimization experienced by immigrants. The services provided to this population and to others seeking to integrate into Canadian society are vitally important. In the final section of this chapter, some of these services, along with the groups, organizations, and agencies that deliver them, will be outlined.

Immigrants as Service Providers

Many newcomers to Canada require immediate access to settlement services. Supported by funds from the various levels of government and, to a lesser extent, from charities and foundations, these services include language training, counselling, employment assistance, translation and interpretation services, housing support, legal assistance, and health and social service referrals (Omidvar & Richmond 2003, p. 7). While families, friends, and members of the immigrant community may help newcomers integrate into their new environment, they also steer them toward the various public and **immigrant service agencies (ISAs)** for support and assistance (Agrawal et al., 2007, p. 110). In Canada, non-governmental ISAs deliver the lion's share of services to newcomers and work hard to ensure that immigrants settle and integrate into Canadian society successfully. They also draw on their everyday experiences and extensive social networks to identify both immigrant needs and service gaps. ISAs have been instrumental in advancing cultural sensitivity in the delivery of services, focusing attention on the need for gainful employment and advocating for public assistance that treats immigrants with dignity. Beyond these specific needs, research has demonstrated that 'immigrants have almost similar needs as the public at large. Whether it is water supply, police protection or social housing, immigrants' needs are similar to those of the Canadian-born' (Agrawal et al., 2007, p. 109).

ISAs provide essential support to immigrants in a fiscal context that is in a perpetual state of flux. As the population of immigrants to Canada has grown and become more diverse, there has been a corresponding expansion in the need for basic immigrant services. For ISAs to keep pace with the various demands would be difficult at the best of times, but as Canada and the rest of the world adjust to the fallout from a global financial crisis, simply retaining their existing funding consumes a great deal of valuable time, energy, and resources. Moreover, ISAs have pointed out that one of the most serious problems of the current immigration system 'lies in the fact that settlement funding and programming is focused on the initial stages of adaptation, in spite of the fact that the process of settlement continues throughout the life of the newcomer' (Omidvar & Richmond, 2003, p. 8). Responding to this gap is virtually impossible in an environment already under stress because of increased demands for services and limited funding.

It is important here to note the contributions that ISAs and other community organizations make to immigrants who have no legal status in Canada. This population, which lives in a shadow world, tends only to reach out for help in the most trying of circumstances. Despite funding constraints and the lack of clear guidance from governments on how to address the needs of this population, service providers have found themselves on the front line of a battle to regularize the status of the undocumented. While a number of municipalities have adopted '**Don't ask, don't tell**' policies when dealing with non-status people, the underlying funding problem remains, as does the problem of this population being unable to access services that require the appropriate legal documentation (see Berinstein, 2006).

ISAs have also played an important role in providing services to immigrants who encounter the criminal justice system. This is particularly true in cases of child abuse, senior abuse, and spousal abuse. For reasons already discussed, ISAs are often the first point of contact for victims because of the agencies' proximity to the community, their ability to understand cultural norms and pressures, and their status as long-standing community partners. Research has shown that specific programs designed for immigrants should try to involve people who have a deep cultural knowledge of the communities they serve (Tyyska & Dinshaw, 2009). The various ISAs are perfectly positioned to provide this knowledge.

ISAs are also trusted sources of information on the policies and practices of various social institutions, including the criminal justice system. ISAs frequently provide their clients with information on the operation of the system, including the role of the various participants, the steps in the criminal justice process, the services provided by the system, and information on how Canadian criminal justice is different from the system of justice familiar to the immigrant. ISAs not only provide much needed support to victims, they also help to educate criminal justice officials through a variety of cross-cultural initiatives. Regular meetings between ISAs, leaders of immigrant communities, and representatives from various agencies of the criminal justice system are now commonplace. Immigrant outreach, multilingual assistance, and special programs tailored to the specific needs of immigrant communities are also increasingly part of the criminal justice landscape.

Unfortunately, the degree to which these various initiatives have succeeded in bridging gaps between immigrant communities and the criminal justice system remains an open question. In the case of policing, Stenning (2003) has identified an extensive list of policies and programs that have been designed over the past two decades to reduce discrimination and improve police relations with immigrant groups and racial and visible minorities in Canada. According to Wortley and Owusu-Bempah, these initiatives have not been successful. Indeed, 'there is evidence to suggest that perceptions of discrimination have actually increased' (2009, p. 465). Heller found that criminal defendants who used an interpreter in shoplifting cases handled by a legal aid clinic in a major Canadian city received sentences that were twice as harsh as those given to defendants who did not use an interpreter. The finding 'suggests that immigrant groups who have not mastered the dominant language are seen as less deserving of justice' (cited in Jiwani, 2002, p. 76).

These examples should serve as a sober reminder of the work that still needs to be done to help immigrants overcome the institutional and structural barriers they face in their newly adopted homeland. This is not a new challenge, but it is one that must be confronted with a sense of urgency. The Canada of the twenty-first century looks very different from the Canada of only 50 years ago. As this chapter has shown, much of this can be attributed to the changing nature of immigration. It is apparent that this population will in large part determine the degree to which Canada is able to harness its full potential in the coming years.

Summary

This chapter has explored the economic, demographic, social, political, and ideological forces that have influenced Canada's relationship with immigration and immigrants. The early history of Canadian immigration is a story of the two charter groups setting the terms and conditions of entry. Clearly the result of attitudes that were biased against those judged not to be of good English or French stock, the poor, the non-white, the non-English, the non-French, and the non-European were systematically prevented from immigrating to Canada during the nineteenth and twentieth centuries. On occasions when this general pattern was not followed, Canada permitted entry under very specific conditions, usually to augment the labour force. Life for those admitted under these circumstances was difficult, with their sense of belonging often undermined by unfair policies and discriminatory attitudes.

Beginning in the 1960s, internal and external pressures led to a liberalization of immigration policy that dramatically changed the makeup of Canada. Spurred by the passage of the Bill of Rights in 1960 and bolstered by the commitment to multiculturalism enshrined in the Charter of Rights and Freedoms in 1982, immigration was advanced as the primary means through which Canada would increase its population, enhance its economic competitiveness, and promote its image as a tolerant nation to the rest of the world. By 2017, fully one-fifth of the Canadian population will be racial or visible minorities, a far cry from the 1 per cent of the population this group represented in 1971.

While the narrative of successful multiculturalism is immensely appealing, it does not capture the lived experience of many immigrants to Canada. Too often, immigrants, particularly those from Africa, the Caribbean, South Asia, and the Middle East, are viewed as the cause for society's ills. This is particularly true for crime and, following the attacks of September 11, terrorism. The impact of this perception is corrosive for the vast majority of immigrants who view Canada as their homeland and for the wider population that should have a keen interest in promoting the successful integration of immigrants into Canadian society. As this chapter has shown, the moral panic over immigrant criminality draws attention away from the serious forms of structural, institutional, and personal victimization experienced by this population. Although non-governmental immigrant service agencies work tirelessly to address a wide array of immigrant needs, much more can and should be done if Canada wishes to be a model of a truly cohesive, diverse, and multicultural nation.

Key Terms

colonization

deportation

discrimination

"Don't ask, don't tell"

four phases of
  immigration

head tax

hidden dimensions
  of victimization

immigration service
  agencies (ISAs)

importation, strain,
  cultural conflict
  and bias models

moral panic

multiculturalism

net-widening

points system

preferred and
  non-preferred
  immigrants

racial profiling

refugee

risk management

security threat

social exclusion

social inclusion

under-reporting of
  victimization

Questions for Critical Thought

1. How does history help us understand the contemporary challenges facing immigrants in Canada?
2. Provide examples both supporting and opposing the 'immigrant-crime connection'. On balance, which position do you feel is strongest and why?
3. Discuss some of the challenges associated with uncovering the true extent of victimization experienced by immigrants.
4. Based on your reading of this chapter, what criminal justice services do you feel would be most helpful to newcomers to Canada?

Additional Readings

Biles, J., Burnstein, M., & Frideres, J. (Eds). (2008). *Immigration and integration in Canada in the twenty-first century.* Kingston, ON: School of Policy Studies, Queen's University.

Gaudet, L., & Jones, C. (Eds). (2009). *Immigration practitioner's handbook 2010.* Toronto: Carswell.

Ginsberg, S. (2010). *Securing human mobility in the age of risk.* Washington, DC: Migration Policy Institute.

Martinez, R., & Valenzuela, A. (Eds). (2006). *Immigration and crime.* New York: New York University Press.

Websites of Interest

Citizenship and Immigration Canada: www.cic.gc.ca

Statistics Canada (Justice Statistics): www.statcan.gc.ca

Canadian Council for Refugees: www.ccrweb.ca

Multicultural Canada: http://multiculturalcanada.ca

The Canadian Community Economic Development Network: www.ccednet-rdec.ca

Endnotes

1. This research was supported by a grant from the Faculty of Arts at Ryerson University. The author wishes to give special thanks to Dean Carla Cassidy and to Neha Patel for her excellent research assistance.

References

Agrawal, S. K., Qadeer, M., & Prasad, A. (2007). Immigrants' needs and public service provisions in Peel Region. *Our Diverse Cities, 4,* 108–112.

Bahdi, R. (2003). 'No exit: Racial profiling and Canada's war against terrorism. *Osgoode Hall Law Journal, 41,* 293–317.

Barnes, A. (2009). Displacing danger: Managing crime through deportation. *Journal of International Migration and Integration, 10,* 431–445.

Berinstein, C., Nyers, P., Wright, C., & Zeheri, S. (2006). *Access not fear: Non-status immigrants and city services.* Report prepared for the 'Don't Ask, Don't Tell' Campaign, Toronto.

Chan, W. (2005). Crime, deportation and the regulation of immigrants in Canada. *Crime, Law and Social Change, 44,* 153–180.

Costelloe, M. (2009). Undocumented immigration as moral panic: Casting difference as threat. In the Criminology and Criminal Justice Collective of Northern Arizona University, *Investigating Difference: Human and Cultural Relations in Criminal Justice* (pp. 214–224). n.p.: Prentice Hall.

Davis, R. C., Erez, E., & Avitabile, N. (2001). Access to justice for immigrants who are victimized: The perspectives of police and prosecutors. *Criminal Justice Policy Review, 12*(3), 183–196.

Esses, V. M., Dovidio, J. F., & Hodson, G. (2002). Public attitudes toward immigration in the United States and Canada in response to the September 11, 2001 'Attack on America'. *Analysis of Social Issues and Public Policy, 2,* 69–85.

Fenlon, B. (2008). Canada's visible minorities top five million. *The Globe and Mail.* Retrieved February 15, 2010, from www.theglobeandmail.com/archives/canadas-visible-minorities-top-five-million/article677116/

French, M. (2007). In the shadow of Canada's camps. *Social and Legal Studies, 16*(1), 49–69.

Hagan, J., Levi, R., & Dinovitzer, R. (2008). The symbolic violence of the crime-immigration nexus: Migrant mythologies in the Americas. *Criminology and Public Policy, 7*(1), 95–112.

Hanley, J., Oxman-Martinez, J., Lacroix, M., & Sigalit, G. (2006). The 'deserving' undocumented? Government and community response to human trafficking as a labour phenomenon. *Labour, Capital and Society, 39*(2), 79–103.

Ismaili, K. (2010). Surveying the many fronts of the war on immigrants in post-9/11 U.S. society. *Contemporary Justice Review, 13*(1), 71–93.

Jiwani, Y. (2002). The criminalization of 'race', the racialization of crime. In W. Chan & K. Mirchandani (Eds), *Crimes of colour: Racialization and the criminal justice system in Canada* (pp. 67–86). Peterborough, ON: Broadview Press.

Kruger, E., Mulder, M., & Korenic, B. (2004). Canada after 11 September: Security measures and 'preferred' immigrants. *Mediterranean Quarterly, 15*(4), 72–87.

Li, P. (2003). *Destination Canada: Immigration debates and issues*. Don Mills, ON: Oxford University Press.

Lucas, A. (2005). Huddled masses: Immigrants in detention. *Punishment and Society, 7*, 323–9.

McCalla, A., & Satzevich, V. (2002). Settler capitalism and the construction of immigrants and 'Indians' as racialized others. In W. Chan & K. Mirchandani (Eds), *Crimes of colour: Racialization and the criminal justice system in Canada* (pp. 25–44). Peterborough, ON: Broadview Press.

Magalhaes, L., Carrasco, C., & Gastaldo, D. (2010). Undocumented migrants in Canada: A scope literature review on health, access to services, and working conditions. *Journal of Immigrant and Minority Health, 12*, 132–151.

Murphy, C. (2007). Securitizing Canadian policing: A new policing paradigm for the post 9/11 security state? *Canadian Journal of Sociology, 32*(4), 449–475.

Omidvar, R., & Richmond, T. (2003). *Immigrant settlement and social inclusion in Canada*. Toronto: Laidlaw Foundation.

Perry, B., Fernandez, L. A., & Costelloe, M. (2009). Exclusion, inclusion, and violence: Immigrants and criminal justice. In the Criminology and Criminal Justice Collective of Northern Arizona University, *Investigating difference: Human and cultural relations in criminal justice* (pp. 88–101). n.p.: Prentice Hall.

Pratt, A. (2005). *Securing borders: Detention and deportation in Canada*. Vancouver: University of British Columbia Press.

Reitz, J. G., & Banerjee, R. (2007). Racial inequality, social cohesion and policy issues in Canada. In K. Banting, T. J. Courchene, & F. L. Seidle (Eds), *Belonging? Diversity, recognition and shared citizenship in Canada* (pp. 489–545). Montreal: Institute for Research on Public Policy.

Sampson, R. J. (2006, March 11). Open doors don't invite criminals. *The New York Times*, p. A27. Retrieved February 15, 2010, from www.nytimes.com/2006/03/11/opinion/11sampson.html

Simon, R. J., & Sikich, K. W. (2007). Public attitudes toward immigrants and immigration policies across seven nations. *International Migration Review, 41*(4), 956–962.

Statistics Canada. (2008). *Immigrants and victimization, 2004*. Ottawa: Ministry of Industry.

Stenning, P. C. (2003). Policing the cultural kaleidoscope: Recent Canadian experience. *Police and Society, 7*, 13–47.

Thobani, S. (2000). Closing ranks: Racism and sexism in Canada's immigration policy. *Race and Class, 42*(1), 35–55.

Tyyska, V., & Dinshaw, F. (2009). Families and violence in Punjabi and Tamil communities in Toronto. *Policy Matters (CERIS), 39*, 1–6.

Vukov, T. (2003). Imagining communities through immigration policies: Governmental regulation, media spectacles and the affective politics of national borders. *International Journal of Cultural Studies, 6*(3), 335–353.

Wayland, S. (1997). Immigration, multiculturalism and national identity in Canada. *International Journal on Group Rights, 5*, 33–58.

Wortley, S. (2009). Introduction: The immigration-crime connection: Competing theoretical perspectives. *Journal of International Migration and Integration, 10*, 349–358.

Wortley, S., & Owusu-Bempah, A. (2009). Unequal before the law: Immigrant and racial minority perceptions of the Canadian criminal justice system. *Journal of International Migration and Integration, 10*, 447–473.

Wortley, S., & Tanner, J. (2006). Immigration, social disadvantage and urban youth gangs: Results of a Toronto-area survey. *Canadian Journal of Urban Research, 15*(2), 18–37.

Yeager, M. (2002). Rehabilitating the criminality of immigrants under section 19 of the Canadian Immigration Act. *International Migration Review, 36*(1), 178–192.

7 Chinese Immigrants in Canada and Social Injustice: From Overt to Covert Racial Discrimination

LI ZONG AND BARBARA PERRY

This chapter provides a historical review of Chinese immigration to Canada, examines the social injustice, criminalization, and structural barriers that **Chinese immigrants** experienced or faced in Canadian society, and analyzes how social injustice and racial discrimination against Chinese emerged and remained in different social and historical contexts. Theoretical debates on the issue of occupational attainment for recent Chinese immigrants and covert racism will be addressed.

Historical Review of Chinese Immigrants in Canada and Overt Racism

Chinese have arrived in large groups in Canada since the Fraser River Gold Rush in 1858. In the latter half of 1800s, the economy of China was suffering badly, spurring many Chinese men to leave their homeland in search for better opportunities in North America. They came, leaving their children and wives behind in China, with initially no plans to stay permanently in Canada. They hoped to go back to China as soon as they earned enough money. The earlier Chinese immigrants in Canada worked as miners in gold mines. Later on, when the gold-mining industry began to decline, over 17,000 Chinese workers were employed in the building of the Canadian Pacific Railway (CPR). They were paid half the wage their white counterparts received, and about 600 Chinese died during the construction of the railway. The rest of them worked as servants, farmers, and laundry and restaurant workers. These earlier Chinese immigrants usually came from the southern part of China. Most were peasants who had great difficulty in making a living in China and who came to Canada to seek an opportunity by 'digging gold'. Between 1858 and 1884, 20,000 Chinese came to Canada, but some returned to China and some died, leaving a Chinese population of 16,000 in 1884 (Lee, 1967, p. 30).

With the completion of the CPR in 1885, the Chinese were out of work. Many were stranded in Vancouver, an environment fuelled with racial hostility and suspicion. According to Li (1998), the British Columbia legislature passed numerous bills restricting the political and social rights of Chinese, including the act prohibiting Chinese from acquiring Crow lands and diverting water from natural channels in

1884, the act excluding Chinese from work underground in coal mines in 1890, the act barring Chinese from admission to the provincially established home for the aged and infirm in 1893, and an amendment preventing Chinese from performing skilled jobs in coal mines in 1903 (Li, 1998, pp. 32–33). Chinese were not entitled to hold a liquor licence in 1899, and they were barred from obtaining a hand-logger's licence in 1903. Chinese were excluded from nomination for municipal office, jury duty, election to the provincial legislature, and the professions of law and pharmacy (Li, 1998, p. 33).

Anti-Chinese sentiments lingered on in British Columbia. In 1907, when a rumour was spread that a mass influx of Chinese, Japanese, and East Indians would arrive in Vancouver to take up jobs in the forest industry and the construction of the Pacific Great Eastern Railway, widespread violence erupted. A racist organization called the **Asiatic Exclusion League** was formed. The league organized a rally, and a mob rampaged through Chinatown, destroying property and goods.

With the growing hostility toward the Chinese in British Columbia at the turn of the century, some Chinese immigrants began moving eastward. However, social injustice and unequal treatment toward the Chinese were similarly prevalent in other provinces. The Chinese in Saskatchewan, for example, were disenfranchised in 1908.

In 1919 the white farmers of British Columbia started a campaign to prohibit Chinese from owning or leasing farmland. In 1920 the Children's Protective Association initiated the removal of Chinese students from the classroom. As a result of pressure exerted by the unions against the competition of Chinese labour, restrictive measures were imposed upon Chinese immigration. Between 1895 and 1923, a series of laws were passed in Canada demanding that Chinese immigrants pay a **head tax**; this tax increased from $50 per head in 1885 to $100 in 1900 and $500 in 1923 (Kung, 1962, pp. 610–620). In 1923 the Canadian Parliament passed the Chinese Immigration Act, which both prevented Chinese from entering the country and controlled those already in Canada. Between 1923 and 1947, only 44 Chinese were allowed into Canada (Kung, 1962, pp. 610–620). Since the Chinese men could not bring their wives and children into Canada, the sex imbalance in the Chinese community remained the highest among ethnic groups in Canada (Li, 1998, p. 67).

From the above discussion, we can see that, historically, **overt racism** against Chinese in Canada was expressed not only at the individual level in civil society, but also at institutional level through governmental policies, laws, and practices. **Institutional racism** refers to racism intentionally perpetrated by government entities such as the federal and provincial parliaments, courts, and school system. Unlike the racism perpetrated by individuals, institutional racism has the power to affect negatively the bulk of people belonging to a racial group.

Recent Chinese Immigrants from China

The **Chinese Immigration Act** of 1923 was repealed in 1947, but even so, the only Chinese allowed into Canada between 1947 and 1962 were those whose family members were Canadian residents. Before 1962, Chinese could not come to Canada as independent immigrants; they could only come if they were sponsored by a wife, husband, or parent who was already a Canadian resident. Immigration from mainland China to Canada was thus light in the 1950s and early 1960s. Those who came were mainly family members joining close relatives in Canada, particularly wives and children coming as family members of Chinese men already in Canada (Li, 1998, p. 96). For example, between 1956 and 1965, only 4,890 mainland Chinese immigrated to Canada. In 1967 Canada changed its immigration policy by adopting a 'point' system (Privy Council, 1967, pp. 1350–1362) in order to screen independent immigrants. The point system provided an equal opportunity for immigration from Asian countries. At the same time, the Cultural Revolution, particularly in its early years (1966–70), brought social turbulence to mainland China, and many mainland Chinese who had relatives in Canada wanted to leave China to seek a more stable future in this country. Both pulling and pushing factors motivated a relatively large number of mainland Chinese (32,534) to immigrate to Canada between 1966 and 1970. However, between 1971 and 1978, the number of immigrants from mainland China decreased because of political pressure and restricted migration control in China. It was not until 1979, after China adopted an open-door policy and began to relax its restrictions on the exit of Chinese citizens, that many mainland Chinese were able to leave for Canada and the immigration flow to Canada began to increase again.

Between 1979 and 1989, 35,366 mainland Chinese immigrated to Canada. The 1989 student protest movement in China, which led to the tragic incident at Tiananmen Square, triggered a sudden increase in mainland Chinese immigrants. The Canadian government enacted a special program (known as OM-IS-339) to protect Chinese students and visiting scholars who were in Canada at the time and who participated in demonstrations in Canada in support of the student movement in China. The policy allowed thousands of Chinese students, visiting scholars, and their family members to obtain landed-immigrant status on compassionate grounds. In the years 1990 and 1991, 22,319 mainland Chinese became landed immigrants in Canada. In the following two years (1992–93), another 21,998 mainland Chinese immigrated to Canada. From 1994 until early in the new century, annual immigration from mainland China continued to increase, reaching 40,315 in 2001. From the year 2000, over 30,000 to 40,000 immigrants from mainland China entered Canada each year (Citizenship and Immigration Canada, 2002, 2004), making China Canada's largest immigration source country. For the decade 1994–2004, a total of 293,680 mainland Chinese immigrated to Canada.

Most recent mainland Chinese immigrants, especially those arriving in the 1990s and 2000s, have been well-trained and experienced professionals seeking new opportunities. Canada welcomes these immigrants mainly because of their potential to contribute to the country's population and economic growth. However, many mainland Chinese immigrants, particularly skilled/professional immigrants, are disappointed and frustrated because they have not been able to achieve a satisfactory social and economic status in Canadian society.

The following section focuses on foreign-trained mainland Chinese professional immigrants and examines the obstacles to their occupational attainment in the Canadian labour market.

Obstacles for Occupational Attainment in Canada

Between 1990 and 2002, over 77,000 well-trained and experienced principal applicants who were skilled workers or professionals immigrated to Canada from mainland China to seek better opportunities in Canada. However, after entering the country, many of them found difficulty in obtaining the professional jobs they expected, and consequently they experienced downward occupational mobility. According to a survey of 1,180 recent mainland Chinese professional immigrants[1] conducted in Vancouver, Toronto, Ottawa, Calgary, Edmonton, and Saskatoon between 1997 and 1999 (the 1997–99 survey),[2] 79 per cent of respondents reported having worked as professionals in China before immigrating to Canada. However, only 31 per cent reported that they worked or had worked as professionals in Canada. Although about 6 per cent of the respondents had become proprietors, managers, supervisors, and administrators, 41 per cent had lower social status in non-professional jobs and 22 per cent had never worked in Canada. About 75 per cent of respondents reported that their occupations in their home country matched their professional qualifications well, while only 23 per cent reported that their current (or last) occupation in Canada matched their professional qualifications. About 41 per cent of respondents reported that they were overqualified for their current occupations, and 29 per cent said they had not worked since their arrival (Zong, 2004, pp. 82–83).

There are two approaches to occupational attainment of immigrants in the literature. The first focuses primarily on individual barriers experienced by immigrants, including the inability to meet occupational entry requirements, a lack of Canadian work experience, and an inadequate command of English (Ornstein & Sharma, 1983). In the 1997–99 survey, 49 per cent of respondents reported that they experienced difficulty with their command of English, and 34 per cent also experienced difficulty in adapting to Western culture. Among those who answered 'difficult' or 'very difficult' with regard to command of English, 70 per cent experienced downward occupational mobility. Among those who answered 'difficult' or 'very difficult' in adaptation to Western culture, 65 per cent experienced downward occupational mobility (Zong, 2004, p. 83). The language barrier can be overcome in time through personal effort. The survey shows that as the length of time in Canada increases, the percentage experiencing downward mobility decreases (Zong, 2004, p. 84). This suggests that the linguistic abilities and level of adaptation of new immigrants improve the longer they stay.[3]

Although the individual approach has elucidated some personal difficulties, it has not explained how the structural factors pertaining to policies, criteria, and procedures for evaluation also contribute to occupational disadvantages for foreign-trained professionals. Failure to locate individual barriers in social conditions and structural arrangements tends to result in the immigrant professionals themselves being blamed for their inability to acquire professional jobs in Canada. A fundamental debate is whether individual attributes or institutionalized barriers are responsible for immigrants' occupational disadvantages.

The second approach stresses structural barriers such as unequal opportunity, devaluation of foreign credentials, and racism. It suggests that control of entry to the professions has caused systematic exclusion of and occupational disadvantages for professional immigrants (Boyd,

1985, pp. 393–445; McDade, 1988; Trovato & Grindstaff, 1986, pp. 569–687; Rajagopal, 1990, pp. 96–105; Ralston, 1988, pp. 63–83; Beach & Worswick, 1989, pp. 36–54). For instance, Boyd provides an analysis of differences between Canadian-born and foreign-born workers in the acquisition of occupational status. She argues that the Canadian born receive a greater return for their education compared to the foreign born because of 'difficulties of transferring educational skill across national boundaries' (Boyd, 1985, p. 405). In their research, Fernando and Prasad (1986) report that among professional immigrants interviewed, particularly doctors and engineers, 71 per cent had perceived barriers to full recognition.

Many Chinese immigrants perceived some structural barriers that affected their occupational attainments in Canada. The 1997–99 survey shows that 73 per cent of respondents believed that they could not enter into the professional occupations in which they were trained because there was unequal opportunity for visible minority immigrants. About 77 per cent reported that it was difficult for them to find professional jobs because of a shortage of opening positions in the Canadian labour market. However, the major systemic barrier identified by respondents was that their foreign credentials and work experience were devalued by professional organizations, government evaluation agencies, and educational institutions (Zong, 2004, p. 84). Sixty-nine per cent of respondents reported that they experienced difficulty in having their foreign credentials recognized in Canada. Based on their own experience and observation, about 78 per cent of respondents reported that 'the difficulty in having their foreign qualifications or credentials recognized' was a major factor that affected or might have affected their chances to practise in their chosen professions (Zong, 2004, p. 83).

Many Chinese immigrants thought that the greater the number of years of professional experience, the better their chance of getting a job in their field in Canada. This assumption, however, turned out to be an illusion. In the 1997–99 survey, 94 per cent of Chinese professional immigrants reported that they had had professional work experience in China before immigrating to Canada, 50 per cent had had 5 to 10 years of professional work experience, and 21 per cent had had more than 10 years of professional work experience. Interestingly, Chinese professionals with more professional experience were more likely to experience downward mobility: 47 per cent of respondents did not believe that 'the foreign work experience is compared to Canadian standards fairly' (Zong, 2004, p. 83). Thus, professional immigrants encounter a difficult situation in the Canadian labour market. On the one hand, non-recognition of their foreign professional work experience disqualifies their entry into professional jobs, leaving them no chance to gain Canadian work experience; on the other, the emphasis on Canadian work experience as a requirement for professional employment makes it difficult for them to qualify for professional jobs.

Covert Racism in Multicultural Society

The racism experienced by recent Chinese immigrants in their everyday life is often expressed in a hidden form known as **covert racism** (Zong, 1997). Covert racism can be defined as a contemporary expression of hostility toward racial minorities that goes undetected by conventional measures (Weigel & Howes, 1985).

Since the implementation of the multiculturalism policy in 1971, there has been a debate on whether or not multiculturalism promotes national unity in Canada. While Canadians generally support the values of equality and democracy, many have exhibited a remarkable degree of intolerance toward the increased presence of visible minorities in their midst. In the past two decades, the dramatic influx of refugees and immigrants from the Third World and a large number of business and professional immigrants from Asian countries have produced renewed racial attitudes and a resurgence of racism. According to the 2003 Ipsos-Reid survey conducted by the Centre for Research and Information on Canada and *The Globe and Mail*, 74 per cent of respondents expressed the view that there is still considerable racism in Canada.

Racism has been generated and reproduced within complex historical and social contexts. Before World War II, overt racism based on the belief in racial superiority was dominant in Europe and North America. It was widely accepted that the Caucasian 'race' was physically and genetically superior to other races and was characterized by an inherent capacity for freedom and the ability to create democratic institutions, capacities that they could impose on many other parts of the world (Horsman, 1976, pp. 387–410; Horsman, 1981, pp. 9–77). With the expansion of capitalism and colonialism, the 'innate superiority' of whites and the 'natural inferiority' of blacks and other non-white peoples were used to legitimate and justify racial oppression. Racism initially arose from unequal relationships as a dominant group sought to subjugate a subordinate group for the purpose of acquiring land, resources, and/or cheap labour. In Canada, racism was maintained toward racialized minorities such as the Aboriginal peoples and Asian immigrants; discriminatory laws, programs, and policies were entrenched in a social order that made prejudicial views appear as though they were natural and justifiable (Zong, 1994, pp. 122–134).

After World War II, many changes contributed to the weakening of notions of racial superiority or inferiority based on biological and genetic factors. These changes included the struggle against colonial rule, the rise of nationalism, the development of sciences, and the abrogation of discriminatory laws and policies in many advanced capitalist countries. Thus, overt racism has become less acceptable in Western societies. The traditional idea of genetic inferiority or superiority may still be important in the fabric of racism (Duster, 1990), but the discourse of racial inferiority has been increasingly reformulated as cultural deficiency, social inadequacy, and technological underdevelopment (Rodney, 1982). An example is cultural ethnocentrism, which is a tendency to evaluate minorities' cultures on the basis of the dominant group's imposed standards (Li, 1994b). According to a survey conducted by the Angus Reid Group, about 13 per cent of Canadians can be considered to be 'ethnocentrists' based on their negative attitudes toward immigrants and refugees. The basis of negative attitudes appeared to be largely cultural, as those expressing them were concerned with a threat to Canadian culture that they perceived to be a consequence of an emphasis on multiculturalism and a rapidly changing population brought about by high immigration levels (Angus Reid Group, 1989, pp. 7–8). In recent years, many scholars in North America (Fleras & Elliott, 1992; Gaertner & Dovidio, 1986; Henry, Tator, Mattis, & Rees, 1995; Katz, Wackenhut, & Hass, 1986, pp. 35–60; McConohay, 1986, pp. 91–126; Weigel & Howes, 1985, pp. 117–138) have drawn attention to the emergence of a form of racism in contemporary social settings that can be described as a 'new racism'.

The new racism often involves an oblique attack on visible minorities in a covert or disguised form. Different from the past, when blatant and stereotypic forms of prejudice and discrimination were routinely directed at racial minorities with explicit hatred, the new racism usually disguises racist attitudes through behaviours that appear non-prejudicial or non-discriminatory on the surface. To avoid embarrassing situations or possible physical or legal retaliation, racism is now usually expressed in somewhat more muted or polite tones that are less likely to provoke outrage or indignation. Some scholars (Fleras & Elliott, 1992; Henry et al., 1995) suggest that this new racism reflects a conflict of interest between opposing values in Canadian society. 'On the one hand is a commitment to abstract equality and justice (egalitarianism); on the other, an equal but often conflicting endorsement of meritocracy and universalism (individualism)' (Fleras & Elliott, 1992, p. 60).

Since World War II, Canada has witnessed the abolition of overt exclusionary policies and laws, such as the repeal of the Chinese Immigration Act in 1947, the adoption of a multiculturalism policy in 1971, and constitutional guarantees of individual rights and freedoms in 1982. These changes have helped to promote a democratic and tolerant society, and the value of equality in Canadian society is widely propagated. However, economic, political, and social inequalities along racial and ethnic lines still exist, and covert expressions of bigotry and stereotyping remain (Bolaria & Li, 1988; Satzewich, 1992). The contradiction between democratic principles and racial inequalities at the structural level is reflected in the conflict between the egalitarian values of justice and racist attitudes. This is the basis of what Henry et al. call **'democratic racism'**—a new ideology prevalent in contemporary Canadian society 'in which two conflicting sets of values are made congruent to each other. Commitments to democratic principles such as justice, equality, and fairness conflict but coexist with attitudes and behaviours that include negative feelings about minority groups and differential treatment of and discrimination against them' (Henry et al., 1995, p. 21).

The 1995 Vancouver survey confirms the coexistence of these contradictory values, and the findings demonstrate the basis of a new ideology shared by many respondents in their attitudes towards Chinese immigrants. Although people generally accept the value of racial equality, many are not prepared to accept non-white immigrants such as Chinese. About 79 per cent of the respondents agreed that 'immigrants should have exactly the same job opportunities as Canadians', and 82 per cent of the respondents agreed that 'minority groups in Canada should have equal opportunity for occupation, education, and promotion in society.' However, European immigrants and Chinese immigrants were not equally supported by the public. About 73 per cent of respondents supported admitting more European immigrants, while only about 47 per cent supported admitting more Chinese immigrants. The negative attitude toward Chinese immigrants was not so much based on colour or biological differences as on perceived cultural differences.

It is widely held that the different cultures brought by immigrants undermine national unity. The 1995 Vancouver survey showed that about 50 per cent of respondents disagreed with the statement that 'the establishment of multiculturalism policy has promoted a democratic and tolerant society in Canada.' Many respondents argued that multiculturalism encourages cultural diversity and denies the existence of Canadian culture, therefore creating and reinforcing separateness and racial conflict. This concern is reflected in public attitudes toward recent Chinese immigrants in Vancouver.

These comments reflect the common belief still held by many Canadians that Anglo-Saxon culture is the one that forms the basis of national unity in this country and that immigrants must make conscious efforts to become 'Canadian' by accepting and adopting behaviours of the dominant group. Most people would deny that race is important and almost unanimously would condemn racism as wrong. In the 1995 Vancouver survey, about 59 per cent of respondents thought that ethnic origin should not be used as a criterion in admitting immigrants to Canada, and over 82 per cent agreed that minority groups in Canada should have equal opportunity for occupation, education, and promotion in society. Yet, at the same time, many people accepted visible minorities and immigrants only if they could adapt to Anglo-Canadian culture. The same survey shows that about 59 per cent of respondents agreed that 'Chinese immigrants should adapt themselves to Canadian culture in order to become a real Canadian.'

Cultural diversity has always been a part of Canadian society; it is an existing fact of Canadian life and not something that can be changed artificially. Despite cultural differences, different racial and ethnic groups in Canadian society share core values such as democracy and equality. Some scholars (Breton, 1984, pp. 123–144; Li, 1994a, pp. 14–33; Li, 1994b, pp. 365–391; Mercer, 1995, 169–84) suggest that although there is no empirical evidence to indicate that immigrants and their cultural diversity are posing any real threat to the dominant culture of Canada, visible minorities and 'immigrants are often perceived as undermining a British-dominated traditional symbolic order, on the grounds that they are seen as carriers of foreign cultures and norms which are believed to be different, if not incompatible, with Canadian heritage and core values' (Li, 1996, p. 24).

Culture is dynamic and complex. The notion of 'Anglo-Saxon Canadian culture' is vague and ambiguous, and the concept of 'acculturation' or 'assimilation' stressed in national unity is misleading and ill-defined. Assimilation implies that social and structural integration is indicated by the achievement of certain objectives and widely agreed-upon standards of behaviour. However, in practice, it is unclear what types of behaviours indicate that a person has been assimilated.

Cultural diversity does not in itself create racial tension and conflict. It is differential power and unequal treatments that do so. Members of the dominant group often use their 'standards' as a frame of reference for interpreting and evaluating behaviours of other groups. As Fleras and Elliott (1992, p. 55) point out, 'Not surprisingly, these groups are rated inferior, backward, or irrational. It can be seen that although favouritism towards one's own group can promote cohesion and morale, it can also contribute to intergroup tension and hostility, [and] to a proliferation of stereotypes about outgroup members.' The real issue is how to promote mutual understanding and a respectful relationship among different racial groups and how to achieve a national solidarity and harmony within a culturally diversified society.

Criminalization and the Social Construction of Crime

Institutional racism in the form of law and order affected Chinese immigrants in Canada in complex ways. Canadian history shows many examples of the law being used for racist ends. Up until 1908, the use of opiates in Canada was unregulated. However, the public's fear of early Chinese immigrants resulted in the implementation of anti-drug policies (Alexander, 1990, p. 50). In the 1850s, a large number of Chinese immigrants came to British Columbia as cheap labour for the railroads, mining, and other industries (Solomon & Green, 1988, p. 89). Many of them were married men who were not allowed to bring their wives to Canada with them. They lived in isolated communities, and the smoking of opium and the presence of opium dens were not initially considered harmful. When the Chinese were considered as an economic threat to other Canadians, they became a bigger target for resentment and fear. Hostility toward Chinese in British Columbia began to be reflected in legislation, which was intentionally designed to end Chinese immigration and drive the Chinese out of Canada's economic mainstream.

During this period, for many white Canadians, particularly government officials and police, opium use and sale were emblematic of the Chinese 'problem.' Chinese immigrants were distinctly labelled and negatively stereotyped. In the 'popular ideology, opium smoking tended to be one among several items exemplifying the alien, inferior, and inassimilable nature of the Chinese' (Giffen, Endicott, & Lambert, 1991, p. 57), though it was not regarded as 'a habit harmful in itself.' Apart from opium being a problem for the Chinese population, it was feared that the practice might spread like a disease to the white population. The common images of Chinese immigrants put forth by many white Canadians were of people who were poor and addicted to opium. One police officer's testimony before an 1885 government commission on Chinese immigration typifies such attitudes: 'Opium is the Chinese evil . . . used in every house without exception. This evil is growing with the whites . . . principally working men . . . and white women prostitutes. . . . I have seen white women smoking in the Chinese dens myself' (Giffen et al., 1991, p. 58). The Canadian government clearly feared that opium was a dangerous expression of Chinese immigrant culture and did not conform to 'Canadian' order and that this vice of bodily pleasure might infiltrate the ranks of the white working class. In 1908 the Opium Act was passed. This was the first anti-drug legislation in Canada. The Act created and reinforced the social stigma of Chinese immigrants, casting them as 'opium evil'. **Social stigma** is an attribute used to separate affected individuals from the normalized social order. The separation implies a process of devaluation and discrimination against the stigmatized group (Gilmore & Somerville, 1994).

Another example of racial discrimination in the Canadian legal system is the **Quong Wing** case, which involved a Saskatchewan law passed in 1912 that made it illegal for a Chinese Canadian to employ a white woman (Li, 1998, p. 33). Any Oriental who violated the law would be fined $100. In 1912 Quong Wing, a naturalized citizen who owned a Chinese restaurant in Moose Jaw, Saskatchewan, was arrested after he hired two Caucasian women to work as waitresses. In so doing, he broke the law (Chapter 17 of the Statutes of Saskatchewan, 1912), and his action led to a charge and a fine. According to the law, no white women can work in a restaurant, laundry, or any other kind of business owned, kept, or managed by any 'Chinaman'. Quong Wing was a 'Chinaman' because he was born in China to Chinese parents. The law was designed to promote morality by 'protecting' white women from the immoral advances of Chinese immigrants.

Quong Wing decided to appeal his conviction. He hired the law firm of MacCraken, Henderson, Greene & Herridge and took his case to court. He argued that (1) the law should not apply to a Canadian citizen like himself; and (2) a province like Saskatchewan could not make laws that applied only to immigrants or that created crimes – that power belonged to the federal government. At that time he did not argue that the law was just plain wrong or a violation of human rights because his lawyers knew that the argument could not work. In 1912 there was not really such a thing as human rights, and most people did not think about the issue in that way.

Quong Wing lost his argument when he appeared before the Supreme Court of Saskatchewan, but he did not give up. He took his case all the way to the Supreme Court of Canada in Ottawa, but on 23 February 1914, four out of five justices judged the law valid and the conviction stood. It did not matter that Quong Wing was a Canadian because he was still from China, and the law was aimed at all people of Chinese origin. The law was repealed in 1918, only to be replaced by the Female Employment Act, which required Chinese businessmen to obtain a special licence from the municipality in order to hire a white female.

The anti-Asian sentiments that underlay the immigration reforms of the 1920s found new purchase during World War II. In response to the Japanese attack on Pearl Harbor, Canada joined the United States in rigidly controlling and containing Japanese residents. Acceding to popular anxieties, Prime Minister Mackenzie King ordered all people of Japanese descent into 10 **Japanese internment** camps. More than three-quarters of the 22,000 Japanese Canadians living primarily in British Columbia were citizens of Canada. Nonetheless, like Americans, Canadians feared the 'patriotism' of Japanese living in the province and presumed that they were more attached to Japan than to Canada—and thus, a security threat.

The Japanese moved to the relocation camps were often given little advance notice. Moreover, in 1943 the 'Custodian of Aliens' sold off the seized assets and property of those who had been interned, leaving most Japanese Canadians with no resources when they were finally released. It was not until the 1980s that the Mulroney administration offered a public apology and financial compensation of $21,000 to the families of those affected by the policies and practices of the war years.

Stereotypes and misperceptions about Asians continue to inform their interactions with the criminal justice system. A key stereotype is that of the mysterious, devious, fearsome Asian. Media, politicians, and social commentators too often confuse this stereotype with the reality of Asian criminal activity. If we were to believe the sensational media images of Asian gangsters portrayed in movies like *Year of the Dragon*, we would think that all Asians are martial arts experts; all were stealthy and silent; all were violent gang members; all were connected by a network of organized crime. These images consistently mark Asians as 'different', as the Other, thereby reinforcing their 'foreign' and alien nature. It also makes them something to be feared and therefore avoided.

What little is known about Asian criminality refutes these images of Asian violence and stealth. On the contrary, the offences for which Asian Americans are most likely to be arrested are public order offences. Asian Canadians are far less likely than any other ethnic group to be involved in homicide, for example (Lee & Martinez, 2006). The contemporary patterns of criminality that have emerged are very much in line with the historical evolution of Asian crim- inality and with discrimination against Chinese and Japanese immigrants in particular. Earlier restrictions on Asian immigration—especially with respect to women—often meant that Asian immigrant labourers were confined to all-male communities. Consequently, '[l]iving in a world of men, Asian laborers sought a sexual outlet and intimacy from prostitutes . . . Most Chinese male sojourners viewed prostitutes as providers of a necessary service to their largely bachelor community' (Espiritu, 1997, p. 31). While there is little Canadian data on these patterns, in the United States over 75 per cent of the nearly 3,000 Chinese women workers in the 1870s identi- fied themselves as prostitutes. In 1900 most Japanese immigrant women were also prostitutes.

With the easing of immigration restrictions later in the century, there was a transition from the importation of prostitutes to the importation of 'picture brides'. Both practices, however, were 'big business'—not so much for the women themselves as for the men who profited from their labours, 'the procurers and importers who brought women to the United States; the brothel owners who controlled the labor of the prostitutes; the high-binders, policemen and immigration officials who were paid to protect the business; and the white Chinatown property owners who charged these brothels exorbitant rents' (Espiritu, 1997, p. 31).

While initially controlled by individual men (and some women), prostitution ultimately fell under the control of emerging Asian 'secret societies', Chinese *tongs* in particular. These organizations were originally created to meet the needs for community and representation of the isolated Asian male immigrants, in the context of a hostile social climate. However, many evolved into criminal organizations or developed links with Chinese triads. Consequently, the tongs came to dominate prostitution, along with gambling, drugs, and other vice crimes. So, in addition to providing sexual outlets, these organizations also created other opportunities for recreation and escapist behaviour.

With respect to the criminal involvement of Asians in public order offences, Mann (1993, p. 133) observes that 'minority people commit the crimes that are created for them.' In other words, particular behaviours come to be criminalized as a means of regulating specific communities. For example, as noted above, turn-of-the-century opium legislation clearly represented an effort to curtail the economic power of Asians. As a result of this discriminatory application of the criminal law, Asians were among the most heavily incarcerated groups on the West Coast. However, in the contemporary era, Asians are consistently under-represented in crime statis- tics, unlike other communities of colour. They consistently represent less than 3 per cent of the prison population at any given time.

The vice crimes for which Asians—especially Japanese, Chinese, and Vietnamese—are most likely to be arrested are lucrative sources of revenue for organized crime groups such as Chinese tongs and triad and Japanese yakuza. There is a consensus among scholars and law enforcement agencies that Asian organized crime is growing more rapidly than organized crime of any other cultural group (Beare, 1996; Lintner, 2004; Hill, 2004). Consequently, the Asian groups are assuming a growing share of illegal markets. It is the effort to protect these market shares that is responsible for the recent increases in violent crime associated with Asian Canadians.

Sometimes connected to and sometimes independent of Asian organized crime are the growing numbers of Asian youth gangs. Flowers (1990) and Mann (1993) both report that Chinatowns across the United States have recently witnessed dramatic and violent increases in Asian gang membership. While triads and yakuza tend to be involved in racketeering, smuggling, and so on, Asian youth gangs are more likely to be involved in localized extortion and robbery, as well as internecine conflicts. The older, more formalized groups tend to include both immigrants and US-born Asians, while the youth gangs are dominated by recent immigrants, leading Parillo (1985) to conclude that

> [t]he growing problem of youthful militancy and delinquency appears to reflect the marginal status of those in the younger generation who experience frustration and adjustment problems in America. Recent arrivals from Hong Kong are unfamiliar with the language and culture, they are either unemployed or in the lowliest of jobs, and they live in overcrowded, slum-like quarters with no recreational facilities. Gang behavior serves as an alternative and a way of filling status and identity needs. (p. 251)

Three characteristics of Canadian youth gangs seem to distinguish the situation here from that in the United States. First, gangs generally and Chinese gangs specifically are not nearly as extensive in Canada, as they tend to be concentrated largely in Vancouver and in Toronto (Gordon, 2000, 1995). Second, unlike the American case, Canadian youth gangs tend to be multi-ethnic rather than ethnically specific (Wortley & Tanner, n.d.). Finally, Canadian gang membership tends to be less closely tied to immigration status. In fact, Wortley and Tanner's (n.d.) study in Toronto found that Canadian-born youth are much more likely than immigrant youth to report gang affiliation.

Asian Canadians as Victims of Crime

Many of the same sentiments that perpetuate anti-Asian discrimination and sensational images of Asian crime also underlie anti-Asian victimization. Moreover, the legacy of discriminatory legislation and activity finds a violent supplement in victimization motivated by anti-Asian bias. The ongoing environment of intolerance has meant that immigrants are often held up as scapegoats, thereby encouraging and legitimating the violent acts perpetrated against these 'foreigners'.

Anti-Asian violence accounts for a relatively small proportion of all **hate crime**. Like violence against South Asians, violence against East and Southeast Asians represents only about 5 per cent of all hate crime and less than 10 per cent of all racially motivated hate crime (Dauvergne, 2010). Nonetheless, there is still reason for concern in particular communities. For example, media reports of ongoing attacks on Asian anglers in the regions north of Toronto began to surface in September 2007. Ultimately, the media glare and the demands of the Asian Canadian community led to an **Ontario Human Rights Commission (OHRC)** inquiry (OHRC, 2007, 2008). The following are among the incidents reported:

- April 27th, Georgina: A man and his 13 year old son were angling on Malone Avenue when they were approached by two men, who pushed the son into the water. A 72-year old man was also pushed, and his fishing gear damaged.
- July 22nd, Georgina: A group of anglers was approached by another group, which pushed one of the anglers into the water.
- August 18th, Georgina: A man who was angling on the Mossington Bridge was approached by two people and pushed from behind into the water.
- September 15th, Westport: Three anglers were assaulted by five men on a bridge on County Road 36, and received minor injuries.
- September 16th, Georgina: Anglers on the Mossington Bridge were approached by a group of men who pushed two of the anglers into the water. In the events that ensued, one of the anglers was very seriously injured.
- September 29th, Westport: Three anglers were threatened by four males.
- October 25th, Hastings: Racial slurs targeting Asian Canadians were found painted under a Trent Severn Waterway bridge. (OHRC, 2007, 6)

This series of incidents represents an interesting phenomenon. Most of the alleged victims were not assaulted in their own geographic communities, but in areas several miles distant from their homes. The incidents tended to occur in the northern part of York Region, while the victims tended to be from the southern part of York Region. Georgina, for example, has a population of about 43,000 but fewer than 300 people who identify as Chinese, Korean, or Japanese.

While research suggests that most hate crime occurs near one's home or work, it is also recognized that such incidents are likely to occur when victims are somewhere they 'don't belong'. In other words, hate crime plays a defensive role. Organized and informal groups or individual perpetrators assert their territorial claims in efforts to purge their neighbourhoods, cities, regions, or nation of the encroaching threats represented by people of colour in particular. Flint, for example, argues that the 'imperatives of the territorial defense of places and spaces result in the adoption of exclusionary visions and practices' (2004a, p. 9), including hate crime. This seems to be the case in the reported incidents, as revealed by the OHRC report. Interestingly, some of the submissions to the human rights inquiry 'excused' the violence on precisely these grounds—that is, that the Asians were 'foreigners' who had no rights to fish in the area. For example:

It is quite clear to me the park I take my kids to is being populated by people not in our neighbourhood . . . The first encounter that led me to look upon people that do not live in our community was when I witnessed an Asian family digging holes in our park to locate worms for their fishing trip. (#17) (OHRC, 2007, p. 10)

Others drew on standard stereotypes to explain away the hate crime. The OHRC report summarizes some of this tendency:

> . . . for example, drawing a distinction between 'Asians' and 'Canadians', and expressing opinions that 'Asians' 'keep everything that they catch', 'have no respect for the country', 'have a reputation for cheating', and have a 'cultural disrespect for Canada's laws and decency standards.' Language and accent appear to be a particular trigger for hostility with some submissions describing individuals as 'pretending not to speak English' or mocking stereotypical speech patterns of persons for whom English is a second language. Some submissions even went so far as to blame Asian Canadian anglers for the assaults that have occurred; for example, one submission stated: Just a note about the articles I read about 'racial hatred on Asians'. I believe it's the end result. Time after time people like me are trespassed against till finally we get to the point where some of us lose it and lash out. (#19) (OHRC, 2007, p. 11)

These few examples are not atypical. Asians—regardless of the longevity of their ties to Canada—are frequent victims of violence ranging from offensive bumper stickers, to verbal harassment, to assault, to murder. Moreover, it is only recently that the problems faced by Asian Canadians have been acknowledged and finally addressed by advocacy groups and state agencies alike. It is to this that we now turn.

Asian Americans as Service Providers

Some efforts have been made by law enforcement agencies to overcome the barriers between Asian communities and police departments. Cultural awareness training has been implemented as a means of improving police officers' understanding and treatment of Asian Americans. Interpreters have been hired where numbers warrant. Community policing initiatives have been implemented as a means of integrating police and public. One of the greatest disappointments in police–Asian relations has been in the area of representation in police departments, where Asians are dramatically under-represented among police officers, even in communities where Asians make up a substantial proportion of the population. Police departments in Vancouver and Toronto, for example, have Asian police officers in proportions far below their relatively high representation in these communities.

Nonetheless, some police departments across the country are making admirable efforts to enhance the accessibility and civility of their personnel. Toronto's police department, for example, has established the Asian Community Consultative Committee, which acts as a conduit for the shared identification of community problems and solutions. The committee brings concerns to the attention of the police and mobilizes community support for the police force.

Like other visible minority communities in Canada, Asian communities across the nation have begun to establish their own advocacy, rights-based, and action groups. This is a dramatic step, given the historical failure of Asian Americans to protest or speak out against their plight. Asian Canadians have discovered the power of their voices and have begun to mobilize their growing numerical strength in a quest for political and social power. In addition to employment, resettlement, and workers' organizations, Asians have established other venues geared toward assisting and advocating for the community. Among the largest—with chapters in most large Canadian cities— is the Chinese Canadian National Council. The council was established in 1979, initially in response to racially insensitive media treatment. It has flourished since then and now has a solid national presence. Its mandate is as follows:

- To promote the rights of all individuals, in particular, those of Chinese Canadians and to encourage their full and equal participation in Canadian society.
- To create an environment in this country in which the rights of all individuals are fully recognized and protected.
- To promote understanding and cooperation between Chinese Canadians and all other ethnic, cultural and racial groups in Canada.
- To encourage and develop in persons of Chinese descent, a desire to know and to respect their historical and cultural heritage; to educate them in adopting a creative and positive attitude towards the Chinese Canadian contribution to society. (www.ccnc.ca/about.php)

In Toronto, the Metro Toronto Chinese and Southeast Asian Legal Clinic provides legal advice and related services in Chinese, Vietnamese, Cambodian, and Laotian, in such areas as social assistance, immigration, and housing. Moreover, the clinic engages in advocacy work for these communities. Most Canadian cities can boast community and cultural centres that provide education, resources, and guidance for Japanese, Chinese, Korean, Vietnamese, and other Asian communities.

Summary

This chapter has shown how racism changed its form from overt to covert. With a strong prevailing history of unjust and unequal treatment of Chinese in Canada, racism has always been an issue. Overt and obvious racial discrimination has become less apparent and less in the realm of the illegal today, but covert racism at institutional and individual levels has remained and is still used to oppress Chinese and other visible minority groups. This study indicates that there are contradictory social values within a multicultural society that form an important ideological basis for covert racism. On the one hand, Canadians generally accept racial equality and democracy as central values in a social democratic society; on the other, cultural ethnocentrism and racial stereotypes prevail in society and are reflected in negative attitudes toward Chinese immigrants. It is often these sentiments that give rise to the criminalization and victimization of Asian individuals and communities.

In the past 25 years, the number of mainland Chinese immigrants to Canada increased dramatically, and they have brought significant financial and human capital resources to this country. However, the study shows that new Chinese immigrants have experienced great difficulty in accessing education-related professions in Canada. Problems in transferring educational equivalences and work experience across international boundaries have resulted in mainland Chinese professional immigrants' taking jobs for which they are over-trained, and this has led to downward occupational mobility relative to the occupations they held before coming to Canada. Recent mainland Chinese immigrants face both individual and institutional barriers to entry into their respective professions. Individual barriers such as linguistic ability and cultural adaptation can gradually improve over time through their personal efforts, community support, and programs and services provided by the Canadian government. However, immigrants themselves cannot resolve institutionalized obstacles, such as the devaluation of foreign credentials and work experience, unequal opportunity, and racism. The chapter criticizes the discourse that cultural diversity threatens national unity and argues that national unity can be achieved in the context of cultural diversity.

Key Terms

Asiatic Exclusion
    League
Chinese immigrants
Chinese Immigration
    Act

covert racism
democratic racism
hate crime
head tax

institutional racism
Japanese internment
Ontario Human
    Rights Commission
overt racism

social stigma
Wing, Quong

Questions for Critical Thought

1. Compare and contrast overt racism with covert racism and explain how racism changed its forms in different social and historical contexts in Canada.
2. Social stigma has been described by US sociologist Erving Goffman as a quality that significantly discredits an individual in the eyes of others. How might this concept be used to understand the racial and cultural stigmatization of visible minorities and Aboriginals in Canadian society?
3. What is meant by the idea that social integration is a two-way street? Analyze structural barriers that affect new immigrants' occupational attainment and upward mobility in Canada.

Additional Readings

Henry, F., Tator, C., Mattis, W., & Rees, T. (Eds). (2009). *The colour of democracy: Racism in Canadian society* (4th ed.). Toronto: Nelson College Indigenous.

Li, P. (1998). *Chinese in Canada*. Toronto: Oxford University Press.

OHRC (Ontario Human Rights Commission). (2008). *Preliminary findings: Inquiry into assault on Asian Canadian anglers.* Toronto: OHRC.

Zong, Li. (1994). Structural and psychological dimensions of racism. *Canadian Ethnic Studies, 26*(3), 122–134.

Websites of Interest

Asian Canadian Communities: www.asian.ca/community

Institute of Asian Research, UBC: www.iar.ubc.ca

Japanese Interment in Canada, Parts I and II: www.youtube.com/watch?v=nyZ3RYlebG8; and www.youtube.com/watch?v=z88zRES6wcw

Endnotes

1. 'Mainland Chinese professional immigrants' refers to those who received their professional training in China and worked as doctors, engineers, school/university teachers, and other professionals; who entered Canada as immigrants; and who were residents in Canada at the time of the survey.

2. The data were obtained through self-administered questionnaires that included 71 questions on credentials, work experience before and after immigration, personal difficulties, perceived structural barriers in accessing professional jobs in the Canadian labour force, opinions on policy issues, and general respondent information. Findings of the survey were reported (Zong, 2004).

3. The result is consistent with previous research findings. For example, Ramcharan (1976), in his study on the economic adaptation of West Indians in Toronto, found that the length of residence is an important factor affecting their economic success.

References

Alexander, B. (1990). *Peaceful measures: Canada's way out of the war on drugs.* Toronto: University of Toronto Press.

Angus Reid Group. (1989). *Immigration to Canada: Aspects of public opinion.* Winnipeg.

Beach, C., & Worswick, C. (1989). Is there a double-negative effect on the earnings of immigrant women? *Canadian Public Policy, 16*(2), 36–54.

Beare, M. (1996). *Criminal conspiracies: Organized crime in Canada.* Toronto: Nelson.

Bolaria, B. S., & Li, P. S. (Eds.). (1988). *Racial oppression in Canada* (2nd ed.). Toronto: Garamond Press.

Boyd, M. (1985). Immigration and occupation attainment in Canada. In M. Boyd (Ed.), *Ascription and achievement: Studies in mobility and status attainment in Canada.* Ottawa: Carleton University Press.

Breton, R. (1984). The production and allocation of symbolic resources: An analysis of the linguistic and ethnocultural fields in Canada. *Canadian Review of Sociology and Anthropology, 21*(2), 123–144.

Citizenship and Immigration Canada. (2002). Landed immigration data system, 1980–2002 [data file] (provided on CD).

Citizenship and Immigration Canada. (2004). *Facts and*

figures 2004: Immigration overview. Catalogue no. Cil-8/2004E-PDF, p. 34.

Dauvergne, M. (2010). Police-reported hate crime in Canada, 2008. *Juristat, 30*(2). Ottawa: Statistics Canada. Catalogue no. 85-002-X.

Duster, T. (1990). *Backdoor to eugenics*. New York: Routledge.

Espiritu, Y. L. (1997). *Asian American women and men*. Thousand Oaks, CA: Sage.

Fernando, K. K., & Prasad, T. (1986). *Multiculturalism and employment equity: Problems facing foreign-trained professionals and tradespeople in British Columbia*. Vancouver: Affiliation of Multicultural Societies and Service Agencies of British Columbia.

Fleras, A., & Elliott, J. L. (1992). *Unequal relations: An introduction to race and ethnic dynamics in Canada*. Scarborough, ON: Prentice-Hall.

Flowers, R. B. (1990). *Minorities and criminality*. New York: Praeger.

Gaertner, S. L., & Dovidio, J. F. (1986). The aversive forms of racism. In J. F. Dovidio & S. L. Gaertner (Eds), *Prejudice, discrimination, and racism*. New York: Academic Press.

Giffen, P. J., Endicott, S., & Lambert, S. (1991). *Panic and indifference: The politics of Canada's drug law*. Ottawa: Canadian Centre of Substance Abuse.

Gilmore, N., & Somerville, M. A. (1994). Stigmatization, scapegoating, and discrimination in sexually transmitted disease: Overcoming 'them' and 'us'. *Social Science and Medicine, 39*, 1339–1358.

Gordon, R. (1995). Street gangs in Vancouver. In J. H. Creechan & R. A. Silverman (Eds), *Canadian delinquency*. Scarborough, ON: Prentice Hall.

Gordon, R. (2000). Criminal business organizations, street gangs and Anna-Be Groups: A Vancouver perspective. *Canadian Journal of Criminology, 42*(1), pp. 39–60.

Henry, F., Tator, C., Mattis, W., & Rees, T. (Eds). (1995). *The colour of democracy: Racism in Canadian society*. Toronto: Harcourt Brace and Company.

Hill, P. (2004). The changing face of the Yakuza. *Global Crime, 6*(1), 97–116.

Horsman, R. (1976). Origins of racial Anglo-Saxonism in Great Britain before 1850. *Journal of the History of Ideas, 37*(3), 387–410.

Horsman, R. (1981). *Race and Manifest Destiny*. Cambridge, MA: Harvard University Press.

Katz, I., Wackenhut, J., & Hass, R. G. (1986). Racial ambivalence, value duality, and behaviour. In J. D. Gaertner & S. L. Gaertner (Eds), *Prejudice, discrimination, and racism*. New York: Academic Press.

Kung, S. W. (1962). Chinese immigration into North America. *Queen's Quarterly, 68*(4), 610–620.

Lee, D. (1967). *A history of Chinese in Canada*. (Text in Chinese.) Taiwan: Hai Tin Printing Co.

Lee, M., & Martinez, R. (2006). Immigration and Asian homicide patterns in urban and suburban San Diego. In R. Martinez & A. Valenzuela (Eds), *Immigration and crime: Race, ethnicity and violence* (pp. 90–116). New York: New York University Press.

Li, P. (1994a). Unneighbourly house or unwelcome Chinese: The social construction of race in the battle over 'monster homes' in Vancouver, Canada. *International Journal of Comparative Race and Ethnic Studies, 1*(1), 14–33.

Li, P. (1994b). A world apart: The multicultural world of visible minorities and the art world of Canada. *Canadian Review of Sociology and Anthropology, 31*(4), 365–391.

Li, P. (1996). *Literature review on immigration: Sociological perspectives*. Ottawa: Citizenship and Immigration Canada.

Li, P. (1998). *Chinese in Canada*. Toronto: Oxford University Press.

Li, P. (2005). The rise and fall of Chinese immigration to Canada: Newcomers from Hong Kong Special Administrative Region of China and Mainland China, 1980–2000. *International Migration, 43*(3), 9–32.

Lintner, B. (2004). Chinese organised crime. *Global Crime, 6*(1), 84–96.

McConohay, J. B. (1986). Modern racism, ambivalence, and the modern racism scale. In J. D. Gaertner & S. L. Gaertner (Eds), *Prejudice, discrimination, and racism*. New York: Academic Press.

McDade, K. (1988). *Barriers to recognition of the credentials of immigrants in Canada*. Ottawa: Institute for Research on Public Policy.

Mann, C. R. (1993). *Unequal justice*. Bloomington: Indiana University Press.

Mercer, J. (1995). Canadian cities and their immigrants: New realities. *Annals of the American Academy of Political and Social Science, 538*, 169–184.

OHRC (Ontario Human Rights Commission). (2007). *Fishing without fear: Report on the Inquiry into Assaults on Asian Canadian Anglers*. Toronto: OHRC.

OHRC. (2008). *Preliminary findings: Inquiry into Assaults on Asian Canadian Anglers*. Toronto: OHRC.

Ornstein, M., & Sharma, R. D. 1983. *Adjustment and economic experience of immigrants in Canada: An analysis of the 1976 Longitudinal Survey of Immigrants*. Report to Employment and Immigration Canada. Toronto: York University Institute for Behavioural Research.

Parillo, V. (1985). *Strangers to these shores: Race and ethnic relations in the U.S.* New York: John Riley.

Privy Council. (1967, August 16). (1967-1616). *Canada Gazette*, Part 2, *101*(17), 1350–1362.

Rajagopal, I. (1990). The glass ceiling in the vertical mosaic: Indian immigrants to Canada. *Canadian Ethnic Studies, 22*(1), 96–105.

Ralston, H. (1988). Ethnicity, class, and gender among South Asian women in Metro Halifax: An exploratory study. *Canadian Ethnic Studies, 20*(3), 63–83.

Ramcharan, S. (1976). The economic adaptation of West Indians in Toronto, Canada. *Canadian Review of Sociology and Anthropology, 13*(3), 295–304.

Rodney, W. (1982). *How Europe underdeveloped Africa.* Washington, DC: Howard University Press.

Satzewich, V. (Ed.). (1992). *Deconstructing a nation: Immigration, multiculturalism and racism in '90s Canada.* Halifax: Fernwood.

Solomon, R., & Green, M. (1988). The first century: The history of non-medical opiate use and control policies in Canada, 1870–1970. In J. Blackwell & P. Erickson, *Illicit drugs in Canada: A risky business* (pp. 88–104). Scarborough, ON: Nelson Canada.

Trovato, C. F., & Grindstaff, F. (1986). Economic status: A census analysis of immigrant women at age thirty in Canada. *Review of Sociology and Anthropology, 23*(4), 569–687.

Weigel, P. W., & Howes, R. H. (1985). Conceptions of racial prejudice: Symbolic racism reconsidered. *Journal of Social Issues, 41*(3), 117–138.

Wortley, S., & Tanner, J. (n.d.). *Criminal organizations or social groups? An exploration of the myths and realities of youth gangs in Toronto.* Unpublished monograph, Centre of Criminology, University of Toronto.

Zong, Li. (1994). Structural and psychological dimensions of racism. *Canadian Ethnic Studies, 26*(3), 122–134.

Zong, Li. (1997). New racism, cultural diversity, and the search for a national identity. In A. Cardoza & L. Musto (Eds), *The battle over multiculturalism: Does it help or hinder Canadian unity?* Ottawa: Pearson-Shoyama Institute.

Zong, Li. (1998). Chinese immigration to Vancouver and new racism in multicultural Canada. In G. Zhuang (Ed.), *Ethnic Chinese at the turn of the centuries.* Fujian: Fujian People Press.

Zong, Li. (2003). Language, education, and occupational attainment of foreign-trained Chinese and Polish professional immigrants in Toronto, Canada. In M. W. Charney, B. S. A. Yeoh, & T. C. Kiong (Eds), *Chinese migrants abroad: Cultural, educational and social dimensions of the Chinese diaspora.* Singapore: Singapore University Press.

Zong, Li. (2004). International transference of human capital and occupational attainment of recent Chinese professional immigrants in Canada. *American Journal of China Studies, 5*(1/2), 81–89.

Crime and Justice: The Experiences of Black Canadians

SCOT WORTLEY AND AKWASI OWUSU-BEMPAH

In a classic analysis of police patrol practices, Skolnick (1966) observes that officers tend to perceive African Americans as 'symbolic assailants'. In this chapter we will argue that members of the black community continue to play the role of 'dangerous other' in contemporary Canadian society. We begin with a brief review of the history of the black community's migration to Canada and the types of institutional discrimination faced by black people throughout Canadian history. We then move to a discussion of media depictions of black crime and how these depictions may contribute to inaccurate perceptions about the relationship between race and criminality. Research documenting patterns of victimization and offending within Canada's black community are then reviewed, followed by an examination of possible racial bias against blacks within the Canadian criminal justice system. The chapter concludes with a brief exploration of the experiences of black professionals working within the justice system.

Migration History

Black people have a long history in Canada. Technically, the institution of slavery never existed in Canada. However, the enslavement of black people was practised in both the French and the English colonies that predate Confederation. Indeed, blacks were introduced to Canadian soil through slavery—and many served as slaves from the early 1600s until the early 1800s. After slavery was abolished in the colonies by England, Canada eventually became the well-known final destination for runaway slaves fleeing America via 'the underground railroad'. Black Loyalists also entered Canada from the United States in the late 1700s, having been promised grants for supporting the British during the American Revolution (Henry & Tator, 2005). Early black settlements were established in Nova Scotia, Ontario, and Western Canada following the opening of the frontier in the mid-1800s (Milan & Tran, 2004). The 1901 Census reports that 17,400 black persons were living in Canada (less than 1 per cent of the population). In the early 1900s Canada's black population remained small and was primarily concentrated in Ontario and Nova Scotia (Milan & Tran, 2004).

In 1967 the introduction of immigration reforms reduced preferences for migrants of European origin. As a result, immigrants to Canada became gradually more diverse and included many black people of Caribbean and African descent (Henry & Tator, 2005). Immigrants from the Caribbean made up the majority of black immigrants during the 1960s, 1970s, and 1980s. Many arrived to fill labour shortages in the domestic services, teaching, and nursing sectors (Milan & Tran, 2004). During the 1970s and 1980s, approximately 40 per cent of all black immigrants to Canada came from Jamaica, with an additional 20 per cent arriving from Haiti. Throughout this period, the majority of Jamaican immigrants settled in the Toronto area, while the majority of Haitians settled in Montreal (Milan & Tran, 2004). However, since the early 1990s, the major source countries for black immigration to Canada has shifted from the Caribbean to continental Africa.

Contemporary Demographics of Black Canadians

Black immigration and settlement in Canada have produced an immensely heterogeneous population. For example, the 2006 Census indicates that 30 per cent of blacks report more than one ethnic origin (i.e., African, French, Jamaican, etc.). There are also huge differences in regional populations with respect to length of time in Canada, reasons for migration, language, religion, and other socio-demographic characteristics (Chui, Tran, & Maheux, 2008). Nevertheless, a number of general observations can be made about Canada's black population.

The 2006 Census puts the black population in Canada at over three-quarters of a million people (783,000). Although the size of the black population increased by almost 20 per cent between 2001 and 2006, blacks still represent only 2.5 per cent of the total Canadian population. Census data also indicate that the black population is highly concentrated within certain regions. Indeed, 84 per cent of Canada's black population lives in either Ontario (60 per cent) or Quebec (24 per cent). Black people represent 4 per cent of Ontario's population, 2.5 per cent of Quebec's population, 2.1 per cent of Nova Scotia's population, 1.5 per cent of Alberta's population, and 1.4 per cent of Manitoba's population. Black representation falls below 1 per cent for all other provinces and territories. Black people in Canada are also highly urbanized; over 90 per cent of the population reside in just six cities: Toronto, Montreal, Ottawa, Calgary, Halifax, and Vancouver. More than half of Canada's black population lives in Toronto (Chui et al., 2008).

Other data indicate that 55.7 per cent of Canada's black population is foreign born. Black immigrants to Canada are most likely to come from Jamaica (25.8 per cent), Haiti (14.9 per cent), Trinidad and Tobago (5.2 per cent), Ethiopia (4.5 per cent), Somalia (4.4 per cent), Ghana (4.4 per cent), Guyana (3.5 per cent), and Nigeria (3.3 per cent). Census data also indicate that (1) Canada's black population is significantly younger than the overall population; (2) black people—especially black males—have a higher rate of unemployment and lower personal incomes than the national average; (3) black children are more likely to live in lone-parent families than children from other ethnic groups; and (4) on average, black people have lower levels of education than other segments of the population. However, it is important to note that Canadian-born blacks are just as likely as others born in Canada to hold a university degree

(Chui et al., 2008). In sum, census data reveal that, at the group level, Canada's black population suffers from relative economic and social disadvantage. Many believe that this disadvantage stems from **institutionalized racial discrimination**.

Institutionalized Discrimination

It must be acknowledged that Canada, despite its international reputation for being a tolerant, multicultural society, was built on a legacy of colonialism and racism. This legacy, not surprisingly, has had a profound impact on the country's black population. To begin with, the enslavement of black people was practised on Canadian soil for over 200 years (see Winks, 1997). Black slavery in Canada was introduced by the French as early as 1609 and lasted until the nineteenth century. It is a little known fact, for example, that 6 of the original 16 legislators of Upper Canada's first parliament owned slaves (Walker, 1980; Hill, 1991; Lampert & Curtis, 1989). While slavery was apparently not as widespread in Canada as it was in the United States or the Caribbean, one cannot deny that this institution both contributed to the wealth and privilege of Canada's early white elite and simultaneously placed the black population in a position of profound social disadvantage. As discussed below, this position of disadvantage has not yet been overcome by the black community—more than a century after abolition.

The historical record also suggests that free blacks in Canada were generally treated with hostility and disdain (Winks, 2008). Black Loyalist soldiers arriving from America, for example, found themselves living in poor conditions and were denied basic rights afforded to other British citizens. The hostility whites felt towards early black settlers led to 'race riots' in Nova Scotia in 1784 (Henry & Tator, 2005). Blacks in Canada were also subject to segregation in schools and other spheres of public life and were restricted from property ownership (Winks, 2008). In Ontario the legislation that mandated segregated schools for blacks and whites remained on the books until 1964 (Henry & Tator, 2005).

Discrimination also took the form of restrictions on racialized groups' ability to enter the country. Potential black immigrants were the first to experience such restrictive measures. Many white residents felt that black people were unsuitable immigrants to Canada on the basis of a variety of racist assumptions. For example, J.S. Woodsworth, superintendent of the Peoples Mission of Winnipeg, commented in 1903 that '[the] very qualities of intelligence and manliness which are essentials for citizens in a democracy were systematically expunged from the Negro race' (Henry & Tator, 2005). Throughout the early 1900s, informal controls were put in place to curtail blacks from entering the country from the United States. Immigration officials, for example, were advised to deny blacks entry on medical grounds rather than for explicitly racist reasons (Winks, 1997). Recently, immigration laws have been modified to facilitate the deportation of unwanted black immigrants. These modifications were fuelled by a moral panic surrounding 'Jamaican' criminality in the wake of high-profile crimes involving black assailants and white victims (Barnes, 2002, p. 194).

The impact of Canada's colonial legacy continues to be felt by members of the black community—in all aspects of their economic and social life. For example, the results of a recent survey show that over one-third of Canadians report being at least slightly racist (Leger Marketing, 2007). Such hostilities also manifest themselves in the form of white supremacist and other hate-based organizations that oppose the presence and continued immigration of blacks and other racialized people to Canada (Siegel & McCormick, 2010). Racial discrimination is also evident in Canada's educational system. Research suggests that black children often fall behind or fail to graduate from high school. The findings of the study by Caldas et al. of the experiences of black children in Montreal's school system indicate that a black achievement gap persists in Montreal and is highly correlated with school socio-economic status, family structure, and the average age of the students' parents (2009, p. 197). Studies in Ontario have found that, in general, black students have lower levels of academic achievement, higher high school dropout rates and are more likely to be suspended or expelled from school. Many experts attribute these findings to institutional racism and systemic problems that include racist teachers, the inappropriate streaming of black students into remedial programs, and culturally biased curriculums (see Codjoe, 2001).

Relatively low levels of academic achievement can eventually have a negative impact on the black community's employment prospects and opportunities. This educational disadvantage is compounded by discrimination within the employment sector. Swidinsky and Swidinsky (2002), for example, provide evidence that black males in Canada face the largest earning deficit and the smallest level of intergenerational improvement in their economic standing. James (2009) also illustrates how Afro-Caribbean Canadians must work harder than other groups to achieve their immigrant dreams.

Black Canadians also face structural barriers in the housing market (Mendez, Hiebert, & Wyly, 2006). Teixeira (2008), for example, examined the experiences of three groups of Portuguese-speaking African immigrants (Angolans, Mozambicans, and Cape Verdeans) in Toronto's rental housing market. While most respondents reported experiencing discrimination from landlords in their housing search, this was less of a problem for the Cape Verdeans, who have lighter skin. This led Teixeira to remark that 'clearly race (the colour of one's skin) still matters in Toronto's rental housing market' (253).

In summary, even the most rudimentary review of the historical literature suggests that black people in Canada have long suffered from racism, oppression, and inequality. Moreover, contemporary social research suggests that Canada's black population still faces racism within the education system, the employment sector, and in most other areas of social life. In the sections that follow, we will further explore the issue of anti-black racism within the Canadian criminal justice system. But first we want to explore how a legacy of racism and social disadvantage in Canada might have impacted patterns of criminal offending and victimization within the black community.

Black Canadians as the Victims of Crime

Due to an informal ban on the release of **race-crime statistics**, it is difficult to fully document the victimization experiences of minorities in Canada. However, the data that are available indicate that, in addition to various economic and social disadvantages, black Canadians suffer from relatively high rates of criminal victimization. Gartner and Thompson (2004) document that between 1992 and 2003 the homicide victimization rate for Toronto's black community (10.1 murders per 100,000) was more than four times greater than the city average (2.4 murders per 100,000). Further investigation reveals that young black males are particularly vulnerable to violent death. In January 2008, the *Toronto Star* published the names and photographs of 113 homicide victims who were murdered in the Greater Toronto Area (GTA) from 1 January to 31 December 2007. An analysis of these names and photos reveals that 44 of the murder victims were African Canadian males. Thus, while African Canadian males represent only 4 per cent of the GTA's total population, in 2007 they represented almost 40 per cent of the city's homicide victims. According to these figures, in 2007 African Canadian males in the Toronto region had a homicide victimization rate of approximately 28.2 per 100,000, compared to only 2.4 per 100,000 for the metropolitan area as a whole (Wortley, 2008).

Survey data also suggests that black Canadians are more exposed to violent victimization experiences than people from other racial backgrounds. The 2000 Toronto Youth Crime and Victimization Survey (YCVS), a study of over 3,300 Toronto high school students, found that black students were significantly more likely than white students to report multiple violent victimization experiences, including serious physical assaults, death threats, weapons-related threats, assault with a weapon, and sexual assault. For example, 13 per cent of black female students reported that they had been sexually assaulted on three or more occasions in their life, compared to 6 per cent of white female students, 4 per cent of Asian female students, and only 1 per cent of South Asian female students (see Tanner & Wortley, 2002).

Other data suggests that black Canadians are particularly vulnerable to hate crime victimization. Hate crimes are those criminal acts in which the perpetrator targets a victim because of his or her perceived membership in a certain social group. These types of crimes are more likely to involve extreme violence and cause greater psychological trauma than crimes in which hate is not a motivating factor (Siegel & McCormick, 2010). Data sources indicate that black people are the most common target of hate crime in Canada. Both police statistics and survey results, for example, indicate that race was the motivating factor in over 60 per cent of all documented hate crimes reported in Canada between 2004 and 2007. Furthermore, official statistics reveal that 48 per cent of the race-related hate crimes reported to the police during this time period involved black victims. In other words, although they represent only 2.5 per cent of the Canadian population, blacks represent half of those victimized by race-related hate crime (Dauvergne, Scrim, & Brennan, 2008; Walsh & Dauvergne, 2009).

The results of the 2000 Toronto Youth Crime and Victimization Survey further underline the fact that black people are more vulnerable to hate crime than the members of other racial minority groups. For example, 74 per cent of black Toronto high school students reported that they had been threatened because of their racial background, and 23 per cent indicated that they had been the victim of a racially motivated physical assault (Tanner & Wortley, 2002).

Imaging Black Criminality

The data reviewed above indicate that black Canadians are significantly more vulnerable to criminal victimization than members of the white majority. However, media analysis reveals that black people in Canada are much more likely to be depicted as criminal offenders than as crime victims (see Wortley, 2002). Indeed, blacks in Canada have long complained that the news media and other forms of popular culture (films, music, etc.) depict their community in a biased, stereotypical fashion. Importantly, empirical research tends to support this argument. For example, Wortley (2002) provided an analysis of all the stories that appeared in Toronto newspapers over a two-month period in 1998. He found that almost half of all the stories depicting black people dealt with crime and violence, compared to only 14 per cent of stories depicting whites. Wortley also found that stories involving the murder of white victims received much more media coverage than stories involving black victims. Finally, he observed major racial differences in the news narratives that sought to explain criminal behaviour. While white crime was almost always explained as the product of individual pathology, black criminality was often characterized as a group or cultural phenomenon (see also Henry & Tator, 2000; Mosher, 1998).

Critics argue that the manner in which black people are depicted in the Canadian media tends to demonize the entire black community and identify blacks as a 'foreign' or 'alien' threat. The negative impact that racialized images of crime can have on the black community is evident in the results of public opinion polls. A recent survey, for example, found that nearly half (45 per cent) of Ontario residents believe that there is a strong relationship between race and criminality. Of respondents who hold this view, two-thirds believe that 'blacks' are the most crime-prone (Henry, Hastings, & Freer 1996). More recently, a 2008 poll asked a random sample of Canadians to estimate the proportion of people in Canada with a criminal record who come from a racial minority group. The respondents' views were hugely distorted. In general, respondents estimated that twice as many minorities have a criminal record in Canada than police records indicate (Rankin & Powell, 2008). Clearly, unbalanced media depictions of minority crime may contribute directly to the formation of racial stereotypes and an exaggerated understanding of the true relationship between crime and racial identity. For a more balanced analysis we must turn to criminological research.

Black Canadians as Offenders

Table 8.1 combines data from the 2006 Canadian Census with 2008 federal correctional data in an attempt to document the representation of various racial groups in the Canadian prison system. The results suggest that both Aboriginals and blacks are grossly over-represented. For example, although they represent only 3.8 per cent of the Canadian population, Aboriginals make up 17 per cent of the population under federal correctional supervision. In other words, the Aboriginal population is represented 4.5 times more in the correctional system than in the general population. Similarly, although they represent 2.5 per cent of Canada's population, black people make up 7.4 per cent of the population within the federal corrections system. Thus, the representation of blacks in federal prisons is three times greater than their representation in the general population. Overall, Aboriginal Canadians have the highest rate of federal corrections supervision (332 per 100,000), followed by black people (215 per 100,000), white people (61 per 100,000), Asians (32 per 100,000) and South Asians (17 per 100,000). Some have argued that the **over-representation** of blacks in the correctional system reflects higher than average levels of criminal offending. Others have argued that it reflects racial bias or discrimination within the Canadian justice system. We will first examine the 'higher offending' hypothesis and then turn our attention to the issue of discrimination.

The ban on race-crime statistics makes it difficult to accurately document patterns of black offending in Canada. Nonetheless, limited data does *suggest* that the black community may be somewhat more involved in some types of crime than other racial groups are. We can infer, for example, that black people are over-represented among homicide offenders—at least in some urban areas. As discussed above, the black homicide victimization rate in Toronto is approximately four times greater than the city average. Since the vast majority of all homicides are intra-racial (i.e., victims and offenders come from the same racial background), many observers have begun to refer to this phenomenon as **black-on-black violence** (Ezeonu, 2008).

Many have argued that the relatively high rates of homicide and gun-related crime among African Canadians are reflective of their over-representation in street gangs. Unfortunately, police statistics on Canadian gangs are almost non-existent. However, in 2003, the solicitor general conducted the first-ever Canadian Police Survey on Youth Gangs (Chettleburgh, 2007).

Table 8.1 The Representation of Ethno-racial Groups in Canada's Federal Corrections System (2008)

Racial Background	National Population[1]	% of National Population	Federal Correctional Population[2]	% Federal Correctional Population	Odds Ratio	Rate of Federal Correctional Supervision (per 100,000)
White	25,000,155	80.0	15,157	66.6	0.83	60.62
Aboriginal	1,172,785	3.8	3,894	17.1	4.50	332.03
Black	783,795	2.5	1,684	7.4	2.96	214.85
Asian[3]	2,090,390	6.7	668	2.9	0.43	31.95
South Asian	1,262,865	4.0	216	1.0	0.25	17.10
Other[4]	931,040	3.0	1,127	5.0	1.67	121.04
Total	31,241,030	100.0	22,746	100.0	1.00	72.80

[1]Population estimates for each racial group were derived from the 2006 Census (Chui & Maheux, 2008).
[2]Federal correctional statistics for 2008 include those in prison and those under community supervision (Public Safety Canada, 2009).
[3]The 'Asian' category includes people of Chinese, Japanese, Southeast Asia, Korean, and Filipino descent.
[4]The 'Other' category includes people with multiple race backgrounds.

More than 264 police agencies from across the nation participated in this study. Between them, they identified 484 different youth gangs operating within Canada and an estimated 6,760 gang members. The majority of the police agencies participating in the survey maintained that racial minority youth are over-represented in gang activity: Asian and South Asian gangs are thought to dominate the West Coast; Aboriginal gangs, the Prairie provinces; and black gangs, central and eastern Canada (Chettleburgh, 2007, pp. 18–20). The Toronto Youth Crime and Victimization Survey (see Wortley & Tanner, 2006) also found that self-reported gang member-ship was twice as high among black (13 per cent) and Hispanic youth (12 per cent) as it was among white (6 per cent) and Asian (5 per cent) youth. It must be stressed, however, that while this study found that black students were more likely to report gang involvement than white students, almost half (40 per cent) of all gang-involved students (over 40 per cent) were white.

Consistent with American findings, survey results from Toronto also indicate that black Canadian youth may be somewhat more involved in some forms of violent behaviour than the members of other racial groups (see Table 8.2). For example, according to the results of the 2000 Toronto Youth Crime and Victimization Survey, 53 per cent of black students indicated that they had been involved in three or more fights in their lifetime, compared to 39 per cent of white students, 32 per cent of Asians, and 28 per cent of South Asians. Similarly, 43 per cent of black students reported that they had been involved in a 'gang fight' (where one group of friends battled another group) at some point in their life, compared to 30 per cent of white students, 28 per cent of Asians, and 27 per cent of South Asians. It is important to note, however, that white students appear to be much more involved with illegal drugs than their black counterparts. For example, 45 per cent of white students reported that they had used marijuana at some time in their life (compared to 39 per cent of black students), 6 per cent had used cocaine or crack (compared to only 2 per cent of black students), and 13 per cent had used other illegal drugs (compared to only 3 per cent of black students). Furthermore, 17 per cent of white students reported that they had sold illegal drugs at some time in their life, compared to only 15 per cent of black students. This last finding is particularly noteworthy in light of other research suggesting that black people are dramatically over-represented with respect to drug possession and drug trafficking arrests and convictions. This discrepancy, therefore, could reflect possible racial bias in the investigation and prosecution of drug crimes in the Canadian context. This issue will be discussed in more detail in the next section.

It is unfortunate that the ban on race-crime statistics in Canada precludes a more detailed analysis of the relationship between race and other forms of criminality. For example, while black people may be somewhat over-represented in certain street-level crimes, it is quite possible that they are grossly under-represented with respect to white-collar and corporate crime. Finally, it must be stressed that any over-representation of black people in criminal activity can likely be explained by their relative social and economic disadvantage. Wortley and Tanner (2008), for example, found that the impact of race on gang membership and criminal offending is greatly reduced after statistically controlling for household income and community-level social disor-ganization. Furthermore, the impact of black racial background on criminal offending becomes insignificant after the introduction of variables that measure **social alienation**. In other words,

Table 8.2 Percentage of Toronto High School Students Who Have Engaged in Selected Deviant Activities at Some Point in Their Life, by Racial Group (Results from the 2000 Toronto Youth Crime and Victimization Survey)

	White	Black	South Asian	Asian	West Asian	Hispanic
Carried a weapon in public	24.7	27.3	13.0	23.3	18.5	27.4
Engaged in robbery or extortion	12.7	17.8	8.6	10.4	7.7	11.0
Tried to seriously hurt someone	19.6	28.1	12.3	19.4	20.6	18.6
Got in a fight	63.9	73.1	50.2	54.7	64.9	59.9
Got in a group or gang fight	30.4	42.5	27.0	28.2	29.0	36.3
Forced someone to have sex	1.1	3.6	0.7	1.0	2.3	2.1
Used marijuana	44.9	38.7	10.9	19.2	20.9	36.5
Used cocaine or crack	5.9	2.3	0.7	2.5	2.3	3.4
Used other illegal drugs	12.5	3.4	0.7	7.1	4.7	7.4
Sold illegal drugs	16.8	14.6	4.1	9.2	8.2	16.9
Stole a motor vehicle	5.4	6.7	2.2	3.8	2.2	8.1
Stole a bike	12.0	18.8	7.1	9.3	8.2	20.3
Engaged in minor theft (less than $50)	50.1	50.3	33.3	48.7	35.1	50.7
Engaged in major theft (more than $50)	16.8	26.2	9.2	16.1	10.4	21.6
Been a member of a criminal gang	6.8	12.6	5.2	5.8	4.4	12.1

respondents who experience and perceive racism against their own racial group—with respect to housing, education, and employment opportunities—are more likely to be involved in crime than those who do not experience or perceive racism. Thus, differences in groups' exposure to racism and disadvantage may explain why black Canadians appear to be more involved in gangs and violent offending than people from other racial groups. Another potential source of racism against the black community lies within the criminal justice system. We turn to this issue in the next section.

Perceptions of Criminal Injustice

Perceptions of racial bias within the Canadian criminal justice system are widespread. In 1994 the Commission on Systemic Racism in the Ontario Criminal Justice System conducted a survey of over 1,200 Toronto adults (18 years of age or older) who identified themselves as either black, Chinese, or white. Over 400 respondents were randomly selected from each racial group. The survey results indicate that 76 per cent of black Torontonians believed that the police treated members of their racial group worse than they treated white people. Furthermore, almost two-thirds of black respondents felt that members of their racial group were treated worse than whites by the criminal courts. Interestingly, the findings indicated that perceptions of bias were not isolated within the black community. Indeed, over half of the white respondents reported that they thought black people were treated worse by the police and a third that blacks were treated worse by the courts (Wortley, 1996). Additional research suggested that a high proportion of black youth perceived that the criminal justice system was discriminatory. A 1995 survey of 1,870 Toronto high school students found that over half of the black respondents felt that the police treated members of their racial group much worse than they treated the members of other racial groups. By contrast, only 22 per cent of South Asians, 15 per cent of Asians, and 4 per cent of whites felt that they were subject to discriminatory treatment (Ruck & Wortley, 2002). It should be noted that, in the studies discussed above, racial differences in perceptions of criminal injustice could not be explained by racial differences in social class, education, or other demographic factors.

Findings such as these have caused various criminal justice officials to admit that the *perception* of discrimination exists. They have also motivated various police organizations to implement programs designed to improve their relationships with various minority communities (see Stenning, 2003). Unfortunately, after more than a decade of race-relations efforts, it appears that black people in Canada continue to distrust the police and criminal courts. In 2007, for example, the 1994 survey (discussed above) was replicated to determine whether minority attitudes towards the justice system had improved over the intervening 13 years. The study found that attitudes had actually gotten worse. For example, in 1994, 76 per cent of black Torontonians felt that the police treated black people worse than whites. By 2007 this figure had risen to 81 per cent. Similarly, in 1994, 48 per cent of black Torontonians believed that a black person would get a longer sentence than a white person charged with the same crime. By 2007 this figure had risen to 58 per cent (see Wortley & Owusu-Bempah, 2009).

Considerable debate remains about the cause of these perceptions of bias. Critics of the justice system feel that perceptions of discrimination reflect reality and are rooted in the lived experiences of black people. Others claim that perceptions of injustice are inaccurate and caused by popular culture and exposure to stories about racism in the media. One popular explanation is that most black people in Canada are immigrants who come from countries where the criminal justice system is corrupt, brutal, and oppressive, and as a result, many black people have based their opinion about the police and the courts on their experiences in their home country. According to this hypothesis, black people who have been raised in Canada will have a much better opinion of the justice system. Research, however, suggests that the opposite is true. Indeed, blacks who were born in Canada tend to have far worse perceptions of the Canadian police and criminal courts than those who were born in other countries (Wortley & Owusu-Bempah, 2009). How can we explain this finding? To what extent are perceptions of discrimination accurate? To answer these questions, we must turn to the empirical data.

Racial Profiling

Racial profiling can be said to exist when members of a particular racial group become subject to greater levels of criminal justice **surveillance** than the 'average' citizen. In the academic literature, racial profiling is commonly defined as (1) significant racial differences in police stop and search practices; (2) significant racial differences in Customs search and interrogation practices; and (3) particular undercover or sting operations that target specific racial/ethnic communities (see Wortley & Tanner, 2005, 2004a, 2004b, 2003; Harris, 2002). It should be stressed that racial profiling is said to exist when race itself—not criminal or other illegal behaviour—is a significant factor in the making of surveillance decisions.

Numerous studies conducted in the United States, Great Britain, and Canada have identified that black people are more likely to be stopped, questioned, and searched by the police than whites (see reviews in Tanovich, 2006; Tator & Henry, 2006; Bowling & Phillips, 2002). For example, James (1998) conducted intensive interviews with over 50 black youths from six different cities in Ontario. Many of these youths reported that being stopped by the police was a common occurrence for them. There was also an almost universal belief that skin colour, not style of dress, was the primary determinant of attracting police attention. James (1998, p. 173) concludes that the adversarial nature of these police stops contributes strongly to black youths' hostility towards the police (also see Neugebauer, 2000). More recently, the Ontario Human Rights Commission (2003) gathered detailed testimonials from over 800 people in Ontario—most of them black—who felt that they had been the victim of racial profiling.

The issue of profiling has also been explored through survey research. A 1994 survey of Toronto residents, for example, found that one-third (30 per cent) of black males had been stopped and questioned by the police on two or more occasions in the past two years. By contrast, only 12 per cent of white males and 7 per cent of Asian males reported multiple police stops. Multivariate analysis reveals that these racial differences in police contact cannot be explained by racial differences in social class, education, or other demographic variables. In fact, two factors that seem to protect white males from police contact—age and social class—do not protect blacks. Whites with high incomes and education, for example, are much less likely to be stopped by the police than whites who score low on social class measures. By contrast, blacks with high incomes and education are actually more likely to be stopped than lower-class blacks (see Wortley & Tanner, 2003; Wortley & Kellough, 2004).

A second survey, conducted in 2001, surveyed Toronto high school students about their recent experiences with the police (Wortley & Tanner, 2005). The results of this study further suggest that blacks are much more likely than people from other racial backgrounds to be subjected to random street interrogations. For example, over 50 per cent of the black students reported that they had been stopped and questioned by the police on two or more occasions in the past two years, compared to only 23 per cent of whites, 11 per cent of Asians, and 8 per cent of South Asians. Similarly, over 40 per cent of black students claimed that they had been physically searched by the police in the past two years, compared to only 17 per cent of their white and 11 per cent of their Asian counterparts. Further analysis of this data suggests that racial differences in being stopped and searched by the police cannot be explained by racial differences in criminal activity, gang membership, drug and alcohol use, or public leisure activities (Wortley & Tanner, 2005).

A second quantitative strategy for examining racial profiling involves the collection of data by the police themselves. In such cases, officers are mandated to record the racial background of all of the people they decide to stop. Although such data collection strategies are quite common in both the United States and Great Britain, the city of Kingston, Ontario, is the only Canadian jurisdiction to conduct such a study. Beginning in the late 1990s, the Kingston Police Service received a number of complaints about racial profiling from the city's relatively small black community. Rather than ignore these allegations, Police Chief Bill Closs decided to engage in a ground-breaking data-collection project. Despite strong resistance from police associations across the country, this pilot project went into the field in October 2003. For the next 12 months, the Kingston police were ordered to record the age, gender, race, and home address of everyone they stopped and questioned—along with the time and location of the stop, the reason for the stop, and the final outcome of the interaction (i.e., arrest, ticket, warning, etc.). Information was ultimately recorded for over 16,500 police stops conducted over a one-year period (Wortley & Marshall, 2005).

In general, the results of the Kingston pilot project mirror the results of racial-profiling studies conducted in the United States and England. During the study period, the black residents of Kingston were three times more likely to be stopped at least once by the police than their white counterparts were. Overall, the individual stop rate for black residents was 150 stops per 1,000, compared to only 51 per 1,000 for whites.[1] The results further indicate that the individual stop rate was highest for the black male residents of Kingston (213 per 1,000), followed by black females (75 per 1,000), white males (74 per 1,000), and white females (29 per 1,000). An additional advantage of the Kingston study is that it gathered information on both traffic and pedestrian stops. Indeed, over 40 per cent of the 16,000 stops conducted during the study period involved pedestrians. Thus, if racial profiling does exist, we might expect that blacks would be over-represented in pedestrian stops to a greater degree than in traffic stops, since the racial background of pedestrians should be more apparent to officers than that of drivers. This is exactly what the results of the Kingston study reveal. While black people were still greatly over-represented in traffic stops (2.7 times), they were even more over-represented in pedestrian stops (3.7 times). Finally, further analysis indicates that the racial differences in Kingston police stops could not be explained by racial differences in age, gender, the location of the stop, or the reason for the stop. Interestingly, neither racial differences in observed or suspected criminal activity nor racial differences in observed traffic violations could explain the higher stop rate for blacks (see Wortley & Marshall, 2005).

Since the release of the results of the Kingston pilot project, no other Canadian city has attempted to collect information systematically on the racial background of people stopped and questioned by the police. However, following a hotly contested freedom of information request that ultimately ended up in the Ontario Court of Appeal, the *Toronto Star* newspaper eventually obtained information on over 1.7 million civilian 'contact cards' that had been filled out by the

Toronto police between 2003 and 2008. It should be stressed that these contact cards are not completed after every police stop; they are only filled out when individual police officers want to record, for intelligence purposes, that they have stopped and questioned a particular civilian. Contact cards contain various pieces of information, including the civilian's name and home address, the reason for the stop, and the location and time of the encounter. These cards also include basic demographic information, such as age, gender, and skin colour. Police argue that this information helps them keep track of who is present on the streets at certain times and at what locations and thus may help them identify potential crime suspects, witnesses and victims.

Critics note that these contact cards provide insight into police surveillance practices and largely reflect the types of civilians who come under enhanced police scrutiny. Interestingly, as with the Kingston data on police stops, black people are grossly over-represented in the Toronto Police Service's contact card database. Although they represent only 8 per cent of the Toronto population, black people were the target of almost 25 per cent of all contact cards filled out during the study period. Furthermore, the data indicate that black people were issued a disproportionate number of contact cards in all Toronto neighbourhoods, regardless of the local crime rate or racial composition (Rankin, 2010a, 2010b). As with the Kingston data, these findings are quite consistent with the racial-profiling argument.

Racial profiling has two potential consequences for the black community in Canada. First, because the black community is subject to much higher levels of police surveillance, they are also much more likely to be caught when they break the law than white people who engage in exactly the same forms of criminal activity. For example, in the Toronto high school survey discussed above, 65 per cent of the black drug dealers (defined as those who sold drugs 10 or more times in the past 12 months) reported that they had been arrested at some time in their life, compared to only 35 per cent of the white drug dealers. In other words, racial profiling may help explain why black people comprise the majority of people charged with drug crimes in North America, even though criminological evidence suggests that the majority of drug users and sellers are white. The second major consequence of racial profiling is that it serves to further alienate black people from mainstream Canadian society and to reinforce perceptions of discrimination and racial injustice. Indeed, research strongly suggests that black people who are frequently stopped and questioned by the police perceive much higher levels of discrimination in the Canadian criminal justice system than blacks who have not been stopped. Being stopped and searched by the police, therefore, seems to be experienced by black people as evidence that race still matters in Canadian society—that no matter how well you behave, how hard you try, being black means that you will always be considered one of the 'usual suspects'.

Police Use of Force

Highly publicized American cases of police violence against black people (e.g., Rodney King, Amadou Diallo, Abner Louima) reinforce the perception that North American police officers are biased against members of the black community. However, high-profile cases of police brutality involving black victims are not limited to the United States. A recent examination of news stories suggests that blacks are highly over-represented among those killed or injured by the police in both Ontario and Quebec (see Pedicelli, 1998).

In addition, a study conducted by Ontario's Special Investigations Unit (SIU) reveals that black people are highly over-represented in **police use of force** cases (Wortley, 2006). The SIU is a civilian law enforcement agency that conducts independent investigations into all incidents in which a civilian is seriously injured or killed by police actions. Between January 2000 and June 2006, the SIU conducted 784 investigations. While black people are only 3.6 per cent of the Ontario population, they represent 12 per cent of all civilians involved in SIU investigations, 16 per cent of SIU investigations involving police use of force, and 27 per cent of all investigations into police shootings. Additional analysis indicates that the police shooting rate for black Ontario residents (4.9 per 100,000) is 7.5 times higher than the overall provincial rate (0.65) and 10.1 times greater than the rate for white civilians (0.48). Finally, if one only includes cases where the death of a civilian was caused by police use of force, the over-representation of blacks becomes even more pronounced. While black people represent only 3.6 per cent of the Ontario population, they represent 27.0 per cent of all deaths caused by police use of force and 34.5 per cent of all deaths caused by police shootings. The black rate of police shooting deaths (1.95) is 9.7 times greater than the provincial rate (0.20) and 16 times greater than the rate for white people (0.12).

These findings, though suggestive, do not constitute proof that the Canadian police are racially biased with respect to the use of force. Indeed, the fact that these cases resulted in few criminal charges against police (and no convictions) could be seen as evidence that these shootings were justified. This interpretation is consistent with American research (see Fyfe, 1998) that suggests that once situational factors (i.e., whether the suspect had a gun or was in the process of committing a violent felony) have been taken into account, racial differences in the police use of force are dramatically reduced. Nonetheless, until such detailed research is conducted within Canada, questions about the possible relationship between race and police violence will remain.

The Arrest Situation

Early American studies of police arrest practices suggests that the racial minorities were much more likely to be arrested for minor crimes (drug use, minor assault, etc.) than whites (see reviews in Gabbidon & Greene, 2005; Walker, Spohn, & Delone, 2004; Bowling & Phillips, 2002). However, recent evidence suggests that racial bias in police arrest decisions may be declining. Contemporary observational studies of police-citizen encounters, conducted in the United States, suggest that, controlling for the seriousness of criminal conduct, race is unrelated to the police decision to arrest (see DeLisi & Regoli, 1999; Klinger, 1997). Nonetheless, a number of recent American studies suggest that it is the race of the victim—not the race of the offender— that may influence the arrest decision. In other words, there is considerable evidence to suggest that police are more likely to make arrests in cases involving white rather than non-white victims and are especially likely to make arrests when the case involves a white victim and a black offender (see Parker Stults, & Rice, 2005; Stolzenberg, D'Alessio, & Eitle, 2004). Some have argued that this is evidence that the police put a higher value on white victims and thus devote more effort and resources to solving such crimes (see Mann, 1993). These findings are also consistent with the 'racial threat' hypothesis that suggests that the police will treat inter-racial crimes involving minority offenders and white victims as particularly heinous.

Unfortunately, studies that examine the impact of the race of both offender and victim on arrest decisions have not yet been conducted in Canada. However, recent Canadian evidence does suggest that race may influence police behaviour once an arrest has been made. An analysis of over 10,000 Toronto arrests—between 1996 and 2001—for simple drug possession reveals that black suspects (38 per cent) are much more likely than whites (23 per cent) to be taken to the police station for processing. White accused persons, on the other hand, are more likely to be released at the scene. Once at the police station, black accused are held overnight, for a bail hearing, at twice the rate of whites. These racial disparities in treatment remain after other relevant factors—including age, criminal history, employment, and immigration status—have been taken into statistical account (Rankin, Quinn, Shephard, Simmie, & Duncanson, 2002a). Studies that have examined the treatment of young offenders in Ontario have yielded very similar results (Commission on Systemic Racism, 1995).

Pretrial Detention

The bail decision is recognized as one of the most important stages of the criminal court process. Not only does pretrial detention represent a fundamental denial of freedom for individuals who have not yet been proven guilty of a crime, it has also been shown to produce a number of subsequent legal consequences. Controlling for factors like type of charge and criminal record, previous research suggests that offenders who are denied bail are much more likely to be convicted and sentenced to prison than their counterparts who have been released (see Walker et al., 2004; Reaves & Perez, 1992). Thus, racial disparities in pretrial outcomes could have a direct impact on the over-representation of racial minorities in American and Canadian correctional statistics.

A number of American (Free, 2004; Demuth & Steffensmeier, 2004) and British studies (Bowling & Phillips, 2002) extensively document the fact that non-whites are more likely to be held in pre-trial detention than whites. A similar situation seems to exist in Canada. An examination of 1,653 cases from the Toronto courts reveals that blacks are less likely to be released by the police at the scene and more likely to be detained following a show-cause hearing. This disparity is particularly pronounced for those charged with drug offences. Indeed, the study finds that almost a third of the black offenders (31 per cent) charged with a drug offence were held in detention before their trial, compared to only 10 per cent of whites charged with a similar offence. This profound racial difference remains after other relevant factors—including criminal history—have been statistically controlled (Roberts & Doob, 1997).

A second Toronto-area study provides additional evidence of racial bias in pretrial decision-making (Kellough & Wortley, 2002). This research project tracked over 1,800 criminal cases that appeared in two Toronto bail courts over a six-month period in 1994. Overall, the results suggest that 36 per cent of black accused are detained before trial, compared to only 23 per cent of accused from other racial backgrounds. Race remains a significant predictor of pretrial detention after controlling for factors associated with both flight risk (e.g., employment status, home address, previous charges for failure to appear) and danger to the public (e.g., seriousness of current charges, length of criminal record). Additional analysis, however, suggests that black accused are more likely to be detained because the moral assessments they receive from arresting officers are much more negative than those for whites. 'Moral assessments' refer to the subjective personality descriptions that the police frequently attach to show-cause documents. The data suggest that police officers, on average, spend more time justifying the detention of black than white accused. Clearly, this is evidence that police discretion extends from the street and into the courtroom, at least at the pretrial level. Finally, the results of this study suggest that, as well as being used to manage risky populations, pretrial detention is a means (along with over-charging) used by the prosecution to encourage guilty pleas from accused persons. Those accused who are not held in pretrial custody, by contrast, are much more likely to have all of their charges withdrawn.

It is interesting to note that, even when they are released on bail, black accused are still subjected to greater court surveillance. Controlling for legally relevant variables, researchers find that black accused out on bail tend to be assigned significantly more release conditions—including curfews, area restrictions, and mandatory supervision requirements—than whites. Since blacks are subject to a greater number of release conditions and are more likely to be stopped and investigated by police, it is not surprising to find that blacks are greatly over-represented among those charged with breach-of-condition offences (Kellough & Wortley, forthcoming).

Race and Sentencing

American and British research on race and sentencing has produced mixed results. Some studies have found that black and other minority defendants are treated more harshly than whites (Mauer, 1999; Hudson, 1989; Shallice & Gordon, 1990; Hood, 1992); some have found that they are treated more leniently (Wilbanks, 1987); and others have found no evidence of racial bias in sentencing outcomes (Lauritsen & Sampson, 1998; Bowling & Phillips, 2002). Recent reviews of the American research (see Johnson, 2003; Ulmer & Johnson, 2004; Spohn, 2000) indicate that racial minorities are sentenced more harshly than whites if they are: (1) young and male; (2) are unemployed or have low incomes; (3) are represented by public offenders rather than a private attorney; (4) are convicted at trial rather than by plea; (5) have serious criminal records; 6) have been convicted of drug offenses; and (7) have been convicted of less serious crimes.

Relatively little Canadian research has focused on the sentencing outcomes of blacks or other racial minorities. Those studies that do exist, however, point to the possibility of racial discrimination. For example, Mosher's (1996) historical analysis of the Ontario courts, from 1892 to1930, reveals that black offenders experienced much higher rates of conviction and harsher sentences than their white counterparts. Multivariate analyses of this data reveal that observed racial differences in sentencing severity cannot be explained by other legally relevant variables (Mosher, 1996, p. 432). More recently, the Commission on Systemic Racism in the Ontario Criminal Justice System compared the sentencing outcomes of white and black offenders convicted in Toronto courts during the early 1990s. The results of this investigation revealed that black offenders—particularly those convicted of drug offences—are more likely to be sentenced to prison. This racial difference remains after other important factors—including offence seriousness, criminal history, age, and employment—have been taken into statistical account. Williams (1999, p. 212) concludes that 'this finding indicates that the higher incarceration rates of black than white convicted men is partly due to judges treating them more harshly for no legitimate reason.' However, Roberts and Doob (1997) caution that the commission's research suggests that the effect of race is statistically weaker at the sentencing stage than at earlier stages of the justice process and may be limited to certain offence categories (i.e., drug offences).

Clearly, research on racial differences in sentencing is at an early stage in Canada. One factor that has yet to be examined is the impact of the victim's racial background. However, American research strongly suggests that, regardless of their own race, individuals who victimize white people are sentenced much more harshly by the courts than those who victimize blacks and other racial minorities (Urbina, 2003; Johnson, 2003; Spohn, 2000; Cole, 1999). This fact might help explain why minority offenders—who usually victimize people from their own racial background—appear to be treated more leniently at the sentencing stage. Finally, the sentencing process appears to be particularly harsh on offenders who have victimized white females. Recent American research, for example, strongly suggests that homicides involving minority males and white females are the most likely to result in a death sentence (see Holcomb, Williams, & Demuth, 2004).

Race and Corrections

As with other stages of the criminal justice system, little Canadian research has examined the treatment of minorities within corrections. However, consistent with studies on the police and the criminal courts, the research that has been conducted suggests that some forms of racial bias exist behind prison walls. The Commission on Systemic Racism in the Ontario Criminal Justice System, for example, found that while racist language and attitudes plague the environments of many Ontario prisons and racial segregation is often used as a strategy for maintaining order, correctional officials do not acknowledge that racism is a significant management problem (Commission on Systemic Racism, 1994). Researchers also found evidence of racial bias in the application of prison discipline. Black inmates are significantly over-represented among prisoners charged with misconducts—particularly the types of misconducts in which correctional officers exercise greater discretionary judgment. This fact is important because a correctional record for such misconducts is often used to deny parole and limit access to temporary-release programs. Indeed, exploratory research suggests that, controlling for other relevant factors, black and other racial minority inmates are more likely to be denied early prison release (Mann, 1993; Commission on Systemic Racism 1995). Unfortunately, researchers have yet to explore possible racial discrimination in parole decisions within Canada's federal correctional facilities. Finally, the commission researchers highlighted the fact that current rehabilitation programs do not meet the **cultural and linguistic needs** of many racial minority inmates (Commission on Systemic Racism, 1994; 1995). The current correctional system, it is argued, caters to white, Euro-Canadian norms. The treatment needs of black and other racial minority prisoners are either unacknowledged or ignored. Ultimately, inadequate or inappropriate rehabilitation services for minority inmates may translate into higher recidivism rates for non-white offenders—a fact that may further contribute to their over-representation in the Canadian correctional system.

Black Canadians as Service Providers

Many believe that one strategy for reducing racial bias in the justice system is to recruit more minorities into policing and other sectors of the justice system (see Stenning, 2003). Unfortunately, very little Canadian research has documented the experiences of black and other minority populations working within the justice system. However, there is some evidence to suggest that diversity is increasing. In 1994, for example, only 6 per cent of Toronto police officers were members of a minority group. By 2009 this figure had risen to almost 19 per cent ('There's still' 2010). There is also evidence to suggest that there is more diversity within the police hierarchy. For the first time in history, two of Toronto's four deputy chiefs are black. It is difficult, however, to determine the overall number of black people in Canadian policing, because police organizations do not release the specific racial background of police recruits. From media releases, we can determine that on 10 September 2009 the Toronto Police Service graduated its most 'diverse' class of recruits ever, and we also know that 38 per cent of this graduating class were members of a visible minority group. However, we do not know what proportion of these visible minorities were black, Asian, South Asian, or the member of another racial minority group (Robertson, 2009). Even less information is available on the racial background of individuals working as lawyers, judges, parole officers, and correctional officers within the Canadian justice system.

American and British research suggests that black police officers often suffer from workplace racism and discrimination (see Bolton & Feagin, 2004; Bowling & Phillips, 2002; Holdaway & Barron, 1997; Holdaway, 1991). Although limited, the evidence suggests that the experiences of black officers have been similarly unpleasant in Canada. In his book *You Had Better Be White by 6 A.M*, Craig Smith, a black Royal Canadian Mounted Police (RCMP) veteran and current diversity policing analyst, chronicles the everyday racism that blacks face within Canada's national police force (Smith, 2006). Similarly, in 2002 a senior officer with the Toronto Police Service held focus group meetings with black officers and discovered that many experienced problems with racism and racial profiling (see Tanovich, 2006). Black correctional officers are also subjected to overt and covert discrimination from both inmates and fellow staff (Commission on Systemic Racism, 1995). In recent years, for example, black correctional officers in Ontario have received racist mail from white colleagues—at both their homes and workplaces—including death threats signed by the Ku Klux Klan (Diebel, 2008).

A 1993 survey of sworn RCMP officers perhaps best captures the types of pressures experienced by black and other racial minority individuals working within Canada's criminal justice system. The results of this survey suggest that, despite official denials of systemic bias, the majority of RCMP officers (69 per cent) believed that racial problems existed within the RCMP. On the one hand, visible minority members often felt that they had to work harder to gain recognition within the RCMP and that their work received more scrutiny than that of their white counterparts. Half of the visible minority officers surveyed also claimed to have heard racist language and seen racist material within RCMP offices—further evidence of a racially intolerant work environment. White males within the RCMP, on the other hand, strongly believed that it was they who were the victim of 'reverse racism'. Indeed, 96 per cent of the white male RCMP officers who took part in the survey felt that it was more difficult for white males to get into the RCMP than for women, racial minorities, or Aboriginals. The majority also felt that white males were discriminated against with respect to promotion and transfers and believed that visible minorities imagined racial harassment and discrimination where none existed (RCMP, 1996).

In response to such experiences, black police and correctional officers have formed organizations such as the Association of Black Law Enforcers (ABLE) to support their interests and provide social support (www.ablenet.ca). A similar organization, the Canadian Association of Black Lawyers (CABL) also exists to support blacks practising within the field of law (www.cabl.ca/pagedisplay.aspx?i=192). Both ABLE and CABL also provide encouragement for young black people—through scholarship and mentoring initiatives—who are interested in criminal justice careers.

The black community has begun to establish its own mechanisms for improving race relations and protecting black people from the various forms of discrimination outlined above. One example is the African Canadian Legal Clinic. Staffed by lawyers, service providers, and volunteers, the clinic was established in 1994 to address anti-black racism and discrimination within the criminal justice system and broader Canadian society. The clinic represents blacks in various legal forums, often participating, for example, in race-based test cases that have the potential to set legal precedents. The clinic also engages in advocacy on the part of black Canadians and provides legal education aimed at eliminating racism—and anti-black racism—in Canada (www.aclc.net).

Conclusion

The history of black people in Canada is marked by a legacy of racism, inequality, and exclusion. The profound economic and social disadvantages faced by the black community have been compounded by their treatment within the Canadian criminal justice system. As in the United States and Great Britain, there is evidence to suggest that black people in Canada suffer from racial profiling as well as from relatively harsh treatment with respect to arrest decisions, police use of force, pretrial decision-making, and sentencing. Explaining the relatively harsh treatment that blacks have received within the Canadian justice system always seems to produce vigorous debate. Some view this treatment as justified—that it stems from the over-representation of black people in criminal offending. Others maintain that this harsh treatment reflects both overt and institutional racism within Canadian society. Few concede that both perspectives may hold some truth. We must ask ourselves, is it possible that the disproportionate economic and social strain experienced by black people within Canadian society has resulted in higher than average rates of criminal offending among members of this racial group? Is it also possible that this over-representation in offending, combined with sensationalistic media coverage, has led to exaggerated stereotypes about the criminality of black Canadians? Are these stereo-types subsequently used to justify racial profiling and other forms of discrimination within the justice system? Is it also possible that racial bias within the criminal justice system has served to further solidify feelings of social alienation among members of the black community and that these feelings of exclusion have provided justifications for additional criminal activity? These are all questions that deserve additional research in the Canadian context. Unfortunately, as the continued ban on the collection and dissemination of race-crime statistics confirms, there is little political will in this country to confront our historical legacy of racism and the manner in which this legacy continues to affect the lives of black residents.

Key Terms

black-on-black violence

cultural and linguistic needs

institutionalized racial discrimination

over-representation

perceptions of racial bias

police use of force

race-crime statistics

racial profiling

social alienation

surveillance

Questions for Critical Thought

1. What are the potential benefits and consequences of allowing the criminal justice system to release statistics on the racial background of criminal offenders and victims?
2. Can racial profiling be justified?
3. How can we explain the over-representation of black people in the Canadian correctional system?
4. History suggests that the first black residents of Canada experienced slavery and other forms of racial oppression. How does this legacy impact the lives of black Canadians today?
5. Critics argue that racism exists with respect to criminal sentencing even when statistics show that minorities sometimes receive more lenient sentences than whites. Do you agree or disagree with this argument?

Additional Readings

Mosher, C. (1998). *Discrimination and denial: Systemic racism in Ontario's legal and criminal justice systems: 1892-1961.* Toronto: University of Toronto Press.

Tanovich, D. (2006). *The colour of justice: Policing race in Canada.* Toronto: Irwin Law.

Tator, C., & Henry, F. (2006). *Racial profiling in Canada: Challenging the myth of a few bad apples.* Toronto: University of Toronto Press.

Walker, S., Spohn, C., & Delone, M. (2004). *The color of justice: Race, ethnicity and crime in America.* Toronto: Wadsworth.

Winks, R. W. (1997). *The blacks in Canada: A history.* Montreal: McGill-Queen's University Press.

Websites of Interest

African Canadian Legal Clinic (2010): www.aclc.net

Association of Black Law Enforcers: www.ablenet.ca

Black Law Students Association of Canada: www.blsacanada.ca

Canadian Association of Black Lawyers: www.cabl.ca/pagedisplay.aspx?i=192

Toronto Star Series on Racial Profiling: www.thestar.com/racematters

Endnote

1. It should be noted that these stop rates were calculated after eliminating all police stops that involved people who lived outside of the city of Kingston. Furthermore, each individual who was stopped during the study period was only counted once. In other words, the rates reported here were not inflated by individuals who had been stopped on multiple occasions.

References

Barnes, A. (2002). Dangerous duality: The 'net effect' of immigration and deportation on Jamaicans in Canada. In W. Chan & K. Mirchandani (Eds), *Crimes of colour: Racialization and the criminal justice system in Canada* (pp. 191–204). Peterborough, ON: Broadview Press.

Bolton, K., & Feagin, J. R. (2004). *Black in blue: African-American police officers and racism.* New York: Routledge.

Bowling, B., & Phillips, C. (2002). *Racism, crime and justice.* Harlow: Longman.

Caldas, S., Bernier, S., & Marceau, R. (2009). Explanatory factors of the black achievement gap in Montréal's public and private schools: A multivariate analysis. *Education and Urban Society, 41*(2), 197–215.

Chettleburgh, M. (2007). *Young thugs: Inside the dangerous world of Canadian street gangs.* Toronto: HarperCollins.

Chui, T., Tran, K., & Maheux, H. (2008). *Canada's ethnocultural mosaic: The 2006 Census.* Ottawa: Statistics Canada. Catalogue no. 97-562-X.

Codjoe, H. M. (2001). Fighting a 'public enemy' of black academic achievement: The persistence of racism and the schooling experiences of black students in Canada. *Race Ethnicity and Education, 4*(4), 343–375.

Cole, D. (1999). *No equal justice: Race and class in the American criminal justice system.* New York: New Press.

Commission on Systemic Racism in the Ontario Criminal Justice System. (1994). *Racism behind bars: The treatment of black and other racial minority prisoners in Ontario prisons—interim report of the Commission on Systemic Racism in the Ontario Criminal Justice System.* Toronto: Queen's Printer for Ontario.

Commission on Systemic Racism in the Ontario Criminal Justice System. (1995). *Report of the Commission on Systemic Racism in the Ontario Criminal Justice System.* Toronto: Queen's Printer for Ontario.

Dauvergne, M., Scrim, K., & Brennan, S. (2008). *Hate crime in Canada—2006.* Ottawa: Statistics Canada. Catalogue no. 85F0033M—no. 17.

DeLisi, M., & Regoli, B. (1999). Race, conventional crime and criminal justice: The declining importance of race. *Journal of Criminal Justice, 27*(6), 549–557.

Demuth, S., & Steffensmeier, D. (2004). The impact of gender and race-ethnicity in the pre-trial process. *Social Problems, 51*(2), 222–242.

Diebel, L. (2008, January 17). Don Jail guards fearful after racist threats. *The Toronto Star.* Retrieved May 17, 2010, from www.thestar.com

Ezeonu, I. (2008). Dudes, let's talk about us: The black 'community' construction of gun violence in Toronto. *Journal of African American Studies, 12*(3), 193–214.

Free, M. (2004). Bail and pretrial release decisions: An assessment of the racial threat perspective. *Journal of Ethnicity in Criminal Justice, 2*(4), 23–44.

Fyfe, J. J. (1988). Police use of deadly force: Research and reform. *Justice Quarterly, 5*(2), 165–205.

Gabbidon, S., & Taylor Greene, H. (2005). *Race and crime.* Thousand Oaks, CA: Sage.

Gartner, R., & Thompson, S. (2004). Trends in homicide in Toronto. In B. Kidd & J. Phillips (Eds), *From enforcement to prevention to civic engagement: Research on community safety* (pp. 28–42). Toronto: Centre of Criminology, University of Toronto.

Harris, D. (2002). *Profiles in injustice: Why racial profiling cannot work.* New York: New Press.

Henry, F., Hastings, P., & Freer, B. (1996). Perceptions of race and crime in Ontario: Empirical evidence from Toronto and the Durham region. *Canadian Journal of Criminology, 38,* 469–476.

Henry, F., & Tator, C. (2000). *Racist discourse in Canada's English print media.* Toronto: Canadian Race Relations Foundation.

Henry, F., & Tator, C. (Eds) (2005). *The colour of democracy: Racism in Canadian society* (3rd ed.). Toronto: Nelson.

Hill, D. (1991). *The freedom seekers: Blacks in early Canada.* Agincourt, ON: Book Society of Canada.

Holcomb, J. E., Williams, M. R., & Demuth, S. (2004). White female victims and death penalty disparity research. *Justice Quarterly, 21*(4), 877–902.

Holdaway, S. (1991). *Recruiting a multi-racial police force.* London: HMSO.

Holdaway, S., & Barron, A. M. (1997). *Resigners? The experience of black and Asian police officers.* London: Macmillan.

Hood, R. (1992). *Race and sentencing: A study in the Crown Court.* Oxford: Clarendon Press.

Hudson, B. (1989). Discrimination and disparity: The influence of race on sentencing. *New Community 16*(1), 23–34.

James, C. (1998). 'Up to no good': Black on the streets and encountering police. In V. Satzewich (Ed.). *Racism and social inequality in Canada: Concepts, controversies and strategies of resistance* (pp. 157–176). Toronto: Thompson.

James, C. E. (2009). African-Caribbean Canadians working 'harder' to attain their immigrant dreams: Context, strategies and consequences. *Wadabagei: A Journal of the Caribbean and Its Diaspora, 12*(1), 92–108.

Johnson, B. (2003). Racial and ethnic disparities in sentencing: Departures across modes of conviction. *Criminology, 41*(2), 449–490.

Kellough, G., & Wortley, S. (2002). Remand for plea: The impact of race, pre-trial detention and over-charging on plea bargaining decisions. *British Journal of Criminology, 42*(1), 186–210.

Kellough, G., & Wortley, S. (Forthcoming). Risk, moral assessment and the application of bail conditions in Canadian criminal courts. *British Journal of Criminology.*

Klinger, D. (1997). Negotiating order in patrol work: An ecological theory of police response to deviance. *Criminology, 35*(2), 277–306.

Lampert, R., & Curtis, J. (1989). The racial attitudes of Canadians. In L. Tupperman & J. Curtis (Eds), *Readings in sociology* (pp. 343–349). Toronto: McGraw-Hill Ryerson.

LaPrairie, C. (1990). The role of sentencing in the over-representation of Aboriginal people in correctional institutions. *Canadian Journal of Criminology, 32*(3), 429–440.

Lauritsen, J., & Sampson, R. (1998). Minorities, crime, and criminal justice. In M. Tonry (Ed.), *The handbook of crime and punishment* (pp. 30–56). New York: Oxford University Press.

Leger Marketing. (2007). Racial tolerance report. Retrieved March 9, 2010, from www.legermarketing.com/documents/SPCLM/070119ENG.pdf

Mann, C. R. (1993). *Unequal justice: A question of color.* Bloomington: Indiana University Press.

Mauer, M. (1999). *Race to incarcerate.* New York: New Press.

Mendez, P., Hiebert, D., & Wyly, E. (2006). Landing at home: Insights on immigration and metropolitan housing markets for a longitudinal survey of immigrants to Canada. *Canadian Journal of Urban Research, 15*(2), 82–104.

Milan, A., & Tran, K. (2004). Blacks in Canada: A long history. *Canadian Social Trends, 72,* 2–7.

Mosher, C. (1996). Minorities and misdemeanours: The treatment of black public order offenders in Ontario's criminal justice system—1892–1930. *Canadian Journal of Criminology, 38,* 413–438.

Mosher, C. (1998). *Discrimination and denial: Systemic racism in Ontario's legal and criminal justice systems: 1892–1961.* Toronto: University of Toronto Press.

Neugebauer, R. (2000). Kids, cops, and colour: The social organization of police-minority youth relations. In R. Neugebauer (Ed.), *Criminal injustice: Racism in the criminal justice system* (pp. 46–59). Toronto: Canadian Scholars' Press.

Ontario Human Rights Commission. (2003). *Paying the price: The human cost of racial profiling.* Toronto: Ontario Human Rights Commission.

Parker, K., Stults, B., & Rice, S. (2005). Racial threat, concentrated disadvantage and social control: Considering macro-level sources of variation in arrests. *Criminology, 43*(4), 1111–1134.

Pedicelli, G. (1998). *When police kill: Police use of force in Montreal and Toronto.* Montreal: Véhicule Press.

Public Safety Canada. (2009). *Corrections and conditional release statistical overview: 2008.* Ottawa: Public Works and Government Services Canada.

Rankin, J. (2010a, February 6). Race matters: When good people are swept up with the bad. *The Toronto Star,* p. A1.

Rankin, J. (2010b, February 6). CARDED: Probing a racial disparity. *The Toronto Star,* p. IN1.

Rankin, J., & Powell, B. (2008, July 21). The criminals among us: Not as many lawbreakers as Canadians believe are members of visible minorities, survey shows. *The Toronto Star,* p. A1.

Rankin, J., Quinn, J., Shephard, M., Simmie, S., & Duncanson, J. (2002a, October 19). Singled out: An investigation into race and crime. *The Toronto Star,* p. A1.

Rankin, J., Quinn, J., Shephard, M., Simmie, S., & Duncanson, J. (2002b, October 20). Police target black drivers. *The Toronto Star,* p. A1.

RCMP (Royal Canadian Mounted Police). (1996). *1993 Members survey: Final report.* Ottawa: Royal Canadian Mounted Police.

Reaves, B., & Perez, J. (1992). *Pre-trial release of felony defendants.* Washington, DC: US Department of Justice.

Roberts, J. V., & Doob, A. (1997). Race, ethnicity, and criminal justice in Canada. In M. Tonry (Ed.), *Ethnicity, crime, and immigration: Comparative and cross-national perspectives.* (Vol. 21, pp. 469–522). Chicago: University of Chicago Press.

Robertson, I. (2009, September 27). Changing of the guard: Today's police force is all about diversity. *Toronto Sun,* p. 4.

Ruck, M., & Wortley, S. (2002). Racial and ethnic minority high school students' perceptions of school disciplinary practices: A look at some Canadian findings. *Journal of Youth and Adolescence, 31*(3), 185–195.

Shallice, A., & Gordon, P. (1990). *Black people, white justice? Race and the criminal justice system.* London: Runnymede Trust.

Siegel, L., & McCormick, C. (2010). *Criminology in Canada: Theories, patterns and typologies* (4th ed.). Toronto: Thompson Nelson.

Skolnick, J. (1966). *Justice without trial: Law enforcement in a democratic society.* New York: John Wiley and Sons.

Smith, C. M. (2006). *You had better be white by 6 A.M.: The African-Canadian experience in the Royal Canadian Mounted Police.* Halifax: C.M.S.

Smith, D., Visher, C., & Davidson, L. (1984). Equity and discretionary justice: The influence of race on police arrest decisions. *Journal of Criminal Law and Criminology, 75,* 234–249.

Spohn, C. (2000). Thirty years of sentencing reform: The quest for a racially neutral sentencing process. In J. Horney (Ed.), *Politics, processes and decisions of the criminal justice system* (pp. 417–501). Washington, DC: National Institute of Justice.

Stenning, P. (2003). Policing the cultural kaleidoscope: Recent Canadian experience. *Police and Society 7,* 21–87.

Stolzenberg, L., D'Alessio, S., & Eitle, D. (2004). A multilevel test of racial threat theory. *Criminology, 42*(3), 673–698.

Swidinsky, R., & Swidinsky, M. (2002). The relative earnings of visible minorities in Canada: New evidence from the 1996 Census. *Industrial Relations, 57*(4), 630–659.

Tanner, J., & Wortley, S. (2002). *The Toronto youth crime and victimization survey: Overview report.* Toronto: Centre of Criminology, University of Toronto.

Tanovich, D. (2006). *The colour of justice: Policing race in Canada.* Toronto: Irwin Law.

Tator, C., & Henry, F. (2006). *Racial profiling in Canada: Challenging the myth of a few bad apples.* Toronto: University of Toronto Press.

Teixeira, C. (2008). Barriers and outcomes in the housing searches of new immigrants and refugees: A case study of 'black' Africans in Toronto's rental market. *Journal of Housing and the Built Environment, 23*(4), 253–276.

There's still fear about reprisals for joining the police. (2010, January 16). *The Globe and Mail*, p. M4.

Ulmer, J., & Johnson, B. (2004). Sentencing in context: A multilevel analysis. *Criminology, 42*(1), 137–177.

Urbina, M. (2003). Race and ethnic differences in punishment and death sentence outcomes: Empirical analysis of data on California, Florida and Texas, 1975–1995. *Journal of Ethnicity in Criminal Justice, 1*(1), 5–35.

Walker, J. (1980). *The history of blacks in Canada: A study guide for teachers and students.* Ottawa: Minister of State and Multiculturalism.

Walker, S., Spohn, C., & Delone, M. (2004). *The color of justice: Race, ethnicity and crime in America.* Toronto: Wadsworth.

Walsh, P., & Dauvergne, M. (2009). *Police reported hate crime in Canada—2007.* Ottawa: Statistics Canada. Catalogue no. 85-002-X.

Wilbanks, W. (1987). *The myth of a racist criminal justice system.* Belmont, CA: Wadsworth.

Williams, T. (1999). Sentencing black offenders in the Ontario criminal justice system. In J. V. Roberts & D. P. Cole (Eds), *Making sense of sentencing* (pp. 200–216). Toronto: University of Toronto Press.

Winks, R.W. (1997). *The blacks in Canada: A history.* Montreal: McGill-Queen's University Press.

Winks, R.W. (2008). Slavery, the Loyalists, and English Canada. In B. Walker (Ed.), *The history of immigration and racism in Canada* (pp.27–40). Toronto: Canadian Scholars' Press.

Wortley, S. (1996). Justice for all? Race and perceptions of bias in the Ontario criminal justice system—a Toronto survey. *Canadian Journal of Criminology, 38*(4), 439–467.

Wortley, S. (2002). Misrepresentation or reality? The depiction of race and crime in the Toronto print media. In B. Schissel & C. Brooks (Eds), *Marginality and condemnation: An introduction to critical criminology* (pp. 55–82). Halifax: Fernwood.

Wortley, S. (2006). *Police use of force in Ontario: An examination of data from the Special Investigations Unit—final report.* Toronto: Attorney General of Ontario (Ipperwash Inquiry), Government of Ontario.

Wortley, S. (2008). A province at the crossroads: Statistics on youth violence in Ontario. In R. McMurtry & A. Curling (Eds), *Review of the roots of youth violence* (Vol. 5, pp. 1–64). Toronto: Queen's Printer for Ontario.

Wortley, S., & Kellough, G. (2004). Racializing risk: Police and Crown discretion and the over-representation of black people in the Ontario criminal justice system. In A. Harriott, F. Brathwaite, & S. Wortley (Eds), *Crime and criminal justice in the Caribbean and among Caribbean peoples* (pp. 173–205). Kingston, Jamaica: Arawak Publications.

Wortley, S., & Marshall, L. (2005). *Police stop search activities in Kingston, Ontario.* Kingston: Kingston Police Services Board.

Wortley, S., & Owusu-Bempah, A. (2009). Unequal before the law: Immigrant and racial minority perceptions of the Canadian criminal justice system. *Journal of International Migration and Integration, 10*(4), 447–473.

Wortley, S., & Tanner, J. (2003). Data, denials and confusion: The racial profiling debate in Toronto. *Canadian Journal of Criminology and Criminal Justice, 45*(3), 367–389.

Wortley, S., & Tanner, J. (2004a). Racial profiling in Canada: Survey evidence from Toronto. *Canadian Review of Policing Research, 1*(1), 24–36.

Wortley, S., & Tanner, J. (2004b). Discrimination or good policing? The racial profiling debate in Canada. *Our Diverse Cities 1*, 197–201.

Wortley, S., & Tanner, J. (2005). Inflammatory rhetoric? Baseless accusations? Responding to Gabor's critique of racial profiling research in Canada. *Canadian Journal of Criminology and Criminal Justice, 47*(3), 581–609.

Wortley, S., & Tanner, J. (2006). Immigration, social disadvantage and urban youth gangs: Results of a Toronto-area study. *Canadian Journal of Urban Research, 15*(2), 1–20.

Wortley, S., & Tanner, J. (2008). Money, respect and defiance: Justifying gang membership in a Canadian city. In F. van Gemert, D. Peterson, & I. Lien (Eds), *Youth Gangs, Migration and Ethnicity* (pp. 192–210). London: Willan.

9 | South Asians and Justice in Canada

Barbara Perry and Shahid Alvi

In this chapter, we explore what is known about the experiences of South Asians with respect to crime in Canada. We begin by emphasizing that the term 'South Asian' is a construction as an identity, not a geographical description, and that in many ways this categorization is relevant only in the Canadian context. For example, in Canada one would call someone from India a South Asian, but in Britain that person would be called black or Asian; in Trinidad, Indian; and in the United States, Asian (Shariff, 2008, p. 457). Moreover, in Canada, those we call South Asian have roots in several distinct nations, primarily India, Pakistan, Bangladesh, and Sri Lanka.

These variations in definition make it difficult to compare the experiences of South Asians in Canada with those of South Asians in other countries. In addition, as we will note below, considerable limitations in the data on South Asian communities in Canada make it nearly impossible to describe their experiences as either victims or perpetrators of crime. Nevertheless, in what follows, we provide a brief history of the South Asian population in Canada and then discuss what little is known about crime among this diverse group, as well as their experiences with victimization.

Migration History

In 1897, several members of the **Sikh** Lancers and Infantry Regiment visited Vancouver after celebrating Queen Victoria's Diamond Jubilee in London, England. These were the first South Asians to reach Canadian shores. Indeed, South Asian **immigration** to Canada was initially shaped by the tripartite colonial relationship between the United Kingdom, Canada, and India—hence the early arrival of Sikhs noted above. As a parallel member of the British Commonwealth, Canada was under pressure to admit its Indian compatriots, in spite of domestic resistance to such entry. Consequently, small clusters of Sikhs, especially, would follow later in search of the opportunities promised by the Canadian government and large corporate entities like the Hudson's Bay Company. However, by 1905, fewer than 5,000 South Asians—virtually all of them from India—could be counted. Their numbers would remain low for most of the first decade of the twentieth century, largely as a result of exclusionary immigration policies and practices. Most notable were the $200 landing fee and the 1909 Order-in-Council commonly known as the **'continuous passage'** policy, whereby entry to the country was 'hereby prohibited of any immigrants who have come to Canada otherwise than by continuous journey from the country of which they are natives or citizens and only through tickets purchased in that country or prepaid in Canada.' Keep in mind, of course, that there were at the time no direct steamship routes between India and Canada—a fact that was well known to Canadian policy makers.

The policy had the intended effect of all but drying up South Asian immigration. In 1909, only 6 were admitted. Between 1910 and 1921 (with the exception of 88 entrants in 1914), fewer than 10 South Asian immigrants were documented in any year. Even into the late 1950s, the numbers remained in the low hundreds. The infamous case of the **Komagata Maru** in 1914 brings into focus the dramatic consequences of Canada's discriminatory policies of the day. In a challenge to the continuous journey policy, a group of 376 East Indians chartered a Japanese ship out of Hong Kong en route for Vancouver. Upon arrival, all but 22—largely dependants of prior immigrants—were denied entry. Upon their return to Calcutta, they were met and detained by representatives of the British government, which had pegged the passengers as anti-colonialists. When they resisted, police opened fire, killing 20, injuring dozens, and arresting dozens more. A report that appeared later, prepared by sympathizers of British rule, sided with the government's actions; this led to further arrests, as well as hangings. Had the migrants been allowed to remain in Canada, such foreseeable consequences could have been averted.

Nonetheless, Canadian immigration policy continued to exclude East Indians and virtually all other Asians well into the twentieth century. Asian immigration was met with corresponding waves of **anti-Asian sentiment**. Labour leaders, temperance activists, and agricultural interests pressed the government to react to the perceived threats that all Asians were thought to represent to employment, morality, and even hygiene. The movement to 'Keep Canada white' would prevail. In thinly veiled words, Prime Minister **Mackenzie King** spoke for the nation:

> We, in Canada, have certain more or less clearly defined ideals of national well being. These ideals must never be lost sight of. Non-ideal elements there must be, but they should be capable of assimilation. Essentially non-assimilable elements are clearly detrimental to our highest national development and should be vigorously excluded. (House of Commons, Sessional Paper No. 360, 1908, 7–8)

These sentiments were institutionalized through increasingly restrictive immigration and naturalization policies that slowed Asian immigration to a trickle throughout the first half of the twentieth century. Even the development of family life—so crucial to any community—was thwarted by restrictions on the entry of Asian and South Asian women. Thus, by the 1920s, most South Asian settlements were male enclaves.

By the closing years of the twentieth century, the trickle would increase to a constant flow, as thousands of South Asians arrived to make Canada their home, lured by the same promises of opportunity and prosperity that had brought South Asians here earlier. The racialized and nation-based quotas of the 1940s and 1950s were replaced by skill-based admissions thanks to extensive immigration reform in the 1960s. Nonetheless, structural patterns continued to restrict South Asian movement to Canada. Notably, immigration offices in countries like India either did not exist or were under-staffed. However, the trend toward more liberal immigration policies continued throughout the 1980s and 1990s, making it much easier for South Asians to immigrate. It was during the 1990s, in fact, that they became the second-largest visible-minority group in Canada at 2.4 per cent of the population, compared to blacks, who represented only 2.0 per cent of the population. Only Chinese ranked higher proportionately (3 per cent) (Chard & Renaud, 1999).

From the outset, South Asians had been lured to Canada largely by employment, educational, and entrepreneurial opportunities. While this initially meant unskilled labour on the railroad or in logging camps, by the middle of the twentieth century, most employment-class immigrants were highly educated and highly skilled. However, migration histories are not shaped by the logic of economics alone, especially with respect to more recent immigrants to Canada like the South Asians. Social and cultural factors such as **family reunification** and **spousal migration** have also helped shape the contours of the South Asian communities in Canada. Indeed, it has consistently been the case that the family class of immigrants accounts for about one-half of all South Asian immigrants and includes predominantly spouses and parents.

Diversity within the South Asian 'Community'

The upshot of 100 years of immigration is that South Asians now represent the largest (approximately one million) and fastest-growing visible minority group in Canada. For example, between 1996 and 2001, the South Asian population grew at a rate of 33 per cent, while the general population grew by only 4 per cent. The implications of this growth have been most dramatic for Ontario and British Columbia, which are home to the largest concentrations of South Asians by far. Nearly two-thirds of all South Asians live in Ontario, and one-quarter live in British Columbia. In both provinces, they represent approximately 5 per cent of the total population. Moreover, Toronto and Vancouver can claim the lion's share of these new Canadians. Approximately half of the one million South Asian residents of Canada can be found in Toronto, and about 200,000 in Vancouver (Statistics Canada, 2007).

Regardless of residence, South Asians in Canada cannot be called a homogeneous community. Rather, they constitute a very diverse population, with regionally and culturally specific languages, dialects, traditions, and beliefs. In short, South Asians belong to a number of communities representing dozens of identities, language groups, and religions. At the last census in 2001, 74 per cent of South Asians self-identified as East Indian, 8 per cent as Pakistani, 6 per cent as Sri Lankan, 5 per cent as Punjabi, and 4 per cent as Tamil. It is no surprise, then, that there was remarkable diversity of languages as well: Punjabi, Tamil, Urdu, Gujurati, Hindi, and Bengali. Notably, in spite of their relatively recent arrival, nearly all South Asians (93 per cent) indicated that they were fluent in at least one official language, and 35 per cent reported that English was their first language (Statistics Canada, 2007).

Interestingly, earlier research on identity by Aspinall (2003) reveals that Asians—South Asians among them—are most likely to self-identify by religion rather than by any notion of 'Asian-ness', which is testimony to the importance of religion in these communities. Indeed, religiosity in South Asian communities tends to be much more salient than in the general Canadian population. This is the case irrespective of South Asians' religious affiliation, which is itself quite diverse, with almost equal distribution across the Sikh, **Hindu,** and **Muslim** faiths (just under 30 per cent each), the bulk of the remainder being Christian. In fact, virtually all Sikhs in Canada (95 per cent) are from South Asia, 60 per cent of Hindus, but only about 20 per cent of Muslims (Model & Lin, 2002).

The processes of immigration can be transformative for the individual, the family, and the communities involved. In particular, when the migration involves a move to a vastly different culture, immigrants often redefine themselves in order to integrate or, at least, to adjust to their new environment. This has disparate implications depending on an array of intersecting factors, with age and gender being paramount.

Age

It is often at either end of the chronological continuum that immigrants face the most difficulty in adapting to their host culture. Recent scholarship has highlighted the experiences of South Asian youth, applying such discursive labels as 'caught between two worlds', 'straddling the divide', or 'bridging the gap'. Collectively, these labels imply anxiety about identity and belonging, especially among young **second-generation** South Asians. And there is some evidence that such struggles are commonplace. Several largely qualitative studies have uncovered sentiments that reflect the difficulty of managing two often-competing value sets (e.g., Abouguendia & Noels, 2001; Reitz et al., 2009) and the struggle to 'fit in', with respect to both the South Asian and the dominant Canadian cultures (e.g., Shariff, 2008; Samuel, 2009).

However, given the heterogeneity of the South Asian community, it is perhaps not enough to focus only on their struggles to 'fit in'. In her own reflections on the South Asian **diaspora**, Banerji (2006) reminds us that

> our own sense of ourselves is not necessarily culturally fractured or marked entirely by the paradigm of a 'clash of civilizations'. The pressures to conform wholly to dominant Eurocentrism, or to dominant conceptions of South Asian ethnicity, are negotiated, accepted, or subverted in a myriad of ways, since we normalize our diasporic consciousness, the assemblage of cultural fragments, the difference and commonalities marking the ground we call home.

In other words, youth are not necessarily overwhelmed by **acculturation** but engaged in processes of negotiating identities for themselves that may in fact be as exciting and stimulating as they are anxiety provoking.

Little attention has been devoted to the acculturative experiences of older immigrants. This is a significant oversight, given the relatively common practice of working-age immigrants sponsoring their parents' entry into Canada. Moreover, just 8 per cent of South Asian seniors live alone, as compared to 11 per cent of Chinese seniors and 29 per cent of all Canadian seniors. Twenty-five per cent live with family members other than their spouse (Tran, Kaddatz, & Allard 2005, p. 22). Adaptation to family life in Canada, however, can be troubling, especially for those coming in their later years. Choudry (2001, p. 376) observes that 'traditional reverence for parents has diminished. They (elders) experience loss of independence and erosion of their traditional power and authority within the family structure.' The themes that Choudry identified among senior South Asian women might also apply to their male counterparts: isolation and loneliness; family conflict; economic dependence; and settling and coping.

Gender

As an extension of the traditional ideologies and practices of patriarchy extant in many South Asian nations, South Asian women—young and old—often face particular barriers to integrating into Canadian society. In an effort to maintain their family attachment to their cultural heritage, parents often demand strict **gender-role conformity** of their teenage girls. Indeed, young girls perceive themselves to be tightly controlled, especially relative to their Anglo-Canadian counterparts. Interviews conducted by Talbani and Hasanali (2000, p. 625) with 22 adolescent South Asian girls uncovered three key dimensions of these practices: (1) boys and girls are treated differently at home; (2) girls are given less decision-making power; and (3) parents exert more control over girls' intermingling with the opposite sex.

In highly traditional families, this rigid control of gender roles continues into adulthood, although it is often mediated by class and culture. Increasing numbers of South Asian women— first and second generation—are empowered by their own employment in Canada. Thus, middle- and upper-class South Asians often step outside the traditional bounds of patriarchal family relationships. However, those immigrant women who remain economically and socially dependent on their husbands, sons, or fathers may be more likely to experience enforced isolation and rigid control by her male sponsor (Shirwadkar, 2004). In short, 'the intersection of gender, ethnicity, culture, and immigration status increases the risk of experiencing adverse manifestations of patriarchy, particularly conflicts in spousal relationships' (Ahmad et al., 2004, p. 263). This vulnerability, in turn, has implications for violence and **abuse** against immigrant women, as we discuss in a later section.

Men, too, face challenges to the extent that their traditional presumption of authority and dominance is challenged by a host nation that has been transformed by successive waves of feminism. Moreover, the traditional role of economic provider is challenged in a context where immigrants are dramatically un- and underemployed. In 2001, for example, nearly 40 per cent of all recent male immigrants with a university degree were employed in jobs requiring less than a university degree; a further 25 per cent were in jobs requiring less than secondary school (Galarneau & Morisette, 2004). As with native-born males, this can be a serious blow to their masculinity and sense of self.

Discrimination and Victimization

As in other chapters in this volume, here we adopt a broad definition of **victimization**, one that goes beyond criminal incidents and includes experiences of **discrimination** in the workplace, in public places, and in accessing services. In this context, we know that South Asians have experienced many such problems. Other than anecdotally, however, we have little empirical data on the exact nature of such discrimination, the context in which it occurs, and consequences of discriminatory practices in South Asian communities. An analysis of aspects of the Ethnic Diversity Survey (EDS), a post-census survey conducted by Statistics Canada in 2002, however, allows us to gain a very basic insight into the level of reported discrimination experienced by South Asians, as well as into reported criminal victimization. Table 9.1 compares the experiences of non–South Asians (all those in the survey data who self-identified as having an ethnic identity other than South Asian, but with those identifying as 'Canadian' or 'French-Canadian' or with some province or territory removed from the analysis) with those of South Asians (those who explicitly reported their ethnic identity as either 'East Indian' or 'Other South Asian').

Table 9.1 Percentage of South Asians and Non-South Asians in Canada Reporting Having Experienced Discrimination and Having Crimes Committed Against Them, in Past Five Years, 2002 Data

Experienced Discrimination in Canada in Past Five Years	Yes	No
South Asians	33.3	66.7
Non-South Asians	18.9	81.1
Experienced Crimes Committed Against Them in Canada in Past Five Years		
South Asians	9.4	90.6
Non-South Asians	14.1	85.9

Note: These data should be used with caution, as Statistics Canada reports the coefficient of variation to be high.

The data in Table 9.1 suggest that about one-third of those self-identifying as South Asian had experienced some kind of discrimination in the five years prior to the year the survey was conducted, compared to approximately one-fifth of non–South Asians. On the other hand, fewer South Asians (about 1 in 10) than non–South Asians (1 in 7) reported being the victim of some kind of crime in the same time frame.

In Table 9.2, we once again draw upon the EDS data to gain some basic understanding of where discrimination against South Asians is occurring. As we can see from this table, of those South Asians reporting that they had experienced discrimination in the past five years in Canada, the majority had encountered discrimination on the street or in stores, banks, or restaurants. Other than this very basic data, we have virtually no understanding of the details of these kinds of discriminatory experiences.

As with other groups discussed in this volume, the paucity of data on South Asian experiences of victimization is due to the fact that, with the exception of Aboriginals, Canada collects virtually no criminal justice data on racialized groups (Sprott & Doob, 2009; Roberts, 2002; Wortley, chap. 8, this volume). One exception is data collected in 2006 from the Hate Crime Supplemental Survey, which relies on police reports of **hate crimes** across the country. According to this survey, 13 per cent of the 502 reported incidents of hate crime in Canada in 2006 targeted South Asians (Dauvergne, Scrim, & Brennan, 2008). The same study also highlighted the fact that of all the hate

Table 9.2 Places or Situations in which South Asians Experienced Discrimination, 2002 (%)

On the street	36
At a store, bank, or restaurant	36
Police or courts	17
Schools or classes	9
Applying for a job or promotion	8
Social situation	0.1
Government or public institution	5
Other	3

Note: These data should be used with caution, as Statistics Canada reports the coefficient of variation to be high.

crimes committed against South Asians, 38 per cent were violent incidents, while 55 per cent and approximately 8 per cent involved property and 'other' crimes respectively. Like many other racialized communities, South Asians have been caught up in the post-9/11 backlash against those *perceived to be* Muslim or Arab. Consequently, there was an identifiable spike of bias-motivated violence against South Asians. For example, in 2002, a survey of Canadian Muslims—many of whom are South Asian, as noted previously—by the Canadian Council on American-Islamic Relations (CAIR-CAN, 2004) found that 56 per cent of respondents had experienced at least one anti-Muslim incident in the 12 months since 9/11. Thirty-three per cent experienced verbal abuse; 18 per cent, racial profiling; and 16 per cent, workplace discrimination. Denise Helly (2004) cites a 2002 CAIR-CAN study finding that 60 per cent of the people of Muslim heritage surveyed reported that 'they experienced bias or discrimination since the 9/11 terrorist attacks', with a third saying their lives had worsened since 9/11 and that they were concerned about their own and their families' safety. The Canadian Islamic Congress (CIC, 2003) noted a 1,600 per cent increase in the annual incidence of anti-Muslim hate crime reported to them in 2002, albeit from a low base of 11 cases in the year prior to 9/11. The CIC, for one, warned of the likelihood of more backlash violence following the arrest of 17 young men for their roles in a plotted terrorist attack in Toronto in June 2006, and indeed, within a day of the arrests, a major Toronto mosque was vandalized.

While we know almost nothing about the victimization of South Asian men, a handful of studies that rely on official statistics partially illuminate the issue of violence against South Asian women in Canada. One of the main problems with these data, however, is that South Asian women are 'hidden' in the category of 'visible minorities'. Johnson (2006, p. 41) for example found that 'visible minority women report lower five-year rates of spousal violence than other women: 4 per cent compared with 8 per cent.' Another study (Smith, 2004) found that 13 per cent of *immigrant and visible-minority* women who reported being physically abused also reported that they received physical injuries as a result of that abuse.

Although we should be cautious about generalizing to Canada the results of studies conducted in other countries, a considerable body of work on violence against South Asian women has been generated in the United States. The general conclusions of these studies are that violence against South Asian women is at least as prevalent as violence against women in mainstream communities and that the nature of the violence against this group is in many ways different from that experienced by mainstream women (Huisman, 1996; Abraham, 1999; Raj & Silverman, 2002).

Thus, there is little to be gleaned on the specificities of violence against South Asian women from the available Canadian data, and only a handful of qualitative studies provide partial information specific to this group. According to Husaini's (2001) study of South Asian women living in Alberta whose partners had sponsored them to come to Canada, not only were many such women physically abused, but they were also economically and psychologically controlled by their husband, through, for example, threats to have them deported if they did not comply with his wishes or by isolating them from the broader cultural community. Similarly, Merali's (2009) examination of the lives of 10 South Asian sponsored women living in Canada reveals that among the non-English-language-proficient South Asian women in her sample, all reported experiencing basic violations of their human rights (severe physical battering; denial of basic subsistence items such as food and clothing; denial of access to opportunities for employment, education, and transportation; and isolation from their cultural and host communities).

Qualitative studies similar to the ones described above point to the unique difficulties encountered by South Asian (and other racialized) women who are victimized by abuse. For instance, many of these women face major obstacles should they try to escape an abusive relationship, such as language barriers, lack of financial resources, and cultural and religious beliefs that perpetuate and often legitimize abuse (Shirwadkar, 2004; Sheehan, Javier, & Thanjan, 2000). Other studies suggest that a considerable degree of stigma is associated with reporting abuse or even talking about it with friends or others in the social support system, and that service providers need to develop greater cultural competence (Preisser, 1999). In order to generate policies and programs tailored to the unique needs of South Asian women, further research is needed to help us better understand the differences and similarities between the abuse experienced by South Asian women and that experienced by their non-South Asian counterparts (DasGupta, 2000; Yoshioka et al., 2003).

Offending

As with victimization, there is very little data available on South Asians as criminal offenders. Roberts (2002) points out that the only area in which racial statistics in the criminal justice system are gathered is in the federal corrections system (see the debate on this issue in *The Canadian Journal of Criminology*, vol. 36, no. 2 [1994]). The Commission on Systemic Racism in the Ontario Criminal Justice System (Gittens et al., 1995) found that 'East Indian' inmates made up just 1.6 per cent of the total adult admissions to Ontario prisons in 1992/93. The only other research report we were able to find that reports data on incarcerated South Asians states that, in November 2002, of the 12,414 incarcerated offenders for whom race data were available, 50 were identified as 'South Asian' and another 27 were identified as 'East Indian', for a total of 77, or less than 1 per cent of incarcerated adults (Trevethan & Rastin, 2004). As noted earlier, there are nearly one million South Asians in Canada, and thus, unlike Aboriginals and blacks, who are over-represented in the criminal justice system, South Asians are under-represented. There is also some data on the ethnic makeup of youth gangs in Canada. The 2002 Canadian Police Survey on Youth Gangs estimates that East Indian/Pakistani youth gangs accounted for 14 per cent of all youth gangs in Canada.

It is well known that crime is not caused by race. However, crime is correlated with a range of social pathologies, such as unemployment, poverty, and low educational attainment, many of which are experienced disproportionately by racialized minorities. As mentioned earlier in this chapter, South Asians are the fastest-growing group of immigrants in Canada. In a study of ethno-racial groups in Toronto (where many South Asians settle), Ornstein (2006) shows that 20.5 per cent of all South Asians were living under the poverty line in 2000. As well, in 1996, 15 per cent of South Asians in Canada were unemployed (Statistics Canada 2001). According to Ornstein's (2006, p. 52) analysis, while the labour force characteristics of South Asian men are close to general population averages, those of South Asian women are more varied, with Bangladeshi and Pakistani women having 'very low rates of labour force participation, below 40 percent, very high unemployment, over 20 percent, and very high rates of part-time work, 36.3 percent for Pakistani and 43.3 percent for Bangladeshi women.'

From these data we can cautiously infer that some subgroups of South Asians may be at more risk of victimization or offending than others because they live in relatively high-risk circumstances. Given that poverty, low employment levels, and other related sociological factors are related to crime, and in the context of rapid growth in the urban South Asian population, there is a possibility that we will see higher levels of victimization or offending in this group in the future. There is some international evidence that may give us pause for reflection in this regard. In the United Kingdom, a nation that has had a very long history of discrimination against South Asian peoples, this group made up just 2 per cent of the incarcerated male population between the ages of 15 and 64 (Goodey, 2001). However, in their study of self-reported offences by British youth, Graham and Bowling (1995) found that 30 per cent of Indian, 28 per cent of Pakistani, and 13 per cent of Bangladeshi youth—males and females—reported committing a criminal offence, compared to 33 per cent of white and 43 per cent of African Caribbean youth. Thus, as Goodey (2001, p. 433) points out: 'Graham and Bowling's research, as with official statistics, points to the need to de-homogenize the category "Asian" and to recognize the diversity in offending rates between, and also within, different Asian categories.'

On the other hand, some research suggests that young people who are firmly attached to their community's cultural or religious values are less likely to engage in delinquent behaviour because those values shield them from other risk factors for deviance (Khondaker, 2007). Again, more research is needed to help us understand the dynamics of risk and protective factors in this community.

Services by and for South Asians

Clearly, there is a need for a better understanding of the nature of the South Asian diaspora in Canada with respect to cultural, religious, and other differences, in relation both to victimization and offending and to the nature of the services these groups may need. Fortunately, it is increasingly the case that the particular needs of South Asian communities, victims, and offenders are being recognized in the context of criminal and social justice concerns. Such recognition, however, is complicated by the distrust of criminal justice agents on the part of many South Asians. One of the contributing factors here is the South Asians' traditional reliance on the private resolution of conflicts, which excludes police involvement. In addition, there is often a great fear of authority figures, especially among recent immigrants from autocratic or wartorn countries. We must also recognize the very real fear, on the part of victims, of retaliation should they point accusing fingers at their offenders.

Some efforts have been made by law enforcement agencies to overcome the barriers between South Asian communities and police departments. Cultural awareness training has been implemented as a means of improving **police** officers' understanding and treatment of South Asians in Canada. Interpreters have been hired where numbers warrant, and community policing initiatives have been implemented as a means of integrating police and public. One of the greatest disappointments in police–South Asian relations has been in the area of representation in police departments. South Asians are dramatically under-represented among police officers, even in communities where Asians make up a substantial proportion of the population. For example, queries to Winnipeg and Vancouver police departments revealed that South Asians and East Indians accounted for only 16 of 1,382 and 72 of 1,344 sworn officers respectively.

Nonetheless, some police departments across the country are making admirable efforts to enhance the accessibility and civility of their personnel. The Toronto Police Service, for example, has a standing South Asian/West Asian Community Consultative Committee. This is one of seven such committees whose mandate is to work together in partnership with identified community representatives in identifying, prioritizing, and problem-solving policing issues by

- being proactive in community relations, crime prevention, education, mobilization, and communication initiatives;
- acting as a resource to the police and the community; and
- developing a strategic long-term vision through building knowledge, education, tolerance, and understanding. (www.torontopolice.on.ca/communitymobilization/ccc.php)

While such efforts represent valuable innovations, they demand long-term commitment to ensure that they do not become merely token initiatives meant to quell public complaint.

To represent and protect South Asian interests, South Asian communities across the nation have begun to establish their own advocacy and action groups as supplements—or, more often, alternatives—to criminal justice agencies. Perhaps buoyed by the gains of other civil rights movements, as well as by the findings of recent civil rights commissions, South Asians have mobilized their growing numerical strength to gain political and social power. **Settlement centres** like those noted by Ismaili in chapter 6 are one such example. Moreover, the South Asian community has established several **legal clinics** geared toward assisting and advocating for the community. The South Asian Legal Clinic of Ontario, for example, was established in Toronto in 1997 with the mandate to 'provide access to justice for low-income South Asians in the Greater Toronto Area. As a specialty clinic funded by Legal Aid Ontario, SALCO provides advice, brief services, and legal representation in various areas of poverty law' (www.salc.on.ca/SALCO%20Website/Home%20SALCO.htm).

There are also a number of umbrella or pan-ethnic organizations that serve the South Asian community in myriad ways. Among these is the Council of Agencies Serving South Asians, which is a 'social justice umbrella organization working with Ontario's diverse South Asian communities.' Its mission statement reads as follows:

> To facilitate the economic, social, political and cultural empowerment of South Asians by serving as a resource for information, research, mobilization, coordination and leadership on social justice issues affecting our communities.
> Create social change by building alliances and working collaboratively with those who share a vision of empowering all communities to participate in defining Canada's future. (www.cassaonline.com)

An example of the council's programming is Trailblazers United: A South Asian Youth Leadership Series, which fosters engagement and leadership—among youth—around issues of bias and violence.

In addition, a number of advocacy and support organizations address the needs of particular South Asian communities. The Pakistani Canadian Cultural Association in British Columbia, for example, is

> a not-for-profit society that works in partnership with community organizations, non-government organizations, the private sector and all levels of government to develop sustainable legacies in inter cultural and social issues. Now actively assisting communities to discover and create unique and inclusive social and economic bridge, especially for new immigrants. (http://pccabc.ca)

The Canadian Sikh Organization seeks to

> promote and strengthen multiculturalism in Canada by encouraging and providing the required platform and resources for active participation in social and political activities that support equality and acceptance irrespective of culture, religion, gender, caste, creed, and race. The Canadian Sikh Association provides assistance to Sikhs and other community groups who have been discriminated against or subject to bias based upon their religious beliefs or Sikh identity. (www.canadiansikhassociation.com)

Significantly, although woman abuse is prevalent in all socio-demographic groups, the unique aspects of South Asian women's experiences—language barriers, labour force exclusion, and their distinctive cultural and religious belief systems—suggest that services for such women should be adapted to their needs. To this end, South Asian women must be educated about the nature of Canadian laws regarding woman abuse and encouraged to turn to agencies for help when they experience abuse. In addition, service agencies must become culturally competent in terms of learning about South Asian culture, customs, and religions, and food and facilities should be responsive to South Asian cultural and religious traditions. In the United States, in response to the unique problems of battered South Asian women, several organizations (e.g., Manavi, Sakhi, and Apna Ghar) have been created to meet these women's needs (Goel, 2005). Manavi was the first agency to specifically address these unmet needs. Its founders recognized that South Asian women facing abuse were unable to access services related to violence prevention from mainstream organizations in the United States owing to cultural, language, and immigration barriers, among others. Consequently,

> as a direct service provider, a social change agent within the South Asian community, and a cultural competency educator and diversity trainer in the mainstream movement to end violence against women in the U.S., Manavi simultaneously addresses both the immediate needs of women facing abuse and the long-term vision of establishing peaceful communities free from gender-based violence. (www.manavi.org)

In Canada, most urban areas have begun to establish South Asian women's centres. Montreal's South Asian Women's Community Centre offers a broad array of services, including language classes, interpretation, and referrals, as well as programs, support systems, and counselling services specifically for South Asian women experiencing family and domestic violence. Cities such as Toronto, Edmonton, Calgary, and Vancouver boast similar resources.

One could go on endlessly. There are literally hundreds of local, regional, and national organizations committed to enhancing the place and power of South Asians in Canada. Given the historical and systemic nature of violence and discrimination against this community, these organizations have correctly recognized that meaningful and lasting change requires activity on the part of the many South Asian communities—singly and collectively.

Summary

This chapter provides an overview of the historical and contemporary migration patterns and experiences of those dubbed 'South-Asian' in Canada. It has also attempted to shed some light on their experiences of victimization and the extent to which members of this diverse group offend. It was noted early in the chapter that the 'South Asian' moniker refers less to geographical point of origin than to cultural and religious identity. In this regard, South Asians are very diverse. They are also one of the fastest-growing immigrant groups in Canada, a trend that should spur further research into the nature of their encounters with social services (including the criminal justice system), their needs, and the contours of their interactions with the broader Canadian social milieu.

The little data we have, while outdated and rudimentary, does suggest that South Asians are under-represented with respect to offending. More reliable evidence, however, suggests that victimization may be another matter. While there is little information on the victimization of South Asian men and boys, there is evidence that the victimization of women and girls may be as prevalent as it is for their non-South Asian counterparts. Moreover, unique cultural and religious differences probably condition these experiences, and women's attempts to escape abusive relationships must be addressed in relation to these differences and the special needs attending them.

Key Terms

abuse	family reunification	Komagata Maru	settlement centres
acculturation	gender-role	legal clinic	Sikh
anti-Asian sentiment	conformity	Mackenzie King	spousal migration
continuous passage	hate crime	Muslim	victimization
diaspora	Hindu	police	
discrimination	immigration	second generation	

Questions for Critical Thought

1. Canada does not collect data on the race of offenders. What are some arguments both for and against collecting such data?

2. Outline some key unique aspects of South Asian culture and religion that might be related to criminal offending and victimization.

3. What is the role of work and employment in relation to South Asian people's historical and contemporary experiences in Canada?

Additional Readings

Khondaker, M. I. (2007). Juvenile deviant behavior in an immigrant Bangladeshi community: Exploring the nature and contributing factors. *International Journal of Criminal Justice Sciences, 2*(1).

Samuel, E. (2009). Acculturative stress: South Asian Immigrant Women's experiences in Canada's Atlantic provinces. *Journal of Immigrant & Refugee Studies, 7*(1), 16–34.

Statistics Canada. (2007). The South Asian community in Canada. Ottawa: Statistics Canada. www.statcan.gc.ca/pub/89-621-x/89-621-x2007006-eng.htm

Tran, K., Kaddatz, J., & Allard, P. (2005, autumn). South Asians in Canada: Unity through diversity. *Canadian Social Trends*. Ottawa: Statistics Canada. Catalogue no. 11-008.

Websites of Interest

Council of Agencies Serving South Asians: www.cassaonline.com/index3

South Asian Legal Clinic of Ontario: www.salc.on.ca/SALCO%20Website/Home%20SALCO.htm

South Asian Women's NETwork: www.sawnet.org

References

Abouguendia, M., & Noels, K. (2001). General and acculturation-related daily hassles and psychological adjustment in first- and second-generation South Asian immigrants to Canada. *International Journal of Psychology, 36*(3), 163–173.

Abraham, M. (1999). Sexual abuse in South Asian immigrant marriages. *Violence against Women, 5*(6), 591–618.

Ahmad, F., Riaz, S., Barata, P., & Stewart, D. (2004). Patriarchal beliefs and perceptions of abuse among South Asian immigrant women. *Violence against Women, 10*, 262–282.

Aspinall, P. (2003). Who is Asian? A category that remains contested in population and health research. *Journal of Public Health Medicine, 25*(2): 91–97.

Banerji, A. (2006). Experiences of South Asian diaspora. *Borders, 3*(2). http://hemi.nyu.edu/journal/3.2/eng/en32_pg_banerji.html

Canadian Council on American-Islamic Relations—Canada. (2004). *Today's media: Covering Islam and Canadian Muslims.* Submission to Standing Committee on Transport and Communications, February 26. www.caircan.ca/downloads/sctc-26022004.pdf

Canadian Islamic Congress. (2003). *Islamic Congress finds most police departments have incomplete data on rising tide of hate-motivated crimes.* www.canadianislamiccongress.com/mc/media_communique.php?id=305

Chard, J., & Renaud, V. (1999, Autumn). Visible minorities in Toronto, Vancouver and Montreal. *Canadian Social Trends.* Ottawa: Statistics Canada. Catalogue no. 11–008.

Choudry, U. (2001). Uprooting and resettlement experiences of South Asian immigrant women. *Western Journal of Nursing Research, 23*(4), 376–393.

Dasgupta, S. D. (2000). Charting the course: An overview of domestic violence in the South Asian community in the United States. *Journal of Social Distress and the Homeless, 9*(3), 173–185.

Dauvergne, M., Scrim, K., & Brennan, S. (2008). *Hate crime in Canada: 2006.* Ottawa: Statistics Canada, Canadian Centre for Justice Statistics. Catalogue no. 85F0033M—no. 17.

Galarneau, D., & Morisette, R. (2004, June). Immigrants: Settling for less? *Perspectives on Labour and Income, 5*(6). Ottawa: Statistics Canada. Catalogue no. 75-001-XIE.

Gittens, M., Cole, D., Williams, T., Sri Skanda Rajah, S.G., Tam, M., & Ratushny, E. (1995). *Commission on systemic racism in the Ontario criminal justice system (full report).* Toronto: Queen's Printer for Ontario.

Goel, R. (2005). Sita's trousseau: Restorative justice, domestic violence, and South Asian culture. *Violence against Women, 11*(5), 639–665.

Goodey, J. (2001). The criminalization of British Asian youth: Research from Bradford and Sheffield. *Journal of Youth Studies, 4*(4), 429–450.

Graham, J., & Bowling, B. (1995). *Young people and crime.* London: Home Office.

Helly, D. (2004). Are Muslims discriminated against in Canada since September 2001? *Journal of Canadian Ethnic Studies, 36*(1), 24–47.

Huisman, K. A. (1996). Wife battering in Asian American communities: Identifying the service needs of an overlooked segment of the U.S. Population. *Violence against Women, 2*(3), 260–283.

Husaini, Z. (2001). *Cultural dilemma and a plea for justice: Voices of Canadian ethnic women.* Edmonton: Intercultural Action Committee for the Advancement of Women.

Johnson, H. (2006). *Measuring violence against women: Statistical trends, 2006.* Ottawa: Minister of Industry, Statistics Canada. Catalogue no. 85-570-XIE.

Khondaker, M. I. (2007). Juvenile deviant behavior in an immigrant Bangladeshi community: Exploring the nature and contributing factors. *International Journal of Criminal Justice Sciences, 2*(1).

Merali, N. (2009). Experiences of South Asian brides entering Canada after recent changes to family sponsorship policies. *Violence against Women, 15*(3), 321–339.

Model, S., & Lin, L. (2002). The cost of not being Christian: Hindus, Sikhs and Muslims in Britain and Canada. *International Migration Review, 36*(4): 1061–1092.

Ornstein, M. (2006). Ethno-racial groups in Toronto, 1971–2001: a demographic and socio-economic profile. Study prepared for Institute for Social Research, York University, Toronto.

Preisser, A. B. (1999). Domestic violence in South Asian communities in America: Advocacy and intervention. *Violence against Women, 5*(6), 684–699.

Raj, A., & Silverman, J. G. (2002). Intimate partner violence against South Asian women in greater Boston. *Journal of American Medical Women's Association, 57*(2), 111–114.

Reitz, J., Banerjee, R., Phan, M., & Thompson, J. (2009). *Race, religion, and the social integration of new immigrant minorities in Canada*. Unpublished manuscript, University of Toronto.

Roberts, J. (2002). Racism and the collection of statistics relating to race and ethnicity. In W. Chan & K. Mirchandani (Eds), *Crimes of colour: Racialization and the criminal justice system in Canada* (pp. 101–112). Peterborough, ON: Broadview Press.

Samuel, E. (2009). Acculturative stress: South Asian immigrant women's experiences in Canada's Atlantic provinces. *Journal of Immigrant & Refugee Studies, 7*(1), 16–34.

Shariff, F. (2008). Straddling the cultural divide: Second-generation South Asian identity and the namesake. *Changing English, 15,* 4, 457–466.

Sheehan, H. E., Javier, R. A., & Thanjan, T. (2000). Introduction to the special issue on domestic violence and the South Asian community. *Journal of Social Distress and the Homeless, 9*(3), 167–171.

Shirwadkar, S. (2004). Canadian domestic violence policy and Indian immigrant women. *Violence against Women, 10*(8), 860–879.

Smith, E. (2004). *Nowhere to turn? Responding to partner violence against immigrant and visible minority women.* Ottawa: Canadian Council on Social Development.

Sprott, J. B., & Doob, A. (2009). *Justice for girls? Stability and change in the youth justice systems of the United States and Canada.* Chicago: University of Chicago Press.

Statistics Canada. (2001). *Visible minorities in Canada.* Canadian Centre for Justice Statistics Profile Series. Ottawa: Statistics Canada. Catalogue no. 85F0033MIE.

Statistics Canada. (2007). *The South Asian Community in Canada.* Ottawa: Statistics Canada. www.statcan.gc.ca/pub/89-621-x/89-621-x2007006-eng.htm

Talbani, A., & Hasanali, P. (2000). Adolescent females between tradition and modernity: Gender role socialization in South Asian immigrant culture. *Journal of Adolescence, 23,* 615–627.

Tran, K., Kaddatz, J., & Allard, P. (2005, Autumn). South Asians in Canada: Unity through diversity. *Canadian Social Trends.* Ottawa: Statistics Canada. Catalogue No. 11–008.

Trevethan, S., & Rastin, C. (2004, June). *A profile of visible minority offenders in the federal Canadian correctional system.* Ottawa: Research Branch, Correctional Service of Canada.

Yoshioka, M. R., Gilbert, L., El-Bassel, N., & Baig-Amin, M. (2003). Social support and disclosure of abuse: Comparing South Asian, African American, and Hispanic battered women. *Journal of Family Violence, 18*(3), 171–180.

10 | Justice and Islam in Canada

Denise Helly[1]

In 1997 the British Runnymede Trust think-tank defined **Islamophobia** as the 'dread or hatred of Islam and therefore the fear and dislike of all Muslims', stating that it also refers to the practice of discriminating against Muslims by excluding them from economic, social, and public life. Are Muslim Canadians experiencing victimization and discrimination as is clearly happening in Europe, where the term 'Islamophobia' is commonly used? Before answering this question, we will describe immigration from Muslim countries into Canada starting in the late nineteenth century and then explicate the social status of Muslims in Canada—that is, their economic perform- ance in the labour market compared to that of other immigrants, the forms of ethnic and religious discrimination they eventually suffered, their particular treatment by the state after September 2001, and the way they are starting to build community institutions.

In Canada, there were 253,260 Muslims in 1991[2] and 579,600 in 2001—that is, in 2001 they made up 2 per cent of the total Canadian population, compared with 43 per cent Catholics, 29 per cent Protestants, and 16 per cent with no religious affiliation. Islam is the fastest-growing religion in Canada; there could be 1.1 million Muslims in 2011 and 1.4 million in 2017 (Jedwab, 2005). In 2002, 40 per cent of Canadians were not very religious, 31 per cent quite religious, and 29 per cent very religious, and from 1982 to 2001 religious beliefs and religious practices were stronger among immigrants. Fifty per cent of Asian immigrants attended a place of worship regu- larly, compared with 20 per cent of European immigrants and 31 per cent of native- born Canadians. But immigrants from the Middle East and western Asia, mostly Muslims, did not show a high level of religiousness: 33 per cent, compared with 65 per cent of immigrants from South Asia and 56 per cent of those from Southeast Asia (Clark & Schellenberg, 2006).

In 2001, 56 per cent of Muslim Canadians (352,000) were living in Ontario, where there were about 100 places of worship (Hamdani, 2002). For all religions combined, 102,155 people identified themselves as Arab[3] (38,440 of whom identified themselves as Lebanese and 14,420 as Egyptian), 38,945 as Pakistani, 43,095 as Iranian, 15,040 as Afghan, 26,850 as Somali, and 9,335 as Turkish.[4] Quebec was home to 17 per cent of Muslim Canadians, or 108,000 people, of whom 100,180 identified themselves as Arab (35,750 as Lebanese, 10,165 as Algerian, 11,470 as Moroccan, 8,655 as Egyptian, 5,940 as Syrian, 7,545 as Iranian, and 6,105 as Pakistani). There were then about 30 Muslim places of worship in Quebec. There were also 56,000 Muslims in British Columbia and 49,000 in Alberta.

History

Emigration from the Arab World and Iran

The first wave of emigrants from Islamic countries came from regions in **Greater Syria** (Syria, Palestine, Lebanon) between 1882 and 1913. They included people of Orthodox or Catholic faith (Melkites, Maronites) fleeing a precarious political and economic future in these areas of the Ottoman Empire. Their main destination was Montreal, then Canada's largest city. This population grew slowly: 2,000 in 1901, 6,500 in 1911, 8,300 in 1921, 10,800 in 1931, and 11,900 in 1941, two-thirds of whom were born in Canada (Abu-Laban, 1980; Haddad, 1983). Few of these immigrants were Muslims: 47 in 1901 (often Druzes from Syria), 797 in 1911, 478 in 1921, 645 in 1931, and 1,800 in 1951 (Hamdani, 1983–1984; Helly, 2004a).

The year 1946 was marked by a **liberalization of immigration**, and from 1946 to 1975, a large migration flow occurred, one-third (37 per cent) of which was from Egypt, another third (34 per cent) from Lebanon, and 15 per cent from Morocco. In 1951, 12,300 Arabs had settled mainly in Ontario; they were Muslims, Christians, or Jews (from Morocco). Restrictions on immigration from the countries of the south were subsequently eliminated, and the annual average of Arab immigrants increased: 181 from 1882 to 1961, 2,900 from 1962 to 1970, and 4,000 from 1971 to 1980. In 1981, 30 per cent of Arab immigrants were Muslims, with Christians from Lebanon and Egypt still representing a majority of this flow, which settled primarily in Ontario (Statistics Canada, 2003). In 1971, of the 28,900 emigrants from Arab countries (excluding Jews from the Maghreb), 16,800 lived in Ontario, 7,500 in Quebec, and 2,000 in Alberta. The numbers of Egyptian Christians arriving then declined as immigration from Lebanon, both Christian and Muslim, increased. When civil war broke out in Lebanon in 1975, more Shiites arrived, coming not only from Lebanon but also from Iraq, Iran, and Syria.

Emigration from Iraq began in 1979 when Saddam Hussein took power. From 1979 to 1992, 6,500 Iraqi emigrants arrived in Canada—Kurds, Assyrians, Chaldeans, and Arabs (Shiites), many of them victims of political persecution. In 1991, 4,800 persons of Iraqi origin were living in Canada, and in 2001, 14,100; their number is currently estimated at 25,000. Two-thirds live in Ontario, especially Toronto, and one-third in Montreal.

Palestinians arrived in Canada in the 1950s, but there is no accurate estimate in their regard until 1981. From 1981 to 1990, of the 21,600 emigrants from Saudi Arabia (7,000), Kuwait (6,600), and the United Arab Emirates (6,000), most were Palestinian, and their numbers grew following their expulsion from the oil monarchies after the Gulf War. Immigrants from Jordan and a small portion of those from Lebanon were Palestinian. In 1991, 4,050 persons were of Palestinian origin, and in 2001, 9,200. But in 1997, an estimated 30,000 Palestinians arrived, including 15,000 in Ontario and 10,000 in Quebec (Shuraydi, 1997b), with some people claiming to be Arab rather than Palestinian. Another wave began after the Algerian civil war: during the 1990s, some 10,000 Algerians came to Canada, mostly to Quebec.

During the 1990s, the average annual migration flow from Arab countries was 24,600 people (8,000 during the 1980s), most of whom were Muslim. Half settled in Quebec (Montreal) and over a third (37 per cent) in Ontario (Toronto, Ottawa, Hamilton, London, Windsor). In 1991, 204,000 permanent residents and 16,500 temporary residents identified themselves as Arabs. In 2001, 238,600 people said that they were Arab (a 20 per cent increase), and of the immigrants of all the religions combined, the Lebanese were still the most numerous (93,900).

The persons of **Arab** origin presented some distinctive traits. In 1991, 75 per cent of the Arabs in Canada were immigrants, compared with 16 per cent of all Canadians. They were younger than other Canadians: 45 per cent of the immigrants from 1981 to 1992 were under 25 years of age and 15 per cent were over 45 years of age. Most were men (127 men/100 women), and most were skilled workers, even among the refugees. Of the 24,800 refugees who, from 1983 to 1992, fled Somalia (9,500 in 1989), Lebanon (5,850), and Iraq (5,000), 16 per cent said, when admitted to Canada, that they were professionals, engineers, or teachers; 9 per cent that they were managers and administrators; and 15 per cent that they were skilled workers. This migration flow also included investors. Three immigration categories allow applicants to gain residence in Canada subject to the depositing of a quarter to a half of a million dollars in a Canadian bank or to the making of a commitment to start up a company offering two jobs. Of the 100,000 emigrants from Arab countries from 1983 to 1992, more than 10 per cent were in these categories; they came from Lebanon, Kuwait, Saudi Arabia, and the United Arab Emirates.

After Iran's Islamic revolution in 1979 and Iraq's attack on Iran in 1981, Iranian emigration increased. It included opponents of the Islamic revolution, well-off individuals, some of whom were connected with the Shah's regime, and members of national, ethnic, or religious minorities (Kurds, Jews, Zoroastrians, Armenians, Baha'is). About 5,000 Iranians came to Canada from 1977 to 1982 and 23,000 from 1982 to 1991. In 1991, Canada's Iranian population numbered 43,000 persons, 8,000 of whom were born in Canada. They lived in Ontario (24,800), British Columbia (7,800), Quebec (6,750), and Alberta (2,100) (Moallem, 1997). In 2001, 73,500 people claimed to be of Iranian origin.

Emigration from Pakistan

There were 5,800 Muslims in Canada in 1961, 33,430 in 1971, and 98,165 in 1981 (Hamdani, 1983–84), most of whom were from the Arab world. Since the beginning of the twentieth century, some 200 Pakistanis had settled in Alberta, where they established Canada's first Muslim place of worship (in Edmonton in 1938). During the 1950s, a flow began to arrive from South Asia, and after the passage of the 1967 Immigration Act, students and skilled workers, followed by their families, came to Canada, especially Montreal. In 1973, 9,709 Pakistanis lived in Canada (Awan, 1976).

In 1972, legislation was enacted that closed Great Britain to nationals from the Indian subcontinent. In the years following, the economic and political situation deteriorated in **Pakistan** (instability, repression, inter-ethnic conflict, government corruption, war in Afghanistan). Migration to North America and to the Gulf States increased. In Canada, this Pakistani immigration was accompanied by racist demonstrations that betrayed Canada's reaction to the new face of immigration since 1967 that whites, both immigrant and native-born, were little prepared to accept.

By the mid-1980s, some 50,000 Pakistani immigrants were in Canada. With the 1991 Gulf War leading to an exodus of Pakistani emigrants from that region, members of the liberal professions and well-off individuals settled in Canada as investors or entrepreneurs. In 1991, people of Pakistani origin numbered 43,150 in Canada, including 25,200 who had been born in Pakistan. This figure does not include the 27,300 people claiming Punjabi origin, some of whom were Pakistani nationals. In 1997 (Israël, 1997), the number of Pakistani immigrants was estimated at more than 100,000, of whom 50 per cent lived in Toronto and 20 per cent in Montreal. In 2001, 54,565 people claimed Pakistani origin and 28,980 Punjabi origin.

Aside from immigrants from the Arab world, Iran, and Pakistan, it is important to mention the arrival of other Muslim groups. After anti-Asian riots in Kenya, Uganda, and Tanzania between 1970 and 1973 and the expulsion of 'Asians' from Uganda by the dictator Idi Amin Dada, Canada accepted approximately 50,000 of the latter as refugees; 15,000 were Ismaili, the descendants of an Indo-Pakistani population established by the British colonial administration in East Africa, for which the current number is estimated to be 70,000. It is also important to mention the arrival of Turks (Bilg, 2000), Bosnians, Albanians, Kosovars (5,000 came in 1999), Afghans, and Somalis, all fleeing wars in their respective countries. Canada also accepted Muslims from other sub-Saharan African countries. In 2001, 13,100 identified themselves as Ethiopians, 6,265 as Erythraeans, and 6,570 as Nigerians.

Community Building

In contrast to other minorities, which have certainly been established in Canada for a longer period of time—Jews, Ukrainians, Italians, Greeks, Chinese, Lebanese Christians—the Muslim population in Canada has not shown any advanced form of community building. By community building, we mean the creation of cultural, social, religious, and recreational institutions, as well as employment and marriage networks. Community building can be seen as a negative process producing **social marginalization** or as a process that helps immigrants learn about their new society of residence, as well as help a minority to mobilize to protect its rights.

Certain factors account for the weakness and slowness of community building by Canada's Muslim population. This population includes a large proportion of newcomers. In 1991, 4 out of 5 Muslim immigrants had arrived after 1971, and in 2001, about 9 out of 10 were foreign-born. This means that the population's links with countries of origin are still quite strong (through the media, the Internet, political debates, family relations, etc.) and that its learning about local institutions, especially political ones, is still underway.

Other factors include substantial socio-economic divisions and difficulties in integrating into the **labour market**. The Muslim population includes professionals and people with considerable financial resources as well as refugees and immigrants who have problems finding jobs, given the labour market changes since the 1980s (see below). There are also religious and national divisions. Unlike the situation in most of the countries of origin and in the Muslim world in general, there are many Shiites in Canada; in Montreal, Lebanese, Iranian, and Iraqi Shiites account for 22 to 24 per cent of the Muslim population. Added to the divisions between Sunnis and Shiites are differences between religious schools and in interpretations of the obligations of Muslims who emigrated to the West. One finds traditionalists/conservatives; modernists who advocate Islam's adaptation to historical contexts and its privatization in secularized societies; Islamic feminists who point to the difference between Islam and patriarchy; progressives who emphasize Islam's universal values of equality, tolerance, and charity; and fundamentalists who are generally apolitical and defend a literal interpretation of the sacred texts. The Salafist movement, though not strongly established, does influence some prayer halls. As for the Wahhabi school, only a single mosque in Quebec officially terms itself as such (its building was financed by Saudi emigrants who left Canada), and in Ontario, the Islamic Society of North America (ISNA), an umbrella group of Muslim NGOs, is said to be linked to Wahhabism.

In terms of countries of origin, unlike the situation in Europe, the Muslim population in Canada is highly diversified. Some 80 per cent of Great Britain's Muslim population comes from Pakistan, India, and Bangladesh; in France, most Muslims are of Maghrebi origin; and in Germany, most are of Turkish origin. In Canada, non-religious NGOs are organized along ethnic lines. Sunni places of worship often bring together people of different origins, whereas Somalis, Afghans, Twelvers Shia Lebanese, Iraqis, and Iranians attend different places of worship. The same goes for Ismailis (Seveners Shia) and Sufis, who attend their own place of worship. In addition, the theological and political influence of the governments of the countries of origin remains relatively weak despite attempts to this effect (Saudi Arabia, Morocco). On the other hand, religious leaders are often trained in Muslim countries.

The final factor is Canadian government intervention. Given Muslims' weak collective capacity to fight the discrimination they may experience, one would have expected governmental interventions similar to those of the 1970s and 1980s **Multiculturalism** Program,[5] which targeted vulnerable immigrant groups. The objectives of multiculturalism, as reaffirmed by 1988 legislation, are twofold: (1) to increase the acceptance of cultural diversity on the part of all Canadians, especially by training staff in the public and para public sectors and by integrating members of visible minorities into these sectors; and (2) to strengthen mono- and multi-ethnic community organizations in order to help them contribute to immigrants' social integration (Helly, 2001, 2004b, 2004c, 2005b).

The Muslim migration flow accelerated in the late 1980s as politicians from the Reform Party and other parties (Liberal, Conservative) claimed that multiculturalism was encouraging **ghettoization**, strengthening communitarianism, stigmatizing non-European minorities, and fostering undue state interference in the cultural sphere. In this climate, the budget for interventions was reduced (Helly, 2004b, 2004c), and since 2001, federal authorities have not intervened as much as they could have to increase Canadians' literacy in religious matters and reduce hostility toward Muslims and other religious minorities. They have, however, made a few symbolic gestures toward recognizing Islam's legitimate presence in Canadian society: for example, in September 2001, the prime minister visited a mosque, and in 2007, Parliament proclaimed October as Islamic History Month Canada (IHMC), an educational project created by Muslims.

But the ruling Conservative Party chose to ignore the positive impacts of the multicul-turalism measures and the fact of their being supported by two-thirds of Canadians (Adams, 2009; Jedwab, 2008; Kymlicka, 2009). It extolled the anti-immigration and anti-multicultur-alism views of the former Reform Party and courted Indo-Canadians and Jews, but clearly not Muslims, given NGOs' positions, different from its own, on international, social, and environ-mental policies and civil liberties. Indicative of this climate were the minister of Citizenship and Immigration's openly hostile remarks to one Arab NGO's freedom of expression (the Canadian Arab Federation)[6] and the intimidation of the Social Sciences and Humanities Research Council in September 2009 regarding the funding of a conference that would supposedly be attended by opponents of Israel.

Not-very-advanced community building does not mean an absence of community NGOs among Muslims in Canada, but rather a fragmentation into a multitude of ethno-cultural and -religious NGOs with little means of intervention. Muslim organizations had existed during the 1930s and 1940s, and as of 1945, Arab NGOs that did not identify themselves as Muslims distrib-uted information on the situation in Palestine to the Canadian public and especially to federal politicians (Asal, 2008). In the 1960s and 1970s, despite a shortage of people able to act as imams, many places of worship were opened and NGOs and newspapers were established, the most important of which were in English, French, and Arabic in Quebec, and in English and Arabic in the other Canadian provinces. Then, with the influx of immigrants since the 1990s, local secular and religious NGOs that bring together people of a single national origin or of the same religious school have increased in number. They tend to include 100 or so individuals at most, have little staff, and are not very structured, all of which limits their opportunities to develop relations with government authorities and their ability to serve their potential clientele. Moreover, the lack of any institutional centrality does not allow them to curtail the expression of extremist groups.

Social, religious, ethnic, cultural, and national divisions reduce the capacity for community mobilization and hardly encourage more well-off members to fund the community sector, as some also keep their distance owing to the often negative image of Muslims in the Canadian public arena. As a consequence, there are few Muslim journalists and politicians—just four federal members of Parliament, including two Ismailis.

The disadvantaged situation of Muslims in Canada—a recently arrived population; frag-mentation along socio-economic, linguistic, cultural, and religious lines; vulnerability in terms of social acceptance; difficulty in creating a representative community sector that is active on the public scene—seems likely to remain, although several activities organized by coalitions of groups concerned with issues related to the Muslim population (e.g., the 2003 Ihya Foundation Toronto Muslim Summit) do hold out the potential for greater mobilization.

Why do we talk about the **social vulnerability** of Muslim Canadians? A group's social vulnerability is linked to an amalgamation of the traits and behaviours of some of its members with those of the entire group—an amalgamation that is equivalent to a denial of individuality. This takes a number of forms: negative stereotypes; distrust and rejection by segments of public opinion, the media, and public discourse; **physical victimization** (people and property); **denial of equal rights**; and **criminalization**.

Stereotypes, Rejection

Over the past 30 years, a series of events has propelled Muslims onto the international political and media scene: the 1975 Lebanese civil war, Iran's 1979 Islamic revolution, Israel's invasion of Lebanon in 1982, the 1987 Palestinian Intifada, the polemic on *The Satanic Verses* in 1988, the 1991 Gulf War, the Algerian civil war in the 1990s, the 1998 terrorist attacks in Kenya, the September 11, 2001, attacks in the United States, the war in Afghanistan in 2001, the second war in Iraq, the attacks in Madrid in 2004 and in London in 2005, the publication of cartoons of Mohammed in Denmark and France in 2005, the arrest of 18 terrorism suspects in Ontario in 2006,[7] and, currently, the military situation in Afghanistan and northwest Pakistan, not to mention the academic writing on the clash of civilizations (Huntington, 1996; Fukuyama, 1994, 1999; Helly, 2002).

These events have led to the dissemination of four main **negative stereotypes** of Islam in Western public opinion and their manipulation by politicians, intellectuals, journalists, and pressure groups: (1) Islam is an intolerant and even dangerous religion; (2) democracy and modernity are impossible in Islamic societies; (3) women's oppression is inevitable in Islam; and (4) immigrant Muslims are archaically religious and beset by the conflicts of their societies of origin (Helly, 2010b).

Canadians' Attitudes

Over the past 10 years or so, annual surveys have shown that Canadians 'do not feel comfortable' with people associated with Islamic culture. In the fall of 2001 (IPSOS-Reid), 82 per cent of Canadians feared that Arabs and Muslims would become the target of prejudice. Nevertheless, in July 2002, according to a CROP poll of people aged 16 to 35, 76 per cent of Quebec respondents and 55 per cent of other Canadian respondents felt that religions are sources of conflict between peoples, and 17 per cent of the former and 13 per cent of the latter felt that Islam fosters conflictive relations (*Le Devoir*, 22 July 2002). Moreover, in August 2002 (IPSOS-Reid), 45 per cent of Quebecers, 37 per cent of Albertans, 33 per cent of Ontarians, and 22 per cent of British Columbians agreed with this statement: 'The September 11 attacks made me more mistrustful of Arabs or Muslims coming from the Middle East.' By November 2002, a survey by *Maclean's* magazine, Global TV, and the *Ottawa Citizen* indicated that 44 per cent of Canadians wanted to see a reduction in immigration from Islamic countries (48 per cent in Quebec, 45 per cent in Ontario, 42 per cent in Saskatchewan and Manitoba, 43 per cent in the Maritimes, 39 per cent in British Columbia, and 35 per cent in Alberta) (Helly, 2004b). This trend continued in the following years. According to a Sun Media poll in December 2006–January 2007, 51 per cent of Canadians insisted that they were not racist at all, but 47 per cent confessed that they were, and while most Canadians polled held a high opinion of the Italian, Asian, Jewish, and black communities, only 53 per cent thought well of Arabs.

Moreover, Canadians have a more positive view of Christians and Jews than of Muslims. According to a July 2006 poll (Association of Canadian Studies), 24 per cent of respondents had a negative view of Muslims (compared with 10 per cent having a negative view of Christians and 9 per cent having a negative view of Jews). Two years later, another poll (Leger Marketing, September 2008) indicated that 36 per cent of Canadians had an unfavourable view of Muslims (increasing from 24 per cent in 2006 and 27 per cent in 2007). In April 2009, according to a Canada-wide poll (Angus Reid Strategies), 72 per cent of Canadians had a favourable opinion of Christianity, 57 per cent of Buddhism, 53 per cent of Judaism, 42 per cent of Hinduism, 30 per cent of Sikhism, and 28 per cent of Islam (17 per cent in Quebec) (Geddes, 2009).

We only have a few indications of the stereotypes disclosed in other areas. In Quebec, it is rare to find judges who show negative prejudices toward Muslim parties bringing family disputes into Quebec courts (Helly & Hardy, 2010). On the other hand, many Quebec and Ontario school texts still contain common stereotypes relating to the history of Islam (McAndrew, Oueslati, & Helly, 2007).

Media Coverage

Media coverage is a factor in the dissemination of negative stereotypes for two main reasons: (1) a mediocre analysis of socio-political contexts in foreign countries and (2) ignorance of the cultures and opinions of immigrants from those countries. The success of the CBC 'Muslim' sitcom, *Little Mosque on the Prairie*, is well known, but studies attest to an anti-immigrant bias in Canadian media: H. Bauder (2008), F. Henry and C. Tator (2002), K. Karim et al. (2007), Mahtani (2008a, 2009), T.Y. Ismael and J. Measor (2003) show how, during debates on immigration, the media convey anxiety-causing rather than informative discourses, creating 'collective anxiety' among Canadians. Immigrants are poorly or under-represented and are often demonized and criminalized—that is, they are presented as sources of problems and disturbing elements (Karim, 2000; Mahtani, 2008a). Moreover, mainstream English-language Canadian TV news does not necessarily offer racialized immigrant audiences a space in which to see themselves reflected accurately as part of Canada's social life, beyond the celebration of ethnic events and festivals (Mahtani, 2008b).

Immigrants arriving in Canada from 1990 to 2000 came at a time when the media were changing. Liberalization of the airwaves and technological advances triggered an explosion in the number of media outlets at the same time as audiences and readerships interested in somewhat deeper analyses were moving over to specialized electronic media. This led to a decrease in the general media's clienteles and advertising revenues, as well as to intense competition among the media and increasingly populist and biased coverage by many local media. The coverage of events in the Middle East since the second Intifada and of the 'war' against terrorism since September 2001 has been harshly criticized by NGOs associated with people of Islamic culture.

The major television networks (CBC, Radio-Canada, CTV, Global) have offered balanced coverage of events in Islamic countries and, since September 2001, have provided less-biased information on Islam and Muslim countries than have other media. The *Ottawa Citizen* and the *National Post* stand out in terms of their anti-Islamic positions, as G. Jonas has demonstrated in one *National Post* article in March 2002: 'The terrorist enemy has no armies to send against us; it has to penetrate our perimeter through fifth columnists' (Elmasry, *The Gazette*, September 5, 2002).

A survey of nine Canadian newspapers by the Canadian Islamic Congress (CIC, 2001, 2002) noted an increase in anti-Muslim stereotypes after September 2001: 'Negative or **biased information** on Islam' appeared 10 times more often than in the previous months in the *Toronto Star*, 18 times more often in the *Globe and Mail*, and 22 times more often in the *National Post*. A similar conclusion was drawn in the study on the *Vancouver Sun* (Enns, 2002), which disseminated a Manichean vision of Muslims. For example, in his August 15, 2009, article titled 'Do Muslims seek to dominate the West? And could they do it?', Douglas Todd stated:

> It is a frightening vision of future Europe, the logic of which Canadians would be wise to monitor. It goes like this: The population of Europe will be 40-per-cent Muslim by 2020. Due to high immigration and birthrates . . . , Muslims from the Middle East and Africa will soon dominate much, if not all, of European politics, education and the courts. Some prophets warn Muslims in Europe will impose shariah law on everyone—banning homosexual relationships, forcing all women to wear headscarves and allowing men (not women) to be polygamous. The continent might as well become known as 'Eurasia'.

French-speaking Quebec written media present more neutral information on Islamic countries and the Israeli-Palestinian conflict (Pietrantonio, 2002; Piché & Djerrahian, 2002). On the other hand, they give only limited coverage to discrimination against Muslims and, in regard to the latter's rights, show themselves to be just as biased as the English-Canadian media. The issue of reasonable accommodation was the most 'inflated' and disproportionate news item of the year. Furthermore, 83 per cent of the media coverage given to ethnic minorities in Quebec was devoted to controversial topics or situations of conflict, and the Quebec press gave 10 times more attention to incidents involving the rights of religious minorities in Quebec than did the press in the rest of Canada (Cauchon, 2007). An analysis of French-speaking Quebec coverage of hate crimes against Muslims shows a strong bias (Helly, 2008a).

Religious Intolerance and Denial of Rights

Hate Crimes

Hate crimes are hostile acts committed against an individual or group because of a personal attribute. These acts include public insults, incitement of hatred, physical violence, and attacks on property; they are infringements of the rights to dignity, safety, integrity, and the peaceful enjoyment of property. In Canada, three categories of hate crimes are defined in the section of the Criminal Code on hate propaganda: advocating genocide (s. 318), public incitement of hatred (s. 319, par. 1), and the wilful promotion of hatred in public (s. 319, par. 2). Hate propaganda has been criminalized since 1971. There are, however, inadequate statistics on the number of hate crimes: such crimes rarely lead to complaints, and police departments are not required to keep statistics—and those that do, do not always record the ethnic origin or religion of those involved.

From being virtually absent before 2001, hate crimes against Muslims rose during the 1991 Gulf War and in the months after September 2001 (Helly, 2004b, 2008a). In Montreal, for example, the police recorded about a dozen complaints from September 11 to September 20, 2001, but according to testimony reported in the media and by NGOs working with immigrants, there were many physical attacks and, especially, insults on the street, on public transit, and in workplaces against Muslims or immigrants from Middle Eastern countries. The Council on American Islamic Relations compiled approximately 50 incidents in Canada between September 11 and November 15, 2001, including death threats and 13 assaults (Nimer, 2001). Municipal police departments in Canada reported an upsurge of (racist) hate crimes, almost all of which were related to the September 2001 attacks. From September 2001 to September 2002, approximately 300 such crimes were committed across Canada, including, in October 2001, 40 hate crimes in Montreal, 44 in Ottawa, and 121 in Toronto (Hussain, 2002, p. 23). In addition, at least one attack on a place of worship occurred in every major Canadian city (Hussain, 2002, p. 15), 16 of which were bomb attacks. A police presence was only provided for a few weeks after 9/11, in front of the most important Muslim places of worship on Fridays and in front of Muslim schools (Helly, 2004b).

The Ethnic Diversity Survey (2002) showed that visible minorities were one and a half times more often the victims of hate crimes than other Canadians (20/1,000 compared with 13/1,000; 31/1000 for members of visible minorities born in Canada) (Silver, Mihorean, & Taylor-Butts, 2004, p. 6). For Muslims, 2.3 per cent said they had been victims of hate crimes or hate incidents since their arrival in Canada or within the last five years (compared with 1.5 per cent of Jews, 2.6 per cent of Hindus, and 2.8 per cent of Sikhs). For people identifying themselves as Arabs, 2.1 per cent said that they had been victims of such crimes or incidents (3.8 per cent of blacks and 2.5 per cent of Arabs from South Asia, a group that includes many Muslims from Pakistan and India).

After 2002, there were fewer hostile acts, as in the United States and Europe, but there were instead more frequent attacks against people or property, actions that are not classified and condemned as hate crimes by Canadian law, which still takes a timid approach in this matter. These kinds of actions increased in 2004 without apparent explanation and in 2006 owing to identifiable events: the publication of caricatures of Mohammed in Denmark, the arrest of 17 presumed Muslim terrorists in Toronto in June, the war in Lebanon in July, the repatriation of Canadian citizens living in Lebanon, and the pope's declarations in Germany in September to the effect that Islam has historically spread through violence. Among these hostile acts were 6 very violent attacks on individuals and 13 attempts to destroy buildings (places of worship, schools) (Helly, 2008a).

'Invasion of the Public Sphere': Places of Worship and Religious Markers

Negative perceptions and biased representations of Muslims, as well as hate crimes, have been accompanied by open attempts to curtail, if not eliminate, the public expression of the Muslim religion. In Canada, as elsewhere in the West, some currents of opinion have been hostile to religious expression, and sometimes even to religious belief, and there are those who would wish to deny equal rights to religious minorities. They would like to reduce, if not eliminate, Muslims' social visibility, that is, their social recognition. This animosity focuses on places of worship and some religious markers rather than on the topics highlighted in Europe, such as excision, polygamy (a practice more often seen among Mormons and Chinese immigrants than among Muslim Canadians), and forced marriages, a custom more often witnessed among Hindu immigrants.

Muslim Canadians have established 47 schools and about 250 associations and places of worship in Canada, including 5 mosques capable of holding over 1,000 people. During the 1960s and 1970s, the opening of such places raised few problems, but the situation deteriorated in the late 1990s when their number grew as the Muslim population increased (Castel, 2009). The Muslim population is an urban one: in 2001, 300,000 Muslims were living in Toronto and approximately 100,000 in Montreal, which since the 1980s had become a centre for the concentration of emigrants from the Middle East and the Maghreb.

Toronto witnessed a bitter conflict in 1998–99 regarding the construction of a dome for a mosque (Isin & Siemiatycki, 2002); in Montreal, the building of two places of worship was denied in 2001 under pressure from non-Muslim residents; and other conflicts arose (Germain et al., 2003; Gagnon, 2005). The arguments invoked referred to traffic congestion on days of prayer, the erecting of a minaret or cupola in an urban setting considered to be Christian or completely secular, and the costs for residents, as places of worship are often exempt from property taxes.

Another form of Muslim visibility is the headscarf (*hijab*) worn by Muslim women. It is despised in some currents of opinion in the public arena, which are sometimes supported by politicians. According to the *hijab*'s opponents, the wearing of a headscarf necessarily means sexist domination and, if freely chosen, the alienation of women through archaic and religious values. In 2007 (Environics Research Group–CBC), almost 60 per cent of Muslim women did not wear any covering, and 72 per cent of Muslim respondents said they were not worried about Muslim women taking on a more modern role in Canadian society. But in defence of religious freedom, 86 per cent of Muslim respondents and 55 per cent of the Canadian general public felt that government should not ban the wearing of headscarves in public.

Revival of the Idea of Assimilation

This atmosphere of contempt, mistrust, and ignorance regarding the Muslim minority and other religious minorities shows the presence in Canada, as elsewhere in the West, of three ideological currents: (1) ethno-national or nativist, which invokes the loss of territory, identity, and culture; (2) modernist and scientific, which promotes a belief in the ineluctability of historical progress and the Western model and prefers to relegate religious expression to the private sphere; and (3) populist, which insists on the threat to popular sovereignty posed by judges and feels nostalgia for pre-1945 democracies when national cultural majorities determined the fate of minorities with complete impunity. These three forms are coming together in a new matrix of the idea of assimilation, one that has been gaining influence over the past 20 years (Helly, 2009a). In this context, 'foreigners'—not only in the cultural sense but also in the religious—provoke hostility, especially since there is no imminent prospect of the secularization of civil societies and the question of the public status of religion is still being asked.

One expression (Laghi, 2008) summarizes the conviction of a majority of Canadians about the social status of cultural foreigners: 'Canada coddles minorities.' This position was present even before there was any public conflict about religious minorities. In 1991 (Angus-Reid, 1992; Helly, 2004b), 58 per cent of Canadians agreed that government should support the preservation of minority cultural customs as long as they respected rights and freedoms and did not involve polygamy, the idea that men were superior to women, or arranged marriages; and 68 per cent felt that discrimination against non-Europeans required government intervention. But 42 per cent of Canadians thought that national unity was weakened by ethno-cultural minorities persisting in their traditions, one-third (32 per cent) that immigrants should forget their culture as quickly as possible, and 39 per cent that if immigrants wanted to preserve their customs, they should do so only in private. Moreover, 15 per cent stated that marriage between people of different 'races' was a bad idea, and 18 per cent thought that multiculturalism was destroying Canadians' way of life. Since then, 40 to 50 per cent of Canadians polled said that new Canadians held on to their customs and traditions for too long (Jedwab, 2008); according to an April 2008 survey (*The Globe and Mail*/CTV News), 61 per cent of those surveyed believed that Canada makes too many accommodations for visible minorities (72 per cent felt that way in Quebec) (Laghi, 2008).

Negative representations of Muslims and other minorities are part of an overall context of hostility to immigration. With immigration coming mainly from the countries of the South, Canadians who feel that there are too many immigrants believe that immigrants should melt into Canadian society, and those who feel that an adequate number of immigrants are arriving every year think that immigrants should preserve their cultural and religious practices or both (adapt to Canadian society, keep their cultural and religious practices) (Jedwab, 2008).

The 'crisis' concerning religious arbitration illustrates this form of hostility. Given the differences in political history and culture, many immigrants would rather the state not intervene in their private lives (which does not mean that they are necessarily mistreating women). In 2007, 53 per cent of Canadian Muslims said that they would like to see an Islamic way adopted for divorce and family disputes, and 34 per cent stated that they would not like this, as did 79 per cent of the Canadian public (Adams, 2009). In Ontario, religious arbitration in family and business matters, legally authorized since 1991, was practised by Christians, Ismailis, Aboriginal people, and Jews. However, in 2004, a power struggle between the different Muslim currents regarding this provision was launched by a conservative group, and a highly publicized debate began on women's domination by imams and spouses. As a result, the legislation was amended in 2006, but religious-conflict resolution bodies are still recognized in Ontario (Cuttings, 2009).

Systemic, Direct, Institutional, and Individual Discrimination

Economic Participation

There are no statistical analyses to tell us whether Muslims and those seen as Muslims experience prejudice in the labour market and whether this prejudice is greater or less than that experienced by Christians, Jews, Hindus, blacks, Chinese, or Latin Americans. The Muslim migration flow increased during a period of relatively weak economic performance by new immigrants. Up to the 1980s, immigrants overcame the handicap of working in a new labour market within a decade; in 1996, however, the earnings of newly arrived immigrant men, which in 1980 amounted to 80 per cent of the earnings of native-born Canadian men, fell to 60 per cent. Employment rates fell as well: the figure was 86.3 per cent in 1980 for newly arrived immigrant men, close to the 91 per cent for native-born Canadian men; and by 1996, it was 68.3 per cent for new immigrant men, as compared with 85.4 per cent for native-born men (Reitz, 2005, p. 3).

Some 60 per cent of adult immigrants arriving since 2000 have a post-secondary degree, compared with 40 per cent of all Canadians, and 35.7 per cent of immigrants arriving from 1996 to 2001 have a university degree, compared with 13.8 per cent of native-born Canadians. Despite this high level of education and a stricter selection of immigrants since the 2002 Immigration Act, the income levels of these immigrants are unsatisfactory (Picot, 2004) and their unemployment rates high. The unemployment rate was 5.5 per cent in Canada in 2006, while, notably, it was 11 per cent for immigrants who had arrived from 2001 to 2006, fluctuating by region of origin: Asia 11 per cent, Latin America 10.5 per cent, Europe 8.4 per cent, and Africa 20.8 per cent (Statistics Canada, 2006). The unemployment rate for immigrants who had arrived from 1996 to 2001 was 7.3 per cent, and for immigrants who had arrived before 1996 it was 5.5 per cent.

Many studies note immigrants' declining earnings and economic performance despite rising skills and education levels (Reitz, 2001, 2005; Sweetman, 2006; Statistics Canada, 2003; Frenette & Morrisette, 2003; Aydemir & Skuterud, 2004; Li, 2000). There are many reasons for this, not just discrimination. They include:

- the tertiarization of the labour market and the elimination of manufacturing jobs often held by low-skilled immigrants (25 per cent industry and manufacturing and 75 per cent services in 2001, compared with 35 per cent to 65 per cent in 1971);
- the increase in highly specialized jobs requiring advanced linguistic knowledge (techniques and materials terminology) and a higher education level, which makes it harder to transfer expertise from one country to another, reduces the effectiveness of degrees obtained outside Canada, and induces employers to require that new immigrants have 'Canadian or North American' experience, a requirement that is difficult to meet;
- the rise in the education levels of native-born Canadians, which in the period 1991–96 accounted for about half of the decline in the earnings of new immigrants (Reitz, 2005, p. 5);

- the difficulty on the part of political authorities, professional associations, and companies in assessing or the refusal to assess the skills obtained outside Canada and not guaranteed by a degree or diploma;
- despite the federal Employment Equity Act (1986), the Embracing Change Initiative to recruit visible minorities (2000), and similar provincial programs, the public sector's failure to absorb a significant proportion of the immigrant labour force given the prerequisite of bilingualism for many positions;
- two periods of recession;
- ethnic, racial, and religious discrimination, which, among other things, seems to be slowing access to managerial positions (*the glass ceiling effect*) and, in the case of religious minorities, may arise from employers' fears of being forced to make reasonable accommodations.

These are clearly factors in the case of Muslims. In 1991, 25 per cent of people of Arab origin[8] had a university degree, compared with 11 per cent of all Canadians and 31 per cent of people holding managerial positions or working in the liberal professions. Despite one-quarter of Arab immigrants having these high qualifications, 39 per cent of them have an income below the poverty level. The average income of families for whom the head of household identifies himself or herself as Arab is $30,000, compared with $50,000 for all Canadians. It is true that this difference is in part due to Arab women's low level of participation in the labour force—52 per cent, compared with 62 per cent for all Canadian women.

In 2001, the Muslim population was young (45 per cent under 24 years of age), mostly immigrant (76 per cent), educated (28.4 per cent with a university degree), and English speaking (72.8 per cent) and less so French (6.4 per cent) or both languages (15 per cent). Muslims were among the most highly educated groups in Canada, but 16.5 per cent were jobless, more than twice the national rate, and among Arabs 38.7 per cent had an annual income of less than $10,000 (Marhraoui, 2009; Moghissi & Rahnema, 2008). In 2006, unemployment rates were highest among Arab and West Asian populations at 14 per cent, followed by blacks at 11.5 per cent. These rates were even higher for Arabs in Quebec (17.7 per cent). But in a 2007 survey (CBC-Environics), 45 per cent of Muslim Canadian respondents had a university degree.

We know that systemic discrimination against new immigrants and members of visible minorities exists. During the 1980s and 1990s, the wages of 'visible minorities', both immigrant and native-born, remained on average 8 per cent below those of people of European origin, with the effects of age, schooling, gender, and time of residence in Canada being controlled for (Pendakur, 2000). Interventions associated with the federal multiculturalism program since 1979 and employment equity programs in government and public agencies since 1986 have given visible minorities social recognition, but have not eliminated racist and xenophobic attitudes in the private sector, except in the case of large corporations recruiting a highly skilled workforce of all origins.

In 2007, 67 per cent of Canadian Muslims surveyed said that they worried about issues of discrimination, and 64 per cent claimed they were concerned about unemployment (Adams, 2009). One known factor affecting the equality of their rights in the labour market is their being rejected when seeking work. In Quebec, people have been excluded since September 2001 because of their family name, a non–French-Quebec accent, the wearing of a veil, or, according to employers, a negative perception of the 'Muslim' group on the part of their clientele (Lubuto Mutoo, 2001). In Ontario, a survey of women who wear the *hijab* and had gone for a job interview indicates that employers are obsessed with the Muslim custom of wearing a headscarf (Women Working with Immigrant Women, 2002). Ninety per cent asked the women about it, and 40 per cent made its removal a condition of employment.

Criminalization

We cannot talk about institutional discrimination, as no Canadian law denies Muslims their rights. Nonetheless, Muslims are vulnerable to **criminalization** under the laws of Parliament. In the aftermath of the 9/11 attacks, Parliament passed the Anti-Terrorism Act (Bill C-36), the Foreign Missions and International Organizations Act (Bill C-35), and the Public Safety Act (Bill C-55, which includes provisions for improving airport and aviation security). About 100 Muslims suspected of terrorist activity have been arrested since 2001.

The Anti-Terrorism Act (7 December 2001)[9] defines and designates terrorist groups and activities, and gives police and security agencies extraordinary powers to fight terrorism. It allows for the conviction of a person for supporting or facilitating terrorism without the knowledge or the intent of doing so, for preventive arrest over a period of 72 hours on suspicion of terrorism without evidence and the laying of criminal charges, and for secret investigative hearings. The Act also allows authorities to conduct secret searches; to extend the period of using electronic listening devices, which was formerly six months; to set up a record of air travel by all Canadians that can be kept for six years; and to listen to individuals' communications with anyone outside the country upon the decision of the Department of Defence and without judicial control. Since the Act criminalizes those who arouse any suspicion that they might be assisting terrorist activities or groups, donations to places of worship and NGOs have been decreasing, as donors fear that the funds could be being used for illegal purposes.

Human rights safeguards are built into the Act, such as a sunset provision of five years for preventive arrest and investigative hearings,[10] but the Act threatens the fundamental freedoms of all Canadians, especially people associated with Islam, whereas the existing legislation would have been adequate to fight terrorism (Ligue des droits et libertés 2004).

Security certificates, for their part, target immigrants from Muslim countries unfairly, as they allow for their continued detention, with the state having no obligation to convict them. These documents are issued under the Immigration and Refugee Protection Act to detain and deport without substantive judicial review non-citizens suspected of threatening national security (spies, etc.). The certificates initiate a process that lacks the procedural safeguards respected in a democratic state (disclosure of evidence, right to confront one's accusers, public trial, right of appeal) (BCCLA 2005), with judges not having the power to stop the procedures. Since September 2001, this provision has been improperly used without any resistance from Parliament. Five immigrants have been arrested and jailed on suspicion of terrorism, but cannot be legally deported because of possible torture in their country of origin. in To protect the information sources and methods of the Canadian Security Intelligence Service (CSIS), criminal procedures have not been followed. The right to a defence is not being respected, and the only possibility for the accused is to launch a constitutionality challenge. In 2007, the Supreme Court found the security certificate process unconstitutional and weighted in favour of the state, as crown lawyers can advance their arguments in secret judge-only hearings. As a solution, Parliament created special advocates to defend detainees, but the judges do not seem to have been impressed by this measure.

One recognized effect of the **Anti-Terrorism** Act is the profiling of Muslims and people associated with Islam (Hurst, 2002; Makin, 2003). A September 2002 IPSOS-Reid poll indicated that 48 per cent of Canadians favour some form of racial profiling. A report by Bourque et al. (2009) examines whether profiling constitutes a valid and effective means for the state to maintain national security. The purpose of criminal profiling 'is to develop correlations between specific criminal activity and certain group-based traits in order to help the police identify potential suspects for investigation.'

> In August 2008, 40 terrorist organizations were recognized by CSIS. Of these 40 organizations, 22 claimed to be Islamist and 19 were aiming for the creation of a Muslim state. More than half came from a country with a Muslim majority. In this context, the use of profiling to fight terrorism involves a racial or religious component. However, there does not appear to be consensus on the definition of terrorism itself and there is no reliable empirical evidence that racial profiling is an effective counterterrorism measure and no solid theoretical reason why it would be. The possibility of recruiting outside the profiled group and of substituting different modes of attack renders the racial profiling in the counterterrorism context suspect. (pp. 60–62)

Moreover, participation in renditions that expose citizens to torture (Maher Arar to Syria)[11] and pressures on Muslims to cooperate with police raise questions about the civil rights of Canadian Muslims. Security certificates, renditions, pressures to denunciate others, and profiling are having negative effects on the social status of Muslims and on their community building (Kundnani, 2009).

Militancy of the NGOs

Wahida Valiante (2009), president of the Canadian Islamic Congress, describes some of the main goals of most Muslim NGOs: 'to remind all Canadian citizens that Islam has contributed greatly to the world, thereby motivating and inspiring Canadian Muslims to take pride in their Islamic identity and their intrinsic worth as citizens'; 'to present a positive contrast to sources that do not objectively represent Islam and Muslims'; 'to motivate Canadian Muslims to become more proactively engaged in national discourse'; 'to reduce or eliminate fear of "otherness" in society; to deter or prevent Islamophobia.'[12] These objectives mean to defend Muslims' civil liberties as well as denounce all forms of political Islamism using violence. The community sector, religious or secular, often accused of being pro-terrorist (for a recent example, see Faith & Media blog, 2009),[13] has condemned the attacks in the United States in 2001 and those subsequently perpetrated in Europe.

The anti-Islamic hostility after 9/11 has prompted the community sector to discuss three questions: how can the community increase its presence in the public arena, how can it mobilize Muslims in defence of their rights, and how should it define the status of religion in secularized society. Is religion a culture, one form of identity among others, a private belief, or a cosmogony orienting a person's every action and involving a particular living environment? A similar debate has taken place in the educational sector: should one simply teach Islamic precepts or should one prepare students to live out these precepts in a secularized society (Zine, 2008)?

Since 2001, many pan-Canadian NGOs have increased their public presence, and local ones have done the same on the provincial scene. The pan-Canadian NGOs include the Canadian Islamic Congress (CIC); the Council of American Islamic Relations (35 chapters in the United States, with an independent Canadian section (CAIR-Can); the Muslim Canadian Congress (MCC); the Canadian Arab Federation (CAF, secular); Muslim Presence (MP); the Canadian Muslim Forum (CMF); the Islamic Society of North America (ISNA); the Canadian Council of Muslim Theologians (CCMT); the Islamic Supreme Council of Canada (ISCC); the United Muslim Students Association; and the Canadian Council of Muslim Women (CCMW)—the activities of which are sometimes supported by the government. These organizations support Muslims' citizen participation, the struggle against discrimination, and the defence of civil liberties (e.g., CAIR publishes know-your-rights trainings, and in 2006 CIC produced six DVDs on Canadian law, history, and politics related to Islamic issues). They also act in other areas: political mobilization, monitoring of rights violations (CAIR-Can, CMF, CAF), Islamic identity, media coverage, voting (in the 2004 elections, CIC graded 400 candidates on 10 issues), education of younger generations, the condition of women (CCMW), Islam and modernity, reform (Ramadan, 2008), dialogue with civil society (MP),[14] secularization of Islam, denunciation of all forms of political Islamism (MCC), explanation of Islam to non-Muslims (ISCC), educational and social programs for Muslims (ISNA) (Khalema & Wannas-Jones, 2003), and inter-faith relations (2008, 2009 CAIR and Canadian Association of Jews and Muslims' 'Twinning of Mosques and Synagogues'; Brodeur 2010). And local NGOs, whether Muslim or ethno-national, given their limited means, are responding to religious and information needs and helping with job searches.

Conclusion

Do Muslims have a more favourable social status in Canada than in Europe, and indeed in the United States? The answer is a positive one, according to Muslims themselves. In 2007, 17 per cent of Muslims in Canada felt hostility toward their religion, compared with 51 per cent in Germany, 42 per cent in Great Britain, 39 per cent in France, and 31 per cent in Spain. Muslim Canadians may consider that they have a better status for three reasons. Being better educated than Muslims in Europe, a portion of them are gaining access to skilled jobs; there is a history of religious pluralism in Canada and violence against minorities (homes burned; public insults by the media; extreme-right politicians; large demonstrations against the presence of mosques, as in Europe; hate crimes and denigration campaigns, as in the United States) occurs less frequently; and most Canadians see US policy as a major cause of Islamic extremism in the world and think that conflicts in Muslim countries are more political and economic than religious. According to a November 2006 Environics Research/*Globe and Mail* poll on Canadians' views of Muslims, 68 per cent of respondents rejected the suggestion that ordinary, law-abiding Muslim Canadians should feel any personal responsibility for violent crimes carried out by others in the name of Islam. And nearly 8 in 10 respondents felt that US foreign policy is a major or minor cause of Islamic extremism and terrorism. Nineteen per cent of Canadians thought it 'very likely' that Canada would experience terrorist attacks in the near future carried out by Canadians with Muslim backgrounds. Forty per cent of Canadians said it was 'somewhat likely'.

Nevertheless, among Western countries, Canada is the only one to claim to be a model of governance of cultural plurality, and it should spearhead state programs to combat Islamophobia and any attempts to deny that Muslims are part of Canadian society. Like Canada's now legendary UN peace missions, its acknowledged generous treatment of refugees and immigrants, its 'peace-oriented' positions on foreign conflicts, and its Charter of Rights and Freedoms, multiculturalism is emblematic of Canadian society and of the Canadian state on the international scene. The government's interventions since September 2001, therefore, have not lived up to this image of Canada, and Muslim Canadians, especially Muslim youth, are not taken in by the myth of Canada being an exception.

In 2001, 67.7 per cent of Canadian Muslims were Canadian citizens, and in 2007, 94 per cent said they were proud to be Canadian, compared with 93 per cent for all Canadians (Adams, 2009), and when asked whether they identified themselves first as Muslim or Canadian, 56 per cent chose Muslim and 23 per cent Canadian, but 77 per cent of Muslims aged 18 to 29 described themselves as Muslim. Some will see in this strong self-identification as Muslims the lack of a desire to 'integrate', but this does not explain why Muslim Canadians say they are so proud to be Canadians. This tendency to claim to be Muslim rather than Canadian closely resembles the valuing of the black identity by American blacks during the 1960s, when they were fighting for equal rights and responded to stereotypes that devalued them with the expression 'Black is beautiful.' Moreover, in 2002 (Ethnic Diversity Survey), 30 per cent of Muslim respondents said that they had had a bad experience because of their race, ethnicity, or religion, and the youngest cohort, raised in Canada, was the most likely to report discrimination: 42 per cent of those aged 18 to 29 reported such an experience (Adams, 2009).

Young Muslim Canadians seem less convinced than their parents by the Canadian model. Perhaps the growing indifference of various federal governments and the open hostility of some toward multiculturalism are having their effects. Two or three symbolic gestures by a prime minister, such as the visit to an Ottawa mosque after September 11, 2001 and the affirmation that 'Islam has nothing to do with the massacre planned and executed in the United States by terrorists', or the statement in the fall of 2002 that the frequent humiliation of Arab countries by Western countries could have led to the 2001 attacks on the United States, cannot make up for the failure of the various governments to facilitate Muslims' participation in public life. The governments could have helped to strengthen the community sector, as was done during the 1980s for other immigrant populations that had been the victims of severe discrimination. They could have tried to reach out to and engage Muslim NGOs and other social and cultural associations that assist immigrants from Muslim countries. They could have enhanced the Canadian population's literacy about Muslim societies and religion, strongly condemn hate crimes against Muslims (as against other minorities), and intervene against the ethnic and racial profiling of Muslims.

Summary

The text describes the diverse flux of immigration from Muslim countries into Canada starting in the late nineteenth century. It then documents the negative social conditions presently experienced by Muslim in Canada: that is, their impaired participation to the labour force market (as other immigrants), different forms of discrimination, their victimization by the state, and their reduced propensity to build a community network in view of their internal divisions along ethnic, social, political, national, and religious lines.

Key Terms

Anti-Terrorism Act	immigration	media	rights
Arab	intolerance	Middle East	security
community building	Islam	multiculturalism	security certificate
discrimination	Islamophobia	Muslim	Syria
hate crimes	labour market	Pakistan	victimization

Questions for Critical Thought

1. Is there a religious minority in Muslin countries?
2. What is meant by freedom of religion?
3. Is it possible to balance national security and individual rights in the context of the 'war on terror'?

Additional Readings

Abu-Laban, B. (1997). Arabs. In P. R. Magocsi (Ed.), *Encyclopedia of Canada's peoples* (pp. 202–212). Toronto: University of Toronto Press.

Boyd, M. (2004). *Dispute resolution in family law, report to the Attorney general of Ontario.* Toronto: Attorney General of Ontario.

Dizboni, A. G. (2008). Muslim discourses in Canada and Quebec. *Australia Religion Studies Review, 21*(1), 17–47.

Helly, D. (in press, 2010). Une nouvelle rectitude politique au Canada: Droits des femmes, laïcité, modernisme et Islam. *La Revue de Tocqueville.*

Helly, D., & Hardy, M. (in press, 2010). Judges and Muslim parties in Quebec. *Diversité canadienne/ Canadian Diversity.*

Institute for Social Policy and Understanding. (2004). *The human capital deficit in the Islamic non-profit sector.* Clinton Township, MI. www.ispu.us/

Kazemipur A., & Halli, S. S. (2000). The colour of poverty: A study of the poverty of ethnic and immigrant groups in Canada. *International Migration, 38*(1), 69–88.

McAndrew, M., Tessier, C., & Helly, D. (2008). From heritage languages to institutional change: An analysis of the nature of organizations and projects funded by the multiculturalism program (1983–2002). *Canadian Ethnic Studies.*

Malik, M. (Ed.). (2009). *Anti-Islam prejudice.* Routledge.

Moghissi, H. (Ed.). (2006). *The Muslim diaspora: Gender, culture and identity.* London: Routledge.

Picot G., & Hou, F. (2002). *The rise in low-income rates among immigrants in Canada.* Research Paper Series 198. Ottawa: Statistics Canada, Analytical Studies Branch.

Poynting, S., & Mason, V. (2008). The new integrationism, the state and Islamophobia. *International Journal of Law, Crime, and Justice, 36,* 230–246.

Poynting, S., & Perry, B. (2007). Climates of hate: Media and state inspired victimisation of Muslims in Canada and Australia since 9/11. *Current Issues in Criminal Justice, 19*(2), 151–171.

Websites of Interest

Islamophobia Watch: www.islamophobia-watch.com

Council on American-Islamic Relations: www.cair.com

Point de Bascule: www.pointdebasculecanada.ca

MEL-net: www.mel-net.ics.ul.pt

Endnotes

1. I would like to thank Frédéric Castel for his critical comments.

2. Unless otherwise indicated, all the demographic data come from censuses.

3. Given the ethnic diversity of the so-called Arab world (including the strong Berber presence in the Maghreb), Arab origin essentially refers to a linguistic practice. In 2001 there were 3,350 Berbers in Canada.

4. In 2001 the most often cited ethno-cultural origins in Canada were Chinese (936,000), Italian (726,000), German (706,000), Portuguese (253,000), Jewish (186,500), and Vietnamese (119,000).

5. Currently under the Multiculturalism and Citizenship Directorate, Citizenship and Immigration Canada.

6. Date: 2009-03-31, Docket: T-447-09, Citation: 2009 FC 333, Toronto, Ontario, March 31, 2009, Canadian Arab Federation Applicant and the Minister of Citizenship and Immigration; http://decisions.fct-cf.gc.ca/in/2009/2009fc 333/2009fc333.html

7. By mid-October 2009, four had pleaded guilty, six

were awaiting trial, and seven had been released.
8. This includes Middle Eastern Christians who have been settled in Canada for three or more generations.
9. This legislation is similar to the Patriot Act adopted in the United States in October 2001 and the Crime and Security Act adopted in Great Britain in December 2001.
10. This can be renewed for a further five years by both Houses of Parliament.
11. Accused of belonging to al Qaeda, Arar was cleared

in 2006 and received financial compensation from the Canadian government.
12. Retrieved October 23, 2009, from www.canadian islamiccongress.com
13. http://blogs.faithandmedia.org/wiseman/2009/04/02/on-the-vapour-trails-of-rumour/
14. MP defines itself as a network promoting universal values and active citizenship based on a contextualized reading of Islam, an open identity, and a harmonious coexistence within society.

References

Abu-Laban, B. (1980). *An olive branch on the family tree: The Arabs in Canada.* Generation Series. Toronto: McClelland and Steward.

Adams, M. (2009). Muslims in Canada: Findings from the 2007 Environics Survey. *Horizons, 10*(2), 19–26.

Angus Reid Inc. (1992). *Le multiculturalisme et les Canadiens: Etude nationale sur les attitudes.* Ottawa: Multiculturalisme et Citoyenneté.

Asal, H. (2008). Les premières mobilisations d'immigrants arabes au Canada, à travers l'exemple du journal *The Canadian Arab*, 1945–1948. *Revue de l'intégration et de la migration internationale, 9*, 1–19.

Awan, S. N. A. (1976). *The people of Pakistani origin in Canada.* Ottawa : Author.

Aydemir A., & Skuterud, M. (2004). *Explaining the deteriorating entry earnings of Canada's immigrant cohorts, 1966–2000.* Ottawa: Statistics Canada. Catalogue 11F0019MIE, No. 225.

Bauder, H. (2008) Immigration debate in Canada: How newspapers reported, 1996–2004. *Journal of International Migration and Integration, 9*(3), 289–310.

BCCLA (British Columbia Civil Liberties Association). (2005). *National Security: Curbing the excess.* Vancouver: BCCLA.

Bilge, S. (2000). *Communalisations ethniques post-migratoires: Le cas des 'Turcs' de Montréal.* Doctoral thesis, University of Montreal.

Bourque, J., LeBlanc, S., Utzschneider, A., & Wright, C. (2009). *The effectiveness of profiling from a national security perspective.* Ottawa: Canadian Human Rights Commission and Canadian Race Relations Foundation.

Brodeur, P. (with D. Helly). (2010). *Les espaces de dialogue inter-religieux au Canada.* Rapport à Citoyenneté et Immigration.

Castel, F. (2009). La dynamique de l'équation ethno confessionnelle dans l'évolution récente du paysage religieux québécois et dans le façonnement des communautés bouddhistes et musulmanes (1941–à aujourd'hui). Doctoral thesis. Montreal: Université du Québec à Montréal.

Cauchon, P. (2007, December 24). *Des nouvelles éphémères qui laissent peu de traces.* Le Devoir, p. B7.

Clark, W., & Schellenberg, G. (2006, Summer). *Les Canadiens et la religion, tendances sociales canadiennes, 2*–9.

Congrès islamique du Canada. *Media Survey Report 2001, 2002.* www.candianislamiccongress.com/

Cutting, C. (2009). *Problematizing public and private spheres: Ongoing faith-based practices in Ontario family law.* Paper presented at American Academy of Religion Conference, Montreal, November 8.

Enns, A. S. (2002). *Assessing the coverage of Islam in the Vancouver Sun after September 11.* Master's thesis, University of British Columbia.

Frenette, M., & Morrisette, R. (2003). *Will they ever converge? Earnings of immigrant and Canadian-born.* Ottawa: Statistics Canada. Catalogue no. 11F0019MIE200—no. 215.

Fukuyama, F. (1994). *La fin de l'histoire.* Paris: Flammarion.

Fukuyama, F. (1999, May). The Great Disruption: Human nature and the reconstitution of social order. *The Atlantic Monthly*, 55–80.

Gagnon, J. E. (2005). *L'aménagement des lieux de culte minoritaires dans la région montréalaise : transactions sociales et enjeux urbains.* Doctoral thesis, INRS, Montreal.

Geddes, J. (2009, April 28). What Canadians think of Sikhs, Jews, Christians, Muslims. *Maclean's.*

Germain, A., Gagnon, J. E., Polo, A.-L., Daher, A., & Ainouche, L. (2003). *L'aménagement des lieux de culte des minorités ethniques: Enjeux et dynamiques locales.* Report. Montreal: INRS-UCS.

Haddad, Y. (1983). The impact of the Islamic Revolution

in Iran on the Syrian Muslims of Montreal. In E. H. Waugh, B. A. Laban, & R. B. Qureshi (Eds), *The Muslim community in North America* (pp. 165–183). Calgary: University of Alberta Press.

Hamdani, D. H. (1983–1984). Muslims in the Canadian Mosaic. *Journal of Institute of Muslim Minority Affairs,* *5*(1), 7–16.

Hamdani, D. H. (1999). Canadian Muslims on the eve of 21st Century. *Journal of Muslim Minority Affairs,* *19*(2), 197–210.

Hamdani, D. H. (2002, May/June). A century of Islam in Canada. *Islamic Horizons,* 18–22.

Helly, D. (2001). Les limites du multiculturalisme canadien. In M. Wieviorka & J. Ohana (Eds.), *La différence culturelle* (pp. 414–427). Colloque de Cerisy. Paris: Balland.

Helly, D. (2002). Occidentalisme et islamisme : Leçons de 'guerres culturelles'. In J. Renaud et al. (Eds.). *Ce qui a changé depuis le 11 septembre 2001: Les relations ethniques en question* (pp. 229–251). Montreal: Presses de l'Université de Montréal.

Helly, D. (2004a). Flux migratoires des pays musulmans et discrimination de la communauté islamique au Canada. In U. Manço (Ed.), *L'islam entre discrimination et reconnaissance* (pp. 257–288). Paris: L'Harmattan.

Helly, D. (2004b). Are the Muslims discriminated against in Canada? *Journal of Canadian Ethnic Studies, 36*(1), 24–47.

Helly, D. (2004c). Le financement des associations mono ethniques par le gouvernement canadien. In A. Manço (Ed.), *La vie associative des immigrés: Quelles valorisations politiques ? Perspectives européennes et canadiennes* (pp. 223–248). Paris: L'Harmattan.

Helly, D. (2005a). Pourquoi créer une instance unitaire musulmane en Belgique, Espagne et France? In S. Lefebvre (Ed.), *Religion et sphère publique* (pp. 274–302). Montreal: Presses de l'Université de Montréal.

Helly, D. (2005b, September). Are the Canadian policies of immigration exportable in France and Europe? Paper 15 bis. Paris: Institut français des relations internationales. www.ifri.org

Helly, D. (2008a). *Crimes haineux et incidents haineux subis par les musulmans au Canada.* Report. Ottawa: Direction de la recherche, Justice Canada.

Helly, D. (2008b). Lutte contre les discriminations au Canada: le secteur privé, la faille du multiculturalisme. In Altay Manço (Ed.), *Diversité culturelle et marché de l'emploi* (pp. 17–36), Paris: L'Harmattan.

Helly, D. (2009a, Summer). Immigration, sécurité, cohésion sociale et nativisme. *Cultures et Conflits, 74,* 42–79.

Helly, D. (2009b). Au miroir de l'immigration: L'Islam révélateur de conflits et tensions. In F. Crépeau (Ed.),

La complexe dynamique des migrations internationales. Montreal: Presses de l'Université de Montréal.

Henry, F., & Tator, C. (Ed.). (2002). *Discourses of domination racial bias in the Canadian English-language press.* Toronto: University of Toronto Press.

Huntington, S. (1996). *The clash of civilizations and the remaking of the world order.* New York: Simon and Schuster.

Hurst, L. (2002, October 20). Who is high risk? *Toronto Star.*

Hussain, S. (2002). *La Voix des Canadiennes-Musulmanes.* Mississauga, ON: Le Conseil Canadien des Femmes Musulmanes.

Isin, E. F. & Siemiatycki, M. (2002). Making space for mosques: Struggles for urban citizenship in immigrant Toronto. In S. Razack (Ed.), *Race, space and the law: The making of a white settler society* (pp. 185–209). Toronto: Between the Lines.

Ismael, T.Y., & Measor, J. (2003, Winter/Spring). Racism and the North American media following 11 September: The Canadian setting. *Arab Studies Quarterly, 25*(1–2), 101–136.

Israël, M. (1997). Pakistanis. In P. R. Magocsi (Ed.), *Encyclopedia of Canada's Peoples* (pp. 1027–1037). Toronto: University of Toronto Press,.

Jedwab, J. (2005, March 30). *Canada's demo-religious revolution: 2017.* Montreal: Association for Canadian Studies. www.acs-aec.ca/Polls/30-03-2005

Jedwab, J. (2008). Receiving and giving: How does the Canadian public feel about immigration and integration? In J. Biles, M. Burstein, & J. Frideres (Eds), *Immigration and integration in Canada in the twenty-first century* (pp. 211–247). Montreal: McGill-Queen's University Press.

Karim K. H. (2000). *The Islamic Peril: Media and Global Violence.* Montreal: Black Rose.

Karim, K., et al., & DiversiPro. (2007). *Research on settlement programming through the media.* Ottawa: Citoyenneté et Immigration Canada.

Khalema, N. E., & Wannas-Jones, J. (2003, April). Under the prism of suspicion: Minority voices in Canada post-September 11. *Journal of Muslim Minority Voices, 23*(1), 25–39.

Kundnani, A. (2009). *Spooked: How not to prevent violent extremism.* London: Institute of Race Relations.

Kymlicka, W. (2009). Current state of multiculturalism in Canada. *Canadian Journal for Social Research, 2*(1), 15–34.

Laghi, B. (2008, April 17). Canada coddles minorities: Poll reveals deeply divided attitudes toward immigrants. *The Globe and Mail.*

Li, P. S. (2000). Earning disparities between immigrants and native-born Canadians. *The Canadian Review of Sociology and Anthropology, 37*(3), 289–311.

Ligue des droits et libertés. (2004). *Nous ne sommes pas plus en sécurité*. Montreal: La Ligue des droits et des libertés du Québec.

Lubuto Mutoo, V. (2001). *Discrimination raciale en milieu de travail dans la région métropolitaine de Québec*. Montreal: La Ligue des droits et des libertés du Québec.

Mahtani, M. (2008a). How are immigrants seen and what do they want to see? Contemporary research on the representation of immigrants in the Canadian English-Language media. In J. Biles, M. Burstein, & J. Frideres (Ed.), *Immigration and integration in Canada in the twenty-first century* (pp. 231–249). Montreal: McGill-Queen's University Press.

Mahtani, M. (2008b). Racializing the audience: Immigrant perceptions of mainstream Canadian English-language TV news. *Canadian Journal of Communication, 33*, 639–660.

Mahtani, M. (2009). The racialized geographies of news consumption and production: Contaminated memories and racialized silence. *GeoJournal* (electronic version), *74*, 257–264.

Makin, K. (2003, January 18). Police engage in profiling, chief counsel tells court. *The Globe and Mail*.

McAndrew, M., Oueslati, B., & Helly, D. (2007). Le traitement de l'Islam dans les manuels scolaires du niveau secondaire, Québec et Ontario. *Canadian Ethnic Studies, 39*(3), 173–188.

Marhraoui, A. (2009). Les conditions socioéconomiques des membres des communautés noires, arabes et musulmanes au Canada. *Revue canadienne des sciences socials, 2*(1), 107–196.

Moallem, M. (1997). Iranians. In P. R. Magocsi (Ed.), *Encyclopedia of Canada's peoples* (pp. 726–732). Toronto: University of Toronto Press.

Moghissi, H., & Saeed Rahnema. (2008). Muslims and multiculturalism in Canada. *Directions* (Canadian Race Relations Foundation), *4*(2), 7.

Nimer, M. (2001, March). *Report*. The Council on American-Islamic Relations.

Pendakur, R. (2000). *Immigrants and the labour force: Policy, regulation, and impact*. Montreal: McGill-Queen's University Press.

Piché, V., & Djerrahian, G. (2002). Immigration et terrorisme: Une analyse de la presse francophone. In J. Renaud et al., *Ce qui a changé depuis le 11 septembre 2001: Les relations ethniques en question* (pp. 81–94). Montreal: Presses de l'Université de Montréal.

Picot, G. (2004). The deteriorating economic welfare of Canadian immigrants. *Canadian Journal of Urban Research, 13*(1), 25–46.

Pietrantonio, L. (2002). Rapports de pouvoir dans le savoir public? Les mots de la mi-septembre 2001. In J. Renaud et al., *Ce qui a changé depuis le 11 septembre 2001: Les relations ethniques en question* (pp. 113–130). Montreal: Presses de l'Université de Montréal.

Ramadan, T. (2008). *Islam: La réforme radicale*. Paris: Presses du Châtelet.

Reitz, J. (2001). Immigrant skill utilization in the Canadian labour market. *Journal of International Migration and Integration, 2*(3), 347–378.

Reitz, J. (2005, February). Tapping immigrants' skills. Institut de recherche en politiques publiques. IRPP *Choices, 11*(1).

Sean, P., & Greenberg, J. (2002). Constructing a discursive crisis: Risk, problematization and illegal Chinese in Canada. *Ethnic and Racial Studies, 25*(3), 490–513.

Shuraydi, M. A. (1997a). Iraqis. In P. R. Magocsi (Ed.), *Encyclopedia of Canada's Peoples* (pp. 732–734). Toronto: University of Toronto Press.

Shuraydi, M. A. (1997b). Palestinians. In P. R. Magocsi (Ed.), *Encyclopedia of Canada's Peoples* (pp. 1037–1043). Toronto: University of Toronto Press.

Silver,W., Mihorean, K., & Taylor-Butts, A. (2004). Les crimes motivés par la haine au Canada, *Juristat, 24*(4). Ottawa: Statistics Canada. Catalogue no. 85-002-XPF.

Song, V. (2007, January 15). Love and Hate. *Toronto Sun*.

Statistics Canada. (2003). *Census of Canada: Religions in Canada: Highlight Tables, 2001 Census*. Ottawa: Statistics Canada.

Statistics Canada. (2006). *Les immigrants sur le marché canadien du travail en 2006: Analyse selon la région ou le pays de naissance*. Ottawa: Statistics Canada.

Sweetman, A. (2006, Spring). Need we pursue immigration objectives one at a time? Economic growth, family reunification and points systems. *Canadian Issues*, 68–71.

Taillefer, G. (2002, September 11). Coupables par association. *Le Devoir*, p. 6.

Valiante, W. (2009, October 16). IHMC: An opportunity to be proud as Canadians & Muslims. Canadian Islamic Congress. *Friday Magazine, 12*(42), 3.

Women Working with Immigrant Women. (2002). *Report*. Toronto.

Zhu, N., Helly, D., & Trudel, M. (2008). Équité et insertion des immigrants au marché du travail canadien. In J. P. Domin (Ed.), *Au-delà des droits économiques et des droits politiques, les droits sociaux?* (pp. 23–36). Paris: L'Harmattan.

Zine, J. (2008). *Canadian Islamic schools: Unraveling the politics of faith, gender, knowledge, and identity*. Toronto: University of Toronto Press.

11 | Zombies in Bel Air: Class and Marginalization in Canada

BRYAN HOGEVEEN

Debates around **class** preoccupy social scientists, yet class itself remains a contested concept. This chapter examines this concept and explores the divergent experiences between the upper and impoverished classes. While the upper classes are moving into fortified communities designed to separate them further from the problems and excesses of capitalist expansion, the working class and marginalized increasingly find themselves disadvantaged. Draconian cuts to social assistance and **neo-liberal** economic restructuring have created conditions ripe for the accumulation of massive wealth—but only for the wealthy. Economic affluence is being won on the backs of a working class that is being asked to work harder and longer for the same remuneration. While worker productivity and corporate profits were soaring, welfare rates were declining to paltry levels and the earnings of workers, those who were fuelling the economic windfall, remained relatively unchanged for 30 years. At the same time that the rich have been buying bigger vehicles that increasingly pollute *our* environment, those among the lowest strata have been forced to make hard choices between paying heating bills and paying the rent.

Regardless of the widening gulf between the rich and poor in Canada, not all social scientists are in agreement about the efficacy of class as a heuristic tool or political concept. Despite its appeal, class analysis has its detractors. Some have called for the 'death' of class analysis, while others maintain that class is a **'zombie' concept**. Authors such as Beck (1999) maintain that wide-ranging social changes (reflexive modernization) have brought about structural alterations that call into question the continued relevance of class analysis.

Even though controversy and debate surround the concept of class, it remains central in the social sciences. For adherents, classes are major social forces that are the product of social structural conditions and that have important consequences for politics, culture, and economics, among many other things. This chapter explores several questions: How can we come to terms with and comprehend the influence, if any, of class in contemporary neo-liberal capitalist societies? How do class relations affect lifestyle, life chances, and criminal justice involvement? What place, if any, does class have in contemporary social science? The chapter suggests that a rigorous analysis of class relations attends to the relative inequalities between groups divided by social, political, economic, and symbolic conditions. It probes how societal structures become embedded in individuals through such processes and institutions as education, socialization, and the media. Behaviours that reproduce the existing social order are the inevitable result.

The Rich Get Richer and the Poor (Still) Get Prison[1]

The disparity between the rich and poor, between the upper strata of the class hierarchy and the impoverished, is widening. A relatively small number of Canadians control much of Canada's total wealth. This fact offers some initial evidence of fundamental class inequality and increasing polarization in this country (Toronto Dominion, 2006). The Canadian Centre for Policy Alternatives (CCPA, 2007) reports that Canadian workers are becoming increasingly efficient, are generating greater revenues for their employers, but are not seeing a return for their hard work. Productivity improved by 51 per cent in the last 30 years, but workers' average wages (as measured in constant dollars) have remained relatively static. Further, the CCPA study finds that workers' wages are at their lowest point in 40 years. Had wages kept pace, Canadians would be earning an average of $10,000 more per year (CCPA, 2007). Predictably, it is the corporations that have been siphoning the increased revenues generated from worker efficiency. The CCPA reports that Canadian corporations are reaping the reward while workers remain on the outside of the profit bonanza. In 2005, 'corporations banked $130 billion more in gross profits than if the profit share had remained at 1991 levels' (CCPA, 2007).

Total economic input by the working class—that is, its rates of productivity—has continued to expand, while the rewards of this labour has been increasingly reaped by those at the very top of the income hierarchy (Osberg, 2008). Lars Osberg (2008) maintains that in the 1990s the incomes at the top of the distribution began to increase rapidly. Those in the top 10 per cent saw their incomes rise 34 per cent. However, the most noticeable and powerful trend has been the large gain in income since the 1990s for those at the highest end of the income scale. Average incomes at the very top (0.01 per cent) increased by 142 per cent in the 12 years between 1992 and 2004. The greater one's income, the greater the increase over time, such that those fortunate few in the top 0.01 per cent continue to reap more rewards from the capitalist economy than any other group.

In 2008 Canada's top 100 CEOs pocketed 22 per cent more money than the previous year (MacKenzie, 2009). Contrast this with the income of the average Canadian, who earned a paltry 3.2 per cent more—the biggest increase in five years. To put this in perspective, consider that these CEOs each banked the average Canadian's annual pay of $39,933 by 9:04 a.m. on 2 January (MacKenzie, 2009). Of particular interest is that 55 per cent of the income of these CEOs came in the form of cashing in stock options. This is important because that part of their salary was taxed as if it were a capital gain—'at half the regular income tax rates paid on wage and salary income' (MacKenzie, 2009, p. 6).

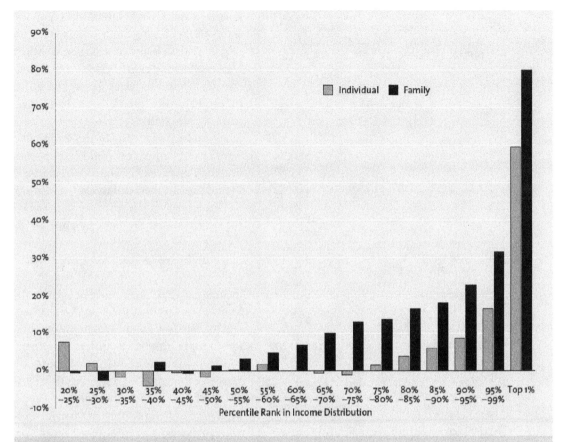

Figure 11.1 Percent Change in Real Taxable Income 1982–2004

Source: Osberg, 2008, p. 9.

While the rich continue to benefit and grow their personal wealth to even greater proportions, the marginalized and impoverished see social assistance subsidies slashed and real incomes erode. Although Canada's gross domestic product has grown by 40 per cent in the last 20 years, fewer are benefiting from it. Social assistance recipients, whose income is adjusted for inflation, are seeing an even lower income than comparable individuals 20 years ago (Osberg, 2008). However, a job is no guarantee of freedom from poverty. Canada is witnessing a growing number of those who have been dubbed the **working poor**. Leach and Sikora (2003, as cited in Fleury & Fortin, 2006) suggest that 'working poor families are families who are "playing by the rules" by working and contributing to the productivity and prosperity (of their country) . . . but yet struggle day-to-day to meet their basic needs.' Thus the working poor, in contrast to low-paid workers, are individuals whose incomes fall below the poverty threshold.[2] In addition to

```
            CARLO'S
    478 CARLINGTON AVE
    NEW YORK, NY 10471
      FRIDAY OCTOBER 30, 2009
      CHECK #976836-4
           TABLE #15
          DUPLICATE

1   MARE MONTE SPAGHETI      $39.00
1   RIGATONI SICILIANA       $36.00
1   MILANESA                 $55.00
1   INSALA.CARCIOFI          $18.00
2   PARMESAN CHUNKS          $28.00
1   LG WATER                 $12.00
5   TAWNY 40                $275.00
2   TRUFFLE CARPACCIO       $200.00
2   ASPARAGUS NELLO          $60.00
3   CAPPUCCINO               $27.00
2   CALAM. FRITTI            $40.00
2   PROSEC. MOZARELLA        $68.00
2   ESPRESSO                 $15.00
1   TIRAMISU                 $15.00
1   MINESTRONE VERDE         $18.00
3   LA TACHE ROMANEE CO  $15000.00
2   CHATEAU PETRUS       $10000.00
2   J.W. BLUE              $150.00
3   TRUFFLE TAGLIOLINI     $585.00
2   CRISTAL ROSE MAGNUM  $10000.00
                        ----------
                        $36631.00
    TAX              :   $3251.89
    SUB-TOTAL        :  $39892.89
    20% GRATUITY     :   $7328.20

TOTAL          $47221.09
           THANK YOU
    347-***-**** & CARLO'S.US
    TIME: 14:39      6 CUSTOMERS
```

Figure 11.2 Sample Receipt of Expenses

receiving low pay and often working more than one menial job, these individuals held jobs with fewer benefits than those of other workers (Fleury & Fortin, 2006). Moreover, the majority in this category worked shifts other than the traditional nine to five workday. Given that the majority of daycare facilities are designed with the traditional workday in mind, the working poor are often at a disadvantage and left to scramble to find care for their children.

It follows that the spending patterns of the very rich and the working poor are at considerable odds. Working-class individuals often have to make very tough decisions at the end of every month, when their income has dried up or been stretched to its limit. To ensure that their children are fed and the rent is paid, the working poor often forgo purchasing items that many others consider necessary. A recent report by Statistics Canada (2007) suggests that they are much less likely to buy sporting goods for their children or to spend their income on eyeglasses, personal computers, or Internet connections. The richest segments of society do not face these spending quandaries. Consider, for example, the following receipt from a dinner enjoyed by billionaire Roman Abramovich and five friends. The total cost for the evening was considerably more than the average Canadian's yearly income. Such extravagance is unfathomable to most Canadians.

Criminalizing Poverty

A considerable gap between the lifestyles and life chances of the working and capitalist classes is palpable in modern society. Those from affluent backgrounds can look forward to quality education, vacations in exotic locations, and a life relatively free of economic restraint. By contrast, the working classes and marginalized populations can expect continuous discomfort and even greater disenfranchisement. Moreover, conventional **crime** is most often concentrated in inner-city neighbourhoods, those spaces that great numbers of poor and marginalized groups call home. To date, research on the interconnection between class and the commission of crime in Canada remains relatively underdeveloped (Hartnagel, 2008; West, 1984). West reports that working-class young people were five times more likely to be arrested by police and 90 per cent more likely to be confined in centres of detention than their more affluent counterparts (West, 1984; Hartnagel, 2008).

While discussions of the amount of crime committed by, and concentrated in, the working and labouring classes are relatively scant, scholarly attention to the regulation of the poor and marginalized through state instruments of control has been more abundant. Starting with Rusche and Kirchheimer (1939) and up to the present with the work of Wacquant (2009), much ink has been spilled documenting the significance and consequences accruing from the over-representation of the poor in capitalist state-sponsored penal institutions (Melossi, 1981). At the same time, commentators have evidenced the relative dearth of the capitalist class in prisons and otherwise as subjects of state control and surveillance. In short, state social-control policies and tactics overwhelmingly target the poor. Police resources are concentrated in the neighbourhoods inhabited by the marginalized and working classes. It is a rare sight to see a police car patrolling suburban streets.

In his recent book *Punishing the Poor*, Wacquant (2009) documents how the social problems emerging from increasing labour insecurity and **social welfare** restructuring have been managed through the prison nexus. Despite stagnating crime rates and even slight reductions in violent crime, governments across the West have implemented extreme and oppressive crime-control policies that target the structurally disadvantaged. Lack of consideration for the poor and economically irrelevant is at the heart of contemporary Western criminal justice policy.

The Canadian state has followed suit. Despite relatively stable crime rates, the federal Conservative Party under Stephen Harper's leadership has stated publicly that it is prepared to be even tougher on crime. Mandatory minimum sentences are central to this government's tough-on-crime strategy. Under the Conservatives' plan, offenders convicted of a whole series of crimes would automatically be sentenced to custody. There remains the problem, however, that academic research has failed to demonstrate conclusively the overall effectiveness of mandatory minimums in protecting the public, deterring crime, or rehabilitating offenders. Indeed, in response to a request from *Maclean's* magazine to explain strict adherence to such a nebulous policy, Justice Minister Rob Nicholson sent a memo that effectively admitted that 'in our opinion . . . the studies are inconclusive particularly with respect to the main debate: do MMPs [mandatory minimum penalties] deter crime?' (Geddes, 2009).

If crime rates are not escalating and mandatory minimums are, by the government's own standards, not particularly effective in deterring crime, why does the Conservative government insist on pushing such punitive measures through the House of Commons? In short, it is politically expedient (Hogeveen, 2005b). Harper's former chief of staff Ian Brodie confirms the value of advocating law-and-order strategies in the face of a paucity of academic support:

> Every time we proposed amendments to the Criminal Code, sociologists, criminologists, defence lawyers and Liberals attacked us for proposing measures that the evidence apparently showed did not work . . . that was a good thing for us politically, in that sociologists, criminologists and defence lawyers were and are all held in lower repute than Conservative politicians by the voting public. (Brodie, cited in Geddes, 2009)

Thus the veracity and effectiveness of punitive criminal justice policies are of little relevance to a political party more intent on securing votes than achieving social justice.

Evidently, whether or not a carceral strategy is effective is of little matter when it comes to garnering votes. It follows, then, that those who are caught up in the penal dragnet are pawns to be moved about in a cruel game of political chess. The tougher, the more intrusive, and the more draconian the interventions the greater the political pay-off. But, who, we should legitimately ask, is the target of such repressive policies? Fundamentally, these interventionist strategies hit poor and marginalized groups the hardest. To wit, **Aboriginal** young people are grossly over-represented at almost all levels of the criminal justice system (Sapers, 2009; Manitoba, 1991). Research suggests that they are more likely to be denied bail, charged when apprehended, and detained in pretrial detention (Carrington & Schulenberg, 2004; Roberts & Melchers 2003; Statistics Canada, 2000). Moreover, while comprising only about 5 per cent of the total youth population in 1999, Aboriginal young people occupied 24 per cent of the beds in Canadian centres of detention (Statistics Canada, 2000). Clearly, law-and-order policies locate their logic and justification in the poor and marginalized, who are subjected to exceedingly harsh punishment.

Notwithstanding a few celebrated and yet isolated cases (Conrad Black, Martha Stuart, and Bre-X), **white-collar crime** and corporate deviance have not received nearly the same level of criminal justice attention. Snider (2000) has lamented that, in comparison to the copious amounts of money dedicated to governing crimes committed by working-class individuals, only limited resources are dedicated to policing and researching corporate criminality—this despite widespread agreement surrounding corporate crime's seriousness and ubiquitous effects. Every year corporate deviance causes considerable harm to economies, consumers, the workplace, the air, the water, and other resources upon which the ecosystem depends for its health (Pearce & Snider, 1995). In 2000 Snider penned an obituary for corporate crime in which she effectively argued that while governments have undertaken an intense strategy of implementing stricter controls over working-class and street-level crime, they have refused to introduce similar levels of control over the activities of the affluent:

> Driven by beliefs that stricter criminal laws, increased chances of conviction and more punitive sanctions will deter criminal behaviour, governments in the developed world have engaged in systematically tightening up criminal justice systems. Criminal law works, is the message, and harsher criminal law works best. However, when it comes to crimes of the powerful—marketing unsafe products, maintaining unsafe workplaces, defrauding workers by insisting on unpaid overtime or demanding 'voluntary' labour, dumping toxic

waste, misrepresenting the benefits or not disclosing the risks of products—criminal law does not work. It is expensive, inefficient, ineffective, a club over the head when a whisper in the ear would suffice. (Snider, 2000, p. 170)

At the same time as governments have taken pains to come down tougher on the working class and marginalized, the state regulation of corporate crime has almost disappeared (Snider, 2000). Now more than ever, the rich are getting richer, while the poor are getting sent to prison (Reiman, 1979).

Theory

Karl Marx: The History of All Hitherto Class Struggle

To this point we have seen how attending to issues of class is useful for understanding the direction of contemporary criminal justice policy. Above that of any other scholar, **Karl Marx**'s name is intrinsically linked to studies of class. He famously concluded:

> The history of all hitherto existing society is the history of class struggles. Freeman and slave, patrician and plebeian, lord and serf, guild master and journeyman, in a word, oppressor and oppressed, stood in constant opposition to one another, carried on an uninterrupted, now hidden, now open fight, a fight that each time ended, either in a revolutionary re-constitution of society at large, or in the common ruin of the contending classes. (Marx & Engels, 1968, pp. 35–36)

This quotation allows us to see how Marx approached and understood class.

Marx was convinced that the forces of production in a capitalist society provide the basic mechanism for social change (Hindess, 1987). It is here that the elemental contradictions of an ontological world are manifest. The incongruence between those who work on machines and those who own them invariably, Marx maintains, leads to acute social conflict that eventually culminates in the overthrow of the contemporary mode of production. History, then, moves according to the settling of accounts. In light of festering contradictions, an exploited class (workers) rises up against its oppressors (the owners).

Marx argues that **class struggle** is central to the movement of history and that the working classes are the agents of social change. But how does Marx conceive of social class? Put simply, Marx maintains that classes are the product of, and defined through, relations to the mode of production. Either one is an owner of machines or, conversely, a subject who works on these machines.[3] The capitalist class owns the machines, buildings, land, and raw materials that are utilized in the production of goods intended for exchange on the market. Capitalists control the production of commodities and benefit from their sale. By contrast, workers have access only to their labour power, which they sell to owners in exchange for a wage.

An asymmetry intrinsic to the commodity and labour markets, Marx maintains, defines the relationship between classes in capitalist society. Marx calls the gap between workers' pay for producing a good and the market price for that good **surplus value**. Since they never receive full value for their labour, workers are exploited and owners get rich in the process. For example, you are working at a local McDonald's for $7 per hour and manage to consistently assemble 35 Big Macs in one hour. If McDonald's sells those Big Macs for $4, the surplus value you create in one hour is $133. At this rate, during an eight-hour shift you are paid $56 (before the capitalist state takes their share in the form of taxes) and earn $1,176 for the company. The result of exploitation on a societal level is massive and expanding profits for the capitalists and **alienation** and frustration for the working classes (Poulantzas, 1978, 1973)

Although class friction may be most evident at the economic level, class antagonism is vividly on display in other domains. Following Marx and his interlocutors, Lefebvre (1996) concluded that **space** is political. Just as capitalism has assimilated everyday life, ideology and politics he maintains that we can add space to this ensemble. One of Lefebvre's (1991) main and lasting contributions is his insistence that space is not a naturally occurring phenomenon, but rather a social construction that has dramatic and important implications for the actors who live out their lives in particular areas. He argues that space is allocated according to class and that, as such, social planning reproduces the class structure (Elden, 2007). Like capital, there is an abundance of desirable space for the affluent, and the poor must scramble for the remaining bits. As well, the quality of space allotted provides obvious clues as to its owners. The inner city's older, crowded, often abandoned, and over-policed sectors are set aside for the impoverished (as well as for the mentally ill, the criminal, and the drug addicted), while sprawling suburbs complete with white picket fences and open 'green' spaces are enjoyed by the rich and affluent. Harvey (1989) claims, alongside Lefebvre, that the history of capitalism is the history of a struggle for command of space: 'the whole history of territorial organization, colonialism and imperialism, of uneven development, of urban and rural contradictions, as well as of geopolitical conflict testifies to the importance of such struggles within the history of capitalism' (p. 237).

Space is a fundamental means through which inequality is expressed and governed. Further, space is increasingly subject to a variety of regulatory forms and a surveillance industry that functions to maintain and bolster class (and racial) boundaries. Thus, as Herbert and Brown (2006, p. 756) argue, 'social divisions are mirrored in spatial ones.'

Pierre Bourdieu: The Field of Dreams

The sociological work of French scholar **Pierre Bourdieu** sheds a somewhat different light on social class. Whereas Marx assumes the existence of class as a social reality readily observable through objective sociological scrutiny, Bourdieu maintains that what exists is not 'social classes' per se, but rather 'a social space in the true sense of the term' (Bourdieu, 1987). He was certain that classes should be understood in the same way we understand other spaces—a class is the 'reciprocal externality of the objects which it encloses' (p. 3). But we're getting ahead of ourselves here.

When pushed to explain his work in two words, Bourdieu responded that it would be 'constructivist structuralism' (Bourdieu & Wacquant, 1992). This phrase points to how this social theorist is attempting to navigate a course between and through the traditional divide in sociology that separates structural or more macro-level theorizing (i.e., Durkheim and Marx) and subjectivist and phenomenological accounts (i.e., Schutz). Instead of an either/or tack, Bourdieu incorporates both into this work. Not content to settle on one or the other side of the structure/agency divide, he sets about to overcome it (Bourdieu, 1989). Since his thinking attempts to braid together perspectives once considered antagonistic, it follows that Bourdieu conceptualizes class rather synthetically (Wacquant, 2007). Thus, as Wacquant (2007) points out, 'it retains Marx's insistence on grounding class in material relations of force but weds it with Durkheim's teachings on collective representations and with Weber's concern for the autonomy of cultural forms and the potency of status as perceived social distinctions' (p. 2).

The idea of **field** is at the heart of Bourdieu's understanding of class. To help us make sense of the concept, it is useful to liken field to a sporting arena. A sports field is a space set apart for competition wherein players boasting different skills and levels of power compete to see who is more adept. To make matters even more difficult, this playing field is uneven. The field is misaligned such that one team is afforded a distinct advantage over its competitors.

People's ability to succeed on this field is dependent upon their **habitus**, which references the actors' feel for the game or rather 'the set of dispositions acquired through experience' that allows them to navigate the social world, (Bourdieu, 1990). An individual lacking the necessary experience and culture to effectively negotiate the social world perpetually toils uphill or rather up*field*. Consider for example the paradigmatic sitcom scene that involves someone of the working classes being invited to a party at the home of the ridiculously affluent. Hilarity ensues as the unexpected dupe quickly realizes that he or she lacks the social graces to navigate the situation comfortably. More accustomed to drinking beer and eating meals in front of the television, this person feels and looks terribly out of place. The 1990s sitcom *The Fresh Prince of Bel Air* is a prime example. After finding himself in considerable trouble on the mean streets of Philadelphia, Will Smith's character is sent by his television mother to live with his uncle in the affluent city of Bel Air. Because Will lacks the necessary culture and upbringing to fit in with this opulence, he is perpetually at odds with his uncle. Behaviour that would be quite acceptable at home in the housing projects of Philadelphia is considered gauche by Bel Air standards. The problem is that Will's 'feel for the game' within the ethos of affluence is skewed by his upbringing.

Those endowed with the greatest quantity of **capital** valued in a particular field (i.e., economic, cultural, symbolic, or linguistic) are much more at ease and better equipped to transmit an aura of competence (Brubaker, 1985). Continuing with our example allows us to see that because Will speaks differently and has a relationship with money different than that of his upscale cousins, he constantly finds himself in trouble with peers, school officials, and family members. Within a given 'game', individuals acquire differing levels of capital (i.e., education, culture, occupation) based on their position in the social structural hierarchy.

Socialization and learning ensure that individuals become capable in their own particular situation; that is, they are predisposed toward certain behaviours and actions. These behaviours and actions are valued in one context, but when individuals perform them in others, they may be perceived to be the proverbial 'fish out of water'. This is a case where the visible (behaviour, conduct) obscures or hides the invisible that determines it (structure) (Bourdieu, 1989). Will's behaviour and conduct in centres of affluence seem alien and obscure, but we must keep in mind that they are a part of his socialization in an ethos of poverty. Individual being in the world is not, then, a product of decisions made in the moment, but the product of embedded social structures. Will lacked upper-class capital because of his upbringing in the housing projects. Bourdieu maintains that it is this context that becomes ingrained in his body and visible through it. His clothes, the way he talked and walked, his taste in music, his comportment, and even his name distinguish him from his affluent cousin Carlton. Agents' dispositions, their habitus, and the mental structures through which they understand and move about the social world 'are essentially the product of the internalization of the structures of that world' (Bourdieu, 1989, p. 18). Thus, 'the socialized body . . . does not stand in opposition to society: it is one of its forms of existence' (Bourdieu, 1989, p. 29).

Affinities of habitus are what account for social classes. Rather than in Marxian relations to machines or in Durkheimian 'social facts,' Bourdieu holds that class is located in *social space.* Social space 'presents itself in the form of agents endowed with different properties that are systematically linked among themselves: those who drink champagne are opposed to those who drink whiskey' (Bourdieu, 1989, p. 18). He goes further to suggest that distinctions manifested in taste are particularly illustrative and instructive for what they reveal about social space and, by extension, class. Bourdieu (1984) claims that even the most insignificant techniques of the body (e.g., ways of blowing one's nose and ways of talking) are direct expressions of the division of labour. Taste functions as a social orientation that guides 'the occupants of a given place in *social space* towards the social positions adjusted to their properties and towards the practices or goods which befit the occupants of that position' (p. 466). Thus, 'the cognitive structures which social agents implement in their practical knowledge of the social worlds are internalized, embodied, social structures' (p. 467). Certainly, these thought processes do not occur at a conscious level, but instead operate 'naturally'.

The division of social space into classes is indicative of the relative distance between individuals such that that those who possess similar amounts of capital will be grouped into one class. These subjects share dispositions and interests in common, and we can suspect that their habitus will be quite similar. Together these individuals hold a sense of what is proper and what is to be reviled. Put simply, members of social classes tend to resemble one another in terms of their shared tastes and, as a result, 'come together as a practical group, and thus to reinforce their points of resemblance' (Bourdieu, 1987, p. 6). It holds that individuals of the upper classes are more likely to congregate together in spaces of shared interest (i.e., the country club, the theatre, the ballet) because of commonly held tastes, capital, and habitus. In summary,

> classes can be characterized in a certain way as sets of agents who, by virtue of the fact that they occupy similar positions in social space (that is, the distribution of powers), are subject to similar conditions of existence and conditioning factors and, as a result, are endowed with similar dispositions which prompt them to develop similar practices. (Bourdieu, 1987, p. 6)

Bourdieu (1984) empirically confirmed these theoretical insights when he argued that despite actors' being relatively free to choose from a range of music, art, and television programs, their preferences demonstrate a strong affinity to their social position. Thus, our tastes in food and leisure are strongly connected to unconscious pushes and pulls conditioned by our place in social space. Our taste in, for example, music (Beethoven vs Jay-Z) and entertainment (the opera vs Jerry Springer) parallels our place in class space. Bourdieu was convinced that our choices are a condition of our having internalized certain social structures and that these social structures not only become manifest in significant and life-altering preferences (i.e., to go to university) but are most 'marked in the everyday choices of everyday existence, such as furniture, clothing, or cooking, which are particularly revealing of deep-rooted and long standing dispositions' (1984, p. 77).

Ulrich Beck's Zombies

Ulrich Beck has been outspoken in his objection to traditional sociological concepts and analysis. He maintains that sociological categories that provided coherence and meaning for decades have lost much of their usefulness of late. Class tops his list. Beck is convinced that social class is dead. He argues that it no longer holds meaning in our late modern, or reflexive modern, society, and he bemoans how social scientists continue to employ class in their attempts to understand and discern modern ways of being. Because this concept has continued to keep on living in the sociological imagination long after it ceased to exist in the contemporary ethos, Beck considers class a 'zombie' category.

To understand Beck's position, we must take a brief detour into his thought processes, particularly how he conceptualizes contemporary times. First, Beck argues that we live in a second modern phase, or reflexive modern epoch, in which core assumptions of modernity have been unravelled and replaced (Beck, 1992, 1994; Atkinson, 2007). Beck maintains that, in this era of reflexive modernization, Marx's ideas and the conception of class are fantastically outmoded. Capitalist expansion and progress have produced unforeseen *risks* to the health and well-being of the entire population—irrespective of class. Western demand for greater and cheaper sources of fossil fuels comes at a significant price to the environment, however. Risks and threats associated with the wanton burning of fossil fuels are widespread and do not discriminate. Thus, Beck believes, class-related problems are no longer the fundamental concerns of our times. Instead, emerging global risks (i.e., greenhouse gas, lack of clean drinking water, nuclear disaster, and pollution) that do not adhere to class logics are at the heart of contemporary concern. He concludes that 'in the water supply all the social strata are connected to the same pipe. . . . In these circumstances, only not eating, not drinking, and not breathing could provide effective protection . . . *poverty is hierarchic, smog is democratic*' (1992, p. 36). In this *risk society,* all are interconnected, and Beck maintains that risk societies are 'not class societies' (p. 47).

Coupled with the emerging risk society is a culture of individualization. In contemporary society, Beck and his collaborators argue, collectivities have dissolved. Instead of having a collective sense of being, individuals are on a never-ending quest for individual fulfilment.

The mass consumption of generic goods—lauded by the media as the fount of gratification—becomes the *sine qua non* of contemporary existence. The quest for happiness and self-fulfilment leads people to spiral into consumerism. For whatever ails you a product or expert is ready at hand to fill the void.

Beck argues that as individuals retreat into the comfort of consumerism and as global environmental risks continue to cut across class lines, the efficacy of class as a heuristic device for dissecting and describing the contemporary condition becomes incredibly hollow. He maintains that despite the death of class, social scientists continue to employ the concept to map the contours of a classless society. If classes have indeed been liquefied by mass individualism and reconfigured logics of risk distribution, what are the sociologists who employ this concept actually measuring or examining? According to this logic, scholars who employ obsolete abstractions are engaged in anachronism. It is for this reason that Beck maintains that class is a zombie category (Beck & Willms, 2004, pp. 51–52). As Beck sees it, employing zombie categories in sociological analysis is counterintuitive and continued adherence and reification of such concepts make us 'blind to the realities of our lives' (1999). Continuing to gather statistics on class, Beck maintains, is akin to feeding zombies.

Beck's critics have been quite outspoken in their opposition. But before we move on to this, it is worthwhile to note that Beck was not the first to suggest the declining relevance of class in and for social analysis. Clark and Lipset (1996) answer the question 'Are social classes dying?' in the affirmative. They maintain that class is an increasingly outmoded concept for anyone employed in contemporary scholarship. These researchers hold that, in light of recent structural shifts, traditional theories that highlight the importance of class demand revision (Clark & Lipset, 2001). Others have claimed that 'class as a concept is ceasing to do any useful work in sociology' (Pahl, 1989, p. 6). Still others have proclaimed the 'death of class' (Pakulski & Waters, 1996).

Recent years have witnessed several scholars come out to rescue class from the obscurity to which Beck and others would relegate it. Among many other criticisms, scholars have claimed that Beck's account suffers from a dearth of empirical support and 'mooring in the social world' (Atkinson, 2007). For his part, Scott (2000) claims that even a cursory glance at statistics provides sufficient evidence of the continued influence of class on income, health, and infant mortality. However—and despite their worsening conditions of life—Scott maintains that 'manual workers have neither the solidarity nor the consciousness that is needed to sustain a strong commitment to collective class action' (2000, p. 46). In place of an inspired dedication to social and political change, Scott holds that the labouring classes have substituted a 'money model' of society that emphasizes consumerism and consumption. Unlike earlier eras in which the working classes fought together for better wages and working conditions, workers no longer live *class* in the same way (Scott, 2000). Instead this group is increasingly fragmented and more interested in spending their well-earned dollars than in struggling for a greater piece of the proverbial pie.

Clearly, the debate about the pertinence of class for social analysis is far from settled. At the same time that Beck is calling class a zombie concept and others are making a case for the death of class, others are *Bringing Class Back In* (McNall, Levine, & Fantasia, 1991), *Reworking Class* (Hall, 1997) and arguing that *Class Counts* (Wright, 1997).

Class, Gender, and Service Provision

Another criticism of existing social theories of class, especially those inspired by Marxist traditions, is their seeming inability or unwillingness to account for women's position in class hierarchies. Crompton (1996) maintains that until very recently the preponderance of class research in Britain considered social class to be tantamount to men's position in the employment structure (Goldthorpe et al., 1969; Goldthorpe, 1987). Social scholars were uncritically accepting of, and in part helped to reproduce, the myth of the male breadwinner.

Except during periods of war, women were largely excluded from the paid labour force (Davidoff, 1986). Evidently, women's 'proper' place was in the home, while men sold their labour power to the highest bidder on the labour market. As Strange (1995) and others (Alexander, 1998; Odem, 1995) have empirically demonstrated, women who stepped outside of the narrowly defined limits of domesticity were subjected to surveillance and scrutiny from state agents interested in enforcing the established **gender** order. In this ethos and as far as many sociologists were concerned, women's labour (whether inside or outside the household) was of little matter (Stacey, 1981).

In their challenge to this silencing of women's experiences, many feminist scholars have attempted to draw particular attention to intersections between class and gender by attending to sexual divisions in the public and private domains (Smart, 1990). Beginning in the 1970s, these scholars examined and revealed how gender is often silently written, but in bold letters, in the entire structural and material conditions of Western industrial societies. Smart (1990), for her part, has brilliantly demonstrated how law is a gendering strategy. She maintains that the law reproduces gender and sex hierarchies through its operation. Smart questions whether law as a masculine domain and misogynist institution can ever be employed in the service of women's interests.

Early feminist scholars did much to draw attention to women's domestic realities. Whereas the mostly male scholars of earlier periods largely silenced women's voices and obscured their ontological being, feminist scholars spilled much ink in getting women's subordinate position in the home and in society on the political and academic map. While women have now moved into traditionally male roles and have won hard-fought political battles for recognition, things are by no means equal. Women continually face discrimination and receive lower pay than their male counterparts. Moreover, when women are employed in paid labour, they are still overwhelmingly responsible for household chores and child care (Gannage, 1986).

Recent years have seen more women enter the labour force. A recent Statistics Canada (2006) report indicates that '[t]he entry of large numbers of women into the paid workforce has been one of the dominant social trends in Canada over the last half century.' In 2006, 58 per cent of all women 15 and over held jobs. This represents a significant increase from 42 per cent in 1976 (Statistics Canada, 2006). Changes in women's employment rates have not, however, eradicated distinctive gender patterns in employment. Women, for example, are much more likely to work part time than their male counterparts. Since the late 1970s, women have accounted for almost 70 per cent of part-time employees (Statistics Canada, 2006). It is important to reconcile this with the reality that part-time work is often underpaid and without health or other benefits. Increasingly, women find themselves in service positions (i.e., domestic services, retail and service jobs)—jobs that are short on pay and even lower on prestige. Furthermore, women continue to be located in occupations traditionally reserved for their sex. In 2006 almost 70 per cent of women were employed in teaching or in health, clerical, or service occupations. While women are making inroads into spheres traditionally dominated by males, they are earning less. 'In 2003, women working on a full-time, full-year basis earned an average of $36,600, or 71 per cent of what their male counterparts make—a gap almost the same as a decade earlier' (Statistics Canada, 2006).

The expansion of the number of mothers (re)turning to the paid labour force is a significant feature of contemporary society. Nearly twice as many women with children under 16 were employed (73 per cent) in the first decade of the twenty-first century than three decades ago (39 per cent). Moreover, many women are returning to work when their children are still very young. By 2006, 64 per cent of women with children under age three were employed. This rate is more than double the 1976 rate of 28 per cent (Statistics Canada, 2006). Evidently, women's labour force participation stands apart from that of their male counterparts, and it follows that their experiences inside and outside the world of work are at odds.

This realization has prompted scholars to claim that class and gender relations 'should be analysed in association and that women [have] their own class position and identity' (McDowell, 2006). Recent shifts at the societal level and women's unique experience therein lend credibility to this position. Indeed, new class divisions between women are emerging and demand attention. But if we attend to women as a whole, the dissimilarities in the realities of, on the one hand, the unattached female law partner and, on the other, the single mother working two equally unpalatable jobs become neglected. Indeed, many middle- and upper-class women depend on their working-class counterparts to care for their children, clean their homes, and serve their food. This new 'servant class' has little, other than their sex, in common with their upper-class sisters (Gregson & Lowe, 1995, as cited in McDowell, 2006). Fundamentally, then, class is a significant concept not only between the sexes but within them. McDowell (2006, p. 842) argues that ungendered class analysis is no 'longer appropriate but then nor is unclassed gender analysis, as women's lives diverge on class lines.'

Women face countless challenges that are not experienced, or not experienced as dramatically, by their male counterparts. On average, women earn less money, have greater trouble finding full-time work, and are more likely to be employed in the service industry than men; women are primarily responsible for raising children; and women are finding it increasingly difficult to locate quality child care (Canada West Foundation, 1997). Indeed, women are much more likely than men to rely on government-funded services. In recent years, funding for these social services has been seriously eroded. Lone-parent families (predominantly led by women) in need of social support in Alberta, Canada's most oil-rich province, received just 48 per cent of the poverty line or a mere $12,000. Given women's heavy reliance on social services, any reduction in social welfare programming and funding will have marked implications for women.

Neo-liberalism and Service Provision

Neo-liberal economic and political restructuring lies at the heart of such repressive reductions in social assistance rates for women. The welfare state that propped up and provided a safety net for the working classes and the downtrodden has weakened dramatically in contemporary times. The welfare state can be summarized in the following way: 'The essence of the welfare state is government-protected minimum standards of income, nutrition, health, housing and education, assured to every citizen as a political right, not as a charity' (Wilensky, 1975). Since the 1970s, commentators have argued that the welfare state is in crisis. Rising levels of unemployment, mounting state debt, and increasing inflation have rendered **Keynesian** welfare policies seemingly obsolete. At the heart of the recent neo-liberal revolution is a trenchant critique of the welfare state. Key opponents, such as von Hayek and the Chicago School, have successfully lobbied for greater freedom for capital investment and movement. Furthermore, these critics maintain that, because of the high taxation levels required to fund it, the welfare state is a deterrent to capital investment and reduces worker motivation (Joppke, 1987).

But what is neo-liberalism? It is important to point out that neo-liberalism is not a monolithic mentality but is most often contoured through immersion in the local conditions of life. Nevertheless, some consistent elements can be identified. Harvey (2005) explains:

> Neo-liberalism is in the first instance a theory of political economic practices that proposes that human well-being can best be advanced by liberating individual entrepreneurial freedoms and skills within an institutional framework characterized by strong private property rights, free markets and free trade. The role of the state is to create and preserve an institutional framework appropriate to such practices. The state has to guarantee, for example, the quality and integrity of money. . . . But beyond these tasks the state should not venture. (p. 2)

The following are among the most archetypal features of neo-liberalism: responsibilization of subjects, concomitant welfare state rollback, privatization of previously public enterprises (including child welfare and imprisonment), tax reductions for the rich, the opening of borders to capitalist investment, and the creation of a climate conducive to the inflow of foreign investment. Indeed, with soaring oil prices, Alberta's oil sands have piqued the interest of foreign investors. Prime Minister Harper has openly invited foreign investors to invest in Canadian energy and has encouraged countries such as Russia to follow suit. At his first G-8 summit in 2006, Harper, in the spirit of the neo-liberal times, stated that 'we [and I think he means Canadians] believe in the free exchange of energy products based on competitive market principles, not self serving monopolistic political strategies' (Anon., 2006). Harper is speaking here on the basis of projected data: it is estimated that foreign investment in the oil sands from Holland, Norway, Japan, and the United States, among others, could amount to as much as $125 billion. Given these figures, paving the way for capitalist investment makes good economic sense.

Oil and gas royalties that pad the provincial coffers encourage officials to find ways to encourage increased foreign investment—even in periods of economic recession. This is why, in the face of a global economic downturn, the province of Alberta recently announced initiatives to stimulate new and continued economic activity, including a drilling royalty credit for new conventional oil and natural gas wells ($200 per metre drilled royalty) and a new well incentive program. Government ventures aimed at creating or conditioning an environment conducive to private economic investment are paramount in neo-liberal capitalism.

If this is not sufficient to indicate the extent of the province's dedication and pandering to big business, consider the rather lengthy debates that centred on the Kyoto Protocol in 2003. Dedicated to altering social and economic conduct so as to have a positive effect on long-term climate change, the protocol was predictably and widely panned in the news media and the Alberta Legislative Assembly for failing to attend to or even recognize the needs of a province heavily dependent on the oil industry. MLA Mary-Anne Jablonski maintained that, 'after all, when you're talking about Alberta, you're talking about the centre of the oil and gas service industry. . . . Our provincial government has reiterated its intention to fight the Kyoto protocol should it prove to be as onerous as first expected' (*Hansard*, Legislative Assembly of Alberta, 20 February 2003). Jablonski's words are illustrative. The Alberta government under Ralph Klein was committed to ensuring that big business—especially the oil and natural gas industries—would enjoy a safe haven no matter the environmental tariff. When the government's promises to big business entail environmental degradation, the outcome is easily foretold.

Ostensibly, the mission of contemporary states is to optimize conditions for capital accumulation and investment—or, to put it crudely, to facilitate a good business environment (Harvey, 2003). When Ralph Klein took office in 1992–93, reducing the provincial debt became his raison d'être. A province with what Albertans were told was an out-of-control debt problem conditioned by, in Klein's mind, big government and overspending on social programs was seemingly unattractive to foreign investors. Three commissioned reports all came to the same conclusion: that expenditure cuts and concomitant revenue increases were necessary to keep the province from spiralling into financial ruin (Laxer, 1995).

In an effort to unfetter capital and encourage competition, Western governments have made a concerted effort to shift responsibility for service provision from the state to the private sector. A claim to more streamlined use of taxpayers' money is central to this assumption. Furthermore, governments have maintained that opening up markets that were once monopolized by crown corporations would encourage competition and thereby effectively drive down consumer prices. Driving this movement is the assumption that only private sector competition can cut prices and ensure cost minimization (Brush, 1987). Few industries were spared as Western governments attempted to off-load their corporations: telephone, prisons, water, airlines, tourism, electricity, and oil were all siphoned to private owners.

In neo-liberal fashion, Conservative MLA Steve West announced on 2 September 1993 that stores now operating under the Alberta Liquor Control Board (ALCB) would be put up for sale.

He suggested that '[a]nybody can apply for a license. We're a free market system' (as cited in Laxer, 1995, p. 102). Despite promises to cut prices and operate more efficiently, liquor stores in the province started charging consumers more for their products, although they generated less income (Laxer, 1995). How does this make coherent sense? Laxer (1995) points out that the public system was surprisingly efficient. He demonstrates that the ALCB had more efficient distribution lines and benefited from economies of sale by buying in bulk. Furthermore, employees were being paid much less for the same work under private ownership, and because they were no longer government employees, they enjoyed fewer, if any, benefits. It is difficult to point to a winner in this matter. Consumers are paying more, employees are worse off, and profits are down. But there is a winner—the private owner. Prior to privatization, this market was closed to all except the government. Deregulation of everything from water to alcohol sales unlocks new zones of 'untrammeled market freedoms for powerful corporate interests' (Harvey, 2006, p. 6).

In addition to off-loading crown corporations to private interests, Western governments have also *seemingly* given up some of their powers with regard to criminal justice. Nevertheless, redistribution of power in this area is a façade. It is only criminal justice *tasks* that are being reallocated. 'A strongly constituted State does not easily give up its diverse powers, which are in turn guaranteed by the institutions it coordinates and dominates' (Lefebvre, 2009, p. 129).

As in other Western nations, Canadian youth justice officials have off-loaded to communities responsibility for the regulation of non-violent and first-time offenders (Canada, Department of Justice, 2004). Under the restorative justice rubric, a great number of community justice programs have been authorized by the state (Woolford & Ratner, 2008; Pavlich, 1996). Included among the restorative approaches endorsed by the Youth Criminal Justice Act are conferencing and youth justice committees (Bala, 2003; Hogeveen, 2005a). In 1997 the standing committee argued that these community-run programs should be 'given a new prominence as a centrepiece in a renewed approach to the youth justice system' and recommended that communities be allowed to 'determine the role to be played by these committees in relation to the coordination and delivery of services to young people' (Canada, House of Commons 1997, chap. 8).

But let us not be fooled by the perceived democratization of the state's powers. While seemingly redistributing its crime control powers through the medium of restorative and community justice, the state maintains a tight grasp on power though setting agendas and mandates, monitoring the efficacy of existing programs and disposing of radical initiatives that may pose a threat to established power (Hogeveen, 2005b). The state curtails community involvement by limiting the tasks available for the community and setting the directives and directions of criminal justice policy. Without any real power, community members are left to do the state's bidding. Furthermore, youth justice committees handle relatively minor forms of deviance like shoplifting, while the important and more serious forms of criminality remain in the hands of the state. For example, of the cases referred to Edmonton youth justice committees in 1996, 97 per cent involved shoplifting, while the remaining 3 per cent included such heinous crimes as vandalism and mischief (Alberta Justice, 1997).

A strongly constituted state does not give up its diverse powers without a struggle.

Targeting the Working Class: Welfare Reform

Cuts to social welfare and alterations to the Keynesian state have continued into the present. On 7 April 2009, in its infinite neo-liberal wisdom, the Alberta government axed its Wild Rose Foundation, a group that, for 25 years, had allocated lottery funds of about $8 million to social service agencies, many of which relied heavily on this source of funding. Community services such as food banks, women's shelters, and inner-city children's programs depended on the grants of up to $50,000 to fund their operations.

But this is the reality that many social services now face. One executive director of an inner-city program acknowledged that she spends between 85 and 90 per cent of her time chasing money to ensure that her programs continue to operate and the vulnerable populations that depend on the services get the help they require. Continual cycles of writing grant proposals and going to funders with her proverbial hat in hand have led her down a road to 'burn out'. Instead of following her passion by assisting inner-city youth directly, she has opted to return to school. I cannot help but wonder how many other dedicated social service workers decamp from the helping industry out of frustration.

Lindsay Blackett, the minister responsible for making this round of cuts, claimed that he was 'proud' that he had not cut money from the Alberta Heritage Foundation, which funds museums; he had been concerned that the arts community would mount a more vociferous outcry than the social service industry could muster, and now he could claim to be protecting funding for culture. Blackett defended himself by saying, '[I]f I was to cut any of their funding . . . the outcry would be louder and rightly so' (*Hansard,* Legislative Assembly of Alberta, 20 April 2009). Further, this $8-million belt tightening occurred alongside a $10-million budget line set aside by the provincial government for its rebranding campaign. The contradictions are obvious, and it is clear what remains important for the province—an attractive image of Alberta that caters to investment capital.

While governments across the West have created ripe conditions for the expansion and accumulation of capital, these have often come at the expense of the working class. The result is that increasing numbers of families are looking for help from a state that seems unwilling to offer any form of meaningful assistance (Hogeveen & Woolford, 2006). Indifference toward the working classes and the structurally disadvantaged is the cold heart of the neo-liberal mentality. Individual problems are deemed pathological rather than the result of structures of oppression and marginalization.

Conclusion: Justice for the Other

Questions about the relevance and importance of class are central to this chapter. I have suggested that attending to class allows for a more nuanced examination of income disparity, spatial segregation, and the unequal distribution of desirable resources. But for class to make conceptual and coherent sense in contemporary times, scholars need to attend to how neo-liberalism and globalization (to name only two issues) reconfigure, buttress, and even fashion new class *relations* and foster even greater inequalities. Instead of jettisoning class altogether, and while recognizing that the concept is not conceptually unproblematic, we should recognize how class relations allow us to think through the relative inequalities existent between groups—especially those at the working and marginalized ends of social hierarchies.

In today's world, while capitalists seem immune to state intervention into their being and business, working-class individuals are frequently at the centre of criminal **justice** and other state-sponsored systems of control. In the neo-liberal ethos, the capitalist state continues to act on behalf of the affluent by freeing up markets and borders, thereby allowing a greater accumulation and investment of capital, while withholding any kind of support and undergirding for the working class and the marginalized. Indeed, state systems of governance and surveillance are deployed in an effort to intrude more deeply and coercively into working-class life. Furthermore, Western governments have undertaken a process of eroding the state-sponsored welfare benefits that propped up the downtrodden in unfortunate times. The neo-liberal world, it seems, functions through oppression and is legitimated through ignorance. Instead of being stoically complacent, we must work away at the edges of possibility and attempt to awaken from the stupor of alienation.

The burgeoning disparity in incomes and the condemnation and vilification of working-class and marginalized populations under neo-liberalism demand justice in the name of the 'Other'. Given the lack of a socialist imagination and a ready-at-hand revolutionary subject, some other form of revolutionary politics is required. Fraser (1997) argues that justice for the Other demands that the deep-seated structures that produce and entrench asymmetries be attacked and eroded. She states: '[T]he project of transforming the deep structures of both political economy and culture appears to be one over-arching programmatic orientation capable of doing justice to *all* current struggles against injustice.' Eyeing justice for the alienated and exploited Other demands that assemblages come together, regardless of status, to struggle against the tyranny wrought by the neo-liberal menace (Minaker & Hogeveen, 2009). As Fraser (1997) suggests, the project of justice is a collective one—for which we must all do our part.

Key Terms

Aboriginal	class	habitus	social welfare
alienation	class struggle	justice	space
Beck, Ulrich	crime	Keynesian	surplus value
Bourdieu, Pierre	field	Marx, Karl	white-collar crime
capital	gender	neo-liberalism	zombie concept

Questions for Critical Thought

1. To what extent is poverty a gendered and a racialized problem?
2. Compare and contrast the conceptions of class set out by Marx, Bourdieu, and Beck. Which perspective best accounts for contemporary marginalization?
3. In what ways can we envision a different and more positive future for marginalized populations, and what alterations to Canadian society are necessary to this end?

Additional Readings

Beck, U. (1992). From industrial to risk society: Questions of survival, social structure and ecological enlightenment. *Theory, Culture and Society, 9*(1), 97–123.

Bourdieu, P. (1984). *Distinction: A social critique of the judgment of taste.* Boston: Harvard University Press.

Lefebvre, H. (1968). *Dialectical materialism.* New York: Cape.

Marx, K. (1976). *Capital: Volume 1.* London: Penguin.

Marx, K., & Engels, F. (1972). The communist manifesto (Manifesto to the Communist Party). In R. Tucker (Ed.), *The Marx-Engels reader* (pp. 469–501). New York: W. W. Norton.

Thompson, E. P. (1964). *The making of the English working class.* London: Gollanz.

Wacquant, L. (2009). *Punishing the poor: The neoliberal government of social insecurity.* Durham, NC: Duke University Press.

Websites of Interest

Canadian Centre for Policy Alternatives: www.policyalternatives.ca

Edmonton Social Planning Council: www.edmontonsocialplanning.ca

Long Sunday: www.long-sunday.net

Marxists Internet Archive: http://marxists.org

Public Criminology: http://contexts.org/pubcrim

Sociological Images: http://contexts.org/socimages

Endnotes

1. Reiman, 1979.
2. In Canada the market basket measure (MBM) of low income is frequently employed to demarcate poverty. To reflect the actual cost of living in vastly different regions of Canada, statisticians use an indexed method. To determine the poverty line for a particular territory, they determine the price of a basket of necessary goods for a reference family of two parents and two children. Food, clothing, shelter, transportation, and miscellaneous household items are included in the 'basket'.
3. Marxism's seeming inability to account for the contemporary growth in the middle class is a trenchant critique often levelled at this perspective (Hindess, 1987).

References

Alberta Justice. (1997). *X-change: News for Alberta's Youth Justice Committees.* Edmonton: Government Printer.

Alexander, R. (1998). The 'girl problem': Female sexual delinquency in New York 1900–1930. Ithaca, NY: Cornell University Press.

Anonymous. (2006). Harper takes jab at Russia's self serving energy policy. *National Post.* www.canada.com/nationalpost/news/story.html?id=d41f238a-db0e-456f-80c8-809875b26aff&k=6322

Atkinson, W. (2007). Beck, individualization and the death of class: A critique. *British Journal of Sociology, 58*(3), 349–365.

Bala, N. (2003). *Youth criminal justice law.* Toronto: Irwin.

Beck, U. (1992). From industrial to risk society: Questions of survival, social structure and ecological enlightenment. *Theory, Culture and Society, 9*(1), 97–123.

Beck, U. (1994). The reinvention of politics: Towards a theory of reflective modernization. In U. Beck, A. Giddens, & S. Lash (Eds), *Reflexive modernization: Politics, tradition and aesthetics in the modern order.* Cambridge: Polity Press.

Beck, U. (1999, March 5). Goodbye to all that wage slavery. *Newstatesman.*

Beck, U., & Willms, J. (2004). *Conversations with Ulrich Beck.* Cambridge: Polity Press.

Bourdieu, P. (1984). *Distinction: A social critique of the judgment of taste.* Boston: Harvard University Press.

Bourdieu, P. (1987). What makes a social class? On the theoretical and practical existence of groups. *Berkeley Journal of Sociology, 32,* 1–18.

Bourdieu, P. (1989). Social space and symbolic power. *Sociological Theory, 7*(1), 14–25.

Bourdieu, P. (1990). *In other words: Essays toward a reflexive sociology.* Stanford, CA: Stanford University Press.

Bourdieu, P., & Wacquant, L. (1992). *An invitation to reflexive sociology.* Chicago: University of Chicago Press.

Brubaker, R. (1985). Rethinking classical theory: The sociology vision of Pierre Bourdieu. *Theory and Society, 14*(4), 745–775.

Brush, L. (1987). Understanding the welfare wars: Privatization in Britain under Thatcher. *Berkeley Journal of Sociology, 32,* 261–279.

Canada, Department of Justice. (2004). Working in partnership. http://canada.justice.gc.ca/en/ps/yj/partner/partner.html

Canada, House of Commons, Standing Committee on Justice and Legal Affairs. (1997). *Renewing youth justice: Thirteenth report of the Standing Committee on Justice and Legal Affairs.* Toronto: Micromedia.

Canada West Foundation. (1997). *Restructuring of social services: The impact on women in Alberta.* www.cwf.ca/V2/files/Women_Social_Services.pdf

Carrington, P., & Schulenberg, J. (2004). Introduction: The Youth Criminal Justice Act: A new era in juvenile justice? *Canadian Journal of Criminology and Criminal Justice, 46*(2), 219–223.

CCPA (Canadian Centre for Policy Alternatives). (2007). *Rising profit shares, falling wage shares.* www.growinggap.ca/files/Rising%20Profit%20Shares%20Falling%20Wage%20Shares.pdf

Clark, T., & Lipset, S. (1996). Are social classes dying? *International Sociology, 6*(4), 397–410.

Clark, T., & Lipset, S. (2001). *The breakdown of class politics: A debate on post-industrial stratification.* Baltimore: Johns Hopkins University Press.

Crompton, R. (1996). Gender and class analysis. In D. Lee and B. Turner (Eds), *Conflicts about class: Debating inequality in late industrialism.* Essex, UK: Longman.

Davidoff, R. (1986). The role of gender in the first developed nation. In R. Crompton and R. Mann (Eds), *Gender and stratification.* Cambridge: Polity Press.

Elden, S. (2007). There is a politics of space because space is political. *Radical Philosophy Review, 10*(2), 101–116.

Fleury, D., & Fortin, M. (2006). When working is not enough to escape poverty: An analysis of Canada's working poor. www.hrsdc.gc.ca/eng/cs/sp/sdc/pkrf/publications/research/SP-630-06-06/SP-630-06-06E.pdf

Fraser, N. (1997). *Justice interruptus: Critical reflections on the post social condition.* London: Routledge.

Gannage, C. (1986). *Double day, double bind: Women garment workers.* Toronto: Women's Press.

Geddes, J. (2009). Are we really soft on crime? *Maclean's.* www2.macleans.ca/2009/11/09/are-we-really-soft-on-crime/

Goldthorpe, J. (1987). *Class structure and social mobility in modern Britain.* Oxford: Clarendon Press.

Goldthorpe, J., Payne, C., & Llewellyn, C. (1969). *The affluent worker in the class structure.* Cambridge: Cambridge University Press.

Hall, J. (1997). *Reworking class.* Ithaca, NY: Cornell University Press.

Hansard. Various dates. *Debates in the Legislative*

Assembly of Alberta. www.assembly.ab.ca/net/index. aspx?p=adr_home

Hartnagel, T. (2008). Correlates of crime. In R. Linden (Ed.), *Criminology: A Canadian perspective*. Toronto: Nelson.

Harvey, D. (1989). *The condition of postmodernity: An inquiry into the origins of cultural change*. London: Blackwell.

Harvey, D. (2003). *The new imperialism*. Oxford: Oxford University Press.

Harvey, D. (2005). *A brief history of neoliberalism*. New York: Oxford.

Harvey, D. (2006). Neoliberalism and the restoration of class power. In D. Harvey (Ed.), *Spaces of global capitalism: Towards a theory of uneven geographical development*. London: Verso.

Herbert, S., & E. Brown. (2006). Conceptions of space and crime in the punitive neoliberal city. *Antipode, 38*(4), 755–777.

Hindess, B. (1987). *Politics and class analysis*. London: Blackwell.

Hogeveen, B. (2005a). Toward 'safer' and 'better' communities? Canada's Youth Criminal Justice Act, Aboriginal youth and the processes of exclusion. *Critical Criminology: An International Journal, 13*(3), 287–305.

Hogeveen, B. (2005b). 'If we are tough on crime, if we punish crime, then people get the message': Constructing and governing the punishable young offender in Canada during the late 1990s. *Punishment and Society, 7*(1), 73–89.

Hogeveen, B., & Woolford, A. (2006). Critical criminology and possibility in neoliberal times. *Canadian Journal of Criminology and Criminal Justice, 48*(5), 681–701.

Joppke, C. (1987). The crisis of the welfare state: Collective consumption and the rise of new social actors. *Berkeley Journal of Sociology, 32*, 237–260.

Laxer, G. (2005). The privatization of public life. In G. Laxer & T. Harrison (Eds), *The Trojan horse: Alberta and the future of Canada* (pp. 101–118). Montreal: Black Rose Books.

Lefebvre, H. (1991). *The production of space*. London: Oxford.

Lefebvre, H. (1996). *Writing on Cities*. London: Blackwell.

Lefebvre, H. (2009). *State, space, world*. Minneapolis: University of Minnesota Press.

MacKenzie, H. (2009). *Banner year for Canada's CEOs: Record high pay increases*. Ottawa: Canadian Centre for Policy Alternatives.

McNall, S., Levine, R., & Fantasia, R. (1991). *Bringing class back in: Contemporary and historical perspectives*. Boulder, CO: Westview Press.

Manitoba. (1991). *Report of the Aboriginal Justice Inquiry of Manitoba*. Winnipeg: Inquiry.

Marx, K., & Engels, F. (1968). *Selected works*. London: Lawrence and Wishart.

Melossi, D. (1981). *The Prison and the factory: The origins of the penitentiary system*. New York: Barnes and Noble.

Minaker, J., & Hogeveen, B. (2009). *Youth, crime and society: Issues of power and justice*. Toronto: Pearson.

Odem, M. (1995). *Delinquent daughters: Protecting and policing adolescent sexuality in the United States, 1885–1920*. Chapel Hill: University of North Carolina Press.

Osberg, L. (2008). *A Quarter century of economic inequality in Canada: 1981–2006*. Ottawa: Canadian Centre for Policy Alternatives.

Pahl, R. (1989). Is the emperor naked? Some comments on the adequacy of sociological theory in urban and regional research. *International Journal of Urban and Regional Research, 13*(1), 127–129.

Pakulski, J., & Waters, M. (1996). *The death of class*. London: Sage.

Pavlich, G. (1996). *Justice fragmented: Mediating community disputes under post-modern conditions*. London: Routledge.

Pearce, F., & Snider, L. (Eds). 1995. *Corporate crime: Contemporary debates*. Toronto: University of Toronto Press.

Poulantzas, N. (1973). On social classes. *New Left Review, 78*(1), 27–54.

Poulantzas, N. (1978). *Classes in contemporary capitalism*. New York: Verso.

Reiman, J. (1979). *The rich get richer and the poor get prison: Ideology, class and criminal justice*. New York: Wiley.

Roberts, J., & Melchers, R. (2003). The incarceration of Aboriginal o enders. *Canadian Journal of Criminology, 45*(2), 170–189.

Rushe, G., & Kirchheimer, O. (1939). *Punishment and social structure*. London: Transaction.

Sapers, H. (2009). *Annual report from the Office of the Correctional Investigator*. www.oci-bec.gc.ca/rpt/annrpt/annrpt20082009-eng.aspx

Scott, J. (2000). Class and stratification. In G. Payne (Ed.), *Social Divisions*. New York: St Martin's Press.

Smart, C. (1990). *Law, crime and sexuality: Essays in feminism*. London: Sage.

Snider, L. (2000). The sociology of corporate crime: An obituary. *Theoretical Criminology, 4*(2), 169–206.

Stacey, M. (1981). The division of labour revisited. In P. Abrams (Ed.), *Practice and progress: British sociology 1950–1980*. London: Allen and Unwin.

Statistics Canada. (2000). *Youth in custody and*

community services in Canada, 1998–1999. Ottawa: Centre for Justice Statistics.

Statistics Canada. (2006). *Women in Canada: Work chapter updates.* www.statcan.gc.ca/bsolc/olc-cel/olc-cel?lang=eng&catno=89F0133X

Statistics Canada. (2007). *Spending patterns in Canada.* www.statcan.gc.ca/pub/62-202-x/62-202-x2006000-eng.pdf

Strange, C. (1995). *Toronto's girl problem: The perils and pleasures of the city.* Toronto: University of Toronto Press.

Toronto Dominion Bank. (2006). Lifestyles of the rich and unequal: An investigation into wealth inequality in Canada. www.td.com/economics/special/dt1206_wealth.jsp

Wacquant, L. (2007). On symbolic power and group making: Pierre Bourdieu's reframing of class. In *Pierre Bourdieu: Et Klassesporsmal.* Oslo: Forlaget Manifest.

Wacquant, L. (2009). *Punishing the poor: The neoliberal government of social insecurity.* Durham, NC: Duke University Press.

West, G. (1984). *Young offenders and the state.* Toronto: Butterworths.

Wilensky, H. (1975). *The welfare state and equality.* Berkeley: University of California Press.

Woolford, A., & Ratner, R. (2008). *Informal reckonings: Conflict resolutions in mediation, restorative justice, and reparations.* London: Routledge-Cavendish.

Wright, E. O. (1997). *Class counts: Comparative studies in class analysis.* Cambridge: Cambridge University Press.

12 Prostituted, Policed, and Punished: Exploring the Victimization, Criminalization, and Incarceration of Women in Canada

GILLIAN BALFOUR

Introduction

Statistics Canada reports the following data regarding criminalized women:

- 'While still quite low compared to male youth, the rate of "serious violent crime" among female youth has more than doubled since 1986 growing from 60 per 100,000 to 132 per 100,000 in 2005. Among female adults, the rate has also grown from 25 to 46 per 100,000' (Kong & AuCoin, 2008).
- 'Although few women commit violent crimes and inflict injury, police-reported data suggest that when they do, females are as likely as males to use weapons. Data from a subset of 121 police services indicate that, overall, 21 per cent of victims of female-perpetrated violence who experienced an injury were injured with a weapon and 76 per cent were harmed through physical force. This distribution was almost identical for victims injured through male-perpetrated violence with 20 per cent being harmed by weapon use and 77 per cent harmed through physical force' (Kong & AuCoin, 2008).
- 'Manitoba and the Northwest Territories were the jurisdictions with the largest proportion of females admitted to sentenced custody for violent crimes. In Manitoba, these females represented 46 per cent of all females admitted in 2006/2007, and in the Northwest Territories, they accounted for 64 per cent of female admissions' (Babooram, 2008).

Yet, these data are also reported:

- 'According to a police-reported data file covering the 11-year time period of 1995 to 2005, 72 per cent of the just over 422,500 females offenders in the file were **one-time** offenders. Repeat offenders, meaning those who had 2 to 4 police contacts, accounted for 21 per cent, and chronic offenders (5 or more police contacts) were **infrequent** at 7 per cent' (Kong & AuCoin, 2008).

- 'Despite decreases in the overall rate of females charged, rates for offences against the administration of justice have been climbing. Such offences under the *Criminal Code of Canada* include bail violations, breach of probation and failure to appear in court. For instance, the rate at which female adults were charged with bail violations tripled between 1986 and 2005, moving from 33 to 103 per 100,000 population' (Kong & AuCoin, 2008).
- 'One in five females who killed were suspected by police as suffering from a mental or developmental disorder (e.g., schizophrenia, depression, fetal alcohol spectrum disorder, etc.) that may have contributed to some degree to the homicide. In comparison, such disorders were suspected with about 1 in 8 males' (Kong & AuCoin 2008).
- 'The growth in the number of women admitted to remand has been greater than the overall growth in remand. The number of adult females admitted to remand rose by 36 per cent between 2001/2002 and 2006/2007 while the total number of adults admitted to remand was up 14 per cent' (Babooram, 2008).
- 'Between 2001/2002 and 2006, the number of adults admitted to provincial and territorial sentenced custody decreased by 9 per cent but the number of females admitted increased by 11 per cent. The share of female offenders admitted to sentenced custody rose from 9 per cent to 11 per cent' (Babooram, 2008)

These data leave us asking many questions about the criminal justice response to women and girls. Are women and girls becoming men's equals in violence and thus held in pretrial custody or sentenced to jail more often? If women are less likely to re-offend, why are a majority of federally sentenced women imprisoned for their first offence? Why have the rates of imprisonment for women increased over the past decade? Have administrative offences become a form of gendered social control that criminalizes disobedience (Sprott, Doob, & Zimring, 2009)? Has the rate of women's imprisonment increased because women have become more serious offenders? Before tackling the complex questions of why women are more likely to be criminalized and imprisoned today than a decade ago, perhaps we should consider biographies of 'women in trouble' (Comack, 1996).

'Women in Trouble'

In the 1960s, **Dorothy Proctor**, a young 17-year-old woman of Aboriginal and black ancestry from Cape Breton, Nova Scotia, was sentenced to three years in prison for robbery. Dorothy's early childhood was marked by experiences of sexual abuse, violence, extreme poverty, and neglect. Once criminalized and imprisoned, she was forced to participate in sensory-deprivation and LSD experiments funded by the CIA for the US military and conducted by McGill University researchers. Throughout her imprisonment, she was held in segregation cells without access to bedding or a proper toilet unless she agreed to participate in the LSD study. When she was released from prison, she was addicted to various drugs and suffered from flashbacks and memory loss. In 1998, she launched a claim against the Canadian federal government for damages resulting from the permanent harm of LSD exposure. In an investigation into the allegations made by Dorothy, McGill University reported that LSD had been used not only for psychiatric medical research but also in the management of defiant inmates (Blanchfield, 1998).

In 1988, **Marlene Moore**, a young woman from Napanee, Ontario, was labelled Canada's first female 'dangerous offender' and was confined indefinitely in Kingston's Prison for Women. Marlene was first institutionalized at age 13 at Grandview School for Girls, where she was sexually abused by staff members. At age 17 she entered the Prison for Women after being convicted of the attempted murder of a man who raped her. While imprisoned, she self-mutilated and attempted suicide numerous times. Finally, at age 31, in chronic pain from infections caused by self-mutilation, Marlene committed suicide. Following her death, a coroner's inquest was held to look into federal prison policy with regard to women with mental health problems and to assess whether such policy was responsible for Marlene's death. The federal government was not found to responsible for her death, but in the following decade, significant reforms were implemented that were aimed toward improving services for imprisoned women in crisis (Kershaw & Lasovich, 1991).

Twenty years after Marlene's tragic death, in 2008, **Ashley Smith** died in her segregation cell inside the newly built Grand Valley Institution for Women in Kitchener, Ontario, touted as a more progressive and woman-centred prison that provided gender-responsive programming. Ashley entered the federal prison system at the age of 18, but initially she had been sentenced to a provincial jail at the age of 15 for throwing crab apples at a postal worker. Within the provincial prison system, Ashley's mental health needs had gone unmet and her behaviour had spiralled downward, leading to assaults against staff. Eventually she was transferred to various provincial institutions in which, it was later reported, she was physically assaulted by guards and not given access to treatment (Ashley Smith Report, 2008). Finally, Ashley was transferred to the federal women's prison in Ontario so that she could receive the specialized treatment she required. However, over the course of her last year in prison, Ashley was held in segregation cells, routinely strip-searched, and forcibly restrained by guards. On the night of her death, several guards watched through the food slot of a segregation door as Ashley self-asphyxiated. Guards asserted after her death that they had been told by senior prison management not to intervene, as Ashley's needs were taking up too many institutional resources (Saper, 2008).

In 1994, **Lisa Neve**, a 21-year-old Aboriginal lesbian woman who worked as a prostitute on the streets of Edmonton, was labelled a dangerous offender. Lisa was never convicted of homicide, but she had lived most of her life on the street, where assault and robbery are means of surviving the extortion by pimps. Lisa was defiant and thus judged unfeminine in court, and she was deemed a sociopath because of institutional charges against her while she was in juvenile detention.[1] At trial, her diary entries were studied for evidence of psychopathy, and her violence against a violent pimp was cast as attempted murder. In 1999, after Lisa had spent nearly six years in maximum-security prisons, her dangerous offender designation was successfully appealed on the grounds that the Crown's expert witness had failed to demonstrate that Lisa's conduct was 'substantially or pathologically intractable' (*R. v. Neve*, 1999). A three-year sentence for robbery was entered upon appeal. Lisa was released immediately from prison and has since gone on to advocate for criminalized women and those with mental health needs (Neve & Pate, 2005).

In 1995, **Pamela George**, a young Aboriginal mother of two children, was brutally raped and murdered by two white male university students in Regina, Saskatchewan. Pamela was working as a prostitute when she was picked up and taken to the outskirts of town, where she was beaten to death. After telling their friends and family about their involvement in the killing of 'the Indian hooker' (Razack, 2002, p. 139), the young men left the province to work in British Columbia or vacation in Banff, Alberta. Two years later, after a lengthy police investigation that focused on male Aboriginal suspects in the killing, the two men were charged. At trial, the accused were described as 'boys . . . who did pretty darn stupid things' (Razack, 2002, p. 124). The two men were eventually convicted of manslaughter and sentenced to six and a half years in prison.

The story of Pamela George's life has been played out countless times across Canada. In October 2004, Amnesty International released a report entitled *Stolen Sisters: A Human Rights Response to Discrimination and Violence against Indigenous Women.*[2] In the report, Amnesty International details the long history of colonialist practices that have criminalized and morally regulated indigenous women's lives, rendering them dependent, poor, and vulnerable to violence. The Native Women's Association of Canada has documented cases of over 500 missing and murdered indigenous women. The stories of missing indigenous women who were murdered or lost to brutalizing poverty in Canada's urban centres have been told again at the trial of Robert Pickton, a white man convicted of murdering six women from Vancouver's Downtown Eastside. For over two decades, anti-poverty activists and anti-violence groups continually demanded that police investigate the dozens of cases of women reported missing from the streets of Vancouver's east side. Criminologist John Lowman (1998) argues that prostitution laws are to blame for the victimization of street prostitutes, as these women must work in obscurity to avoid arrest. Throughout the Pickton trial, women of the Downtown Eastside were 'disappeared' from political discourse through voyeuristic and erotic representations of drug addiction and prostitution (Culhane, 2003, p. 595), rather than analyzed through a lens of poverty and sexual violence.

How can we begin to make sense of Dorothy's, Marlene's, Lisa's, Ashley's, and Pamela's personal narratives of criminalization, imprisonment, victimization, and death? Are these women's lives connected to each other across time and place? Are these isolated tragedies that could have been prevented through proper staff training and cultural sensitivity? Common sense tells us that only guilty people go to prison, that lawyers must protect public safety and uphold principles of fundamental justice, and that prisons are supposed to ensure the control of inmates who are potentially dangerous. And yet, these biographies of women in trouble reveal lives lived along a victimization-criminalization continuum.

The relationship between women's victimization and their criminalization was first theorized by feminist criminologists who argued that women's behaviour, such as drug abuse or violence, could be understood as a response to, or strategy to deal with, the impact of sexual violence (Heney, 1990; Comack, 1996). Thus, victimization was a 'pathway' into crime (see Ritchie, 1996). This analytical approach was criticized as essentializing and pathologizing women as damaged by their victimization (Sudbury, 2005; Pollack, 2000, 2004), and as lending credence to the anti-feminist charge that violent women offenders receive lenient treatment because of the 'abuse excuse' (Comack & Balfour, 2004; Comack & Brickey, 2007). However, an empirical connection between violence against women and their criminalization persists. In this chapter, we will examine how the criminal justice system structures the relationship between women's victimization and their punishment. Rather than considering how women are affected by violence, we should ask how the criminal justice system obscures the relationship between violence against and punishment of women. Thus, our gaze shifts away from how women cope with violence and turns toward how law, policy, organizations, institutions, and professionals respond to violence against women.

In this chapter, we will explore trends in the victimization, criminalization, and imprisonment of women in Canada and consider the systemic practices of punishment of poor and racialized women that challenge our sensibilities of justice. From these data, we can begin to theorize women in trouble as subjects constituted through legal discourse (Smart, 1990), governed through disciplinary power (Howe, 1994), and therapeutically managed through risk discourses (Hannah-Moffat, 2004). A central aim of this chapter is to consider the analytical concept of intersectionality (discussed throughout this book) in perhaps a different light, one that tries to theorize how the state governs (women) through material and ideological practices. Through a review of Canadian feminist criminology and socio-legal studies, we can perhaps locate how gendered discourses of 'need as risk' and 'punishment as healing' constitute the criminalized and victimized woman in trouble and the role of feminists in designing, reforming, and resisting the criminal justice response to women. Finally, we will explore the possibilities of restorative justice for women who are both criminalized and victimized.

Austerity and Penalty: Women under Neo-liberalism

The criminal justice response to public safety over the past 20 years is marked by the material and ideological scaffolding of **neo-liberalism**. Free-market fundamentalism has played out to varying degrees across most Western countries. In Canada, Keynesian principles of public expenditures and services—to regulate markets and ensure access to universal social programs as a right of citizenship—have been dismantled through privatization and deregulation, resulting in deepened class cleavages buttressed by neoconservative ideologies of law and order. Despite austere social policies, the criminal justice system has grown, with more laws criminalizing and regulating welfare dependency (Chunn & Gavigan, 2004), addiction (Boyd, 2006), homelessness (Hermer, 2002), and mental illness (Neve & Pate, 2005). More police are deployed with more sophisticated weaponry (Gordon, 2006), more prisons are being built, and more prisoners are being confined (Sudbury, 2005). Snider (1998) refers to neo-liberalism as 'the second great confinement,' reminiscent of the eighteenth-century rise of industrial capitalism across Western Europe during which peasants were forced off the land and denied means of subsistence, then forced into mills as wage labourers. Twenty-first-century post-industrial capitalism's neo-liberal practices have required a concomitant ideological shift that has mobilized the censure of the working poor as morally blameworthy, criminalized the mentally ill rather than promote the delivery of services in the community, and designated prisons to be places of healing where therapeutic discipline is administered in segregation cells.

Neo-liberal policies have had a particularly gendered impact. The auditor general of Canada reports that 77 per cent of Canadians who access the programs of social service agencies, such as income assistance, public housing, and daycare, are women (Canada, Auditor General, 2003). Thus, as neo-liberal governments claw back social services and income assistance, create new crime categories of welfare fraud, set up 'snitch lines' so that neighbours can report on welfare recipients, legislate expansive definitions of 'spouse' that inhibit those on welfare from creating supportive relationships, and grant case workers the power to monitor the conduct of the poor, women are becoming increasingly vulnerable to criminalization (Chunn & Gavigan, 2004, cited in Balfour, 2006b). The tragic death of Kimberly Rogers in Sudbury, Ontario, has come to symbolize how poor single mothers have been victimized and criminalized by neo-liberal reforms. Rogers—eight months pregnant and a single mother of a young child—was convicted of welfare fraud for collecting welfare and accepting student loans while attending college (*Rogers v. Sudbury*, 2001). She received a lifetime ban from collecting welfare, lost her right to Pharmacare benefits to pay for her prescribed medications, and was sentenced to six months of house arrest. She died while housebound in a one-bedroom apartment during a heat wave. It was revealed during the inquest into her death that she and her young child lived on a monthly food budget of $18. Regardless of the Ontario provincial government's actions and inactions leading up to her death, the government's policies were not found to be directly responsible for her death (see Chunn & Gavigan, 2004).

Another paradox of neo-liberalism's austere social policies and its ballooning crime control expenditures is the federal government's 'war on drugs'. Long denounced in the United States as an ineffective and racist anti–drug strategy that has disproportionately targeted young African American men (Cole 1999), in Canada the war on drugs has contributed to increased rates of imprisonment for women over the last decade, particularly of poor and racialized women. The Ontario Commission on Systemic Racism in the Ontario Criminal Justice System reports that admissions of African Canadian women for trafficking/importing charges to the Vanier Centre for Women increased by 5,200 per cent between 1986 and 1992. More recent data shows that 'charges against females for drug trafficking/importation have increased by 11 per cent between 1994–1998. Furthermore, amongst serious crimes generally, only charges for these major drug crimes show an upward trend between 1994 to 1998' (Boe, Olah, & Cousineau, 2000). In another study, researchers found that as of March 2001 approximately 24 per cent of all women in Canada's penitentiary system were primarily serving sentences for drug offences (Statistics Canada, 2002).

The moral panic associated with the war on drugs has specifically affected women through moralizing discourses of motherhood, femininity, and sexual promiscuity (Boyd, 2004; Boyd & Faith, 1999). For example, missing and murdered women in Vancouver's Downtown Eastside are portrayed in the media as women who chose to work as prostitutes to feed a heroin addiction, rather than as prostituted women addicted to drugs and not able to access drug treatment. Similarly, women criminalized for importing drugs do so because they are unable to support their children properly on a minimum-wage job, but they are described by police and Crown prosecutors as criminals who prey on young people in schoolyards.

The case of Marsha Hamilton (*R. v. Hamilton,* 2000) reveals how race, class, and gender intersect in discourses on public safety. In 2000, Hamilton—a young, black single mother criminalized for drug importation—was arrested at Toronto's international airport for trafficking when she was found in possession of pelletized cocaine, which she had ingested prior to boarding her plane in Jamaica on return to Canada. In handing down a non-custodial sentence in the case, the provincial court judge recognized the feminization of poverty and racial discrimination as the context of Hamilton's involvement in drug trafficking. However, the sentence was overturned on appeal on the grounds that Hamilton should be imprisoned to set an example that would serve to denounce drug trafficking and deter others from seeking financial gains through drug trafficking.

Each of these cases (*Rogers* and *Hamilton*) reveals how race, class, and gender intersect in the administration of justice. We need to understand why, in Canada, court rooms, police cells, deportation centres, welfare offices, jail cells, and morgues are increasingly filled with women of colour, poor women, and single mothers.

What Happens When She Is Both Victimized and Criminalized?

Women like Ashley Smith, Marlene Moore, and Kimberly Rogers were marginalized and condemned as being dangerous or undeserving because of their choices and conduct. Feminist criminologists and activists have been confronted by the challenges of political work that recognizes how the structural inequalities of race, class, and gender intersect in the victimization and criminalization of women. As feminist activists, front-line staff, and scholars struggled against the distortions and silences about women's lives as victims and offenders, it became clear that gendered violence was an experience common to women as a group, but especially to poor, racialized, and institutionalized women. Feminist activism focused on the prevalence and impact of rape and domestic violence so as to break through the 'add woman and stir' hegemony of criminal justice policy and to condemn the invisibility of gendered violence in the public discourse of crime. Throughout the 1980s, **standpoint feminism** called for women's lived experiences to be the epistemology of a feminist ontology. 'Theory building [was to be] informed by women's experiences of oppression to avoid reductionist explanations of women's lives' (Balfour, 2006a, p. 748).

For feminist criminologists, standpoint offered theory and praxis to counter the distortion of women's lives and their exclusion from male-centred theories of crime and male practices of social control. For example, orthodox criminological theories of strain theory, differential association, and subcultural theory constituted the criminal subject as exclusively young, black, urban, and male. As Heidensohn (1985) pointedly argues in her review of male-stream criminologies, if one believed Merton's claim that criminal conduct is an adaptation to structural strain (unemployment, relative deprivation), then surely women would be over-represented in crime data given the concentration of poverty among single mothers and the prevalence of gendered violence. Yet, the gender ratio remained decidedly masculine: despite media accounts, charges against girls and women represented approximately 20 per cent of crimes cleared by charge. Women could not be 'added and stirred' into the theoretical mix. Rather, the social control of women in spaces outside the criminal justice system (such as welfare offices, doctors' offices, and psychiatric hospitals), and their conformity to cultural norms of hetero-femininity, had to be theorized from the standpoint of women.

Despite its important contributions to feminist criminology, standpoint theory was challenged on numerous fronts. First, critical race scholars denounced standpoint theory's inattention to the disparate rates of imprisonment of black people, and liberal feminists called for the compulsory criminalization of men who batter. For example, black and indigenous women experience much higher rates of domestic violence than Caucasian women do, yet they hesitate to look to the state for protection. Thus, victimization and criminalization is 'colour-coded and class compounded' (Daly, 1994, p. 451). Second, standpoint theory tended to frame women's victimization as the cause of her criminal behaviour, thus 'sidestepping the question of why the state responds to abused women with punishment' (Sudbury, 2005, p. xv). Finally, by the 1990s, standpoint theory was rejected by post-structuralist feminists such as Carol Smart (1995), who called on feminists to 'denounce modernist criminology's focus on race, class, and gender, as an endeavour inescapably bound up by greater and greater complicity with the mechanisms of discipline' (cited in Balfour, 2006a, 745). Analyses of violence against women and the feminization of poverty were replaced by an exploration of an identity-based politics, or what Fraser (2005) refers to as the politics of recognition of difference. Postmodern feminists sought to destabilize modernist categories as social fictions (Butler & Scott, 1992) 'and to abandon the state and gender as limited conceptual tools. Yet, in the process, postmodern feminists have forsaken women whose lives are inextricably linked to the state' (Currie, 1992, cited in Balfour, 2006a, p. 745).

Feminist criminology appeared to be at a crossroads. Postmodernist feminism's critique of standpoint asserted that women's voices could not stand as truth, as they are unmediated by analyses of history and context, and standpoint theory assumes that women are politically engaged in their own self-analysis. Some postmodern feminists argued that liberal and radical feminists were using women's experiences to further their own political agenda (criminalizing men for violence against women, censorship of pornography). Liberal and radical feminists were, therefore, anti-intellectual at worst and an example of false consciousness at best. 'The project of making experience visible precludes critical examination of the workings of the ideological system itself; its categories of representation (race, class, gender, sexuality) as immutable fixed identities' (Scott, cited in Mardorossian, 2002, p. 745). Postmodernist feminists argued that standpoint theory assumes the confessional act of telling about one's own experience to be knowledge production. Yet, as feminists engaged in scholarly debate over the meaning and authenticity of experience, violence against women continued, low prosecution rates for sexual assault persisted, and rates of women on welfare and in prison grew.

Bringing the State Back In: Feminist Engagement with Retributive Justice

Although most feminists seek to address gendered violence through the achievement of substantive equality and social justice through the empowerment of women, other feminists ally themselves with the law-and-order state to utilize police, courts, and prisons to combat male violence against women. The consequences of such alliances, however, have been the erasure of feminists as 'authorized knowers' (Snider, 2003). Instead, feminists working inside government research offices as policy advisors have not been able to mobilize political resources. As a result, feminist analyses of structural gendered inequality are stripped away from policy development and implementation. As noted by feminist scholars Fraser and Gordon (1994), women's accounts of sexual violence and domestic assault 'have been redefined away from the socio-political reality of gender inequality and into a new expert discourse' (cited in Balfour, 2000, p. 100). Thus, feminist criminology's 'punishable woman' (Snider, 2003) came into being, constituted through expert discourses that have transformed her needs for addiction treatment, trauma recovery, housing, employment, and mental health services into risk factors for violence and criminality.

An example of an expert discourse that has been championed by psychologists working with women in conflict with the law is 'relational psychology', which explains women's offending behaviour as being caused by 'damaged disconnections and violations such as child sexual abuse, rape and male violence which leave some women susceptible to drug abuse, street life and [criminal behaviour]' (cited in Pollack, 2007, p. 161). In Canada, security classification and parole eligibility are determined by a woman's history of victimization and how she has coped with the assault(s). The goal of prison programming is to encourage healthy relationship choices (as it is the woman who seeks to be in an abusive relationship), proper parenting skills (despite living in poverty), and anger management (so that she does not respond inappropriately to threats against her).

Through this psychological discourse, we see glimpses of feminist clarion calls about the prevalence and impacts of sexual violence. However, the policy language and the practice of law have pathologized women for their dependency on abusive men, drugs, and welfare. For example, in 1990 the Supreme Court of Canada recognized the battered woman's syndrome defence in the case of Angelique Lavallee, a young Aboriginal woman accused of murdering her abusive common law husband (*R. v. Lavallee*). The court agreed that the legal doctrine of self-defence allowed consideration of an accused woman's own subjective fears based on her experiences of chronic abuse. Defence lawyers in the case introduced expert testimony about Lavallee's psychological state because of ongoing abuse, successfully arguing that she suffered from learned helplessness—a belief that there was no way to escape the ongoing violence. In law, a battered woman's decision to kill her abusive spouse can be excused if the woman has been clinically diagnosed to suffer from battered woman's syndrome (Comack, 1988).

Despite Lavallee's 'victory' in court, the battered woman's syndrome defence has rarely been applied in cases where women have killed to defend themselves against male violence. Tragically, between 1994 and 2003, females aged 15 to 24 had the highest rate of spousal homicide (22.5 per million female spouses). This rate is nearly three times the rate of males aged 15 to 24 (8.5 per million male spouses) (AuCoin, 2005). While femicide rates have dropped significantly over the past 30 years, young women remain four times more likely than young men to be killed by an intimate partner (Beattie, 2005, p. 48). These data reveal the severity of intimate partner violence against young women, yet before the law, women's own defensive violence remains cast as irrational, pathological, and rarely justified. These data also suggest the importance of an intersectional analysis of how women's own violence relates to their rate of victimization. Law and correctional policies constitute victimized women as being at risk of re-offending because of their history of being in abusive relationships; they fail to contextualize women's own violence at the nexus of victimization and poverty.

The socio-political context of the anti-feminist backlash and the erasure of feminists as 'authorized knowers' plays out in media accounts of women charged with violence against intimate partners as evidence of gender symmetry between women's and men's violence. Government research reports discuss family or spousal violence, not violence against women, making claims that there are too many services for women and a lack of recognition of husband abuse because feminists have controlled the cultural scripts of intimate personal violence (Minaker & Snider, 2006). Given the data discussed here, how has the moral panic of 'husband battery' become so entrenched in the official discourse of family violence? Minaker and Snider (2006) suggest that making claims like these is a form of **anti-feminist backlash** rather than a significant social problem. As Snider pointedly states:

> Such developments underline the perils of good intentions—in a culture of punitiveness reforms will be heard in ways that reinforce rather than challenge dominant cultural themes; they will strengthen hegemonic not counter-hegemonic practices and beliefs. . . . She [the female offender] is a direct relative of the violent self-maximizing, voluntary underclass criminal, raised on welfare by a single mother, lacking in self control, unable to defer gratification. (2003, p. 369)

Anti-Feminist Backlash: Feminist Conspiracies and Lying Sluts

A troubling impact of the feminist-inspired reforms that have focused on violence against women is a spiralling anti-feminist backlash. Conservative social commentators (here in Canada the likes of the *Globe and Mail*'s Christie Blatchford and Margaret Wente, the *National Post*'s Donna LaFramboise, and independent author Patricia Pearson) have effectively captured the public imagination and discourse about sexual violence: women can want and desire coercive sex, feminists make them call it rape, and rape statistics are an anti-male conspiracy. Within academe, scholars in the fields of cultural studies and psychology have taken up this anti-feminist backlash sentiment as well, publishing texts such as *Moral Panic: Biopolitics Rising* (Fekete, 1997), *Big Sister: How Extreme Feminism Has Betrayed the Real Fight for Equality*

(Boyd, 2004), and *Rethinking Domestic Violence* (Dutton, 2006). Each of these texts assails feminist research as misleading and biased, but each is also a form of censorship, as feminism precludes discussion of certain topics. Furthermore, through feminism, the discovery of true knowledge has been thwarted by political correctness (Skeggs, 2008). While many feminists would argue that 'manning up' the criminal justice system cannot address gendered violence (Snider, 1994), the result of the feminist alliance with the neo-liberal state has been an appropriation of feminist knowledge claims about the prevalence of gendered violence, especially among poor and racialized women, to justify policy tactics that have increased surveillance of poor women through welfare requirements and the imprisonment of mentally ill and addicted women so that they might be therapeutically managed. Cultural scripts about violence against women have responsibilized women who have failed to make appropriate relationship choices or who are damaged and in need of therapeutic discipline. It should come as no surprise, then, that anti-feminist discourse has retrenched the narrative of raped women as liars, temptresses, or irresponsible party girls.

Despite decades of feminist-inspired criminal law reforms directed toward denouncing sexual assault as a serious crime, according to police report data, only 10 per cent of rape cases are reported (Brennan & Taylor-Butts, 2008). Thus, the prevalence of sexual assault remains uncertain. However, earlier self-report victimization data have shown that approximately 30 per cent of adult women in Canada have experienced sexual assault (Statistics Canada, 1993). The General Social Survey reported that in 2004 there were 512,000 incidents of sexual assault, yet only 24,200 rapes were reported to the police (Brennan & Taylor-Butts, 2008). How do we make sense of women's unwillingness to report sexual assault? Consider this finding by Statistics Canada: 'sexual offences are less likely to be cleared by police (charges laid) than other types of violent offences. In 2007, charges were laid in over a third of sexual offences reported to police compared to almost half of other types of violent crime' (Brennan & Taylor-Butts, 2008, p. 10). Victimization data also show that women are more likely to be sexually assaulted by someone with whom they share an intimate personal relationship than by strangers (Du Mont & Myhr, 2001), yet studies of sentencing indicate that intimate partner violence is treated less seriously by the courts regardless of the severity of violence or the perpetrator's lack of remorse (Du Mont, 2003).

Women recognize that calling the police will likely lead to a humiliating process. Research has shown that women are treated as 'lying sluts' under cross-examination by defence lawyers (Comack & Balfour, 2004). Lawyers appear to rely on cultural scripts or rape myths such as 'Yes to one then yes to all', 'No means maybe', 'A woman who resists cannot be raped', 'Women enjoy rough sex', 'Rape is a sexual act that results from a woman arousing a man', and 'Rape doesn't hurt anyone' (Comack, 1999, cited in Comack & Balfour, 2004, p. 111). Rape trials have typically been sites of 'pornographic vignettes' or 'celebration[s] of phallocentrism' (Smart, 1989, p. 35) by portraying women as liars and temptresses. Yet, Gotell's studies (2001, 2007, 2008) of rape trials reveal that defence lawyers will also cull together evidence of a victim's emotional instability or history of mental illness from third-party confidential documents and even the victim's personal diaries. Gotell found that such tactics are most often used in cases involving women with histories of involvement with child protection or mental health systems, or who are prostituted and homeless with histories of addiction.

Despite the research findings of the prevalence and seriousness of gendered violence within intimate partner relationships and for the most marginalized and vulnerable women, the official version of law imposes the meaning and identity of the 'real' victim of gendered violence: a middle-class white woman is attacked by a stranger; she is appropriately upset but not psychologically traumatized; her body provides forensic evidence of penile vaginal or anal penetration or bruising, she has not been drinking; and she is in a monogamous heterosexual relationship. Is it possible, then, for the criminal justice system to accept an intersectional analysis of criminalized women's lives that takes into account poverty, systemic racism, and gendered conditions of endangerment?

Intersectional analysis has been recognized by some feminists as a means to contextualize women's lives by identifying cultural, political, and economic conditions of 'gender entrapment' (Ritchie, 1996). Let us consider the case of Marsha Hamilton, who was arrested and criminalized for drug trafficking. We see intersections of racial inequality and the feminization of poverty in the neo-liberal context: a young black immigrant woman with few means of financial support for her young children agrees to swallow 93 pellets of cocaine worth $70,000 and cross into Canada for a few hundred dollars. She almost dies from a drug overdose and is sentenced to three years in prison on appeal by the Crown. Smart's article 'The Woman of Legal Discourse' (1992) helps us understand the law as a gendering process: 'woman is a gendered subject position which legal discourse brings into being' (p. 34). This analytical approach allows us to consider victimization and criminalization as embodied experiences that are discursively constituted through legal, psychiatric, neo-liberal, and feminist discourses. For example, Lisa Neve experienced sexual violence and exploitation on the streets of Edmonton, yet her violence against those who abused her (pimps, dangerous johns, etc.) was constituted through expert discourses of psychiatrists as evidence of her dangerousness to others. In turn, strategies of Crown prosecutors were structured by cultural scripts of 'law and order', resting upon psychological and psychiatric discourses to justify their application for a dangerous offender designation. Thus, her victimization enabled her criminalization.

So far we have seen some of the unintended consequences of feminist-inspired law and policy reforms and the impact of neo-liberal austerity on the lives of women in trouble. But what have been the roles of the women who have acted as professionals, activists, researchers, and volunteers working with victimized and criminalized women in the context of neo-liberalism?

'Their Sisters' Keepers'

The roles of women as 'their sisters' keepers' (Freedman, 1981) within the bureaucracies of the criminal justice system—as lawyers, police officers, prison guards, probation officers, psychologists, and volunteers—have been critically debated by various feminist criminologists (Freedman, 1981; Hannah-Moffat, 2004; Howe, 1994; Hayman, 2006; Kendall, 2002). In an earlier study of feminist psychologists working inside the Prison for Women, I found that institutional frameworks of a paramilitary institution would often over-determine the strategies of the women whose work involved supporting prisoners in crisis, but would also malign the work done by feminists, as expressed here by a feminist therapist reflecting on how she was blamed for causing a prisoner's suicide:

> It is such hard and deeply difficult work. That is why it felt like such a slap in the face to be attacked by CSC [Correctional Services of Canada]. There was actually an article printed in the local newspaper in which the warden made clear statements about too much therapy in the prison and it was causing emotional upheaval and suicides. It was devastating for us. Walking into the prison one day after a suicide a staff person saying to us, "so you've done it again—lost another one." They have no idea what we do. (Balfour, 2000, p. 95)

Feminist principles of empowerment, which contextualize women's lives and help us understand that women's self-injurious behaviour is a means of coping with punitive practices such as strip searches and segregation cells, clearly challenge the orthodoxy of paramilitary institutions. Thus, feminists working in prisons work under hegemonies of risk management and correctionalism that individualize and responsibilize women for their choices and conduct.

> "When there is a crisis, everyone runs around trying to point the finger. But when things are quiet, no one talks about the outbreak of mental health. It is like housework, you only notice it when it's not done. . . . Certainly I have spent a lot of time being called a con lover. In some way I suppose if I was not a feminist, I would blend in more. So I guess my feminism is a problem." (Balfour, 2000, p. 95)

Women advocates and professionals who chose to work from an abolitionist standpoint challenge state regimes that seek to criminalize and imprison women rather than deliver services in communities. The place of women in the policing, punishment, and regulation of women has been seen by some as necessary for reform, yet remains a contested debate among feminists. Snider (1994), for example, asserts that feminist-inspired attempts to utilize compulsory criminalization of domestic violence to protect women have resulted only in dual charging of women who call police for help, putting more men in jail with no or little access to programming, and increasing welfare dependency among women with young children. Kim Pate of the Canadian Association of Elizabeth Fry Societies—a national prisoner advocacy organization that achieved significant prison reforms in the 1990s—reflects on the damaging effects of reforms that have created more prisons for women rather than more resources in communities. Snider (2006) later argues that the punitive law and policy reforms often sought out by feminist criminologists, bureaucrats, and reformers have resulted in the incarceration spiral of racialized and poor women. For example, in Canada, women are more likely to be held in pretrial custody than men, the rate of women's federal imprisonment doubled between 2001 and 2008, and Aboriginal women represent 72.5 per cent of women prisoners (Babooram, 2008; Pollack, 2009). Women's prison reforms in Canada have been a sobering lesson for feminists working in government offices, in communities, and in institutions with criminalized women. Yet feminists have been active in other sites of the criminal justice system, such as restorative justice, investigating and documenting prisoners' human rights abuses and conditions of confinement, and transnational alliance building across anti-poverty, anti-violence, anti-racism, and prison abolition networks.

Making Change: Social and Political Action

The life and death of Ashley Smith inside one of Canada's 'women-centred prisons' reveals the challenges facing those working for reform within the correctional system in the absence of an intersectional analysis of mental illness, victimization, and punishment. Some feminists who have worked for change experience tension between the need to seek alternatives to incarceration and the need to denounce violence against women. Similarly, advocating for street-involved prostitutes has meant working between the lines of supporting women's right to choose sex trade work and recognizing the realities of sexual violence and exploitation on the street. How do we resolve these political tensions in our work for change? How do we achieve the protection of women by the state without entrenching their powerlessness and dependency on police and prisons for their safety? How do we prevent women from being imprisoned under the laws intended to end their victimization?

The surge of victims' rights groups and their growing political influence have had a decidedly negative impact on the work of feminists seeking to challenge how the state punishes. Ideologically in line with neo-liberal governments, these groups assert that more police officers and prisons mean a safer community. Yet court and prison data suggest that women—despite high rates of victimization—are increasingly criminalized and incarcerated, especially poor and Aboriginal women and women living with mental illness. Because of the increasing punitiveness of neo-liberal social and criminal justice policies, feminists have begun to establish new alliances with prison abolitionists and anti-violence and social justice groups. The Canadian Association of Elizabeth Fry Societies (CAEFS), for example—a national prisoner advocacy and prison abolition organization—works nationally and internationally with women's groups and human rights organizations, and has appeared before the United Nations with regard to the treatment of women prisoners in Canada.[3] Such alliance building, as well as this global perspective, is necessary in a socio-political context of a 'culture of control' (Garland, 2001) that 'governs through crime' (Simon, 1997) to utilize retributive criminal justice policies to protect the interests of wealthy and middle-class people through the increased criminalization and surveillance of the poor.

Other efforts to reform the criminal justice system have sought to introduce restorative justice as a new paradigm of criminal justice to denounce harms without imprisonment, emphasizing instead a human rights perspective that seeks to restore the victim's security, self-respect, and dignity.

> Restorative processes and practices, therefore, should empower offenders and victims by
> giving them a sense of inclusion in and satisfaction with these processes and practices; they

should enable victims to feel better as a result of participating in them; and they should hold offenders accountable in meaningful ways by encouraging them to make amends to their victims. If all these occur, we might expect the restorative justice processes to impact on reoffending and reintegration and to heal victim's hurt. (Morris, 2002, cited in Balfour, 2008, p. 108)

Yet, many feminists remain skeptical of the implications of restorative justice in cases of sexual and domestic violence, asserting that its practices can be 'cheap justice' (Coker, 2001, cited in Balfour, 2008, p. 109; Cameron, 2006). Restorative justice relies upon community capacity and resources to supervise the offenders and ensure that the needs of victims are respected. However, many offenders come from impoverished and socially marginalized communities that are unable to provide such services. Cook (2006) asserts that the ideals of restorative justice—empowerment, remorse, and reintegration—are more 'elusive than anticipated' (p. 107), as the process reproduces race, class, and gender relations. Others, however, are cautiously optimistic about the possibilities of restorative justice if the social exclusion of women in their communities caused by poverty and racism is recognized as a barrier to full and meaningful participation (Curtis-Fawley & Daly, 2005; Daly & Stubbs, 2006).

Feminist discussions of restorative justice are partial and incomplete, as the criminalization and punishment of victimized women are not theorized or debated. Feminists have not taken up the question of restorative justice for women criminalized and punished coercively for violent offences, despite the growing rates of women's imprisonment. The victimization-criminalization continuum is not recognized within these feminist claims of restorative justice. Thus, if we limit the use of restorative justice in cases of domestic violence because we fear it will silence and further victimize women, we run the risk of abandoning those women for whom policies of mandatory charging and vigorous prosecution have not worked and who live in conditions of endangerment compounded by poverty and racism.

Given the demonstrated impacts of retributive justice reforms and the uneasy questions of restorative justice practices for women, Hudson (2006) suggests that feminists should reposition women's violence strategically as relational to the gendered conditions of endangerment enabled by the community and the state. Feminist scholarship and activism require a more complex and nuanced understanding of the intersectionality of victimization and criminalization 'as embodied in a network of relationships, which include the community and state failures to guarantee the safety of women' (Hudson, 2006, p. 37).

Summary

Sentencing practices and correctional policy are examples of how gendered conditions of endangerment cultivated by systemic discrimination and relative deprivation have become criminogenic risks justifying the incarceration and surveillance of women. While feminist-inspired prison reforms were intended to limit the imprisonment of women given their low risk to re-offend and the need for community resources and supports to deal with sexual violence, addiction, and poverty, the conditions of women's confinement continue to worsen, especially for women living with mental illness, such as Ashley Smith. Similarly, the establishment of family violence courts and vigorous prosecution policies, while intended to condemn male violence against women, have resulted in the dual charging of women who call the police for help, as well as the criminalization of women who use violence to resist their own victimization.

Feminist-inspired reforms to the criminal justice response to gendered violence have relied on a victim narrative that has not taken up women's own violence. Furthermore, feminist engagement with the criminal justice system has increased the power of the state to prosecute women vigorously and build more prisons for them. Yet rates of victimization have not slowed significantly, and as we have read in the personal narratives of women like Lisa, Marlene, and Ashley, young women living in poverty with mental health problems continue to be prostituted, policed, and punished.

Key Terms

anti-feminist backlash

George, Pamela

Moore, Marlene

neo-liberalism

Neve, Lisa

Proctor, Dorothy

Rogers, Kimberly

Smith, Ashley

Questions for Critical Thought

1. What is the victimization-criminalization continuum? How does it allow for an intersectional analysis of women in conflict with the law?

2. How have neo-liberalism's economic and social policies created gendered conditions of endangerment for women?

Additional Readings

Cunliffe, E., & Cameron, A. (2007).Writing the circle: Judicially convened sentencing circles and the textual organization of criminal justice. *Canadian Journal of Women and the Law, 19*(1), 1–35.

Hugill, D. (2010). *Missing women, missing news*. Halifax: Fernwood.

Kline, M. (1994). The colour of law: Ideological representations of First Nations in legal discourse. *Social and Legal Studies, 3,* 451.

McGillivray, A., & Comaskey, B. (1999). *Black eyes all the time: Intimate violence, Aboriginal women, and the justice system*. Toronto: University of Toronto Press.

Maurutto, P., & Hannah-Moffat, K. (2006). Assembling risk and the restructuring of penal control. *British Journal of Criminology, 46,* 438–454.

Murdocca, C. (2006). National responsibility and systemic racism in criminal sentencing: The case of *R. v. Hamilton*. In *Law Reform Commission, The place of justice*. Halifax: Fernwood.

Murdocca, C. (2009). From incarceration to restoration: National responsibility, gender, and the production of cultural difference. *Social and Legal Studies, 18*(1), 23.

Wiebe, R., & Johnson, Y. (1999). *A stolen life: The journey of a Cree woman*. Toronto: Random House Canada, Vintage Canada.

Websites of Interest

Canadian Association of Elizabeth Fry Societies: www.elizabethfry.ca

Native Women's Association of Canada: www.nwac.ca

Amnesty International: www.amnesty.ca

prisonjustice.ca: www.prisonjustice.ca

Endnotes

1. Institutional charges against prisoners are not typically criminal charges (assault, etc.); they are more often associated with non-compliance with an order issued by a correctional officer, such as taking extra food from the meal line back to the cells. Neve's record of institutional charges included

insubordination (swearing at an officer) as well as threatening staff.

2. Retrieved December 21, 2009, from www.nwac-hq. org/en/sisresearch.html

3. See www.elizabethfry.ca/un/canrep5.pdf

References

Ashley Smith Report. (2008). Office of the Ombudsman and Child and Youth Advocate, Province of New Brunswick, June.

AuCoin, K. (Ed.). (2005). Family violence in Canada: A statistical profile. Ottawa: Statistics Canada, Canadian Centre for Justice Statistics. Catalogue 85-224-XIE.

Babooram, A. (2008). The changing profile of adults in custody, 2006/2007. *Juristat*. Statistics Canada, December. Retrieved September 6, 2009, from www.statcan.gc.ca/pub/85-002-x/2008010/article/10732-eng.htm#a6

Balfour, G. (2000). Feminist therapy with women in prison: Working under the hegemony of correctionalism. In K. Hannah-Moffat & M. Shaw (Eds), *An Ideal Prison? Critical Essays on Women's Imprisonment* (pp. 94–102). Halifax: Fernwood.

Balfour, G. (2006a). Reimagining a feminist criminology. *Canadian Journal of Criminology and Criminal Justice* (special ed.), 48(5), 741–757.

Balfour, G. (2006b). Regulating women and girls. In G. Balfour & E. Comack (Eds), *Criminalizing women: Gender and (in)justice in neo-liberal times* (pp. 154–173). Halifax: Fernwood.

Balfour, G. (2008). Falling between the cracks of retributive justice and restorative justice: The victimization and punishment of Aboriginal women. *Feminist Criminology, 3*(2), 101–120.

Beattie, K. (2005). Family homicides. In *Family violence in Canada: A statistical profile*. Ottawa: Statistics Canada: Canadian Centre for Justice Statistics.

Blanchfield, M. (1998, March 4). LSD experiment subjects may get assistance. *Ottawa Citizen*, p. A5.

Boe, R., Olah, C.L., & Cousineau, C. (2000). Federal imprisonment trends of women 1994–95 to 1998–99. Correctional Service of Canada, Research Branch.

Boyd, N. (2004). *Big sister: How extreme feminism has betrayed the fight for sexual equality*. Vancouver: Greystone Books.

Boyd, S. (2006). Representations of women in the drug trade. In G. Balfour & E. Comack (Eds), *Criminalizing women* (pp. 131–153). Halifax: Fernwood.

Boyd, S., & Faith, K. (1999). Women, illegal drugs and prison: Views from Canada. *International Journal of Drug Policy, 10*, 195–207.

Brennan, S., & Taylor-Butts, A. (2008). *Sexual assault in Canada 2004 and 2007*. Ottawa: Statistics Canada, Canadian Centre for Justice Statistics.

Butler, J. (1990). *Gender trouble: Feminism and the subversion of identity*. New York: Routledge.

Butler, J., & Scott, J. (Eds). (1992). *Feminists theorize the political*. New York: Routledge.

Cameron, A. (2006). Stopping the violence: Canadian feminist debates on restorative justice and intimate violence. *Theoretical Criminology, 10*(1), 49–66.

Canada, Auditor General. (2003). *Report of the Auditor General of Canada to the House of Commons.* Ottawa: Minister of Public Works and Government Services.

Canadian Association of Elizabeth Fry Societies. (2000). Dangerous offender designation denounced. In *Annual Report.* Retrieved October 20, 2009, from www.elizabethfry.ca/areport2000e/page17.htm

Chunn, D., & Gavigan, S. (2004). Welfare law, welfare fraud, and the moral regulation of the 'never deserving poor'. *Social and Legal Studies, 13,* 219–243.

Coker, D. (2001). Crime control and feminist law reform in domestic violence law: A critical review. *Buffalo Criminal Law Review, 4,* 801–860.

Cole, D. (1999). *No equal justice: Race and class in the American criminal justice system.* New York: New Press.

Comack, E. (1988). Justice for battered women? The courts and battered woman syndrome. *Canadian Dimension, 22*(3), 8.

Comack, E. (1996). *Women in trouble.* Halifax: Fernwood.

Comack, E. (1999). New possibilities for a feminism 'in' criminology? From dualism to diversity. *Canadian Journal of Criminology, 41*(2), 161.

Comack, E., & Balfour, G. (2004). *The power to criminalize: Violence, inequality, and the law.* Halifax: Fernwood.

Comack, E., & Brickey, S. (2007). Constituting the violence of criminalized women. *Canadian Journal of Criminology and Criminal Justice, 49*(1), 1–36.

Cook, K. J. (2006). Doing difference and accountability in restorative justice conferences. *Theoretical Criminology, 10*(1), 107–124.

Culhane, D. (2003). Their spirits live within us: Aboriginal women in Downtown Eastside Vancouver emerging into visibility. *American Indian Quarterly, 23*(3/4): 593–606.

Currie, D. (1992). Feminist encounters with post-modernism: Exploring the impasse of debates on patriarchy and the law. *Canadian Journal of Women and Law, 5,* 63–86.

Curtis-Fawley, S., & Daly, K. (2005). Gendered violence and restorative justice. *Violence against Women, 11*(5), 603–638.

Daly, K. (1994). Criminal law and justice system practices as racist, white, and racialized. *Washington and Lee Law Review, 51*(2), 431.

Daly, K., & Stubbs, J. (2006). Feminist engagement with restorative justice. *Theoretical Criminology, 10*(1), 9–28.

Du Mont, J. (2003). Charging and sentencing in sexual assault cases: An exploratory examination. *Canadian Journal of Women and the Law, 15,* 305–40.

Du Mont, J., & Myhr, T. (2001). So few convictions: The role of client-related characteristics in the legal processing of sexual assault. *Violence against Women, 6*(10), 1109.

Dutton, D. (2006). *Rethinking domestic violence.* Vancouver: University of British Columbia Press.

Fekete, J. (1997). *Moral panic: Biopolitics rising.* Montreal: R. Davies.

Fraser, N. (2005). Mapping the feminist imagination: From redistribution to recognition to representation. *Constellations, 12*(3), 295–307.

Fraser, N., & Gordon, L. (1994). A genealogy of dependency: Tracing a key word of the U.S. welfare state. *Signs, 19*(2), 309–366.

Freedman, E. (1981). *Their sister's keepers: Women's prison reform in America: 1830–1930.* Ann Arbor: University of Michigan Press.

Garland, D. (2001). *The culture of control: Crime and social order in contemporary society.* Oxford: Oxford University Press.

Gordon, T. (2006). *Cops, crime, and capitalism: The law and order agenda in Canada.* Halifax: Fernwood.

Gotell, L. (2001). Colonialization through disclosure: Confidential records, sexual assault complainants and the Canadian law. *Social and Legal Studies, 10*(3), 35–46.

Gotell, L. (2007). The discursive disappearance of sexualized violence: Feminist law reform, judicial resistance and neo-liberal sexual-citizenship. In D. Chunn, S. Boyd, & H. Lessard (Eds), *Reaction and resistance: Feminism, law, and social change.* Vancouver: University of British Columbia Press.

Gotell, L. (2008). Tracking decisions on access to sexual assault complainants' confidential records: The continued permeability of subsections 278.1–278.9 of the Criminal Code. *Canadian Journal of Women and the Law, 20*(1), 111–154.

Hannah-Moffat, K. (2004). Criminality, need, and the transformative risk subject: Hybridization of risk/need in penalty. *Punishment and Society, 7*(1), 29–51.

Hayman, S. (2006). *Imprisoning our sisters: The new federal women's prisons in Canada.* Montreal: McGill-Queen's University Press.

Heidensohn, F. (1985). *Women and crime.* New York: New York University Press.

Heney, J. (1990). *Report on self-injurious behaviour in the Kingston Prison for Women.* Ottawa: Correctional Services Canada.

Hermer, J. (2002). The shrinking of the public and private spaces of the poor. In J. Hermer & J. Mosher (Eds), *Disorderly people: Law and the politics of exclusion in Ontario* (pp. 41–53). Halifax: Fernwood.

Howe, A. (1994). *Punish and critique: Towards a feminist analysis of penalty.* New York: Routledge.

Hudson, B. (2006). Beyond white man's justice: Race, gender and justice in late modernity. *Theoretical Criminology, 10*(1), 29–47.

Kendall, K. (2002). Time to think again about cognitive behavioural programmes. In P. Carlen (Ed.), *Women and punishment: The struggle for justice*. Cullompton, UK: Willan.

Kershaw, A., & Lasovich, M. (1991). *Rock-a-bye baby: A death behind bars*. Toronto: McClelland and Stewart.

Kong, R., & AuCoin, K. (2008). Female offenders in Canada. *Juristat, 28*(1).

Lowman, J. (1998). Prostitution law reform in Canada. In Institute of Comparative Law in Japan (Ed.), *Toward comparative law in the 21st century* (pp. 919–946). Tokyo: Chuo University Press.

Mardorossian, C. (2002). Towards a new feminist theory of rape. *Signs: A Journal of Women in Culture and Society, 27*(3), 743–777.

Minaker, J., & Snider, L. (2006). Equality with a vengeance? *Canadian Journal of Criminology and Criminal Justice, 48*(5), 754–779.

Morris, A. (2002). Critiquing the critics: A brief response to critics of restorative justice. *British Journal of Criminology, 42*(3), 596–615.

Neve, L., & Pate, K. (2005). Challenging the criminalization of women who resist. In J. Sudbury (Ed.), *Global lockdown*. New York: Routledge.

Pollack, S. (2000). Dependency discourse as social control. In K. Hannah-Moffat & M. Shaw (Eds), *An ideal prison? Critical essays on Canadian women's imprisonment* (pp. 72–81). Halifax: Fernwood.

Pollack, S. (2004). Anti-oppressive practice with women in prison: Discursive reconstructions and alternative practices. *British Journal of Social Work, 34*, 693–707.

Pollack, S. (2007). 'I'm just not good in relationships': Victimization discourses and the gendered regulation of criminalized women. *Feminist Criminology, 2*(2), 158–174.

Pollack, S. (2009). You can't have it both ways: Punishment and treatment of imprisoned women. *Journal of Progressive Human Services, 20*(2), 112–128.

Razack, S. (2002). Gendered racial violence and spatialized justice. In S. Razack (Ed.), *Race, space, and the law: Unmapping a white settler society*. Toronto: Between the Lines.

Ritchie, B. (1996). *Compelled to crime: The gender entrapment of battered black women*. New York: Routledge.

Sapers, H. (2008, June). *A preventable death*. Office of the Correctional Investigator, Canada. www.oci-bec. gc.ca/rpt/oth-aut/oth-aut20080620info-eng.aspx

Simon, J. (1997). Governing through crime. In L. Friedman & G. Fisher (Eds), *The crime conundrum: Essays on criminal justice* (pp. 171–190). Boulder, CO: Westview.

Skeggs, B. (2008). The dirty history of feminism and sociology: Or the war of conceptual attrition. *Sociological Review, 56*, 4.

Smart, C. (1989). *The power of law*. London: Routledge.

Smart, C. (1990). Law's power and the sexed body, and feminist discourse. *Journal of Law and Society, 7*(2), 194–210.

Smart, C. (1992). The woman of legal discourse. *Social and Legal Studies, 1*, 29–44.

Smart, C. (1995). *Law, crime and sexuality: Essays in feminism*. London: Sage.

Snider, L. (1994). Feminism, punishment, and the potential for empowerment. *Canadian Journal of Law and Society, 9*(1), 75–104.

Snider, L. (1998). Towards safer societies: Punishment, masculinities, and violence against women. *British Journal of Criminology, 38*(1), 1–39.

Snider, L. (2003). Constituting the punishable woman: Atavistic man incarcerates postmodern woman. *British Journal of Criminology, 43*, 343–378.

Snider, L. (2006). Making change in neo-liberal times. In G. Balfour & E. Comack (Eds), *Criminalizing women* (pp. 323–342). Halifax: Fernwood.

Sprott, J., Doob, T., & Zimring, F. (2009). *Justice for girls? Stability and change in the young justice systems of the United States and Canada*. Chicago: University of Chicago Press.

Statistics Canada. (1993). The Violence against Women Survey: Survey highlights. Ottawa.

Statistics Canada. (2002, November). Police reported incidents by most serious offence, Canada and the provinces/territories 2001. Canada Justice, Questions and Answers 2000: Appendix B, Tables 11, 12.

Sudbury, J. (Ed.). (2005). *Global lockdown: Race, gender, and the prison industrial complex*. New York: Routledge.

Legal Cases

R. v. Lavallee [1990] 1 S.C.R. 852
R. v. Neve, Alberta Court of Appeal, 29 June 1999
Rogers v. Sudbury (2001) 57 O.R. (3d) 460 (Ont. Sup. Ct. J).

13 | Sexualities and Difference: The Criminalization of Lesbian, Gay, Bisexual, Transgendered, and Queer (LGBTQ) People in Canada

ELLEN FAULKNER

Introduction

This chapter explores the social construction of lesbian, gay, bisexual, transgender, and **queer** (**LGBTQ**) people as offenders and victims through their engagement with criminal justice systems. It also explores discrimination faced by LGBTQ people in service provision. By exploring the parallel treatment of LGBTQ people along lines of sexuality, race, gender, and class, this chapter emphasizes that difference—in this case LGBTQ difference—has been socially constructed through practices of victimization, aggression, hostility, negativity, and violence. The introduction provides a historical context/overview by exploring the criminalization and legal exclusion of LGBTQ people. Empirical research on **homophobic** and heterosexist violence in Canada sets the context for a discussion of the gaps in service provision within criminal (in) justice systems that typically socially control, regulate, and repress LGBTQ people of diverse backgrounds. An examination of the use of the **defence of homosexual panic** provides an example of how power and authority are used to socially control/regulate and re-inscribe deviant status on LGBTQ people, effectively criminalizing them and denying them personhood and human rights. Discrimination in service provision to those seeking redress from non-lethal forms of **hate crime** shows that the majority of LGBTQ fail to report anti-gay/lesbian violence owing to a perception that nothing can or will be done by police. Based on a history of mistrust and fear because of aggression on the part of police toward sexual and racial minorities, victims fear secondary victimization should they report attacks. They are more likely to report victimization to gay and lesbian organizations and to seek support from within their own communities.

The aim in exploring the various ways in which people are affected by homophobic and heterosexist violence is to show how criminal justice systems and those who work within them have reproduced relations of power and powerlessness through criminalizing LGBTQ people and promoting injustice toward those subject to victimization. Nevertheless, as agents of resistance, LGBTQ people have engaged in social and political action to redress previous historical forms of discrimination.

Canadian Hate Crime Legislation

'Hate crime' as currently defined in Canada was added to the Criminal Code in 1970 for the first time through Bill C-3, creating specific criminal offences such as 'advocating genocide', 'public incitement of hatred', and 'willful promotion of hatred' (Kaplan & McRae, 1993, pp. 243–44). Additional provisions were added to the Criminal Code in 1995 through Bill C-41 (section 718.2(a)(i)) (House of Commons, Canada, 1995). Unlike Bill C-3, Bill C-41 did not create any new criminal offences. Section 718.2 (C-41) prescribed that longer sentences be imposed by the courts if 'bias, prejudice or hate' were elements of or motivating factors for a crime. Section 718.2 (enhanced sentencing) dealt with aggravating or mitigating circumstances relating to a crime or a criminal upon sentencing if 'bias, prejudice or hate' were found in the commission of a crime. These provisions remain unchanged in the current Criminal Code (Canadian Human Rights Reporter, 1998). In short, the Canadian hate crime offence provisions introduced through these two bills constitute the current Criminal Code position (Faulkner, 2007).

The History of Legal Responses to LGBTQ Murders

Historically, killings of LGBTQ people have been legally sanctioned (Robson, 1992; Boswell, 1980). While excesses of violence stemming from religious and racial hatred have resulted in the international legal protection of human rights for traditionally disadvantaged groups, irrational hatred of sexual minorities has not, until recently, been perceived as warranting the same attention (CBA, 1995, p. 1; Amnesty International, 1995, 1997, 2001). While laws proscribing death to those who practise homosexuality still exist in some countries, more recently in North American society moral and ethical values are utilized to facilitate the social control of sexual minorities through harassment, detainment, intimidation, physical assault, murder, and denial of personhood (Harvard Law Review, 1989; Lahey, 1989; Brenner, 1995; Shilts, 1982). Murders of LGBTQ people are the tip of the iceberg; underneath are everyday experiences defined by fear, harassment and actual victimization. For this reason it is important to explore how murders of LGBTQ people are legally sanctioned.

While violence against LGBTQ people is not a new phenomenon, attempts to explain it are relatively recent. Early examinations of murders of gay men relied on newspaper reports, which sensationalized the killing of men in pick-up situations (Miller & Humphries, 1980). The seedy side of the closeted gay culture was played up in these reports, and the victim who had allegedly paid for the services of a young 'hustler' was blamed for his own demise. Early theorists assumed that violence against gay people was somehow deserved because gay men or lesbian women were engaging in illegal activities. It was also assumed that the victim must be mentally ill. Typically, the attacks were attributed to outbursts of uncontrollable sadistic sexual aggression. Like abused women, blame was often laid on gay male victims who were thought to be masochistic, provocative, or sexually promiscuous. The subversive nature of same-sex love was used to rationalize the violence and exploitation that took place within the gay subculture. Not only did hustlers have an edge on blackmailing closeted gay men, police had the ability to target bars and bathhouses to arrest those who ran bawdy houses as well as anyone who was a 'found-in' (McCaskell, 1988; Maynard, 1999). In such cases, police often engaged in brutal acts of retaliation against gays who resisted arrest. The closeted nature of gay relationships in pre-sixties Canada meant that if a person were harassed, beaten, or even killed because someone assumed or knew him or her to be gay, society, the law, and police often justified the violence on the basis of the presumed illegal actions of the parties involved. All activities of LGBTQ people were sexualized, and sexual perversion was seen to be the reason and justification for the violence. While LGBTQ people had the legal right to charge a person with assault, they knew well that their sexual orientation could be dragged through the courts. If they contacted police, they risked experiencing secondary victimization. With no lesbian or gay organizations they could turn to for support, fear about revealing their sexuality forced victims to remain silent (Smith, 1990; Lesbian and Gay History Group of Toronto, 1981; Morand Report, 1976).

Over the past three decades, these assumptions have been widely criticized, as researchers have found that LGBTQ people are not sexual deviants who suffer from psychological disorders. In Canada, the gay and lesbian liberation movement has had a large impact on two issues: the declassification of homosexuality as a psychiatric condition in the *Diagnostic and Statistical Manual of Mental Disorders* (*DSM-IV*) and the decriminalization of homosexuality (Kinsman & Gentile, 2010; Warner, 2002; Smith, 1999). Slowly, attitudes about LGBTQ people changed as they were granted more legal rights. In the 1980s HIV-AIDS activism and resistance to bath house raids and police brutality mobilized LGBTQ communities (McLeod, 1996; Adam, 1995; McCaskell, 1988). Queer Nation organized in many large urban centres in the United States and Canada to protest anti-gay/lesbian violence (Maynard, 1994, 1991). LGBTQs drew attention to the lack of awareness given to murders as well as to an increase in gay-bashing events documented by gay community groups. Public protests against police brutality and lack of follow-up on gay-bashing incidents became more and more common (Comstock, 1991, pp. 152–162). With the advancement of gay and lesbian organizations and businesses and demands for increased rights, LGBTQ people began to protest unequal treatment and document the various forms of victimization that members of their communities experienced. Early grassroots responses to anti-LGBTQ violence led to an understanding of patterns of victimization (Janoff, 2005; Mason & Tomsen, 1997; Herek, 1992; Comstock, 1991). Further, as more sophisticated techniques for measuring the prevalence of violence against LGBTQ people have evolved, it has become apparent that violence against LGBTQ people is far too prevalent to be attributable to a small group of deviant men on the prowl on a Saturday night.

Lethal and Non-Lethal Violence Experienced by LGBTQ Canadians

Little is known about the prevalence of anti-LGBTQ homicide in Canada. While there is no national organization in Canada that compiles data on homophobic homicides, there have been a few attempts to document and analyse violent attacks on LGBTQ people on the basis of analysis of judicial records and newspaper accounts. For example, in the 1980s Miller and Humphries conducted an analysis of Canadian and American newspaper accounts of the brutal murders of gay men (Miller & Humphries, 1980). In the 1990s the Quebec Human Rights Commission, prompted by a number of unsolved murders of numerous Montreal gay men since 1989, held hearings on violence against gays (Corelli, 1995, p. 43; Burnett, 1998, p. 19). Based on analysis of legal cases involving the provocation defence of homosexual panic, the Canadian Bar Association (CBA) in June 1995 was able to determine patterns and trends in the types of murders committed mainly against gay men. Murders of LGBTQs have been documented in other countries. In the United States, Comstock (1991) monitored and researched news-media coverage of 17 anti-LGBTQ murders from the mid-1970s to the present. The National Coalition of Anti-Violence Programs (NCAVP, 2010a) documented 232 anti-LGBTQ murders in the United States since 1998 (NCAVP, 2010a, p. 30). There were a total of 22 hate-motivated murders in 2009, 'the second highest rate in a decade reflecting a pattern of severe and persistent violence against LGBTQ communities' (NCAVP, 2010b, p. 1). Bell and Vila (1996) compared the number and extent of injuries of homosexual and heterosexual victims and found that LGBTQ victims were often subject to overkill. Van Gemert (1994) and Comstock (1991) both studied the perpetrator population to determine its characteristics. Trends from American anti-violence programs that collect data on incidents of anti-LGBTQ violence suggest that, while murders provide tragic and sometimes very visible examples of anti-LGBTQ violence, they represent a small portion of its incidence overall (NCAVP, 1999, 11).

Janoff (2005) notes a striking trend in the Canadian homicide cases in which LGBTQ people have been murdered: the minimization of responsibility on the part of the perpetrators. Altogether, 81 homicides involving gay victims and 7 homicides involving lesbian victims have been documented between 1990 and 1999 in Canada (Janoff, 2005, p. 55). Of these, 64 (72.5 per cent) were classified as unambiguously anti-gay by local groups or police. The remaining 24 murders were identified as 'gay related' (i.e., killings in which the victim's sexual orientation appeared to have been a relevant factor but the motivation was uncertain and anti-gay prejudice was not clearly manifest). Some of these (11 cases or 13.5 per cent) and other homicides documented in legal cases in recent years appear to have been sex related. These figures are believed to sharply underestimate the magnitude of the hate crime murders.

In 1995 the Canadian Bar Association (CBA) published a report documenting findings from its research on the provocation defence of homosexual panic in cases where gay men and lesbian women have been murdered in Canada. From examples drawn from a number of reported judicial cases and newspaper accounts that document the level of violence against both lesbian women and gay men in Canada, the CBA 'found that the viciousness of attacks was often extreme, and that the violence took place in everyday contexts' (CBA, 1995, pp. 9–12). Provocation was often used as a defence for attacks on gay men on the basis of 'homosexual panic' or 'frenzy' associated with a 'homosexual pass'. In all of the Canadian cases, the assailant attempted to use the defence of provocation or some other version of the defence. In the majority of the cases in which the defence was used, the sentences were reduced to second-degree murder on the basis of provocation. Some of the cases were dismissed because of technicalities involving improper presentation of evidence.

The cases researched by the CBA involved the murder of a total of 18 gay men. Of those not murdered, 5 gay men were seriously injured and 3 lesbian women were attacked and seriously injured. In many of the cases involving the use of the provocation defence, the testimony of the respondent was relied upon, since the deceased could not provide information. Some of the attackers verbalized their hatred of LGBTQs during the attacks or murders. All of the attackers were men, either singly or in groups. Some of the gay men and lesbian women who were murdered were attacked by people they knew or people they had met after spending an evening in a bar or at a party. As well, some gay men were murdered when they were in situations in which they would have no chance to defend themselves against their attackers. Lesbian women were most likely to be attacked by male family members. Most survey research on anti-gay/lesbian violence indicates that, compared to gay men, lesbian and bisexual women are more likely to be attacked by someone they know rather than by a stranger (Robson, 1992, p. 156; Comstock, 1991; Faulkner, 1997; Von Schulthess, 1992).

In one of the cases researched by the Canadian Bar Association, two gay men were murdered in their homes after drinking with their assailant in a bar. In two other cases, the perpetrator murdered or critically maimed the victim and then bragged to friends about the assault and showed off the victim to friends. In some of the cases the perpetrator(s) exerted extreme violence, with multiple stabbings. Three lesbian victims were attacked by male relatives who stated that they did not accept the lesbian relationship. In two of the cases 'expert witnesses' described the assailant's attack on a gay or lesbian person to have occurred in a 'frenzy,' diminishing the premeditation of the attack. In only two cases did the judge comment on the sexual orientation of the victims in sentencing.

These assaults and murders are only the tip of the iceberg in terms of the experience of anti-LGBTQ violence. Other forms of harassment and victimization take place on a daily basis. The findings from North American and international **victimization surveys** reveal the experiences of LGBTQ people and those who support them (Herek, 1992; Comstock, 1991; Faulkner, 1999). Granted, the surveys are based on unrepresentative samples using the purposive sampling method, but despite this limitation, the findings reveal trends across LGBTQ populations. These trends support the claims made by sexual minorities that they are stigmatized, stereotyped, ostracized, and verbally and physically harassed. The degree and extent of this victimization has yet to be explored on a national basis in Canada.

Trends from Victimization Surveys: Anti-LGBTQ Violence in Canada

Although victimization against sexual minorities and their supporters is now recognized as a social problem in North America, social science data concerning the prevalence and consequences of such crimes are limited. Survey data from a convenience sample of 1,992 participants who self-selected their involvement in community-based studies across Canada reveal that LGBTQ people experience a variety of non-lethal forms of hate crime during their lifetime (Faulkner, 2009). Current estimates indicate that the mean proportion of Canadian participants (N=1,992) who were verbally harassed was 68.8 per cent; 39.9 per cent were threatened with violence; 21.2 per cent had objects thrown at them; 31.6 per cent had been chased or followed; eight per cent had been spat at; 18.9 per cent had been punched, kicked, or beaten; 6 per cent had been assaulted with a weapon; 22.3 per cent had been sexually harassed; 9 per cent had been sexually assaulted; 14.0 per cent had been harassed by police (or subject to police misconduct); 3 per cent had been beaten or assaulted by police; and 19.2 per cent had been harassed/abused at school at least once since the age of 16 because someone presumed them to be LGBTQ. These Canadian findings are somewhat comparable to the findings obtained from American research on anti-LGBTQ violence (Herek & Berrill, 1992, pp. 270–281; Berrill, 1992, p. 20; Herek, Gillis, Cogan, & Glunt, 1997, p. 210; Pilkington & D'Augelli, 1995, p. 40; Faulkner, 2009, p. 130; Comstock, 1991).

My Canadian study found that men are more likely to experience homophobic and **hetero-sexist** victimization than women, although in some instances, such as sexual harassment, women experience equal or higher percentages of victimization (Faulkner, 2009). Those who are most vulnerable—youth, those from low socio-economic backgrounds, and those who are single—indicate higher percentages of lifetime experiences of victimization. Those who are more 'out' are more likely to experience anti-LGBTQ victimization. Most crimes are perpetrated in public settings by one or more strangers, but victimization also occurs in other locales and perpetrators include neighbours, co-workers, and relatives. Participants identified a wide range of locations of victimization, showing that they are targets of anti-LGBTQ victimization in ordinary circumstances of work and life. Victims' concerns about police bias and public disclosure of their sexual orientation were important factors in their deciding whether to report anti-gay/lesbian crimes. Many participants knew of others who had been victimized. Women were more likely than men to indicate that fear of future anti-lesbian victimization affects their day-to-day behaviour. Participants were more likely to seek help from friends and partners than from formal institutions primarily because of fear of secondary victimization.

While approximately 80 per cent of Canadian survey participants identified themselves as Caucasian, those who identified their race/ethnicity as other than Caucasian experienced higher lifetime percentages of homophobic and heterosexist victimization compared to their Caucasian counterparts. Transgendered participants also experienced higher percentages of lifetime experiences of victimization compared to gays, lesbians, bisexuals, **two-spirited**, and heterosexual participants. This finding suggests that the combined experience of being a visible minority/queer and transgendered increases the likelihood of experiencing homophobic and heterosexist violence, hostility, aggression, and negativity. Canadian surveys of anti-LGBTQ violence did not ask participants about how being differently abled affects the experience of homophobic and heterosexist violence, and this was noted by critics of the survey.

The above trends are consistent with findings from the Canadian 1994 General Social Survey (GSS). The 2004 GSS found that gays, lesbians and bisexuals experienced higher levels of violent victimization, 'including sexual assault, robbery and physical assault, than did their heterosexual counterparts' (Beauchamp, 2004, p. 8). 'When all factors are held constant, being gay, lesbian, or bisexual significantly increased the odds of being a victim of violent crime'

(Beauchamp, 2004, p. 8). 'Compared to heterosexuals, the odds of being victimized were nearly 2 times greater for gays and lesbians and 4.5 times greater for bisexuals' (Beauchamp, 2004, p. 8). It was also noted that 'members of traditionally marginalized communities continue to be disproportionately targeted for severe violence' (NCAVP, 2010b, p. 1). For example, 'of the 22 reported hate murder victims in 2009, 79 per cent were people of colour, and most were transgender women or were feminine presenting' (NCAVP, 2010b, p. 1). There was a spike in anti-LGBTQ violence at the time of the passage of the federal hate crimes law, suggesting a correlation between increased visibility and increased targeting of LGBTQ people (NCAVP, 2010b, p. 1).

In all Canadian and American studies, gender differences in rates of victimization are evident. As with American trends (Berrill, 1992, pp. 26–27; Herek, Gillis, & Cogan, 1997; Pilkington & D'Augelli, 1995) males in Canada generally experienced greater levels of anti-gay verbal harassment (by non-family members), threats, victimization in school and by police, and most types of physical violence and intimidation (including weapon assaults and being pelted with objects, spat upon, and followed or chased). Women generally experienced equal or higher percentages of sexual harassment and attacks by family members and people they knew, and reported greater fear of anti-lesbian violence.

In four (Toronto, Halifax, Calgary, and Fredericton) Canadian studies, women were found to be more likely to provide qualitative data suggesting they experienced greater fear of future victimization and were more likely to modify their behaviour than were men, although several women mentioned modifying their behaviour because they faced sexism as well. In order for levels of fear to be assessed within the victim population, participants were asked whether the potential for future victimization owing to their sexual orientation affected their behaviour. While women and men reported equal percentages of being somewhat and greatly affected (73.3 per cent women, 73.5 per cent men, 72 per cent transgender), women were much more likely to provide qualitative data on how they modified their behaviour to prevent attack.

The threat of anti-gay/lesbian violence had a major impact on the attitudes and behaviour of those surveyed. Participants in the Toronto (76 per cent), Calgary (69.7 per cent), Nova Scotia (68 per cent), and Fredericton (58.3 per cent), studies reported having modified their behaviour to reduce the risk of attack (Faulkner, 1997; Faulkner, 1999, p. 107; Faulkner, 2001a; Smith, 1993, p. 42; Samis, 1995, pp. 85, 76–77; Faulkner, 2004).

Canadian survey participants noted that their fear of potential anti-LGBTQ victimization led them to alter their behaviour in various ways. The qualitative data reveals the following themes: not being openly gay and lesbian; practising closetry; limiting public displays of affection; modifying dress and behaviour; developing street wariness; and practising political advocacy, resistance, and 'fighting back'.

Canadian survey participants consistently demonstrated that the majority were somewhat affected by the potential for anti-LGBTQ violence (59 per cent men, 56.4 per cent women, 48 per cent trans). They took self-defence classes, avoided certain locations, censored their speech and dress, or avoided contact with friends or lovers in public places (Faulkner, 1999, p. 174). Canadian participants used terms such as 'fearful', 'hesitant', 'uncomfortable', 'worried', 'anxious', 'secretive', 'angry', 'more cautious', 'careful', 'nervous', 'wary', 'embarrassed', 'defensive', 'more covert', 'conservative', 'constantly alert', 'more attentive', and 'guarded' to describe their behaviour when they felt they might be at risk because others perceived them to be LGBTQ (Faulkner, 1999, p. 174; Faulkner, 2001a, 2004). Trans-identified participants were more likely to be greatly affected by the perception of future victimization than women and men (24 per cent trans, 16.9 per cent women, 14.6 per cent men).

Many of the LGBTQ survey participants and some of the heterosexual participants surveyed also reported they feared anti-LGBTQ harassment and violence and that they anticipated such victimization in the future. In studies about these concerns, the median proportion reporting that they modified their behaviour to prevent future victimization (from the Toronto, Calgary, and Nova Scotia studies) was 71.2 per cent; a median proportion of 63.5 per cent of Vancouver respondents expected to be the target of anti-gay/lesbian violence or harassment in the future. At least half of the women and half of the men in the Vancouver study thought it very or somewhat likely they would be bashed in the future because of their sexual orientation (Samis, 1995, p. 85). Half of the men and women in the Vancouver study believed they might be victimized in the future, and more women (80 per cent) than men (75 per cent) said they feared that they would experience some form of institutional discrimination. Similarly, Berrill's analysis of findings from nine American victimization studies (excluding those conducted on American campuses) found that 'the median proportion of LGBTQs reporting that they feared for their safety was 66 per cent; a median proportion of 80 per cent expected to be the target of anti-gay violence or harassment in the future' (Berrill, 1992, p. 24).

A high percentage of Toronto (82 per cent), Calgary (82 per cent), and Fredericton (84.4 per cent) survey participants knew of at least one other person who had been attacked (Faulkner, 1999, p. 168; Faulkner, 2001a, 2004). Men in all three studies showed higher percentages of knowing at least one person who had been a victim of anti-LGBTQ violence than did women (48.5 per cent men, 37.6 per cent women, 2.3 per cent transgendered). The Toronto (Faulkner 1999, p. 168) study showed that those somewhat affected by fear of anti-LGBTQ violence were more likely to have been attacked in the past, suggesting that previous experience of victimization increases one's fear of future attack. Over half of Torontonians who were somewhat affected by fear of future victimization had been victimized two times or more since the age of 16 (Faulkner 1999, p. 168).

The data reveal that, based on previous experience of some form of anti-LGBTQ violence and harassment, respondents were sensitive to future attacks and also had expectations that such a situation could recur. The expectation of those who had been attacked that they might be harassed or assaulted in the future because of their perceived sexual orientation is not unreasonable in terms of the high lifetime incidence of victimization experienced by the samples overall.

Survey participants were considerably less likely to report an incident of anti-LGBTQ violence to police than to victim assistance programs such as the 519 Church Street Community Centre in Toronto (Faulkner 1991a, 1997). The qualitative data clearly show that concern about secondary victimization is an important reason for non-reporting, but not the sole basis for it. The reasons cited by participants suggest a complex calculus in which victims considered the costs and benefits of reporting (e.g., whether or not the perpetrators could be apprehended and punished) and whether the crime could appropriately be considered a police matter. Participants were asked to rate police responses to incidents of anti-LGBTQ violence and were given the opportunity to provide their own written responses about their experiences with police. While some responses were positive, a majority of Canadian participants provided evidence of discrimination and harassment on the part of police. Given that the police are often the first point of contact for victims, such negative experiences have an impact on the ability of police to gain the trust of LGBTQ communities.

Discrimination Experienced by LGBTQ People within Criminal Justice Systems: The Defence of Homosexual Panic

This section draws on Canadian research on the use of the defence of homosexual panic to reduce murder charges from first-degree murder to manslaughter or even acquittal in cases where LGBTQs are murdered. The underlying premise of the defence of homosexual panic in the psychological literature and in its application in Canadian legal discourse shows that this defence underpins and supports heterosexist roles and relations within the Canadian legal system. Judicial events that accept the defence are situated within the structure of more extended social processes that support homophobic and heterosexist violence.

Medical science has in effect supported the homosexual panic defence in criminal cases where LGBTQs have been battered and murdered because of their sexual orientation. Homosexual panic (also known as the 'gay' or 'trans panic' defence [NCAVP, 2010a]) has for a long time been considered to be a medical psychological condition (Waldinger, 1990; Campbell, 1989; Chuang & Addington, 1988). However, there is little empirical evidence to back up the claims made by the homosexual panic diagnostic category. Medical and psychological theories about trauma to heterosexual people have been used to perpetuate prejudicial ideologies. For example, while 'homosexual panic' is not a mental disorder recognized by the psychiatric profession in *DSM-IV*, nevertheless this prejudicial theory has historically been used in criminal trials to show that a medical condition was responsible for a male heterosexual's act of assault upon or murder of a gay man (American Psychiatric Association, 1994). Expert witnesses were regularly called to testify on the validity of the defence in murder trials where heterosexual men were alleged to have killed gay men.

The homosexual panic disorder is described as a psychotic reaction to latent homosexual desire. The term was coined by psychiatrist Edward J. Kempf in 1920 and later became known as Kempf's disease, or Kempf's syndrome (Kempf, 1920, pp. 477–515). On the basis of 17 anecdotal cases involving 2 female and 15 male members of the US armed forces, Kempf formulated his principal symptomatology (Glick, 1959, p. 24). Kempf suggests that homosexual panic is due to the 'pressure of uncontrollable perverse sexual cravings' that forces the patient to offer himself as a sexual object, which he then disowns via the mechanism of projection (Glick, 1959, p. 28). The concept of projection is based on the bisexual theory of sexual development and latent homosexuality, a theory no longer considered tenable within psychiatry (Chuang & Addington, 1988, p. 616). While the theory is mentioned in case histories, teaching seminars, and case discussions, a review of the concept in 1959 revealed that it was not recognized as existing in many of the standard psychiatric and psychological dictionaries of the time (Glick, 1959, p. 20). However, definitions of homosexual panic can be found in contemporary psychiatric textbooks and dictionaries, suggesting that the concept is still accepted within the discipline (Waldinger, 1990, p. 470; Campbell, 1989; Leigh, Pare, & Marks, 1977, p. 213). Chuang and Addington suggest that it is more likely that the concept of homosexual panic is a result of religious, medical, social, and legal homophobic attitudes (1988, p. 616).

As a result, LGBTQ victims of violence experience blame, alienation from the larger heterosexual mainstream community, and denial about the seriousness of the violence. Like women who are abused, LGBTQ people may fear the stigma of deviance if they complain about heterosexist attacks. Many are forewarned that they will encounter only secondary victimization if they interact with police or courts, and so keep the violence hidden within LGBTQ communities. LGBTQs who remain closeted may feel they would jeopardize their identity if they complained about anti-LGBTQ attacks, with the result that perpetrators go free. Sadly, many attacks that begin as verbal taunts or physical harassment become life threatening if there is no intervention.

Brian Shein's (1986) analysis reveals three parts to the symptomatology of homophobic violence: (1) a typical homophobic attack involves males who deliberately travel to an area identified with gay men, select a victim whom they do not know but presume is gay, outnumber him and attack him with intense violence; (2) Many in the legal and counselling professions ignore or minimize the role of homophobia in these assaults sometimes resulting in grotesque miscarriages of justice; and (3) the victim, either directly or by implication, is himself blamed for the attack, much in the way that a female rape victim is often presumed to have been 'asking for it'.

Comstock (1991) notes that, in the majority of cases in which the gay panic defence is used, the defence attempts to minimize the damage done by the perpetrator and blame the victim by discrediting him or her on the basis of the victim's sexual identity. Second, judges and/or juries often recognize the merit of such a defence by acquitting or lightly sentencing the defendants, suggesting that killing LGBTQ people is not regarded with the same seriousness as is criminal activity in general. In fact, in many of the trials, evidence was produced to convey that the perpetrators were average 'noncriminal' people whose actions were neither serious nor unusual (Comstock, 1991, p. 92).

The Canadian Bar Association found that in numerous Canadian criminal cases the provocation defence of homosexual panic has been used successfully (CBA, 1995). Common characteristics in Canadian trials reveal a trend on the part of courts indicating that they fail to give appropriate sentences for hate-motivated violence perpetrated against those identified as lesbian women and gay men (CBA, 1995, p. 16). Trial courts consistently entertain claims that the violence was provoked by victims, a defence that supports the dominant ideology that sees LGBTQ people as pathological (CBA, 1995, p. 16). The CBA notes that the 'gay panic defense is used in most cases where a gay person has been battered or killed, except when there is uncontroverted evidence of consensual sex or when groups of attackers had been motivated by the express purpose of finding and killing gay men' (1995, p. 16). Gay men are considered to have provoked their own murder or battery simply because they are gay or are in circumstances associated with their sexual orientation, in contrast to other defences where provocation has to be serious and the response of the accused has to be reasonable and proportionate to the perceived threat. The CBA notes, for example, the high test of abuse used in the 'battered woman syndrome' (such as that used in *R. v. Lavallee, 1990*), in which the battered woman who murdered had to produce evidence that she had been injured so seriously in previous beatings by her ex-male partner that she had required repeated hospitalizations (CBA, 1995, p. 16). None of the acts that constituted the alleged provocation of homosexual panic found by the CBA 'were at all proportionate to the viciousness or deadliness of the attacks that gave rise to the criminal charges in question' (1995, p. 17). In fact, there was no factual evidence for the violence, and most of the attacks occurred in situations where the attackers had the option of leaving the premises of homes, parks, or other public places, but yet chose to 'attack their victims with unrestrained violence, and in most cases killed them' (CBA, 1995, p. 17).

In analyzing 83 Canadian homicide cases that took place between 1990 and 1999, Janoff (2005) notes trends in the discourse of the suspects during the trial. In 12 per cent of the cases (10 homicides), the male suspect or his lawyer blamed the gay victim or someone else for the death (60). In 11 per cent of the cases (9 homicides), the lawyer mentioned childhood or teenage abuse as a factor contributing to the actions of the suspect. In 8 per cent of the cases (7 homicides), the presumably heterosexual male suspect performed other homophobic acts or revealed homophobic attitudes during the trial. In 7 per cent of the cases (6 homicides), the lawyer attempted to lie in court in order to distort the events surrounding the gay male victim's death. In 6 per cent of the cases (5 homicides), the male suspect bragged about the victim's death, minimized or rationalized the victim's death, and made homophobic comments. In 5 per cent of the cases (4 homicides), the male suspect or his lawyer implied that the gay male victim either wanted or deserved to die. In 25 per cent of the cases, or 21 homicides out of 83, the suspect alleged that a sexual advance had taken place. Another unsettling trend found in the homicide cases was the diminished sentence given to the perpetrator. In the majority of cases, the male suspect was convicted of manslaughter (42.5 per cent) or second-degree murder (36.5 per cent). Only two cases resulted in a conviction of first-degree murder. Out of the 31 known sentences, almost a third (10) of the men were eligible to apply for day parole within two years.

A Case Study of LGBTQ Murders in Canada

In the following Canadian cases researched by the Canadian Bar Association (1995), the actions of the accused were minimized through allegations that the deceased gay man made a 'homosexual pass'. In some of the cases, 'experts' were called upon to give evidence on the exemplary character of the accused. As well, there is evidence of overkill in some of the murders. These cases are just a few of the examples of ways in which stereotypes about LGBTQ people are utilized to diminish the crime of murder to a crime of passion and thus reduce the sentence given to perpetrators of hate crime.

In the first case, three men—Charles Reid, Dominic Ginell, and Cribbin—and a woman—Betty Gates—had been drinking beer while driving around in a car in southern Ontario. At one point in the early morning they stopped on a deserted road. An argument ensued when Cribbin hit Ginell after perceiving him to have made a 'sexual proposition' toward him. At that point Reid attacked Ginell, and the three then left him to die. While Reid and Cribbin stated that they believed at the time that the injuries to Ginell were not life-threatening, the victim drowned in his own blood. The two men and Betty Gates took Ginell's credit cards and used them. The men turned themselves in after reading of Ginell's death in a newspaper article. Reid and Cribbin were charged with second-degree murder. Cribbin claimed self-defence on the basis that a sexual proposition had been made toward him. In the course of the trial, Reid pleaded guilty to second-degree murder and Cribbin was convicted of manslaughter and sentenced to eight years' imprisonment and a ten-year firearm prohibition. Cribbin appealed his conviction and asked for an appeal of his sentence. The appeal was allowed, and a new trial was ordered on the charge of manslaughter (*R. v. Cribbin*, 1994).

A taxi driver, Kenneth Spoonheim, was murdered by Edward Hansford, a passenger, who assumed he had made homosexual advances toward him. Spoonheim had reached back with his hand as if to obtain his fare, but Hansford presumed the action to be an inappropriate 'homosexual pass'. Hansford was eventually convicted of second-degree murder (*R v. Hansford*, 1987, p. 74). Hansford relied on the defence of provocation at his trial, arguing that 'the driver reached back and at this time the accused stabbed him as he believed he was going to be subject to a 'homosexual advance' (*R. v. Hansford*, 1987, p. 74). Hansford stated that he had just previously experienced a homosexual advance from another person, from which he had been traumatized. The test of whether an ordinary person would have reacted in the way that Hansford did was used to assess whether 'there had been a wrongful act of such a nature as to be sufficient to deprive an ordinary person of the power of self-control within the meaning of s. 215 of the *Criminal Code*' (*R. v. Hansford*, 1987, p. 74). The jury was instructed not to consider what the intention of the deceased might have been and that it was of no relevance to this case that the accused may have been subjected to a sexual advance the day before. The accused appealed the conviction of second-degree murder, but the appeal was dismissed on the grounds that there was no proof that Hansford's previous experience of a 'homosexual advance' had put him into a state of 'mindless reaction'. Rather, it was determined that there was more probability in this case that Spoonheim had been involved in a drunken attempt to rob the taxi driver (*R. v. Hansford*, 1987, p. 76).

While the defence of provocation was not successful in the Spoonheim case, it is often used to bolster the unstated assumption that it would indeed be an insult for a normal heterosexual man to be propositioned by a gay male. However, the reasons why someone could be justified in murdering another man on the basis of such an insult are never investigated in these Canadian trials, and thus the issue of homophobic attitudes is not addressed. It is presumed that there is justification for using lethal force in a situation where such an insult is perceived by the accused. There is also a presumption that the deceased was in the wrong.

The defence of provocation was used to justify the murder of Verne Pegg, a 32-year-old gay man. Pegg was murdered with a hatchet and two knives by Hill, a 16-year-old youth who claimed the victim had made a 'sudden and uninvited homosexual advance which caused the accused to strike the deceased' (CBA, 1995, p. 15). Hill first denied knowing Pegg but later confessed to police, 'indicating that he had killed Pegg in the early morning hours after Pegg had made uninvited sexual advances toward him' (*R v. Hill*, 1986, p. 342). In this case, as in many cases involving the defence of provocation, we must rely on the testimony of the respondent, since the deceased could not provide information.

The question in this case was whether an ordinary person would have lost self-control in such a situation (*R. v. Hill*, 1986, p. 343). In the appeal to the Supreme Court of Canada, the test of the 'ordinary person standard' used in the defence of provocation was reviewed in order to assess whether its use was consistent with the requirements of the Criminal Code. The respondent argued that his age was directly related to his mental state at the time in that his response to the 'offensive sexual advances' was that of an immature person (*R. v. Hill*, 1986, p. 349). However, the Supreme Court judges felt that 'sex is not relevant to the standard of self-control of the ordinary person, but it was obviously relevant in this case to the nature and gravity of the provocation claimed by the accused' (*R. v. Hill*, 1986, p. 353). The judges declared that the age of the respondent should not have been considered by the jury in assessing whether an ordinary person of that age would have reacted similarly to the alleged sexual advances. Because the trial court judge did instruct the jury to take into account the mental, emotional, and physical characteristics, as well as the age, of the accused, the Supreme Court judges allowed the appeal on behalf of the deceased on the basis that the reference to age may have been misleading for the jury, and restored the conviction of second-degree murder.

The way in which the defence of provocation is discussed in *R. v. Fraser* (1980) reveals a blatant homophobia and defence of masculinity on the part of the judge, lawyer, and jury. In 1978 Fraser, a 28-year-old taxi driver, killed Gordon Bjornson in his own home by severely beating Bjornson's head, face, and neck with a brass-headed cane that belonged to the deceased. After administering 27 wounds to the body, Fraser left Bjornson on the floor of his apartment and fled. Afterwards Bjornson was able to make a 911 telephone call in which he stated he had been beaten and robbed. Police arrived and took him to a hospital where he died later that morning. During the trial it was 'the theory of the defense and two psychiatrists called by the defense that the respondent lapsed into what was described in psychiatric terms as homosexual panic' (*R. v. Fraser*, 1980, p. 507). The trial judge accepted the defence of provocation and rejected the defence of robbery put forward by the Crown, although the homosexual panic allegation was based solely on the evidence and statement given by the respondent (**R. v. Fraser,** 1980, p. 507). The judge likened the defence of homosexual panic to that of a normal reaction to a disaster, which could set a person to 'act in a rather implausible manner. . . . This might consist of striking out at the object of the perceived attack and doing anything within their power to repulse such an approach' (*R. v. Fraser*, 1980, p. 507). The judge believed that the respondent experienced some sort of 'an attack of a homosexual nature' and then went on to say, 'I am of the opinion that the accused perceived this as a real threat and as a danger to him, both physically and emotionally, in his perceived image of himself as a male person' (*R. v. Fraser*, 1980, p. 507). The judge linked a fear of homosexual attack with a man's sense of identity as a male, perceiving such an advance as an insult to the respondent that justified self-defence. For this reason he decided that the excessive use of force did not constitute murder but constituted manslaughter or a crime of passion. While Fraser was originally acquitted of second-degree murder by the jury on the basis of provocation and self-defence, the Crown obtained a conviction by getting an order for a new trial with proper instructions from the appellate court (CBA, 1995, pp. 3, 15–16).

In another case, a Guy S. murdered a Dennis McDonald, who had befriended him and his brother in Toronto and offered them a job. Guy was a 17-year-old youth at the time of the murder of Dennis McDonald, and therefore there was a question about his eligibility for support under the Young Offenders Act. Guy applied under section 16(10) of the Act for a review of the decision to transfer him to adult court. He presented fresh evidence from a psychiatrist who had examined him 19 months after the murder. The report stated that the victim had made sexual advances toward Guy, which he claimed he had not reported earlier because 'he was ashamed that a man had touched him' (*R. v. Guy S.*, 1991, p. 97; indexed as *R. v. S. (G)*). It was Dr Meen's opinion that at the time of the murder Guy experienced a panic attack, 'possibly a homosexual panic, and that he was now suffering remorse, guilt and shame' (*R. v. Guy S.*, 1991, p. 97).

The psychiatrist was called to give expert testimony and repeated his conclusion that at the time of the assault and murder Guy had suffered from a 'panic attack'; the attack included a state of 'being disoriented, confused, disconnected and perhaps disassociated at times during that night' (*R. v. S. (G)*, 1991, p. 101). Dr Meen said that this state was not a psychosis in which Guy was out of touch with reality. It was the opinion of the learned Dr Meen that Guy suffered from a 'personality disorder immature type with some hysterical features' (*R. v. S. (G)*, 1991, p. 101). He concluded that Guy should be tried under the Young Offenders Act and treated in a youth facility. Although Dr Meen had spent only six hours with Guy, he believed Guy 'has the capacity for insight, has a tremendous sense of remorse and guilt, shame, and bewilderment secondary to the horrific event in his life' (*R. v. S. (G)*, 1991, p. 102). Guy wanted to be tried in youth court rather than ordinary court and used the expert witness testimony of the psychiatrist to buttress his claim for a transfer. However, this appeal for a transfer of the case from ordinary court to youth court was rejected in the Court of Appeal for Ontario on 8 October 1991 (*Regina v. Guy S.*, 1991); indexed as *R. v. S. (G)*.

Douglas Moses, a 70-year-old gay retired schoolteacher was beaten and strangled in his apartment by a friend with whom he had spent the night drinking. The 27-year-old assailant showed enough self-control to clean up the blood in the apartment and take a shower to wash the blood off himself after the killing; nevertheless, he was acquitted of all charges on the basis that he was insane by reason of 'homosexual panic' (*R. v. Hatt*, 1988).

Finally, Gary Roberts was brutally murdered by a male stranger he had taken home with him one evening. The stranger, Carifelle, murdered Roberts with a hammer, leaving him to die. Soon after, he bragged about the murder and returned to the scene of the crime to show his dead body to a male friend. Carifelle claimed he had reacted to a homosexual advance by Gary Roberts, as a result of which he hit Roberts over the head with a hammer and stabbed him numerous times (*R. v. Carifelle*, 1988, p. 317). Carifelle was charged with first-degree murder but was sentenced to second-degree murder with 15 years' parole ineligibility. He used the defence of alleged provocation based on a homosexual advance, claiming that Gary had touched him on the knee. The jury rejected the defence because of the gravity and severity of the murder and the fact that Carifelle had taken his friend to view Roberts's dead body. The lengthy criminal record of the appellant, which included convictions for robbery, armed robbery, arson, and other lesser offences, was also a factor in the sentencing. Carifelle appealed the sentence of second-degree murder on the basis that his right to counsel had been infringed. On 4 November 1988 the appeal was dismissed, and the second-degree conviction stood (*R. v. Carifelle*, 1988).

Recent Canadian Applications of Section 718.2 Enhanced Sentencing

Recent applications of section 718.2(a)(i) enhanced sentencing may indicate there is hope that social justice may be obtained for LGBTQ people in the future. Sandler (2010), for example, documents four Canadian convictions since 1995 in which sentences were enhanced as a result of proof of motivation on the basis of sexual orientation. Unlike earlier cases involving the assault and murder of LGBTQ people, in these cases there was recognition of hate, bias, or prejudice as aggravating factors. In all cases, section 718.2(a)(i) was used to impose more severe punishment.

In *R. v. Howald* (1998) the accused was given an enhanced sentence of five months' custody for assault based on proof that 'the offence was motivated by prejudice based on sexual orientation' (Sandler, 2010, p. 7). The assault occurred when 'Howald and the victim were held in the same drunk tank when the victim momentarily touched Howald's buttocks. Howald responded by beating the victim until he lost consciousness. After administering a final kick to the unconscious victim, Howald told police: "I hope I killed the fucking faggot"' (Sandler, 2010, p. 7).

In *R. v. Demelo* (1999), the accused was given an enhanced sentence of 60 days' custody and 18 months' probation. Demelo was charged and convicted of sexual assault after sexually assaulting a lesbian woman in her residence. 'The sentencing judge found that Demelo was seeking sexual gratification, but noted the "significant amount of evidence to suggest that he violated [the victim] as well because of her sexual preference"'. The judge found that 'part of Demelo's motivation in committing the sexual assault was the victim's sexual orientation' (Sandler, 2010, p. 5).

In *R. v. M.D.J.* (2001), '[t]he victim and his friends were confronted by M.D.J. and Wilton outside a convenience store. The offence was unprovoked. The offenders referred to the victim's group as 'fucking faggots' and 'queers' and then attacked the victim. After his arrest, M.D.J. informed several inmates that he had 'beat up some freak"' (Sandler, 2010, p. 4). An enhanced sentence was imposed on M.D.J. and Wilton.

In *R. v. J.V.* (2006), a sentence of life imprisonment was imposed for second-degree murder and assault with a weapon in the murder of J.V.'s ex-girlfriend, given that the 'offence was vicious, premeditated and motivated in part by J.V.'s "bias against homosexuals"' (Sandler, 2010, p. 2). 'J.V. believed that she had left him to pursue a lesbian relationship. He broke into the victim's home, slashed her female companion with a knife, and stabbed the victim to death. After J.V.'s arrest, he made reference to what he believed was the victim's gay lifestyle, stating that the victim had "turned dyke on him"' (Sandler, 2010, p. 2). An officer posing as a prisoner in an adjoining cell asked J.V. why he had been charged with murder, to which he responded, 'Don't know, fucking goofs, dykes, slutties, choke 'em, stomp 'em, fuck ' em, deserve it' (Sandler, 2010, p. 2).

In 2010 Michael Kandola, 'who pleaded guilty to a violent gay bashing[,] was sentenced to 17 months in jail for an act a B.C. Supreme Court judge deemed a hate crime' (CBC News, 30 April 2010). Kandola had lashed out at Jordan Smith, who had been holding hands with another man as they walked on a downtown Vancouver street in September 2008. Smith suffered jaw fractures (CBC News, September 29, 2008). 'Smith had to have surgery and his jaw was wired shut for six weeks after the attack' (CBC News, April 30, 2010). The victim and witnesses said that Kandola had uttered a string of homophobic slurs during the attack. 'Calling Kandola's actions vicious, unprovoked and cowardly, BC Supreme Court Judge Joel Graves said hatred of Smith's sexual orientation was a motivating factor in the attack, and for that reason, he was meting out a harsher penalty' (CBC News, 30 April 2010).

Conclusions and Recommendations

Victimization survey data and General Social Survey estimates suggest that LGBTQs are targeted because of their perceived sexual orientation and experience victimization at a rate higher than heterosexuals. Since 2000, many police departments in Canada have taken measures to respond to the problem of hate crime, often with assistance from provincial and federal government agencies. Police officials increasingly are working with minority communities to improve their response to hate crimes. Undoubtedly, police personnel in many provinces still need clearer policies and better training for dealing effectively with hate crimes based on sexual orientation. But to the extent that non-reporting persists as a problem, effective remedies will have to come from LGBTQ communities as well as the criminal justice system. Outreach to LGBTQs is necessary to overcome their long-standing suspicions of the police. Such efforts will have to originate not only in criminal justice agencies but also through community organizations.

The National Coalition of Anti-Violence Programs (2010a, p. 9) recommends the expansion of the efficacy of the criminal justice system to support restorative justice strategies such as (1) providing rehabilitation and alternatives to incarceration, including restorative justice; (2) prohibiting the gay and trans panic defences; (3) increasing meaningful police training in responding to LGBTQ-specific violence, including deterring and remedying police violence against LGBTQ communities; and (4) reforming of sexual assault laws to end the silence and stigma around LGBTQ sexual assault.

There have been some police and medical reforms in Toronto that specifically address anti-LGBTQ violence. Victim assistance programs exist in some Canadian cities, although they are extremely underfunded and understaffed (Roberts, 1995; Hierlihy, 1996; Faulkner, 2001b). The chances of victimized LGBTQ people being treated sympathetically are much greater now than they were 10 years ago. Those working to change policies within institutions may believe that it is only a matter of time before the reforms that have been institutionalized take effect so that all victims of anti-LGBTQ violence who report are guaranteed proper treatment at the hands of doctors and police and victim assistance programs. However, Roberts (1995) estimates that only 1 in 10 victims of anti-LGBTQ ever report. Reforms lead us to believe that something may be done about anti-LGBTQ violence. Because there is a perception that police, doctors, and victim assistance programs are doing everything they can, to not report is considered to be contributing to the problem. In the end, reforms are only as good as the attitudes of the individual police, doctors, lawyers, and judges working within institutions. The assumption that everyone should report ignores many of the real reasons why LGBTQs choose not to report anti-LGBTQ violence. There are fears related to their safety, their jobs, and families as well as their own sense of guilt, shame, and humiliation. While reforms may suggest that LGBTQs are now safe, the truth is that these reforms will not stop anti-LGBTQ violence or the use of the provocation defence of homosexual panic. Institutions cannot stop the violence; they can only make it easier for LGBTQs who are attacked because of their perceived sexual difference. This includes making the system fairer through examination of the existing heterosexist attitudes in law.

The provocation defence of panic exists in our society because men are socially conditioned to think that they have the right to control women's bodies and exert power over the women and men who step out of their gender roles and threaten their social position. The National Coalition of Anti-Violence Programs reports that trans and gay people who display femininity were more likely to be murdered in 2009. It therefore becomes clear that unless the trial courts and police come to understand how sex- and gender-role stereotyping affects attitudes toward LGBTQ people and that the use of such homophobic defences is a result of these attitudes, the murder and attack of LGBTQ people will continue and their murderers will receive light sentences.

Homophobic and heterosexist attitudes have to be dismantled. It is true that LGBTQs can help by telling people how it feels to live with the fear of attack and to see and hear about attacks on friends daily, everywhere they work. This information can help heterosexual men and women comprehend the damage created by their attitudes and show what needs to be changed. In terms of altering power relations, the actual burden of changing attitudes rests with society. Today there is no mandatory program for perpetrators to attend. At best, perpetrators who are brought to trial receive a reduced sentence and criminal record. At worst, the crimes are ignored and tolerated as a fact of everyday life in Western society and the victims—who are, more often than not, dead—are thought to have brought the assault upon themselves. These horrific stories are only a few that can be told about the experiences of LGBTQ people.

The legal context in which the innocence of male perpetrators, all presumably heterosexual, is tested in trial courts must be considered in order to understand the links between the defence of gay panic and trans panic and the presumption of consent claimed by rapists. Lawyers, judges, and parliamentarians are primarily white, middle-class heterosexual men whose conscious and unconscious biases influence the law and whose actions and attitudes reflect the system's sexism, racism, and classism, which calls for a reorganization of the whole legal system. In sexual assault cases, a woman's sexual history becomes the focus of judgments from the jury, the judge, and the defence attorney. Since sexual assault is considered to be a crime against the state, the Crown takes the case and can drop it if it sees fit. 'Founded' or 'unfounded' cases are labelled by police and Crown attorneys on the basis of evidence. Within Canadian law, before 1983 a woman could not be raped by her husband. A limited test was used so that an assault was rape only if the woman's vagina had been penetrated, a stipulation that ignored other forms of sexual assault. The onus was on the woman to prove that she fought back. The law placed rape under Section IV of the Criminal Code along with public, moral, and disorderly conduct laws, enabling the judge to make moral judgments of the victim. Therefore, the conviction rate was and remains very low; the onus is on the woman to report, there is very little support for women to do so, and rehabilitation programs for those convicted of sexual assault are limited.

Like sexual assault victims, LGBTQ victims of violence are subject to discrimination. Lawyers and judges make or imply moral judgments on victims without analysis of systemic homophobia and heterosexism within the judicial system itself. For this reason, there have been cases where the defence of provocation was used and the jury or judge acquitted the perpetrator, having been convinced that the perpetrator perceived they would be sexually assaulted and were provoked into defending themselves. The overkill of many of the defenceless victims in these cases suggests that the attacks were not motivated by mere self-defence but by a desire to vent anger and hatred on LGBTQ people. Such hatred, which is often the reason for the murder itself, is paralleled by the heterosexism LGBTQs frequently face when seeking justice from institutions. The inclusion of sexual orientation in Canada's Criminal Code sentencing provisions means that sentencing may be enhanced if it is determined that a hate element was involved in a murder. However, to date, Canada's enhanced-sentencing provisions have been used in only a few cases where LGBTQs have been attacked or murdered (Sandler, 2010). Still in other cases, the aggravating factor of hate bias is ignored. For example, in the recent sentencing of three males found guilty in the murder of Aaron Webster in British Columbia, the judge at sentencing did not recognize the hate-motivated elements of the crime even though a group of young men had stalked and beaten Webster to death with pool cues, golf irons, and baseball bats in a parking lot near an area where gay men cruised (R. v. Cran, 2005).

Trial courts continually accept the argument that fear of potential homosexual liaison—whether consensual or not—is enough to throw a stable, heterosexual male into a 'frenzy'. The same justification has been made for male rape of women when it is assumed that uncontrollable male sexual desire throws a heterosexual man into a frenzy of aggressive sexual passion. In such cases, a woman's sexual history, dress, actions, and appearance are blamed. The notion that a man cannot control his sexual desire is transformed in the homosexual panic defence to support the idea that a man's fear of homosexual desire could equally lead him to kill or maim. There is hardly ever any evidence in such cases, other than the defendant's testimony, of a 'homosexual pass' having been made, since the gay men are usually dead. On the basis of testimony by the assailant and the previous sexual history of the victim, perpetrators are often given a socially sanctioned justification for murder. The resulting charges of homosexual passes or advances as provocation are taken seriously by trial courts and contribute to the lenient sentencing of the perpetrator. The sexual history of the gay man is often commented upon but not the sexual history of the perpetrator. Plea bargaining on the basis of 'fear of rape' may be attempted if the accused can prove he perceived his safety was in jeopardy, though his attitude toward gay men is seldom questioned.

With few examinations made of the underlying hatred toward gay men in such cases, much is left to the discretion of judges and juries. Where there is obvious consent, sexual assault cannot be used as a motivating factor. But lawyers still try to use lack of consent as a motivating factor in murders of gay men where the two men are strangers or have never had sexual relations. Like the justification of consent for a male's sexual assault of a woman, if a man had an 'honest and reasonable belief' that he had been subjected to a 'homosexual pass', then the act is considered not murder but self-defence on the basis of provocation, which means that the act becomes a crime of passion and thus qualifies for a lesser sentence.

Despite legal protections and acknowledgment of LGBTQ personhood, LGBTQs continue to experience victimization, aggression, hostility, negativity, and violence. The most extreme form of this aggression is found in the murders of LGBTQ people. The high percentage of lifetime experiences of victimization indicated by participants in Canadian surveys of anti-gay/lesbian violence suggests that LGBTQ people are justified in being fearful of future attacks. Given the negative experiences with police reported by LGBTQs who have been victimized, there is a need to challenge homophobic attitudes in police training. The sad history of acceptance, on the part of judges and lawyers, of the provocation defence of homosexual panic in Canada's criminal justice system demonstrates the need to challenge heterosexist and homophobic attitudes and educate both lawyers and the judiciary.

Key Terms

hate crime	homosexual	LGBTQ	victimization surveys
heterosexism	homosexual panic	queer	
homophobia	defence	two-spirited	

Questions for Critical Thought

1. How have laws and social sanctions (medical, legal, religious) contributed to the social control and regulation of LGBTQ people in Canada?

2. What connections may be made between legal discrimination against female sexual assault victims and discrimination against LGBTQ victims of hate crime in the criminal justice system?

3. Given the lack of funding for victim assistance programs in Canada, what kinds of educational outreach initiatives would you and your classmates recommend to counteract anti-LGBTQ hate crime?

Additional Readings

Amnesty International. (2004, March 30). *Human rights and sexual orientation and gender identity*. Amnesty International. Retrieved July 9, 2010, from www.amnesty.org/en/sexual-orientation-and-gender-identity

Goldberg, J. M. (2002). *Trans people in the criminal justice system: A guide for criminal justice personnel*. British Columbia: Trans Alliance Society. Retrieved July 14, 2010, from www.iiav.nl/epublications/2004/trans_people_in_the_just.pdf

Janoff, V. D. (2005). *Pink blood: Homophobic violence in Canada*. Toronto: University of Toronto Press.

Kinsman, G., & Gentile, P. (2010). *The Canadian war on queers: National security as sexual regulation*. Vancouver: University of British Columbia Press.

Lahey, K. (1999). *Are we 'persons' yet?: Law and sexuality in Canada*. Toronto: University of Toronto Press.

MacDougall, B. (2000). *Queer judgements: Homosexuality, expression and the courts in Canada*. Toronto: University of Toronto Press.

Namaste, V. K. (2000). *Invisible lives: The erasure of transexual and transgendered people*. Chicago: University of Chicago Press.

Websites of Interest

CBC News Online. (June 2004). In depth—Hate crimes: What is a hate crime? CBC News Online. Retrieved July 25, 2010, from www.cbc.ca/news/background/hatecrimes

Equality for Lesbians and Gays Everywhere (EGALE) Canada. (n.d.) Weblink: www.egale.ca

519 Church Street Community Centre. (n.d.). Anti-violence program. Toronto. Retrieved July 16, 2010, from www.the519.org/programsservices/the519anti-violenceprogram

Media Awareness Network. (2010). Criminal Code of Canada: Hate provisions—summary. Media Awareness Network Online. Retrieved July 25, 2010, from www.media-awareness.ca/english/resources/legislation/canadian_law/federal/criminal_code/criminal_code_hate.cfm

NCAVP (National Coalition of Anti-Violence Programs). (n.d.) National advocacy for local LGBT communities. New York, NY. Retrieved July 23, 2010, from www.ncavp.org/about/Contact.aspx

Perry, B. (2010). Reading hate: Hate crime research and scholarship in Canada. Toronto: University of Ontario Institute of Technology. Retrieved July 14, 2010, from www.criminologyandjustice.uoit.ca/hatecrime/gov.html

Tremblay, P. J., & Ramsay, R. F. (2010). Gay, lesbian, bisexual, queer, transgender and two-spirit info site. Calgary: University of Calgary. Retrieved July 15, 2010, from clubs.ucalgary.ca/~ptrembla/gay-lesbian-bisexual/01b-full-text-lesbian-transgender.htm

References

Adam, B. D. (1995). *The rise of a gay and lesbian movement*. New York: Twayne.

American Psychiatric Association. (1994). *Diagnostic and statistical manual of mental disorders: DSM-IV*. Washington, DC: American Psychiatric Association.

Amnesty International. (1995). *Breaking the silence. Human rights violations based on sexual orientation*. New York: Amnesty International.

Amnesty International. (1997). *Breaking the silence: Human rights violations based on sexual orientation*. London, UK: Amnesty International Publications UK Section.

Amnesty International. (2001). *Crimes of hate, conspiracy of silence: Torture and ill-treatment based on sexual identity*. London, UK: Amnesty International Publications. Retrieved March 20, 2008, from www.amnesty.org/en/library/info/ACT40/016/2001/en

Beauchamp, D. (2004). *Sexual orientation and victimization.* Catalogue no. 85F0033M – no. 016. Ottawa: Canadian Centre for Justice Statistics Profile Series.

Bell, M. D., & Vila, R. I. (1996). Homicide in homosexual victims: A study of 67 cases from the Broward County, Florida, medical examiner's office (1982–1992), with special emphasis on 'overkill'. *American Journal of Forensic Medicine and Pathology, 17*(1), 65–69.

Berrill, K. T. (1990). Anti-gay violence and victimization in the United States: An overview. *Journal of Interpersonal Violence, 5*(3), 274–294.

Berrill, K. T. (1992). Anti-gay violence and victimization in the United States: An overview. In G. M. Herek and K. T. Berrill (Eds), *Hate crimes: Confronting violence against lesbians and gay men* (pp. 19–24). Newbury Park, CA: Sage.

Berrill, K. T., & Herek, G. M. (1992). Primary and secondary victimization in anti-gay hate crimes: Official response and public policy. In G. M. Herek & K. T. Berrill (Eds), *Hate crimes: Confronting violence against lesbians and gay men* (pp. 289–305). London: Sage.

Boswell, J. (1980). *Christianity, social tolerance, and homosexuality: Gay people in Western Europe from the beginning of the Christian era.* Chicago: University of Chicago Press.

Brenner, C. (with H. Ashley). (1995). *Eight bullets: One woman's story of surviving anti-gay violence.* Ithaca, NY: Firebrand Books.

Burnett, R. (1998, April 23). Interview with a murderer: Danny McIlwaine calls priest's death 'accidental'. *Xtra!, 352*(19), 5.

Campbell, R. J. (1989). *Psychiatric Dictionary* (6th ed.). New York: Oxford University Press.

Canada Law Book. (1987). *Canadian criminal cases.* Toronto: Canada Law Book.

CBA (Canadian Bar Association). (1995, June). *Addendum to submission on Bill C-41: An Act to Amend the Criminal Code (Sentencing) and Other Acts in Consequence Thereof.* Toronto: Lesbian and Gay Issues and Rights Committee of the Canadian Bar Association, Ontario Branch.

CBC News. (2008, September 29). Gay-bashing suspect facing aggravated assault charge. CBC News on the Web. Retrieved September 29, 2008, from www.cbc.ca/canada/british-columbia/story/2008/09/29/bc-gay-bashing-community-court.html

CBC News. (2010, April 30). B.C. gay basher gets 17-month sentence. CBC News on the Web. Retrieved April 30, 2010, from www.cbc.ca/canada/british-columbia/story/2010/04/30/bc-kandola-sentence.html

Chuang, H. T., & Addington, D. (1988). Homosexual panic: A review of its concept. *Canadian Journal of Psychiatry, 33*(77), 613–617.

Comstock, G. D. (1991). *Violence against lesbians and gay men.* New York: Columbia University Press.

Comstock, G. D. (1992). The police as perpetrators of anti-gay/lesbian violence. In G. T. Herek & K. Berrill (Eds), *Hate crimes: Confronting violence against lesbians and gay men* (pp. 152–162). Newbury Park, CA: Sage.

Corelli, R. (1995, August 14). Justice: A tolerant nation's hidden shame. A federal study suggests that thousands may be victims of hate crime. *Maclean's,* 41–43.

Equality for Gays and Lesbians Everywhere (EGALE). (2005, September 16). *EGALE applauds conviction of trans teen killers. Calls on parliament to amend the Canadian Human Rights Act.* Retrieved from www.egale.ca/index.asp?lang=E&menu=38&item=1167

Faulkner, E. (1997). *Anti-gay/lesbian violence in Toronto: The impact on individuals and communities. A project of the 519 Church Street Community Centre Victim Assistance Program, Toronto.* Ottawa: Department of Justice Canada, Research and Statistics Division/Policy Sector. TR1997-5e.

Faulkner, E. (1999). *A case study of the institutional response to anti-gay/lesbian violence in Toronto.* Unpublished doctoral dissertation, University of Toronto.

Faulkner, E. (2001a). *Anti-gay/lesbian violence in Calgary, Alberta: The impact on individuals and communities. A project of the Calgary Gay and Lesbian Communities Police Liaison Committee.* Calgary: Calgary Police Services.

Faulkner, E. (2001b). Empowering Victim Advocates: The Community Response to Anti-Gay/Lesbian Violence in Canada. *Critical Criminology: An International Journal, A Special Theme Edition on Criminology, Empowerment and Social Justice, 10*(2), 123–135.

Faulkner, E. (2004). *Anti-gay/lesbian violence in Fredericton, New Brunswick: The impact on individuals and communities. A project of the Fredericton Pride Committee.* Fredericton, NB.

Faulkner, E. (2009). Anti-lesbian, -gay, -bisexual, and -transgendered victimization in Canada and the United States: A comparative study. In B. Perry (Ed.), *Victims of hate crime* (Vol. 3, pp. 121–151). Westport, CT: Praeger.

Glick, B. S. (1959). Homosexual panic: Clinical and theoretical considerations. *Journal of Nervous and Mental Disease, 129*(1), 20–28.

Goldberg, J. M. (2002). *Trans people in the criminal justice system: A guide for criminal justice personnel.* British Columbia: Trans Alliance Society. Retrieved December

2002 from www.iiav.nl/epublications/2004/trans_people_in_the_just.pdf

Harvard Law Review. (1989). *Sexual orientation and the law.* Cambridge, MA: Harvard University Press.

Herek, G. M., & Berrill, K. T. (Eds). (1992). *Hate crimes: Confronting violence against lesbians and gay men.* Newbury Park, CA: Sage.

Herek, G. M., Gillis, R. J., & Cogan, J. C. (1999). Psychological sequelae of hate-crime victimization among lesbian and gay bisexual adults. *Journal of Consulting and Clinical Psychology, 67*(6), 945–951.

Herek, G. M., Gillis, J. R., Cogan, J.C., & Glunt, E. K. (1997). The impact of victimization among lesbian, gay, and bisexual adults: Prevalence, psychological correlates, and methodological issues. *Journal of Interpersonal Violence, 12*(2), 195–215.

Hierlihy, D. (1996). Educational manual to support the gay bashing protocol. In *Behind the bruises: Confronting hate motivated crimes against lesbians and gay men: A community coordinated response.* Toronto: Wellesley Central Hospital Urban Health Initiative.

Janoff, V. D. (2005). *Pink blood: Queer bashing in Canada.* Toronto: University of Toronto Press.

Kempf, E. J. (1920). The psychology of the acute homosexual panic. In *Psychopatholgy* (pp. 477–515). St Louis: C. V. Mosby Company.

Kinsman, G., & Gentile, P. (2010). *The Canadian war on queers: National security as sexual regulation.* Vancouver: University of British Columbia Press.

Lahey, K. (1999). *Are we 'persons' yet?: Law and sexuality in Canada.* Toronto: University of Toronto Press.

Leigh, D., Pare, C. M. B., & Marks, J. (1977). Kempf's syndrome. In *A concise encyclopedia of psychiatry* (pp. 213–214).

Lesbian and Gay History Group of Toronto. (1981, August 18). A history of the relationship between the gay community and the Metropolitan Toronto Police. A brief presented to Arnold Bruner for his Study of Relations between the Homosexual Community and the Police. Toronto: Lesbian History Group of Toronto.

McCaskell, T. (1988). The bath raids and gay politics. In F. Cunningham et al. (Eds), *Social movements/social change: The politics and practice of organizing* (pp. 169–188). Toronto: Between the Lines Press.

MacDougall, B. (2000). *Queer judgements: Homosexuality, expression and the courts in Canada.* Toronto: University of Toronto Press.

McLeod, D.W. 1996. Lesbian and gay liberation in Canada. A selected annotated chronology 1964–1975. Toronto: ECS Press/Homewood Books.

Mason, G., & Tomsen, S. (1997). *Homophobic violence.* Sydney, Australia: Hawkins Press.

Maynard, S. (1991). When queer is not enough: Identity and politics in Queer Nation. *Fuse Magazine, 15*(1/2), 14–18.

Maynard, S. (1994). Through a hole in the lavatory wall: Homosexual subcultures, police surveillance, and the dialectics of discovery, Toronto, 1890–1930. *Journal of the History of Sexuality, 5*(2), 207–242.

Media Awareness Network. (2010). *Criminal Code of Canada hate provisions—summary.* Retrieved July 12, 2010, from www.media-awareness.ca/english/resources/legislation/canadian_law/federal/criminal_code/criminal_code_hate.cfm

Miller, B., & Humphries, L. (1980). Lifestyles and violence: Homosexual victims of assault and murder. *Qualitative Sociology, 3,* 169–185.

Morand Report. (1976). Prepared for the Toronto Metropolitan Police Complaints Bureau by Justice Morand. Toronto: Metropolitan Toronto Police Services.

NCAVP (National Coalition of Anti-Violence Programs). (1999). *Hate violence against lesbian, gay, bisexual, and transgender people in the United States.* New York: National Coalition of Anti-Violence Programs.

NCAVP. (2006). *Hate violence against lesbian, gay, bisexual, and transgender people in the United States.* New York: National Coalition of Anti-Violence Programs.

NCAVP. (2010a). *Hate violence against lesbian, gay, bisexual, transgender,and queer communities in the United States in 2009.* New York: National Coalition of Anti-Violence Programs. Retrieved July 14, 2010, from www.avp.org/documents/NCAVP2009HateViolenceReportforWeb.pdf

NCAVP. (2010b, July 13). Media release: Report of hate violence against lesbian, gay, bisexual, transgender and queer (LGBTQ) communities released today. New York: National Coalition of Anti-Violence Programs. Retrieved July 14, 2010, from www.avp.org/documents/2009HVReportMediaReleaseFINAL_000.pdf

Pilkington, N. W., & D'Augelli, A. R. (1995). Victimization of lesbian, gay, and bisexual youth in community settings. *Journal of Community Psychology, 23,* 33–56.

Roberts, J. (1995). *Disproportionate harm: Hate crime in Canada, an analysis of recent statistics.* Ottawa: Department of Justice.

Robson, R. (1992). The violence against us. In *Lesbian (Out)Law* (pp. 146–150). Ithaca, NY: Firebrand Books.

Samis, S. M. (1995). *An injury to one is an injury to all: Heterosexism, homophobia, and anti-gay/lesbian violence in greater Vancouver.* Unpublished master's thesis, Simon Fraser University.

Sandler, J. (2010, February). Hate motivation as an aggravating factor on sentence: An overview of the legal landscape. Toronto. Retrieved 14 July 2010 from www.law.utoronto.ca/documents/conferences2/CombatingHatred10_Sandler.pdf

Shein, B. (1986, April). Gay-bashing in High Park. *Toronto Life, 37*–39, 64–69.

Shilts, R. (1982). *The mayor of Castro Street: The life and times of Harvey Milk.* New York: St Martin's Press.

Smith, C. G. (1993). *'Proud but cautious': Homophobic abuse and discrimination in Nova Scotia.* Nova Scotia Public Research Group. Halifax: Dalhousie University.

Smith, M. (1999). Lesbian and gay rights in Canada: Social movements and equality-seeking, 1971–1995. Toronto: University of Toronto Press.

Van Gemert, F. (1994). Chicken kills hawk: Gay murders during the eighties in Amsterdam. *Journal of Homosexuality, 26*(4), 149–174.

Von Schulthess, B. (1992). Violence in the streets: Anti-lesbian assault and harassment in San Francisco. In G. M. Herek & K. T. Berrill (Eds), *Hate crimes: Confronting violence against lesbians and gay men* (pp. 65–73). London, UK: Sage.

Waldinger, R. J. (1990). Homosexual panic. In *Psychiatry for Medical Students* (2nd ed., p. 470). Washington, DC: American Psychiatric Press.

Warner, T. (2002). *Never going back: A history of queer activism in Canada.* Toronto: University of Toronto Press.

Legal Cases

R. v. Carifelle A.J. No. 1024 Alta. C.A. 317 (1988) per Laycraft, McClung, and Berger JJ.).

R. v. Cran 171 BCSC (2005). Found in *(CanLII) Reasons for Sentencing.* Retrieved March 15, 2010, from Canlii: www.canlii.org/eliisa/highlight.do?text=hate+crime&language=en&searchTitle=Search+all+CanLII+Databases&path=/en/bc/bcsc/doc/2005/2005bcsc171/2005bcsc171.html

R. v. Cribbin 17 O.R. (3d) 548 O.J. No. 477 Ont. C.A. (1994), per Morden A.C.J.O. Catzman and Arbour JJ.A.).

R. v. Demelo O.J. No. 3952 Prov. Div. (1999).

R. v. Fraser 55 C.C.C. (2d) 503 Alta. C.A. 507 (1980) per McDermid, Lieberman, and Moir JJ.A.).

R. v. Hansford 33 C.C.C. (3d) 74, 1 W.C.B. (2d) 270 Alta. C.A. 74-76 (1987) per Kerans and Hetherington JJ.A. and Hutchinson J.

R. v. Hatt as reported in *Atlantic Regional News* (March 30 and 31, 1988).

R. v. Hill 25 C.C.C. (3d) 322 S.C.C. 342-353 (1986) per Chouinard, Lamer, Wilson, Le Dain, and La Forest JJ.).

R. v. Howald O.J. No. 3121 Gen. Div. (1998).

R. v. J.V. O.J. No. 2392 Sup. Ct. (2006).

R. v. Lavallee 1 S.C.R. 852 (1990). Retrieved March 15, 2010, from http://ca.vlex.com/vid/r-v-lavallee-37666924.

R. v. M.D.J. B.C.J. No. 2110 Prov. Ct. (2001).

R. v. S. (G) 5 O.R. (3d) 97, [1991] O.J. No. 1731 Ont. C.A. 97-102 (1991), per Dickson C.M. (also referenced as *R. v. S. (G)*).

14 Older People, Crime, and State Intervention

Joan Harbison

Introduction

Older people, like other groups in society, fear being the victims of crime much more than evidence appears to warrant (Webb, 2006). This is especially notable given that statistics indicate that they are the least likely group to suffer from criminal acts (Ogrodnik, 2007). Their public image as people vulnerable to crime may be one reason for these fears (Luu & Liang, 2005–06; Yin, 1985). However, other norms pervasive in our society lend support to older people's fear of mistreatment. This chapter begins with a discussion of what it means to be old. It examines why negative views of aging as decline and negative portrayals of older people as in a state of physical and mental deterioration support the aged's apprehension about how others may treat them (McPherson & Wister, 2008). It traces how older people have come to be viewed as homogeneous, deficit-ridden objects of various expert assessments and interventions, rather than as unique subjects in their own dynamic lives (Cheal, 2002). It explores how the foregoing constructions of aging contribute to discrimination against older people through a societal preoccupation with the burden that they are said to have on resources (Gee & Gutman, 2000). It discusses how challenges to their capacities also have an impact on their rights (Wahl, 2009). In the light of this understanding of older people, the nature of their victimization—of crimes against them, how they are interpreted, and how many are addressed differently than similar crimes against younger people—is discussed. Specifically, the phenomenon of 'elder abuse and neglect', under which many criminal or illegal acts against older people are subsumed, is explored and assessed. The criminality of the relatively few older people who are criminals is examined. The final section of the chapter considers service and resource issues for those who are identified as victims of elder abuse and neglect, or of crime, and those who are criminals.

The discussion leads to a number of conclusions. First, the very diversity of older people—in their health, wealth, class, and education, and in their ethno-cultural backgrounds and values and beliefs—militates against coordinated efforts to challenge the powerful myths that surround aging and older people. Second, negative constructions of older people and their contributions to society lead us to an understanding of difference that legitimates the inadequacy of their treatment both as victims and as perpetrators of crime.

Who are Older People? Their Historical and Contemporary Context

The idea of old age has been acknowledged throughout Western history (Cole & Winkler, 1994). Its importance varies widely from society to society as does the value assigned to those in their later years (Vincent, 1999; de Beauvoir, 1970). The understanding of old age, and hence the place of older people in society, has evolved to reflect ongoing societal change. For instance, important to our understanding of old age today is the growth of a secular modern society in which science rather than spirituality is the dominant force. The wane of spirituality and the cultural hegemony that accompanied it have brought the meaning and purpose of life, and especially of old age, into question, even as science extends the number of years lived (Cole & Winkler, 1994). This search for meaning is occurring in the context of a globalization within which societies have become preoccupied with materialism associated with economic productivity in a market economy and with the importance of the individual as both producer and consumer (Estes, 2001). It is in these conditions that those designated as older people must find their place (Phillipson & Biggs, 1998).

Demography and Old Age

Just how many years at the end of life are considered part of old age is a matter not only of chronology and the biophysical but of socio-economic and political forces. In the twentieth century, industrialization led to the displacement of older workers from the labour market, forcing them into retirement (Townsend, 1981). This was accompanied by the introduction of both the mandatory retirement policies and the old age pensions that now provide a marker for the onset of old age. Currently one officially becomes a senior citizen in Canada at age 65 with eligibility for Old Age Security—a universal financial benefit administered by the federal government. It is also the age at which people become eligible for the full amount of the Canada Pension Plan and many other contributory pensions (Chappell, Gee, McDonald, & Stones, 2003).

In 2005 more than 13 per cent of the Canadian population (4.2 million people) were over 65 years of age (Schellenberg & Turcotte, 2007). However, the fact that people are living longer and healthier lives than previously, in combination with declining birth rates, means that the proportion of those in old age in comparison with other age groups in our population is increasing. It is projected that the over-65 population may reach 24.5 per cent in 2036 and 27.2 per cent in the year 2056 (Statistics Canada, 2007). Meanwhile research has shown that many older workers retain the capabilities of mind and body that constitute a valuable employee (Novak & Campbell, 2001). In concert with demographic trends, this has brought pressure for mandatory retirement policies to be altered or abandoned so that older people can work beyond age 65, the pensionable age pushed upwards, and demands on pension schemes lessened (Denton & Spencer, 2002; Ibbot, Kerr, & Beujot, 2006).

How Old Age Is Characterized

There is therefore plenty of support for the notion that the economic dependency of older people on the state follows from the needs of a capitalist market economy—in other words, that the dependency itself is part of the structure of the economy (Townsend, 2007, 1981). In addition, some economists point to the economic decisions of governments that have resulted in the depletion of state pension funds even as the need for them has increased (Gee, 2001). Moreover, the fact that the 'impact of population aging on health-care costs has been greatly overstated' has long been noted in the literature (Evans, 1987; Evans, McGrail, Morgan, Barer, & Hertzman, 2001; McGrail et al., 2000). However, these facts have not inhibited the public outcry that declares older people to be an unproductive burden on society whose pensions and demands for services will bankrupt the economy (Gee & Gutman, 2001).

When older people are shown in a positive light, it tends to be that of 'successful aging' (Rowe & Kahn, 1999). This conceptualization of old age emerged with the research that demonstrated that old age was not a disease; nor, for many people, was it a period of inevitable slow decline of mental and physical abilities. Instead, for older people their later years may offer a prolonged period of relatively good health—one in which they might expect to actively enjoy retirement (Chappell et al., 2003). This group of older people also make contributions to society and to the market economy through volunteerism; caring for and assisting family, peers, and grandchildren; investing in markets; and sometimes through financial contributions to younger generations. However, in a market economy 'it does not matter what your contribution to society has been, if you are linked to the market only as a vulnerable end-point consumer' (Vincent, 1999, p. 128).

The two views of old age that have dominated the socio-political landscape in recent years—of burdensome frailty and successful greed—may at first appear contradictory. In tandem they have supported government policies that separate older people into two major groups—those who increasingly will be expected to fend for themselves and those who will become the objects of care by the state (Gilleard & Higgs, 1998). Only a select group of older people are eligible for government-funded services based on their frailty and on their ability to mobilize family or community members to provide the necessary support (Chappell et al., 2003). Yet it is remarkable that in our society the pervasive notion is that most older people are frail in mind and body, with the successful agers being the exceptions. Phillipson and Biggs suggest that 'modern living undercuts the construction of a viable identity for living in old age' (1998, p. 21). On the one hand, older people may internalize their construction as lacking in various capacities and acquiesce to the views and wishes of others with regard to their lives. On the other, they may fight against such a view by denying their own aging.

What few older people and their organizations do is to become active in representing their own interests. Many scholars argue that age is so linked to power through mainstream social institutions that separation from these institutions leads older people to accept that in old age they will have 'power exercised upon [them] as they increasingly appear to be a drain on limited resources and a burden upon society' (Bytheway, 1995, p. 58). While they may hope that this exercise of power will be benign, there are many instances when their acquiescence allows them to become exploited, abused, and the objects of crime.

Chronology, Terminology, and Old Age

Two matters concerning the designation of old age are worthy of further specific consideration here: chronology and terminology. So far, it has been noted that old age in Canada begins officially at 65 years, after which Canadian governments refer to those individuals as senior citizens. The period between 65 years and death can last for many years and is increasing for most groups (Markson, 2003). However, while in the past social theory put forward the concept of 'age-as-leveller'—one that assumed that old age is characterized by 'poor physical health and economic problems' (Markson, 2003, p.110)—it is now understood that chronology-based distinctions have only limited usefulness. Older age groups have the same dimensions of diversity as other adults. In other words, they are distinguished by their social class and income, their gender, their mental and physical state, their ethno-cultural background, the activities they engage in, their social political views, and so forth (Vincent, 1999). It is readily apparent that while some 70-year-olds may already be frail in mind and body, many 90-year-olds are mentally and physically fit and active, so that some make the case for ignoring chronological age (Bytheway, 2005). Moreover, lifetimes of poverty and hardship have a major effect not only on longevity but also on quality of life in later years. For instance, it is notable that for many reasons Aboriginal peoples in Canada encounter ill-health relatively early in life and have average life expectancy rates considerably lower than those of other groups (McPherson & Wister, 2008). Similarly, it is not without reason that much of the research on aging in prisons use 50 years as the entrance to old age.

The tendency to refer to older people as 'the old' or 'the elderly' has been sustained despite much evidence that the 'the' fails to address differences among older people (Bytheway, 1995; McPherson & Wister, 2008). The term 'senior citizen'—often shortened to 'senior'—is used by Canada's federal, provincial and territorial governments. However, some older people do not appreciate their arbitrary inclusion in a group that seems to have so much negative baggage attached—one that is pensionable and not part of the mainstream of society. As currently used, the designation 'old'—for instance an 'old' person—is likely to be seen as a chronological assignment to deep old age and hence a pejorative term, although Calasanti and Slevin (2001, p. 10) suggest that in the future it may be possible to reclaim the term 'old' as a term of respect—just as the term 'black' has been reclaimed. The term 'elder' is used for different groups in different ways. Specifically in Canada, it is used with regard to a select and honoured group of older people notably in Aboriginal communities, but also in some immigrant communities. The term 'older people' is deemed most appropriate for use in this chapter, although on occasion 'old', 'old age', or 'senior' will be used where these terms better fit the context in which they are used.

All these components of how older people are viewed in society, as well as their individual characteristics and experiences, contribute to whether an older person has a good old age or not. However, societal norms may well trump individual characteristics and experiences. In a society where older people both lack positive self-regard and are viewed by many as lacking the positive attributes of other adults, their treatment is frequently less than exemplary—in other words, their vulnerability is not intrinsic but may lie in their victimization.

Crimes against Older People

Although contested by some (Brogden & Nijhar, 2006), the overall evidence is strong that people over 65 years of age living in individual households are much less likely to be victims of most crimes than members of younger age groups in Canada. An analysis of the data collected through self-reports from the 2004 General Social Survey (GSS) on eight types of offences (including 'physical assault, sexual assault, robbery, theft of personal property, break and enter, motor vehicle theft, theft of household property'), as well as through 'police-reported crime data from the Incident-based Uniform Crime Reporting Survey', yielded the following information (Ogrodnik, 2007, p. 7). Seniors are less likely than other age groups to be victims of violent crime—for instance, according to the GSS, 4 times less likely than those 55 to 64 years of age and 20 times less likely than the most victimized group, those aged 15 to 24 (the youngest age group surveyed). Moreover, when violence does occur older people are 'no more likely to sustain injuries' (Ogrodnik, 2007, p. 6). Seniors are also much less likely to experience theft of personal property—half as likely as the next highest age group and eight times less likely than the youngest age group—and 'three times less likely than all Canadian households to experience a break and enter, a property theft, a motor vehicle theft or vandalism' (Ogrodnik, 2007, p. 6). One area where the evidence suggests that seniors are in much greater likelihood of victimization than other groups is that of telephone fraud perpetrated by telemarketing schemes.

When seniors are the victims of violent crime, they are, much as other age groups, likely to know the perpetrator. Family members are more likely to be the perpetrators of violence against older people than against other age groups, including 'adult children (35 per cent) and current or previous spouses (31 per cent)' (Ogrodnik, 2007, p. 11). Thirty-eight per cent of their 'victims sustained a minor injury' while 2 per cent 'sustained a major physical injury that required physical attention' (Justice Canada, 2009). Women are most likely to be the victims of violent crime in those over 65, at 62 per cent. However, men constitute a considerable minority given that they are estimated to be victims of 38 per cent of violent crime against seniors.

Not only have these findings been consistent over time in Canada, but they are also similar to those reported in the United States (Luu & Liang, 2005–06). There are a number of possible explanations for these apparently low crime rates. First, more crimes against seniors may go unreported to police or any other authority than those perpetrated against the general population (Brogden & Nijhar, 2006). Second, even when crimes against seniors are reported, they might be difficult to prosecute or the older person might be unwilling to cooperate in the prosecution. In fact, these are some of the assumptions on which the introduction of adult protection and guardianship legislation are predicated (Wolhuter, Olley, & Denham, 2009). For instance, it is claimed that in order to maintain their familial affiliations older people are unwilling to report a variety of mistreatment and neglect (Beaulieu, Gordon, & Spencer, 2005). Or they are reluctant to reveal themselves as victims of exploitation by family or others because of the shame involved (Barer, 1997) or alternatively because they take pride in their positive identity as copers (Podnieks, 1992b). There are some parallels here with the noted reluctance of younger women to bring charges against their male partners and the arguments for and against the criminalization of the violence of males against women (Currie, 1998; Montminy, 2005; Straka & Montminy, 2006). Another argument that reflects societal **ageism** is that older people fear revealing exploitation and fraud because that will bring into question their mental capacities and therefore threaten their autonomy (Harbison et al., 2005).

While some research supports these varied explanations, it is not extensive. In addition, we do not have comparisons about the extent to which similar or different considerations dissuade other age groups in society from reporting crimes. What we can say is that the reasons for the non-reporting of crimes by older people appear to be reflections of an ageist society in which older people fear that, by reporting their victimization, yet more revelations about their inadequacies will be made.

Crime versus Elder Abuse

Differentiation between crimes against seniors and elder abuse is not well developed and is sometimes confusing. A case in point is a recent publication entitled *Abuse of Older Adults: Department of Justice Canada, Overview Paper* (Justice Canada, 2009), which is intended to make the connections between the Criminal Code and 'elder abuse'. In the overview paper, elder abuse is named as a family violence topic, notwithstanding the fact that within the paper reference is made to abuse perpetrated by non-family members and outside of the family context, including 'at the hands of … caregivers, service providers or other individuals' who both are and are not 'in a position of power and trust' (p. 1). Six differing types of abuse—physical abuse, sexual abuse and exploitation, neglect, psychological or emotional abuse, economic or financial abuse, and spiritual abuse—are identified. The Criminal Code might apply to these named abuses with reference to 'physical and sexual abuse', 'neglect', 'psychological or emotional abuse', 'economic or financial abuse', and 'institutional abuse' [that occurring in care facilities] (pp. 3–4). For instance, physical abuse might in fact involve assault (ss. 265–268) but is more likely to be named as 'abuse' if perpetrated by a family member or an institutional caregiver. Sexual abuse is for the most part sexual assault (ss. 271–273) involving some form of coercion 'to participate in any unwanted, unsafe or degrading sexual activity' (Justice Canada, 2009, p. 3). 'The unnecessary use of or misuse of restraints (physical or pharmaceutical) or confinement' (Justice Canada, 2009, p. 3)—both of which are known to occur in institutional care—could constitute assault, unlawfully causing bodily harm (s. 269), or forcible confinement (s. 279) (Justice Canada, 2009, p. 2).

Altogether, it is said that nearly 40 provisions of the Criminal Code might be applied to what is named as elder abuse and neglect (Justice Canada, 2009). What this demonstrates is that many actions and inactions that are termed elder abuse and neglect are in fact crimes, and some of them are serious crimes. Of particular concern is the inclusion in the overview of manslaughter and murder under the heading of physical and sexual abuse. This raises profound questions of just how crimes against older people are being considered (Justice Canada, 2009, p. 3).

There are many degrees of neglect, from those that cause some form of emotional stress or mild physical discomfort to those that constitute severe harm. The latter might be prosecuted under the Criminal Code as criminal negligence causing bodily harm or death (ss. 219–221) or as a failure to provide the necessities of life (Justice Canada, 2009, p. 3). It is important to recognize that in private homes sometimes those charged with the care of an older person are both physically and mentally incapable of providing adequate care—especially without supports—for instance, in the case where the child or spouse is physically or mentally challenged (Anetzberger, 2005). In residential care facilities, psychological or emotional abuse and neglect may occur because of lack of appropriate resources for care (Baltes, 1996). For instance, the facility may be understaffed and the staff may have insufficient time to spend with residents or may lack education and training in how to assist them (McDonald et al., forthcoming, n.d.).

'Economic or financial abuse' is most often mentioned by seniors as the form of abuse with which they are familiar. In the Justice Canada (2009) paper, these abuses are said to refer to various forms of financial and legal transactions, including 'acting without consent in a way that financially benefits one person at the expense of another . . . stealing or using older adults' money or property in a dishonest manner, or failing to use older adults' assets for their welfare.' Many of these actions could be prosecuted as various forms of 'theft', 'misappropriation of funds' (ss. 322, 328–332, 334, 342), 'extortion' (s. 346), 'forgery' (s. 366), and 'fraud' (s. 380) (p. 4). The willingness of older people to bring charges may depend on their relationship with the perpetrator (Tomita, 1990). The willingness of the police to support older people in bringing charges before the courts to convict perpetrators may depend on whether or not they view older people through an ageist lens.

Abuse within residential institutions may consist of all of the interpersonal forms of abuse/crime discussed above—those that emanate from personal relationships between staff and residents or between residents and other residents (Spencer, 2008). However, there are other forms of abuse that are primarily a consequence of the resourcing, administration, and regulation of the institution. These include 'inadequate care and nutrition, low standards of nursing care, inappropriate or aggressive staff-client interactions, or substandard, overcrowded or unsanitary living environments' (Justice Canada, 2009, p. 4). One form of mistreatment that has been widely noted and censured is a likely outcome of inadequate staffing—that is, the use and 'misuse of physical or chemical restraints' to control residents' behaviours (Justice Canada, 2009, p. 4; Spencer et al., 2008). These forms of mistreatment within institutions are sometimes referred to as systemic abuse and are widely regarded as reflective of societal ageism (Payne, 2005). Internal and professional regulation of standards of care in institutional facilities, even where protective legislation exists, means that the laying charges under the provisions of the Criminal Code is rare. Further, claims are increasingly being made that residents are 'out of control', because they sometimes attack staff or one another, although the reasons for this may relate directly to the deficits in care and environment named above (Banarjee et al., 2008, p. 3).

The Justice Canada overview paper also speaks to the fact that 'the law has largely protected older adults' interests in terms of physical or mental deterioration' through measures contained in provincial and territorial legislation, including adult protection legislation itself, as well as 'guardianship, health law, substitute decision-making and succession and legislation directed at family violence and abuse within care facilities' (2009, p. 4; Gordon, 2001). What is referred to as 'elder abuse' therefore may subsume many crimes against older people in addition to many other different types of acts of commission and omission. The fact that elder abuse is not a single phenomenon—but is made up of many and diverse phenomena—is often overlooked in discussions of how to address it (Harbison et al., 2008). These difficulties in definition also make quantification of elder abuse very difficult, and it not surprising that given its complexities and the lack of boundaries on the topic, few studies attempting to measure elder abuse have been carried out and estimates of the size of the problem vary considerably (McDonald et al., 2006). Beaulieu et al. suggest that based on the available evidence the 'abuse or neglect of older adults in community settings is conservatively estimated at between four and ten percent' (2005, p. 204). However, there is currently no viable research to determine the levels of abuse in institutional care facilities in Canada.

Elder Abuse as a Social Problem

Despite uncertainties in definition and quantification, it has long been demanded that elder abuse be accepted as a major social problem (Leroux & Petrunik, 1990; Phillipson, 1993). These demands have come mostly from professionals and academics in the field of gerontology who insist that the amount of abuse and neglect and the needs of older people for protection are much greater than evidence suggests. Wahl and Purdy (n.d.) refer to 'Elder Abuse: The Hidden Crime'. Payne (2005) states that the statistical evidence does not represent the true picture—that is, it fails to demonstrate the extent of the problem of mistreatment and neglect of older people.

Thus the literature in effect sidesteps the lack of conceptual clarity about what constitutes a crime against an older person versus what constitutes elder abuse and neglect. Instead, it concentrates on reinforcing the importance of elder abuse as a social problem. Payne suggests that 'because many abuses against older adults are not universally defined as illegal, a social harm conceptualization of crime offers a broader base from which we can begin to understand abuses against older adults' (2005, p. 5). Beaulieu et al. (2005) would add to this 'broader social harms', which might include the older person's 'dignity and autonomy . . . adequacy of pensions . . . disrespect and ageist attitudes . . . as well as marginalization, neglect and abandonment' (p. 201)—in other words, measures that would include older people in the 'common good', as suggested by Brogden and Nijhar (2006, p. 48). Further, they suggest that 'the social and legal thresholds for identifying situations as "abusive" are dynamic and will likely continue to evolve' (p. 202).

Just why the problems of older people as opposed to those of other groups should be treated differentially as 'social harms' rather than as illegal is not clearly addressed. What can be inferred is the explanation is connected to the discourse that constructs older people as frail and vulnerable in mind and body. It is taken for granted that the characteristics with which older people are imbued are sufficient indication that they are unable to protect themselves and their interests. Thus they have been treated as a group for whom a variety of interventions under the aegis of the state are justified (Coughlan et al., 1995; Robertson, 1995; Wolhuter et al., 2009). The fact that this constructs older people as children was discussed with apprehension when the idea of elder abuse began to develop nearly 30 years ago (McDonald et al., 1991; Poirier, 1992). This concern did not prevent the introduction of adult protection and guardianship legislation—targeted mostly at older people—in both Canada and the United States (Harbison et al., 1995, 2008). So far, this chapter has discussed how perceptions of aging and older people may have led to their differential treatment under the law—treatment that raises the question of whether older people are at least potentially subject to oppression through laws that are intended to protect them. The next section expands on how and why this differentiation evolved.

Critical Theory and the Construction of 'Elder Abuse and Neglect'

Contributing factors identified in accounts of the evolution of elder abuse and neglect, for instance, in those by Baumann (1989) and Leroux and Petrunik (1990), help answer the question of why older people are held to be in need of protection. Baumann takes a contextual constructionist approach to elder abuse and neglect—that is, she suggests that it is not the intrinsic qualities of elder abuse and neglect that have determined its increasing acceptance as a social problem but events within its societal context, in concert with claims made by members of expert groups. Thus Baumann (1989) argues that it is highly relevant that the concept of elder abuse and neglect emerged in the 1980s at a time when greater attention was beginning to be paid to demographic aging. Researchers and professionals developed the discipline of gerontology—the study of aging—in response to the aging of the population and began to establish themselves as experts on the aging process.

Ongoing research has established that most older people are independent and competent and therefore not vulnerable (Chappell et al., 2003). Further, where families are stressed by caregiving, there is little support for the idea that this leads to abuse (Pillemer, 1986; Pillemer & Finkelhor, 1989). In addition, older men and women do not necessarily seek escape from abusive situations, although they would like assistance on their own terms (Harbison, 2008; Older Women's Network, 1998; Podnieks, 1992b). Nevertheless the perceptions of older people and their need for professional intervention, which Baumann (1989) discusses, maintain their presence in a system of care that now concerns itself predominantly with the right to risk—that is, with whether the older person is sufficiently competent to make the decisions to stay in a situation that experts identify as containing risks to their safety and best interests (Harbison et al., 2008).

Leroux and Petrunik (1990) investigated the construction of 'elder abuse and neglect' in Canada through a study of activities surrounding the issues, using Blumer's model of the development of social problems. They concluded, as had Baumann (1989) in the United States, that underpinning the attempt to construct elder abuse and neglect as a social problem was a 'public perception of old age as a social problem' based on the construction of old people as frail and incompetent (1990, p. 162).

While it is unlikely that elder abuse and neglect will ever become a social problem in the sense of a now past era of social welfare—one that commands substantive national and provincial resources (Leonard, 1997)—it has nevertheless caught the attention of governments as they strive to gain the support of an aging population. Activities both within and between the provincial and federal governments with regard to policy development and awareness raising have been ongoing for a number of years, as have those of lobby organizations such as the Canadian Network for the Prevention of Elder Abuse (CNPEA). An increased interest in elder abuse was signalled by the appointment of Marjory Le Breton, government leader in the Senate, as minister of state for seniors and the creation of the National Seniors Council, which Le Breton chairs and which produced a report on elder abuse (National Seniors Council, 2007). Also of note is the Federal Elder Abuse Initiative (2008). Led by Human Resources and Skills Development Canada with the participation of the Public Health Agency of Canada, the Department of Justice, and the Royal Canadian Mounted Police, this initiative acknowledges that responses to elder abuse include criminal and justice as well as personnel and health issues, although its activities are mainly focused around awareness campaigns, training, and research.

Diversity and Elder Abuse and Neglect

Throughout its documented history, elder abuse has consistently been described in homogeneous terms—for instance, as *a* social problem of *the* elderly (see also Neysmith & Macadam, 1999). This is notwithstanding the fact that definitions include the many diverse problems potentially affecting older people, from those who are mentally fit and physically healthy to those who are frail in mind and body. Physical abuse by an intimate surely requires a very different response than fraud by a stranger or systemic neglect in a residential institution. Moreover, as we have seen, there are no clear distinctions, chronological or otherwise, that can tell us how the elderly should be defined or who should have protection. In addition, the concept of elder abuse has been treated as if it was gender neutral (Neysmith, 1995). This not only desexualizes older people, but also serves to mask important gender differences in patterns of mistreatment and responses and the general lack of interest that feminists have demonstrated in assisting their older peers (Marshall, 2006; Whittaker, 1997; Harbison, 2008). As with the study of aging in general, the approach is also 'heteronormative' and leaves little room for the attempt to explore and understand the experiences of older lesbian, bisexual, gay, and transgendered older people (Cronin, 2006).

Ethno-cultural diversity as a unique factor in the mistreatment of older people has recently begun to be recognized within individual Western states (Tatara, 1998). In Canada this was first recognized in service agencies through their efforts to assist their clients of both sexes from diverse cultural backgrounds, including rural and Aboriginal older Canadians (Spencer, 2000) and recent immigrants (see Cornwell, 2000; Hansell, 1999; Zaman & Shakir, 2000; Ward-Hall, 2001). These service initiatives have continued and have been followed by an interest in researching the issues in diverse communities (Older Women's Network, 1998; Tam & Neysmith, 2006).

The idea of elder abuse itself has been internationalized through the International Network for the Prevention of Elder Abuse (INPEA). INPEA originated in North America but now has members from many countries in the Americas, Europe, the Middle East, Africa, Asia, and Australia (Lowenstein, 2009). There is little doubt that the Westernization through globalization of many states has led to the breakdown of traditional norms of behaviour with regard to older people, resulting in their mistreatment. In addition, the research indicates that, in any case, negative stereotypes of older people are transcultural (Cuddy, Norton, & Fiske, 2005). Some argue, however, that bringing a Western, medicalized perspective to aging and the problems subsumed under elder abuse is simply another form of colonization (Katz, 1996; Truscott, 1996).

An Emerging Rights Discourse

More recent Canadian discussions in the field of elder abuse have emphasized the need to strike a balance between rights and protection (Beaulieu et al., 2005; O'Connor, Hall, & Donnelly, 2009; Watts, 2009). This new focus may be seen as an important development in moving beyond the ageism of seeking only the protection of older people. However, many issues are raised with regard to legislation that claims both to protect older people and to ensure their rights (Robertson, 1995; Coughlan et al., 1995; McDonald et al., 1991; Poirier, 1992, 1995):

> These include whether legislative solutions support a tendency to undermine the rights and autonomy of older people by providing more intrusive solutions than would otherwise be the case [and] whether mistreated and neglected older people may be further marginalized by legal interventions which are by their very nature paternalistic: that is, that they take as a starting point the question of whether or not a person has the capacity to make decisions for him or herself . . . [failing to] address the difficulties inherent in assessing capacity. (Harbison et al., forthcoming, n.d.)

In other words, shifting the ground to a legal rights perspective, especially one that places so much emphasis on a determination of capacity, leaves power in the hands of professional and legal 'authorities' (O'Connor et al., 2009).

These concerns are reinforced by a further issue in the attempt to understand the victimization of older people—that is, that we know so very little about what older people themselves want. There are very few studies in Canada (or indeed elsewhere) that ask older people who are victims of crime and abuse about their experiences and about how they would like to have them addressed. The few studies that do mostly give voice to older women and indicate that most older women want to remain in their situation of mistreatment, but that they would like to have it ameliorated through support and services and want to be reassured that should their situation deteriorate, they would have access to emergency assistance (Hightower, Smith, & Hightower, 2006; Older Women's Network, 1998; Podnieks, 1992b).

Older Offenders

The literature discussing seniors' crime is sparse. According to a profile prepared by Statistics Canada (2001), 'seniors are much less likely than younger age groups to be involved in criminal activity as offenders, [accounting for] less than 1 per cent of all persons accused of a Criminal Code offence in 1999.' However, of those accused of crimes in that year, 40 per cent were accused of a violent crime, including 12 per cent who were accused of assault causing bodily harm or assault with a weapon and 13 per cent who were accused of sexual assault. Older women made up only 23 per cent of those accused of a Criminal Code offence and only 12 per cent of those accused of a violence offence.

Of those cases that were taken to court, 56 per cent 'resulted in a conviction'. The most common sentence imposed on those found guilty was a fine (50 per cent), with 27 per cent being placed on probation. Only 14 per cent of all cases resulted in a prison sentence. It is notable that seniors appeared to be treated differently from other groups with regard to sentencing in that they were 'more likely to receive a fine (50 per cent versus 33 per cent), less likely to receive a prison term (14 per cent versus 35 per cent), and equally likely to receive a term of probation (27 per cent). This more lenient sentencing may be due to a reverse form of ageism whereby the older offenders are seen as less likely to reoffend or as less of a danger to society.

A further issue relating to the fair treatment of aging offenders is reflected in a Statistics Canada report: 'the relatively high incidence of sexual offences . . . appears to be due in part to a growing willingness of adult victims to report incidents which allegedly occurred years earlier' (2001, p. 11). In the intervening period, many high-profile cases have involved the conviction of old men for sexual offences that took place when the victim was a child. The ethical and legal implications of sentencing and imprisoning old offenders for crimes that are so abhorrent to the general public are challenging.

Services for Older Victims

There is a strong connection between the construction of social problems and the services offered to address them. Harbison and Morrow (1998) identified four major constructions of the mistreatment and neglect of older people: **'adults in need of protection'**, 'subjects of illegal acts', 'victims of domestic violence', and 'agents for their own lives'. In this section, these ways of viewing the problems associated with mistreatment and neglect provide the framework for a discussion of the assistance offered to older people who are victims. Older offenders are considered separately.

Adults in Need of Protection

The predominant legal response to the needs of older people suffering mistreatment and neglect involves some form of adult protection or guardianship legislation (Beaulieu et al., 2005; Gordon, 2001). While the use of such legislation does not preclude additional legal remedies—including criminal charges against perpetrators—for the most part the focus is on protecting the older person. There are several weaknesses in this approach. Given an individual's rights under law, legislation can only impose solutions to the mistreatment and neglect on those who are mentally incapacitated with respect to decisions that affect their safety or best interests. Yet few older people, including those that are referred as in need of protection, are mentally incapacitated in this way (Wahl, 2009), and many refuse assistance that is offered (Vinton, 1991).

A number of reasons centring on the older person's need for autonomy are commonly offered for their refusal of assistance. These include the wish to live as they choose and to protect their sense of positive identity, including their relationships with abusers. For example, the older person may want to protect a family member or caregiver to whom they are emotionally attached but who has perpetrated or been complicit in their abuse or neglect (Beaulieu et al., 2005). Further, severe limitations in the quantity and diversity of the assistance that is provided may discourage older people from taking it up. If they do, they may find that the assistance offered does not suit their own perceptions of their needs (Harbison et al., 2005). Older clients therefore have the well-founded fear that those in professional roles who enter their home will engage in surveillance of their mental state and their capacity to manage their household and that if they are found wanting, the only alternative will be residential care (Harbison et al., 2008).

It is nonetheless important not to discount the fact that some of the people referred for protection do indeed lack various capacities that would allow them to care for themselves or to make provision to care for themselves in a manner that would have been in accord with their previous wishes. There is a very real dilemma about how the needs of these relatively few older people should be met and on what legal grounds (O'Connor et al., 2009). For instance (citing issues raised by the Canadian Charter of Rights and Freedoms), Nova Scotia's Adult Protection Services, which is one of the pioneers of provincial adult protection legislation, has moved over time toward applying its legislation to fewer and fewer older adults, to the point where it presently includes only the 'most vulnerable' (Harbison et al., forthcoming). In addition, guidelines and regulations associated with adult protection legislation generally focus on procedural rights, including processes that are the least intrusive and that acknowledge older people's wishes. However, these provisions are not intended to override the primacy given by intervenors to an older person's 'best interests' when the older person is assessed as not having the capacity to act in his or her own best interests (Harbison et al., 2008).

Some jurisdictions have attempted to focus their legislation on issues of rights, acknowledging that even when people's mental capacities have limitations, they can and should be supported in making decisions that meet their wishes (Wahl, 2009). However, once again limitations in the availability and diversity of services mean that there is frequently little chance of meeting older people's wishes. Theoretically, this response to the needs of older people for services is captured in the notions of the 'risk society', which is one where the role of the state is to ensure that risks are avoided through measures of surveillance and the role of citizens/consumers is to provide for their own necessary services with the support of a notional community (Biggs & Powell, 1999; Webb, 2006). One of the participants in one of our studies of the relationship between legislation and services echoed the comments of many others when she said that, quite simply, 'everything's downloaded to the community' (Harbison et al., 2005).

Persons Subject to Illegal Acts

Casting older people as the subjects of illegal acts—as opposed to objects of care—suggests that older people should receive the same types of responses and services from the legal system as other adults. However, to date there have been many barriers to proceeding in this way. In the literature, much has been made of the fact that older people are likely to be unwilling to bring charges because of concerns such as those that have been discussed above. For instance, it is said that older people may be ashamed of and embarrassed by their own mistreatment, including crimes against them. If the abuse or crime is perpetrated by an intimate, they may wish to maintain the relationship whatever the cost. If it is perpetrated by a stranger, then they may fear that others will question their ability to manage their lives, or they may fear emotional or physical repercussions (Payne, 2005). While these may well be the valid considerations of older people, it is important to recognize that older individuals live within an ageist society, one that asks them to question their own values and abilities constantly, and supports the negative stereotypes that others may have of them (Bytheway, 1995). This alone discourages older people from asserting their legal rights.

Should older people attempt to follow a legal path, they may be discouraged in doing so by friends and family and sometimes by police. There is some evidence, however, that police are increasingly involved in efforts to support older people in their wish to maintain their rights (Harbison et al., 2005). There is also anecdotal evidence that some police discourage older people from bringing criminal charges, citing uncertainty of conviction and suggesting instead civil charges. However, civil action has the potential to incur huge costs that older people cannot meet or shy away from. In effect, by attempting to assert themselves, older people may become subject to secondary victimization: 'victim-blaming attitudes, reactions, behaviours and practices by service providers that result in further violation of victims' rights and/or additional trauma' (Wolhuter et al., 2009, p. 55).

These concerns are compounded by the fact that legal aid focuses on younger age groups and has very limited funding, and within Canada there are few legal clinics devoted to serving older people (see, however, the British Columbia Centre for Elder Advocacy and Support and the Advocacy Centre for the Elderly in Ontario). Thus, despite the establishment of elder law as a specialty area of practice within the Canadian Bar Association (Soden, 2005), most older people still have little access to legal advice that is affordable, knowledgable about their interests, and able to transcend ageism in responding to their needs.

Should older people take part in a criminal investigation of those who have perpetrated crimes against them, or join a civil action that attempts to redress fraud or other matters, the process may be affected by ageism. For instance, age alone may affect the credibility of the older person's statements with jurors (Hodell et al., 2009) and the supports that they need to understand the court processes and to deal with the emotional and psychological stress are not always available (Payne, 2005). One means of supporting victims of crime is through victims' services. In Canada these may be associated with provincial/territorial departments of justice or with police or non-profit agencies. However, most victims' services focus on younger people rather than on those who are older, although when the problems of older people are brought to the attention of the services, they make considerable efforts to provide assistance (personal communications with professionals involved). The importance of providing cultur-ally appropriate services is recognized in the provision of services for specific cultural groups. The government of Ontario, for instance, has recently announced a grants program that will assist support groups for First Nations women as well as First Nations, Metis, and Inuit people who are victims of crime.

One alternative means of addressing mistreatment, including actions that could be subject to criminal charges, is restorative justice. This approach involves the diversion of cases brought to the courts. Instead of punishment, there is a process that focuses on the hurt that the victim has suffered, the needs that have been engendered by the hurt, and the ways in which these needs can be met by those who have inflicted the hurt. An important element is the restoration of relationships within a process that respects the rights and dignity of all parties involved. Given what we understand of the reluctance of older people to reveal their abuse, especially because they do not want to lose relationships they value, restorative justice seems to be an appealing solution. It is also widely recognized that restorative justice has historically been associated with many cultures—notably, Canada's First Nations (Groh, 2003). Thus the needs of diverse groups of older people, including members of Aboriginal and new immigrant communities, might be served. However, some people question whether issues of power can be adequately addressed within this intervention framework, especially with regard to groups already embedded in negative stereotypes (Wolhuter et al., 2009). Winterdyk and King argue that many issues need to be researched and addressed before the restorative approach has widespread implementation, including the inappropriateness of its application for many crimes and, for some locations, cost effectiveness, the rights of both offender and victim, and the question of whether this approach would result in 'a better quality of justice' (1999, p. 292).

Older People as Victims of Domestic Violence

Power in relationships has long been a central consideration in attempts to deal with domestic violence. On the one hand, as a stand-alone solution, the use of the criminal justice system, with the possibility of the incarceration of offenders, may be an important means of communi-cating to 'violent men' that their behaviour is unacceptable to society; on the other, it fails to deal with the relationship aspects of the violence (Snider, 1998, p. 148). Currie points out that 'framing male violence against women as a criminal justice response was facilitated by white, professional feminists who, over time, increasingly claimed ownership of the issue of violence against women' (1998, p. 45). Some people therefore favour a restorative justice approach to domestic violence. Others are more wary (Snider, 1998). It is generally acknowledged that where some form of mediation is used—such as conferencing or restorative justice—measures and services must be in place to empower the victim and ensure that the agreement that has been worked out is honoured, especially by those perpetrating the abusive or criminal acts (Wolhuter et al., 2009).

Older women rather than older men constitute the majority of victims of family violence (Neysmith, 1995). However, feminists in general, as well as those associated with the systems that respond to domestic violence against younger women, by their own acknowledgment have shown little interest in the difficulties of older women until recently (Calasanti, Sleven, & King, 2006; Hightower et al., 2006; Marshall, 2006; Straka & Montminy, 2006). Even when they do so, older women are sometimes characterized as those over 50 years of age, and there is no recognition of the gulf of experiences, needs, and interests that are present in the 30 or 40 years that follow (Harbison, 2008).

While older women are, like younger women, more likely than men to be victims of domestic violence, older men, as we have seen, are also victims. This may be a consequence of the lessening of their power in the family owing to physical or mental deterioration or to loss of status. In response to the needs of older men, a number of jurisdictions have introduced programs that respond to both men and women. These include Kerby House in Calgary, which offers shelter and services; safe housing in the city of Edmonton; and the newly developed Pat's Place in Toronto, all of which offer shelter and services to both men and women.

Cultural and ethno-cultural considerations are central to the provision of meaningful services for diverse older people. Ideally, leadership will come from members of the communities involved. Aboriginal women, for example, have developed culturally congruent ways of responding to what they refer to as 'senior abuse' (thus avoiding the duality of the meaning of 'elder'); these approaches frame older abused women not as victims but as women of wisdom and strength, and focus on restoring their positive roles in their communities. However, this is not always possible, especially in the initial stages of consciousness raising because of issues or politics internal to the community (Tam and Neysmith, 2006; Ward-Hall, 2001). Finally, in Canada many older people live relatively isolated lives in rural communities and need special consideration for services (Spencer, 2000). The attachment to place is very strong within these communities, and rural older people have higher thresholds for what they consider abuse than those who live in urban communities (Stones & Bedard, 2002).

Agents for Their Own Lives

To date, those designated as older people have not been a major driving force behind responses to the mistreatment and neglect of other older people. A number of reasons for this may be hypothesized, based on the ongoing evolution of elder abuse and neglect as a social problem. As previously discussed, at its inception elder abuse was perceived as a clinical phenomenon related to family dysfunction, and hence it became part of the territory claimed for expert intervention by a number of gerontological disciplines, including, most prominently, social work, medicine, and nursing (Anetzberger, 2005; Baumann, 1989; McLean, 1995). Later it became evident that elder abuse and neglect occurred not just in families, but in many different contexts, and was perpetrated by people in many different relationships with older people, including strangers (CNPEA, 2007). This period coincided with one in which governments began demanding that the activities they funded demonstrate their relevance to what became known as 'stakeholders' (Aronson, 1993). As a consequence, older people were invited to become involved in efforts to address issues of elder abuse, primarily efforts intended to raise awareness of the many types of abuse that they and their peers might suffer. Thus older people are now represented on federal, provincial, and territorial committees and advisory boards focused on the prevention of abuse. More recently, as we have seen, the federal government has demonstrated an interest in taking a leadership role in the issue and has been judicious in ensuring that seniors' representatives are included—for example, by means of the National Seniors Council. For the most part, these actions are yet further instances of seniors being invited to sit at the elder abuse table rather than to become leaders and take charge. The revitalized Canadian Association of Retired Persons (CARP), which invites membership from those aged 45 and up and appears to speak for the relatively well-off, is encouraging its members to take an interest in elder abuse.

Services for Older Offenders

The sparse literature on seniors' crime points to the lack of knowledge about issues surrounding older criminals, both those who are incarcerated and those who are serving sentences in the community (Codd & Bramhall, 2002; Stojkovic, 2007). The point is made repeatedly that because of the aging demographic of our Western societies, and given present trends, there is likely to be an increase in the number older prisoners and it is therefore important to consider their needs (Fazel et al., 2009; Loeb & Steffensmeier; Stojkovic, 2007). However, Wahidin and Cain point to research in British prisons that suggests an uncaring environment and little interest in addressing older prisoners' needs (2006, p. 3). Studies on the subject provide a sometimes inconsistent picture of older incarcerated men, raising questions about the accuracy of the information, given that most of it is based on self-reports (Fazel et al., 2001). However, for the most part, what the inmates report agrees with evidence contained in medical records. Overall they are said to be in poor health relative to those not imprisoned (Loeb & Steffensmeier, 2006). Over 80 per cent in one study were found to have at least one chronic illness (Fazel et al., 2001). In a study of men over 50 years of age, 85 per cent had 'multiple chronic health conditions' (Loeb & Steffensmeier, 2006, p. 269). While in some instances their poor health may have been related to a lifetime of poverty and deprivation, in most cases the prison environment itself is seen as providing few opportunities for healthy living, and as a consequence older prisoners neglect their health (Loeb & Steffensmeier, 2006). Indeed, Loeb et al. (2001) found that physiologically 'the health of many inmates in this study was found to be comparable to that of community-dwelling men who are 15 years older' (p. 247).

One outcome of an aging prison population is that some prisoners are likely to develop dementia. Fazel et al. (2002) use case examples to highlight the ethical and legal implications of continuing incarceration for those with dementia. They conclude that besides issues centring on 'deterrence', 'punishment', and 'retributive punishment' or 'punitive justice', there are human rights issues that need to be considered. Specifically, the European Convention on Human Rights 'forbids inhuman or degrading treatment or punishment of those in detention' and 'the lack of appropriate health care for sick prisoners has been declared as a form of inhuman or degrading treatment' (p. 158). Whether Canada holds itself to a similar standard is not known. Stojkovic (2007) sees old prisoners as themselves the victims of 'systemic abuse and neglect . . . [both] while they are incarcerated and when they are released from prison' (p. 97).

Conclusion

Older people in Canadian society, as elsewhere, are ascribed negative, stereotypic characteristics. As a consequence, they are both marginalized and discriminated against (Townsend, 2007). In seeking to avoid further discrimination, they often fail to draw attention to, or even acknowledge, their victimization through criminal or illegal acts, as well as the mistreatment and neglect with which discrimination is frequently associated. The available evidence indicates that older people are the least likely group to be the victims of crime or to commit crimes. However, it is uncertain how many criminal or illegal acts against older people go unreported or are diverted to the limited services available under the aegis of 'elder abuse and neglect'. Where older people themselves are criminals, they appear to receive both positive and negative discrimination from the state. Older people have so far had only a limited role in societal efforts to address issues relating to their mistreatment and neglect. Whether they will become more involved as the baby boomers move into old age is difficult to predict.

The author wishes to acknowledge with thanks the ongoing support of her interdisciplinary research colleagues Stephen Coughlan, Jeff Karabanow, and Sheila Wildeman at Dalhousie University and Madine VanderPlaat of Saint Mary's University, as well as Dominique Zipper, who assisted with the background research for this chapter.

Key Terms

adults in need of protection   ageism

Questions for Critical Thought

1. Based on the discussion in the chapter, identify some of the ways in which ageism is manifest in Canadian society. Consider the ways in which you may be ageist and the impact this may have on older people.

2. Using evidence discussed in the chapter, debate the following statement: 'Crimes against older people should be dealt with in the same way as those against younger people and not through special adult protection and guardianship legislation.'

3. Identify ways in which services for older offenders should be improved.

Additional Readings

Harbison, J., McKinley, P., & Pettipas, D. (2006). Older people as objects not subjects: Theory and practice in situations of 'elder abuse'. In R. Alaggia & C. Vine (Eds), *Cruel but not unusual: Violence in Canadian families, a sourcebook of history, theory and practice.* Waterloo, ON: Wilfrid Laurier Press.

Katz, S. (2005). *Cultures of aging: Life course, lifestyle, and senior worlds.* Peterborough, ON: Broadview Press.

Wahl, J. (2009). Capacity and capacity assessment in Ontario. Toronto: Advocacy Centre for the Elderly. Retrieved May 24, 2009, from www.acelaw.ca

Websites of Interest

Advocacy Centre for the Elderly, Ontario: www.advocacycentreelderly.org

Canadian Centre for Elder Law, BC: www.bcli.org/ccel

References

ACE (Advocacy Centre for the Elderly). (n.d.). *The Advocacy Centre for the Elderly: A celebration of twenty-years of operation, 1984–2004.* Toronto: Holly Street Advocacy Centre for the Elderly.

Anetzberger, G. J. (Ed.). (2005). *The clinical management of elder abuse.* New York: Haworth Press.

Aronson, J. (1993). Giving consumers a say in policy development: Influencing policy or just being heard. *Canadian Public Policy, 19*(4), 367–378.

Bachman, R., & Meloy, M. L. (2008). The epidemiology of violence against the elderly. *Journal of Contemporary Criminal Justice, 24*(2), 186–197.

Baltes, M. M. (1996). *The many faces of dependency in old age.* Cambridge, UK: Cambridge University Press.

Banarjee, A., Daly, T., Armstrong, H., Armstrong, P., Lafrance, S., & Szebehely, M. (2008). *'Out of control': Violence against personal support workers in long-term care.* Canadian Women's Health Network. Retrieved May 22, 2008, from www.cwhn.ca/resources/kickers/outofcontrol.htm

Barer, B. M. (1997). The secret shame of the very old: 'I've never told this to anyone else'. *Journal of Mental Health and Aging, 3*(3), 365–375.

Baumann, E. A. (1989). Research rhetoric and the social construction of elder abuse. In J. Best (Ed.), *Images of issues: Typifying contemporary social problems* (pp. 55–74). New York: Aldine de Gruyter.

Beaulieu, M., Gordon, R., & Spencer, C. (2005). The abuse and neglect of older Canadians: Key legal and related issues. In A. Soden (Ed.), *Advising the older client* (pp. 197–233). Markham, ON: LexisNexis, Butterworths.

Biggs, S. (1993). *Understanding ageing: Images, attitudes and professional practice.* Buckingham, UK: Open University Press.

Biggs, S., Lowenstein, A., & Hendricks, J. (Eds). (2003). *The need for theory: Critical approaches to social gerontology.* Amityville, NY: Baywood.

Biggs, S., Phillipson, C., & Kingston, P. (Eds). (1995). *Elder abuse in perspective.* Buckingham, UK: Open University Press.

Biggs, S., & Powell, J. (1999). Surveillance and elder abuse: The rationalities and technologies of community care. *Journal of Contemporary Health, 4*(1), 43–49.

British Columbia Adult Abuse/Neglect Prevention Collaborative. (2009). Vulnerable adults and capability issues in BC. Provincial strategy document.

Brogden, M., & Nijhar, P. (2006). Crime abuse and social harm: Toward an integrated approach. In A. Wahidin & M. Cain (Eds), *Ageing, crime & society* (pp. 35–52). Devon, UK: Willan.

Bytheway, W. (1995). *Ageism.* Buckingham, UK: Open University Press.

Bytheway, W. (2005). Ageism and age categorization. *Journal of Social Issues, 61*(2), 361–374.

Calasanti, T. M., & Slevin, K. F. (Eds). (2001). *Gender social inequalities and ageing.* Walnut Creek, CA: AltaMira Press.

Calasanti, T., Slevin, K. F., & King, N. (2006). Ageism and feminism: From 'Et cetera to center'. *National Women's Studies Association Journal, 18*, 13–30.

Chappell, N., Gee, E., McDonald, L., & Stones, M. (2003). *Aging in contemporary Canada.* Toronto: Prentice Hall.

Cheal, D. (Ed.). (2002). *Aging and demographic change in Canadian context.* Toronto: University of Toronto Press.

CNPEA (Canadian Network for the Prevention of Elder Abuse). (2007). *Outlook 2007: Promising approaches in the prevention of abuse and neglect of older adults in community settings in Canada.* Ottawa: Public Health Agency of Canada.

Codd, H., & Bramhall, G. (2002). Older offenders and probation: A challenge for the future. *Probation Journal, 49*(1), 27–34.

Cole, T. R., & Winkler, M. G. (1994). *The Oxford book of aging.* Oxford: Oxford University Press.

Cornwell, L. (2000). 'Nobody knows our sorrow': Working to eliminate elder abuse affecting immigrant women from ethno-racial communities. *Proceedings of the Ontario Elder Abuse Conference,* April 13 and 14. Toronto: Institute for Human

Development, Life Course and Aging, University of Toronto.

Coughlan, S., Downe-Wamboldt, B. D., Elgie, R. G., Harbison, J., Melanson, P. M., & Morrow, M. (1995). *Legal responses to elder abuse and neglect.* Vol. 2 of *Mistreating elderly people: Questioning the response to elder abuse and neglect.* Halifax: Dalhousie University, Health Law Institute.

Cronin, A. (2006). Sexuality in gerontology: A heteronormative experience, a queer absence. In S. O. Daatland & S. Biggs (Eds), *Ageing and diversity: Multiple pathways and cultural migrations* (pp. 107–122). Bristol, UK: Policy Press.

Cuddy, A. J. C., Norton, M. I., & Fiske, S. T. (2005). This old stereotype: The pervasiveness and persistence of the elderly stereotype. *Journal of Social Issues, 61*(2), 267–285.

Currie, D. H. (1998). The criminalization of violence against women: Feminist demands and patriarchal accommodation. In K. Bonnycastle & G. S. Rigakos (Eds), *Unsettling truths* (pp. 41–51). Vancouver: Collective Press.

de Beauvoir, S. (1970). *Old age.* Harmondsworth, UK: Penguin Books.

Denton, F. T., & Spencer, B. G. (2002). Some demographic consequences of revising the definition of 'old age' to reflect future changes in life table probabilities. *Canadian Journal on Aging, 21*(3), 349–356.

Estes, C. L. (Ed.). (2001). *Social policy and Aging: A critical perspective.* Thousand Oaks, CA: Sage.

Evans, R.G. (1985). Illusions of necessity: Evading responsibility for choice in health care. *Journal of Health Politics, Policy and Law, 10*(3), 439–467.

Evans, R. G., McGrail, K. M., Morgan, S. M., Barer, M. L., & Hertzman, C. (2001). Apocalypse no: Population aging and the future of health care systems. *Canadian Journal on Aging, 20*(supplement 1), 160–191.

Fazel, S., Hope, T., O'Donnell, I., Piper, M., & Jacoby, R. (2001). Health of elderly male prisoners: Worse than the general population, worse than younger prisoners. *Age and Ageing, 30,* 403–407.

Fazel, S., McMillan, J., & O'Donnell, I. (2002). Dementia in prison: Ethical and legal implications. *Journal of Medical Ethics, 28,*156–159.

Foot, D., & Stoffman, D. (1996). *Boom bust and echo: Profiting from the demographic shift in the new millenium.* Toronto: Macfarlane, Walter and Ross.

Gee, E. (2000). Population and politics: Voodoo demography, population aging, and social policy. In E. Gee & G. Gutman (Eds), *The overselling of population aging: Apocalyptic demography, intergenerational challenges, and social policy* (pp. 5–25). Don Mills, ON: Oxford University Press.

Gee, E., & Gutman, G. (2000). *The overselling of population aging: Apocalyptic demography, intergenerational challenges, and social policy.* Don Mills, ON: Oxford University Press.

Gilleard, C., & Higgs, P. (1998). Old people as users and consumers of healthcare: A third age rhetoric for a fourth age reality? *Aging and Society, 18,* 233–248.

Gordon, R. M. (2001). Adult protection legislation in Canada, models, issues and problems. *International Journal of Law and Psychiatry, 24,* 117–134.

Groh, A. (2003). *A healing approach to elder abuse and mistreatment.* The Restorative Approaches to Elder Abuse Project. Kitchener, ON: Community Care Access Centre of Waterloo Region. www.mcmaster. ca/mjtm/5-1b.htm

Hansell, E. (1999). Multi-cultural brochures on elder abuse. *Proceedings of the Second National Conference on Elder Abuse Conference.* Toronto: Institute for Human Development, Life Course and Aging, University of Toronto.

Harbison, J. (2008). Stoic heroines or collaborators: Ageism, feminism and the provision of assistance to abused old women. *Journal of Social Work Practice, 22*(2), 221–234.

Harbison, J., Beaulieu, M., Coughlan, S., Karabanow, J., VanderPlaat, M., Wildeman, S., & Wexler, E. (2008, August 31). Conceptual frameworks: Understandings of 'elder abuse and neglect' and their implications for policy and legislation. Background paper for Human Resources and Skills Development Canada (HRSDC).

Harbison, J., Coughlan, S., Downe-Wamboldt, B. D., Elgie, R. G., Melanson, P. M., & Morrow, M. (1995). *Societal frameworks and responses to elder abuse and neglect.* Vol. 1 of *Mistreating elderly people: Questioning the response to elder abuse and neglect.* Halifax: Dalhousie University, Health Law Institute.

Harbison, J., Coughlan, S., Karabanow, J., & VanderPlaat, M. (2004). Offering the help that's needed: Responses to the mistreatment and neglect of older people in a rural Canadian context. *Rural Social Work, 9,* 147–157.

Harbison, J., Coughlan, S., Karabanow, J., & VanderPlaat, M. (2005). A clash of cultures: Rural values and service delivery to mistreated and neglected older people in eastern Canada. *Practice: A Journal of the British Association of Social Workers, 14*(4), 229–246.

Harbison, J., Coughlan, S., Karabanow, J., VanderPlaat, M., Nassar, C., Koskela, R., & Wexler, E. (2007). Adult protection legislation: Offering solutions or removing rights. Invited paper for the Canadian Bar Association Elder Law Conference, Fredericton , NB, June 15–16. Published online by Canadian Bar Association.

Harbison, J., Coughlan, S., Karabanow, J., VanderPlaat,

M., Wildeman, S., & Wexler, E. (Forthcoming). Understanding 'elder abuse and neglect': A critique of assumptions underpinning responses to the mistreatment and neglect of older people. *Journal of Elder Abuse and Neglect.*

Harbison, J., McKinley, P., & Pettipas, D. (2006). Older people as objects not subjects: Theory and practice in situations of 'elder abuse'. In R. Alaggia & C. Vine (Eds), *Cruel but not unusual: Violence in Canadian families, a sourcebook of history, theory and practice.* Waterloo, ON: Wilfrid Laurier Press.

Harbison, J., & Morrow, M. (1998). Questions and contradictions: A re-examination of the social construction of elder abuse and neglect. *Ageing and Society, 18,* 691–711.

Higgs, P. (1995). Citizenship and old age: The end of the road?*Ageing and Society, 15,* 535–550.

Hightower, J., Smith, M. I., & Hightower, H. C. (2006). Hearing the voices of abused older women. In M. J. Mellor & P. Brownell (Eds), *Elder abuse and mistreatment: Policy, practice and research* (pp. 205–228). New York: Hawthorne Press.

Hodell, E. C., Golding, J. M., Yozwiak, J. A., Bradshaw, G. S., Kinstle, T. L, & Marsil, D. F. (2009). The perception of elder sexual abuse in the Courtroom. *Violence against Women, 15*(6), 678–698.

Holstein, M. B., & Minkler, M. (2007). Critical gerontology: Reflections for the 21st century. In M. Bernard & T. Scharf (Eds), *Critical perspectives on aging societies* (pp. 13–26). Bristol, UK: Policy Press.

Ibbott, P., Kerr, D., & Beujot, R. (2006). Probing the future of mandatory retirement in Canada. *Canadian Journal on Aging, 25*(2), 161–178.

Justice Canada. (2009). *Abuse of older adults.* Department of Justice Canada, overview paper.

Katz, S. (2005). *Cultures of aging: Life course, lifestyle, and senior worlds.* Peterborough, ON: Broadview Press.

Katz, S. (2006). *Disciplining old age: The formation of gerontological knowledge.* Charlottesville: University Press of Virginia.

Kelley, M. L., & MacLean, M. J. (1997). 'I want to live here for the rest of my life': The challenge of rural case management. *Journal of Case Management, 6*(4), 174–182.

Kosberg, J., Lowenstein, A., Garcia, J., & Biggs, S. (2003). Study of elder abuse in diverse cultures. *Journal of Elder Abuse and Neglect, 15*(3/4), 71–89.

Laws, G. (1995). Understanding ageism: Lessons from feminism and postmodernism. *Gerontologist, 35*(1), 112–118.

Leonard, P. (1997). *Postmodern welfare: Reconstructing an emancipatory project.* London: Sage.

Leroux, T. G., & Petrunik, M. (1990). The construction of elder abuse and neglect as a social problem: A Canadian perspective. *International Journal of Health Services, 20*(4), 651–663.

Loeb, S. J., & Steffensmeier, D. (2006). Older male prisoners: Health status, self-efficacy beliefs, and health promoting behaviours. *Journal of Correctional Health Care, 12*(4), 269–278.

Loeb, S. J., Steffensmeier, D., & Lawrence, F. (2008). Comparing incarcerated and community-dwelling older men's health. *Western Journal of Nursing Research, 30*(2), 234–249.

Lowenstein, A. (2009). Elder abuse and neglect—'Old phenomenon': New directions for research legislation, and service developments. *Journal of Elder Abuse and Neglect, 21,* 278–287.

Luu, A. D., & Liang, B. A. (2005–06). Clinical case management: A strategy to coordinate detection, reporting, and prosecution of elder abuse. *Cornell Journal of Law and Public Policy, 15,* 165–196.

McDonald, L., Beaulieu, M., Harbison, J., Hirst, A., Podnieks, E., & Wahl, J. (Forthcoming). Institutional abuse of older adults: What we know, what we need to know. *Journal of Elder Abuse and Neglect.*

McDonald, L., Collins, A., & Dergal, J. (2006). The abuse and neglect of older adults. In R. Alaggia & C. Vine (Eds), *Cruel but not unusual: Violence in Canadian families, a sourcebook of history, theory and practice.* Waterloo, ON: Wilfrid Laurier University Press.

McDonald, L. P., Hornick, J. P., Robertson, G. B., & Wallace, J. E. (1991). *Elder abuse and neglect in Canada.* Toronto: Butterworths.

McGrail, K., Green, B., Barer, M. L., Evans, R. G., Hertzman, C., & Normand, C. (2000). Age, costs of acute and long-term care and proximity to death: Evidence for 1997–88 and 1994–95 in British Columbia. *Age and ageing, 29,* 249–253

MacLean, M. J. (Ed.). (1995). *Abuse and neglect of older Canadians: Strategies for change.* Toronto: Thompson Educational Publishing.

McMullin, J. A., & Marshall, V. W. (2001). Ageism, age relations, and the garment industry in Montreal. *Gerontologist, 41*(1), 111–122.

McPherson , B. D., & Wister, A. (2008). *Aging as a social process: Canadian perspectives.* Don Mills, ON: Oxford University Press.

Manthorpe, J., Cornes, M., Moriarty, J., & Rapaport, J. (2007). An inspector calls for adult protection in the context of the NSFOP review. *Journal of Adult Protection, 9*(1), 4–14.

Markson, E. W. (2003). *Social gerontology today: An introduction.* Los Angeles: Roxbury.

Marshall, L. (2006). Aging: A feminist issue. *National Women's Studies Association Journal, 18,* vii–xiii.

Montminy, L. (2005). Older women's experiences of psychological violence in their marital relationships. *Journal of Gerontological Social Work, 2,* 3–22.

Mullaly, R. (1993). *Structural social work: Ideology, Theory and Practice.* Toronto: McClelland and Stewart.

Mullaly, B. (2002). *Challenging oppression: A critical social work approach.* Don Mills, ON: Oxford University Press.

National Seniors Council. (2007, November). *Report of the National Seniors Council on Elder Abuse.* www. seniorscouncil.gc.ca/en/home.shtml

Neysmith, S. (1995). Power in relationships of trust: A feminist analysis of elder abuse. In M. J. MacLean (Ed.), *Abuse and neglect of older Canadians: Strategies for change* (pp. 43–54). Toronto: Thompson Educational Publishers.

Neysmith, S., & Macadam, M. (1999). Controversial concepts. In S. Neysmith (Ed.), *Critical issues for future social work practice with aging persons* (pp. 1–26). New York: Columbia University Press.

Novak, M., & Campbell, L. (2001). *Aging and society: A Canadian perspective* (4th ed.). Scarborough, ON: Nelson, Thomson Learning.

O'Connor, D., Hall, M. I., & Donnelly, M. (2009). Assessing capacity within a context of abuse or neglect. *Journal of Elder Abuse and Neglect, 21,* 156–169.

Ogrodnik, L. (2007). *Seniors as victims of crime.* Ottawa: Statistics Canada, Canadian Centre for Justice Statistics, Ministry of Industry. Catalogue No. 85F0033MIE. www.statcan.ca/

O'Keefe, M., Hills, A., Doyle, M., McCreadie, C., Scholes, S., Constantine, R., Tinker, A., Manthorpe, J., Biggs, S., & Erens, B. (2007). *UK study of abuse and neglect of older people: Prevalence study report.* London: National Centre for Social Research and King's College London.

Older Women's Network/Kappel Ramji Consulting Group. (1998). *Study of shelter needs of abused older women.* Toronto: Author.

ONPEA (Ontario Network for the Prevention of Elder Abuse). Conference brochure and presentations. www.onpea.org/conference09

Payne, B. K. (2005). *Crime and elder abuse: An integrated perspective* (2nd ed.). Springfield, IL: Charles C. Thomas.

Phillipson, C. (1993). Abuse of older people: Sociological perspectives. In P. Decalmer & F. Glendenning (Eds), *The mistreatment of elderly people* (pp. 76–101). London: Sage.

Phillipson, C., & Biggs, S. (1998). Modernity and identity: Themes and perspectives in the study of older adults. *Journal of Aging and Identity, 3*(1), 11–23.

Pillemer, K. A. (1986). Risk factors in elder abuse: Results from a case-control study. In K. A. Pillemer & R. S. Wolf (Eds), *Elder abuse: Conflict in the Family* (pp. 239–263). Dover, MA: Auburn House.

Pillemer, K., & Finkelhor, D. (1989). Causes of elder abuse: Caregiver stress versus problem relatives. *American Journal of Orthopsychiatry, 59,* 179–87.

Podnieks, E. (1992a). National survey on abuse of the elderly in Canada. *Journal of Elder Abuse and Neglect, 4*(1/2), 5–58.

Podnieks, E. (1992b). Emerging themes from a follow-up study of Canadian victims of elder abuse. *Journal of Elder Abuse and Neglect, 4*(1/2), 59–111.

Podnieks, E. (2008). Elder abuse: The Canadian experience. *Journal of Elder Abuse and Neglect, 20*(2), 126–150.

Poirier, D. (1988). Models of intervention for the guardianship and protection of elderly persons in Canada. In M. E. Hughes & E. D. Pask (Eds), *National themes in family law.* Toronto: Carswell.

Poirier, D. (1992). The power of social workers in the creation and application of elder protection statutory norms in New Brunswick and Nova Scotia. *Journal of Elder Abuse and Neglect, 4*(1/2), 113–133.

Poirier, D., & Poirier, N. (1999). *Why is it so difficult to combat elder abuse and, in particular, financial exploitation of the elderly?* n.p.: Law Commission of Canada.

Prager J. (2002). Aging and productivity: What do we know? In D. Cheal (Ed.), *Aging and demographic change in Canadian context* (pp. 133–189). Toronto: University of Toronto Press.

Robertson, G. (1995). Legal approaches to elder abuse and neglect in Canada. In M. J. MacLean (Ed.), *Abuse and neglect of older Canadians: Strategies for change* (pp. 55–62). Toronto: Thompson Educational Publishers.

Rowe, J. W., & Kahn, R. L. (1998). *Successful aging.* New York: Pantheon Books.

Rozanova, J., Northcott, H. C., & MacDaniel, S. A. (2006). Seniors and portrayals of intra-generational and inter-generational inequality in the *Globe and Mail. Canadian Journal on Aging, 25*(4), 376–386.

Schellenberg, G., & Turcotte, M. (2007, February). *A portrait of seniors in Canada.* Ottawa: Ministry of Industry. Catalogue no. 89-519-XIE. www.statca. gc.ca/pub89-519-x/89-519-x2006001-eng.htm

Scourfield, J., & Welsh, I. (2003). Risk, reflexivity and social control in child protection: New times or the same old story'. *Critical Social Policy, 23*(3), 398–420.

Snider, L. (1998). Struggles for social justice: Criminalization and alternatives. In K. Bonnycastle & G. S. Rigakos (Eds), *Unsettling truths* (pp. 144–154). Vancouver: Collective Press.

Soden, A. (2005). *Advising the older client.* Markham, ON: LexisNexis, Butterworths.

Special Senate Committee on Aging. (2008). *Final Report: Canada's Aging Population: Seizing the Opportunity.*

Spencer, C. (2000). Abuse and neglect of older adults in rural communities. GRC *News, 19*(1), 7–11.

Spencer, C. (2008). *A way forward: Promising approaches to abuse prevention in institutional settings.* Toronto: Institute for Life Course and Aging, University of Toronto.

Statistics Canada. (2001, June). *Seniors in Canada.* Ottawa: Canada Centre for Justice Statistics Profile Series. Catalogue no. 85F0033MIE.

Stiegel, L. (2000, Summer). The changing role of the courts in elder abuse cases. *Generations.* American Bar Association.

Stiegel, L. (2006). Recommendations for the elder abuse, health and justice fields about medical forensics issues related to elder abuse and neglect. *Journal of Elder Abuse and Neglect, 18*(1), 41–81.

Stojkovic, S. (2007). Elderly prisoners: A growing and forgotten group within correctional systems vulnerable to elder abuse. *Journal of Elder Abuse and Neglect, 19*(3/4), 97–117.

Stones, M. (1995). Scope and definition of elder abuse and neglect in Canada. In M. J. MacLean (Ed.), *Abuse and neglect of older Canadians: Strategies for change* (pp. 111–115). Toronto: Thompson Educational Publishers.

Stones, M. J., & Bedard, M. (2002). Higher thresholds for elder abuse with age and rural residence. *Canadian Journal on Aging, 21*(4), 577–586.

Straka, S. M., & Montminy, L. (2006). Responding to the needs of older women experiencing domestic violence. *Violence against Women, 12*(3), 251–267.

Tam, S., & Neysmith, S. (2006). Disrespect and isolation: Elder abuse in Chinese communities. *Canadian Journal on Aging, 25*(2), 141–151.

Tatara, T. (Ed.). (1999). *Understanding elder abuse in minority populations.* London: Brunner/Mazel.

Tindale, J. A., Norris, J. E., & Abbott, K. (2002). Catching up with diversity in intergenerational relationships. In D. Cheal (Ed.), *Aging and demographic change in Canadian context* (pp. 224–244). Toronto: University of Toronto Press.

Tomita, S. K. (1990). The denial of elder mistreatment by victims and abusers: The application of neutralization theory. *Violence and Victims, 5*(3), 171–184.

Townsend, P. (1981). The structured dependency of the elderly: The creation of social policy in the twentieth century. *Ageing and Society, 7*(1), 5–28.

Townsend, P. (2007). Using human rights to defeat ageism: Dealing with policy-induced structured dependency. In M. Bernard & T. Scharf (Eds), *Critical perspectives on aging societies* (pp. 27–44). Bristol, UK: Policy Press.

Truscott, D. (1996). Cross-cultural perspectives: Toward an integrated theory of elder abuse. *Policy Studies, 17*(4), 287–298.

Vincent, J. A. (1999). *Politics, power and old age.* Buckingham, UK: Open University Press.

Vinton, L. (1991). Factors associated with refusing services among maltreated elderly. *Journal of Elder Abuse and Neglect, 3*(2), 89–103.

Viriot Durandel, J.-P. (2004). The new forms of 'grey power' in the public arena. *Les cahiers de la FIAPA: Action Research on Aging: Grey Power? Volume 2: Economic and Social Influences, 3*, i–iii.

Wahidin, A., & Cain, M. (Eds). (2006). *Ageing, crime & society.* Devon, UK: Willan.

Wahl, J. (2009). Capacity and capacity assessment in Ontario. Toronto: Advocacy Centre for the Elderly. Retrieved May 24, 2009, from www.acelaw.ca

Wahl, J., & Purdy, S. (n.d.). *Elder abuse: The hidden crime.* Ontario: Advocacy Centre for the Elderly and Community Legal Education Ontario.

Ward-Hall, C. (2001, July). *Educating seniors and others about abuse: A decade of experience from a provincial organization.* Paper presented at the meeting of the 17th Congress of the International Association of Gerontology, Vancouver.

Watts, L. (2009). *From elder abuse to elder justice: The Canadian landscape.* Plenary Presentation at the Ontario Network for the Prevention of Elder Abuse Conference, Toronto, November 2–5.

Webb, S. A. (2006). *Social work in a risk society: Social and political perspectives.* Basingstoke, UK: Palgrave Macmillan.

Whittaker, T. (1997). Rethinking elder abuse: Towards an age and gender integrated theory of elder abuse. In P. Declamer & F. Glendenning (Eds), *The mistreatment of elderly people* (2nd ed.). London: Sage.

Williamson, J. B. (1998). Political activism and the aging of the baby boom. *Generations 22*(1), 55–59.

Winterdyk, J. A., & King, D. E. (1999). *Diversity and justice in Canada.* Toronto: Canadian Scholars' Press.

Wolhuter, L., Olley, N., & Denham, D. (2009). *Victimology: Victimization and victims' rights.* London: Routledge-Cavendish.

Yaffe, M., Wolfson, C., Lithwick, M., & Weiss, D. (2008). Development and validation of a tool to improve physician identification of elder abuse: The Elder Abuse Suspicion Index (EASI). *Journal of Elder Abuse and Neglect, 20*(3), 276–300.

Yin, P. (1985). *Victimization and the aged.* Springfield, IL: Charles C. Thomas.

Zaman, B., & Shakir, U. (2000). Elder abuse in the South Asian community. *Proceedings of the Ontario Elder Abuse Conference,* April 13 and 14. Toronto: Institute for Human Development, Life Course and Aging, University of Toronto.

15 | Putting Youthful Offending and Victimization into Context

Carla Cesaroni

Age often acts as an important societal division, a marker for a particular type of social stratification. It differentiates young people from adults in ways that often have important social consequences for youth. For example, children and youth have fewer rights and fewer institutional protections than their adult counterparts (Giroux, 2003). They have often become a focal point for the Canadian public's anxiety regarding law and order (Tanner, 2010). Youth have sometimes been isolated, treated with suspicion, and subjected to diminished rights of privacy and civil liberties (Giroux, 2003). As Tanner (2001, p. 2) suggests, young people are seen as both 'troubling and troubled'. The public is often given a fractional view of youth crime that tends to be biased against all youth, but particularly against the marginalized and disadvantaged (Schissel, 1997).

Youth crime and antisocial behaviour are together a complex social phenomenon. How we choose to respond to youth in conflict with the law, especially the most vulnerable, has ramifications for all youth, all communities, and society as a whole.

A Brief History of Youth Justice Legislation in Canada

The public's ambiguity regarding youth is particularly evident in the area of youth justice. There has been a long public debate over the best strategy to deal with young persons in conflict with the law. On the one hand, youth have been viewed as vulnerable and in need of protection; on the other, they have been viewed as individuals who are entitled to full adult legal protection, rights, and responsibilities. The history of youth justice legislation in Canada reflects these two conflicting views. For instance, the way in which we respond to youth crime has changed substantially over the past century. There has been a shift from legislation based on welfare principles toward legislation that focuses on criminal law principles and proportionality. There has also been a concomitant shift away from the assumption that youth crime problems can be solved through the formal youth justice system (Doob & Sprott, 2004). Successive changes in legislation have provided more structure in governing key decisions in the youth justice system.

Prior to the nineteenth century, most of the Western world, including Canada, provided no allowances for the special needs of children and adolescents in conflict with the law. Any youth over the age of seven could be charged and dealt with under the same criminal law as adults. By the turn of the twentieth century, however, the needs of children and youth were receiving increasing social and legal recognition (Bala, 2003). The **Juvenile Delinquents Act** (JDA) (1908) was based on a **child welfare** orientation. Under the JDA, notions regarding young people's vulnerabilities, together with the need to avoid stigmatization, were the impetus for the establishment of youth custody facilities (Leon, 1977). Separate custodial facilities were part of a larger move toward separate courts and a separate justice system (Trépanier, 1999).

The scope of the JDA was very broad (Doob & Sprott, 2004). It was focused on such values as protection, guidance, education, supervision, and treatment of misguided children. These values overshadowed the importance of **due process** and young people's fundamental rights. A youth who committed any criminal offence or breached any provincial law or municipal bylaw could be sent to a provincial training school or reformatory (Doob & Sprott, 2004). During this era of youth justice history, it was the intention that the 'best interests' of the child were to be balanced by justice concerns, but this was often not the case. There was no distinction between neglected and delinquent youth. The focus of the courts was not on whether a crime had been committed, but on whether a young person was in a 'condition' of delinquency and/or in need of assistance. The JDA allowed for indeterminate sentences in order for training-school officials to hold youth until they were deemed cured of their condition of delinquency or were seen as rehabilitated (Bala, 2003).

The **Young Offenders Act** (YOA, 1984) moved youth justice legislation away from welfare principles toward criminal law principles. The act narrowed the scope of federal law pertaining to youthful offenders to only include federal offences. The Act's other important provisions included the standardization of the age of criminalization, definite lengths for all dispositions, the stipulation of maximum sentence lengths, and certain legal protections (e.g., the right to a lawyer, provisions governing statements) (Doob & Cesaroni, 2004). Although the new Act was oriented more toward a justice model, including clear legislation on due process and the elimination of **status offences**, it attempted to strike a balance between the commission of the offence and the needs and interests of society. The YOA attempted to narrow its mandate to include only criminal offences and signalled that child welfare issues were best handled within the child welfare system.

The lack of clear legislative direction in the general principles of the YOA contributed to a number of problems that would later be identified by provincial governments and advocacy groups (Barnhorst, 2004). For example, ambiguity in the language of the YOA regarding when to impose custody, such as 'whenever appropriate' and 'reasonable in the circumstance', allowed for enormous latitude in interpretation from judges (Doob & Sprott, 1999). In addition, there is considerable consensus that, under the YOA, custodial dispositions were overused for minor and non-violent offences and that the rate of placing youth in custody in Canada was higher than in many Western countries (Bala, 2003; Department of Justice Canada, 1998; Sprott & Snyder, 1999). There was also a great deal of provincial variation in the use of the courts and custody, as well as evidence to suggest that Aboriginal youth were over-represented in custody (Doob & Sprott, 2004).

As a response to the perceived inadequacies of the YOA, the **Youth Criminal Justice Act** (YCJA) (2003) was created with the intent of decreasing the use of courts and restricting the use of custody (Bala, Carrington, & Roberts, 2009; Barnhorst, 2004). The Act includes much more guidance for judges in regard to sentencing. The YCJA provides a detailed set of sentencing principles to apply, including proportionality and restraint, with the greatest emphasis on proportionality (Bala et al., 2009). Additionally, the YCJA creates significant hurdles for the use of custody. The government chose to emphasize the legislation's criminal law nature by putting 'Criminal' in the Act's name (Sprott & Doob, 2009).

While custody was over-utilized under the YOA, **alternative measures/diversion** programs were under-utilized. The YCJA, in contrast, encourages the diversion of cases from youth court through extrajudicial measures and extrajudicial sanctions. **Extrajudicial sanctions** are community-based measures that may include restitution and family group conferencing. Extrajudicial measures may include warnings and cautions by the police or referrals to a community agency. The Act affirms the importance of extrajudicial measures and notes that '[e]xtrajudicial measures are presumed to be adequate to hold a young person accountable for his or her offending behavior if the young person has committed a non-violent offence and not been previously been found guilty of an offence' (s. 4 (c)). For extrajudicial measures it recognizes that 'extrajudicial measures are often the most appropriate and effective way to address youth crime (s. 4 (a)).'

Since the enactment of the YCJA there has been a significant decline in the use of courts and custody for Canadian youth and an increase in various methods of police diversion (Bala et al., 2009; Doob & Sprott, 2005; Milligan, 2008). It appears that police, prosecutors, and judges have responded to the Act as intended, reducing the over-reliance on custody for youthful offenders (Bala et al., 2009). The level in the **remand** population, however, does not appear to have been affected by the YCJA, and the proportion accounted for by remand of all youth in custodial facilities across Canada appears to have increased (Bala et al., 2009; Calverley, 2007; Milligan, 2008). There has therefore been a shift in the incarcerated population from one comprised of (largely) sentenced youth to one comprised of a larger proportion of youth being held on remand or pretrial detention. This change in the proportion of a custody to a detention population may have implications for the management of the youth correctional population and is worrisome given the conditions that often exist in detention facilities.

Youth as Offenders

The discussion of youthful offending should be approached with some caution. Most of what we read about and have access to regarding 'youth crime' does not reflect all actual youth crime per se, but instead gives us a picture of the end of a filtering process rather than the beginning. The cases that go to court, or perhaps more importantly, the findings of guilt, should not be thought of as representative of all youth crime—just a subset. Though official statistics are one important measure of youth crime, they are subject to discretionary practices. Additionally, a certain number of crimes either are never reported or are handled informally by the police. One of the problems of estimating youth crime is that youths, unlike older people, are more likely to offend in groups. Perhaps this is the reason they are more likely to be apprehended or caught (see Sprott & Snyder, 1999). Therefore, relative to their offending, youth may actually be over-represented in official crime statistics (Doob & Cesaroni, 2004).

Official statistics suggest that adults commit the majority of crime. Adults represented, for instance, 85 per cent of all persons accused of homicide in 2006 (Li, 2007). While a total of 84 youths were implicated in 54 homicides in 2006, it is important to remember that this represents 84 youths of over 2 million youths living in Canada at the time. Data from Statistics Canada (2010) seem to suggest that for 2008 adults represented the majority of those charged with crimes against the person (85 per cent) and of those charged with property crimes (82 per cent). Indeed, there is sufficient evidence to suggest that within any offence category youth crime is less serious than adult crime of the same category (Feld, as quoted in Roberts, 2004).

The best alternative to official statistics is **self-report studies**. Self-report studies are useful in that they provide a comparison of adolescents who have been officially charged to those who have not. In other words, they tell us something about the representativeness of those who have been officially charged both in the types of crime and in the types of young people charged. In these types of studies, young people are asked (anonymously) whether they have committed any series of acts that could be considered crimes. The more specific and numerous the questions the more offending will be reported.

The Toronto Youth Crime and Victimization Survey is a self-report survey of 3,000 high school students and 500 street youth (Tanner & Wortley, 2002). It probes youth on their friendships, family life, leisure activities, fear of crime, victimization experiences, and deviant behaviour. The majority of high school respondents had not been involved in deviant or illegal behaviour. Furthermore, among the sample of high school students, deviance was minor. While a quarter of respondents reported engaging in minor theft (under $50) in the past year, only 4 per cent reported that they had tried to break into a home or business. For all offence categories, street youth reported higher levels of deviant or illegal activity. Thirty-four per cent of street youth had tried to break into a home of business. Additionally, 54 per cent of street youth reported selling illegal drugs in the past year, compared to only 11 per cent of high school students.

Street youth reported much higher levels of violence than high school students. For example, 72 per cent of street youth reported they were in a physical fight in the past year, compared to only 30 per cent of high school students. Street youth were more likely (44 per cent) than high school students (10 per cent) to report that they had attacked someone with the intent to cause serious harm. Finally, gender differences in violent behaviour were small or non-existent among street youth. Female street youth were just as likely as their male peers to fight or carry weapons and reported higher levels of violence than male high school students.

Though not all youth involved in illegal activity are apprehended, charged, and found guilty, a small but significant number of youthful offenders will find themselves in the 'deep end' of the system, having been sentenced to custody. As a group, incarcerated young offenders are characterized by multiple forms of familial, socio-emotional, and academic disadvantage (Bortner & Williams, 1997; Goldson, 2005, 2006). In addition, many of the indicators of family adversity are associated with incarceration status, including physical abuse, family breakup, and violence between parents (Bortner & Williams, 1997). Young offenders are also likely to have come in contact with the child welfare system prior to custody (Johnson-Reid & Barth, 2000).

Research on youth in custody mirrors more recent research on adult inmates, focusing on **risk** as it relates to recidivism and the impact of the **new penology**. As Simon (2000) argues, there has been a switch from an interest in the adjustment of inmates and the state's role in rehabilitation to a focus on **responsibilization**, whereby individuals must take responsibility for their own actions, the consequences of their actions, and ultimately, their own rehabilitation. It has been argued that this perspective has led some authorities responsible for young inmates to see maladjustment to custody as being predicted by the 'weaknesses' of individual youths (Goldson, 2005, 2006) rather than a consequence of systemic problems. However, there is research that calls into question the ethos of punishment and responsibilization (i.e., that children need to be treated as adults when they do something wrong) that currently prevails when youth are having difficulties within state-run institutions.

Youth as Victims

Public anxiety about youth crime tends to concentrate upon young people as offenders; much less attention is paid to young people's experiences as victims. Young people are particularly vulnerable to violent crime (Gannon & Mihovean, 2005). Canada's 2004 General Social Survey (GSS)[1] suggests that the rate of violent victimization is highest amongst 15- to 24-year-olds. In fact, it is 1.5 to 19 times higher than the rate recorded for other age groups (Gannon & Milhovean, 2005). Ironically, the adults who are often quickest to express fears about violent crime tend not to be its principal target (Tanner, 2010), as young people are more likely to victimize other young people (AuCoin, 2005). While adults are more likely to be victimized at home, young people are more likely to be victimized on the streets or in public or commercial places (Gannon & Milhovean, 2005). This is not to suggest that the family home is a safe haven for all youth. Between 1998 and 2003, there were 401 homicides of children and youth, 87 per cent of which were solved (AuCoin, 2005). Two-thirds of (solved) homicides involving children and youth were committed by family members, the majority (60 per cent) by the father. Sexual assaults are largely committed against children and youth, and overall, children and youth account for 61 per cent of sexual assaults reported to police and 21 per cent of all physical assaults (AuCoin, 2005).

There are important differences between youthful victims, however. In a recent survey of 3,000 high school students and 500 street youth (Tanner & Wortley, 2002), young people's self-reported victimization rates appeared to be quite high. For example, 72 per cent of high school students reported that they had been a victim of a minor theft (under $50) and 70 per cent reported that they had been physically assaulted. Rates of serious victimization, however, were much lower (12 per cent for sexual assault, 16 per cent for assault with a weapon). Street youth reported much higher rates than high school students. For example, 69 per cent of street youth reported that they had been physically assaulted in the past 12 months, compared to 39 per cent of high school students. Moreover, 29 per cent of street youth claimed they had been sexually assaulted in the past year, compared to 6 per cent of high school youth.

With the exception of sexual assault, male high school students reported higher victimization rates than female high school students. Gender differences in victimization were smaller among street youth. In fact, female street youth often reported higher rates of victimization than their male counterparts. For instance, 71 per cent of female street youth reported that they had been physically assaulted in the past year, compared to 68 per cent of male street youth. In general, females reported higher levels of sexual assault among both the high school and street youth samples. However, according to Tanner and Wortley (2002), male street youth also appeared to be vulnerable to this type of victimization. Male street youth reported much higher rates of sexual assault than female high school students.

A considerable amount of evidence suggests that there is an overlap between delinquency and victimization and therefore a belief that some victims are not 'worthy' (Tanner, 2010). As Tanner (2010) argues, however, an exclusive focus on the offending behaviour of young people neglects their suffering as victims and deflects attention away from the non-trivial social harm caused by all manner of adult crime.

Special Populations and Emerging Issues

Female Offenders

One of the strongest and most consistent correlates with offending is the gender of the offender. On self-report measures, girls typically report lower levels of offending than boys. Canadian data for 2005/06 suggest that girls are less likely to be involved in youth court than boys, especially regarding serious offences. At the 'found guilty' stage, girls are involved in 34 per cent of minor assaults but only 21 per cent of more serious assaults (Sprott & Doob, 2009). The same is true of property offending, where 25 per cent of girls were found guilty of theft but only 9 per cent of break-and-enter (Sprott & Doob, 2009).

In recent years, there has been speculation regarding the apparent increase in violence concerning girls, yet there has never been any credible evidence that girls' involvement in violence has substantially changed (Sprott & Doob, 2009). Indeed, the reasons for increases in girls' arrest rates for violence are many, ranging from 'zero tolerance' policing to an increase in the use of the criminal justice system to deal with family conflict (i.e., physical fights within the family) (Sprott & Doob, 2009). Sprott and Doob (2009) present compelling data to suggest that the seemingly large increase in the percentage of minor assault cases involving girls (in contrast to boys) has been driven not by changes in girls' behaviour, but by decreases in the arrests of boys. In other words, if boys offending decreases and girls offending remains stable, girls proportion of overall offending appears to have gone up.

Concern has often been raised over the way in which girls have been processed by the criminal justice system in Canada. There is a general consensus that under the JDA female young offenders have been discriminated against by being disproportionately punished for status offences such as immorality, incorrigibility, and promiscuity (Corrado, Odgers, & Cohen, 2000). Under the YOA there was an increase in the use of custody for minor offences or administration of justice offences (e.g., failure to appear). Corrado et al. (2000) maintain that this was an attempt by youth justice professionals to protect female young offenders from high-risk environments and to address the inability of community-based organizations to get young women to participate in rehabilitation programs (e.g., for substance abuse). Sprott and Doob (2009) suggest that failure-to-comply cases constitute a larger proportion of girls' caseloads than boys' at every stage of the proceedings. They argue that this is most dramatic at the custody stage, where, in 1999–2000, 34 per cent of girls were sentenced to custody for failure to comply compared to 17 per cent of boys. Custody could be used for failure to comply (even under the YCJA) because failing to respect the court is seen as requiring a harsh response (Sprott & Doob, 2009). Or as the authors maintain, these might be 'simply status offences in disguise, and the high use of custody reflects the desire to intervene and "help"' (p. 148).

Girls have perhaps been the most marginalized, the least studied, and the least understood of custodial populations (Dohrn, 2004). They comprise an addendum or footnote to the study of adult populations and even of adolescent boys in custody (Dohrn, 2004). The small number of girls within custodial institutions has produced the same problems that have often characterized women's prison populations. Female young offenders are often overlooked in a system designed to hold young men (Chesney-Lind & Pasko, 2004). Perhaps even more than their adult female counterparts, they are 'the forgotten few' (Chesney-Lind & Pasko, 2004). Notably absent from a record of over a century of incarcerating girls have been the voices and experiences of the girls themselves (Dohrn, 2004). A general lack of understanding regarding the experiences of female young offenders in custody perhaps explains the reluctance of staff to work with girls and the perception among practitioners that girls in custody are complex and demanding (Cernkovich, Lanctot, & Giordano, 2008).

Research on female young offenders in custody tends to focus on pathways to custody, the need for gender-sensitive programs, and peer-on-peer violence (see Belknap & Cady, 2008; Belknap & Holsinger, 1997, 1998; Chesney-Lind, 1988; Dohrn, 2004; Macdonald & Chesney-Lind, 2001; Viljoen, 2005). Several studies have shown that girls share many of the same pre-existing vulnerabilities as boys, such as poverty, dysfunctional families, and problems with school, delinquent peers, and substance abuse. However, they have also identified vulnerabilities that are unique to adolescent girls, including histories of sexual abuse, sexual assault, dating violence, unplanned pregnancy, and motherhood (see Acoca, 1998; Corrado et al., 2000; Chesney-Lind & Pasko, 2004; Gavazzi, Yarcheck, & Chesney-Lind, 2006; MacDonald & Chesney-Lind, 2001).

Additionally, girls in custody have been found to have a higher incidence of self-harm, post-traumatic stress disorder, and depression (Dohrn, 2004). The impacts of social control during female adolescence may be quite different from those of boys (Medlicott, 2007). Institutional practices that are routine in boys' facilities—strip searches, for example—may be problematic for girls with a history of victimization (Chesney-Lind & Pasko, 2004). The use of isolation/segregation for girls with a history of suicidal ideation is also worrisome (this has been a problem for adult women in prison).

Mental Health

The Canadian youth justice system has had a history of incarcerating youth as a means of giving them access to **mental health** treatment. The high number of youth with mental health disabilities who at later stages are involved in the criminal justice process reflects a cumulative bias at earlier stages (Vandergoot, 2006). There is a disproportionate number of youth with disabilities on probation or in youth custody facilities owing to the fact that youth with disabilities are more likely to be caught, arrested, and formally processed (Vandergoot, 2006). Often youth justice personnel do not understand or misread their behaviours and capabilities (Vandergoot, 2006).

The prevalence of psychiatric disorders in incarcerated youth is known to be high (Ulzen & Hamilton, 1998). These disorders include, but are not limited to, unipolar and bipolar depression, alcohol dependence, attention deficit hyperactivity disorder, conduct disorder, post-traumatic stress disorder, and separation anxiety disorder (Duclos et al., 1998; Ulzen & Hamilton, 1998). Although prevalence rates for mental disorders are variable across studies, even with the most conservative estimates the rate is approximately four times higher among incarcerated young offenders than in community samples (Kazdin, 2000). Research has also demonstrated that up to 75 per cent of incarcerated young offenders have learning problems (Henteleff, 1999). Concern has been raised over the high prevalence of fetal alcohol spectrum disorders (FASD) among the young offender population, which often go undiagnosed (Vandergoot, 2006). Vandergroot (2006, p. 68) notes that for youth with FASD-related disabilities 'the criminal justice system is the final common pathway resulting from complex interactions among developmental, environmental, medical and psychiatric conditions.'

Youth Gangs

There is considerable disagreement in the research literature about what constitutes a **youth gang**. The issue is that if a restrictive definition is utilized, there is a chance that the true number of gangs in a community is underestimated (Wortley & Tanner, 2007). Conversely, a broad definition runs the risk of overestimating the true number of gangs in a community (Wortley & Tanner, 2007). Young people often claim to be members of a gang, but when they are probed further, their gang activity is really about social group activity rather than criminal gang activity (Tanner & Wortley, 2002). According to Schissel (1997, p. 58), the word 'gang' often remains undefined by the media 'but is used loosely to refer to kids who "hang around" in twos or threes and have an identifiable ethnicity or class.' Schissel (1997) argues that the media discourse on gangs not only suggests the potential danger of kids who hang around in groups, but also tends to link gangs and gang violence to racialized and immigrant groups.

A study of 102 gang members in Toronto[2] (Wortley & Tanner, 2007) reveals some of the important characteristics of criminal gang members and the reasons for joining gangs. Almost all of those interviewed came from disadvantaged backgrounds; they included those from single-parent homes (61 per cent), those who grew up within the child-protection system (11 per cent), and those who were raised in housing projects (60 per cent). Many of the interviewees grew up under circumstances of poverty and in homes marked by violence and verbal abuse. Though the majority of gang members (70 per cent) were born in Canada, many came from diverse ethnic backgrounds; for example, 41 per cent of respondents self-identified as black, 37 per cent as white, 9 per cent as Hispanic, 7 per cent as Native, 3 per cent as Asian, and 3 per cent as South Asian.

Wortley and Tanner (2007, p. 109) note that 'what eventually became a gang often began as a loose informal friendship grouping of kids who grew up in the same, invariably, tough neighbourhood and went to the same schools.' The reasons given for joining a gang included protection, social support, companionship, status, respect, and financial gain. However, Wortley and Tanner (2007) indicate that through the course of their interviews it became apparent that many respondents felt alienated or isolated from mainstream society:

> These youth often expressed the belief that social injustice was widespread in Canada and that they were the victim of social inequality, racism and oppression. Some offered a rudimentary view of the inequalities of Canadian society, seeing gangs as an outcome of those structural inequalities, a cultural response to alienation and estrangement. Contained in this world view is the depiction of gangs as expressions of protest and defiance: a statement about how not all Canadians had equal access to the benefits of Canadian society, good schooling, decent housing or reasonable jobs. (pp. 123–124)

Minority Over-representation

Decades of research have documented the severe economic, social, and cultural disadvantages that have characterized the lives of Aboriginal peoples in Canada since colonization by European peoples. Several studies on adult offenders suggest that Aboriginals are over-represented at each stage of the criminal justice system (see La Prairie, 2002). The YCJA states that 'with particular attention to the circumstances of Aboriginal young persons, all available sanctions other than custody should be considered.' Despite the YCJA directive, there is an **over-representation** of Aboriginals who have been sentenced to custody in all provinces and territories in Canada (Milligan, 2008). In British Columbia in 2005/2006, for example, Aboriginal youth were five times more likely to be sentenced to custody than non-Aboriginal youth (Milligan, 2008). In 2005/2006, Aboriginal youth comprised 31 per cent of all admissions to sentenced custody in Canada, 23 per cent of all admissions to remand, and 22 per cent of all admissions to probation, even though they represent only 6 per cent of the population of youth in Canada (Milligan, 2008). Poverty, substance abuse, high rates of victimization, family dysfunction, and discrimination within the criminal justice system may be factors that in combination contribute to Aboriginal youth's higher rate of incarceration (Latimer & Foss, 2004).

There is evidence to suggest that black adults in the criminal justice system are over-represented in admissions to prison (Ontario, Commission on Systemic Racism in the Ontario Criminal Justice System, 1995). This issue has not been sufficiently researched, however. The author's own work on youth in custody and detention in Ontario would suggest that among adolescent male youth, black males (and Aboriginal males) are over-represented (Cesaroni & Peterson-Badali, 2005; Cesaroni, 2009; Cesaroni & Peterson-Badali, 2010). A recently concluded study of youth in detention, for example, found that 48 per cent of the 137 youths interviewed self-identified as black, though they represent only 7 per cent of the population in the province (Cesaroni, 2009). This is a critical area of research that needs to be addressed.

Lesbian, Gay, Bisexual, and Transgender Youth

There is a paucity of research on LGBT youth and their experiences with the Canadian criminal justice system. However, research in the United States suggests that LGBT youth are over-represented in both the child welfare and youth justice systems (Estrada & Marksamer, 2006). LGBT youth's offending behaviour is often tied to survival strategies connected to homelessness, such as shoplifting and prostitution (Estrada & Marksamer, 2006). They often remain invisible in the criminal justice system because they have been socialized to hide their identities and therefore fail to receive support and appropriate services (Estrada & Marksamer, 2006).

LGBT youth in custody and detention facilities are disproportionately the victims of harassment and violence, including rape (Ray, 2006). There is evidence that lesbian and gay girls are often forced to live with other incarcerated females who are violently homophobic (Ray, 2006). Because of a lack of empathy and understanding, the staff in youth correctional facilities often presume that gay and lesbian girls are sexual predators and desire sexual relations with other girls (Estrada & Marksamer, 2006). Accordingly, they do not protect gay youths and lesbian girls from unwanted advances. Gay male youths are often victimized both by staff and other inmates. This includes emotional, sexual, and physical victimization (Ray, 2006).

Youth as Service Providers

As noted previously, the Youth Criminal Justice Act has reduced the use of custody for youth in Canada through the use of extrajudicial measures and extrajudicial sanctions. It has also provided for a more formal set of protocols to help youth reintegrate back into home communities. The federal government has funded a number of innovative programs that support these two important aspects of the YCJA. Two of these initiatives are significant for their involvement of peers as mentors and service providers. It is important to recognize the special kind of emotional support, consensual validation, identification, and modelling that adolescent peers can provide (Seiffge-Krenke, 1995). The following two illustrations demonstrate the altruism and empathy that youth are capable of and counter the often negative images of youth embraced by the public and media alike.

The **Youth Restorative Action Program** (YRAP) is the first of its kind in Canada. It is a youth justice committee made of entirely of youth members (15 to 24). The youth members range from honours students, to former young offenders, to recovering drug addicts. The idea for YRAP came from a young girl who arrived in Edmonton after fleeing from her home of Serbia. She approached Mark Cherrington, a youth-care worker with Edmonton Youth Court Defence Office, hoping to develop a group that would deal with youth and racism (Purdy, 2004). Her idea inspired YRAP, and at first the group only handled young offender cases for race-related crimes. The group's first coordinator, a 16-year-old girl who lived on the streets, later expanded the mandate to include other social issues: homelessness, addiction, sexual abuse, mental health, and prostitution (Purdy, 2004). In the context of a group conference (with the offender, victim, and family members of both parties present), YRAP members decide on a resolution. A judge must formally agree to the sentence/resolution in court, and YRAP members then provide the mentorship and support needed to complete the terms of the resolution.

That **National Network for Youth in Care** is an organization driven by youth and alumni from the child welfare system. It is among the longest-running child welfare organizations in Canada and the oldest national youth-directed organization. Recently, the organization was awarded a grant to pilot the Youth for Youth Reintegration Project. This program will be tested in four pilot communities and is intended to provide peer support for youth who are attempting to reintegrate back into their home community following incarceration. Mentorship will include assisting youth in building healthy relationships, encouraging them to attend pro-social events, and helping them cope with important institutions that affect their lives (such as school).

Summary

The public is often given a fractional view of youth crime, one that tends to be biased against all youth, but particularly against marginalized and disadvantaged young people. It is important to place youth crime in context by exploring the diversity of young people who may find themselves in conflict with the law. Youthful offenders are often drawn from vulnerable populations. Youth crime and anti-social behaviour are complex phenomena.

Key Terms

alternative measures	Juvenile Delinquents Act	new penology	Young Offenders Act
child welfare		remand	Youth Criminal Justice Act
diversion	mental health	responsibilization	
due process	over-representation	risk	youth gang
extra-judicial measures	National Network for Youth in Care	self-report studies	Youth Restorative Action Program
		status offence	

Questions for Critical Thought

1. If the public knew that youth are more likely to be victims than adults, do you think they would be more sympathetic to the general youth population?

2. Do you think the fact that youth cannot vote impacts on their ability to have their voices and concerns heard?

3. Do you think it is more important to spend money on youth after they have offended (i.e., there should be more programs in youth custody facilities) or to spend money on prevention for high-risk youth (i.e., there should be a greater investment in social programs, education, and jobs)?

Additional Readings

Gleason, M., Myers, T., & Paris, L. (2010). *Lost kids: Vulnerable children and youth in twentieth century Canada and the United States.* Vancouver: University of British Columbia Press.

Minaker, J. C., & Hogeveen, B. (2008). *Youth, Crime & Society: Issues of Power and Injustice.* Toronto: Pearson.

Endnotes

1. A survey of 24,000 Canadians aged 15 and older from 10 provinces. Violent victimization includes sexual assault, robbery, and physical assault.

2. The Toronto Street Gang Project was conducted in consultation with the Toronto Police Service and various community organizations. Though Wortley and Tanner allowed their respondents to self-identify as gang members, their findings suggest that the people they interviewed tended to meet even the most stringent of gang criteria (i.e., based on size of crew, criminal activity, fighting over territory, use of colours, weapons, etc.).

References

Acoca, L. (1998). Outside/Inside: The violation of girls at home, on the street and in the juvenile justice system. *Journal of Research in Crime & Delinquency, 44*(4), 561–589.

AuCoin, K. (2005). *Children and youth as victims of violent crime.* Ottawa: Juristat Centre for Justice Statistics.

Bala, N. (2003). *Youth criminal justice law.* Toronto: Irwin Law.

Bala, N., Carrington, P., & Roberts, J. (2009). Evaluating the Youth Criminal Justice Act after five years. *Canadian Journal of Criminology and Criminal Justice, 51*(2), 131–168.

Barnhorst, D. (2004). The Youth Criminal Justice Act: New directions and implementation issues. *Canadian Journal of Criminology and Criminal Justice, 46*(3), 231–250.

Belknap, J., & Cady, B. (2008). Pre-adjudicated and adjudicated girls' reports on their lives before and during detention and incarceration. In R. T. Zaplin (Ed.), *Female offenders: Critical perspectives and effective interventions* (pp. 251–282). Sudbury, ME: Jones and Bartlett.

Belknap, J., & Holsinger, K. (1997). Understanding incarcerated girls: The results of a focus group study. *Prison Journal, 77*(4), 381–404.

Belknap, J., & Holsinger, K. (1998). An overview of delinquent girls: How theory and practice have failed and the need for innovative change. In R. T. Zaplin (Ed.), *Female offenders: Critical perspectives and effective interventions* (pp. 31–64). Gaithersburg, MD: Aspen.

Bortner, M. A., & Williams, L. M. (1997). *Youth in prison: We the people of Unit Four.* New York: Routledge.

Calverley, D. (2007). *Youth custody and community services in Canada, 2004/2005.*Ottawa: Juristat Centre for Justice Statistics.

Cernkovich, S. A., Lanctot, N., & Giordano, P. C. (2008). Predicting adolescent and adult antisocial behavior among adjudicated delinquent females. *Journal of Research in Crime & Delinquency, 54*(1), 3–33.

Cesaroni, C. (2009, October). *The experiences of adolescent males in secure detention.* Discussion paper prepared for the Ministry of Children and Youth Services (Ontario) Research and Outcome Measurement Branch.

Cesaroni, C., & Peterson-Badali, M. (2005). Young offenders in custody: Risk and adjustment. *Criminal Justice and Behavior, 32*(3), 251–277.

Cesaroni, C., & Peterson-Badali, M. (2009). Understanding the experiences of incarcerated male youth: The importance of a developmental framework. In A. Renshaw & E. Suarez (Eds), *Prisons: Populations, health conditions and recidivism* (pp. 1–27). New York: Nova Science.

Cesaroni, C., & Peterson-Badali, M. (2010). Understanding the adjustment of incarcerated young offenders: A Canadian example. *Youth Justice: An International Journal, 10*(2), 1–19.

Chesney-Lind, M. (1988). Girls in jail. *Journal of Research in Crime & Delinquency, 34*(2), 150.

Chesney-Lind, M., & Pasko, L. (2004). *The female offender: Girls, women, and crime.* Thousand Oaks, CA: Sage.

Corrado, R., Odgers, C., & Cohen, I. (2000). The incarceration of female young offenders: Protection from whom? *Canadian Journal of Criminology, 42*(2), 189–207.

Department of Justice Canada. (1998). *A strategy for the renewal of youth justice.* Ottawa: Department of Justice Canada.

Dohrn, B. (2004). All ellas: Girls locked up. *Feminist Studies, 30*(2), 302–324.

Doob, A. N., & Cesaroni, C. (2004). *Responding to youth crime in Canada.* Toronto: University of Toronto Press.

Doob, A. N., & Sprott, J. B. (1999). Changes in youth court sentencing in Canada. *Federal Sentencing Reporter, 11*(5), 262–268.

Doob, A. N., & Sprott, J. B. (2004). Changing models of youth justice in Canada. In M. Tonry & A. N. Doob (Eds), *Youth justice: Comparative and cross-national perspectives* (pp. 185–242). Vol. 31 of *Crime and Justice.* Chicago, University of Chicago Press.

Doob, A. N., & Sprott, J. B. (2005). *The use of custody under the Youth Criminal Justice Act.* Ottawa: Department of Justice.

Duclos, C. W., Beals, J., Novins, D. K., Martin, C., Jewett, C., & Manson, S. M. (1998). Prevalence of common psychiatric disorders among American Indian adolescent detainees. *Journal of the American Academy of Child and Adolescent Psychiatry, 37*(8), 866–873.

Estrada, R., & Marksamer, J. (2006). The legal rights of LGBT youth in custody. *Child Welfare, 65*(2), 171–194.

Gannon, M., & Mihavean, K. (2005). *Criminal victimization in Canada.* Ottawa: Juristat Centre for Crime Statistics.

Gavazzi, S. M., Yarcheck, C. M., & Chesney-Lind, M. (2006). Global risk indicators and the role of gender in a juvenile detention sample. *Criminal Justice and Behavior, 33*(5), 597–612.

Giroux, H. A. (2003). Racial intolerance and disposable youth in the age of zero tolerance. *Qualitative Studies in Education, 16*(4): 553–565.

Goldson, B. (2005). Child imprisonment: A case for abolition. *Youth Justice, 5*(2), 77–90.

Goldson, B. (2006). Damage, harm and death in child prisons in England and Wales: Questions of abuse and accountability. *Howard Journal, 45*(5), 449–467.

Henteleff, Y. (1999, September). The learning disabled child-at-risk: Why youth service systems have so badly failed them. Paper presented at the Working Together for Children: Protection and Prevention Conference, Ottawa.

Johnson-Reid, M., & Barth, R. P. (2000). From placement to prison: The path to adolescent incarceration from child welfare supervised or group care. *Children and Youth Services Review, 22*(7), 493–516.

Kazdin, A. E. (2000). Adolescent development, mental disorders, and decision making of delinquent youths. In T. Grisso & R. G. Schwartz (Eds), *Youth on trial: A developmental perspective on youth justice* (pp. 33–65). Chicago: University of Chicago Press.

LaPrairie, C. (2002). Aboriginal overrepresentation in the criminal justice system: A tale of nine cities. *Canadian Journal of Criminology, 44*, 181–208.

Latimer, J., & Foss, L. (2004). *A one day snapshot of Aboriginal youth in custody across Canada.* Ottawa: Department of Justice.

Leon, J. S. (1977). The development of Canadian juvenile justice: A background for reform. *Osgoode Hall Law Journal, 15*(1), 71–106.

Li, G. (2007). *Homicide in Canada, 2006.* Ottawa: Juristat Centre for Justice Statistics.

Macdonald, J. M., & Chesney-Lind, M. (2001). Gender bias and juvenile justice revisited: A multiyear analysis. *Crime & Delinquency, 47*(2), 173–195.

Medlicott, D. (2007). Women in Prison. In Y. Jewkes (Ed.), *Handbook on Prisons* (pp. 245–268). Portland: Willan.

Milligan, S. (2008). *Youth custody and community services, 2005/06*. Ottawa: Juristat Centre for Justice Statistics.

Ontario, Commission on Systemic Racism in the Ontario Criminal Justice System. (1995). *Report*. Toronto: Queen's Printer of Ontario.

Purdy, C. (2004, January 19). Kids help in innovative programme. *Edmonton Journal*.

Ray, N. (2006). *Lesbian, gay, bisexual and transgendered youth: An epidemic of homelessness*. New York: National Gay and Lesbian Task Force Policy Institute and the National Coalition for the Homeless.

Roberts, J. (2004). Harmonizing the sentencing of young and adult offenders. *Canadian Journal of Criminology and Criminal Justice, 46*(3), 301–326.

Schissel, B. (1997). *Blaming children*. Halifax: Fernwood.

Seiffge-Krenge, I. (1995). *Stress, coping and relationships in adolescence*. Mahwah, NJ: Lawrence Erlbaum.

Simon, J. (2000). The 'society of captives' in the era of hyper-incarceration. *Theoretical Criminology 4*(3), 285–308.

Sprott, J. B., & Doob, A. N. (2009). *Justice for girls?: Stability and change in the youth justice systems of the United States and Canada*. Chicago: University of Chicago Press.

Sprott, J. B., & Snyder, H. N. (1999). A comparison of youth crime in the U.S. and Canada, 1991 to 1996. *Overcrowded Times, 10*(5), 1, 12–19.

Statistics Canada. 2010. Data downloaded from the University of Toronto, Statistics Canada website on January 21, 2010.

Tanner, J. (2010). *Youth and deviance in Canada* (3rd ed.). New York: Oxford University Press.

Tanner, J., & Wortley, S. (2002). *The Toronto Youth Crime and Victimization Survey*. Toronto: Centre of Criminology, University of Toronto.

Trépanier, J. (1999). Juvenile courts after 100 years: Past and present orientations. *European Journal on Criminal Policy and Research, 7*, 303–327.

Ulzen, T., & Hamilton, H. (1998). Psychiatric disorders in incarcerated youth. *Youth Update, 16*, 4–5.

Vandergoot, M. E. (2006). *Justice for young offenders: Their needs our responses*. Saskatoon: Purich.

Viljoen, J. L. (2005). Bullying behaviors in female and male adolescent offenders: Prevalence, types, and association with psychosocial adjustment. *Aggressive behaviour, 31*(6), 521–536.

Wortley, S., & Tanner, J. (2007). *Criminal Organizations or Social Groups?: An Exploration of the Myths and Realities of Toronto Youth Gangs*. Ottawa: Solicitor General.

Statutes Cited

Juvenile Delinquents Act, R.S.C. 1970, c. J-3.
Young Offenders Act, R.S.C. 1985, c. Y-1.
Youth Criminal Justice Act, S.C. 2002, c. 1.

16 | Individuals with Disabilities

DICK SOBSEY AND HEIDI JANZ

Definition and Social Construction of Disability

There is no single, universally accepted definition of **disability**. Concepts of disability evolve over time and differ according to context. Definitions of a disability may differ greatly for different purposes, such as definitions that determine whether students will receive special funding and services in schools, definitions that determine if drivers receive special parking privileges, or definitions that determine who is identified as having a disability during a census. Medical models of disability view disability exclusively or primarily as a deficit in an individual's physical or mental capacity, while social models consider disability as partially or even exclusively a product of the environment.

Most current definitions of disability consider three essential dimensions: (1) impairment of an individual's physical or mental performance, (2) the resulting limitations in the individual's ability to carry out common activities of daily living, and (3) the characteristics of the environment that contribute to increasing or decreasing these limitations. Being blind (an impairment of vision), for example, may result in significant limitations in travelling independently in the community (activity limitations), which may be ameliorated by the presence of audio-signal crosswalk lights or Braille on elevator buttons or may be aggravated by the introduction of electric cars that are silent (environmental characteristics). According to the World Health Organization:

> *Disabilities* is an umbrella term, covering impairments, activity limitations, and participation restrictions. An **impairment** is a problem in body function or structure; an **activity limitation** is a difficulty encountered by an individual in executing a task or action; while a **participation restriction** is a problem experienced by an individual in involvement in life situations. Thus disability is a complex phenomenon, reflecting an interaction between features of a person's body and features of the society in which he or she lives. (World Health Organization, 2001)

The interaction between the individual and culture becomes apparent when one considers how the changing definitions and concepts of disabilities influence their observed incidence. For example, while a small number of individuals with very severe intellectual disabilities were known throughout history, milder intellectual disabilities went largely unnoticed until the late nineteenth century, when intelligence testing was developed. The development of the concept of IQ (intelligence quotient) in the late 1800s led to many people being categorized as having intellectual disabilities and the perception that there was a large increase in the number of people with intellectual disabilities. The belief that the number of people with intellectual disabilities was increasing rapidly combined with other social prejudices in Canada and many other countries. In response, these countries established restrictive immigration policies, massive institutionalization programs, and involuntary sexual sterilization in attempts to stem the rising tide of 'feeblemindedness' that they feared. As late as 1972, about 16 per cent of the population was defined as having some degree of 'mental retardation', the term then used for intellectual disability. Then with a change in the definition, moving the cut-off point from one to two standard deviations below average, most of that 16 per cent of the population became 'normal', leaving only about 2 per cent who met the new definition (Grossman, 1973).

Currently, the rapid increase in the prevalence of autism is also, at least in part, due to changing definitions and diagnostic criteria. While there remains considerable controversy over whether the actual percentage of individuals with a specific impairment has changed, there is no question that the very large increase in diagnosed cases follows changes in the diagnostic criteria.

Disability in Canada

Canada generally follows a common, internationally recognized approach to defining disability. Statistics Canada (2007b) bases its definition on the World Health Organization framework, stating, 'Disability is an activity limitation or participation restriction associated with a physical or mental condition or health problem' (p. 8). It is important to remember, however, that in collecting data Statistics Canada relies on self-reports or reports of family members. As a result, responses are sensitive to socially determined values, attitudes, and beliefs about disability. The increasing number of Canadians who report mild disabilities has been interpreted as reflecting increasing social acceptance of disability in addition to the effects of an aging population (Statistics Canada, 2007a).

Contemporary Demographics

According to Statistics Canada (2007a), there were 4,417,870 Canadian children and adults with disabilities in 2006, a number comprising just over 14 per cent of the total population. This percentage, however, varies significantly by age group. Only 3.7 per cent of individuals under the age of 15 were identified as having disabilities, while 11.5 per cent of those ages 15 to 64 were identified as having disabilities, and 43.4 per cent of those 65 and older were identified as having disabilities. As a result, the percentage of the total population with disabilities is increasing with the aging population. While 63.9 per cent of individuals under the age of 15 with disabilities are

Table 16.1 Percentage of Canadian Children and Adults with Various Categories of Disabillity, as Reported by Statistics Canada (2007b)

Category of Disability	Per cent of Children Age 0 to 4	Per cent of Children Age 5 to 14	Per cent of Adults Age >15
Agility	Not included	1.0	11.1
Chronic health condition	1.2	3.1	Not included
Delay	1.1	Not included	Not included
Developmental	Not included	1.4	0.5
Hearing	0.2	0.5	5.0
Learning	Not included	3.2	2.5
Memory	Not included	Not Included	2.0
Mobility	Not included	0.6	11.5
Pain	Not included	Not included	11.7
Psychological	Not included	1.6	2.3
Seeing	0.2	0.4	3.2
Speech	Not included	2.1	1.9
Other	0.1	0.2	0.5

Note: Categories are not exclusive and many individuals appear in more than one category.

males, 61.0 per cent of individuals age 75 and older with disabilities are females. The percentage of females who have disabilities and males who have disabilities is about equal for the 15-to-24-year-old age group, greater for males younger than 15, and greater for females age 25 and older.

Statistics Canada categorizes disabilities into 13 different groups: agility, chronic health condition, delay, developmental, hearing, memory, mobility, learning, pain, psychological, seeing, speech, and other. As seen in Table 16.1, not all of the categories have been applied to all age groups. For example, speech disabilities are not included in the 0-to-4 age group because young children are typically just starting to develop speech around the end of their first year and there is considerable variability in normal development, making it meaningless to attempt to enumerate speech disabilities in this age group. In the youngest age group, *delay* is used to describe significant deficits in meeting developmental milestones. This term is not used for older children or adults because some delays in infancy resolve and others manifest themselves clearly as developmental or physical disabilities as the child grows older.

Equal Treatment and Reasonable Accommodation

The treatment of people with disabilities at various times in history has been inconsistent. There is some anthropological evidence that prehistoric communities and families provided special care for at least some children with disabilities during the earliest days of humankind. Infants with obvious signs of disability were abandoned to die in ancient Greece. Under the Nazi regime, about 300,000 individuals with disabilities were systematically killed and another 300,000 were sterilized.

In Canada, some prominent experts argued for a formal euthanasia policy as late as 1982, and two provinces, Alberta and British Columbia, enacted sterilization laws. In Alberta, involuntary sterilizations of people were carried out under this law until 1972. These laws were at least partially fuelled by **eugenics** and the fear that 'mental defectives' would overrun Canada. While only two provinces carried out sexual sterilization, these same fears led to massive institutionalization programs designed to prevent the sexual expression of people with mental disabilities throughout their reproductive years, as well as restrictive immigration policies designed to keep 'inferior stock' out of Canada.

In spite of many negative events, there has been a general trend toward improvement in the acceptance and treatment of people with disabilities in Canada since the end of World War II. Improving conditions in Canada reflect a global trend toward improved social conditions for people with disabilities and other marginalized groups, but clearly more progress is required. Many developments in law and policy have contributed to the growing acknowledgment of the rights of individuals with disabilities. Only three of these will be discussed here.

The Canadian Charter of Rights and Freedoms ('Canadian Charter of Rights and Freedoms: Part I of the Constitution Act', 1982) specifically protects the rights of persons with mental or physical disabilities under the Equality Rights section (s. 15) of the Charter. This guarantee of equal protection and benefit of the law, however, is not absolute and is subject 'to such reasonable limits prescribed by law as can be demonstrably justified in a free and democratic society', as specified in section 1. These limits remain open to interpretation by the courts.

In 1989 the Convention on the Rights of the Child was passed by the United Nations, and in 1991 Canada became one of 193 nations to ratify the convention, the most widely supported human rights treaty in human history. In addition to establishing the universal rights of all children, it identifies the special rights of several groups of marginalized children, including children with disabilities. Special rights do not actually provide children with disabilities with more fundamental rights than other children, but rather require governments to take special actions to ensure that children with disabilities can access the same universal rights as other children. For example, all children have the same right to an appropriate education, but without accessible schools and transportation, some children with disabilities would be unable to exercise this universal right.

While Canada played a leadership role in developing the Convention on the Rights of the Child, it has not been a leader in meeting its obligations under the convention. Canadian law takes a dualistic approach to international treaties. This means that the provisions of Canada's international treaties have no effect on internal federal or provincial law unless they are enacted by the passage of specific statutes (Howe, 2007). This has not occurred. The convention has little force in Canada, and evaluations of Canada's compliance, particularly in regard to children with disabilities, have not been very positive (Howe & Covell, 2007). An evaluation in 1999 of Canada's compliance with the Convention on the Rights of the Child concluded that Canada's 'most glaring failure [is] its treatment of disabled children' (Picard, 1999). The 2003 update on this report found progress had been made in some areas for children with disabilities (e.g., immigration restrictions), but that much more work is needed. Howe and Covell (2007) conclude that children with disabilities continue to face a situation in which their basic right to life and survival is under threat and in which segregated classrooms and schools compromise their right to education and equality.

The **Convention on the Rights of Persons with Disabilities** was passed by the United Nations in 2006 and came into force in May of 2008. The government introduced the convention to Parliament on December 3, 2009, and Canada officially ratified it on March 11, 2010. This convention affirms the rights of all individuals with disabilities, regardless of age, and requires governments to take actions to reduce inequities. It is also more specific than the Convention on the Rights of the Child in some areas (e.g., the requirement for inclusive education). The real test of this new convention will be its implementation. Under Canadian law, international treaties such as this convention do not have the force of law within Canada unless their provisions are enacted into Canadian law. Therefore, the ratification of the Convention on the Rights of Persons with Disabilities can be viewed as a commitment by Canada and its provinces to enact law and policy consistent with its mandate. Until these steps are taken within Canada, ratification of the convention remains a symbolic gesture.

Medical Discrimination

Access to appropriate medical care is essential to optimized health and in some cases essential to survival. Infants and young children with severe disabilities in Canada frequently are not provided with the medical treatment required for survival and are allowed to die by agreement between parents and physicians. In one study conducted at a Canadian hospital, about 40 per cent of deaths in a paediatric intensive-care unit occurred in spite of vigorous attempts to save the baby's life, while the remaining 60 per cent died because of a decision to withhold treatment. The physicians indicated that, of those who died because of a decision to withhold treatment, about 69 per cent probably could not be saved, but the other 31 per cent would be expected to survive if treated. They died because of a decision that death was preferable to survival with a severe disability.

Educational Discrimination

For decades many children with disabilities were denied equal access to education. In some cases, that meant total exclusion from school, and in many others, it meant segregation in special classes.

For two decades, Canada has been a party to the United Nations Convention on the Rights of the Child, and as of early 2010, it has signalled its intention to adopt the Convention on the Rights of Persons with Disabilities. Each of these international treaties commits Canada and its provinces to recognizing that children with disabilities have a right to inclusive education in their local schools, with appropriate accommodations to facilitate access and full participation. This right has not been fully implemented in Canada, and the Canadian Supreme Court has ruled that school boards have the right to determine whether students with disabilities are educated in inclusive classrooms with their peers or in special segregated facilities *(Eaton v. Brant County Board of Education,* 1997).

Generally, Canadians with disabilities receive less education than Canadians without disabilities. Many factors appear to contribute to this difference, including individual differences in aptitude, socio-economic differences, competing demands (e.g., more frequent health-related interruptions), and inadequate accommodations to support successful academic achievement.

Social Inclusion and the Independent Living Movement

In response to various kinds of systemic discrimination, people with disabilities and their allies started the independent living movement in the early 1970s (Hutchison, 1996). Independent living, as seen by its advocates, is a philosophy, a way of looking at disability and society, and a worldwide movement of people with disabilities who work for self-determination, self-respect, and equal opportunities for people with disabilities. It is thus fundamentally based on the principle of the social inclusion of people with disabilities. **Social inclusion**, the converse of social exclusion, is a systematic strategy that seeks to ensure that disenfranchised groups of people, including people with disabilities, have greater participation in decision making that affects their lives, allowing them to improve their living standards and their overall well-being. In the case of the independent living movement, this includes the creation of affordable, accessible housing and in-home personal attendant care services as required. The independent living movement is a social movement that evolved as a struggle for civil liberties by persons with disabilities who used self-help tactics. Independent living is really about interdependence, not living in isolation.

Prior to the 1970s, many more Canadian children and young adults with disabilities lived in institutional settings, and many more community environments and services were inaccessible to people with special needs. Life in large, isolated institutions was commonly associated with harsh living conditions, abuse, and neglect. A report from the Law Commission of Canada (1999) focused on the institutional abuse of children but its conclusions can also be applied to adults. It noted that institutionalization for people who were deaf or had intellectual disabilities resulted in disconnection from society, powerlessness, and degradation. While the report found that these outcomes were common in Canada's institutions for Aboriginal children, orphans, and others, it also pointed toward the special vulnerabilities of institutionalized children with disabilities: 'The isolation and powerlessness referred to earlier are more marked in their case, because the disability itself may cause or contribute to those conditions. Thus the very characteristic that makes institutionalization more necessary for disabled children also makes them easier targets for abuse once there' (p. 15).

In some cases, former residents of these institutions have been compensated for a variety of abuses they suffered while in care. For example, a group of more than 800 former residents of Alberta institutions for children and adults with developmental disabilities, primarily the Provincial Training School at Red Deer, received approximately $150 million in compensation for abuse, neglect, and wrongful sterilization (Thomson, 2000). Former residents of Jericho Hill School for the Deaf received about $23 million in compensation from the Province of British Columbia for emotional, physical, and sexual abuse (Matas, 2004). In December 2009, a tentative settlement was announced whereby $3,000 to $150,000 would be awarded to 1,100 former residents of British Columbia's Woodlands, an institution for people with developmental disabilities (Woo, 2009). Individual compensation amounts for Woodlands residents are based on the nature and extent of abuse experienced by individuals. An additional approximately 500 survivors who left the institution prior to 1974, however, have been determined to be ineligible for compensation. Woodlands opened in 1878 and closed in 1996.

Other provinces have also downsized or closed institutions over the last 40 years, and many people have left institutions to live in community settings. For example, Ontario made a commitment to close its institutions for people with intellectual disabilities in the 1970s. That commitment led to decades of downsizing and developing of community services before the doors of its last three such institutions closed in March 2009, 160 years after Ontario opened its first institution (Puzic, 2009).

In spite of the continued trend toward community-based care, many Canadians with disabilities continue to live in institutions. According to Statistics Canada (2008), as of 2007, more than 200,000 Canadians lived in residential care for the aged, for individuals with psychiatric disorders, for individuals with intellectual disabilities, and for individuals with substance abuse disorders. Although considerable efforts have been made to effect institutional reform and improve the quality of care, abuse and neglect continue to be problems in some facilities. As part of the efforts to minimize the risk for institutional abuse or neglect, several provinces have passed **Protection for Persons in Care Acts** (Protection for Persons in Care Act, Alberta, 1995; Protection for Persons in Care Act, Manitoba, 2000; Protection for Persons in Care Act, Nova Scotia, 2004). These laws include a variety of provisions, such as a requirement to report abuse, protection for whistleblowers (those who report abuse), and background checks for staff. In spite of these and other efforts, abuse and neglect continue to be problems in Canada's residential care facilities for people with disabilities.

Immigration and Citizenship

Historically, individuals with disabilities and their families have frequently faced obstacles when attempting to immigrate to Canada. Canada's first immigration act, passed in 1869, required that individuals who were deaf, blind, physically impaired, intellectually impaired, or psychiatrically impaired had to be identified so that a determination could be made as to whether or not they were likely to become dependent upon public welfare (Hanes, 2009). If crews did not screen out passengers who lacked medical clearance before departing for Canada, the shipowners could be held financially responsible for the care of passengers with disabilities who reached Canada. While this provided a strong motivation for carriers to screen out passengers with disabilities, these passengers were not explicitly prohibited from entering the country.

Canada's 1910 Immigration Act established **'prohibited classes'**, which referred to people with mental and physical disabilities, and with the growing influence of an international eugenics movement, Canada's 1929 Immigration Act blurred the distinction between disability and criminality, categorizing people with intellectual and mental disabilities along with conspirators, criminals, prostitutes, and revolutionaries. Hanes (2009) points out that there was some leniency in admitting people with physical or sensory disabilities but little or no leniency in admitting people with intellectual or psychiatric disabilities.

This distinction continued in post-war Canada with the 1952 Act, which unconditionally prohibited the entry of people with intellectual or psychiatric disabilities or seizure disorders, while permitting people with physical or sensory disabilities to enter if they could demonstrate that they could be self-supporting or if they had a family that would support them. In spite of several reports recommending changes to the exclusion of people with disabilities, there was little change prior to the coming of the twenty-first century, except that epileptics were removed from the prohibited classes in 1976.

In 2001, Canada established a new immigration act that eliminated much of the offensive language of the previous acts. While the new act does not define 'prohibited classes', it does include an **excessive demand** section. This section allows immigration officials to refuse entry to anyone who they reasonably believe is likely to add to waiting lists for health care or social services or to anyone who is likely to exceed the average per capita health care costs over the next 5 to 10 years. While this approach appears to eliminate the obvious discrimination issues raised by the old prohibited classes, the effect is to allow immigration officials to deny entry to almost anyone with a significant disability.

In 2005, two cases of exclusion reached the Supreme Court of Canada (*Hilewitz v. Canada* [Minister of Citizenship and Immigration]; *De Jong v. Canada* [Minister of Citizenship and Immigration], 2005). The Hilewitz family immigrated to Canada under 'investor' provisions, and the de Jong family immigrated under 'self-employed' provisions. Both families had children with disabilities, and both applied for permanent residence. Both were rejected because their children were considered to be excessive burdens. In each case, the families had substantial assets and they represented no excessive costs to provincial or federal programs. The families' willingness and ability to cover any costs, however, was not considered relevant to the excessive-burden decisions that had been made. In appealing their rejection, these families argued that since their financial circumstances were factors in their consideration for investor and self-employed status, these circumstances should also be factors in the consideration of whether their children should be considered to be excessive burdens. The Supreme Court agreed in a split decision. The two dissenting opinions suggested that while considering all of the circumstances would be fair, that the intent of the Act is to base decisions solely on the basis of the nature and severity of the condition.

The majority decision supports a broader reading of the Act, one that allows exclusion but considers all circumstances in determining when an individual is likely to be an excessive burden. Nevertheless, the 2005 Supreme Court decision has not provided clarity and the discretionary judgments of excessive burden act as a strong disincentive for individuals with disabilities or their families from even considering entering Canada.

Former British police officers Paul and Barbara-Anne Chapman decided to move their family to Canada and bought a farmhouse in Fall River, Nova Scotia. After a six-hour transatlantic flight to Halifax, however, they were sent back to the United Kingdom as undesirables by a border guard who told them that their seven-year-old daughter, Lucy, who has Angelman syndrome, is banned for life from entering Canada (Tibbets, 2008).

The Barlagne family immigrated to Montreal from Paris in 2005. David Barlagne, a francophone who runs a successful computer software business, and his wife, Sophie, who teaches French, were encouraged by officials at the Canadian Embassy in Paris to come to Quebec. Four years later, his business had become very successful, and the family applied for permanent residence. In 2009, however, the Barlagnes were told they are unwelcome in Canada. Their seven-year-old daughter has cerebral palsy and developmental delays. According to Immigration Canada, she is potentially an excessive burden, and she and the rest of her family were asked to leave (Derfel, 2009). According to the papers filed in court, Immigration Canada claims that the excessive burden that would be imposed would be $5,200 per year in special education costs, although her family has repeatedly offered to pay this cost (Wilton, 2010).

At best, as of 2010, the issue of immigration to Canada for people with disabilities and their families remains uncertain and unresolved. Future guidance may be found in Article 18 of the Convention on the Rights of Persons with Disabilities, which proclaims that individuals with disabilities shall '[h]ave the right to acquire and change a nationality and are not deprived of their nationality arbitrarily or on the basis of disability'.

Perhaps ironically, the notion that people with disabilities will impose a special burden on the Canadian economy is based in part on the belief that they will be unemployable and will therefore require social assistance throughout much of their lives. While it is certainly true that individuals with disabilities are more likely to be unemployed and, if employed, often work in low-paying jobs, the reasons for their employment difficulties are not always clear. In many cases, their lack of employment appears to result from systemic bias rather than individual limitations.

Employment and Income

Canadians with disabilities are much less likely to be employed than their counterparts without disabilities. While the precise percentages vary by age and gender, the proportion of individuals with disabilities who have jobs is well below the proportion in the general population. Both men and women with disabilities are much less likely to be part of the labour force, much more likely to be unemployed if they are part of the labour force, and if employed typically earn much less than Canadians without disabilities. For example, Canadian men and women with disabilities aged 55 to 64 were only about half as likely to have jobs as their counterparts without disabilities.

Sixty per cent of Canadians with disabilities who are not considered to be part of the workforce report that they are unable to work because of their disabilities, while another 20 per cent report that they are limited in the kind or amount of work that they can do. About 20 per cent report that they do not participate in the workforce because they would lose benefits if they were employed. Canadians with disabilities who are in the workforce are approximately 40 per cent more likely than those without disabilities to be unemployed.

Considering these employment factors, it is not surprising that Canadians with disabilities typically have incomes that are well below average. Although many Canadians with disabilities receive disability-related income supplements, the total income for Canadians with disabilities is only 60 per cent to 80 per cent that of their non-disabled peers, depending on age and gender (Statistics Canada, 2001).

People with Disabilities as Victims of Crime

Canadians with disabilities are at particular risk for becoming victims of violence throughout their lifespan. Studies of child maltreatment and of various forms of violence against adults suggest that people with disabilities are much more likely to be victims of violent crime than people without disabilities, although they experience about the same rate of property crime as people without disabilities.

Children with Disabilities as Victims of Abuse and Neglect

Large-scale studies from the United States and the United Kingdom provide strong evidence that children with disabilities are much more likely to be abused than children without disabilities. Data from Canada is consistent with these findings, but the nature of the Canadian data makes it difficult to establish firm conclusions.

Sullivan and Knutson (2000) studied a very large cohort of Omaha schoolchildren, merging school records of disability with child abuse registry, foster care review, and police records. They found that children with disabilities were 3.4 times as likely as children without disabilities to have a known history of maltreatment. Among children without disabilities, 9 per cent had a known history of abuse, while 31 per cent of children with disabilities had a known history of abuse.

Spencer et al. (2005) followed a cohort of 119,729 children in West Sussex for 19 years. They found that most categories of children with disabilities had an increased risk of being listed on the child maltreatment registry. However, the degree of increased risk differed substantially across categories of disability. For example, children with conduct disorders were 11.5 times as likely to be registered as abused, those with moderate or severe intellectual disabilities were 6.5 times as likely to be registered as abused, and those with non-conduct psychological disorders were 5.24 times as likely to be registered as abused. Children with sensory disabilities and autism were not found to be at increased risk in this study.

Canadian research appears to be consistent with these findings, but the available information does not allow direct comparison. Trocmé and Wolfe (2001) reported on 'child functioning issues' in a very large sample of maltreated Canadian children. While many of these issues correspond closely to disabilities (e.g., developmental delay, physical or developmental disability), others do not (e.g., negative peer involvement, running away). As a result, one can only generally conclude that there appear to be more disabilities among maltreated children than one might expect based on the prevalence of disabilities in the general population. Sobsey and Sobon (2006) attempted a rough estimate of the extent of this over-representation by comparing the data from this study to census data, and found that disabilities were noted about 3.7 times as frequently among maltreated Canadian children as among the general child population of Canada. Trocmé and Wolfe concluded that 26 per cent of all children who were the focus of child maltreatment investigations had one or more health-related child functioning issue and that 33 per cent of all children who were the focus of child maltreatment investigations had one or more behaviour-related child functioning issue.

Bullying is a general term that is commonly used to refer to a variety of behaviours, such as teasing, name-calling, threatening, harassment, intimidation, and physical violence. While bullying exists at every age level, childhood bullying is commonly discussed as a specific problem. Children with disabilities are frequently the targets of bullying. In spite of limited research, both Canadian and international studies suggest that children with disabilities are bullied at least twice the rate of children without disabilities.

A group of Winnipeg children aged 8 to 11, pushed a 14-year-old with spina bifida into a wooden shed, locked the door, and set the shed on fire before he was rescued by a passerby (Santin, 2006). A group of Pickering elementary school children proudly posted their taunting and tripping of a 7-year-old partially paralyzed schoolmate on YouTube (Kalinowski, 2007).

Adults with Disabilities as Crime Victims

Statistics Canada data suggest that the annual rate of violent crimes against people with activity limitations is 147 victims per 1,000 individuals, significantly higher than the rate of 101 victims per 1,000 individuals determined among individuals without activity limitations.

Each year Statistics Canada conducts the General Social Survey, and the 2004 cycle of this study, based on data from interviews with 23,766 Canadian adults (age 15 and older), included questions on crime victimization. In 2009, the Canadian Centre for Justice Statistics released its analysis of the data collected in this cycle, comparing victimization of individuals with disabilities to victimization of individuals without disabilities. The following are some of the report's findings:

> In 2004, the rate of violent victimization, including sexual assault, robbery, and physical assault, was 2 times higher for persons with activity limitations than for people without limitations.

The personal victimization rate, which is violent victimization including theft of personal property for persons with mental of behavioural disorder, was 4 times higher than the rate for persons with no mental disorder.

Persons with activity limitations were 2 to 3 times more likely to be victims of the most severe forms of spousal violence, such as being sexually assaulted, beaten, struck or threatened with a weapon. (Perrault, 2009)

These Canadian findings were very similar to those in the Crime against People with Disabilities report from the Bureau of Justice Statistics based on the US National Crime Victimization Survey of 2007 (Rand & Harrel, 2009). The Canadian report also found that while the absolute rates of victimization decreased with advancing age, individuals with disabilities continued to have approximately twice the rate of victimization as that of individuals of corresponding age without disabilities. In addition to the greater likelihood of being victimized at least once, 46 per cent of Canadians with disabilities who were crime victims were victimized on more than one occasion in the last year compared to 35 per cent of crime victims without activity limitations.

Hate or Bias Crimes

The topic of **hate crimes** against individuals with disabilities is extremely controversial. According to a 2008 report, *Hate Crimes in Canada,* from the Canadian Centre for Justice Statistics, Canada's police agencies recorded only two hate crimes against people with disabilities in a recent one-year period (Dauvergne, Scrim, & Brennan, 2008). The following year, a report from the same agency based on interviews with Canadians with and without disabilities estimated that 36,000 hate- or **bias**-motivated violent crimes were committed against people with disabilities per year (Perrault, 2009). These crimes comprised 12 per cent of all violent crimes against people with disabilities. It should be pointed out that the sentencing-enhancement provisions of section 718.2 of the Canadian Criminal Code allow for harsher sentences for any crime motivated by 'bias, prejudice or hate' based on mental or physical disability or other specific marginalized characteristics. Bias is a broader concept than hatred and may allow for more prosecutions. For example, offenders might suggest they were motivated by pity for rather than hatred of people with disabilities when they attempted to kill them. While pity might not fit the narrower definition of hatred, it would still likely meet the broader definition of bias, since it is based on the false assumption that people with disabilities have worse lives than those without disabilities.

The apparent discrepancy between cases identified by police and cases identified by victims demonstrates, at least in part, the stringent requirements necessary for official designation as a hate crime. While 36,000 Canadians with disabilities may have concluded that they were singled out for victimization because of their disabilities, official categorization as a hate crime requires stronger evidence not only that the victim was targeted because of a disability but also that the offender was motivated by hatred of individuals with disabilities.

People with Disabilities Employed in the Justice System

In spite of some high-profile exceptions and some undeniable progress over the last few decades, individuals with disabilities appear to be substantially under-represented in Canada's justice system. The exact extent of participation seems to be difficult to determine. An article published in the *Lawyers Weekly* (Allen, 2006) indicates that 'disabled lawyers continue to face significant barriers to entering the legal profession and practising law.' Discriminatory practices may continue even after entering the profession. A 2004 survey of 7,600 lawyers in Alberta reported that 40 per cent of lawyers with disabilities had personally experienced discrimination in their careers (Marron, 2004).

In 1994, Ontario Justice Fernand Gratton fought attempts to remove him from office in Federal Court after a stroke left him with substantial disabilities. The Canadian Judges Conference supported his position because the only statutory ground for removing a judge from office was misconduct (Bindman, 1994). He lost his case in Federal Court and later resigned his position. In 1998, however, Heather Robertson was sworn in as a justice of Nova Scotia's Supreme Court and became Canada's first federally appointed judge who used a wheelchair. Her appointment required considerable accommodation, since many of Nova Scotia's courtrooms were not accessible to people with mobility impairments.

Of course, the under-representation of people with disabilities as lawyers and judges is not in itself sufficient to demonstrate bias. In some cases, bona fide occupational requirements may be difficult to meet for individuals with certain disabilities, even after **reasonable accommodations** are in place. This is also true for police officers. Typically, Royal Canadian Mounted Police (RCMP) officers are required to meet stringent health, physical fitness, and mental standards. Most other Canadian police agencies follow this model, which assumes that each officer should have the same basic abilities and would theoretically be able to manage the responsibilities of any assignment. Officers who acquire significant disabilities while in service are generally retired with a disability pension. Nevertheless, there has been some increase in the number of Canadian police officers with disabilities in active service and indications that further accommodations will be made to facilitate further increases (Corley, 2006). This trend follows the lead of countries such as the United States, where numerous changes implemented under the Americans with Disabilities Act have greatly increased the hiring of police officers with disabilities.

People with Disabilities as Witnesses

The right of individuals to participate in the justice system as witnesses is critical to their participation as full citizens in society and essential for equal protection of the law. For example, during the slavery era in the United States, slaves were considered incapable of performing civil acts, such as giving testimony in court (DeLombard, 2007). This resulted in the inability of slaves who were victims or witnesses to crimes to testify against slave owners and any other offenders. As a result, many crimes became invisible to the justice system. Similarly, the exclusion of individuals with intellectual and communicative disabilities has resulted in invisible crimes against people with disabilities.

People with Disabilities Investigated, Accused, or Convicted of Crimes

Like other Canadians, individuals who have mental or physical disabilities may be suspected or, in some cases, actually convicted of crimes. The issues raised concerning people with various disabilities under criminal investigation or as inmates in jails or prisons are too numerous and too complex to discuss fully here. Hassan and Gordon (2003) offer a much fuller Canadian perspective and an excellent review of mental and intellectual disabilities among individuals who are suspected or convicted of committing offences. This chapter provides only a brief discussion of a few of these issues.

First, many factors associated with increased risk for offending are also associated with increased risk for disabilities. Lower socio-economic status, for example, is associated with increased risk for disability and higher crime rates. These factors may account for the over-representation of people with disabilities as suspects or convicts in the Canadian justice system.

Second, while difficult to measure, it is likely that criminals with mental disorders typically are more likely to be apprehended than other criminals. This may have the effect of magnifying their perceived contribution to crime and increasing their presence in the criminal justice system.

Third, many individuals with intellectual and mental disabilities may be compliant with others and in some cases exploited by more sophisticated offenders. In some cases, they may not even be aware that they are committing a crime. In others, they may be easily threatened or manipulated into compliance by more sophisticated offenders who exploit them.

Fourth, regardless of innocence or guilt, individuals with intellectual or mental health disabilities may be unaware of their rights and have diminished capacity to defend themselves. About 30 per cent of confessions that are later proven to be false come from people termed 'vulnerable suspects', who have developmental or psychiatric disabilities (Drizin, 2004).

Fifth, while research suggests that crime victims with developmental disabilities receive sympathetic treatment from police, the same study suggests that police tend to view crimes as more serious when suspects have developmental disabilities than when suspects of similar crimes are without disabilities (McAfee, Cockram, & Wolfe, 2001). Suspects with developmental disabilities are reported to receive harsher treatment.

Sixth, while numerous studies suggest that the actual association between psychiatric disorders and violence is very weak, the public perception that mental illness frequently contributes to violence exaggerates the strength of this association (Stuart, 2003). As a result, individuals with mental disabilities may be more likely to be suspected when crimes occur.

Seventh, individuals who commit crimes, particularly those who commit violent crimes, frequently have high-risk lifestyles that can substantially increase the risk of injury or illness and subsequent disability. As a result, spinal cord injuries, brain injuries, and other forms of acquired disabilities occur frequently among offenders.

Since about 17 per cent of Canada's population is considered to have some degree of disability, it is not surprising that people with disabilities make up a significant proportion of the incarcerated population. The exact percentage is unclear, but there is some evidence of over-representation of people with certain specific disabilities among the prison population.

One Canadian study of pretrial detainees in a Quebec facility found that 19 per cent had intellectual disabilities and another 30 per cent functioned in the 'borderline range'. Of those assessed as having intellectual disabilities, 85 per cent had previous convictions, compared to 90 per cent of detainees assessed as having normal intelligence (Crocker, Cote, Toupin, & St-Onge, 2007).

Estimates of the percentage of prisoners with intellectual disabilities from the United States and the United Kingdom range from less than 1 per cent to almost 10 per cent of prisoners, and estimates of intellectual disabilities among prisoners on America's death row are as high as 20 per cent (Crocker et al., 2007). A study from New South Wales in Australia reported that 10 per cent of prisoners had intellectual disabilities and another 20 per cent tested in the borderline range (Vanny, Levy, Greenberg, & Hayes, 2009).

A study of jail inmates in two American states found serious mental illness in 14.5 per cent of male inmates and 31.0 per cent of female inmates (Steadman, Osher, Robbins, Case, & Samuels, 2009). Attention deficit disorders and reading difficulties have also been reported at very high rates in prison populations (Rasmussen, Almvik, & Levander, 2001). Little research is available on impairments of vision, hearing, or mobility among prison populations, but these also appear frequently among prison populations. Likewise, little data is available from Canadian prisons, but among 80 inmates polled by Corrections Canada, 64 reported having at least one disability, and of these, 10 reported intellectual disabilities, 12 reported hearing impairment, 21 reported visual impairment, 24 reported psychiatric disabilities, and 30 reported mobility impairments (Correctional Service of Canada, 2006).

Prisoners with disabilities are at high risk of being physically and sexually abused in prison. According to the US National Prison Rape Elimination Commission (2009), 'Physical and developmental disabilities and mental illnesses can significantly affect an individual's ability to function and remain safe in a correctional facility. Individuals with severe developmental disabilities are at especially high risk of being sexually abused' (p. 71).

While other prisoners are typically responsible for most of the abuse of inmates with disabilities, prison staff also has been implicated in many offences. One study concluded that inmates with intellectual disabilities are at least twice as likely as other prisoners to commit suicide while in prison (Shaw, Appleby, & Baker, 2003).

Summary

Approximately one in six Canadians report having disabilities. While there is vast diversity among these individuals, as a group they continue to experience significant social, educational, vocational, and economic disadvantages. They are over-represented both among victims of crime and among those accused or convicted of crimes. Individuals with disabilities continue to face barriers to immigration. Canadians with disabilities are under-represented among the ranks of the employed, particularly among those employed in the justice system.

Key Terms

activity limitation

Convention on the
   Rights of Persons
   with Disabilities

disability

eugenics

hate crimes and bias
   crimes

impairment

participation
   restriction

prohibited classes
   and excessive
   demand

Protection for
   Persons in Care Act

reasonable
   accommodation

social inclusion

Questions for Critical Thought

1.   What standards can be used to determine when a request for a 'reasonable accommodation' for a person with a disability becomes an unreasonable request?

2.   The claim of excessive demands on health care or social services has been used to block immigration of individuals with disabilities and their families from immigrating to Canada. What arguments can be made for or against this policy?

3.   What criteria should be used to determine when crimes against people with disabilities should be considered to be hate or bias crimes?

Additional Readings

Clements, L., & Read, J. (Eds). (2008). *Disabled people and the right to life: the protection and violation of disabled people's most basic human rights.* London: Routledge.

Fitzsimons, N. M. (2009). *Combating violence & abuse of people with disabilities: A call to action.* Baltimore: Brookes.

Sherry, M. (2010). *Disability hate crimes: Does anybody really hate people with disabilities?* Burlington, VT: Ashgate.

Websites of Interest

Access to Justice for People with Communication Disabilities: www.accpc.ca/ej-backgroundinfo.htm

Preventing Violence against People with Disabilities, *Abilities Magazine:* www.abilities.ca/agc/article/article.php ?pid=&cid=&subid=147&aid=802

2006 Participation and Activity Limitation Survey: Disability in Canada: www.statcan.gc.ca/bsolc/olc-cel/olc-cel?catno=89-628-XWE2008005&lang=eng

References

Allen, J. (2006, December 8). Disability diversity continues to take a back seat—especially in private sector. *The Lawyers Weekly*. Retrieved from www.lawyersweekly.ca/index.php?section=article&articleid=392

Bindman, S. (1994, July 12). Disabled judge drops fight to keep job; Ontario justice opts for retirement after his health worsens. *The Gazette*, p. B1.

Canadian Charter of Rights and Freedoms: Part I of the Constitution Act. (1982).

Canadian Coalition for the Rights of Children. (2003). *How does Canada measure up? 2003 update of Canada's report to the UN Committee for the Rights of Children*. Ottawa: Canadian Coalition for the Rights of Children.

Corley, C. R. (2006). *The future of disability programs and services for RCMP members & their families: Needs assessment*. Ottawa: Occupational Health and Safety Branch.

Correctional Service of Canada. (2006). *Accommodating the needs of offenders with disabilities: Audit report*. Ottawa: Correctional Service of Canada, Performance Assurance Sector. Document no. 378-1-195.

Crocker, A. G., Cote, G., Toupin, J., & St-Onge, B. (2007). Rate and characteristics of men with an intellectual disability in pre-trial detention. *Journal of Intellectual and Developmental Disabilities, 32*(2), 143–152.

Dauvergne, M., Scrim, K., & Brennan, S. (2008). *Hate crimes in Canada*. Ottawa: Statistics Canada, Canadian Centre for Justice Statistics. Catalogue no. 85F0033MWE—no. 17.

DeLombard, J. M. (2007). *Slavery on trial: Law, abolitionism, and print culture*. Chapel Hill: University of North Carolina Press.

Derfel, A. (2009, December 31). Illness may force family out of Canada. *The Gazette*, p. A6.

Drizin, S. (2004). The problem of false confessions in the post-DNA world. *North Carolina Law Review, 82*, 891–1007.

Eaton v. Brant County Board of Education, 1, 241 (S.C.C. 1997).

Grossman, J. J. (Ed.). (1973). *Manual on terminology and classification in mental retardation*. Washington, DC: American Association on Mental Deficiency.

Hanes, R. (2009). None is still too many: From prohibited to excessive, an historical exploration of Canadian immigration and citizenship for people with disabilities. *Developmental Disabilities Bulletin, 37*(1/2), 91–126.

Hassan, S., & Gordon, R. M. (2003). *Developmental disability, crime, and criminal justice*. Burnaby, BC: Simon Fraser University, Criminology Research Centre. (C.R.C. Simon Fraser University. Document Number 2003-01).

Hilewitz v. Canada (Minister of Citizenship and Immigration); *De Jong v. Canada* (Minister of Citizenship and Immigration), 2, 706 (S.C.C. 2005).

Howe, B. (2007). Introduction. In R. B. Howe & K. Covell (Eds), *Children's rights in Canada: A question of commitment* (pp. 1–19). Waterloo, ON: Wilfrid Laurier University Press.

Howe, B., & Covell, K. (2007). Conclusion. In R. B. Howe & K. Covell (Eds), *Children's rights in Canada: A question of commitment* (pp. 395–411). Waterloo, ON: Wilfrid Laurier University Press.

Hutchison, P. (1996). *Impact of independent living resource centres in Canada*. Ottawa: Canadian Association of Independent Living Centres.

Kalinowski, T. (2007, February 14). Bullying of disabled boy put online. *The Toronto Star*, p. A2.

Law Commission of Canada. (1999). *Minister's reference on institutional child abuse: Discussion paper*. Ottawa: Law Commission of Canada.

McAfee, J. K., Cockram, J., & Wolfe, P. S. (2001). Police reactions to crimes involving people with mental retardation: A cross-cultural experimental study. *Education and Training in Mental Retardation and Developmental Disabilities, 36*(2), 160–171.

Marron, K. (2004, April 19). Equality struggle remains in law. *The Globe and Mail*, p. B15.

Matas, R. (2004, April 3). B.C to compensate sexually abused students. *The Globe and Mail*, p. A11.

National Prison Rape Elimination Commission. (2009). *National Prison Rape Elimination Commission report*. Washington, DC: National Prison Rape Elimination Commission.

Perrault, S. (2009). *Criminal victimization and health: A profile of victimization among persons with activity limitations or other health problems*. Ottawa: Statistics Canada, Canadian Centre for Justice Statistics.

Picard, A. (1999). Report critical of way disabled children treated. *The Globe and Mail*, p. A7.

Protection for Persons in Care Act (1995). Statutes of Alberta.

Protection for Persons in Care Act (2000). Statutes of Manitoba.

Protection for Persons in Care Act, c. 33 (2004). Statutes of Nova Scotia.

Puzic, S. (2009, April 1). Community living celebrated;

Disabled mark end of institutionalization in Ontario. *The Windsor Star,* p. A2.

Rand, M. R., & Harrel, E. (2009). *National crime victimization survey: Crime against people with disabilities, 2007.* Washington, DC: US Department of Justice, Office of Justice Programs, Bureau of Justice Statistics.

Rasmussen, K., Almvik, R., & Levander, S. (2001). Attention deficit hyperactivity disorder, reading disability, and personality disorders in a prison population. *Journal of the American Academy of Psychiatry and Law, 29*(2), 186–193.

Santin, A. (2006, October 16). Disabled boy trapped in burning shed saved by man, two girls. *National Post,* p. A4.

Shaw, J., Appleby, L., & Baker, D. (2003). *Safer prisons: A National Study of Prison Suicides 1999–2000 by the National Confidential Inquiry into suicides and homicides by people with mental illness.* London, UK: Department of Health.

Sobsey, R., & Sobon, S. (2006). Violence, protection and empowerment in the lives of children and adults with disabilities. In R. Alaggia and C. Vine (Eds), *Cruel but not unusual: Violence in Canadian families* (pp. 49–78). Waterloo, ON: Wilfrid Laurier University Press.

Spencer, N., Devereux, E., Wallace, A., Sundrum, R., Shenoy, M., Bacchus, C., et al. (2005). Disabling conditions and registration for child abuse and neglect: a population-based study. *Pediatrics, 116*(3), 609–613.

Statistics Canada. (2001). *Canadians with disabilities.* Ottawa: Statistics Canada, Canadian Centre of Justice Statistics.

Statistics Canada. (2007a). *Participation and Activity Limitation Survey 2006: Analytical report.* Ottawa: Statistics Canada, Social and Aboriginal Statistics Division.

Statistics Canada. (2007b). *Participation and Activity Limitation Survey 2006: Technical and methodo-logical report.* Ottawa: Statistics Canada, Social and Aboriginal Statistics Division.

Statistics Canada. (2008). *Residential care facilities 2006/2007.* Ottawa: Statistics Canada.

Steadman, H., Osher, F., Robbins, P., Case, B., & Samuels, S. (2009). Prevalence of serious mental illness among jail inmates. *Psychiatric Services, 60*(6), 761–765.

Stuart, H. (2003). Violence and mental illness: an overview. *World Psychiatry, 2*(2), 121–124.

Sullivan, P. M., & Knutson, J. F. (2000). Maltreatment and disabilities: A population-based epidemiological study. *Child Abuse & Neglect, 24*(10), 1257–1273.

Thomson, G. (2000, February 13). Sterilization settlements 'essentially done', lawyer says. *Edmonton Journal,* p. A6,

Tibbets, G. (2008, August 8). Canada refuses entry to disabled girl. *The Daily Telegraph,* p. 7.

Trocmé, N., & Wolfe, D. (2001). *Child maltreatment in Canada: Canadian incidence study of reported child abuse and neglect: Selected results.* Ottawa: Health Canada.

Vanny, K. A., Levy, M. H., Greenberg, D. M., & Hayes, S. C. (2009). Mental illness and intellectual disability in Magistrates Courts in New South Wales, Australia. *Journal of Intellectual Disability Research, 53*(3), 289–297.

Wilton, K. (2010, February 24). French father makes public appeal: 'Allow us to stay'; Ottawa wants disabled daughter out. *The Gazette,* p. A7.

Woo, A. (2009, December 15). B.C. settles with 1,100 school-abuse survivors: Mentally disabled. *National Post,* p. A9.

World Health Organization. (2001). *International Classification of Functioning, Disability and Health.* Geneva: World Health Organization.

Justice for Diversity

As noted in chapter 2, if difference is socially constructed, then it can also be *re*constructed. Thus, with the nature and dynamics of disparate experiences within the criminal justice system established, this concluding section addresses means by which those disparities can be minimized. Some, but not all, of the initiatives are grounded in criminal justice reform. However, these must also be contextualized within concrete efforts to reconstruct difference in positive relational terms and within a social justice framework.

One way to minimize disparities in the criminal justice experiences of different groups is to enhance communication and thus understanding between communities and to break down damaging and disparaging stereotypes. Chapter 17 emphasizes that it is also imperative that those working with diverse communities be aware of culturally distinct patterns of verbal and non-verbal communication (e.g., eye contact) and thus of the potential barriers to effective intercultural communication. Thus, the chapter highlights the nature of these barriers, as well as ways to overcome them. Importantly, it also suggests the impact that these verbal and non-verbal practices have for intercultural communication—and miscommunication—within the justice system specifically.

Over the past couple of decades, there has been a growing awareness of the need for focused pre- and in-service education for criminal justice personnel. This includes broad approaches to diversity generally, through what has come to be called 'social context education', but also more specialized training relevant to particular crimes (e.g., hate crime). Chapter 18 provides a brief overview of the background to current approaches to diversity and anti-racism training in Canada and explores some of the important caveats learned to date with respect to various means of delivering such training to various constituents in the justice sector. Interestingly, the discussion is contextualized within the framework of multiculturalism, thus bringing us back to our starting point. It becomes clear that the sorts of training explored in this chapter were intended to support the programmatic goals of the ideology of multiculturalism.

The concluding chapter returns to the theme of social equity as a prerequisite for reducing disparity in criminal justice. It encourages the reader to think about alternative ways to respond to offending, victimization, and service provision. Thus, the chapter pays some attention to criminal justice reform—such as legislative reform, changes in hiring and training, and the development of culturally specific programming—but it also recognizes the need to intervene in broader cultural and social contexts to alter the conditions that give rise to victimization and criminalization. In particular, the concluding chapter stresses the importance of *social* justice (economic, political, and cultural) for enhancing the likelihood of *criminal* justice.

17 | Communicating from the Margins: Exploring Intercultural Communication

VALERIE PRUEGGER

Introduction

Many languages are spoken in Canada. First Nations people alone speak over 60 different languages (Statistics Canada, 2006). In 2006, one in five Canadians had a mother tongue that is neither English nor French—20.1 per cent of the population, up from 18.0 per cent in 2001 (Statistics Canada, 2007). The proportion of francophones decreased from 22.9 per cent to 22.1 per cent, while the proportion of anglophones in 2006 was 57.8 per cent, down from 59.1 per cent in 2001. Canadians reported speaking more than 200 languages, many of these long associated with immigration to Canada, such as German, Italian, Ukrainian, Dutch, and Polish. However, between 2001 and 2006, language groups from Asia and the Middle East recorded the largest gains. These language groups include the Chinese languages, Punjabi, Arabic, Urdu, Tagalog, and Tamil, with the Chinese languages as Canada's third most common language group after English and French (Statistics Canada, 2007). Despite this richness in languages, 9 out of 10 Canadians speak English or French in the home. But communication is not only about language, it is about learned communication patterns. This chapter will explore cultural aspects of barriers to effective communication, communication in the criminal justice system, ways to work effectively with different communication patterns, and the consequences of miscommunication.

Case example: A traditional First Nations man sat in the witness box looking very uncomfortable. The clerk approached, asked him to hold up his right hand and swear to tell the truth, the whole truth, and nothing but the truth. Looking even more uncomfortable, the witness said softly, hesitantly: 'I cannot tell you the whole truth. I only know my truth. What I saw and heard. That is what I can tell you.'

This example speaks to the contextual and cultural nature of communication and language. In Western European contexts, we speak of truth as an absolute, an unchanging, fixed, and universal property. In other cultural contexts, truth is socially constructed: my truth may be different from your truth, but both may be true. In **individualistic** cultures like Canada and the United States, people focus on the communicator and it is important that he or she be clear, credible, intelligent, and have expert knowledge of the subject matter (Triandis, 1994). The word 'I' is used frequently, and the speaker often tries to discuss different viewpoints objectively, using logic, proofs and linear arguments. The emphasis is on *what* is said, and the communication is expected to be precise and to the point. Silence is regarded as disagreement, hostility, shyness, and is not valued. In **collectivist** cultures, such as many Asian, African, and Aboriginal cultures,[1] what is unspoken is valued and saying too much may confuse. The focus is on the receiver of the communication, and *how* something is said is more important than *what* is said. The goal is to preserve harmony, so 'we' is heard much more than 'I' and probabilistic terms like 'maybe' and 'perhaps' are common. Age, status, and family background all factor into the communication and how it is presented, and context is of utmost importance. Silence implies feeling comfortable, thinking, or having nothing important to say, and is valued. From these differences, we can see how the seeds of miscommunication and misunderstanding can be sown.

To communicate well, we need to be able to understand these complexities of language, our own assumptions, and how these create barriers to effective ***inter*cultural communication**. Communication is a continuous, ongoing process between two or more people. It relies on symbols that represent things, processes, ideas, or events that make communication possible. Effective communication depends on those involved in the communication process agreeing on the symbols and linguistic conventions used, such as tone and pitch of voice, turn-taking cues, appropriate topics, and directness of speech. All of these conventions are created in a particular cultural context. When we come into contact with individuals from other cultural contexts, we may find that our symbols and linguistic conventions no longer apply and miscommunication can result.[2]

For most people born and raised in Canada, Euro-Canadian assumptions and expectations about behaviour, values, and communication styles are presumed, unconsciously, to be the norm across all human beings. If we see someone speaking with a loud voice and broad arm gestures, we may assume that the person is agitated or angry; we rarely think that we may be misinterpreting his or her behaviour because of our own cultural norms. Our culturally based assumptions and interpretations are so completely ingrained that we experience them spontaneously—and invisibly. And we expect others to share these ingrained patterns. When they do not, we often make negative judgments about those individuals. We may think they are pushy, arrogant, cold, excitable, inscrutable, aggressive—any number of negative attributes, and all of these judgments create barriers to effective communication. Let's look at some of these barriers.

Barriers to Communication

To have an effective communication, there needs to be a sender who encodes a message and sends it through a channel (either verbal or non-verbal) and a receiver who decodes the message sent. The receiver must be able to decode the message accurately and encode a return message (feedback) to the original sender. This is what we mean by interaction. However, all sorts of 'noise' can occur in this interaction, be it physical, psychological, or cultural. And this noise may prevent us from sending and receiving our messages accurately.

For example, think about trying to have a conversation while a jack-hammer clatters away close by. You will find it very difficult to hear and to understand your partner without a lot of shouting, repetition, and clarification. We can think of psychological and cultural noise the same way. **Psychological noise** may be in the form of bias, prejudice, or defensiveness, among many other influences. This type of noise makes it difficult for us to concentrate on the communication act itself, as we are more focused on our own thoughts and needs rather than those of the receiver. Similarly, **cultural noise** may present language barriers or value barriers that become the focus of our communication rather than the topic itself. When we are concerned with things that lie outside the message, this noise prevents us from having an effective and accurate communication experience.

Barriers to effective communication include the following (Matsumoto & Juang, 2008, p. 245):

a. Assumptions of similarities
b. Language differences
c. Misinterpretation of non-verbal behaviour
d. Preconceptions and stereotypes
e. Tendency to evaluate
f. High anxiety or tension

Each of these potential barriers is discussed in turn below.

a. Assumption of Similarities

Assumption of similarities is the process by which we assume that our communication pattern is the same as that of others. As such, when our patterns are violated, we tend to make often negative personal evaluations about our communication partner, rather than recognizing that the misunderstanding is rooted in different patterns of communication.

Case example: A man and a woman are out for a drive. She looks at him and asks, 'Do you want a cup of coffee?' He replies, 'No', and keeps on driving. She becomes angry with him and he is confused as to what has caused her anger.

This example highlights the difference between direct and indirect speech. Men and women, as well as different cultural groups, have different norms around direct speech. Many cultures go to great lengths not to be direct. The risk of disharmony with other group members is too great to allow one to be outspoken and blunt. It is better to agree to somebody's face and negotiate with him or her afterwards than to disagree blatantly. Direct communicators may consider this indirectness deceptive, manipulative, two-faced, and lacking in integrity. Indirect communicators may find direct communication bossy, arrogant, rude, and cold. Direct communication tends to occur in cultures that value task over relationship, while indirect communication occurs where relationship takes precedence over task, at least in the early stages. While both men and women of all cultures can and do communicate in both modes, most people have a dominant style in certain contexts. Neither indirect nor direct speech is better than the other; each has a role to play, but each can lead to a negative evaluation of the other (him—rude, unfriendly, unresponsive; her—passive, manipulative). The chance to understand what is being communicated by both parties is lost when anger and mistrust get in the way of the message.

In the criminal justice system, where direct, often confrontational, and even adversarial speech is the norm, people who display indirect styles of communication—for example, traditional Aboriginal people—are at a disadvantage. Their speech may appear to be evasive, non-responsive, unfocused, and deceptive, leading to an interpretation that they are hiding something or being deliberately obstructive, rather than to the recognition that this pattern is an appropriate communication style or pattern.

b. Language Differences

Language differences present a number of unique structural and cultural obstacles. Language is composed of several **features**, including (Matsumoto & Juang, 2008):

- The lexicon or vocabulary of a language
- The syntax or grammar of a language that defines rules about how to form meaningful sentences
- Phonology, a system of rules about how words should sound or be pronounced in a given language
- Semantics, which refers to the meaning of words
- Pragmatics, which goes beyond linguistic knowledge to the ability to interpret meaning, which in turn depends on a social and environmental context. Being able to understand another's meaning is called 'pragmatic competence'. For example, 'you have a green light' could mean something different in traffic, in a work situation, or when hanging Christmas decorations.

In the criminal justice system, there are obvious constraints when a person does not speak the host language as his or her first language. Even the use of interpreters is not always effective because while it is fairly easy to find interpreters who can deal with the lexicon and syntax, very few have pragmatic competence. Phonology is also an issue for those with differentially accented speech. One area where police and justice workers become frustrated or suspicious is when witnesses or suspects, who in other contexts appear to be quite fluent in the language, suddenly are inarticulate and revert to their mother tongue. While this can be an evasive manoeuvre, it more often represents the effects of stress and anxiety on second-language users. When people are stressed, the natural tendency is to revert to their own language where they can more easily express their thoughts and emotions. You, too, may have had a similar experience, when, say, you were pulled over by a police officer for speeding. You may have found yourself becoming quite inarticulate even if English (or French) is your first language!

Case example: An Arabic immigrant businessman and his Canadian-born son attended court to settle a small claims dispute. On the first day of the trial, the businessman struggled to understand witnesses and state his case, but his son was available to help, holding whispered conversations with his father. On the second day, the son could not attend and the father asked for an interpreter (a guaranteed right under Section 14 of the Canadian Charter of Rights and Freedoms). However, the judge would not grant this request as he held that the individual had been communicating in English the previous day.

c. Misinterpretation of Non-verbal Behaviour

Misinterpretation of non-verbal behaviour is a minefield for miscommunication, and particularly of concern in law enforcement. Members of all cultures tend to internalize and become consciously unaware of their own norms, especially in terms of non-verbal or **paralinguistic** behaviour. Some cultural and vulnerable groups are very attentive to non-verbal communication, while others attend more to the content of communication. While it is impossible to know the communication norms and styles of everyone you may encounter, there some common dimensions of non-verbal behaviour where misunderstandings often occur. These are: emotional expressivity and gestures; eye contact; touch; loudness and pitch; personal space; and the use of silence. Each of these will be discussed later in the chapter.

d. Preconceptions and Stereotypes

Preconceptions and stereotypes about a group of people, their values, and their behaviours are often damaging and disparaging and based on very little knowledge about what underpins those behaviours. Rather, stereotypes become broad generalizations that are applied to every member of the group. We learn our biases from an early age from parents, societal leaders, the media, teachers, faith leaders, and peers. Think back to what you learned or did not learn about people from diverse backgrounds when you were growing up. How were they (or were they?) portrayed in history books? What authors did you read in school? How much were you exposed to people from different backgrounds in school, in your neighbourhood, in clubs, in the workplace? Who were the bad guys in TV shows and movies?

The sum total of all of these experiences leads us to internalize our own biases and preconceptions about others, biases that, because they are unconscious, are very hard to unlearn without first learning to be aware of them. The criminal justice system, like any other system, is full of people with these biases. This is not to say that they are bad people or that they deliberately discriminate, but, like the rest of us, they have learned often negative stereotypes about various groups of people. Unlike the rest of us, they have power and authority granted by the state, and thus their acting on their unconscious or conscious biases can have more far-reaching and serious consequences. Their unconscious preconceptions, for example, often underlie **racial profiling**, which results in unequal treatment in the criminal justice system.

Case example: A 24-year-old man claims to have been handcuffed six times by police since he was 13 years old. In the latest incident, he and two other drivers ran a yellow light but he was the only one pulled over. He believes it was because he was the only black driver and was driving a new Audi. When detained by police, he called his family. His mother and 74-year-old grandmother arrived, and they too were detained (Smith, 2007, p. 102).

The literature abounds with similar stories from Canada, the United States, and the United Kingdom (see Cryderman & O'Toole, 1986; Smith, 2007; Tanovich, 2006; Tator & Henry, 2006). That racial profiling exists can no longer be questioned, hence the current emphasis by many police services and in the courts on **articulable grounds** and **bias-free policing**. In 2003 an inquiry was held into the inordinate number of police-involved deaths and injury for Aboriginal people across Canada (Hannum, 2003). While records are poor, the study found that over a 20-year period, 43 per cent of people shot and killed by the Royal Canadian Mounted Police (RCMP) in Alberta were First Nations, and in British Columbia 60 per cent of all First Nations deaths while incarcerated occurred in police custody. The figure for non-Aboriginal people is 25 per cent.

> In several days of hearings . . . we heard many complaints from Native people relating to their treatment by police. There was a general feeling of frustration and alienation. . . . Many believe it is ineffective to register a complaint. . . . There is a perception that many reactive incident-driven policing methods used in the area are not appropriate to the community situation. . . . One person interviewed commented, 'Just being Native is reason enough for police to stop an individual.' (p. 9)

This study noted lack of communication as one of the key issues in these tragic events. It recommended that communications training be improved and that solutions be devised to overcome systemic discriminatory practices and address attitudes based on racial or cultural prejudice.

e. Tendency to Evaluate

The tendency to evaluate involves how our cultural values influence our **attributions** about other people and the world around us. Different value systems may generate negative evaluations of others, as their different ways of life may impede our ability to communicate with them in a respectful and open manner. In law enforcement, this tendency may lead to frustration, impatience, or hostility on both sides.

Case example: A police officer pulls over a car with a broken headlight. The driver, a woman, appears to be of South Asian origin. Before the officer has a chance to say anything, the male passenger asks, 'Is something wrong?', his tone one of concern. The officer responds that the headlight is broken and asks the driver if she knew this. She looks very nervous and glances over at the male passenger. Before she can respond, the male passenger states, 'No, it was fine yesterday.' The officer asks the woman for her licence and notices that she is not looking directly open to new ways by increasing our knowledge of different cultural patterns, and taking opportunities to adapt our communication styles (Matsumoto & Juang, 2008).

The Global People website and resource bank (see www.globalpeople.org.uk) offers a number of excellent tips and tools to improve intercultural communication skills (Spencer-Oatey & Stadler, 2009). A number of critical skill areas and the components necessary to achieve intercultural communication literacy are offered. These include the following:

- Communication management—The individual can choose the appropriate mode of communication.
- Language learning and language adjustment—An effective intercultural communicator will be motivated to learn and use other languages or adapt language use to the proficiency of the recipient.
- Active listening—The effective communicator is attentive and regularly checks for and clarifies meaning, notices potential misunderstandings, and negotiates for common understanding.
- Attuning—The individual is adept at observing non-verbal language and learns to interpret it appropriately in different cultural and communicative contexts.
- Building shared knowledge and trust—The individual discloses and elicits background information necessary for mutual understanding and can apply visual or written aids. The goals of the communication are clear to both parties.
- Stylistic flexibility—The effective intercultural communicator pays attention to different styles and can flex his or her own style to suit different purposes, contexts, and audiences.

The goal is not to walk into any relationship with any cultural assumptions. The capacity to look beyond someone's race, ethnicity, gender, sexual orientation, family status, or disability to find out who she or he really is, is at the core of cultural competence or cultural literacy in communication. Ultimately, becoming an effective intercultural communicator is more than recognizing and understanding our biases; it is about being able to harness different perspectives to create understanding.

It is imperative that, along with understanding the historical underpinnings of systemic discrimination and the real barriers faced by racialized, Aboriginal, and other marginalized people in our society, criminal justice system personnel be trained to recognize their own communication patterns and to recognize and respect different communication patterns so as to avoid misunderstandings and increase trust in the communities they serve. Effective communication helps police officers to identify additional, alternative courses of action when responding to calls for service. Many police services are incorporating diversity units and training into their organizations to ensure that cultural literacy becomes a tool for good judgment and better decisions. Being good listeners and understanding the importance of verbal and non-verbal communication differences allow officers to defuse potentially violent situations and resolve them in a peaceful manner. Police officers, probation officers, and lawyers adept at interpreting the non-verbal behaviours of others will be more effective interviewers and interrogators. Similarly, effective communication enables criminal justice workers to better support the at him when he speaks to her. Becoming frustrated, he asks her again if she was aware that the headlight was broken. Again the male passenger interrupts and repeats that it was fine yesterday. The officer asks the passenger if this is his vehicle. He responds, 'No, I am her uncle.' Angry now, the police officer tells the passenger to be quiet and asks the woman to get out of the car.

Here we have a clash between law enforcement's expectations that all business will be conducted with the driver of the car and this family's cultural values and norms around gender roles and modesty. The police officer appears rude and impatient, the occupants of the car uncooperative and evasive. Both parties are acting within acceptable parameters of their communication protocols, but both end up with negative evaluations of the other owing to the failure of each to understand these different goals and expectations.

f. High Anxiety or Tension

High anxiety or tension arises often in intercultural communication which can lead to dysfunctional thought process and behaviours—including holding on stubbornly to one's own preconceptions and stereotypes. It is easy to perceive each misstep by the communication partner as affirmation of one's own biases.

These barriers demonstrate that culture and language are intimately related. Culture influences both the structural and functional uses of language. It also reinforces our cultural values and world view, which has implications for understanding different cultural perspectives. For example, in English, the pronoun 'I' is used whenever we are talking about ourselves, regardless of to whom we are speaking, that is, that person's role or status. But in Japan, there are several 'I' pronouns and the one to use depends on our status in relation to the other person, our sex, the degree of politeness expected, our familiarity with the person, and so on. These differences reflect fundamental cultural differences in the importance of group relationships and status. In individualist countries like Canada, there is less emphasis on these variables than there is in a collectivist country like Japan. This is not to say that group relationships and status are not important in both countries, but that the degree of importance varies on a continuum.

In *intra*cultural communication (between people from the same cultural background), people implicitly share the same ground rules and can focus on the content of messages, as they use the same cultural codes to decode the message. If people violate these ground rules, they may be seen as abnormal, bad, or stupid, but more often the violation will be ignored, overlooked, or explained away—'Oh, that's just Paul. He likes to shock people.'

But when we enter an *inter*cultural communication environment (between people from different cultural contexts), we need to be aware that we may not share the same communication ground rules and may thus make negative assumptions about the other person that reinforce our biases. Until we learn to communicate effectively, we will find it difficult to focus on content, since we are too busy trying to code or decode according to different rules. Without effective communication, conflict and misunderstanding are inevitable and can lead to negative reactions. Often we may think or hear that people from a particular cultural background are loud, aggressive, and pushy. What this usually reflects is not a personality pattern, but a different communication pattern, one where louder voice tones, expansive gestures, expressive emotions, and perhaps different proximity needs all combine to be interpreted by someone who does not share these communication patterns as a negative aspect of the *person* or *group* rather than as communication differences. However, instead of making assumptions and negative evaluations, we can use our awareness of different communication patterns to move beyond the *style* of communication to the *content* of the communication.

Acquiring a genuine intercultural communicative capability requires more than learning new ways of saying things; it requires learning new ways of seeing things. The term **'accommodation'** means adjusting our habitual expressive habits in order to facilitate communication with other people. We make our modes of representation converge with theirs. Seasoned international negotiators, for example, routinely adjust their communicative behaviour to people of other cultures by adapting their words, speaking style, cultural references, eye contact, use of silence, and so on. The extent of such accommodation varies greatly from case to case, and it is a two-way street. But you do not have to be a diplomat to accommodate other patterns; this is a skill you already have and practise everyday. When you speak to your grandparent differently than you do to your friends—that is, you choose different words, you speak a little louder and slower, and you avoid jargon and discuss different topics—you are accommodating a communication pattern difference, in this case, a generational difference.

How might these barriers impact the criminal justice system and how can we learn to work with differences, especially non-verbal differences, to foster good communication and community relations? The next sections deal with these questions.

Communication and the Criminal Justice System

Historically, there has been a mutual distrust between various **racialized** and **marginalized** (e.g., gay and lesbian) communities in Canada and the criminal justice systems. The roots of this distrust are systemic and deep (e.g., see Cryderman & O'Toole, 1986; Smith, 2007; Tanovich, 2006; Tator & Henry, 2006), and for some immigrants may reflect their experiences with a corrupt justice system in their homelands. Factors that have influenced this distrust include overt discrimination, racial profiling, police insensitivity, differential policing and criminal justice outcomes, lack of representation of racialized people in the criminal justice system, and poor communication. The latter is what interests us in this chapter. All of the elements that have been discussed that vary from culture to culture, both in verbal and non-verbal behaviour, come into play in interactions with police and justice personnel. To this we add the issue of power.

> Police officers expect individuals to display respectful behaviour towards them. A recent report showed that the police subculture places an emphasis on respect: A good officer demands respect and is able to quickly establish his or her legal authority when dealing with civilians. The subculture also reinforces the belief that it is sometimes okay for

officers to respond to citizen hostility, disrespect or disobedience with violence. Within the police subculture, 'contempt of cop' is an offence that deserves punishment. (Wortley, 2006, p. 11)

For example, police officers attempting to control a hostile situation may establish themselves as the authority and expect or demand that everyone comply with their orders. Those who 'flunk the attitude test' may be more vulnerable to police violence than those who are passive or compliant (Wortley, 2006). In such cases, poor communication or a misreading of communication patterns may only inflame the situation and provoke a violent reaction, thus limiting the officers' options for resolving the incident.

The repercussions of these misunderstandings are critical in situations involving power and authority. Those in positions of power have the authority and mandate to impose on others their values and expectations of appropriate norms and behaviours.

Case example: An African American police officer in Texas relates the response of his white colleagues to the communication styles of young African-American men. He says that when officers enter the community, the young men will come right up into their face, talk loudly with broad gestures, and 'jive' with them. He himself is comfortable with this communication pattern, as he understands it. But it makes his white colleagues very nervous, they stand back, with a hand on their weapon, and have remarked that if he were not there, they would handcuff the young men and take them downtown.

An exercise: Can the above example suggest one reason for the over-policing and over-charging of black youth? A simple communication difference? Debate this issue with your classmates.

One way to minimize disparities in criminal justice experiences is to enhance communication and thus understanding between communities, and to break down damaging and disparaging stereotypes. It is imperative that those working with diverse communities be aware of culturally distinct patterns of verbal and non-verbal communication and barriers to effective intercultural communication. The next section will discuss the non-verbal communication differences we noted earlier, for it is often through this form of communication that misunderstandings arise, particularly in the criminal justice system.

Non-verbal Communication[3]

Emotional Expressivity and Gestures

Cultural differences in facial expression and the amount of emotional expressivity one displays are called **'display rules'**. All cultures have learned norms that govern the display of emotions. In individualist cultures, such as Canada, we have fairly loose cultural display rules; that is, all emotions can be expressed in public spaces, but we value moderate emotional expressivity.

So laugh, but not too loudly; cry, silently; get angry, but don't raise your voice. We may show a wide range of emotions on our faces, but we tend to keep our expression of emotion low-key. In collectivist cultures, such as those in many parts of Asia or in Canada's Aboriginal communities, cultural norms suggest that the mature person shows little facial expression or emotional expressivity in public. Cultures like those found in southern Europe, the Caribbean, and Latin or South America have broad and open emotional expressivity. Attend an Italian wedding or a Jamaican gathering, and you will find loud laughter and voices, lots of hugging, broad expansive gestures, and maybe even people openly weeping. These differences can lead us to think that people are cold or overly emotional, passive or aggressive, shy or obnoxious, when all that is occurring is a difference in display rules. In the criminal justice system, knowledge of different display rules prevents justice workers or juries from misinterpreting emotional cues when listening to a suspect or witness.

Case example: One day at the Multicultural Centre in Calgary, a number of senior East African males were playing cards. They were getting very loud, shouting at each other and slamming fists on the table. The staff became afraid that a fight was about to break out and phoned the police. The police arrived to find a very perplexed group of men who were having fun and saw their boisterous behaviour as normal in this context.

Gestures are also part of emotional expressivity and will differ as cultural display rules vary. In addition, some gestures that we take for granted, like nodding the head for 'yes' or shaking it for 'no', do not mean these things in more collectivist cultures. For example, a lawyer working with a Japanese client recalls all the 'uh-huhs', 'nods', and 'yeses' she observed in a meeting. She believed that her client agreed with her proposal as he nodded and smiled. But what he was doing was expressing understanding and encouragement rather than agreement.

In the criminal justice system, it is easy to see how these different gestures, especially around perceived agreement, could be problematic. The likelihood of misinterpretation increases if the person's first language is not English or French. And, under stressful conditions, as any contact with the justice system tends to be, normative cultural gestures are more likely to be displayed. To ensure that we understand what is intended, it is critical that we check for feedback.

Eye Contact

Eye contact also differs across cultures. Behaviour such as infrequent eye contact or looking down are seen in white Euro-Canadian culture as a signs of dishonesty, lack of confidence, deceit, or timidity. But, in many cultures, people avoid eye contact, especially with authority figures, as a sign of respect, modesty, or deference. This may be especially true of traditional First Nations people, Asian women, and children from many traditional backgrounds. In Canada, we prefer intermittent and direct eye contact. We look at who we are speaking to but look away at intervals. Some Middle Eastern groups may find this disconcerting, as their cultural norm is to maintain steady, direct, and unwavering eye contact to demonstrate interest and respect. A

Euro-Canadian may see this behaviour as threatening or hostile. In the criminal justice system, much emphasis is placed on a person's eye contact. Is the person hostile, threatening, frightened, evasive, lying, disrespectful? Not being aware of different patterns can and does lead to erroneous assumptions about people's intentions, especially with such peoples as African blacks or Middle Eastern individuals, among whom very direct eye contact is often mistaken for hostility, anger, or a threat. The first impulse should be to assess if there is a different cultural, generational, or gender norm in play.

Case example: A Korean man is stopped by the police and questioned, as he fits the description of someone who robbed a corner grocery store. The man politely and quietly answers their questions but avoids eye contact. The police officers feel that he is evasive, fidgety, and is lying, and they take him in for questioning.

In this example, the respectful pattern of communication learned in Korea does not serve this individual well. His lack of eye contact in a Western communication situation, in which direct eye contact is valued, signals evasiveness and dishonesty to police officers unaware of the difference. Note also that the description given to police would likely be of 'an Asian male', an overly broad term in a society that has difficulty distinguishing between people from different parts of Asia.

Touch and Gestures

Groups differ in how and when it is appropriate to touch others, especially women and children. In North America, a firm handshake denotes confidence and good will. In many other cultures, a soft hand laid in yours is a more proper greeting. It should not be construed as 'wimpy' or disinterested. Some cultures, even in business, greet with hugs or kisses on the cheek. This can be between two men, two women, or between opposite sexes. By recognizing these differences in touch as cultural and reserving judgment about the individual with different norms, we can avoid miscommunication and misunderstanding. These sorts of differences are important to community police officers and justice workers when interacting with these communities.

Case example: A police officer was invited to attend a Laotian food festival. While there, he spoke with many people in the community and was enjoying himself immensely. The people were very glad to see the police represented and went out of their way to offer the utmost hospitality. At one point, a young mother approached the officer with a baby in her arms. The officer reached over to stroke the baby's hair as was customary in his culture. The room went silent, with horrified onlookers staring at the officer. He became flustered, not knowing what had changed or why.

In many Southeast Asian cultures, including Laotian, touching a child on the head is taboo, as it is believed to make the child vulnerable to evil spirits or illness. The head is the repository of the soul. For many Euro-Canadians, patting children on the head is a sign of affection.

Loudness and Pitch

In Canada, a person talking very loudly is assumed to be angry or upset. A person speaking very quietly is seen to be timid, passive, or not confident. However, rules about the volume of one's voice differ across cultures and often have little to do with emotion or confidence. But as seen in the example above with the police officer in Texas, if a person uses a tone and volume that is outside of the cultural norms of our criminal justice system, he or she can be viewed as angry, hostile, or threatening.

Personal Space

For Euro-Canadians, the comfort zone in casual conversation is about an arm's-length all around our bodies (except for close friends and family). People who move into that zone are seen as aggressive, pushy, and rude. In other cultures, standing close conveys warmth and sincerity. The result is that the person whose zone has been 'violated' moves away, appearing to the other as standoffish, rude, and unfriendly. How can we communicate effectively if we are worrying about our comfort zone?

> When someone comes too close in an undesirable way, it triggers a physiological reaction in the other person—as heart rate and galvanic skin responses increase. The other person then tries to restore the 'proper' distance by looking away, stepping behind a barrier (desk, chair, table), crossing their arms to create a barrier, pulling back to create space, or tucking in their chins as an instinctive move of protection. They may even rub their neck so that an elbow protrudes sharply toward the invader. (Goman, 2009)

In order to ensure that communication can proceed smoothly, negotiate your personal space needs. If someone is too close or too far for comfort, say, 'It is nothing personal, but I feel more comfortable standing a little closer/further apart', or you can sit down, which creates a different dynamic.

An exercise: Find a partner and have him or her walk toward you, face to face, and ask your partner to stop when you feel you are a comfortable distance apart for conversing. Raise your arms to see how far apart you are. Ask your partner to step closer. See how you both feel. Ask your partner to step farther away. Examine how that feels. Can you communicate when your space is violated?

Outside of cultural differences, those who feel powerful and confident will usually control more physical space, extending their arms and legs and generally taking up more room (Goman, 2009). In doing so, they may unknowingly infringe on another person's territory. Someone may also purposefully stand too close in order to make the other person feel self-conscious or insecure. Police interrogators often use the strategy of sitting close and crowding a suspect. This theory of interrogation assumes that invasion of the suspect's personal space (with no chance for defence) will give the officer a psychological advantage. Police officers also have a proximal safety zone that ranges from three to eight feet depending on the context. If someone invades that zone, a threat may be perceived. This safety procedure may appear to the ordinary citizen as standoffish or rude.

Silence

Gaps and lapses in conversation play a crucial role for allowing the conversation to flow and transition smoothly. However, cultures vary considerably with respect to the conventions where gaps are possible and how long a gap or lapse should be. As a consequence of this, several problems may arise with regard to the communication partners' differing expectations of what constitutes normal behaviour. A speaker, for example, may take his or her turn either too slowly or too quickly owing to miscues. In Canada, we tend to start speaking almost immediately after the first speaker has finished a sentence, whereas for some cultural groups, the pause at the end of a sentence may be longer but may not signify that a person is finished speaking. And so, sometimes, we jump in too quickly and interrupt his or her process. This can lead to a negative evaluation. When communicating with a speaker from another culture, it is useful to slow down your turn-taking and allow for longer gaps until you can observe the flow of speech that will work best for the two of you.

There are many ways in which communication can go awry and lead to misunderstanding. But this review of some common non-verbal communication differences demonstrates how, with awareness, we can become effective intercultural communicators. There is a simple checklist on the next page which can help us stay on track.

The consequences of miscommunication in the criminal justice system can lead to tragedy, as we have seen. However, lesser but still important consequences arise from poor communication. The lack of trust that is engendered by failing to recognize and respect intercultural communication patterns can hurt the recruitment and retention of personnel from racialized, Aboriginal, and other marginalized communities. Victims of crime may be reluctant to report incidents to the police. This is especially true in the case of hate crimes (e.g., see Stewart, 2007). Moreover, individuals in these communities are unlikely to give information to police, report suspicious incidents, or testify in court. In the most extreme cases, these communities may become actively hostile to police, leading to tension and the potential for violence.

Case example: The family of a teen shot by police on the weekend said they were upset to see that a peaceful demonstration against the shooting turned into a riot. Fredy Villanueva, 18, was shot by police on Saturday after officers encountered him and his friends in a park. The officers said they felt threatened and opened fire. . . . Montreal police chief Yvan Delorme has come under fire for the shooting. . . . 'I'd say we never saw anything like this in Montreal,' he said. 'We have to continue the dialogue with the leaders of the community to find solutions. I don't want this to repeat in the future.'

The riot left three police officers and one ambulance worker injured. Among the injured was one female police officer who was shot in the leg. Delorme said she was in stable condition and

A Checklist for Respectful Communication

- Treat all people as individuals. Try to look beyond the cultural background and see the person, but use your cultural knowledge as a guide to avoid misunderstanding.

- Respect personal names. Call people by the name they want to be called. Learn the correct way to pronounce it, the correct order to say it, and the appropriate titles of respect.

- Avoid making generalizations about a whole group based on one or two members.

- Just because one member of a group avoids eye contact doesn't mean they all do! Try to be open to new information about a culture or group of people. We tend to devalue or ignore information that does not agree with our view of the world.

- Avoid making judgments based on the accent, timing, or pace of someone's speech. Different ways of speaking may strike you as stupid, arrogant, passive, or even insulting. Try to view the person objectively, be patient, and don't interrupt.

- Find out how disagreements are handled in the other person's culture. It may be considered unacceptable to say 'No' directly, or 'No' may simply mean that further negotiation is expected.

- Pay attention to gestures. Be careful about the gestures you use and how they might be interpreted. If you are puzzled by someone else's gestures, ask questions. Tell people if they are using inappropriate gestures, but do so in a way that does not make them 'lose face.'

- Adjust your personal space requirements if necessary. People in different cultures may feel very uncomfortable if you stand too close or too far away (by their standards). Notice how closely they stand after they approach you. Pay attention to how they react if you move closer or further away, and find something that works for both of you.

- Be very careful about touching in any way, but don't be surprised if in some cultures strangers greet you with hugs or kisses. You are responsible for establishing comfortable boundaries with respect to these differences.

the bullet didn't cause serious damage. The ambulance worker had a bottle smashed on his head and the other police officers suffered minor injuries. Pierreson Vaval, director of a community outreach group, said the riot was the result of pent-up anger against police. 'The people of this community are complaining about how they are treated,' he said (*The Gazette*, 2008).

Failure to communicate effectively does not only have an impact on racialized and Aboriginal people; it is also of concern to people with physical or mental disabilities. Persons with disabilities are much more likely than persons without limitations to be very dissatisfied with police response to complaints (Statistics Canada, 2009).

Case example: An 18-year-old man was arrested in April 2009 after being mistaken as being intoxicated by police. The man was walking home from a video store at midnight in Mount Pearl, Newfoundland. Police asked him to walk on the sidewalk, and when he failed to comply, he was taken into custody. His mother reported that he was not allowed to make a phone call when he was arrested, nor was he allowed to make a phone call at the police station. At 5:00 a.m. after the family exhausted attempts to locate him, the mother contacted the police to file a missing-person report. She was informed that her son had been arrested for public drunkenness. After she informed the police that her son had autism (and did not drink), he was released. Since this time, Royal Newfoundland Constabulary Chief Joe Browne has made a public apology (CBC News, 2009).

Physical and mental disabilities can be misconstrued as lack of attention, intoxication, aggression, resistance, non-compliance, or a range of other behaviours considered to be suspect in our society. Often these non-verbal behaviours can lead to communication miscues and result in conflict with the criminal justice system.

There is also the intersectionality of identities to consider in communication. We all belong to many different groupings, which become more or less salient given the context. Some of these groupings include sex, socio-economic class, ethnic or socio-racial identity, physical and mental ability, age, and gender/sexual identities. And all of these groupings come into play in our interaction with others. People respond to us based on our membership in various groups and on their own internal attitudes toward members of that group.

Take the example of people who have fetal alcohol spectrum disorder (FASD). The symptoms of this disorder can range from mild to severe, and the impact on communication ability can be profound. Persons with this disorder often come into contact with the criminal justice system. The ability of those with FASD to comprehend may be lower than would be expected, and their inability to read social cues accurately may interfere with their ability to understand the expectations of others (Kellerman, n.d.). They may understand rules and consequences, but still may not understand why they are in trouble. The ability to process information is sporadic and unpredictable. Now add to this mix belonging to the identity group of young, Aboriginal male, a group that is often over-policed and over-represented in the criminal justice system. In a policing context, this intersectionality can easily lead to misunderstandings. First, the bias is set up by the individual's age and ethnicity. Then, the communication difficulties attendant to FASD can lead law enforcement to view the individual as uncooperative, hostile, impulsive, and anxious—all presumed signs of guilt.

A good understanding of the various ways in which communication can go wrong across diverse groups is essential to professional practice. We have seen in this chapter the often severe consequences of miscommunication based on different cultural norms and values and different physical or mental capabilities.

Summary

This chapter has only scratched the surface of the complexities of intercultural communication. To improve communication and avoid conflict, we need to develop mindfulness and reduce uncertainty by becoming aware of our own cultural expectations in communication, being

goals of justice through more accurate witness testimony or assessment of the merits of a case. Readers interested in learning more about this area are encouraged to explore the additional resources provided at the end of this chapter.

Key Terms

accommodation

articulable grounds

attributions

bias-free policing

collectivist

cultural noise

display rules

features of language

individualistic

intercultural communication

intracultural communication

marginalized

paralinguistic

psychological noise

racial profiling

racialized/ racialization

Questions for Critical Thought

1. How can you use this information on the importance of effective intercultural communication in your day-to-day practice as a student, in your home life, or where you work?

2. Can you find examples of instances where poor communication, owing to different communication expectations, has led to serious consequences?

3. What changes, if any, would you make to the criminal justice system (police, courts, corrections) to ensure that justice workers develop effective communication practices to better serve a diverse community?

Additional Readings

Axtell, R. E. (1998). *Do's and Taboos around the World.* New York: John Wiley.

Gudykunst, W. B. (Ed.) (2003). *Cross-cultural and intercultural communication.* Thousand Oaks, CA: Sage.

Hall, E. T. (1981). *Beyond culture.* New York: Anchor Books.

Hall, E. T. (1981). *The silent language.* New York: Anchor Books.

Hall, E. T. (1990). *The hidden dimension.* New York: Anchor Books.

Harris, P. R., & Moran, R. T. (1996). *Managing cultural differences.* Houston: Gulf Publishing.

Lewis, R. D. 1996. *When cultures collide.* London: Nicholas Brealey.

Morrison, T., Conway, W. A., & Borden, G. A. (1994). *Kiss, bow or shake hands, how to do business in sixty countries.* Holbrook, MA: Bob Adams.

Novinger, T. (2001). *Intercultural communication: A practical guide.* Austin: University of Texas.

Tannen, D. (1990). *You just don't understand: Men and women in conversation.* New York: HarperCollins.

Websites of Interest

Global People website and Resource Bank: www.globalpeople.org.uk

Cultural Savvy: www.culturalsavvy.com/index.htm

Culture Briefings: www.culturebriefings.com/index.html

Endnotes

1. Please note that not all people from these regions will reflect these characteristics. There are many language groups, cultures, and ethnicities across these groups, each with its own social norms and patterns, but as a general rule, these characteristics may apply.
2. There are a number of terms used to discuss different communication patterns. 'Intercultural' often refers to communication between members of two different cultures, while 'diversity' is a more general term, indicating differences owing both to cultural factors and to other factors such as gender, socio-economic status, ability, etc. The term 'cross-cultural' is generally used in the United States to describe 'intercultural' interactions. This chapter will use the term 'intercultural' to refer to communication that occurs between people from different ethno-cultural communities as well as diverse communities.
3. It should be noted that these are broad generalizations only and should be used as a tool to guide you. Every member of a cultural group will display aspects of his or her culture in different ways, and some of the traditional communication patterns noted here may not hold true for any given individual.

References

CBC News (2009). *Can't trust police yet, arrested autistic man says.* Retrieved September 27, 2010, from www.cbc.ca/canada/newfoundland-labrador/story/2009/04/24/spurrell-autism-apology-424.html

Cryderman, B. K., & O'Toole, C. N. (1986). *Police, race and ethnicity: A guide for law enforcement officers.* Toronto: Butterworths.

The Gazette. (2008, August 11). Family of Montréal teen shot by police upset about riots. Retrieved October 13, 2009, from www.canada.com/story_print.html?id=9ec92305-9cb6-493a-9271-dd569f0c50bd&sponsor

Hannum, N. (2003). *Aboriginal deaths and injuries in custody and/or with police involvement: An initial survey of information and incidents in British Columbia, Saskatchewan, Manitoba and Ontario.* Report to Native Courtworker and Counselling Association of British Columbia.

Kellerman, T. (n.d.). *Fetal alcohol spectrum disorders: Fact sheet for personnel in law enforcement.* Retrieved August 15, 2009, from www.faslink.org/FASD%20Law%20Enforcement%20Fact%20Sheet.htm

Goman, C. (2009). *Importance of space in a business relationship.* Retrieved October 13, 2009, from http://m.workcabin.ca/index.php?option=com_content&task=view&id=1248&Itemid=153

Matsumoto, D., & Juang, L. (2008). Culture, language and communication. In D. Matsumoto & L. Juang, *Culture and psychology* (4th ed.). Belmont, CA: Thomson Wadsworth.

Smith, C. C. (2007). *Conflict, crisis and accountability: Racial profiling and law enforcement in Canada.* Ottawa: Canadian Centre for Policy Alternatives.

Spencer-Oatey, H., & Stadler, S. (2009). *The Global People competency framework: Competencies for effective intercultural interaction.* Warwick Occasional Papers in Applied Linguistices #3. University of Warwick, Centre for Applied Linguistics.

Statistics Canada. (2006). *2006 Census: Aboriginal peoples in Canada in 2006: Inuit, Métis and First Nations, 2006 Census: Métis.* Catalogue no. 97-558-XIE2006001. Retrieved July 3, 2009, from www12.statcan.ca/census-recensement/2006/as-sa/97-558/p19-eng.cfm

Statistics Canada. (2007, December 4). 2006 Census: Immigration, citizenship, language, mobility and migration. *The Daily.* Retrieved July 3, 2009, from www.statcan.gc.ca/daily-quotidien/071204/dq071204a-eng.htm

Statistics Canada. (2009). *Persons with activity limitations less satisfied with police response.* Canadian Centre for Justice Statistics Profile. Catalogue no. 85F00033M—no. 21. Retrieved August 13, 2009, from www.statcan.gc.ca/pub/85f0033m/2009021/f-r/f-r4-eng.htm

Stewart, C. (2007). *Combating hate and bias crime and incidents in Alberta.* Alberta Hate Crime Committee. Available at www.kanataint.ca/hatecrimereport.pdf

Tanovich, D. (2006). *The colour of justice: Policing race in Canada.* Irwin Law.

Tator, C., & Henry, F. (2006). *Racial profiling in Canada.* Toronto: University of Toronto Press.

Triandis, H. C. (1994). *Culture and social behaviour.* New York: McGraw-Hill.

Wortley, S. (2006). *Police use of force in Ontario.* Toronto: University of Toronto. Retrieved October 13, 2009, from www.attorneygeneral.jus.gov.on.ca/inquiries/ipperwash/policy_part/projects/pdf/African CanadianClinicIpperwashProject_SIUStudybyScot Wortley.pdf

18 | Anti-Racism Training in the Criminal Justice System: A Case for Effective Social Context Education

KAREN R. MOCK

There is an increased awareness of the need to provide focused pre- and in-service education for criminal justice personnel. This includes broad approaches to diversity generally, through what has come to be called social context education, but also more specialized training relevant to particular crimes (e.g., hate crime). This chapter will provide a brief overview of the background to current approaches to diversity and anti-racism training in Canada, and will explore some of the important caveats learned to date with respect to various means of delivering such training to various constituents in the justice sector.

Background and Rationale for Anti-Racism Training

When **multiculturalism** was declared an official policy of Canada in 1971, the government began to support heritage languages and activities of ethnocultural communities, as well as continuing its earlier programs designed to enhance long-term integration. Throughout the 1970s, the emphasis of multicultural programming was on cultural retention and cultural sharing—that is, on 'celebrating our differences'—with the initiative for the direction of the programs coming from the groups themselves. At the same time, removal of some of the systemic barriers in our immigration policy began to allow fairer access to Canada, and the voices of racial minorities began to be heard. There was a greater push nationally and internationally for equality and justice for all minority groups. Along with the multiculturalism policy, there were several related developments in the early 1970s. **Hate propaganda**, the promotion of hatred against identifiable groups, became a criminal offence in Canada in 1970, when the **hate crime** laws were adopted as amendments to the Criminal Code (sections 318–320). That same year, Canada ratified the **International Convention on the Elimination of All Forms of Racial Discrimination**, which had been adopted by the United Nations (UN) in 1965 and signed by Canada in 1966. The Canadian government began to give more attention to equality issues. **The Canadian Human Rights Act** of 1977, and various provincial human rights codes were also enacted to provide greater protection of minority rights.

In 1982 the **Canadian Charter of Rights and Freedoms** entrenched multiculturalism and equality rights in the constitution and called on the whole Charter to be interpreted in a way that 'preserves and enhances the multicultural heritage of Canada'. The Charter guaranteed equal protection and benefit of the law, free from discrimination on the basis of race, national or ethnic origin, colour, and religion. In the 1980s, amendments to various **human rights codes** provided the provincial human rights commissions the power to monitor and enforce those rights, strengthened in Ontario, for example, by the Race Relations Division of the Human Rights Commission. In 1984 the National Association of Japanese Canadians (NAJC) published *Democracy Betrayed,* making public the history of Japanese Canadians, and launched the campaign for redress for the complete abrogation of human and civil rights of Japanese Canadians (National Association of Japanese Canadians, 1984). And the *Equality Now!* Task Force (1984) and **Employment Equity Commission** (1984) pointed out **systemic racism** in education, the media, health services, the criminal justice system and employment across the country (Canada, 1984a, 1984b). Their reports called for the immediate implementation of measures to combat discrimination and increase equity for disadvantaged and vulnerable groups. In 1985 the Urban Alliance on Race Relations and the Social Planning Council published *Who Gets the Work?* (Henry & Ginsberg, 1985), and their research was unequivocal in finding blatant discrimination in both hiring practices and the workplace. And, all the while, there were ongoing rumours and reports of harassment of minorities by the police and differential treatment by the justice system as a whole.

By the mid-1980s, evaluation of the implementation of earlier policies and practices (in school boards and other public institutions) was disappointing indeed. Any attempt at real organizational change was met with resistance and resulted in further marginalization of the staff, who were trying to combat racism and effect change. Research and evaluation studies in education, media, policing, health, and justice revealed very little movement in this area. It was also clear that effective race relations training in each of these sectors was sorely lacking. Parents and community groups were becoming more vocal in their demands for equitable treatment in schools. Backlogs were increasingly jamming up the human rights commissions. And all the while alleged police harassment and even shootings of minorities, in particular black youth, increased. Clearly, celebrating our differences was not enough. Many of us knew what had to be done, and having the courage to name the problem and use the language was a start.

A report by Masemann and Mock titled *Access to Government Services by Racial Minorities* (1987) reveals that differential treatment of minorities appeared to be the norm, resulting in lack of equal access to services, as well as in frustration, alienation, and continued feelings of marginalization and helplessness among racial minorities. My *Race Relations Training Manual* (Mock, 1988), developed for the Ontario Race Relations Directorate in 1988, outlines training strategies for the various sectors. And our study titled *Implementing Race and Ethnocultural Equity Policy in Ontario School Boards* (Mock & Masemann, 1990) documents the barriers to implementation and the key factors in success, and calls on the government to mandate such policies and to begin so by cleaning up its own act in the area of equitable practices and multicultural **anti-racist education**. We could now use the words. The multiculturalism policy and its programs had enabled us to do the research, gather the data, and have the conferences—but then what? Many of the task forces, commissions, and research studies of the 1980s, and all their recommendations, represent the collective voices of many marginalized and victimized Canadians, voices summarized and then silenced in reports on shelves.

But the concerns of the 1980s were heard loudly and clearly, and it was eventually recognized that equality issues were the results of systemic inequalities—of power imbalances—and therefore beyond the capability of individuals or communities to resolve. In other words, the cooperation and active involvement of government and institutions were required to achieve such goals as employment equity and the acceptance (not just tolerance) of all communities as part of the so-called mainstream. These concepts are at the core of the 1988 Canadian Multiculturalism Act.

It is clearly stated in the Act that it 'recognizes the diversity of Canadians as regards to race, national or ethnic origin, colour and religion as a fundamental characteristic of Canadian society.' And embedded in the Act is the notion that it is also 'designed to preserve and enhance the multicultural heritage of Canadians while working to achieve the equality of all Canadians in the economic, social, cultural and political life of Canada.' As an act of Parliament, the Multiculturalism Act is directed at *all* Canadians, not just at ethnocultural or racial minority communities. The 1988 Act gave government institutions responsibility to implement multicultural organizational change, and the Department of Multiculturalism provided programming not just for community groups, but also for so-called mainstream institutions (police, health care facilities, education, social service, the arts), to develop and implement multiculturalism policies and programs to address equality of access and service delivery. The Act explicitly recognized the special status of Aboriginal peoples. In addition, it resulted in multiculturalism being no longer embedded within a bilingual framework, but each now had its own legislative and constitutional basis. With the policy enacted into legislation in 1988, there was indeed cause for celebration.

In 1988 there was also celebration among Japanese Canadians and all those who were part of the coalition lobby when redress was achieved. The NAJC negotiated the creation of the Canadian Race Relations Foundation (CRRF) as part of the Japanese Canadian Redress Agreement, and the **Canadian Race Relations Act** was passed in 1990. Through the redress agreement and the creation of the CRRF, the government reaffirmed the principles of justice and equality for all citizens in Canada and pledged to ensure that such violations would not happen again.

But in 1989 yet another police shooting in Toronto's black community created such an outcry that the Task Force on Race Relations and Policing was convened in Ontario to receive public deputations. Within in a very short time the task force came up with concrete recommendations to improve police/community relations. The work was intense, the stories gut wrenching, the recommendations concrete—these included strong recommendations for cross-cultural and race relations training at all levels of the criminal justice system, echoing those in *Equality Now!* Some recommendations were implemented, but most were not, so it was not surprising that several years later, in May 1992, after the so-called riot on Yonge Street, the Stephen Lewis commission (Lewis, 1992) on anti-black racism heard deputation after deputation on the very same issues. In fact, the League for Human Rights of B'nai Brith's testimony to the Metropolitan Toronto Police Services Board that I delivered on May 28, 1992, contained excerpts from our brief to the Task Force on Race Relations and Policing and to the Standing Committee on the Administration of Justice that had been delivered fully two and three years earlier; that is, very little change, if any, had occurred. The task of turning theory and policy into practice was and remains challenging indeed.

Since it is beyond the scope of this chapter to provide a detailed history of this work, fast forward 15 years and many task forces and reports later—from the 1995 report of the Commission on Systemic Racism in the Ontario Criminal Justice System, chaired by David Cole, to the report of the Hate Crimes Community Working Group, *Addressing Hate Crime in Ontario*, which I chaired for the attorney general and minister of community safety and correctional services in 2006, and several in between from jurisdictions across the country. The common denominator in all reports related to the justice system was the call for effective education and training to better prepare professionals and practitioners in all sectors of the system to meet the needs of our diverse society and thus enhance and ensure fairness and justice for all.

From Multiculturalism to Anti-Racism to Equity

According to research conducted by the Canadian Race Relations Foundation (2003), the difference between a diversity or multicultural program and anti-racism training is sometimes blurred. Generally, anti-racist work addresses issues of **power** and **privilege**, while a multicultural approach may focus on understanding, acceptance, and even celebration of diversity as a primary means for achieving harmonious communities. While anti-racist training acknowledges the need to respect differences, it also tries to address the more complex issues of how people are treated unfairly as a result of their racial identity. An anti-racist approach explores the reasons why so-called visible or racialized minorities often have greater difficulty finding work and housing, and are less likely to be treated fairly, respectfully, and equitably. Ultimately, the goal of anti-racism work is the elimination of racial **discrimination** in all its forms—individual and systemic. Anti-racism training acknowledges that different people, in different parts of Canada, experience and feel the impact of racism differently. Anti-racism training is more overtly politicized than a cross-cultural approach. It acknowledges the historical oppression of people of colour and calls for overt action against racism and other barriers to equality.

In the early years of police and judicial education in Canada's multicultural society, the emphasis was on intercultural or cross-cultural communication, that is, on dealing with difference rather than on identifying and removing the barriers to equality and justice. Racism was rarely named or addressed in a meaningful way. Guest speakers would be invited from various ethno-racial groups to describe their experiences, backgrounds, and culture, with the goal of increasing awareness and understanding differences.

There was often resistance to these programs, a common complaint being that they were 'soft' and did not deal with substantive law. Some participants would undercut the credibility of presenters, regardless of their expertise, by alleging that they were from special interest groups. There was a tendency in those days (and sometimes there still is) to undervalue the kind of experience, expertise, and skill required to do effective diversity, anti-racism or hate crimes training. Police and judges usually prefer to have in-house personnel deliver the programs and workshops. But when skilled professionals from diverse communities have reviewed the training materials and case studies prepared by inexperienced trainers who have jumped on the bandwagon, they often find stereotypical descriptions of minorities. On a few occasions police officers have asked me if I can give them a two- or three-day course so they can learn to 'do what I do'. I smile and answer, 'Yes!—if you can give me a two- or three-day course so I can be a police officer!'

There is no question that there is value in learning about the impact of culture and ethnicity on behaviour. As Justice Katherine Swinton puts it (1996), the programs that provide cross-cultural awareness training are designed to provide background to help raise judicial awareness about issues in future cases; and while some judges fear that this is an inappropriate way of acquiring evidence outside the courtroom, it should not be seen in this way. Rather, Swinton concludes, such training is only one of the many ways that judges' knowledge of our society and legal system can be enriched, in much the same way as reading, television viewing, or personal conversations with friends and family help shape attitude and awareness. I had a participant in a training session suggest to me that if he spent time with members of a particular minority community, it might compromise his judicial independence, and he therefore shouldn't become too familiar with a particular group. When I asked him who he played cards with, or attended church with, and then asked if anyone ever suggested he was unsuitable to adjudicate cases when the accused was a member of his own ethnic or religious group, it was as if a light went on in his head. It had never occurred to him that, as a member of the so-called dominant group, he was immersed in and very familiar with one particular racial/cultural/religious group— and his unbiased adjudication of members of his own group was never questioned or even considered an issue.

For the most part, the early programs did not address structural or systemic discrimina-tion. However, today there is strong consensus that at the core of most effective training programs is an understanding of history and context; a grasp of the principles, dynamics, and impact of power and powerlessness; and practical applications relevant to the work-place, social context, and/or political climate. In other words, as can be seen below, we have moved from multicultural education to training grounded in anti-racism—or anti-oppression—theory and practice. As others have indicated (Hier, Lett, & Bolaria, 2009), we find ourselves at a unique historical moment. Unlike any other time in Canadian history, the institutional infrastructure is now in place to push ethno-racial equality in employment and service delivery to a level that was difficult to imagine even 10 years ago, including in the justice system.

The Development of Social Context Education

In her paper for the National Judicial Institute on *Judicial Impartiality and Social Context Education*, Swinton (1996) points out that in our society, where equality is a constitutional norm, members of some groups have challenged the alleged impartiality of the justice system, suggesting that 'social context education' (sometimes called 'judicial awareness education') needs to deal with the social setting within which judicial decision-making occurs, with particular attention to equality concerns of groups that have suffered discrimination, including women, racial minorities, those with disabilities, and Aboriginal people. In spite of the challenges this poses, particularly from naysayers who feel it may compromise judicial independence, Swinton argues for such education as a way to pursue greater impartiality in the justice system.

Many well-designed studies have shown unexplained discrepancies in the treatment of racial minorities and Aboriginal peoples within the criminal justice system. Thus, it is reasonable to conclude that there is a measure of unconscious bias or systemic racial discrimination in the system that affects decisions about, for example, pretrial release or incarceration rates (Commission on Systemic Racism in the Ontario Criminal Justice System, 1995, chap. 5). It has also been shown that women face greater obstacles than men in credibility assessments in courts (Schafran, 1995). There is consensus that religion, family history, relationships, region, career experiences, financial circumstances, physical or mental condition, and gender—among many other factors—have some impact on the fact-finding process and the interpretation of the law. As Swinton (1996) explains in her overview, which is summarized in the section below, it is precisely the impact of these factors that is addressed in **social context education**.

The Case for Social Context Education

The Canadian Judicial Council passed a unanimous resolution in 1994 approving the concept of a 'comprehensive, in-depth, credible program on social context issues which includes race and gender'. Many efforts have been made to provide this kind of judicial education, with programs offered by the Canadian Institute for the Administration of Justice, the Western Judicial Education Centre, the Canadian Association of Provincial Court Judges, and the courts of various jurisdictions. In 1996 the federal Department of Justice agreed to fund an ambitious effort by the National Judicial Institute (formerly the Canadian Judicial Centre) in Ottawa to develop social context programs for delivery throughout the country. The institute was created in 1988 to provide educational programs for federally and provincially appointed judges.

As Swinton's (1996) overview describes, social context education can perform a number of functions. At its basic level, the objective is to ensure non-discriminatory conduct by judges and court personnel, emphasizing the use of appropriate language (such as gender neutrality), the use of proper forms of address for those from different cultural groups, an avoidance of improper references (such as the assumption that all members of visible minority groups are immigrants), and facility in cross-cultural communication methods. Other issues that might be covered relate to appropriate behaviour—for example, the use of various oaths or affirmations and the role of interpreters. This kind of education is provided in the National Judicial Institute videos *Judicial Awareness: Race, Culture and the Courts and Gender Equality*, as well as by panels at various conferences on sexist language.

A second objective of social context education is to broaden a judge's base of knowledge. Here, the emphasis is on increased awareness of the characteristics, needs, and values of a group or of the magnitude of the legal problems confronting them. Examples could include information about Aboriginal spirituality, the incidence of domestic violence or its impact on children, the belief structures of various religions, or the problems of those with disabilities in gaining access to the legal system. The information presented ranges from the empirical (e.g., the incidence of female poverty or the changing demography of Canada) to the interdisciplinary and the personal (e.g., presentations by specialists in fields other than law, by individuals from these groups, or by those who work with them—specialists in psychology might talk about battered women's syndrome; Aboriginal elders might discuss spirituality and community traditions; victims of sexual assault might describe their experience with the justice system).

A further objective of social context education requires judges to evaluate the meaning of equality, both within the Charter and as a broader social norm. This can lead to discussions of equality in relation to a range of legal issues, in an extrapolation from the decisions of the Supreme Court of Canada.

These objectives can be pursued through a variety of educational techniques. One possible method is **self-teaching**, whether through reading or through the use of materials specially designed for judges. The National Judicial Institute, for example, provides videos on race and culture and on gender issues, along with manuals of readings and questions, to all newly appointed federal and provincial judges. This approach focuses on new judges rather than incumbents, and it does not provide a forum for discussion of issues that often warrant examination in light of judges' practical experience.

A second model for delivery can be called the **integration** approach, where social context issues are featured as part of a larger program of judicial education. This might take the form of one panel on equality issues within a larger conference dealing with a full range of issues—for example, a discussion of family violence as one element of a program that included recent developments in civil procedure, criminal law, or evidence. Alternatively, a conscious effort can be made to bring out equality issues in every panel where these issues are relevant.

A third model is what Swinton (1996) refers to as the **immersion** approach, pioneered in Canada by the Western Judicial Education Centre (WJEC) and emulated in a number of other jurisdictions internationally. Under the leadership of Judge Douglas Campbell, then of the British Columbia Provincial Court, assisted by Judges David Arnot and Gerald Seniuk of Saskatchewan and Professor Peter Mackinnon, then dean of the College of Law of the University of Saskatchewan, the WJEC organized a series of 'full immersion' courses on gender, Aboriginal, and race issues, primarily for western provincial court judges.

An Innovative and Exemplary Model

I was honoured to serve as a principal advisor and program consultant (along with Mobina Jaffer) for the development and delivery of the WJEC's Seminar on Racial, Ethnic and Cultural Equity, held at the University of Saskatchewan, Saskatoon, June 1992. The overall goal of the seminar is described in the introduction to the binder of resource materials as follows: 'To begin the process of examining and understanding the nature and extent of racism in Canada and its impact on the justice system, and to examine strategies to address racism in all its forms' (Western Judicial Education Centre, 1992).

The WJEC's innovative programs were different in scope and approach from other judicial education courses. They were based on the openly articulated philosophy that there is systemic discrimination in Canadian society and the legal system against women, Aboriginal people, and racial and ethnic minority groups. The clearly expressed goal was to examine and address equality issues in the hope that this would increase public faith in the judicial system by creating a more empathetic judiciary.

The WJEC's programs ran for several days in a residential setting, as they were designed to be immersion, not conference, learning. The premise of the organizing team of judges, academics, practising lawyers, and other resource persons was that it was necessary to bring judges together for a significant period of time in order to promote effective communication of and appropriate reflection on the material. Utilizing **adult learning principles**, the programs included a variety of formats, including dramatizations, videos, panels, speakers, and small discussion groups. The latter were a central element of the WJEC approach. While the plenary sessions of panels or presentations involved judges, academics, individuals able to present facts about and concerns of the groups under study, and others offering various kinds of expertise, it was in the small discussion groups that the judges had the opportunity for frank discussion in a safe setting.

The WJEC planning process included a diverse team and a 'training of trainers' component, so that specially trained members of the judiciary could facilitate the discussion groups. For the program on gender equality, two pre-trained judges (one male and one female) worked with each discussion group, but for the course on race and ethnicity, because of the additional expertise required, a trained judge was joined by an experienced anti-racism practitioner to facilitate the breakout sessions. Participants remained with the same small group throughout the five-day seminar. As expected, reactions were mixed, but an evaluation report by Professor Norma Winkler described the WJEC model for judicial social context education as 'extraordinarily successful . . . the most in-depth and sophisticated treatment on this subject that I have observed in either the United States or Canada' (Winkler, 1992).

Perhaps an excerpt from our foreword to the binder of resource materials best explains the values of the program and the key elements that led to its success:

> As far as we knew, there had never been a major conference for judges in Canada on the topic of racism, but we accepted the challenge for several reasons. First, it appeared the leaders of the planning committee were genuinely interested in consultation with and participation

by the community. During our initial meetings it was clear that community concerns and suggestions were to be taken seriously and that they would be part of the ongoing planning, developing a partnership in the process. Indeed, even *we* were brought into the process on the basis of community referrals. Secondly, the seminar model developed by the WJEC is one that is conducive to effective learning—a combination of stimulating plenary sessions, innovative and enjoyable programs, and ongoing small group discussions where ideas can be shared and discussed openly—and supplemented by an excellent collection of readings and resources, providing an opportunity for greater depth and ongoing development.

And thirdly, we agreed to accept the challenge because there was a commitment to our being able to model what this work is really about—breaking down the barriers to equality; that is, the program would be delivered by an eclectic team of women and men from diverse racial, cultural and professional backgrounds as facilitators, resource persons and concerned community members, using a planning process that emphasized co-operation and consensus building. . . . Such a model of shared power and partnership ultimately provides the strongest program and the greatest commitment to and understanding of the issues. (Jaffer & Mock, 1992, p. iii)

Various other groups have emulated the WJEC model, including the Ontario Provincial Court Judges Association at their May 1996 annual meeting, a three-day conference on 'The Court in an Inclusive Society'. Again, the format was a mix of panels, speakers, and discussion groups, with the latter offering a forum for judges to speak mainly to each other about issues related to judging in a racially diverse society. However, in recent years, with funding and workload challenges, most training programs (where they exist at all) have reverted to one-day programs of primarily plenary sessions or breakout workshops (as opposed to in-depth discussion sessions), or two-and-a-half-day courses or annual conferences that integrate one or two sessions on topics related to anti-racism and equity or other social context issues. Even where outstanding programs have been developed, their continuity and success usually rest on the enthusiasm and dedication of one person. When he or she moves on, the program often wanes if it has not been institutionalized and made an ongoing part of the business of the system. We see this happening over and over again in every sector of the justice system—police, corrections, government, academia, the judiciary, and the court system.

Choosing (and Sustaining) the Optimum Model

There is value in offering social context education in a variety of forms, both as an element of any judicial education program, where equality issues are relevant, and as a larger immersion program closer to the approach of the WJEC. The integration model emphasizes that equality issues are pervasive in the practice of law and judging today, rather than being some problem detached from judging and of concern only to interest groups. However, there is a real advantage in the immersion model, because it gives judges time to discuss and reflect on what can be troubling and difficult issues affecting groups disadvantaged by the legal system. There is consensus among those who have given this topic significant thought that some period of immersion is important for judges who have not confronted the equality issues that arise with respect to gender, race, or disability. A single panel on or periodic references to equality issues would be a much less effective way to educate judges on these issues, especially if the information is presented in a fairly passive format, with speakers and listeners provided little chance for interchange (Swinton, 1996). Regretfully, many jurisdictions still rely on this latter format of panels and speakers, usually rushed through with little or no opportunity for meaningful discussion, although there are many more effective models available.

Overcoming Resistance

Experienced anti-racism practitioners, along with several members of the judiciary with experience in this area, have concluded that there are a number of factors to address in order to maximize the success of training programs. Some judges remain resistant to this type of education, the most extreme claiming that it is indoctrination for the purpose of 'political correctness', which they think unwarranted at best and an interference with judicial independence at worst. Negative reaction is especially strong when seminars or courses are deemed to be compulsory.

There is no question that little can be achieved if the audience is fiercely resistant. However, recently, several models of judicial leadership and peer commitment have encouraged reluctant individuals to participate. For example, social context sessions have been increasingly incorporated into the annual meetings of judges in particular courts and introduced by the chief justice. Additionally, compulsory training for judges in both gender and racial issues was recommended by the Canadian Bar Association's Task Force on Gender Equality in the Legal Profession (Canadian Bar Association, 1993).

As described above, concerns about independence must be recognized as an important consideration. And it must also be emphasized that judges have to act on the evidence and law before them, so that some of the changes sought by groups and individuals may have to come from either the highest level of court, legislative action, or societal change. One safeguard for judicial independence is provided by close judicial control of the training programs. For example, the National Judicial Institute's initiative was co-directed by two judges working with an advisory panel and curriculum groups that reached beyond the judiciary to bring in various forms of expertise.

It is important to note that the delivery of high-quality social context education is a long-term process, while judicial time available for educational program is limited. The Canadian goal of 10 days of education for each judge annually is often not feasible, given the pressures from crowded dockets. And judges perceive a wide range of topics in which they would like educational programming, so competition is great for scarce available time. Several judges have suggested that key topics warrant relief from their sitting time, rather than encroaching on their judgment-writing days or vacation, thereby demonstrating the judicial system's commitment to this important and timely area of education.

As Swinton (1997) concludes, social context education, well designed and sensitive to the judicial task, is an important instrument to lessen the appearance of judicial partiality and move us toward an inclusive method of judging that will, in the end, make for greater impartiality in the system.

National Justice Institute—Social Context Education Project

In 1996 the National Judicial Institute (NJI) initiated the Social Context Education Project (SCEP), envisaged as a national program that would build on earlier work begun by the Western Judicial Education Centre (WJEC). Then chair (now Justice) Lynn Smith (1996) explained that the NJI has been assisted in this work by a number of important factors, factors that anti-racism practitioners have deemed to be essential to the success of such training programs—law/policies, commitment, long-term integration, community involvement, and leadership. The key factors to the success of the NJI's Social Context Education Project can be summarized as follows:

• *Mandated by law*
Equality and contextual judicial inquiry are not optional but are mandated by law in Canada through our constitution and accession to relevant international conventions. It is an explicit ethical obligation of Canadian judges to 'conduct themselves and proceedings before them so as to assure equality according to law' (*Ethical Principles*). Increased judicial awareness of social context, then, is not only essential to good judging, but required by law.

Note: Last year the Ontario Court of Justice developed and adopted a 'discrimination and harassment policy'. The policy applies only to contacts between judicial officers. As a result, in October 2009, 30 judges and justices of the peace attended a two-day seminar to prepare them to act as advisors and mediators for the implementation of this new policy and to give some insights into the social context of discrimination. This year I was pleased to contribute to a half-day seminar on 'equity and inclusiveness in the justice system' that was provided to all deputy judges in Ontario as part of the annual compulsory Caswell Seminar and based on the articulated Ethical Principles.

• *Complemented by judicial commitment to contextual inquiry*
Senior judges, including members of the Supreme Court of Canada, have expressed their view that social context is a legitimate and necessary part of judicial decision making and judicial education. Justice Iacobucci has argued that 'understanding the Canadian social context and incorporating this into the process of adjudication requires that we always bear in mind the moral underpinnings of our Constitution and in particular the fundamental principle of equality' (2001). Justice L'Heureux-Dubé, has pointed to 'the importance of ensuring that courts remain attentive to historical patterns of discrimination in determining whether a particular rule, inference, or presumption is based on myth or stereotype and therefore violates constitutional guarantees of equality' (2001a). In her view, 'contextual inquiry is an attempt to attack the problem of privilege and to understand the diversity of people's experiences.' When issues are examined in context, it becomes clear that some so-called objective truths may only be the reality of a select group in society and may, in fact, be completely inadequate to deal with the reality of other groups' (2001b).

• *Based on the premise that this is a long-term process that has integration of social context as the long-range goal*
Further to the emphasis provided by Swinton, it is agreed by the leadership of NJI that social context education should not be regarded as 'an inoculation' to be received through stand-alone or 'one off' conferences; but

rather it is a long-term and continuing process, the long-term goal of which is to make social context factors 'automatically part of the landscape, in the same way that discussion of tax implications would automatically form part of any program on estate planning' (Smith, 1996). Smith also pointed out that this would require efforts to reach all judges 'to create a common base of information and understanding' and to develop a cohort of judicial education leaders.

- *Enhanced by community involvement*
An important principle of judicial education pioneered by SCEP was outreach to the community and efforts to foster a two-way dialogue between judges and communities outside the adversarial setting of the courtroom. This took three forms:

1. *Using non-judges as faculty members*. This included drawing on non-lawyer community members as faculty members and, in some cases, as members of planning committees. This began a long-term shift at NJI away from a model of judicial education as 'J3' (judges talking to other judges about judgments) and foreshadowed acceptance at NJI of the 'three pillars' principle of judicial education (involvement of judges, academics, community practitioners). Having a broadly representative planning group and a range of faculty members helps to ensure appropriate understanding of issues, high-quality content, and widespread credibility of programming.
2. *Significant efforts at community consultation*. Two formal community consultations were undertaken to enhance two-day dialogue between judges and communities. This initiative has been piloted further in Phase II of the project with Nova Scotia initiating a permanent community–judicial liaison process.
3. *Working closely with advisors*. The NJI convened a National Advisory Committee comprised of judicial leaders, academics, and community members, and works with the committee throughout its activities.

- *Fostered by judicial leadership*
Successful social context education for judges requires the commitment of chief justices and chief judges, the involvement of respected judicial leaders in each court in program planning and delivery, and close coordination with judicial education committees. In Canada, chief justices supported the social context initiative through resolutions of the Canadian Judicial Council, through constituting education committees in their courts to plan and deliver social context seminars, and through dedicating court-based education meetings to the subject of social context. This high-level of judicial leadership sends the strong message that this work is considered to be credible and of a high priority for all judges.

NJI's Seminar on Race, Law and Judging

The National Judicial Institute develops and delivers education programs for federally appointed judges across Canada, including for provincial superior court judges. Provincially appointed judges are also able to attend many of these programs. To illustrate the significant progress that has been made in the implementation of what can be deemed to be anti-racism training in the judiciary, the following description was offered during the NJI's three-day seminar on race, law, and judging held in Halifax last year:

> This seminar will explore the relevance of race to what judges do, paying attention to the past and present of racial equality in Canada, and to the role of law and the judicial system

in either hindering or enhancing racial equality. The situation and experiences of both immigrant and indigenous racialized communities will be addressed. The program will also examine key terminology and concepts such as race, racialization, racial stereotyping and discrimination, systemic discrimination, identity construction, race consciousness and racial literacy. Using active learning formats, the seminar will consider whether, when and how judges might take account of racial context in a variety of areas, likely including the Charter and law enforcement (racial profiling), credibility and risk assessment, child protection and civil damages. Issues of judicial notice and expert evidence will be addressed. The seminar will take advantage of the educational resources of the local environment including, for instance, the Pier 21 Immigration Museum. Continuing the tradition of the NJI 'Emerging Issues' seminars, participants will also be invited to participate in a movie club with a Canadian film-maker whose work engages race issues. Throughout, the seminar will focus on skills, applications and practical approaches for judging. (National Judicial Institute, 2009)

The language used to describe the NJI seminar illustrates the facility with which anti-racism/anti-oppression terminology, concepts, and techniques are used and taught. Presenters in Halifax included several senior judges as well as anti-racism and diversity practitioners from school boards, policing services, and Aboriginal organizations, and several academics with relevant expertise from various law faculties. A review of the curriculum of this important course reveals how current the material is in terms of anti-racism/anti-oppression theory and practice. For example, the introduction includes such topics as 'Race in Canada: Facts and Figures' and 'Race and Judging', prompting judges to offer personal reflections on their experiences involving race in the courtroom and participants to reflect on their own experiences. And a session on 'First Nations: Colonialism, Racism, Inequality & Identity' provides detailed information on the impact of colonialism and racism on First Nations peoples. The main segment is a case study on the residential schools policy, the experience of Aboriginal peoples under that policy, and the resulting legacy, with consideration of the implications of this legacy for tasks of judges.

The session on 'Racism, Race Consciousness and Racial Literacy' is described in the syllabus as including learning exercises and providing information on key concepts and terminology, addressing questions such as the following:

- What do we mean by the terms 'race', 'racism', and 'racialization'?
- How is language 'raced'?
- Why do we experience discomfort when issues of race and racism are raised?
- How can we become more comfortable?
- What is 'white privilege'?

The course description also specifies that the session would seek to identify and define appropriate means by which judges might enhance their capacity to approach race issues effectively, and that concepts such as 'colour-blindness', 'race consciousness', and 'racial literacy' would be explored.

The session on 'Recent Inquiries and Research' provided information on studies of the impact of racial stereotyping and discrimination on the experiences of people and their attitudes toward the justice system. The session also explores the extent to which racialized youth 'trust' the legal system and the implications of this for the legal system, courts, and judges.

The case study on 'Racial Stereotyping and Bail' begins with a video of a mock bail hearing and invites discussion of what action a judge might take and why. This is followed by a presentation on recent research on racial stereotyping and the administration of criminal process. Participants are then invited to reflect on their earlier discussions in light of this research.

A presentation on 'Race, Profiling, Judicial Notice, and Proof' is followed by a case study on 'Sentencing, Systemic Discrimination, and Racial Stereotyping' that provides an opportunity to explore the relevance of systemic discrimination to judicial decision making in the context of sentencing of Aboriginal offenders and non-Aboriginal racialized offenders.

The remaining sessions in this innovative and timely course include 'Restorative Justice and Racialized Youth', which emphasizes the role of the judge in youth justice matters involving racialized youth, both in court and in community justice processes more generally; 'Race, Children, and Families', which explores the significance of race in child protection, child custody, and access matters, including legal and social work perspectives; and 'Racial Discounting and Deflation (Damages)', which explores the role of racial criteria in the assessment of civil damages.

It is important and also gratifying to note that the National Judicial Institute's course on 'Race, Law, and Judging' also examines the profession itself. The concluding session of the seminar devotes a half day to 'Racism and the Legal Profession: Issues and Anti-Racism Initiatives', which addresses the systemic nature of racism, how professional development assists in understanding and identifying systemic racism, and remedial programs to overcome systemic discrimination. This session also addresses the experiences of racialized lawyers in the courtroom and in the legal profession generally. In the Halifax course, practical illustration of these phenomena included an overview of two Nova Scotia anti-racism initiatives: the Indigenous Blacks and Mi'kmaq Initiative at Dalhousie Law School and the Equity Program of the Nova Scotia Barristers' Society. The speakers discussed the programs and indicated how successful they have been in increasing the number of practising lawyers from racialized groups. They also provided a frank discussion of the response to the programs by lawyers and the difficulties experienced in having the programs accepted.

Hate Crimes Training

One of the specialized forms of training in the criminal justice system that involves an anti-racism component is training that is designed to raise awareness of and enhance skills in identifying hate crime and bringing criminals who perpetrate them to justice. The Hate Crimes Community Working Group (HCCWG) was convened in 2005 by the attorney general and the minister of community safety and correctional services and reported to the Ontario govern-ment in 2006. The group's work, including extensive community consultations, is summar-ized in two volumes, which also include local, national, and international resources in this important area (Ministry of the Attorney General, 2006). The HCCWG determined that there were several ongoing initiatives, including training programs, in Ontario and across Canada.

Police-Based Initiatives

Policing Standards Guidelines: Section 29 of the Adequacy and Effectiveness of Police Services regulation under the Police Services Act (PSA) requires that police services boards have policies on investigating hate propaganda and hate- or bias-motivated crime. Section 12(1) (h) also requires the chief of police to develop and maintain procedures on and processes for under-taking and managing these investigations.

Ontario Police College (OPC): Under the Police Services Act, officers are required to complete an initial period of training within six months of being appointed to a police service. The OPC is responsible for administering provincial basic training to all new recruits in Ontario. The 13 topics include anti-racism, community policing, and federal and provincial statutes. There is mandatory training related to hate crimes as part of the community policing module.

Ontario Provincial Police (OPP): The OPP has a Hate Crime/Extremism Unit, mandated to conduct multi-jurisdictional strategic and intelligence operations targeting individuals or organized groups involved in hate crime activity and criminal extremism. They collect, evaluate, collate, analyze, disseminate, and utilize intelligence on targeted activities; provide specialized investigative support; contribute to and maintain a database; share information with other law enforcement and/or government agencies; and assist with the training of officers.

Hate Crime/Extremism Investigative Team (HCEIT): The HCEIT is a joint forces team of 10 large police services, funded by the Ministry of Community Safety and Correctional Services, mandated to collect, evaluate, and disseminate information and intelligence on targeted activ-ities and to provide specialized investigative support for matters involving hate propaganda, the promotion of genocide, hate-motivated crimes, and the diverse variants of criminal extremism. They assist with officer training and produce front-line educational materials. Each of the services also has its own training programs, usually under the auspices of its own Hate Crimes Unit or Community Relations Unit.

While some police-based, court-based, and community-based services seek to provide assistance to all victims of crime, victims of hate crime require additional services, as well as specialized and culturally appropriate support that takes into account their status as victims of hate-motivated crime. Some victims may not have contact with, or access to, police-based services that require police referral, and thus may have to turn to others for help and support.

Many victims are unaware of the services that exist to help them, or they may be unable to reach services for a variety of reasons. It is for this reason that community-based services and training programs are recommended as essential partners to police, prosecutors, and judicial-based education programs in this area.

Community-Based Programs

Community organizations, often at the front line in providing services to victims of hate incidents and hate crime, differ from government-based initiatives in several ways. First, community-based initiatives tend to enjoy higher visibility because they are based in the demographic constituencies that they serve. Second, community-based victim support is likely to be integrated into a broader mandate to offer assistance in areas of social and economic equity and justice. Third, these agencies identify the need for culturally and linguistically specific tools to support victims through the healing process and to assist them as they navigate the criminal justice system. Community organizations enjoy a certain level of trust among the clients they serve, although it is crucial to recognize that issues such as gender, class, sexual orientation, and gender identity affect access and delivery—as they do in the society at large.

Because of funding challenges, community-based programs are usually, of necessity, short-term. However, the HCCWG identified several very effective community projects to raise awareness and to counter hate crime victimization:

- The *Safety in the Streets* program by the Grand Council Treaty 3 Justice Initiative is designed to build trust and break down barriers that prevent First Nations people from bringing incidents of racism and hate crime to the attention of police or other authorities, and to promote healing between Aboriginal and non-Aboriginal communities in Kenora and the Treaty 3 area.
- The *Say No to Hate* campaign of the Council of Agencies Serving South Asians is a video and training program aimed at youth and produced and conducted by youth.
- *Taking Action against Hate (Protection, Prevention and Partnerships)* is a training of trainers program prepared by the League for Human Rights of B'nai Brith Canada, aimed at community groups, schools, and law enforcement and government agencies.
- *Stand Up, Speak Out*, a resource kit produced by the Federation of Muslim Women, provides resources to empower victimized members of the community.
- The *Scadding Court Community Centre* provides a model for police/community partnerships to counter hate crimes and also to facilitate the police complaints process.
- *Choose Your Voice* is the initiative of FAST (Fighting Antisemitism Together) in cooperation with the Canadian Jewish Congress.
- The *Anti-Violence Programme at the 519 Community Centre* provides model programming and services for victims of homophobic harassment and assault.
- *Deconstructing On-Line Hate* by the Media Awareness Network (MNet) helps parents, children, and schools recognize and react to hate on the internet.

These and many other programs and services offered by not-for-profit groups are continually at risk of being discontinued because of lack of ongoing funding, making it impossible to sustain initiatives, with the result that ongoing dissemination of the information and services is almost impossible.

Non-governmental organizations (NGOs) are also typically overextended and under-resourced, resulting in lack of sustainability of culturally appropriate victim services and programming. As the first point of contact for victims—outside of circles of family and friends—these organizations are charged with providing emotional and physical support as well as guidance and referrals. A review of the services of NGOs in Ontario reveals that very few of these organizations have developed a dedicated anti-hate crime support function. Instead, most offer broad-based programs aimed at developing community capacity. Those organizations that do offer services specific to victims of hate crime have tended to focus their attention on public education and awareness, direct assistance, reporting, and monitoring. The need for recognition of community expertise and the importance of capacity building in enabling community groups to contribute to educational programs remain significant concerns for victims of hate and bias crime across the country.

The recommendations of the Hate Crimes Community Working Group are in various stages of implementation, although a great deal remains to be done. Among the 196 recommendations, the HCCWG recommended that the Ministries of the Attorney General and of Community Safety and Correctional Services work with the municipal police service boards and the Ontario chiefs of police to ensure

- the development, in collaboration with representatives from communities vulnerable to hate, of comprehensive programs for training in diversity and in hate incident recognition and response;
- the provision of such training, on a regular basis, to all police officers, provincial corrections officers, provincial Crown prosecutors, and their supervisory staffs and all front-line victim service providers employed by the provincial government or by provincially funded community agencies; and
- that demonstration of ongoing competence in these matters be, for all these individuals, a part of his or her annual performance review.

Further, the HCCWG recommended that the Ministry of Education work with, as appropriate, school boards, institutions involved in educating system professionals, and accreditation bodies to design and deliver, in collaboration with community members, ongoing training (i.e., at all stages of their careers) in anti-racism/anti-oppression practice and, more specifically, in recognizing and reporting hate- and bias-related incidents, and diversity training for teachers, counsellors, and administrative staff to better equip them to support victims and witnesses of hate- and bias-related incidents, and to link performance plans/appraisals to successful completion of this training.

Finally, given the important role of the judiciary in matters related to offences associated with hate crime, the HCCWG requested that its report be forwarded for review to the Offices of the Chief Justices of each level of court in Ontario and to the National Judicial Institute so that it might inform consideration of judicial education in this area. The NJI has offered a course on hate crimes, in addition to its seminar on 'Race, Law and Judging'.

Conclusion

Countless reports and task forces within and outside of the criminal justice system have concluded that social context education in general and anti-racism training in particular are essential for professionals in all sectors of the justice system to raise awareness, increase knowledge, and enhance the likelihood of fair and equitable delivery of justice. There are several examples of outstanding policing and judicial education programs in this important area, with consensus that the most effective programs are (1) integrated into ongoing educational requirements, (2) include an immersion component, (3) provide discussion opportunities in safe surroundings, and (4) involve facilitators and faculty from both the justice system and wider professional community.

Community-based organizations and other NGOs can and should offer assistance and should be consulted in planning, included in the implementation of programs, and involved in an ongoing advisory capacity. Anti-racist education workshops and guidance on policy development and implementation should ultimately be compulsory and system-wide. Courses and materials for use in policing services and judicial education programs are now widely available and do not need to be reinvented.

The most successful programs in any organization or profession have strong leadership from the senior management. In recent years, the judiciary's leadership in this area has been exemplary in several jurisdictions. However, anti-racism training still remains optional in most areas and is dependent on enthusiastic individuals, rather than being part of the ongoing system. The challenge remains for more consistent and sustainable implementation of the most effective models of anti-racism training so that the goals of fairness and equitable treatment articulated by the trailblazers in the field might be achieved.

Key Terms

adult learning principles

anti-racist education

Canadian Charter of Rights and Freedoms

Canadian Human Rights Act

Canadian Race Relations Act

discrimination

Employment Equity Commission

Equality Now!

hate crime

hate propaganda

human rights codes

immersion

integration

International Convention on the Elimination of All Forms of Racism and Discrimination

multiculturalism

power

privilege

Race Relations Training Manual

self-teaching

social context education

systemic racism

Questions for Critical Thought

1. How is 'anti-racist' education different from 'cross-cultural' education? Is this a significant distinction?

2. Mock describes three models of social context education. Which of these do you think might be most effective? Why?

3. What challenges face non-profit and non-governmental organizations' efforts to confront racism?

4. Aside from hate crime, in what other areas might anti-racist education be useful? Can you provide examples of existing programs in these areas?

References

Canada. (1984a). *Equality now! Report of the Special Committee on Visible Minorities in Canadian Society.* Ottawa: House of Commons.

Canada. (1984b). *Report of the Commission on Employment Equity.* Ottawa: Supplies and Services.

Canadian Bar Association. (1993). *Touchstones for change: Equality, diversity and accountability.* Ottawa: Canadian Bar Association.

Canadian Race Relations Foundation. (2003). *Educating against racism—An annotated bibliographic tool of anti-racist resources for activists and educators.* Toronto.

Commission on Systemic Racism in the Ontario Criminal Justice System. (1995). Report (chap. 5). Toronto: Ministry of the Attorney General.

Henry, F., & Ginsberg, E. (1985). *Who gets the work?* Toronto: Social Planning Council and the Urban Alliance on Race Relations.

Hier, S. P., Lett, D., & Bolaria, B. (2009). *Racism and justice.* Halifax: Fernwood.

Iacobucci, F. (2001, June). *The broader context of social context.* Remarks at Social Context Education Faculty and Curriculum Design Program, Victoria.

Jaffer, M., & Mock, K. (1992). Foreword to *WJEC Seminar on Racial, Ethnic and Cultural Equity.*

Lewis, S. (1992). *Stephen Lewis Report on Race Relations in Ontario.* Ministry of Citizenship.

L'Heureux-Dubé, C. (2001a). What a difference a decade makes: The Canadian constitution and the family since 1991. *Queen's Law Journal, 27,* 363.

L'Heureux-Dubé, C. (2001b). *Beyond the myths: Equality, impartiality and justice. Journal of Social Distress and Homelessness, 10*(1), 94.

Masemann, V., & Mock, K. R. (1987). *Access to government services by racial minorities.* Ontario Race Relations Directorate, Ministry of Citizenship.

Ministry of the Attorney General. (2006). *Addressing hate crime in Ontario: Report of the Hate Crimes Community Working Group.* Karen R. Mock, chair.

Mock, K. R. (1988). *Race relations training: A manual for practitioners and consultants.* Ontario Race Relations Directorate, Ministry of Citizenship.

Mock, K. R., & Masemann, V. L. (1990). *Race school boards and ethnocultural equity policy development and implementation in Ontario.* Ministry of Education.

National Association of Japanese Canadians. (1984). *Democracy betrayed.* Winnipeg: NAJC.

National Judicial Institute. (2009). Seminar on Race, Law and Judging, Halifax (syllabus handout).

Schafran, L. H. (1995) Credibility in the courts: Why is there a gender gap? *ABA Judges' Journal,* 34, 5.

Smith, L. (1996). *Statement of needs and objectives for continuing judicial education on the social context of judicial decision-making.* Ottawa: National Judicial Institute.

Swinton, K. (1996). *Judicial impartiality and social context education.* Ottawa: National Judicial Institute.

Swinton, K. (1997). Judicial impartiality and social context education. In T. Camwell, D. Penard, & H. Duraont (Eds). *Human rights in the 21st century: Prospects, institutions and processes* (pp. 253–266). Montreal: Edition Thèmis.

Western Judicial Education Centre. (1992). *Judicial education program on racial, ethnic and cultural equity.* Resource Binder. Saskatoon.

Winkler, N. (1992). *Western Judicial Education Centre Program evaluation report.* Ottawa: Department of Justice.

19 | *Criminal Justice/Social Justice*

Barbara Perry

The contributors to this volume have powerfully demonstrated the extent to which identity shapes individual and collective experiences with the justice system. It is evident that disparities grounded in difference have been and continue to be perpetuated by practices, patterns, and policies associated with the way we do business within the criminal justice arena. Our task, then, is to develop strategies by which these disparities might be mitigated. Central to this are projects by which we might undo the damages associated with the ways in which we 'do difference' in our society. Recall my assertion in chapter 2 that

> [t]o the extent that difference is socially constructed, it can also be socially reconstructed. In other words, as a society, we can redefine the ways in which difference 'matters'. We can strive for a just and democratic society in which the full spectrum of diversity addressed here is re-evaluated in a positive and celebratory light. (Perry, this volume, chap. 2, p. 26)

Interestingly, this parallels the observation of a First Nations man in previous research I had conducted on the community impacts of hate crime. He, too, recognized that the beliefs, patterns, and practices that contribute to justice disparities can be reversed: 'I think it is learned. It is learned partly in our educational system, it is learned in the home and is learned through the media culture. I would suggest that the only good news is that hate can be unlearned.' Indeed, this is the flip side of the social construction of difference. The key is to labour toward a reconstructed politics of difference that **empowers** rather than disempowers. In a just society, difference would not be the foundation of criminalization, marginalization, or victimization. On the contrary, difference would be the foundation of **inclusion** and **equity** in all areas of social life. Some, but by no means all, of the related initiatives would be grounded in criminal justice reform. However, these must also be contextualized within a **social justice** framework. My goal in this concluding chapter, then, is to point the way by briefly highlighting some of the key means by which this might be accomplished. I begin with a discussion of needed reforms within the criminal justice system and conclude with suggestions for social justice.

The importance of this chapter—and the two previous chapters (17 and 18) cannot be overstated. Too often we devote all of our attention to identifying and critiquing the problems embedded in the criminal justice system without then offering constructive suggestions for how to address them. Indeed, as I began this chapter, I reviewed a number of relevant texts, looking for some inspiration on how to categorize and describe the myriad approaches to reform. Sadly, few of these offered much in this context. Only one (Winterdyk & King, 1999) devoted a full section—five chapters—to 'Prevention and Intervention Strategies'. This chapter, then, is intended to confront head on the question of what is to be done.

Criminal Justice

Legislative Reform

It is evident from the material presented throughout this text that the law has played a crucial role in enabling disparate experiences across groups in Canada. From exclusionary immigration law, to discriminatory criminalization of cultural practices, to lack of criminal regulation of corporate 'wrong-doing', legislation has historically served to defend dominant race, class, and gender privileges in particular. Consequently, organizing around challenges to existing legislation is vital.

A concrete example of how effective such movements can be is to be found in the work of Egale, a national organization that 'advances equality and justice for lesbian, gay, bisexual, and trans-identified people and their families across Canada' (http://egale.ca). The website makes it clear how extensively Egale has been engaged in court and parliamentary actions that enhance the place and legal standing of the LGBT community in Canada. The organization led the campaign for same-sex marriage and has been actively involved in virtually all of the Supreme Court gay rights cases, including *Egan v. Canada, Vriend v. Alberta, Little Sisters Book and Art Emporium v. Canada Customs,* and *B.C. College of Teachers v. Trinity Western University.*

A second example is LEAF—the Women's Legal Education and Action Fund. Established in 1984, this organization is committed to ensuring that the equality rights enshrined in section 15 and section 28 of the Charter of Rights and Freedoms are realized in practice. LEAF has been a key actor in more than 150 cases and 'has helped establish landmark legal victories for women on a wide range of issues from violence against women, sexual assault, workplace inequities, socio-economic rights, and reproductive freedoms' (www.leaf.ca/about/index.html#target). Through both law reform advocacy and litigation, the organization has been successful in establishing and upholding key equality rights. Among the most significant cases in recent years have been those around so-called rape-shield laws and around women's right to control their own bodies.

The African Canadian Legal Clinic, founded in 1994, is also involved in law reform and litigation, especially around test cases that are likely to set important precedents. The mission of the clinic is to act 'as an advocacy agency, and as a resource centre for individuals and other organizations dealing with racial discrimination' (www.aclc.net/about-us). It has transformed criminal justice responses to black citizens at the local and national level through interventions in such areas as racial profiling, police use of force, and hate crime.

Organizations such as these will continue to be vital in challenges to unjust policy and practice. Given the complexity and expense of litigation and lobbying, reform-based bodies are necessary conduits for launching campaigns against injustice. They have the legal expertise and typically the funding to enable them to represent the interests of disadvantaged groups and individuals. Without these committed groups, the movement toward justice within the *criminal* justice system would be even slower and more arduous than it is. Advocacy organizations will continue to lead the way in dismantling unjust policies.

Equally important, however, is challenging *proposed* changes that would exacerbate current disparities in the experience of justice. At the time of writing, Canada is at a criminal justice crossroads. The Conservative Harper administration has articulated a reform agenda that would seriously jeopardize any progress toward a more just and humane justice system. Even the British newsmagazine *The Economist*—hardly a left-wing publication—recognizes the contradictions inherent in the proposals, asking, 'But what is a politician to do when the crime rate is at a 30-year low and both the rate and severity of reported crime has been dropping?' (*The Economist*, December 19, 2009). In spite of overwhelming evidence of the lack of effectiveness, and in fact counterproductivity, of US-style justice reform, the Conservatives seem determined to push through a series of bills that would create new offences, lengthen sentences, and constrain prisoners' rights. And we know from the American and British examples that the 'war on crime' typically constitutes an assault on those who are already disadvantaged. Importantly, there are organizations that are challenging these initiatives. The John Howard Society, for example, publicly opposes such proposals as mandatory minimum sentences for drug offences. The society, along with many other Canadian and American organizations, provided evidence-based testimony at the public Senate hearings on Bill C-51. Importantly, many such organizations have a relatively open membership or utilize volunteers on a regular basis, thereby providing ample opportunity for individual engagement in confronting the problems identified throughout this text.

Hiring

Discussions revolving around efforts to increase the cultural awareness and sensitivity of criminal justice practitioners often skip over the most crucial stage of agency acculturation. Many assume that the place to begin is with training. But in fact the key to more aware and thus effective personnel is to hire wisely at the outset. In policing, for example, the practice if not the policy is to hire well-educated recruits, particularly those with liberal arts and social science degrees. The proportion of those working in policing with at least some post-secondary education is generally well over 75 per cent (Goudreau & Brzozowski, 2002). In fact, after legal personnel, police officers are currently among the highest educated of all justice personnel.

Ironically, traditional criminal justice or justice administration students are not necessarily the best choice in this context. The mainstream and often conservative education they receive typically reinforces the problematic 'us versus them' mentality that marginalizes and stigmatizes the 'Other'. Recent surveys of criminal justice students, for example, have found them to be more homophobic and racist than peers from other programs (Wimshurst, Marchetti, & Allard, 2004; Cannon, 2005; Owen & Wagner, 2008). One team of researchers has found that criminal justice majors tend to be both more punitive and less empathetic than their peers in other majors (Mackey & Courtright, 1998; Courtright, Mackey, & Packard, 2005). In contrast, more broadly defined programs grounded in the liberal arts and/or social sciences tend to graduate students who have had more sympathetic exposure to themes of diversity and multiculturalism, as well as to the crucial skills of critical thinking and inter-personal and intercultural communication. This kind of education tends to better prepare them for subsequent interactions with diverse communities. As an example, consider my own faculty, which offers a very comprehensive interdisciplinary Criminology and Justice major. In addition to standard theory, methods, and criminal justice courses, the program requires that students take an array of classes that highlight cultural difference: Issues in Diversity; Social Justice and Conflict; Violence against Women; and even Hate Crime. Consequently, by the time they have left our classrooms, they are well attuned to the values of tolerance, respect, and equity.

Another potential avenue in the context of hiring would involve aggressive recruitment from the communities most vulnerable to the problems identified in this text and thus empathetic to them. Again, in the context of policing, justice reformers in recent years assumed that the inclusion of officers from communities of colour would ensure the success of not just commun-ity policing, but policing generally. Many believed that this would bridge the divide between officers and the communities they served and that officers' knowledge of 'their' communities would enhance their effectiveness. Sadly, this has not generally been borne out by experi-ence. Rather, minority officers are often plagued by 'double marginality', whereby they are not deemed fully a part of either their racialized community or the world of policing. On one side of the equation of double marginality, members of minority groups who choose a career in law enforcement fear being perceived as having betrayed their community, while on the other, of course, they are apprehensive about how white officers will react to them. The very realistic fear of racism—both individual and systemic—within the profession is a major prohibiting factor to recruitment (Bolton, 2003; Bolton & Feagin, 2004). The difficulty, then, is that the existing culture of racism, homophobia, and sexism that permeates many police organizations must be whittled down. Again, effective hiring of majority and minority officers with a keen grasp of progressive social dynamics will, in the long term, go a long way toward this. We saw in chapter 4 how strategic recruitment within minority communities has begun to subtly change the face of many Canadian police agencies.

Training

Once hired, officers need to be immersed in the values that mitigate against apathy or outright hostility toward difference. We have largely failed in this area as well. In Canada and the United States, new recruits receive from 12 weeks to 6 months of formal training prior to going into the field. Yet they typically receive less than 20 hours of diversity training and little subsequent in-service training. Moreover, what is available does not appear to be of the highest quality.

This assessment, however, is speculative, as there have been virtually no systematic evaluations of police-training modules.

Since at least the 1960s, some form of cultural awareness or sensitivity training for law enforcement has been seen as a panacea to the hostile relationships between police and racialized communities. Interestingly, cultural awareness training programs have been supported by both liberal and conservative reformers, albeit for reasons that are diametrically opposed. For the former, cultural awareness training is seen as a potential inoculant against problems of discrimination, harassment, and violence perpetrated by police against racialized and other minority groups. Effective diversity training, they argue, would sensitize police to the impacts of their actions, thereby making subsequent changes in their behaviour more likely. In contrast, conservative supporters contend that the behavioural changes wrought by such programming have positive implications with respect to issues of police liability and reduced lawsuits. Additionally, they see more harmonious police–community relations as an effective means of reinserting the legitimacy and thus the authority of the police in minority communities (Barlow & Barlow, 1993). It is a daunting task to attempt to synthesize the array of cultural diversity training initiatives. There are nearly as many approaches as there are police departments, each with its own set of assumptions and related content and delivery style. However, perhaps the most concise means of categorizing cultural training is to follow Rowe and Garland's (2003) typology of cognitive, behavioural, and affective/attitudinal approaches. The first has arguably been the most common strategy historically, perhaps because it appears at first blush to be the simplest.

It is not only police officers, however, that must become attuned to the disparate experiences of the communities they serve. Any agency that serves the needs of victims, offenders, and even witnesses must be aware of the particular needs of all who come in contact with the justice system. For example, just as police officers should enter the field with some sensitivity to difference, so too should practising attorneys be outfitted with the necessary tools to assist their diverse clients. Yet Canadian law schools let them down in this respect, in that questions of disparity and the other consequences of difference are not firmly embedded in existing law degree curricula. It is no wonder, then, as Mock's discussion in chapter 18 suggests, that by the time they reach the bench, the judiciary are also in need of enhanced training.

Culturally Specific Programming

Many contributors to this volume have recognized the inherent inability—if not unwillingness—of criminal justice organizations to address the complex needs and experiences of diverse communities. Two distinct types of initiatives are typically suggested as a means to overcome this: (1) embedding culturally specific programs within the agencies in question or (2) establishing adjunct organizations that can facilitate 'justice' outside the bounds of the criminal justice system.

Victims of crime may experience their victimization differently, depending on their personal and cultural biographies. Thus, those 'victimized because of their difference, or those who experience victimization differently because of their difference, or those who are uncomfortable with the criminal justice system because of their difference, often require culturally sensitive services' (Jones, Perry, & Nielsen, 2009, p. 294). By now, we are all familiar with victim services developed for women who are victims of violent crime, especially intimate partner violence. These have been developed in recognition of the unique trauma, risk, and frequency of violence perpetrated against women by their male partners. As Canadian demographics shift, the onus is on the justice system to provide similarly concentrated victim services to other communities. Most provincial governments, for example, feature a victims' services office that typically develops programs oriented toward vulnerable communities in their regions. Locally, police departments and Crown attorneys' offices also provide specific services to the diverse communities they serve. These might include translators, counselling services, disability accommodation, or community liaison panels.

Similarly, offenders come into the system with distinct experiences and needs. We clearly recognize this in the context of youth, for example, to the extent that we have explicitly established separate policies and institutions for dealing with young offenders. Increasingly, the acknowledgment of difference is impacting the services available to offenders from other communities. Correctional Services Canada claims to address the growing religious diversity of those incarcerated:

> Religion, or spiritual beliefs and practices, often the predominant indicator of one's culture is an important need to respond to. Religious customs vary widely and, in institutional settings particularly, can be difficult to accommodate. To fulfil these requirements CSC considers a number of factors including traditional dress (e.g. turbans), religious diets (e.g. pork free diet), sacred scriptures (e.g. the Quran), different days of worship, and diverse religious and/or spiritual leaders. (www.csc-scc.gc.ca/ethnoculture/srvc-eng.shtml)

Canada's Aboriginal offenders have been the focus of culturally specific strategies for addressing the unique factors giving rise to crime in their communities. Prisons and jails, especially in the western provinces, have begun to implement an array of services that reflect Aboriginal values. The Aboriginal Corrections Continuum of Care model, for example, incorporates cultural practices as a means of enhancing community reintegration. The model

- starts at intake to identify Aboriginal offenders and to encourage them to bridge the disconnect with their culture and communities;
- leads to paths of healing in institutions to better prepare Aboriginal offenders for transfer to lower security and for conditional release;
- engages Aboriginal communities to receive offenders back into their community and support their reintegration; and
- ends with the establishment of community supports to sustain progress beyond the end of the sentence and prevent reoffending. (www.csc-scc.gc.ca/text/prgrm/abinit/plan06-eng.shtml#6)

Whether victims or offenders, or even witnesses, people from distinct communities come into the justice system with similarly distinct needs. Programs designed with elders in mind are not likely to be effective for gay adolescents or for middle-aged Muslims. Similarly, those that target Muslim victims of hate crimes may not be appropriate for Jewish victims. To be effective, just, and humane, services must take into account the varied histories and contemporary experiences of their 'clientele'.

In the absence of this recognition, affected communities often establish initiatives outside the formal system of justice. Most contributors to this volume have illustrated this trend, providing concrete examples of community organizing around particular forms of crime and victimization. Such initiatives will continue to be important mechanisms for identifying community-specific problems and seeking just solutions to them. Related activities will include those of community-run organizations, as well as public lobbying for recognition and government intervention where appropriate.

Restorative Justice

Several Western nations have slowly come to realize that the many strategies associated with **restorative justice** may be a viable alternative means of dealing with crime, particularly for low-level offences and juvenile offenders. The restorative justice model goes beyond victim–offender mediation to promote involvement of the victim, the offender, *and* the community in the justice process. In particular, restorative justice interventions help to restore victims' and communities' losses by holding offenders accountable for their actions by making them repair the physical and emotional harm they have caused. Such interventions also focus on changing the behavioural patterns of offenders so that they become productive and responsible citizens. The restorative justice model places emphasis on everyone affected by the crime—the community and the victim as well as the offender—to ensure that each gains tangible benefits from their interaction with the criminal justice system.

Academics Umbreit, Lewis, and Burns (2003) highlight two particularly important elements associated with restorative justice initiatives: 'The entire community is engaged in holding the offender accountable and promoting a healing response to the needs of victims, offenders, and the community as a whole'; and 'While it is important to address the immediate needs of crime victims and offenders, involving community members in the process of doing justice helps to build stronger, more connected, caring communities.' This alternative, then, is significant in that it allows any affected party a place at the table. Moreover, who comes to the table is variable and depends on the incident in question. Ordinarily, the dialogue begins with victims and offenders and the key support persons they may bring with them. Additionally, however, it is as likely to include representatives of the larger community or neighbourhood, people who can speak precisely to the nature and intensity of how the incident affected them as well.

An outstanding resource for Canadians interested in restorative justice is Simon Fraser University's Centre for Restorative Justice (www.sfu.ca/cfrj). In part, the centre acts as a clearing house for literature and links associated with restorative justice in this country and abroad. It also provides background on the key principles and practices of this approach. One thing that is immediately apparent from a review of the website is that it is in the areas of Aboriginal justice and youth justice that restorative justice has made the greatest inroads. The former should come as no surprise in that many practitioners claim that the movement is derived from principles similar to those that inform many Aboriginal communities' 'holistic peace and justice-making' orientations. Dickson-Gilmore, in chapter 5, highlights both the limitations and the contributions of sentencing circles within Aboriginal communities. The use of restorative justice models in youth justice finds its footing in the Youth Criminal Justice Act, which emphasizes the application of 'extrajudicial' measures. Restorative justice seems an apt approach here, for it demands that youth both take responsibility and make amends for the consequences of their actions. One program derived from this understanding is the Chilliwack Restorative Justice and Youth Advocacy Association in British Columbia. According to the website, the mandate of the organization is to

> bring offenders and victims together in order to discuss criminal incidents and to find ways to repair the harm caused. The Association has been in operation since 1998 and during this time we have been extremely successful in connecting youth with their community, providing mentoring to young offenders, providing a forum for victims, and facilitating the payment of monetary restitution to victims by offenders. (www.gov.chilliwack.bc.ca/ main/page.cfm?id=178&CFID=244468&CFTOKEN=35899836)

Education/Prejudice Reduction

Somewhere in the grey area between *criminal* and *social* justice initiatives lie educational programs, with a special emphasis on **prejudice reduction**. This volume has highlighted the consistency with which the Other has been stigmatized, demonized, and subsequently criminalized and/or victimized. Stereotypes of the 'promiscuous woman', for example, have consistently served to enable violence against women, just as stereotypes of gay men as pedophiles have consistently served to enable violence against them. In each of these illustrative cases, the stereotypes disempower those who are different, since their difference is assumed to be immutable and deviant. Consequently, the key to empowerment is to eliminate the discriminatory and/or privileging effects of difference.

It is not enough to provide services for the victims of such hostility. The other side of the equation must also be addressed, so that the pool of offenders is reduced through treatment and prevention strategies. As a condition of probation, some judges across the country have attempted to prevent secondary offending by helping the offender to see the humanity of the victims' community. This is often accomplished by requiring that the offender engage in community service with the victim community: an anti-Semite might work with the Anti-Defamation League (ADL), or a gay-basher might work with a local gay and lesbian advocacy group (Levin & McDevitt, 1993).

As a means of preventing hate crime victimization, bullying, and other forms of discrimination, anti-prejudice and anti-violence projects have begun to spring up across the country, especially in elementary and secondary schools. This is an initiative that federal, provincial, and local governments must continue to support through promotional and funding activities. The website www.safehealthyschools.org is a valuable clearing house with information about healthy and safe schools, providing 'links to research, reports, how-to manuals, planning & assessment tools, lesson plans and student webquests.' Of particular interest is its inventory of anti-racism and multicultural educational programs and initiatives across Canada. This inventory highlights policies as well as school-based initiatives intended to reduce stereotyping, prejudice, bullying, and other exclusionary practices. The United Nations Association in Canada has involved youth in the creation of *The Kit: A Manual by Youth to Combat Racism through Education* (www.unac.org/yfar/The_KIT.pdf). In language that is accessible to students, the manual provides background and history on racism experienced by diverse racialized communities in Canada, as well as insight into 'myths and misconceptions' that have shaped these experiences.

Yet it is not only youth who are vulnerable to the adoption of damaging stereotypes and prejudices. Indeed, it is often the adults around them who teach these in the first place. Thus, broader public campaigns against racism and other forms of discrimination are also important. Some time ago, I was part of a team exploring the potential for media campaigns against racism (Sutton, Perry, Parke, & John-Baptiste, 2007). We found that the few media-based initiatives to reduce racial prejudice that have been conducted varied considerably in terms of how they sought to influence subjects. Building upon Pate's (1981) work, initiatives to reduce racial prejudice using the media sought to

1. reduce racially prejudiced beliefs, often by general awareness raising;
2. reduce specific types of racial discrimination in specific settings (violence, harassment, intimidation, threatening or derogatory physical attitudes); and
3. reduce specific types of victimization—often by victim empowerment or by encouraging reporting by the public.

Each of the aims and mechanisms employed in the initiatives described in the typology above has a number of strengths and weaknesses. Those that seek to use media to change racially prejudiced beliefs must utilize knowledge from studies of the social psychology of attitude change. Initiatives that aim to alter physical and social situational elements in the precise locations where discrimination takes place may be effective in particular places at particular times. However, they may not take into account the fact that discrimination may simply be displaced to another place and time because the root causes of prejudice are not being addressed. Finally, campaigns that aim to reduce victimization may place responsibility for confronting discrimination in the hands of those who are on its receiving end rather than in the hands of those who are wrongfully acting upon their prejudices (Sampson & Phillips, 1992). Consequently, such initiatives might be better employed as part of a wider campaign of initiatives to reduce the incidence of discriminatory behaviour and/or beliefs rather than as a stand-alone program. Nevertheless, there may be situations where there is a clear need for prioritizing the empowerment of potential victims in order to address a particular vulnerability, an increase in discriminatory activity, or some other trend.

Media campaigns have been used in Canada to address problems of violence and discrimination. For example, in an effort to stem the tide of domestic violence, a recent series of television advertisements encourages men to teach their sons respect for women; another series focuses on encouraging women of colour, and especially immigrant women, to report their victimization; and yet another highlights the abilities as opposed to the disabilities of those living with vision, mobility, or hearing limitations. The hope is that, if widely dispersed and repeated, the message of respect for difference will have some impact on public perceptions.

Social Justice

Coincident with social action for reform of legislation, education, and victim services, we also have a responsibility to work toward social change that mitigates the negative effects of difference more broadly. Access to adequate housing and medical care, education, full-time employment, income support, child care, and other crucial social services should be acknowledged as the inalienable rights of all, not just as the privilege of a few. At bottom, 'the goal should be to make sure that every child, whoever his or her parents and whatever their race or class, has a reasonable chance to live a satisfying, productive and law-abiding life' (Tonry, 1995, p. 208). In short, the way forward is through social justice initiatives. Rothenberg and Michalowski, respectively, offer their assessments:

> A society that distributes educational opportunities, housing, health care, food, even kindness, based on the color of people's skin and other arbitrary variables cannot guarantee the safety or security of its people. In this sense, all of us, both the victims and beneficiaries, pay a terrible price. (Rothenberg, 2002, p. 4)
>
> The justice system helps many people, but it alone cannot produce *justice* in the society. Real justice is *social justice*. A large criminal justice system cannot compensate for a lack of social justice. (Michalowski, 2009, p. 70)

In short, the realization of criminal justice is dependent upon the realization of social justice. Most of the contributors in Part 2 of this text illustrate quite forcefully the ways in which social injustice leaves disadvantaged communities disproportionately vulnerable to both victimization and criminalization. Those who are marginalized by virtue of stigmatization or powerlessness, for example, are easy prey for those seeking to enhance their own sense of privilege by harming others. Similarly, these same communities often live in the sorts of dire economic conditions that provoke criminal activity as a mode of adaptation. Perhaps the clearest illustration of this comes from chapter 5, this volume, which discusses the ways in which the life conditions of Aboriginal people leave them vulnerable to over-representation as both victims and offenders. The history of colonization and marginalization has left many Aboriginal communities without the individual or collective resources to flourish, resulting in impoverishment, substance abuse, poor health, and generally substandard living conditions—all of which are correlated with crime and victimization. Clearly, then, reducing the risk of disparate experiences of victimization and offending will also require transforming the conditions that give rise to both.

Many consider John Rawls to be the inspiration for contemporary understandings of social justice. The two key principles that have become the starting point for defining its meaning are

1. Each person is to have an equal right to the most extensive total system of equal basic liberties, compatible with a similar system of liberty for all.
2. Social and economic inequalities are to be arranged so that they are both:
   a. to the greatest benefit of the least advantaged, consistent with the just savings principle, and
   b. attached to offices and positions open to all under conditions of fair equality of opportunity. (Rawls, 1971, p. 302)

These dual principles of liberty and difference have been operationalized in diverse ways since Rawls's writing. For example, they provide the underpinnings for the UK Commission on Social Justice (1993), which highlights four central tenets of social justice:

- The foundation of a free society is the equal worth of all citizens
- All citizens are entitled, as a right of citizenship, to be able to meet their basic needs— for income, food, shelter, education and health
- Self-respect and personal autonomy are inherent in the idea of equal worth, but their fulfillment depends on the widest possible spread of opportunities and life-chances
- Inequalities are not necessarily unjust—but those which are should be reduced and where possible eliminated. (Commission on Social Justice, 1993, p. i)

In 1992 the Canadian National Anti-Poverty Organization issued a draft 'Social Charter' for Canada, which also adopted a Rawlsian approach:

1. In light of Canada's international and domestic commitment to respect, protect and promote the humans rights of all members of Canadian society, and, in particular, members of the most vulnerable and disadvantaged groups, everyone has an equal right to well-being, including a right to:
   a. A standard of living that ensures adequate food, clothing, housing, child care, support services and other requirements for security and dignity of the person and for full social and economic participation in their communities and in Canadian society;
   b. Health care that is comprehensive, universal, portable, accessible, and publicly administered, including community-based non-profit delivery of services;

    c. Public primary and secondary education, accessible post-secondary and vocational education, and publicly-funded education for those with special needs arising from disabilities;

    d. Access to employment opportunities; and

    e. Just and favourable conditions of work, including the right of workers to organize and bargain collectively.

Interestingly, one month prior to the release of the Anti-Poverty Organization's charter, Ontario premier Bob Rae's provincial administration floated a proposal for a social charter that was very similar in content (see Bakan & Schneiderman, 1992).

Despite the myriad and often competing conceptualizations of social justice (Burchardt & Craig, 2008; Cook, 2006), it is possible to tease out a number of common factors that emerge within progressive agendas for social justice. Among them:

- Equity/**egalitarianism** (not necessarily *equality*)
- Equitable distribution of resources
- Satisfaction of basic needs
- Personal autonomy
- Inclusiveness

Traditionally, social justice initiatives have revolved around social and economic rights in particular. These rights are evident in the Canadian example highlighted above. Here, the emphasis is on ensuring the satisfaction of basic human needs and the capacity for self-determination. However, recognition of social and economic rights should also be accompanied by efforts to integrate difference into our cultural repertoire. The values and practices of alternate cultures must also be recognized for what they contribute. Black Canadians find in their traditional communities, which refer to their members as 'brother' and 'sister', a sense of solidarity absent from the calculating individualism of white, professional, capitalist society. Feminists find in the traditional female values of nurturing a challenge to a militarist world view, and lesbians find in their relationships a confrontation with the assumptions of complementary gender roles in sexual relationships. From their experience of a culture tied to the land, Aboriginal people formulate a critique of the instrumental rationality of European culture that results in pollution and environmental destruction (Young, 1990, p. 205). Indeed, in my Social Justice and Conflict course, I typically ask students to complete an exercise I call 'What Do They Bring?' Confronted with a social policy problem, they are asked to think about what a diverse array of people bring to the table in terms of experience, perspective, and expertise. Such an exercise highlights the important fact that, regardless of background or identity, virtually everyone has something to contribute to our understanding and resolution of social problems.

From a pragmatic standpoint, Connell (1990, 1992) provides a useful model for what he calls the 'practical politics' involved in eliminating gender inequality. We would do well to mimic this approach in setting the agenda for the broader 'practical politics' of social justice, which may provide alternative ways of doing difference that give rise to choice rather than to violence or criminalization. Consider the following 'different' bill of rights and freedoms:

In the context of labour: Equity of wages across race and gender categories; freedom from workplace harassment and violence; elimination of job segregation patterns; democratic decision making in the workplace; equitable distribution of household labour; affordable and available child care.

In the context of power: Democratic and equitable representation and participation in state, workplace, and household politics; freedom to voice dissent; autonomy of thought and action; freedom from public and private forms of violence; freedom to live in the place and conditions of one's choice.

In the context of sexuality: Control over one's sexuality and reproductive capacity; freedom to choose sexual partners and activities; freedom from sexual violence.

In the context of culture: Freedom from stereotypical imagery and expectations; ability to respond to and overturn negative imagery; freedom to define one's own individual and collective identity.

In achieving these ends, the foundations that support social disparities will be weakened, and so too will the links to parallel disparities in the criminal justice system. Ultimately, the **mobilizations** around these four axes must provide the basis for collective struggle in the interests of social justice.

Key Terms

advocacy	equity	mobilization	restorative justice
egalitarianism	inclusion	prejudice reduction	social justice
empowerment			

Questions for Critical Thought

1. Which of the categories of criminal justice reform noted here do you think is the most important area of intervention? Why?
2. How does social injustice shape diverse experiences within the context of criminal justice? Illustrate your response by examining the links as they are experienced by one particular community/group.
3. Which of the five common factors of social justice identified by Perry do you think is most important? Why? What concrete policy or practice might facilitate the realization of that element?

Additional Readings

Capeheart, L., & Milovanovic, D. (2007). *Social justice: Theories, issues and movements.* New Brunswick, NJ: Rutgers University Press.

Cook, D. (2006). *Criminal and social justice.* London: Sage.

Craig, G., Burchardt, T., & Gordon, D. (Eds). (2008). *Social justice and public policy.* Bristol, UK: Policy Press.

Websites of Interest

Centre for Social Justice: www.socialjustice.org

Ontario Project for Inter Clinic Community Organizing, Social Justice Links: www.opicco.org/?q=links

Statistics Canada: Exploring Social Justice Issues: www.statcan.gc.ca/edu/edu05_0022-eng.htm

References

Bakan, J., & Schneiderman, D. (1992). *Social justice and the constitution: Perspectives on a social union for Canada.* Ottawa: Carleton University Press.

Barlow, D., & Barlow, M. (1993). Cultural diversity training in criminal justice: A progressive or conservative reform? *Social Justice, 20*(3–4), 69–84.

Bolton, K. (2003). Shared perceptions: Black officers discuss continuing barriers in policing. *Policing, 26*(3), 386–400.

Bolton, K., & Feagin, J. (2004). *Black in blue: African American police officers and racism.* New York: Routledge.

Burchardt, T., & Craig, G. (2008). Introduction. In G. Craig, T. Burchardt, & D. Gordon (Eds), *Social justice and public policy* (pp. 1–16). Bristol, UK: Policy Press.

Cannon, K. (2005). 'Ain't no faggot gonna rob me!' Anti-gay attitudes of criminal justice undergraduate majors. *Journal of Criminal Justice Education, 16*(2), 226–245.

Commission on Social Justice. (1993). *The justice gap.* London: IPPR.

Connell, R. (1990). The state, gender and sexual politics: Theory and appraisal. *Theory and Society, 19*(4), 507–544.

Connell, R. (1992). Drumming up the wrong tree. *Tikkun, 7*(1), 31–36.

Cook, D. (2006). *Criminal and social justice.* London: Sage.

Courtright, K. E., Mackey, D. A., & Packard, S. H. (2005). Empathy among college students and criminal justice majors: Identifying pre-dispositional

traits and the role of education. *Journal of Criminal Justice Education, 16*(1), 125–144.

The Economist. (2009, December 19). Prisoners of politics: Less crime, more punishment. www.economist.com/node/15127510?story_id=15127510

Goudreau, J., & Brzozowski, J. (2002). *A Statistical profile on persons working in justice-related professions in Canada.* Ottawa: Statistics Canada, Canadian Centre for Justice Statistics. Catalogue no. 85-555-XIE.

Jones, L., Perry, B., & Nielsen, M. (2009). Reinvestigating difference. In Criminology and Criminal Justice Collective of Northern Arizona University (Ed.), *Investigating difference: Human and cultural relations in criminal justice* (pp. 286–300). Upper Saddle River, NJ: Prentice Hall.

Levin, J., & McDevitt, J. (1993). *Hate crimes: The rising tide of bigotry and bloodshed.* New York: Plenum Press.

Mackey, D. A., & Courtright, K. E. (1998). Assessing punitiveness among college students: A comparison of criminal justice majors with other majors. *The Justice Professional, 12,* 423–441.

Michalowski, R. (2009). Social class, crime and justice. In Criminology and Criminal Justice Collective of Northern Arizona University (Ed.), *Investigating difference: Human and cultural relations in criminal justice* (pp. 56–73). Upper Saddle River, NJ: Prentice Hall.

Owen, S., & Wagner, K. (2008). The specter of authoritarianism among criminal justice majors. *Journal of Criminal Justice Education, 19*(1), 30–53.

Pate, G. (1981, January). Research on prejudice reduction. *Educational Leadership,* 289–291.

Rawls, J. (1971). *A theory of justice.* Oxford: Oxford University Press.

Rothenberg, P. (2002). Introduction. In P. Rothenberg (Ed.), *White privilege: Essential readings on the other side of racism* (pp. 1–8). New York: Worth.

Rowe, M., & Garland, J. (2003). 'Have you been diversified yet?' Developments in police community and race relations training in England and Wales. *Policing and Society, 13*(4), 399–411.

Sampson, A., & Phillips, C. (1992). *Multiple victimisation: Racial attacks on an East London estate.* Crime Prevention Unit Series. Paper no. 36. London: Home Office.

Sutton, M., Perry, B., Parke, J., & John-Baptiste, C. (2007). *Getting the message across: Using media to reduce racial prejudice and discrimination.* London: Home Office.

Tonry, M. (1995). *Malign neglect.* New York: Oxford University Press.

Umbreit, M., Lewis, T., & Burns, H. (2003). A community response to a 9/11 hate crime: Restorative justice through dialogue. *Criminal Justice Review, 6,* 383–391.

Wimshurst, K., Marchetti, E., & Allard, T. (2004). Attitudes of criminal justice students to Australian indigenous people: Does higher education influence student perceptions? *Journal of Criminal Justice Education, 15*(2), 327–350.

Winterdyk, J., & King, D. (Eds). (1999). *Diversity and justice in Canada.* Toronto: Canadian Scholars' Press.

Young, I. M. 1990. *Justice and the politics of difference.* Princeton, NJ: Princeton University Press.

Glossary

abuse A single action or a combination of psychological, physical, emotional, and economic actions that is done by someone to hurt or mistreat someone else.

accommodation (1) Accommodation means adjusting one's habitual expressive habits to facilitate communication with people with different communication patterns. (2) In another context, it occurs when adjustments are made to policies or practices so that someone is not disadvantaged or discriminated against on the basis of any of the prohibited grounds of discrimination. The *duty to accommodate* is an obligation within a human rights context that arises where requirements or qualifications, which may be imposed in good faith, have an adverse impact on, or provide an unfair preference for, a group of persons based on a protected ground under the Human Rights Code. There is an obligation to accommodate unless to do so would create undue hardship.

acculturation A process by which individuals or groups coming into contact with another culture gradually adopt that culture.

activity limitation A difficulty experienced by an individual in independently carrying out a typical day-to-day function owing to an impairment or health condition.

adults in need of protection Older people who are perceived as vulnerable and therefore subject to a variety of mandated forms of intervention.

ageism Discrimination based on a person's chronological age or on the perception of his or her chronological age.

alternative measures Under the Young Offenders Act, young persons charged with relatively minor criminal offences, such as shoplifting, were eligible for alternative measures programs unique to each province. If approved, the criminal charges would be withdrawn or stayed upon the young person's undertaking to do community work, write apologies, make restitution, write papers, or perform some other public service.

anti-Asian sentiment Attitude or reaction that reflects resentment or hostility toward people of Asian descent. It was especially strong in Canada once the transnational railway was finished and Asian labourers were no longer required.

anti-feminist backlash Feminist-inspired denunciations of gendered violence, campaigns to achieve pay equity, and legal challenges against the state to protect the rights of women have been met in response with (mostly male) critics who see feminist politics and policies as a threat to family values, as underestimating violence against men and the seriousness of women's own violence, and as undermining the rights of men before the law.

anti-racist/anti-racism education A current practice that permeates a wide array of subject areas and school practices, aimed at the eradication of racism in all its various forms—individual, institutional, and systemic. Anti-racism can also be taught/learned in informal or formal education settings.

anti-Semitism Latent or overt hostility or hatred directed toward individual Jews or the Jewish people, leading to social, economic, institutional, religious, cultural, or political discrimination. Anti-Semitism has also been expressed through individual acts of physical violence, vandalism, the organized destruction of entire communities, and genocide.

articulable grounds Reasonable grounds that allow one to suspect an individual of wrong-doing beyond a mere suspicion. Articulable grounds constitute a belief that is justified by meaningful, relevant evidence that exceeds a 'hunch'.

Asiatic Exclusion League The Asiatic Exclusion League was formed in 1905 in San Francisco, California, and was followed by a parallel Canadian branch in Vancouver, British Columbia, in 1907. The group's stated aims were to spread anti-Asian propaganda and influence legislation restricting Asian immigration. Throughout the opening decades of the twentieth century, the league fomented extensive anti-Asian sentiment and activity, including extreme acts of violence against Japanese and Chinese immigrants.

Assembly of First Nations A national political body representing on-reserve and status Indians in Canada through their elected band chief and council. There are over 630 First Nations communities in Canada. The AFN Secretariat is designed to present the views of its membership in areas such as Aboriginal and treaty rights, economic development, education, languages and literacy, health, housing, social development, justice, taxation, land claims, environment, and a whole array of issues of common concern that arise from time to time.

assimilation With 'civilization', assimilation was the official policy of the Canadian government toward Aboriginal people for most of the nineteenth and twentieth centuries. This policy advocated the relocation of Aboriginal communities to reserve lands where the people were to be weaned from their indigenous habits and institutions and adopt instead their 'civilized' non-Aboriginal equivalents. Residential schooling and the eradication of indigenous social, political, and spiritual institutions were pivotal tools in this effort to end the 'Indian problem' by eradicating the 'Indian in the man'.

bias A subjective opinion, preference, prejudice, or inclination that is formed without reasonable justification and that influences an individual's or group's ability to evaluate a particular situation objectively or accurately—a preference for or against. *Reasonable apprehension of bias* exists when there is a reasonable belief that an individual or group will pre-judge a matter and therefore cannot assess a matter fairly because of bias.

bias-free policing This refers to the provision of police services to individuals and communities in an equitable manner, without detriment on the basis of characteristics such as race, religion, place of origin, age, sex, disadvantaged social or economic status, sexual orientation or gender identity, or disability.

black-on-black violence A term used in the media and increasingly within academic forums to describe black intra-racial violence.

Canadian Charter of Rights and Freedoms Enacted in 1982, the Charter institutionalizes the legal, civil, and political rights that flow to citizens, residents, and even visitors to Canada. Specifically, the classes of rights that are enshrined in the Charter are Fundamental Freedoms, Democratic Rights, Mobility Rights, Legal Rights, Equality Rights, Language Rights, and Minority Language Education Rights.

Canadian Multiculturalism Act The Multiculturalism Act of 1988 established multiculturalism as 'official' policy in Canada. According to the Act, one of its key objectives is to 'recognize and promote the understanding that multiculturalism is a fundamental characteristic of the Canadian heritage and identity and that it provides an invaluable resource in the shaping of Canada's future.'

child welfare Each province in Canada has a well-established system of child welfare services to prevent or help remedy problems that may result in children being neglected, abused, exploited, or in trouble with the law; to provide out-of-home care (i.e., foster care, group home care, residential care, and adoption services) for children removed from their homes; and to provide a variety of support services for families who experience difficulties caring for their children.

Chinese Immigration Act Chinese immigration was heavily constrained by the Chinese Immigration Act of 1885, which imposed a hefty head tax on all immigrants from China. The later Chinese Immigration Act of 1923, known in the Chinese Canadian community as the Chinese Exclusion Act, banned Chinese immigrants from entering Canada except those classified as merchants, diplomats, and foreign students until 1967.

collectivist This term refers to a society wherein the needs of the group or family unit are more important than those of the individual; it emphasizes the importance of interdependence.

colonization The process of claiming lands, usually foreign lands, by sending in people to occupy and settle on those lands, thereby establishing a colony that remains in contact with the country of origin and its government.

community building The creation of cultural, social, religious, and recreational institutions, as well as of employment and marriage networks, intended to establish or re-establish capacity and empowerment within a group or geographical area.

continuous passage This reflects that idea (passed into Canadian law in 1908 and remaining in effect till 1947) that immigrants would be prohibited from entering the country unless they had an uninterrupted or continuous journey from their original country.

Convention on the Rights of Persons with Disabilities An international treaty developed by the United Nations that commits the states that are party to the convention to recognize, protect, and actively promote the rights of individuals with disabilities.

covert racism A contemporary expression of hostility toward racial minorities that goes undetected by conventional measures. Covert racism, a much less public and obvious form of racism than simple racism, is hidden in the fabric of society, covertly suppressing the individuals being discriminated against. Covert, racially biased decisions are often disguised or rationalized with an explanation that society is more willing to accept.

cultural noise 'Cultural noise' suggests the impediments to successful communication between people of different cultures. Sources of cultural noise include differences in languages and non-verbal cues.

culture Culture refers to the way groups of people have learned to live together by sharing certain historical experiences, including ideas, beliefs, values, knowledge, and historical, geographical, linguistic, racial, religious, ethnic, or social traditions. Culture is a complex and dynamic organization of meaning, knowledge, artifacts, and symbols that guides human behaviour, accounts for shared patterns of thought and action, and contributes to human, social, and physical survival. Culture is the total of everything an individual learns by being immersed in a particular context, and it results in a set of expectations for appropriate behaviour in similar contexts. It is transmitted from generation to generation, reinforced, passed on, and changed.

deculturation The process whereby communities are stripped of their cultural uniqueness and often their cultural heritage, typically through coercion and policy that criminalizes their traditional practices.

democratic racism A new ideology held by people in contemporary society in which two conflicting sets of values are made congruent to each other. Commitments to democratic principles such as justice, equality, and fairness conflict but coexist with prejudice and discrimination against Others.

deportation The expulsion of a legal or unauthorized immigrant from Canada to a receiving nation, usually the nation of birth of the person expelled.

diaspora The term, literally meaning a 'scattering of seeds', refers to a people of the same ethnic identity moving away from their original homeland.

disability disadvantage Disability disadvantage results when an individual cannot meet the environmental requirements for full participation in typical activities of daily living. Since disability is a product of both individual capabilities and environmental requirements, it cannot be defined solely by either of these factors.

discrimination The denial of equal treatment, civil liberties and opportunity to individuals or groups. It is the result of prejudiced attitudes of individuals or institutions and leads to inequitable outcomes for persons perceived as different.

disparity Unequal treatment that cannot be accounted for by differences between groups. Disparity is understood to be capricious and unfair and to result in disadvantage. In the context of criminal justice, it generally refers to inequity in arrests and sentencing for certain groups of people; it nearly always refers to racial and ethnic disparity.

dispossession The act of undermining the possession of land, property, rights, and opportunities of a people. It reflects much of the history of Canadian policy in regard to Aboriginal and First Nations peoples.

diversion A term that refers especially to youthful offenders who are diverted away from formal criminal justice processing and the courts, and instead are given informal sanctions outside of the court.

diversity This refers to the presence of a wide range of human qualities and attributes within a group, organization, or society. The dimensions of diversity include—but are not limited to—ancestry, culture, ethnicity, gender, gender identity, language, physical and intellectual ability, race, religion, sex, sexual orientation, and socio-economic status.

due process According to the principle of due process, the government must respect all of the legal rights that are owed to a person according to the law. Due process protects individual persons from the state and guarantees such rights as the right to a lawyer.

egalitarianism The doctrine that sees equality of condition, outcome, reward, and privilege as a desirable goal of social organization.

empowerment The processes and strategies by which individuals, groups, or communities may enhance their capacity to exercise their rights. It typically involves resisting and overcoming oppressive conditions.

equity A condition or state of fair, inclusive, and respectful treatment of all people. Equity does not mean treating people the same without regard to individual differences.

ethno-national Ethno-national (or nativist) refers to an ideology invoking the territory, identity, and culture said to be linked exclusively to an ethnic group.

eugenics A belief system and the practices resulting from that belief system that promote intentional actions to improve the quality of human stock through selective reproduction or selective mortality. **Positive eugenics** attempts to increase the number of people considered to be of superior quality, while **negative eugenics** attempts to decrease the numbers of people considered to be of inferior quality.

extrajudicial measures Extrajudicial measures under the Youth Criminal Justice System consist of all forms of diversion from the formal judicial system, including the decision not to lay a charge and programs known as alternative measures under the YOA. These measures include taking no further action, informal police warnings, police cautions, police referrals to a program or agency in the community, pre-charge screening programs, youth justice committees, conferences, and extra-judicial sanctions.

family reunification Family reunification reflects the idea, often crystallized in immigration law, that families have a right to live together and thus if a member or members of a family live in one country, they have the right to join other family members living in a different country.

gender 'Gender' describes those characteristics of women and men that are socially constructed; 'sex' refers to those characteristics of males and females that are biologically determined.

gender identity This constitutes an intrinsic sense of self, particularly one's sense of being male or female. A person's gender identity may not conform to his or her birth-assigned sex. It is different from and does not determine a person's sexual orientation.

gender-role conformity The notion that one's performance of gender roles matches social expectations of a particular sex. An example would be when a girl 'acts' like a girl is 'supposed' to act, according to social norms and expectations.

ghettoization Residential, economic, and/or social exclusion, typically manifested in segregation.

hate crimes Hate crimes (also known as bias-motivated crimes) occur when a perpetrator targets a victim because of his or her perceived membership in a certain social group, usually defined by racial group, religion, sexual orientation, disability, class, ethnicity, nationality, age, gender, gender identity, or political affiliation. They are associated with criminal acts that are seen to have been motivated by hatred of one or more of the types above, or of their derivatives. Incidents may involve physical assault, damage to property, bullying, harassment, verbal abuse or insults, or offensive graffiti or letters (hate mail).

head tax The Chinese head tax was a fixed fee charged for each Chinese person entering Canada. Between 1895 and 1923, a series of laws were passed in Canada demanding head tax from Chinese immigrants; the tax increased from $50 per head in 1885 to $100 in 1900 and $500 in 1923. The head tax was one of the most racist laws ever passed by the Canadian government, as it was meant to discourage Chinese from entering Canada after the completion of the Canadian Pacific Railway. The head tax was ended by the Chinese Immigration Act of 1923, which stopped Chinese immigration except for business people, clergy, educators, students, and other categories.

hegemonic masculinity The preferred and privileged form of masculinity that is dominant in a culture. In Canadian society, hegemonic masculinity typically stresses such traits as competition, aggression, dominance, strength, wealth, material possessions, and sexual prowess vis-à-vis women.

heterosexism The privileging of heterosexual (opposite sex) attraction and activity over all other sexualities. This is the dominant sexuality in most Western cultures.

hierarchy A mechanism of social organization in which members are divided by status or, especially, authority. Most societies are characterized by multiple social hierarchies, ranging from family, tribe, and clan groupings to genders, races, classes, and castes, to city-states, empires, and nation-states, to bureaucratic organizations, including corporations, guilds, unions, political parties, and other civic associations. All hierarchies are comprised of relationships of superiority-inferiority or domination-subordination. On a daily basis, each individual in a modern society is likely to be a member of several distinct hierarchies with multiple and overlapping jurisdictions.

ideology The world views that shape our perception and evaluation of our social contexts. Ideologies offer justifications and explanations of social patterns such as the distribution of wealth, status, and power.

impairment Any abnormality of a person's body part that results in loss of function.

inclusion Inclusion refers to the patterns and practices by which individuals or communities are perceived to be valued members of their society. It involves a commitment to fostering the full and equal participation of all individuals and communities in the economic, social, cultural, and political dimensions of life in their country of residence.

Indian Act First passed in 1876 and subject to extensive amendments over time, the Indian Act governs virtually every aspect of the lives of status Indians. The Act spells out certain federal obligations to Indians and regulates the management of Indian reserve lands (R.S.C., 1985, c-I-5).

individualistic An individualistic society values the individual over the group. Such a society emphasizes the importance of independence.

inequality The condition whereby people have unequal access to valued resources, services, and positions in society. It is reflected across multiple dimensions, including race, class, gender, and sexuality, to name just a few. Inequalities are upheld by a system that reproduces and maintains the status of the dominant group socially, economically, politically, and psychologically. In other words, inequality implies that access to resources and goods is overwhelmingly denied to subordinate groups because of systemic practices rather than individual traits.

institutional racism The established policies, practices, and procedures of an institution that systematically reflect and reproduce racial inequalities. Institutionalized racism may be conscious or unconscious, direct or indirect, overt or covert. Unlike the racism perpetrated by individuals, institutional racism has the power to affect the bulk of people belonging to a racial group.

intercultural communication The process of exchanging meaningful and unambiguous information across cultural boundaries.

intersectionality The interconnected nature of forms of oppression (e.g., cultural, institutional, and social) against identifiable groups, such that they operate in compounded ways (e.g., gender and race, race and religion, sexual orientation and race, and so on).

intracultural communication The process of exchanging meaningful and unambiguous information among individuals or groups who share similar coding strategies and understandings of the features of language in a shared context.

Islamophobia The dread or hatred of Islam and therefore the fear and dislike of all Muslims.

Japanese internment The confinement of Japanese Canadians in British Columbia during World War II. The internment began in December 1941 following the attack by the Japanese air force on the American base at Pearl Harbor, Hawaii. The leaders of the push for internment justified it on grounds of national security. The property of the Japanese Canadians was confiscated, and the people were transported to camps in various locations in the interior of the province.

Juvenile Delinquents Act Passed in 1908 by the Canadian government, the Act was the first youth justice legislation in Canada. At that time, there was no Charter to protect a juvenile's rights and no right to a lawyer. Problems with the Act led to demands for changes, and it was revised in 1929. In 1984 the Young Offenders Act replaced the Juvenile Delinquents Act.

Komagata Maru The Japanese steamship that sailed from Hong Kong to Canada via China and Japan carrying passengers (all of them British subjects) from India. The ship was not allowed to land in Vancouver and was forced to return to India. The incident is regarded as an example of the ways in which immigrants were prevented from entering Canada and the United States.

marginalization/marginalized The condition of not having access to the same level of influence, power, privilege, opportunities, and advantages as others in a society.

multiculturalism A set of legal and cultural norms that recognize, advance, and protect the reality of pluralism in Canada.

neo-liberalism An ideology constituted by fiscal and social policies that eschew public spending and taxation in favour of privatization and deregulation of government. It is grounded in the free market ideology of unfettered competition, individualism, and regulation of the working poor through criminalization of welfare or deskilling of labour. Neo-liberal governments rely heavily upon corporate welfare (e.g., subsidies and tax cuts for corporations such as General Motors).

new penology The study, theory, and practice of prison management and criminal rehabilitation. The old penology focused on a sociological perspective, whereas the new penology focuses on risk management and the system itself. The old penology looked at social reforms and the relationship between individuals and communities, while new penology relies more on information related to imprisonment, surveillance, and custody.

net-widening This refers to policies and practices that expand the social control of individuals and communities either intentionally or unintentionally.

over-representation With over-representation, members of a certain group are represented in the population in a proportion that is greater than might be statistically expected or warranted. For example, if the Aboriginal population in a province is 12 per cent but Aboriginal people make 50 per cent of the province's prison population, they would be considered to be well above their expected representation in the latter.

points system The points system represents an effort to apply non-discriminatory and selective criteria to determine eligibility for immigration, with points awarded for occupation, education, language, skills, and age.

police use of force The use of physical force or violence by the police undertaken while carrying out their duties. Excessive use of force occurs when a police officer uses more force than deemed necessary for the situation.

preferred and non-preferred immigrants This recurring theme in Canadian immigration refers to groups that are viewed as acceptable for admission versus those that are deemed not to be. Historically, these distinctions were usually based on race and ethnicity.

prejudice The tendency to prejudge, typically in negative terms. Prejudicial attitudes tend to be unfavourable judgments of people because of their group membership.

privilege Privilege refers to advantages that accrue to individuals by virtue of their group membership rather than through their own individual effort. Typically, privilege refers to unearned advantages that work to maintain or reinforce the systematic systems of power described in chapter 2. This is in contrast to earned advantages that are in fact garnered by dint of effort.

prohibited classes Any identified group barred from immigrating to Canada by law or policy. Previous laws restricted the immigration of prohibited classes to Canada. Current law has eliminated the discriminatory language of prohibited classes but denies entrance to many members of the previously identified prohibited classes based on potentially excessive demands.

Protection for Persons in Care Act Embodied in laws enacted in several Canadian provinces, this Act is intended to protect individuals in health or social care facilities from abuse and neglect. Provisions vary across provinces, but examples include mandatory reporting of abuse and neglect, whistleblower protection, and background checks for caregiving staff.

psychological noise The preconceived notions we bring to conversations, such as racial stereotypes, reputations, biases, and assumptions.

race Race is a social construct that refers to a group of people of common ancestry, distinguished from others by characteristics such as colour of skin, shape of eyes, hair texture, and/ or facial features. The term is also used to designate the social categories into which societies divide people according to such characteristics. The various types of broad-based groups (e.g., racial, ethnic, religious, and regional) often intersect and are rarely mutually exclusive, with the degree of discrimination against any one or more of them varying from place to place and over time.

racialized/racialization These terms refer to the social construction of race that creates a hierarchy based on superficial physical characteristics in population groups. This hierarchy, over time, becomes systematized and institutionalized, creating social and economic inequities, power differentials, and discrimination against population groups viewed as undesirable because of their perceived 'racial' origin. These groups are referred to as 'racialized' to convey this system of oppression.

racial profiling Racial profiling exists when the members of a particular racial or ethnic group become subject to greater criminal justice or institutional surveillance than others. Profiling occurs when racial characteristics—rather than behaviour— contribute to surveillance decisions.

racism Racism is comprised of a set of erroneous assumptions, opinions, and/or actions stemming from the belief that one race is inherently superior to another. Racism may be present in organizational and institutional structures and programs as well as in the attitudes and behaviour of individuals. It results from the combination of racial prejudice and power and is manifested through individual action and/or institutional or organizational policies or practices.

reasonable accommodation This entails an adjustment or change in the social environment to permit participation of an individual or group of individuals with exceptional needs that does not result in extreme hardship for the organization making this adjustment or change.

refugee A person who has a well-founded fear of being persecuted in his or her home nation and seeks refuge from this persecution in a different nation.

reserves Lands that are held by the federal Crown and 'reserved' for the use of Indian bands.

residential schools Treaties struck with Aboriginal nations by the federal government made general promises of schooling that the Indian leadership commonly construed as involving community schools similar to those in non-Aboriginal communities. In an effort to economize and isolate Aboriginal children from their families and communities, and thereby from informal education in their own culture, language, and traditions, the Indian department implemented a system of boarding schools, distant from the home communities, where children could be 'civilized' and thereby 'assimilated'. As is now well known, many children experienced only violence, trauma, and death in the schools.

responsibilization A term developed to refer to the process whereby the state downloads the responsibility for behaviours and activities that are usually the responsibility of the state. For example, individuals are held responsible for their own safety and security and their own health and welfare.

restorative justice An approach to justice that centres on bringing together victims, offenders, and their communities of care in a collaborative project to acknowledge, account for, and make amends for the harms caused by conflict or crime, and to restore and repair those harms and the relationships among those touched by them.

R. v. Gladue The first case in which the Supreme Court of Canada, in 1999, interpreted section 718.2(e), which directs judges to consider the 'special circumstances' of Aboriginal people in sentencing and, where possible, alternatives to imprisonment that are restorative in nature and focus on healing.

self-report studies A type of survey, questionnaire, or poll in which respondents read the question and select a response by themselves, without researcher interference. Some criminologists favour self-report studies as an alternative method of collecting crime statistics. For example, a representative sample of individuals are asked, under assurances of confidentiality, whether they have committed any offences of a particular kind.

sentencing circles Sentencing circles represent a restorative process in which the determination of sentence following an admission of guilt by an offender for a criminal act is handed over to the community. After considering the nature of the act, the harms it caused, and the needs of the parties to the crime event, the community makes a recommendation for a sentence to a judge, who may or may not follow it.

settlement centres Settlement centres provide services to newcomers—typically immigrants—enabling them to integrate into their new communities.

sexism Sexism stems from a set of implicit or explicit beliefs and erroneous assumptions and actions based on an ideology that views one gender as superior to another. It may be evident within organizational or institutional structures or programs, as well as within individual thought or behaviour patterns. Sexism includes any act or institutional practice, backed by institutional power, that subordinates people because of gender.

social exclusion Social exclusion refers to a variety of barriers that prevent individuals and communities from participating fully and equally in their country of residence.

social stigma Social stigma refers to the severe social disapproval of personal characteristics or beliefs that are perceived to be against cultural norms. Stigma comes in three forms: (1) overt or external deformations, such as scars, physical manifestations of anorexia nervosa, leprosy (leprosy stigma), or a physical disability or social disability, such as obesity; (2) deviations in personal traits, such as mental illness, drug addiction, alcoholism, and criminal backgrounds; (3) 'tribal stigmas', such as traits, imagined or real, of ethnic groups, nationalities, or religions that are deemed to constitute a deviation from what is perceived to be the prevailing normative ethnicity, nationality, or religion. Stigma is generally based on stereotypical and uninformed impressions or characterizations of a given subject.

social stratification Social stratification refers to the system of inequalities within and between societies, the processes of assignment to positions within a social hierarchy, and the means by which resources are allocated.

spousal migration The process by which a legally married spouse of a person who has migrated to a country can also immigrate to the country because of his or her status as a spouse.

standpoint feminism In response to male-stream social theories and methodologies, feminists sought to have women's lived experience of poverty, sexual violence, and mothering incorporated as the basis of truth or epistemology of social theory. In this way, experience narratives reveal the intersection of dimensions of oppression, power, and resistance.

status Indian According to the Indian Act, a status Indian is an individual who is 'registered as an Indian, or eligible to be registered as an Indian' (hence the terms status or registered Indian, used interchangeably) and who is thus entitled to live on reserves.

status offence A delinquency or crime that can only be committed by people occupying a particular status. The Juvenile Delinquents Act (replaced in 1984), for example, created the criminal offences of school truancy, incorrigibility, sexual immorality, and violations of liquor laws. Only young people could be charged with or found to be in a state of delinquency because of these behaviours.

stereotype A mental picture or image of a group of people ascribing the same characteristic(s) to all members of the group, regardless of their individual differences. A stereotype is an over-generalization in which the information or experience on which the image is based may be true for some of the individual group members but not for all members. Stereotyping may be based on misconceptions, incomplete information, and/or false generalizations about race; age; ethnic, linguistic, geographical, or national groups; religions; social, marital, or family status; physical, developmental, or mental attributes; gender or sexual orientation; or other similar factors.

surveillance Taken from the French word for watching over, 'surveillance' commonly refers to the close observation of an individual's or a group's behaviours and activities. In the law enforcement context, surveillance can take various forms, such as observation via closed circuit television (CCTV) monitoring and the interception of telecommunications and cellular communications.

underemployment Underemployment occurs when workers with high skill levels are employed in low-wage jobs that do not require such abilities. In Canada, this is most evident among highly trained immigrants whose foreign credentials or experience may not be recognized or accepted in their new country. As a result, doctors or engineers immigrating from other countries may be unable to work in their profession and may be compelled to seek menial work.

Young Offenders Act The Young Offenders Act (YOA) was enacted in 1984 to replace the Juvenile Delinquents Act. The Act established the national age of criminal responsibility at 12 years old and stipulated that youths could only be prosecuted if they broke a law of the Criminal Code (previously, youths could be prosecuted or punished solely on the grounds that it was in their 'best interests'). The Act also indicated that the rights established in the Canadian Charter of Rights and Freedoms applied to youths as well. The YOA was repealed in 2003 with the passage of the Youth Criminal Justice Act.

Youth Criminal Justice Act The Youth Criminal Justice Act (YCJA) came into effect on April 1, 2003. It covers the prosecution of youths for criminal offences. The YCJA replaced the Young Offenders Act, which was a replacement for the Juvenile Delinquents Act.

Index

Aboriginal peoples: Aboriginal Corrections Continuum of Care, 354–5; Aboriginal sovereignty, 59; col-lectivist cultures of, 312; criminogenic nature of, 64; culturally specific programs, 74, 354–5; direct vs. indirect speech, 313–14; dispossession, as state-induced marginalization, 76–7; domestic violence, 66; education levels, 7; employment opportunities, 22; ethno-racial groups in federal corrections system, 131t; languages and cultural groups, 75; life expectancy rates, 256; Native Women's Association of Canada, 213; offence and prior history data, 80; over-representation of in criminal justice system, 8–9, 77–81, 192, 285–6; police treatment of, 77–8, 87n1, 87n2; racial profiling, 10; recidivism rates, 79; restorative justice, 82–5, 267; Royal Commission on Aboriginal Peoples (1996), 9; Safety in the Streets program, 345; sentencing circles, 77, 82–5, 356; social justice reforms, 358–9; 'Starlight Tours', 77, 87n1; stereotypes, and racial profiling, 45; *Stolen Sisters* (Amnesty International), 213; Stolen Sisters Project, 77, 87n2; suicide rates, 76; Third World conditions on reserves, 75–7; 'Two Spirited' view of sexual diversity, 18; victims' services, 267; violence against Aboriginal women, 7

Abramovich, Roman, 190

Abuse of Older Adults: Department of Justice Canda, Overview Paper, 258–60

Access to Government Services by Racial Minorities (Masemann & Mock), 331

accommodation, 318

accountability, 19

acculteration: age and gender, role in societal integration, 152–3

Addington, D., 239

Addressing Hate Crime in Ontario (Hate Crimes Community Working Group), 333

Advocacy Centre for the Elderly (ON), 266

advocacy groups. *see also groups by name*: as alternatives to criminal justice agencies, 11, 158–9; Asian Canadians, 119–20

Afghani immigrants, 164

Africa: as the 'dark' continent, 47; as immigration source region, 126

African Canadian Legal Clinic, 143, 350

Agamben, G., 51–2

age: as determinant of risk, 7, 129; and societal integration, 152–3

ageism, societal, 258, 259, 264, 266

Agocs, C., 69

Alberta, 202–3, 204

Altheide, D.L., 50

Amnesty International: on racial profiling, 9–10; *Stolen Sisters*, 213

anti-racism training: background and rationale for, 330–3; *The Kit: A Manual by Youth to Combat Racism through Education*, 357; multicultural programs, differences between, 333–4; overcoming resistance to, 339–40; Seminar on Racial, Ethnic and Cultural Equity, 337–8; social context education, 335–6

anti-Semitism, 25, 91; Choose Your Voice, 345

Anti-Terrorism Act (Bill C-36), 178–9, 184n9, 184n10

Anti-Violence Programme at the 519 Community Centre, 345

Arab immigrants: Arab ethnic diversity, 164, 183n3; Canadian Arab Federation, 169; migration history, 165–6

Arar, Maher, 179, 184n11

Arnot, David, 336

Asian Canadians. *see also* South Asian Canadians: domestic violence, 66; ethno-racial groups in federal corrections system, 131t; hate crime, and anti-Asian violence, 8, 117–19; racial profiling, 135; sexual assault, female students, 129

Asiatic Exclusion League, 107

Aspinall, P., 152

Assembly of First Nations: Third World conditions on reserves, 75–7

assimilation: ideological currents of, 174–5

Association of Black Law Enforcers (ABLE), 143

attributions, and tendency to evaluate, 316–17

Australia: Aboriginal people, incarceration rates, 75, 80; sentencing circles, 84–5

Azocar, C.L., 45

Banerjee, R., 93

Banerji, A., 152

Barlagne family, 299

battered woman's syndrome, 218–19, 240

Bauder, H., 171

Baumann, E.A., 261

B.C. College of Teachers v. Trinity Western University, 350

Beaulieu, M., 260

Beck, Ulrich, 187, 197–9

Bell, M.D., 233

Berrill, K.T., 237

bias model of immigrant criminality, 94–5

Biery, R., 18

Biggs, S., 255

bigotry, obvious, 29